M. P. Shiel

A Biography

Harold Billings

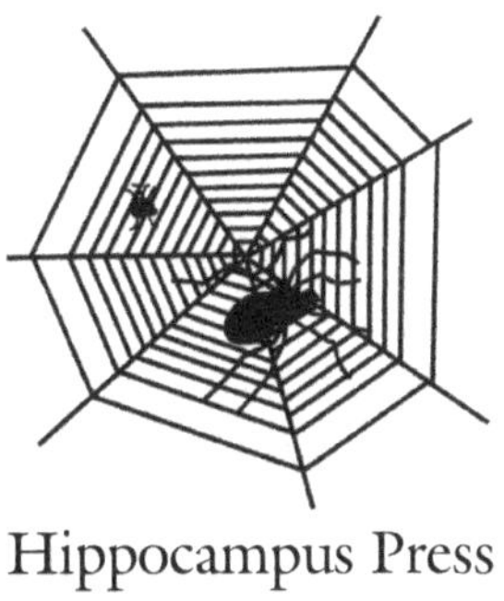

Hippocampus Press

New York

Published by Hippocampus Press
P.O. Box 641, New York, NY 10156.
www.hippocampuspress.com

Hippocampus Press logo designed by Anastasia Damianakos.
Cover design by Dan Sauer Design, dansauerdesign.com

1 3 5 7 9 8 6 4 2
ISBN 978-1-61498-492-4 trade paperback
ISBN 978-1-61498-496-2 ebook

M. P. Shiel: A Biography

CONTENTS

Publisher's Preface 9
Introduction 11
The Early Years 15
Chapter 1. "Whose glossy black to shame might bring . . ." 17
Chapter 2. "'a flushed brown' harmony" 38
Chapter 3. "I shall have to be content with becoming a teacher" .. 91
Chapter 4. "I have begun writing, writing, writing" 106
Chapter 5. ". . . an island in the sea of London" 122
The Middle Years 1897–1923 161
Chapter 6. ". . . as a bud for the sunshine" 163
Chapter 7. "the fictional serial trade" 184
Chapter 8. "The Empress of the Earth" 204
Chapter 9. "a lovely Spanish girl of sixteen" 212
Chapter 10. "Will you come to the wedding, will you come?" ... 232
Chapter 11. 45 Acton Street 259
Chapter 12. ". . . on account of the Spanish Squall" 292
Chapter 13. Re-Enter Louis Tracy 302
Chapter 14. Mary Price and Elizabeth Price Sircar 326
Chapter 15. "Love's language . . ." 337
Chapter 16. "My dear Chesson" 381
Chapter 17. "rather in distress . . ." 397
Chapter 18. Restoring a Career 419
The Final Years 1923–1947 433
The African Tale 437
The Barbara Brennan Memoir 441
The Knopf Tale 447
"My Dear Fytton": The Letters of M. P. Shiel to John Gawsworth... 458
Shiel's *Book of Luke* 468
Refusing Corruption: A Shape in the Fire 472
The Disposition of L'Abri 477
Envoi 478
References 479
The Works of M. P. Shiel 485
Index 493
The Author 503

Illustrations

Phipps as Master at Hunt Bridge House, 1886 10
Topographical Map of Montserrat.. 51
Plymouth, Montserrat, as seen from the sea.................................... 52
Matthew Phipps Shiell about 14, Montserrat, ca. 1880 53
Shiel's Home, Montserrat, ca. 1929 54
Parliament Street (looking south), Plymouth, Montserrat 73
Launching of new schooner, Montserrat 74
The Montserrat Spectator, Friday, 15 December 1876 75
Henry Dyett, Percy Trott, Paddy Burke, Harry Dyett—Montserrat friends of Phipps, ca. 1885 76
Augusta Shiell Horsford, Devonshire, ca. 1880............................ 115
Cyril Horsford, London, ca. 1891 [ca. 1890], age 15 116
Isle of Redonda 117
Harrison College, Bridgetown, Barbados, ca. 1880....................... 117
Sarah Ann ("Sallie") Shiell, possibly Barbados, ca. 1887 118
Phipps as Junior Master, Matlock, 1886 145
Shiel at King's College, Strand, interpreters school, ca. 1891 146
Prince Zaleski title page, 1895 147
Ella D'Arcy, ca. 1895 148
M. P. Shiel.. 160
Lina and servant Jeanne, 1898.. 197
Lina in Paris, 1898 198
Phipps and Lina in Paris, 1898.. 199
Ella D'Arcy, ca. 1896 200
Salvadore, Micaela, and Carolina Gomez in Convent School......... 219
Wedding Menu for Phipps and Lina, 1898 220
Love child Ada Phipps Seward Shiel in Cheltenham, 1899 221
Lina and Baby Lola Shiel on Keppel St., 1901. 222
Baby Lola Shiel on Keppel St., 1901 223
Lina with cigarette, dog, seated Mica, servant Louise, 1903.......... 224
Ada Phipps Shiel on chair in Cheltenham, 1904........................... 225
Ada Phipps Shiel with dog in Cheltenham, 1904 226
Poster for *The Evil that Men Do* serial, 1904 331
Surja Fumar Sircar, common-law husband of Elizabeth Price........ 332

Elizabeth Price Sircar, mother of Caesar Kenneth Shiel 333
Caesar Kenneth Price Shiel (born 1914), ca. 1950.......................... 334
Mica Gomez in Artist Atelier Paris, ca. 1903 {1898?} 349
Esther Lydia Furley at age 12 350
Lydia Furley (age 18), ca. 1890 in London 351
William Arthur Jewson in his late teens, ca. 1870 352
William Arthur Jewson (age 48), 1904.. 363
Gerald Arthur Jewson, January 1918 364
Gerald Arthur Jewson, December 1918 365
Lydia Furley Jewson winter, 1907/08 366

Abbreviations

JG	John Gawsworth
MDS	Matthew Dowdy Shiell
MPS	Matthew Phipps Shiel
HRC	Harry Ransom Humanities Research Center, University of Texas, Austin
Works	A. Reynolds Morse, *The Works of M. P. Shiel* (1979–83)

Publisher's Preface

The present work was written by Harold Billings (1931–2017), a distinguished librarian who worked at the library of the University of Texas at Austin for nearly fifty years (1954–2003), culminating in his appointment as Director of General Libraries (1978–2003). His articles on library science were collected in the volume *Magic and Hypersystems: Constructing the Information Sharing Library* (2002). In 2003 he received the Hugh C. Atkinson Award from the American Library Association.

To devotees of weird fiction, Billings is best known for his tireless work in gathering up documents relating to M. P. Shiel, many of them obtained from Shiel's literary executor John Gawsworth, and depositing them in the Harry Ransom Center at the University of Texas. Using this material, Billings wrote two volumes of biography, *M. P. Shiel: A Biography of His Early Years* (2005) and *M. P. Shiel: The Middle years 1897–1923* (2010), published by Roger Beacham, Publisher (Austin). He was unable to complete the third and final volume, and the extensive notes for it were published as *An Ossuary for M. P. Shiel: The Final Years, 1923–1947* (Bucharest: Mount Abraxas/Ex Occidente, 2016).

Hippocampus Press is proud to publish this biography in a single volume. We have made some modest revisions—such as the placement of separate introductions to each volume at the beginning of the book—to facilitate reading, and we have also consolidated the bibliographical references and placed them at the end of the volume. We hope that this omnibus edition of a landmark biography will foster interest and scholarship on a neglected master of weird fiction and also demonstrate Harold Billings's lifelong scholarship on and devotion to M. P. Shiel.

Phipps as Master at Hunt Bridge House, 1886
Courtesy of the Harry Ransom Humanities Research Center
The University of Texas at Austin

Introduction

M. P. Shiel, West Indian–born British novelist and short story writer, will be remembered for several enduring prophetic novels and a handful of supernatural stories that can stand with anyone's best. He is an especially interesting literary figure whose life embraced the final effects of slavery in the West Indies, the culture of the British Empire at its most refulgent, and the sobering years of Edwardian England.

Shiel was a masterful stylist. His writing still trembles with a wild imagination and an adoration for words that are made to sing. At times he was regarded as a cult figure, as self-indulgent as Corvo. The broad scope of his novels and stories continues to attract new cycles of readers, who relish the apocalyptic vision of *The Purple Cloud,* the decadent tales from *Shapes in the Fire,* that great adventure *The Lord of the Sea,* or the detective, fantasy, or Edwardian adventure-romances that are encompassed in some thirty books. *The Yellow Danger* established a genre almost by itself. Withal, there is a philosophical and provocative depth to Shiel's work that defies genre. Some call this literature.

The first section of the present work is devoted to the forces that shaped his character and his writing, those early years in the life of Shiel that led him from birth and youth in the West Indies to a point of major change in his writing career in London at the end of 1897. He had already written profusely, but this was the year that saw him commence writing serial novels—wildly imaginative and stylish beyond any expectation of the publication source—that would provide an immediate income and that he could rework for book publication. The second part selects a few facts from the early years, and with fresh information, more fully develops Shiel's career as an author of serial fiction, supernatural short stories, and prophetic novels by which he is recalled today.

This is the story of the families that shaped him, the Irish generation that reaped unholy benefits from the bondage and concubinage constructed around the slave-based sugar industry in the West Indies, and the family that represented the white and olive-blooded illegitimate cast-offs from the demise—in just a generation's time—of the plantation wealth and society built by their fathers. This is the story of his youth on a beautiful, volcanic-peaked island that was struggling to survive the poverty left by the death of its sugar industry and the social structure built upon it. This is the story of Shiel's sail-away to England and how he began a fascinating life of his own in the glory of another empire, fading in its most colorful days.

Access to correspondence from Shiel's personal archives, from family records of persons closely associated with him, and the archives of his publishers and literary agents has provided the basis for a deeper look into this man whose publisher, Grant Richards, described as "extraordinarily clever and a little mad."

His wild imagination as an author, several deeply human love affairs, a supremely intense ego, and a revealed decadence mark this period in his life and are shaped in this biography. The rich detail in the present volume answers questions that have existed a hundred years, surprising, not always pleasant.

This is a biography and not a critical study. Studies of his works are elsewhere, especially in some depth on the World Wide Web and increasingly in monograph literature.

HAROLD BILLINGS

Acknowledgments

Since my initial effort at preparing a biography of M. P. Shiel was preempted by career, family, and other personal interests around 1961, the huge archive of books, manuscripts, correspondence, photographs, and other material relating to Shiel that I had donated to the collections of the University of Texas–Austin starting in 1956 lay fallow. But the ongoing interest of A. Reynolds Morse in Shiel remained and was fanned into new life in the late 1970s by the indefatigable young scholar John D. Squires, whose biographical, bibliographical, and critical research regarding Shiel was joined by other fresh hands soon thereafter. This has been enhanced by the significant genealogical research into the Shiell family by Richard Shiell and Dorothy Anderson of Australia, whose family origins derive also from the island of Montserrat and a likely common ancestor in a great-grandfather of M. P. Shiel.

Were it not that Shiel's original literary executor, John Gawsworth, gathered copies of family letters and jotted notes relating to family lore on anything within his reach as Shiel shared memories with him, much of what we know of M. P. Shiel would have been forever lost. Alan Gullette, a Shiel enthusiast in his own right, is making much of this effort available on a worldwide basis through Internet presentation.

In digging afresh in the vaults of the Harry Ransom Humanities Research Center and in exchanging facts with a new generation of admirers of M. P. Shiel's writing, it has been possible to add new information about the life and works of Shiel, to make corrections to an older piece of this book, and to publish it greatly enlarged and anew where its wider availability may lead to the unearthing of further facts about this fascinating writer and the worlds from which he grew.

"The Early Years" is a considerably revised and enlarged version of a contribution with the title "The Shape of Shiel" published in A. Reynolds Morse, ed., *Shiel in Diverse Hands: A Collection of Essays* (Cleveland: Reynolds Morse Foundation, 1983), 77–105. The letters quoted are in the Harry Ransom Humanities Research Center, The University of Texas at Austin, and are used with the permission of the Ransom Center and Javier Marías (The Estate of M. P. Shiel).

The second part of my efforts to gather the life of M. P. Shiel owes a great deal to the assistance of the longtime troopers who have provided a chase after details that have been hidden in many cases for a hundred years or more: Douglas A. Anderson, Victor Berch, Barbara Brennan, Tim Brennan, Gracelyn Cassell, Roger Dobson, Grace Eckley, Benjamin Franklin Fisher, Alan Gullette, Antonio Iriarte, Kirsten MacLeod, Richard Shiell, William Holman, and the modern master of Shiel studies, John D. Squires.

Gratitude is expressed to the Ransom Center for access to and use of original photographs, correspondence and other research materials in its collections. The assistance of Linda Briscoe, Tara Wenger, and Richard Workman of the Center's staff is gratefully appreciated. Ann Hartness and Margo Gutiérrez of the UT Nettie Lee Benson Latin American Collection have been especially helpful. Jim Retherford of the UT Libraries has provided graphic assistance in a number of ways, and his retouching of the frontispiece warrants special recognition. Artwork for the title page is from Aubrey Beardsley's title page border design for *Prince Zaleski.*

The assistance of the following individuals in developing the content of this work is gratefully acknowledged: Dorothy Anderson, Victor Berch, Roger Dobson, Alan Gullette, Antonio Iriarte, Claudia Semper, Richard Shiell, John D. Squires, Richard Wildman—and the memory of John Gawsworth, Adrian Goldstone, and A. Reynolds Morse. William R. Holman has not only guided the production of this book, he has been a prime mover for much of my career. I appreciate it. Any mistakes in this work are my own.

The Shiel Collection at The University of Texas at Austin, with its spectacular holdings, has been the source of most of the primary materials that supported this study, including correspondence of Grant Richards, Lydia Furley Shiel, and others as referenced, including the letters from Shiel to John Lane in the John Lane Firm Archives. (A number of the documents are transcriptions originally made by John Gawsworth of material now lost or located in other repositories.)

Many of the Ransom Center staff contributed warmly to my requests. I must thank Pat Fox, Molly Schwartzburg, Rich Oram, and Richard Workman.

And thanks to Loraine Fletcher for information regarding the friendship of her husband, Ian Fletcher, with John Gawsworth.

To Maggie Parry, daughter of Kenneth Shiel, for sharing family photographs, much gratitude. Warm thanks to Barry Humphries for use of the only known letter from Ella D'Arcy to Shiel. And thanks to the University of Iowa, Iowa City, for use of the rare photograph of D'Arcy from Shiel's own archives (Gawsworth (Armstrong) / Shiel / Redonda Papers).

Thanks to The Henry W. and Albert A. Berg Collection of English and American Literature, The New York Public Library, for use of a note from M. P. Shiel to John Gawsworth relating to Theodore Wratislaw (A.L.S. to [Terence Ian Fytton] [Armstrong] [Horsham, England] penciled 10 September 1935); Bruce Kellner of the Estate of Carl Van Vechten, has made the Machen note available.

For access to the A. P. Watt and Company Records at the University of North Carolina at Chapel Hill, as well as the W. H. Chesson Collection at Brown University, I am extremely indebted.

There are others whom I have surely overlooked, but who will understand the many thanks they deserve. Thank you all!

H. B.

The Early Years

The collaboration of John D. Squires
is gratefully acknowledged

Chapter 1

"Whose glossy black to shame might bring . . ."

It was on Montserrat, in the port of Plymouth, now ravaged and buried by recent volcanic eruptions—where even the dead were covered again—that Matthew Phipps Shiell was born on 21 July 1865.[1] (He shortened his surname to "Shiel" after he commenced writing in London.) For five hundred years Montserrat was recognized as the loveliest of that sunlit chain of islands known as the Lesser Antilles (or Leeward Islands), even when storm-drenched or shaken by earthquake. Thirty-nine square miles of green, ragged mountains, long ago limned with forest and savannah, lime orchards and fields of cane, Montserrat was wracked at the end of the twentieth century by volcanic destruction. Its raw verdant beauty still holds in the north. Its south is sodden with ash.

Discovered by Columbus in 1493, Montserrat later was heavily settled by Irish, as were St. Christopher (more generally called St. Kitts) and Antigua. And increasing numbers of African slaves were imported to those islands throughout the eighteenth century to provide labor for the sugar industry. For years it was reputed that the Irish influence was so strong on Montserrat that the dark descendants of the island's white plantation owners and those who worked in bondage for them spoke with an Irish brogue. Linguists disagree. This was simply Caribbean Creole English. The lingering surnames were the chief legacy of the Irish.

Phipps's father, Matthew Dowdy Shiell, was a ship-owner, trader, shopkeeper, and lay Methodist minister. He appears to have been an

---

1. There has been some uncertainty as to whether Matthew Phipps Shiell was born on 20 or 21 July 1865. A copy of MPS's birth certificate that A. Reynolds Morse located on Plymouth, Montserrat, on his first trip "in quest of Redonda" in 1978 indicated that MPS was born on 20 July 1865, as listed by Christopher Skerrett, District Registrar. However, MPS consistently listed his birthday as 21 July throughout his life. His enrollment record at Harrison College bears the date 21 July. And on 21 July 1887, his father wrote him that his birthday had again arrived and apologized for not mentioning it in advance. A transcription of the birth certificate is pictured in A. Reynolds Morse, *The Quest for M. P. Shiel's Realm of Redonda* [23]; rpt. in his *Works* 3.606.

apprentice tailor in his youth. He was born 18 September 1824 and died 7 January 1888.[2] The history of his family is important in understanding the background from which M. P. Shiel grew.

Phipps's mother, Priscilla Ann Blake, was identified as "free" on her birth record, indicating that she was, at least to some degree, a descendant of slaves. (Her parents were William and Sarah (Harman) Blake, family names of long history in the Leeward Islands.) Priscilla was born 13 April 1828 and died 14 April 1910.[3] Phipps's sister Harriet Shiell later wrote of her:

> My mother's maiden name was Blake, hence "Cousin Blake" (Lilian's father). She, like myself, was dark and the wonder is that my father, a most prejudiced man, should have picked her out, but we know, don't we, that love will not be hindered. Her mother, Granny Blake, was I think what you call an octoroon, with hair hanging below her waist, "Whose glossy black to shame might bring the plumage of the raven's wing," as my brother was to say of mine once.
>
> And this old lady was very intellectual—for her day. She composed little poems by the hour and on a spur of the moment would criticize Captain Piper's poorer attempt to compose. Hear what she says, "Like fruit that's wanting to be riper are the lines of Captain Richard Piper."

The only formal information that is available regarding the birth

---

2. MDS wrote his son on 10 September 1887 that he would be 63 years old on 18 September. There is no other record extant that confirms or contradicts this information. "Burials in the Parish of St. Anthony in the Island of Montserrat 1888," where Matthew D. Shield [*sic*] is recorded as buried 7 January 1888, abode Plymouth, 63 years, ceremony performed by A. Jamison. Original holograph letter from MDS to his son 10 September 1887 (HRC). Photograph of burial record in Morse, *The Quest for M. P. Shiel's Realm of Redonda* [77]; rpt. in his *Works* 3.660.

The most detailed account of MPS's family is contained in a letter from MPS's sister Harriet Garry Shiell to her niece, Olive Horsford, of 2 February 1932 (typed copy, HRC). This letter answers many of the questions raised over the years—including those by MPS himself!—about their ancestry. All references in this work attributed to Harriet Shiell about these family details are based on that document.

3. Photograph of birth certificate for Priscilla reproduced in Morse, *The Quest for Redonda,* and burial record information provided in same source ([77]; rpt. in his *Works* 3.660). The details that follow about her are contained in Harriet's letter to Olive Horsford mentioned above.

and death dates of Matthew and Priscilla exist in the few parish records that have survived when A. Reynolds Morse and Jon Wynne-Tyson were able to photograph them in 1979. When T. Savage English tried to search out the "records of Montserrat" in the Court House of Plymouth to compile his typescript history of the island in the 1920s, he noted: "Many of these documents are in fragments eaten by insects and rotted by the soakings they have had when the roof over them has been wrecked by the hurricanes . . ." Subsequent hurricanes and volcanic destruction have left these records only extant in this work by English. The originals have been destroyed. With the recent destruction of Plymouth by volcanic fire and ash, it can only be hoped that the remaining records of church and court have been moved to a place of security elsewhere on Montserrat.

Both of Phipps's parents may have been of a mixed racial heritage, although there is not enough evidence regarding his father to be certain of this. No birth record for him has survived and his children did not appear to know who his mother was. Harriet Shiell said that her father "was of course illegitimate—a rather intellectual man for his day but with a temper of the devil and so stuck up he was called the 'Governor.'" "His father," she said, "was Irish, James Phipps Shiell, by name, an aristocrat, I think." From what she had to say of her father, including his selection of Priscilla Blake for a wife, he was likely "white" in appearance, if his blood in part of color.

Some bloodlines had so thinned by the time of Phipps's birth that shade of color and financial circumstances were not as distinctive arbiters for accepted social levels as once they were. By this time, only some fifty white families remained on Montserrat, but there were hundreds of free men of color who carried the same family name as generations of interred white West Indians.[4] It is not known what definition of "white" was used for this census. As the number of whites decreased, through emigration and intermarriage, the island's population began darkening again, so that the one-time presence of the white Irish majority and the children of concubinage might never have been.

---

4. *Caribbeana: Being Miscellaneous Papers Relating to the History, Genealogy, Topography, and Antiquities of the British West Indies*, ed. Vere Langford Oliver (Toronto, ON: CanDoo Creative Publishing, 2000; 8 vols.). This set was originally published at the beginning of the 20th century and is an indispensable resource for West Indian studies and genealogical research.

One thing is apparent from these family histories: many of the black antecedents from which the mixed-blood West Indians emerged were absolutely brilliant people, for all their differences in culture, their superstitions, and their obeisance to the rules of captivity forced upon them.

Many travel writers visited the West Indies during the early years of Matthew Shiell's and Priscilla Blake's youth, and each added description and dimension to the earth in which the Shiell family was born and now lies at rest. When Henry Coleridge, the nephew of Samuel Taylor Coleridge, visited Montserrat on a trip to improve his health in 1825, he complained loudly at the ducking he endured at Plymouth while trying to get from his ship onto the shore. There was no deep-water port to ease the passage. "Though a jetty or pier might be constructed with a trifling expense by simply rolling a few large blocks of the stone, which abounds on the spot, into the water, yet these provoking people would rather that themselves and every human being, who visits or leaves their island, should get drenched, than stir one step towards erecting it."

Coleridge liked the turtle soup that lay like a feather on one's stomach. It required serving up in a capacious tin shell, well lined with a thin crust of pastry. He decried the refusal of religious instruction for most of the island's 6,396 slaves, especially those the property of "a noted Papist of great influence."[5] But he complimented Mr. Luckcock, who was able to teach the catechism to some few of the slaves and "who also preaches and expounds portions of Scripture" with a frequency depending on the slaves' proximity to Plymouth. (Benjamin "Luckock" signed the birth record for Priscilla Blake.) Coleridge commented, without apology, on the evil that "the Methodists . . . have done upon the long run both at home and abroad." The Anglican faith was being overwhelmed.

He admired the cloud-topped peaks sliding into meadow-green savannahs and the miraculous soufrières, where water boiled and clouds of sulfur fumed. The scarlet-feathered hibiscus and drooping amaryllis were lusher than the flowers of home, and the lime and orchard trees that lined the paths added a darker green as contrast. This was the place and the years in which Matthew Dowdy Shiell and Priscilla Blake were born.

5. Coleridge 171. It is likely the "noted Papist" he mentions was Dudley Semper, who had all his slaves baptized by Fr. O'Hannan, a Catholic priest, in 1824.

Harriet's comment and other evidence indicates that Matthew Dowdy Shiell was a natural son of James Phipps Shiell whom M. P. Shiel identified in the 1929 version of his "About Myself" as "Sir" James Phipps Shiel, his "great-grandfather," a doctor and namesake. (In fact, James Phipps Shiell had no title, nor was he a doctor. He was the son of a wealthy progenitor of the family, Queely Shiell, of St. Kitts and Montserrat, and was Phipps's grandfather.)

The most interesting description of M. P. Shiel(l)'s possible origins has proceeded from the genealogical research of Richard Shiell and Dorothy Anderson, of Australia, on the Shiell family.[6] Their great-grandfather was William Shiell (1823–1899), natural son of William Shiell (1785–1853), longtime member and president of the Montserrat Legislative Council and a prominent, if insidious, plantation manager. He too was a son of Queely Shiell. Mary McNamara, probably William's mistress, who operated a ships' chandler store on Plymouth, was young William's mother. (Her sister, Lucy, was a schoolteacher—"Headmistress" according to Anderson and Shiell—on the island in 1841.) After apprenticeship as a West Indian seaman, the younger William Shiell emigrated to London and sailed on to Australia in 1853.[7] Mary had probably died by 1853, perhaps in this same year that William's father and his wife died, a period marked by vicious attacks of smallpox and cholera in the Indies.

William might well have crewed on his own relatives' vessels. Before the death of young William's grandfather, Queely Shiell, in 1847, and his own departure from Montserrat for Australia in 1853, a ship, the *Queely Shiell,* is recorded as having arrived 24 March 1841 at Bermuda (nationality Bermuda) under Captain John T. Watlington. The ship stopped at Montserrat in 1842 and arrived August 19, 1843 at Vera Cruz (nationality England) under Captain Watlington.[8] One must assume this was the property of the Shiell we know, and that given these distant ports of call it was a larger vessel than those that were con-

6. Richard Shiell and Dorothy Anderson, *Shiell Genealogy: Essays.* The Possible Origins of Matthew Phipps Shiell. web.archive.org/web/20050221194412/alangullette.com/lit/shiel/family/PossibleOrigins.htm

7. Anderson and Shiell, *Montserrat to Melbourne: The Story of a Shiell Family* 9.

8. "Magellan—The Ships Encyclopedia," www.cimorelli.com/magellan/default.htm This source lists the 1841 and 1843 visits. Dorothy Anderson observed that the *Montserrat Water Journals* notes the ship's arrival in Montserrat sometime in 1842 under Captain Watlington.

structed simply to ply the Antilles. Its call at Montserrat seems significant. This could help corroborate the Australian Shiell family tradition that William had opportunities to visit South America, California, and other distant ports before he left Montserrat for London.

Taking advantage of family shipping to provide an occupation for the young William would have made good sense, and could have provided the background that enabled him to pass so easily the nautical Master's Certificate in London. His father William Shiell could have helped place him before the mast. The shipping business of his mother and her seafaring McNamara family could also have helped provide an opportunity for him to learn a skill that was lacking for so many in those impoverished islands at the time.

To sort out this confusion of family relationships, it is useful to understand a well-accepted practice of human property owners during that time. Concubinage was simply another ugly product of West Indian slavery, routinely practiced by plantation owners and managers but widely condemned by the increasingly influential young Methodist Church. In place of the Roman Catholicism to which the original white Irish population clung, and the official Church of England that lay over the populace, Methodism rapidly expanded from its original island base in Antigua and began to dominate the religious life of slaves and the increasing number of free persons of African descent in the West Indies—"people of colour," as they were willing to describe themselves.

It was from the practice of concubinage that many young West Indians found themselves of obvious mixed bloodlines from the end of the eighteenth century until late in the nineteenth. This represented a precarious economic and social situation for everyone. English law forbade the right of inheritance for illegitimate children. Some were provided an education and moved into apprenticeships or basic service positions. Young women might hope for positions as household servants. Others were simply dropped back into plantation stews or given wooden hoes. Before the middle of that century, most of the "white" plantation owners, managers, and their family members had removed to England or elsewhere, leaving an increasingly "colored" population, and sons from illegitimate lines, to assume power, responsibility, and enormous problems throughout the economically distressed West Indies.

The Rev. John Horsford, of St. Vincent (a self-described "man of colour" and likely relative of Samuel Horsford, who married into the Shiell family), wrote in his book, *A Voice from the West Indies* (1856), that even at that late date, "Concubinage exists still in the West Indies. The antiquated and iniquitous system adopted by the planters, for every overseer or manager to keep a mistress, still largely prevails . . ." The situation was improving, however, said Rev. Horsford, thanks in large measure to the missionary-driven Methodist church and a growing sense of morality among the former slaves and their families.[9]

> Respectable coloured gentlemen generally marry their equals in point of intellect and character. The fact is, a just and honourable ambition has for a long time fired the coloured classes, to be as well qualified for society, or for business, as are the whites, who have long monopolized every situation of any emolument or influence. Complexional differences being now swept away by statute, and, in our older Colonies at least, the recollection of them being detested by all the whites possessed of high-mindedness and honour . . .[10]

It was within these moral and social conditions that members of the Shiell and other West Indian families originally engaged in this heinous practice, within which the complications of family relationships must be understood, though they confuse us still.

William (1785–1853), John (1788–1847), and James Phipps Shiell (1790–1834) were the known sons of Queely Shiell (1755–1847), the major plantation and slave owner on Montserrat in the early nineteenth century. In 1824, Queely owned 656 slaves, by far the most of any plantation proprietor on Montserrat. He had been comptroller of customs from 1805 to 1827. His parents, the great-great-grandparents of M. P. Shiell, were very probably William Shiell and Margaret Queely (daughter of John Queely, attorney), who married by license in Basseterre, St. Kitts, on 17 June 1756. An earlier Shiell, Luc (or Lucan) Shiell, was a major slaver out of France. Some of the Queely Shiell family wealth may have come from traffic in slavery. Slaves from some source continued to pour into the West Indies until the trade's abolishment by Great Britain in 1807.[11]

---

9. John Horsford, *A Voice from the West Indies* 55.

10. Ibid.

11. Shiell and Anderson, *Shiell Genealogy: Essays.* Queely Shiel (1755–1847). William Shiell (1785–1853). John Shiell (1788–1847). James Phipps Shiell (1790–

The mother of these three sons was most likely Ann Gordon, from an exceedingly prominent family, who married Queely about 1783. In addition to the three known sons, a daughter Maria died from smallpox a few months after birth (on 16 September 1792), and daughter Eleanor married an Allen, probably William. Since Ann Gordon Shiell was deceased, Eleanor inherited most of what was left of her father Queely's actual wealth when he died at age ninety-two at his Clarges Street residence in London. His debt-ridden estates were left to his two sons, William and John (James was deceased), with William assuming their management, since John had died a few months earlier than his father.[12]

When Quakers Joseph Sturge and Thomas Harvey visited the West Indies in 1836 to review the condition of the "negro population" following the advent of manumission, Sturge could only exclaim over a situation in which the president who administered the government of Montserrat was also a planter and apprentice holder. He controlled all appointments, including those of well-paid magistrate and serjeant of police. These positions oversaw one another and could be held *by the same person,* a fit situation for abuse. And the freed slaves "had no voice to plead their own wrongs."[13] The worst results of such inbred excesses are visible in the machinations of William Shiell, Phipps's great-uncle.

William served on the Montserrat Council for many years, from 1808 to 1850, when he resigned because of insolvency (and several charges hanging over his head). He served as elected council president from 1834 to 1846, and as appointed administrator of the Island Government from 1840 to 1846. He managed his father Queely's plantations after Queely left to live in London sometime after 1827. Shiell and Anderson describe his duties and own property thus:[14]

> William Shiell was listed as the manager of 16 sugar estates and a number of stock estates (H of C 1848, V45). These included 7 belonging to his father Queely valued at £44,700 and 5 belonging to

---

1834) alangullette.com/lit/shiel/. T. Savage English reported that Queely owned 655 slaves on Montserrat and one attending his daughter in St. Vincent (280).

12. Ibid.

13. Sturge 87–88.

14. Shiell and Anderson, *Shiell Genealogy: Essays.* William Shiell (1785–1853) alangullette.com/lit/shiel/family/Shiell_William.htm

the "Heirs of Dudley Semper," valued at £27,500 (these heirs would probably have included William's wife and his surviving children). William was Lessee of another 5 estates valued at £28,500. He was Executor for another 3 properties valued at £23,200. These prices were quite unrealistic as the properties all carried heavy debts and were virtually un-saleable. He personally owned only one small stock estate (Morris's) valued at £1000.

It appears that William Shiell never got too far from questionable financial practices. Professor Douglas Hall has described how in 1846 after the president of Montserrat, Edward Dacre Baynes, went to London on leave, William Shiell was named acting president in his place. A Friendly Society, established under auspices of the Anglican clergyman on Montserrat, had foundered and a review of the Society's accounts by President Baynes indicated its accounts were short £300.[15]

Mr. Shiell was asked by the governor of the Leewards to investigate. He produced papers showing that the shortage was only £4 17s 7d. During the same year, President Baynes had reported to the Colonial Office that an inspection of the island's treasury accounts revealed that £3,000 sterling was missing; the treasurer, a merchant, had substituted bills of exchange for cash from time to time against accounts he held against a London firm. Shiell was again asked to investigate.

He reported, "For more than a year past, a very irregular system of conducting the affairs of the Treasury seems to have prevailed at Montserrat. I mean by this, that the Treasurer has resided at a distance of ten miles from town, in a mountainous [part of the] country, and managed the estates of a Merchant, which Merchant in return transacted the affairs of the Treasury in his own Country House." (The treasurer was replaced in office by Edmund Semper, a *relative* of a member of the investigating committee!)

Professor Hall's explanation for how these numerous travesties of morality and responsibility could develop was that it was not a matter of political differences among groups; it was a matter of getting along in a tiny island society, where everyone was known to one another, and indeed were (as Baynes said) "generally connected either by blood, or marriage."

15. Hall 159–60.

"The prizes here were not administrative authority and legislative power, but rather personal privilege and perquisites," Hall states.[16]

A good sense of William's reputation and the workings of financial, economic, and political enterprises on the tiny island, and the relationships between families and individuals, can be found in this letter that Anderson and Shiell obtained from official colonial records. By this time the value of sugar had so heavily declined, as had the value of land, that William was beginning to feel the weight of heavy losses from the debt-burdened estates left to him by his father Queely Shiell.[17]

President Baynes alerted the governor of the Leeward Islands regarding William's problems and his ambition:

> Letter from Edward D. Baynes President, to the Governor in Chief of the Leeward Islands (Mr. I. M. Higginson Esquire)
>
> Government House Montserrat 9th April 1850
> Confidential
> Sir,
>
> Circumstances have occurred since I addressed Your Excellency my confidential despatch of the 28th ultimo that render it, I think advisable that I should communicate again with Your Excellency on the subject. An overwhelming number of executions have been recorded against Mr. Shiell the President of the Council, and the Marshal has in consequence levied on the stock of every property belonging to, or rented by him in the island. The result will be, that as he is, under one designation, or another, proprietor, lessee, attorney, Receiver, or Executor, in possession of 17 out of the 35 Sugar Estates in the island that what from the want of cattle and want of means half of the growing crops will not be taken off and the cane in all probability will be left to perish on the ground. At the mean time the labourers remain unpaid and have such large sums due to them while there is not the remotest chance of their ever obtaining even their half of the sugar belonging to the negroes on the properties marked on the metayer system has been seized. It is to be feared with this example of bad faith before their eyes; the labourers on the other properties conducted on this plan will throw up the work on their hands.

16. Ibid.

17. Shiell and Anderson, *Shiell Genealogy: Essays.* William Shiell (1785–1853) alangullette.com/lit/shiel/family/Shiell_William.htm.

This man is possibly the evil genius of the colony, not only has he by bad management ruined himself but he drags down the island by him. It would be hazardous under any circumstances to allow him ever again to administer the government.

I stated in my last that he interfered too much with the Treasury. I have since learned that during my absence he was not only in the habit of forcing the Treasurer to pay the Treasury paper in his hands before all other demands but even in preference to the prior lien prescribed by law such as the amounts allotted for the maintenance of the poor on one of which occasions Mr. Burns a Member of the Board of Guardians resigned his seat.

When I returned here in August 1847 I found that the people refused to pay the cattle tax then due. Mr. Shiell the Administrator of the Government in conjunction with Mr. Armstrong and others having spread about a report that the tax was illegal. Under the resistance manifested against this impost when Your Excellency was in the island, Mr. Shiell had actually encouraged the people to oppose it by suffering his name to be included in the levy warrant, for every estate under his charge.

Before he left Montserrat in August 1847 and whilst still in the Administration of the Government he drew on his father the late Mr. Queely Shiell for £419-13-7 to pay the interest on the loan from Government. Being in London when the Bill arrived, he went to Messrs Kensington of Mincing Lane who had it in possession, and there accepted the bill which he himself had drawn as his father's attorney in Montserrat, which he was, alleging that he was also his father's attorney in England, which he was not. I send a copy of the original bill which is in my possession. It was of course protested and returned unpaid. I however compelled him to pay the Commissioners on his return.

I wish specially to observe that in communicating these facts, they are by no means to be received in the light of charges now brought against Mr. Shiell, but as given simply in order to afford Your Excellency the fullest information on Your Excellency's question as to the expediency of Mr. Shiell being again allowed to administer the Government.

I may however remark in conclusion that setting aside the additional and immediate blow, the country is likely to receive from the failure of Mr. Shiell and the too probable destruction in consequence of half the crop spared by the drought his removal and that of Mr. Trott who is in similar circumstances from the list of proprietors both of them so long the drawback and the deadweight of the colony and the inveterate opposers of everything in the shape of improvement will be the most fortunate event that can befall the country supposing their large and valuable estates pass into the hands of parties possessed of capital to carry on the cultivation on a wiser system and more liberal scale.

I have the honor to be
Edward D. Baynes
President

William's derelictions are so well documented, and provide such a vivid picture of Montserrat life in the early nineteenth century, that it is useful to include these legal records of the man who was M. P. Shiel's great-uncle. While President Baynes was cautioning against the reappointment of William as president of the Legislative Council, William was busily soliciting several important positions, while claiming to have been swindled out of his property at a mere fraction of its value. Anderson and Shiell discovered that to help establish that claim, he was anonymously posting the following announcement in newspapers throughout the West Indies in late 1850.[18]

Montserrat

. . . .

Lately sold in this Island, by Marshal's Sale, the following undermentioned Sugar and Cotton Estates, including Stock of every description, with a variety of Furniture, Silver and Plated articles, &c., &c., three Houses in the Town of Plymouth, with Plantation Stores attached, and Lumber Yards to two of them, Twenty hogsheads of Sugar, and Three puncheons Molasses, the whole of which did not exceed the amount, or realize more than twelve hundred pounds sterling.

Six Sugar Estates comprising by estimation, 1000 acres of cane, pasture and provision land, with two Wind Mills and two Horse Mills, in complete repair, three sets of Works, all recently repaired, with Clarifyer and Coppers in them, sufficiently capable of boiling off annually, 400 heavy hogsheads Sugar, with large Still, Condenser, and Worm attached to one of them, also a Dwelling House, containing large dining room and drawing Rooms, five bed Chambers, with a Marble Gallery around the house with Out offices attached, all recently repaired, and

18. Ibid.

a large Garden contiguous.

Four of these Sugar Estates gave the late Proprietor, when Sugar was very high, £20,000 sterling in one year, and for several consecutive years, upwards of £5000 per annum after deducting expenses.

Two Cotton and Provision Estates, situated at the South part of the Island, containing upwards of 600 acres of Land, with fifty Mules, one hundred and fifty head of Cattle, forty Asses, several Horses, and a flock of Sheep, with Furniture, Silver and Plated articles, an extensive and valuable Library, a four wheel Carriage and Gig with Harness complete to the former, twenty hogsheads of Sugar, three puncheons Molasses, the whole of which did not sell for more than £1200 Sterling. This enumeration of Property specified, and which has been sacrificed for one fortieth part of its value, is only brought under the notice of the Public to shew the manner in which property is confiscated in this island, when sold and brought under the hammer of a Marshal's Sale.

This generation of the Shiell family had not been wanting for a long time. But William now faced absolute ruin. Richmond Estate, the luxurious likely homesite of Queely when he was a resident of the island, was probably the most valuable of the plantations sold.

Queely's second son, John Shiell (1788–1847), commenced studies in law at Lincoln's Inn, London, in 1808 and was admitted to the bar in 1813; he served on the Montserrat Assembly, later as King's Council, Antigua, and became chief justice of Antigua in 1844.[19] He appears to have been the most responsible of Queely's sons.

James Phipps Shiell, grandfather of Phipps, brother of John and William (the "evil genius of the colony"), was appointed customs search officer in 1811 and acting comptroller of customs in 1828, and later comptroller until his death in 1834. His father was pensioned off from that position in 1827 at the age of 72. In 1831, James also carried the title of "Tide Surveyor." He served as an elected member of the Legislative Assembly (the Lower House) from 1823 to his death. A once-extant local record indicated that James attended the marriage of his brother William Shiell and Mary Cabey Semper in 1826. This would have been two years after Matthew Dowdy Shiell was born. James married Elizabeth Carey in either late 1825 or early 1826, and

19. Ibid.

they had two known legitimate children, Henry (b. 1826) and Mary Ann (b. 1830). Both migrated in later years to Australia.

Apparently, however, James Phipps Shiell was never a doctor or naval officer, as some Shiell family descendants believed, nor was he a knight, as his grandson, Matthew Phipps Shiell, said.[20] Neither does he appear to have ever accumulated the wealth of his brother William prior to the bankruptcies that began to ruin the absentee landowners and plantation managers after the decline of the sugar industry and following the manumission of slaves in 1834, the year that James Phipps Shiell died. There is no doubt, however, that James was able to use the power of the offices he held to gather a number of personal benefits, including all the privileges of concubinage.

Anderson and Shiell have gathered documents from Colonial Office and other records that suggest, with imaginative detective work, that Phipps's father, Matthew Dowdy Shiell, was the son of James Phipps Shiell and a slave child, Priscilla, one-time property of Mrs. Sarah Dowdy.[21] Matthew's parentage could have derived from a more ordinary relationship between James Phipps Shiell and a mistress, but the facts gathered by Anderson and Shiell provide compelling support for the tragic story that follows.

Priscilla's mother took her daughter and ran away with other slaves to the Dutch island of St. Eustatius early in 1823, apparently to escape the ownership of Dudley Semper who had acquired them from foreclosure on Mrs. Sarah Dowdy's property. Some were captured and returned to Montserrat in the fall of 1823. Others were not found and returned until January 1824, when they were placed in the custody of Edmund and Dudley Semper and James Phipps Shiell, who said they could identify the runaway slave Priscilla from personal knowledge. This suggests that the slave girl might have been attractive enough to catch James's attention earlier at the Dowdy home, south of Plymouth. She would have been of mixed blood, but very fair to have had a son with Matthew's appearance, and very handsome to have captured the attention of James so strongly. There were certainly

20. Shiell and Anderson, *Shiell Genealogy: Essays.* James Phipps Shiell (1790–1834) alangullette.com/lit/shiel/family/Shiell_James_Phipps.htm.

21. Shiell and Anderson, *Shiell Genealogy: Essays.* The Possible Origins of Matthew Phipps Shiell. https://web.archive.org/web/20050221194412/alangullette.com/lit/shiel/family/PossibleOrigins.htm

hundreds of other young black slave girls on Montserrat that had no escape from ravishment or concubinage.[22]

Captain J. M. Saba played an official part by transferring the captured slaves from Dutch government hands into those of Captain Allers of the British sloop *Dasher,* who delivered them into the official, but unscrupulous, hands of Montserrat authority. He provided for the record the following document:

Letter from the Governor of St. Eustatius,
regarding the return of several runaway slaves.

27th January 1824
Government House St Eustatius.
Sir,

I have delivered over to Captn Allers of the British Sloop "Dasher" four Slaves by name Simon, Ino Matthews, Ned and William which it appears are the same of whom Your honor gave me Notice under date the 24th July last and which were at the time searched for in vain.

The three first were concerned with nine other Slaves of this Colony in cutting out of the Road of the Dutch Sloop "John and Anna" in the Night of the 30th November last. They were pursued and fortunately taken by an Expedition, fitted out by this Government, off Porto Rico, and brought back to this place where they have been tried and punished according to our Laws.

William did not go with them and returns without having been in anywise punished. Three Slaves complain much of ill treatment and some of them bear evident marks of the truth of their assertions.

There is likewise aboard the "Dasher" a female Child, Slave to Mr. D. Semper of your Island, whom it appears, had been clandestinely brought here by Her Mother, a Slave formerly of Mrs. Dowdy. She is sent up to her Master by his Attorney here.

Capt Allers has my direction to report to Your Honor immediately on his arrival and you will direct him farther how to proceed.

I have the Honor to be
Sir, Your Honor's Most Obedient Servt
(signed) J. M. Saba
Post Captain in His Netherland Majesty's Navy
Governor of St. Eustatius

---

22. Ibid.

The slave child Priscilla and the other slaves could not have been delivered into worse hands. If Matthew Dowdy Shiell's mother was indeed the slave Priscilla, she figured as a victim in a matter of sophisticated thievery as well as possible rape. The matter would have been masterminded by some of the most prominent men in the Lesser Antilles, all for the sake of owning and victimizing human property. As Shiell and Anderson develop the story from Colonial Office records and the correspondence from the governor of St. Eustatius regarding the capture of the runaways, the most unsavory aspects of the punishment of slaves and their degradation are apparent from the governor's description of their treatment. They were formally received just as matter of fact by officers of Montserrat and, as valuable property, simply disappeared back into the circumstances from which they had tried to escape.[23]

James Phipps Shiell and the brothers Semper were more than glad to receive these runaway slaves and to swear as to their version of who owned them:

Certificate acknowledging the receipt
of runaway slaves from St. Eustatius and signed by
Edmund and Dudley Semper and James Phipps Shiell

Montserrat 30th January 1824

Mr. Dudley Semper, Edmond Semper Junior and James Phipps Shiell of the Island of Montserrat. Do swear. That the Negroe Slaves just arrived in the Sloop Dasher Ino D. Allers Master are truly and Bonafide the same Slaves as are described in the several Certificates of Registration herewith produced. And that the said Slaves did in the Month of July last 1823 Elope without leave, from this Island taking with them the Boat the Property of a Mr. John Brambles of this Island. And upon receiving advice from a Mr. Martine of the Island of St Eustatius informing us of the Arrest and Detention of the said Slaves did Hire and dispatch the Aforesaid Sloop for the Purpose of bringing them to this Island. So help me God.

(signed and sworn)
Ed. Semper
James Phipps Shiell. (Attorney to the Representatives of James Neave, Deceased)
Dudley Semper

23. Ibid.

The slave child Priscilla then disappears from official record, but confirming the basic facts of this incident, the West Indian scholar Riva Berleant-Schiller describes the story in this manner:

> Despite Dudley Semper's high standing with the Colonial Office, neither he nor his brother (Michael), both of whom were merchants, come across as savory or principled persons. They had a reputation for bill-buying and lending at high interests, and appear in many contexts as sharp operators motivated by political or financial expedience.[24]

She continues:

> In a suspicious succession of events in 1823 the two brothers foreclosed a mortgage on the property of Sarah Dowdy. She had put it up as security for a loan from the Sempers to one of her relatives, who was also kin to the Sempers. When the loan was not paid, the Sempers claimed Dowdy's property. Fearing destitution and arrest, she fled with her twenty slaves on an uncleared vessel to St. Eustatius, pursued by Dudley Semper. Dowdy was defying the laws abolishing the slave trade, but the Sempers appear to have conspired with their common kinsman to do her out of her property.[25]

The identity of this common kinsman of the Sempers and Mrs. Dowdy is intriguing, but unknown. The loan was apparently made in 1822 or earlier. It would be especially interesting if the Shiell family was involved, but that does not appear to be the case. Dudley Semper would soon become a relative in-law to William Shiell when his daughter, Mary Cabey Semper, married Queely's son William. But Dudley hated William so strongly that he expressly stipulated in his will that

> it is my intention that no children or child of the said William Shiell shall have any part of my property . . . because of the increasing hostility and opposition of the said William Shiell . . . upon all occasions to one and mine notwithstanding my earnest endeavors to be upon that kind and friendly footing with him that our near and intimate connection required . . ."

Mary Cabey Semper Shiell and her children could not benefit from

24. Riva Berleant-Schiller 270–71, 277–78.

25. Ibid.

her father's estate while William Shiell was alive.[26]

There was no religious dispute involved. The heavily Irish white population on Montserrat had Catholic roots, if sometimes hidden ones, for the Anglican Church was the only officially recognized faith on the islands. There was not even an official recognition of the Catholic Church until 1826. The Sempers were Catholic, as Queely Shiell has been identified at times, but the burial of his infant daughter Maria is commemorated by a monumental inscription in the St. George Church of Bloomsbury, a Church of the Establishment.

In 1824, Fr. O'Hanan, a Catholic priest who was on the island from 1824 to 1828, baptized all slaves of the Kirwan, Cannonier, Semper, and Hamilton families. The omission of the Shiell slaves is significant, since Queely was the major slave owner. This is another indication that the Shiell family was not Catholic. Also, in 1840 "Shield, His Honour the President, Montserrat" contributed 10/8/8d to the Wesleyan Mission Fund.[27] So William Shiell endorsed Methodism, if not all its moral tenets. It appears that it took only one generation for many of the white residents of the Lesser Antilles to change their religious affiliation from Anglican or Catholic to Methodist, but many never changed the ill way they treated slaves or free men of color. Meanwhile, both slaves and freemen were flocking into Wesleyan churches, and it became the religious haven for the olive-blooded descendants of the original Irish settlers.

Dudley Semper most likely never forgot the fact that he was relieved in 1816 of the choice offices that he held on Montserrat, that of island treasurer and a seat on the Bench of Justices. And neither William Shiell nor several other members of the island Legislative Council supported him in his financial loss and embarrassment. The Colonial Office soon restored the offices to him, but the most odious offense that William offered Dudley was not political, economic, or a difference over religion, but his marriage to Dudley's daughter, Mary, in June 1824, with the birth of a son two months later![28] This combi-

---

26. Semper, "Last Will," 3–4.

27. Wheeler 35; Demets 5. Original source for President's contribution misplaced.

28. Shiell and Anderson, *Shiell Genealogy: Essays.* William Shiell (1785–1853) [and] John Shiell (1788–1847). alangullette.com/lit/shiel/family/Shiell_William.htm alangullette.com/lit/shiel/family/Shiell_John.htm.

nation of circumstances clearly represents the backdrop to Dudley Semper's will that excluded William or any of his children from Dudley's estate.

Both versions of the story of the Dowdy slaves' escape and capture, and of related events, complement each other pretty nicely. Michael Semper claimed that his brother Dudley had purchased Priscilla from Mrs. Dowdy in September 1822. Riva Berleant-Schiller suggests that this was a fiction to establish prior ownership of Priscilla by Dudley so that he could claim her following her capture. Matthew Dowdy Shiell's birth date (18 September 1824) follows by almost nine months the date of the slaves' capture and their return to Montserrat in January 1824. That appears to validate the possibility that Matthew could have been the son, whether by ravishment or concubinage consent, of James Phipps Shiell and Priscilla of the Dowdy household as speculated by Anderson and Shiell. Even if Matthew were aware of these facts, he might not have wanted to describe such sordid details to his children, but might have suggested instead a grander picture of their grandfather as an alleged distinguished descendant of old Irish kings. It is also quite possible that Sarah or another member of the Dowdy household was either mistress to or concubine of James Phipps Shiell and the mother of Matthew. His middle name, Dowdy, did not come to him by accident. It was frequently the name of the mother's family that was bestowed on sons.

In any event, William Shiell (b. 1823), the illegitimate son of William Shiell and Mary McNamara, and Matthew Dowdy Shiell (b. 1824), the illegitimate son of James Phipps Shiell, would have been cousins.[29]

As a young man, M. D. Shiell apparently trained as an apprentice tailor. He then became involved in the shipping trade, partnering with Peter Irish to carry goods between St. Kitts, Antigua, Nevis, Montserrat, and Barbados. Based on research undertaken in Montserrat's Shipping Registers in the Public Record Office by Shiell and Anderson relating to the Shiell family, the 24-ton schooner *Jane* was constructed on Montserrat in 1850 by Anthony Meade, was owned by Matthew Dowdy Shiell, "a tailor of the Parish of St. Anthony (Town of Plymouth)," and was registered in Barbados in 1851.[30] The only ship regis-

29. Anderson and Shiell, *Montserrat to Melbourne.*

30. Notes by Dorothy Anderson, gathered from Colonial Office records for re-

tered on Montserrat in 1852 was the 59-ton schooner *Agnes,* previously registered on Barbados 11 May 1852, but transferred to the ownership of Peter Irish and Matthew Dowdy Shiell, "merchants of Plymouth."[31]

The establishment of a shipping partnership with Peter Irish would have helped Matthew develop his own trading and merchandise store business. The cost of acquiring interests in such a vessel is unknown, but since James Phipps Shiell died in 1834, when Matthew was ten, he had no opportunity to help even if he had wished. Grandfather Queely and Uncle John had both died in 1847, and would have had no interest in this possible dropping of a slave girl. The finances of his uncle, former Council President William Shiell, were in ruins, and he was more concerned with finding an appropriate position for his legitimate eldest son, a teenager, and re-establishing a means for his own livelihood.

If Matthew Dowdy Shiell were the illegitimate child of James Phipps Shiell and a slave or concubine, he would probably have been left in the care of his mother and her family, even though James Phipps Shiell might have contributed in some way to his support. If Matthew's mother had ties to Mrs. Sarah Dowdy or her family, it might well be that he spent his childhood and youth with them, possibly apprenticing as a tailor until that contract was done and an opportunity for betterment appeared.

The leap from making a livelihood as a "tailor" to that of shipowner and merchant appears to be a formidable one. It only seems possible with financial assistance from some relative who had an interest in young Matthew Dowdy Shiell, the product of an illegitimate line. There is no known candidate unless it was the Dowdy family or the family of his wife, Priscilla Blake. Since it appears that Matthew and Priscilla were married about 1846, the latter is a possibility. There is no information available about this particular Blake family, except that there was a link to slavery through it as indicated on Priscilla's birth record. The white Blake family had a long and major role in the history of the Leeward Islands. However, there is nothing in the contemporary records to indicate that William Blake owned either property or slaves. An intriguing possible answer as to how these events

---

search relating to her great-great-grandfather, William Shiell (1823–1899), and shared by Richard Shiell with Harold Billings by fax on 23 April 2004.

31. Ibid.

and relationships developed, consistent with the known facts, is suggested by Dr. Richard Shiell, the Australian descendant of William Shiell, the young cousin of Matthew Dowdy Shiell.

Dr. Shiell speculates that William Blake may have been a tailor to whom the young Matthew Dowdy Shiell was apprenticed. Since William Blake is not listed as having owned property or slaves, and as a probable man of color, the role of tailor would have been appropriate for him. If Matthew were apprenticed to Blake at the usual age of fourteen, the completion of a seven-year contract at age twenty-one would have allowed him to accept an apprentice of his own and permitted marriage. This would have occurred in 1846, consistent with my own speculation regarding the possible date of his marriage to Priscilla Blake. Their relationship might have been fostered through Matthew's closeness to her family during his apprenticeship.

Perhaps there was some resource that came to Matthew through the Blake family, igniting the financial spark that allowed him to partner with Peter Irish in the purchase of a boat and a move into shipping and other commercial enterprises. The lack of facts simply does not allow for more than imagining such intriguing possibilities.

These suggestions of fatherhood and kinship are probably as close as we can come at the present in determining the family origins of Matthew Phipps Shiel.

Chapter 2

"'a flushed brown' harmony"

Phipps says that he was told (with perhaps more than a faint intimation of divine portent) that his birth was a day of earthquake and storm. "The sheet lightning, like a sheeted ghost, came peering into the chamber, winking a million to the second. And with lullaby rough enough, this mixture of Heaven and Earth and Hell which I call 'I,' and sometime 'We,' came out and began to cry."[1] This was his fate, that all events betokened (to him) the tap of Favor's finger on his shoulder. His family bears the blame for spoiling him as they did.

Phipps described his father as a strong, turbulent man who roared about like a Methodist prophet, ruling his house in an Old Testament manner. Harriet Shiell's memory certainly confirmed this description. My own impression is that it must have been of men like him that the Psalmist sang: "They that go down to the sea in ships, that do business in great waters; these are the works of the Lord, and his wonders in the deep." Let his son describe him further:

> Never can be effaced from my memory that red, heroic figure, as of Prometheus, those outcries of his, those mutterings, and, I should like to add, cursings; but, to tell the truth, my poor father would not curse, though could not but have wanted to, having the extraordinary taste to be a Methodist preacher, not by profession, be it said, but of that kind they call "local preachers," his trade being that of shipowner, and many ships he had on the sea . . .[2]

To the boy it appeared that his father was willing to engage the very elements and take pride in challenging the worst of West Indian storms. He must have assumed mythological dimensions to the boy, while he also must have appeared in his Methodist guise to commune with God himself:

> When there was a storm and all men cowered awe-struck, and the bounds of Heaven and Earth were lost, ah, then was my father's heyday! *His* heart alone was strong: for the storm was his brother, and

1. MPS, "About Myself" (1901) 630.

2. Ibid.

own father's son with him. I, though then very young, can remember him stalking in a loose robe up and down the travailing house, in the very mood of that bellowing throat without, like Lear himself, with "That's right! How grand! Crack your cheeks, then—rage! blow!" while we others, and my poor mother, had our hands on our mouths, and our mouths in the dust.[3]

Famed anthropologist Margaret Mead, writing field notes on Montserrat in 1966, wonders about the singular effects that living on this island might have on those who dwelled there:

> I have had a chance also to experience some of the extraordinary physical aspects of this island which, no matter how well they are explained, you still don't quite believe. I've had three weeks to get used to a world in which the temperature shifts from five minutes to five minutes, in which you may have your own private rainstorm beating down and half a mile away in three directions you see the bluest sky and the calmest sea and sunlight resting on the hilltops. The formation of the mountains changes all the time, as the shifting clouds bring out the different patterns, and no one knows whether it will rain here or there or nowhere at all in the next ten minutes as the sea suddenly turns winedark and threatening from your viewpoint, floating on its surface. On no island I have ever lived has there been such simultaneity of microclimates, all visible at once.
>
> We sit and speculate about how the character of the island may have affected the people who came to live here and how differently they fragment memory from the way most people do . . . It is a world in which at any moment you may not be able to tell what time it is, what day it is, what season it is . . .[4]

Did such conditions help construct a distraction from reality? Shiel himself said, "No one born in such a place can be quite sane."[5] He mentioned another characteristic of his father that would take on a special significance in the development of a legend that would cloak Phipps's life some fifty years in the future: "He had also the Irish foible of thinking highly of people descended from kings, and *had,* in truth, about him some species of Kingship, aloofness, was called by all 'the Governor.'"[6]

3. Ibid.

4. Margaret Mead, *Letters from the Field 1925–1975* 291.

5. MPS, "About Myself" (1901) 630.

6. MPS, "About Myself" (1948) 2.

This conceit of "kingship" could have been applied to the family from the late eighteenth century through the early years of Phipps's boyhood, when there would still have been a legacy of family importance throughout the Lesser Antilles. The idea of an inherited "kingship" could have furthered the desire for a son as heir (and possibly a claim to royalty). In any event, his father kept Shiel's mother Priscilla bound to a birth-locked bed for many years.

Shiel was clearly very fond of his mother, who must have been an attractive woman. He freely admitted that several of the women he later loved resembled her.[7]

Priscilla apparently accepted her role as mother with the expected habit of women in those days, when death was a threat at every birth, although she eventually took a more aggressive role with Matthew after he became virtually helpless following a series of strokes in 1887.[8] If she had borne twenty girls in a row she could only have hoped the twenty-first would be a boy. Shiel seems to have been uncertain whether eight or nine girls preceded him. It probably made little difference to his father.

> His children, too, he knew by name, though it was something of a feat, for there were nine girls, and then, lastly, I. At each birth of a girl, a prayer-meeting gathered in the house, attended by everybody . . . the meeting being intended to thank God for the child, but with a mental reservation, a 'but' of disaffection, and a hint to Heaven that it would be graceful to make the next a boy. For many years no boy would come, for I was ever stubborn; but my father, a true Irishman, kept plodding on, like the present Czar of Russia, and by a last effort I was evolved, taken to the lamp-light, and discovered to be male. Then, while the earth shivered, the storm raved, and Heaven's lightning blinked to see me, there was an added grand racket of prayer and thanksgiving: though why they should have been so very thankful, I, "in the light of maturer experience," cannot tell, cannot tell. But God knows best.[9]

---

7. MPS, "About Myself" (1901) 630.

8. MDS wrote MPS and Augusta both in June 1887 about their mother's impatience with him. Using his own religious pronouncements against him must have been particularly galling: ". . . she pharisees like prides herself on her religion . . ." Holograph letter from MDS to MPS, 10 June 1887 (HRC).

9. MPS, "About Myself" (1901) 630.

Indications are that Phipps and his sisters were extremely close, but we know the names of only four of them: Alberta Augusta ("Gussie," 11 January 1852?–1927), Ada Catherine (1855–10 October 1886), Harriet Garry ("Harrie," 7 January 1862–August/September 1946), and Sarah Ann ("Sallie," 1864?–February 1913).[10] If there were others they might have died either in childbirth or at a very early age. More likely, Phipps exaggerated to make his story more dramatic, although there appears to be enough spacing between the births of the known daughters to have allowed for the birth of others. And, in fact, during that period of time, it would have been rather unusual for every baby born to survive. Mortality rates at birth reached as high as 50 percent.

Matthew and Priscilla would probably have married about 1846, since it seems unlikely that Priscilla would have been any older than eighteen before marrying, while Matthew would then have been twenty-two. Birth and death dates for the known daughters, as listed above, are uncertain, as few formal records have survived. Evidence of their West Indian racial heritage is also ambivalent.

Photos of Augusta and Sallie, in the possession of M. P. Shiel at the time of his death, reveal both women with light complexions—Sallie, brown-haired, and Gussie, the prettier one, dark-haired. Gussie might be no older than thirty in her portrait (made in Tiverton, Devon), while Sallie appears to be younger, but their photos are undated.[11] Gussie was most likely married in the summer of 1872 to Samuel Lamartine Horsford of Nevis; their first son, Reginald, was born 1 May 1873. Giving an estimated birth date for Augusta of 1852, this would have made her about twenty at the time of her marriage. (Her husband was born in 1849.)[12]

---

10. There is no single source for the names and dates of birth and death for the Shiell sisters. Until late in 2004 it was presumed, for instance, that Augusta must have had a middle name as is known for the other three sisters. As it develops, "Horsford's," the newly adopted contemporary name for S. L. Horsford & Co. Ltd., has provided online a brief history of the firm, noting that the Shiell interests in the firm were sold early in 1929 following the death of Alberta Augusta Horsford. So, Augusta was the middle name of Gussie, never previously mentioned in Shiell family correspondence, records or by JG. Horsford's also lists the full name of Samuel Lamartine Horsford, previously identified only as Samuel L. One can only presume that the names of the Shiell sisters were likely based on maternal family members, probably Blake or Harman.

11. These photographs are located in HRC.

12. The "Horsfords" firm web site provides online the following history of

Harriet Shiell told her niece Olive Horsford that Matthew Dowdy Shiell "thought no end of his two eldest daughters in particular who were not allowed to even look at a man. When your father asked for Gus, he was accepted as you know, but was told that he was born with a silver spoon in his mouth and under a lucky star. The impertinence of it and your father one of the best men under the sun!!"

Ada was probably born in 1855, since she was thirty-one at the time of her death in October 1886.[13] If John Gawsworth's note that says Sallie died at age forty-eight in February 1913 is accurate, she would have been born in 1864 and was twenty-three when she married in 1887.[14]

The 1901 Census of England notes that Harriet was thirty-nine at the time the census was taken, suggesting a birth date of 1862, since her birthday was in January. She died in late August or early September 1946. Although no photograph of Harriet has survived, she bears the brunt of being described as the most racially marked of the children. The distinguished British author Sir Arthur Ransome, who visited Shiel several times as a young man starting a career in journalism, recounted a dinner party given by Shiel at which Harriet was present—a "smiling negress," Ransome described her, who entertained

---

S. L. Horsford & Co. www.horsfords.com/about-us/our-history/. "The business was founded in 1875 when the Firm of Geo. W Bennett & Co of St John's, Antigua opened a branch in Basseterre, St. Kitts. Mr. Samuel Lamartine Horsford who was at that time the Accountant at Geo. W Bennett & Co was appointed as Manager of the St. Kitts branch. In February 1880 the business traded under the name 'The Estates Agency Depot' and was a partnership between Messrs Geo. W. Bennett & Co. and Mr. John Hardtman Berkeley, planter of Shadwell Estate, St. Kitts. In 1885, Mr. Samuel Lamartine Horsford purchased the business from its previous owners and started trading as S. L. Horsford and Co. On the 31st day of January 1912, a Company Limited By Shares and named S L Horsford and Co. LTD was registered on the island of St. Christopher under The Companies Act 1884 (No. 20 of 1884) of the Leeward Islands. In January 1929, Mr. B. Marshall purchased the shares owned by the late Mrs. Alberta Augusta Horsford (widow of Mr. S. L. Horsford Dec'd) and the four surviving offspring of Mr. & Mrs. Horsford." [Cyril, Olive, Muriel and either Leonard or Reginald were still alive.]

13. The black-edged funeral card for Ada Catherine Shiell is located in HRC.

14. The note that JG made regarding Sallie's death date is mentioned in a footnote by A. Reynolds Morse in his *Works* "Shielography Updated" 3.421. Morse says he noticed the information in London in a notebook among the mass of disorganized material JG left to Jon Wynne-Tyson.

him with stories of her childhood with Phipps on Montserrat.[15]

Harriet has already acknowledged in this work the darkness of features that she and her mother shared. As an elderly woman, she wrote Olive, "I think my traveling days are over. I would hate to go about with white hair, with my dark complexion. It would be so ugly. I remember your Ma saying she had not met any one quite as vain as Harriet—is this another proof of it—?" Harriet seems to have had no embarrassment revealing her dark features in London.

The same census that lists Harriet's age as thirty-nine lists Phipps as being only thirty-four, when he should have been listed as thirty-five at census taking on the night of 31 March 1901, when he, his sister Harriet, his first wife Carolina (Lina), and his daughter Dolores (Lola) were all living at 11 Keppel Street. A specific date for Augusta's death has not been determined, although it is certain that it was in summer 1927, and apparently in London.[16] Shiel had written her in 1924 in a manner that suggests he could visit her and the girls.[17] The Horsford

---

15. JG indicated that Harriet Shiell died in 1946. MPS wrote Olive Horsford on 6 September 1946: "My Olive / The enclosed will explain itself. I am sending to Miss Winifred Manchester, Sandy Point, St. Kitts, a contribution towards the funeral expenses . . ." (Holograph copy by JG of this note in HRC). Ransome's description of Harriet is in his *Autobiography* 81.

16. The sale of the Shiell family interests in the SL Horsford & Co firm in early 1929 followed Augusta's death in June or July 1927. Harriet wrote Olive from Montserrat on 15 July 1927, thanking her for the details of her "Ma's" illness and death. She had even "tried to picture how she looked lying there silent in death, but I have failed, and I do envy your uncle, and all, who had the privilege of having a last look on the poor dead face . . . I should say that your home now should be with Muriel. Ada is quite well and was of course very grieved to hear of your Ma's death." It appears that Gussie was living in London with her daughters when she died, so Harriet had probably gone to stay with her niece Ada on St. Kitts. She wrote MPS on 16 November 1928 that she had just returned to "the old place" on Montserrat after "a never to be forgotten six months in St. Kitts." The devastating hurricane of 12 September 1928 that killed 42, injured 100, and left hundreds homeless on Montserrat probably made the Shiell home in Plymouth uninhabitable. But Harriet would then have already been at St. Kitts for several months. Because of the devastation, Harriet could not have returned earlier if she had wished (Wheeler 50). Typed copies of letters by Olive Horsford are in HRC.

17. Holograph copy of letter from MPS to his sister, Augusta, 19 October 1924, 88 Grand Park Terrace, Chiswick W. (HRC). Did she hear of Montserrat's hurricane? Just to have been there, "to see that wind and feel it in my hair!" Harriet had been in St. Kitts at the time, he tells Gussie. (This storm was not the devas-

family interests in the S. L. Horsford Company were sold in early 1929, with Gussie listed as deceased. Harriet's thanks to Olive in July 1927 for describing her Ma's death seems to confirm June or early July of that year for Gussie's death.

Presuming Matthew and Priscilla married as early as 1847, and that Augusta was not born until 1852, it is probable that another child preceded her. Similarly, if Ada was born in 1854 and Harriet in 1862, there is another lengthy period within which there might have been other births. These possibilities suggest that Phipps might not have been exaggerating when he says there were eight or nine daughters that preceded him, with only four of them having survived to adulthood. Of course, Phipps's parents could have married several years later than 1847, but that seems unlikely. There will probably never be a documented answer to these issues.

Augusta ("Gussie") affectionately called Phipps "brother-uncle" and "uncle," as her children grew to know him. Phipps was always ready to give advice to his sisters, advice that veered from the elevated philosophical to the lowest practical level (the best coital position, for instance, to conceive the finest children). While Phipps seems to have always treated his sisters with rather straightforward respect, his personal relations with other women seem to have been, with few exceptions, purely (and voraciously) physical. Women and their functions were taken for granted. He afterwards generalized: "Women are all beast below the navel; above, all peri: and thus you get a very decent blend."[18]

It is doubtful whether Phipps ever really loved anything (or wrote anything) in which he could not see a reflection of himself. He was too self-centered. However, he recognized the importance of parents and grandparents ("even unto the third generation") and loved and respected his family in his own way. Some hint of this is cast in a letter he wrote his sister Augusta ten years after he left home, when the question of his ancestry began to be an issue:

> By the way, I want to know the name of my father's mother, and also the maiden name of our old Granny. Will you write and let me know, and if you yourself don't know, try and find out for me. It is

---

tating one of 1928 that almost obliterated every church on the island. Augusta was then dead.)

18. The circumstances that elicited this remark are discussed in MPS's letter of 12 February 1895 to his sister Augusta.

> from the old folk, darling, that we get all we are; they fiz in our blood, and beat in our brain; it is they who stand at my shoulder and dictate to me the very words I am now writing.[19]

It is interesting that Shiel would ask for the names of "my father's mother, and also the maiden name of our old Granny." This suggests that he knew at least the surname of his father's father (if not his forename), but not the maiden name of his paternal grandmother; and that he knew who his maternal grandfather was, but not the maiden name of his maternal grandmother, "our old Granny," Sarah Harman Blake.

If his father's mother was a slave, he probably would not have heard her mentioned in his boyhood. His grandfather, James Phipps Shiell, would have been dead for fifty years and apparently romanticized in family memory. On the other hand, references to the Blake name occur frequently in Shiell activities. This suggests an ongoing closeness of his family to the Blakes. Both of Phipps's maternal grandparents might have been a major presence in his boyhood, cer-

---

19. Typescript copy by JG of letter by MPS to his sister, Augusta, Rugby Chambers, Bedford Road, W.C., 14 January 1895 (HRC). JG notes that this letter was written on embossed dove grey paper—suggesting better quarters? The letter regarding MPS's race is from Walter Goldwater, "Shiel, Van Vechten and the Question of Color," in Morse, *M. P. Shiel in Diverse Hands* 75–76.

John D. Squires has pointed out an important passage in MPS's novel *The Yellow Wave* that forecasts the evolution of the races and is certainly a significant hint that MPS was aware of being "flushed brown":

> ". . . I wonder what it will all end in!"
>
> "Intermarriage, no doubt," said Mr. England. "Remember, Peterson, that Man is not a white animal: white men are a freak, like white mice or white horses, and will soon disappear. I have heard M[urino] make the same remark, and Schopenhauer, too, you remember makes it: that is why, says Schopenhauer, a fair woman likes dark men, because she has an instinct to return, in her offspring, to the original dark type of the race; but dark women have no corresponding impulse to marry fair men; in fact, often shrink from them. We fair types are a temporary accident, only human by courtesy. So I look forward three hundred years to one universal race, highly evolved, of a flushed brown as clear as the ruby, with melting, almond eyes, and a thick little coral mouth, with little pearls for teeth." [*The Yellow Wave* 250.]

John D. Squires, "Some Contemporary Themes in Shiel's Early Novels," in Morse, *Diverse Hands* 280.

tainly at least the striking "Granny." It is unlikely that Gussie knew any more than Harriet about their ancestors, and Harriet knew little more than what it appears that Phipps knew.

Over the years, a number of questions have been raised about what Phipps actually knew of his racial heritage. Several "critics" have accused him of vicious racial slurs against Jews and other minorities in his fiction and of efforts to hide any self-knowledge of his own likely black forebears. As already noted, there were early references on Montserrat to "negroes" (slaves, plantation blacks, freedmen), "men of color," and white men. It is likely that the "men of color" only designated themselves with this appellation after being several generations removed from African slaves, and it is just as likely that those white men, or men of color, who engaged in concubinage accepted such relationships with those women most attractive to them, or those closest to them in color and in personal and moral values, as the Rev. Horsford described.

But the vast majority of the Montserratian population were African slaves in the early part of the nineteenth century or freedmen after manumission in 1834. After the white population started deserting the West Indies as economic conditions worsened through the middle of the century, the men of color, through intermarriage, including marriage with the remaining "white" populace, and with the freedmen population, saw a rapid darkening of their children and grandchildren, so that by the late nineteenth century the population of the West Indies was exactly that: West Indian.

Thus, the intermixing of races probably meant very little to Phipps as a boy. He apparently saw himself as "white," with a sharp distinction between his lighter family and the generally black mass of those in the West Indies removed just a few years from slavery. He also probably paid little attention to casual differences in color. By the time he spent a few years in England, however, and started to achieve attention as an author, questions developed regarding his "race" (meaning, perhaps, nationality as much as race).

Perhaps for the first time in his life, Phipps began to recognize that there were major distinctions as to how such issues were treated in the West Indies and how they were treated among social, cynical literary circles in England. He freely acknowledged his West Indian birth. The fact that his father was a local "Methodist minister" was in itself an obvious indication of that man's closeness to people of color. There was the fact that his mother's dark attractiveness was a feature that quickly drew him to women; and his sister, Harriet, as he made her welcome to friends and dinner guests, was quite "dark." He never made much of the issue; he seems to have simply shunted the matter aside.

When asked directly by the bookseller Walter Goldwater in the 1930s about his race, after his books were shelved with "Negro" authors, Shiel answered: "Dear Mr. Goldwater: Yours to hand. I'm afraid I am an Irish Paddy—very mixed blood—Andalusian, Moorish—but perhaps no 'Negro' except in so far as Roosevelt, the Mikado, that so 'Aryan' Hitler, are Negro, each of them having had four grandparents, each of those four by which geometric progression one soon gets to the population of the globe. Andalusian girls have brown skin, light-brown hair, pretty green eyes—deucedly pretty. One of my sisters has jet-black hair, brown eyes—a throw-back perhaps to some dim Negro, while I, after a gold-haired youth, have nearly-black hair (but Irish-gray eyes). Thanks so much for your interest."

His West Indian heritage became extremely important to him years later, since he developed very outspoken ideas regarding the future of the races, just as he did on issues of land ownership and the concept of the "overman." He saw evolution leading all races toward a human physiological blend just as he had observed in the West Indies—"a flushed brown" harmony, as he wrote in his novel *The Yellow Wave*. He saw the "overman" as a development of the entire human race accomplished through better educational systems and a more scientific bend of mind, not for a single "overman" race against other races, but for all humankind.

But these ideas lay years ahead in his career. Far more important to his early development than his color were two personal characteristics that he demonstrated early on, a gift for language and a genius for imagination.

There apparently were few boys as light-skinned as he for companions on Montserrat, so that racially darker youths were his closest friends. They too treated him with affection and curiosity. No wonder he was spoiled and egoistic, the long-awaited son and heir, the youngest and brightest, a handsome sturdy lad with crisp dark curls crowning his head. Possibly the main connecting personal thread throughout his life, one that he fully recognized, was the development, expression, and occasionally attempted suppression of a vast megalomania; it is obvious how it began.

Little god or no, the darker youths on the island were drawn to this boy who loved to scale the ridges of La Soufrière, to climb about the cragged and forested sides of Silver and Centre Hills, to display his agility at acrobatics and dancing. Shiel frequently had black friends who followed him agape at his antics, who sat in astonishment to hear him expound on some subject of interest to him, but alien to his "mulatto" companions—"as credulous as priests are, for whom fancies have the same weight as ascertained facts."[20]

It would be foolish to think that it was only male companions that engaged the attention of the young Phipps. An inscription by Shiel in a copy of *The Purple Cloud* acknowledges the early presence of females among his interests: "The 'heroine' in this is a representation of the personality of my first sweetheart Xena, a girl of Montserrat in the West Indies, who, when I was five years old, taught me how to love, she being eight. Two of her sons have quite easily nonchalantly and as a matter of course surpassed by far all competition in the race of intellect. So that she was a fit mother of a race, as (before I knew of these sons) I made her in the book. 'Our mothers make us most.' 1924, M. P. Shiel."[21]

There was comparatively little on the tiny island to engage his interest besides exploring its undefiled wildness and capturing the rapt attention of descendants of slaves. He described Montserrat as a "mountain-mass, loveliest of the lovely, but touchy! uncertain! dashing into tantrums—hurricanes, earthquakes, brooks bubbling hot, 'Soufrières' (sulphur-swamps), floods—'fit nurse to a poetic child.'"[22] And again:

> I have an idea that at the moment of my death it will sink: I do not know if it is true. I have passed on the calm sea some vast, blazing day, like an Eternity of light (whether in the body I know not), close under its piled augustness of crags, and my eyes have filled with tears of love and pity for it, and all its turbulent epilepsies, and its despondent manias, and wayward Orestian frenzies, and coming doom. It has souffraires (hot sulphur springs), and sometimes, after one of its tantrums, passing invisible ships many a mile out at sea can smell that fume of Hell it sends.[23]

---

20. MPS, "About Myself" (1948) 3.

21. This is referenced in Morse, *Works* 2.27. Told to Morse by George Locke and quoted in Locke's *A Spectrum of Fantasy: The Bibliography and Biography of a Collection of Fantastic Literature* (London: Ferret Fantasy, 1980) 194.

22. MPS, "About Myself" (1948) 1.

23. MPS, "About Myself" (1901) 630.

When Rev. John Horsford visited the Wesleyan outposts throughout the Caribbean just ten years before Phipps was born, it was not only concubinage that concerned him. Although he detested the use of lashing to punish the practices of Obeahism, he also granted that this "evil in all its obstinacy continues."[24] With hardly a generation between the dark superstitions that crept out of the slave plantations and the folk practices of Methodism, it is understandable how as a boy Phipps could observe superstitious reaction to the religious practices of one belief as well as another, and feel no contradiction between them:

> I was born in a small island, so, as a boy, had to go to funerals, and press the dead hand in farewell—one old lady who had prominent teeth I still see.
>
> There was a belief that if the funeral moved along the seashore the sea, at some point, would smell the dead, would be drawn, would sweep up once and wet everyone's feet—which thing I once saw and, ah! The awe of it, that haunted all the heart's hollows.
>
> Awesome, too, to a boy's heart was when the funeral-pace quickened a little (as is natural), and one mourner would murmur to another, "Ah, poor thing, ain't she eager to get home?"
>
> "True, true," would be the answer; "she's hurrying home, she's hurrying home."[25]

This theme of African superstitions, of "obeah" or "obiah," is most visible in a story that Shiel probably wrote about 1899 but that first appeared in the *Pictorial Magazine* of 24 October 1903. Although Shiel wrote the story as though the events occurred in the American South, it reeks of the West Indies, of stories that he might have heard from his dark companions or from family members sitting in the gloom remembering events from the days of slavery, not too far past, and superstitions still present among them. "A Shot at the Sun" is worth including for the smell it carries of the worst practices on the plantations, some still undoubtedly very close to Phipps as a boy.

---

24. Horsford, *A Visit* 93.

25. MPS, "On Panic," *Science, Life and Literature* 198.

A SHOT AT THE SUN

A WEIRD STORY BY M. P. SHIEL

I tell you something which I have seen with my own eyes; you believe it or not, as you like.

I am an old fellow now at this date of writing, and what I tell of happened forty years ago, in the old slavery days, down South.

Charles K. Brownrigg at that time was the owner of two hundred and forty-five niggers, not to mention fifteen hundred acres of cotton plantation. And I take it upon me to state that he was the worst-feared man in the Southern States of America.

He was a big, red man, with hard, hairless jaws and a goat-beard, and continually went about with a gun on his shoulder. His estate-house, a rambling place, lay a little outside of Cliftonville (in South Carolina), and looked directly upon his plantations. That gun which he carried had shot, at one time or another, five separate niggers—nobody had the least doubt of it in Cliftonville—yet by some strange power which was in him, or about him, Brownrigg had escaped justice.

One day—it was in "the hot" of the year '59—a maroon rushed into the shed where Brownrigg was overseeing the reaping, with the words:

"Massa, massa, Brams and Jess done gone run 'way!"

Brams was a negro youth of twenty, and Jess a mulatto girl, shapely as Venus, both slaves of Brownrigg. Brams and Jess, from the first mutual glance some months before had loved; and now, by concert, had taken to the woods and wilds in some mad hope of finding free happiness.

Brownrigg's Panama hat was low on his forehead that morning, and his face even before this announcement had worn a scowl, for he was in money difficulties; and he had two bad years with the cotton, and as the news of the flight passed the lips of the maroon Brownrigg sent the long lash of a shorthanded cowhide coiling about the man's legs with the crack of a Maxim gun, while the slave skipped in a dance of pain.

There was something very queer about Brownrigg—he was no ordinary slave-owner. Now, for instance, when he threw down the whip, and the slave lay writhing in the "long-grass," it was natural to expect that he would have rushed instantly away, hurried together dogs and horses, and set out after the fugitives. But he did nothing of the sort.

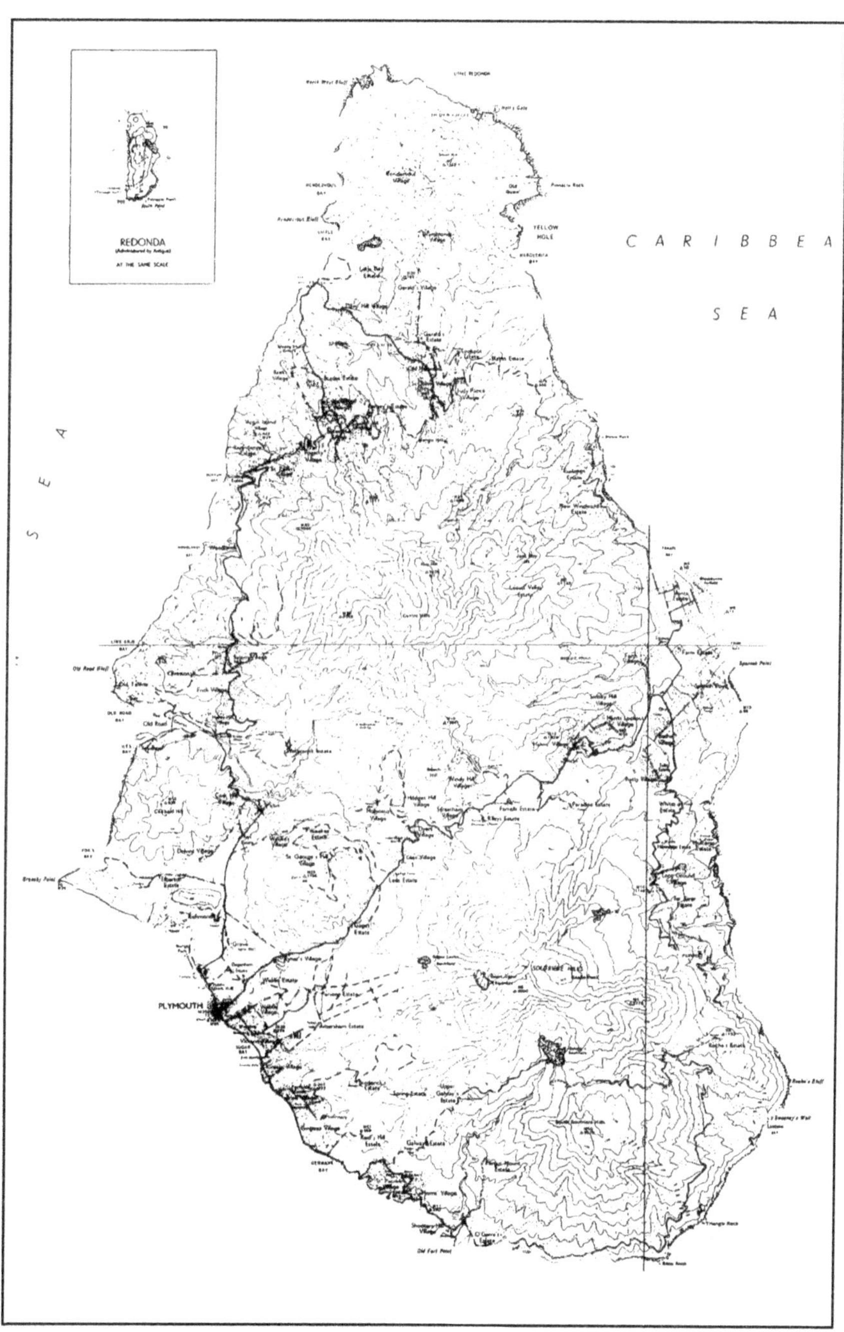

Topographical Map of Montserrat

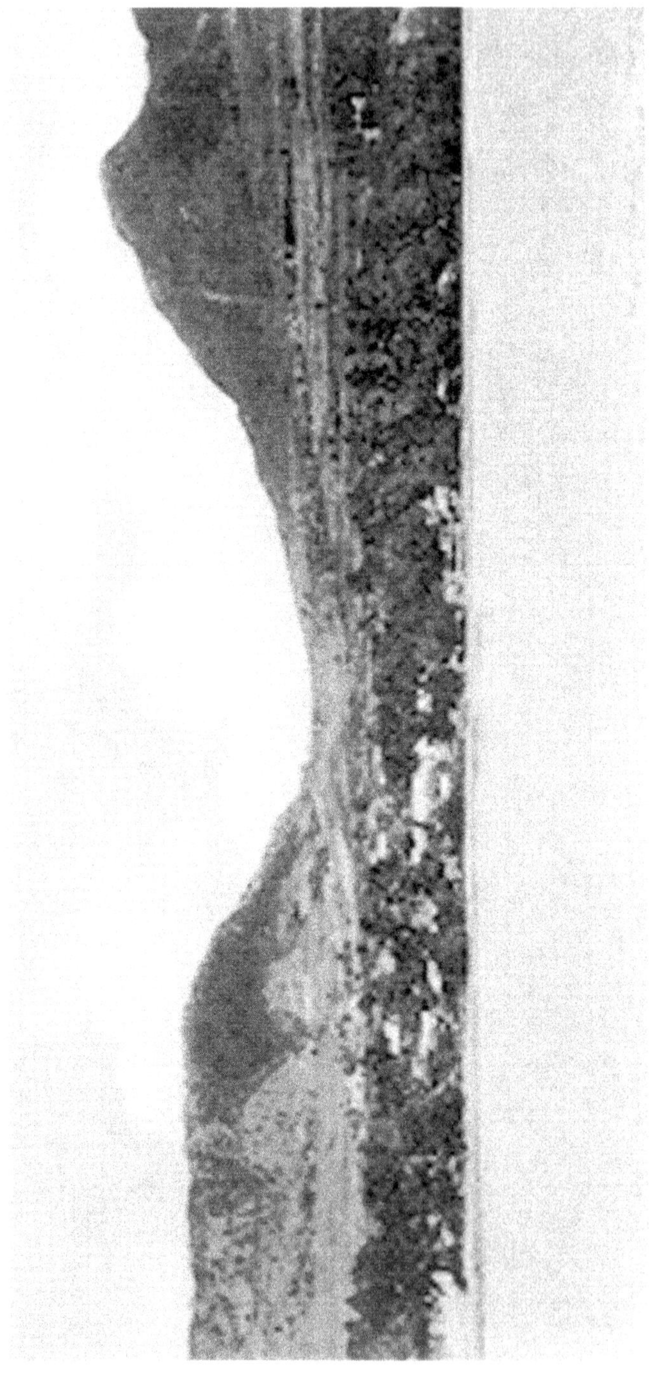

Plymouth, Montserrat, as seen from the sea

Matthew Phipps Shiell about 14, Montserrat, ca. 1880
Courtesy of the Harry Ransom Humanities Research Center
The University of Texas at Austin

Shiel's Home, Montserrat, ca. 1929
Courtesy of the Harry Ransom Humanities Research Center
The University of Texas at Austin

What he did do was to put his hand into his waistcoat pocket, draw out three little black stones, deposit them in his left palm and stare at them for some three minutes. They were obiah-stones.

Brownrigg, standing with his knickered bowlegs apart, put a finger-tip to his lips, touched each of the stones with spittle, and rattled them in his left hand. Then he opened the hand, put the middle stone back into his pocket, and with two fingers of the right hand struck down smartly upon the two remaining stones. They started away from his palm in divergent directions; Brownrigg noted the directions and picked them up.

Only then did he set out. He hurried to the estate house, blowing a whistle. In ten minutes two pursuing parties had started in the directions which the stones had indicated, and in less than an hour Brams and Jess were safely lodged in the estate ward-house. It may have been only chance, or it may have been Brownrigg's obiah-stones, that caught them; of course, I do not know—I merely state facts.

Brams and Jess were to be pitied that day, if ever two poor mortals were to be pitied. I say that day, meaning that day above all other days whatsoever; for on that day Brownrigg had in him the humour of ten demons. I am going to tell you why. Perhaps you are aware that there are three special days (sometimes it is four, or even five, but usually it is three) when, during the cotton-reap, it is of the greatest importance that the sun shine strongly and steadily without rain or even cloud. Clouds means loss, rain disaster, the reason being that the new-plucked fruit needs just at that time the swelter of the sun for what is called its "fibring." Now this particular day when Brams and Jess ran away and were captured was the second of the three critical days in that year, and the sun was not shining too well, and Brownrigg was angry with it.

You may imagine perhaps that the sun did not care so very much about Brownrigg's anger, but this was the very point which was in doubt all through Cliftonville that day; and it is no exaggeration to say that positively hundreds of bets were being made in the saloons, in the Exchange, at the store doors, as to whether the sun would shine, and, if not, as to whether Brownrigg would command it to shine, and, in that case, as to whether or not it would obey Brownrigg.

The fact is that during the previous year's reap, one afternoon, when the sun had gone behind a cloud, Brownrigg had been clearly seen to do an extraordinary thing. Standing in midfield he had hurriedly loaded his gun; he had then cocked the hammer ready for shooting; then he had taken his massive silver watch in his left hand, and three niggers near had heard him say, with a nod at the sun, these strange words:

"I give you five minutes!"

And one minute, two, three minutes passed, and the sun had remained hidden; and four minutes had passed, and it had remained hidden; and as the five minutes ended it had walked out into open sky with clear, blistering face.

Now Cliftonville was not a bit more superstitious than anywhere else, and in another man such conduct would have seemed to it simply silly. But in Brownrigg it somehow did not seem silly. He was felt to be a genuinely diabolical and dreadful man. It was known for a certainty that with blackened face he had attended the rites and midnight orgies of the negro obiah-men in the depths of the forest. All Cliftonville knew it. And at the top of his estate house was some sort of cupola in which at night his light was seen to shine, no one knowing in the least what Brownrigg was doing there—whether he was star-gazing, or whether he was holding intercourse with who can say what or whom.

And therefore, I say, the bets in Cliftonville were many that day, and a thrill of excitement filled the town; and when, about two in the afternoon, the sun went definitely behind a spread of cloud, looking as if it meant to stay there and casting a shade over the land, all the lanes leading to Brownrigg's plantation were covered with groups of twos and threes, of fives and tens, slouching out innocently that way to see what there was to see.

At that hour, Brownrigg was with the two runaways in a foul hole of the estate ward-house—he and they were alone. He had tied them together with many whorls of rope which entered the flesh, and he had laid them so upon the mud floor, with outstretched arms. At his feet were two pails of boiling water, whose surface still bubbled, and in his hand his gun.

"Now, you two young niggers!" was all he said.

Upon the two forms he tossed in three spurts the contents of one pail, the tied mass on the floor filling the cell with yells and flinging itself about in wriggling spasms. Then he put down the pail, took from his waistcoat-pocket one of the little obiah-stones, spat on it, dropped it into the other pail, and said these words aloud:

"I give the lives of these two young niggers for a good reap. The moment that water cools, let 'em die, Bam, let 'em die, O Bam."

Then Brownrigg put his gun to his shoulder and took aim. He

had not the least intention of killing, for slave justice, though crude, was not an existent fact, and he had been too often suspected of murder already. But he took aim; he was a good shot, and though the den was dark he could see. He sighted the fleshy parts of the now quietly-groaning mass.

He pierced the shoulder of Brams; a minute, then ping!—he pierced the thigh of Jess; another minute, then ping!—he pierced he knew not what, for at this third shot the gun gave such a jarring to kick at this shoulder that he staggered backward. The shock was very unexpected. He frowned.

"Why, what's matter with the old gun?" he muttered.

He cast a glance at the pail containing the stone, shouldered his gun, and ascended. As he mounted the light shone on a hideous face distorted with passions.

The first thing he saw now was that the sun was not shining as it should.

He at once went down the back lane toward the plantation, around he cast his lurid eyes, and must have observed that every path and niche of foliage was thronged with people from Cliftonville. But they took no interest in him. All along the cotton overseer and nigger were at work—but in shadow—the sun was behind a cloud.

Every minute Brownrigg was losing seventy-five dollars.

All eyes were fixed upon Brownrigg. All about him was a murmur of tongues. Bets ran high. Brownrigg seemed unconscious of it all.

Suddenly with a jerk, he moved. He put his left hand to his waistcoat pocket.

This was a signal for a general crowding round him; through field and path, they came, every-one, however, keeping a respectable distance.

There was a rock near to Brownrigg, and on the top of this he put his watch, together with the leather strap which attached it to his waist-coat. Face upward he settled it, just under his eye; and he put his gun to his shoulder, and with a face of diabolical wickedness he pointed it at the sun.

As he did so he said these words:

"Three minutes—I give you three."

The words were heard by an overseer who at that moment had happened to approach Brownrigg. And the overseer, holding down his little finger with his thumb, lifted on high three fingers behind Brownrigg's back to show the crowd how the matter stood.

At once hundreds of watches were snatched from hundreds of pockets, and held in hundreds of palms. A minute passed. Not a sound now but the soft rush of the breeze in the cotton leafage, every man feeling his heart beat thickly in his bosom.

The second minute is gone. The sun remains clouded, and steadily points Brownrigg's muzzle at it. Every five or six seconds he gives a downward glance at his watch. In all that crowd of onlookers there is hardly now a single face not pallid with excitement.

Suddenly there is a stirring—there is the widest sensation! The sun is re-adjusting itself—there is a working, a movement yonder on high—the clouds are giving way, as when a crowd opens for the passage of Royalty! He has won his way—he shines triumphantly—the world is sweltering in his blaze.

From the fields and lanes there went up a shout. Brownrigg was seen to nod, as if to say, "Ah, so much the better for you!" There were still fifteen seconds lacking to the completion of his three minutes.

During the next five minutes there ensued an agitated scene among the crowd; bets were being settled, comments made; on the outskirts there was a tendency toward departure for Cliftonville. It seems probable that the saloons would do a brisk trade that day, for considerable sums had changed hands.

Brownrigg had again put on his watch. He was talking to the overseer who had approached him. In the midst of his talk he was seen to snatch up his cow-skin "cart-whip," and crack it around the bare legs of a negro who had happened to pass too near.

All at once those who had sauntered from the outskirts of the crowd to return to the town stopped, and ran back with cries to their former stations. With a strange suddenness the sun had buried itself into cloud involving the land in shadow.

Expectation now stood more wildly on tiptoe than ever. The betting instinct at this fresh impetus was on the point of manifesting itself with tenfold vigour; but, as a matter of fact, not a single bet was made, for Brownrigg left them no time. With a gesture of horrible rage he snatched away his watch, placed it on the stone, snatched up his gun, and pointed it upward.

The overseer, still near him, drew away, and holding down his third and fourth fingers with his thumb, lifted on high his first two behind Brownrigg's back for the information of the crowd. Brownrigg had said:

"Two minutes—I give you two."

And once more the hundreds of watches lay flat in the hundreds of palms. And in silence a minute passed.

It must have been about this time, as the Cliftonville folk said afterwards, that the negro Brams drew himself along the mud floor of his cell, wounded as he was, dragging with him his companion in misery. He had heard the curse pronounced against him and seen the obiah-stone dropped into the hot water. With a push he upset the pail, and took out the stone. That is what he afterwards asserted.

But whatever truth is to be credited to the statement of the black, the fact remains that Brownrigg stood with his gun pointed at the sun; and a minute passed and the sun remained hidden.

Obstinately this time. A minute and a-half—and no one dared to breathe; a sense of the awful oppressed the heart; the waiting air seemed crowded with something momentous. The breeze died away, as if holding its breath to watch that blasphemy.

Then—at last—with a shock of fear everyone knew that the two minutes were over, and the sun remained a mere blotch.

Bang! Brownrigg fired.

He vanished. He perished. Never could one have conceived such a thing. To say that his gun burst and sent him into eternity is to put it very feebly; he disappeared. Gun and Brownrigg and watch were wiped out. The folk at Cliftonville used to tell that not a single trace was left of him—that he was clean eaten up and swallowed by the wrath of heaven. That is an exaggeration—but not much of one; some traces were found—but wonderfully few. I state facts.

THE END

Those superstitions remained with Shiel throughout his life, while the sight of the sea and surging surf, its relentless crest and roar, the feel of the Caribbean sun and wind, the black magnetic sand of Montserrat's beaches, burned themselves into Phipps's character and left a pantheistic impression on his later writing.

> . . . this worship of wind—which to me is the worthiest of the works of God, as fog the ugliest, which I worship as the Persian the sun—I having learned when a nipper of ten in the West Indies; where, as you know, it is hot; yes, but anon there blow hurricanes that raise a body's hair like a ghost with their gloomy mood, and about Christmas, too, gales of a delicious chill come to blow and mouth about one's brow—bleak! bleak!—of a morning, when one walked to bathe

in the sea. Was I aware that those gales came to me from England and the Glacial Sea? I forget. I know that they spoke to me of the moon, of moons that no telescope ever explored; and if I possessed a thousand pens, and then ten thousand mouths to tell, still, heaven knows, I'd be far enough from uttering half of all their holy psalmodies told to me.[26]

A boy's character is malleable in its reaction to the pressure of nature or event. But, unlike clay, it cannot easily be reshaped: any or all impressions may someday appear in some fashion. So it was that years later Shiel remembered and revealed the presence of panic in boyhood activities:

> I once felt that real presence when a boy of fourteen, sitting small on a massive stallion that was stepping down a ledge, precipice above, precipice below—sedately stepping, when those same devils that entered the Gadarene hogs got into him, and began to gallop him—down and round the curves; then there was prayer without words.
>
> Nothing, in fact, can be quicker than a boy's panics, more delicate than his mental poise. I remember being terror-struck by some sudden text of Scripture: "he goeth after her, and knoweth not that the dead are there . . ." and, on jumping into mid-ocean from a schooner becalmed—just to bathe—no danger—panic suddenly took me at my loneliness, at a malignancy and ghostliness in the sea.[27]

The last two events were used in stories he wrote some thirty years later. And that long-distant terror of the author was powerfully re-created in the reader.

Many events of those early years turned up in later books. Shiel was particularly impressed by the escapades of his young black friends. A fight between one of those acquaintances and the police, and the subsequent hunt-and-chase, were used as scenes in several stories. And the attributes of various novel-characters were based on these figures he knew in his youth.[28] He was so fond of several (especially of Paddy

---

26. MPS, "On Reading," *This Knot of Life* 68–69.

27. MPS, "On Panic," *Science, Life and Literature* 197.

28. In addition to the characters that are based on MPS's boyhood friends that are mentioned here, there are undoubtedly many others scattered throughout his novels and short stories if one were familiar enough with the individuals to spot them in the fiction. In some cases, like that of Mary Semper, in *How the Old Woman Got Home* (1927), he simply attached a familiar

Burke, who virtually adopted him, Phipps said) that he saved photographs of several of them through the miles and events of over sixty years, and based fictional characters on them: Henry Dyett, on whose image Shiel based his character Baron Kolar in *The Last Miracle;* Harry Dyett, the nephew of Henry and son of a local preacher, who impressed Phipps with the fact that he had once gotten a girl to give him a dozen kisses; Percy Trott, basis for the character "Shan," the gamekeeper in *The White Wedding;* and Paddy Burke.[29]

Paddy was the son of a local grocer and once took Phipps to the shop where the latter deformed a toe on a wheel located there. This story, told to John Gawsworth by Shiel and recorded on the back of an old photograph by Gawsworth, says that Paddy's mother promptly smashed his head with a soapbox as punishment.[30]

Several of Shiel's stories written long afterwards concern a fear of being buried alive; perhaps this had its genesis in the habit of an old family servant to shut him in a dark cupboard when one of his sisters became ill.[31] It may also account for his lifelong habit of staying up at night and sleeping by day.

Young Phipps was left chiefly to his own devices, to find his own pastimes and make his own pleasures with local companions as told above. His feel for the natural life of Montserrat must have entered into the heart of much of what he later wrote. One of his most mem-

---

name to a character without there being any specific known characteristic that belonged to both the real and fictional person.

Perhaps even more so than characters, were the geographic locations that he frequented in his personal life that he used in his fiction. Even in short stories, like "Many a Tear" (published in *Pearson's* [New York], September 1908), wherein there seems little to relate the location to the fictional events, the story is placed near Woolaston where a young love of his, Mary Price, lived in the years just before 1908. The accuracy with which out-of-the-way but real physical locations are described in *The Purple Cloud* has attracted the interest of literary geography scholars.

29. From holograph notes by JG of information told him by MPS that he recorded on the backs of old photographs (HRC). One of MPS's several women friends insisted that "there is much of your own personality" in the character Shan in *The White Wedding,* so she had started thinking of him as "Shan." (Holograph letter from Margaret Bertram Hobson to MPS, Gordon House, Billinghay, Linc. [1908], HRC.)

30. Note by JG on photograph of Paddy Burke (HRC).

31. MPS, "About Myself" (1948) 2–3.

orable characters, "Skin-the Goat," an albino youth attached to gypsies and the woods of England, was a favorite of Shiel's, used and abused as he was, but redolent of possible youthful adventures on Phipps's part. One can see him with one of Montserrat's unusual large frogs, offering it bread and tapping its head: "Eat, frog. Eat!" Those of a psychological bent can make what they want of this albino character.

He could occasionally accompany his father on trips to Cuba, Barbados, and Martinique—at least, so he said. And it was a special day for Phipps and his friends when a traveling troupe of acrobats, or clowns, or a conjuror came to entertain the island.

> Once when a troupe came, I saw a conjuror break eggs into a hat, put on the hat, take it off, and now round his brow was a row of roses. So the next day I, entranced—I was eleven—said to Paddy—lad of twenty, wedded to me—"I can do it!" Now he was a mulatto—a sort of people as credulous as priests are, for whom fancies have the same weight as ascertained facts—and, shaken in his faith in Nature by my faith in myself, he said, "Well, we'll see." So he gets eggs, breaks them into a hat; and I can see again his keen stoop, his stare of interest, as I raised the hat toward my head, and can again hear his glad out-cry of laughter, as the universe rallied to re-establish his old view of her, while I stood foolish, with fluids raining down my face . . . But how ill-educated for eleven! How foreign to the cosmos. I had been reading Caesar, you see, the prick of my intellect "let down" (as we say when we soften steel) forever.[32]

This reading of the classics was a normal thing for a well-educated boy of the period. ". . . by the time I was eleven and at school in Devonshire I had devoured I should think, most of what is written in Greek." How his earliest education was conducted is not known. Much of that learning came in biblical form. Every day for years Phipps and his father sat on a little couch and read together from the Bible. For years, too, the boy took these readings completely to heart, imagined himself a preacher like his father, and stood "preaching in a night-dress over my clothes, of Jonah-in-the-whale's belly, shouting 'Lazarus, come forth!' and Lazarus came; but no sooner was I fourteen than I began to name the Methodists 'the Methodies,' making sad a man." Several of his books include a firebrand evangelist among their characters.

32. Ibid.

Probably the most prominent of these is the wild-stalking, thundering pastor Mackay, in *The Purple Cloud,* who warned of disaster to the human race if foot were set on the North Pole.

Job and the Jehovist were Phipps's biblical favorites, and always afterwards he thought the finest passage of literature ever created was that mouthed by Jacob (as Shiel rephrased it): "Few and evil have the days of the years of my life been, and have not attained to the days of the years of the lives of my fathers in the days of their marches."[33]

Actual details of his father's business activities are generally lacking, although we know of references to his trading ships and store. A description of a brief stop-off at Montserrat by a traveling New York journalist just a few months after Phipps left Montserrat for the final time in 1885 provides colorful anecdotes of the townspeople and descriptions of a shop that might well be that of the elder Shiell. None of the several shopkeepers in Plymouth was prepared for visits by tourists.

William Drysdale wrote of this brief visit in the *New York Times,* 29 December 1885.[34] In sailing for Montserrat south from St. Kitts, the boat passed Redonda, "an immense rock rising up almost perpendicularly out of the water to a height of perhaps 200 feet . . . The rock is almost 25 miles from St. Kitts and the same distance from Montserrat. And it is a sight worth seeing, this great rock standing out by itself, with nothing else near it, and the water breaking up against the sides into white foam." Drysdale goes on:

> It was 3 o'clock in the afternoon when we dropped anchor in front of Plymouth, Montserrat's capital city. We were not more than a quarter of a mile away, and close enough to see that it was a small town, with no buildings of much size and with streets that were short and narrow and crooked. Of course such an out-of-the-way place as Montserrat must be visited when occasion offered, and Capt. Fraser told me the ship would be there till dark at the least. So, accompa-

33. MPS, *This Knot of Life* 51. From the introductory essay "On Reading," reprinted somewhat revised and as "On Reading" and "On Writing" by JG in *Science, Life and Literature* and also in Morse, *Diverse Hands.* (It is difficult to understand how MPS was able to convince the publisher to include this dense essay in an Edwardian romantic novel.)

34. William Drysdale, "A Visit to Montserrat: Two Hours in Plymouth, Its Capital Town. Where Steamers Do Not Often Land and Strangers Are as Good as a Circus—A Reception in the Market Place," *New York Times* (29 December 1885): 4.

nied by two New York ladies, I took advantage again of the permission to use the ship's boat, and "Sunny" and his companion rowed us ashore. There were no vessels in the harbor—only two or three little fishing smacks—and the arrival of a steamer seemed to be an event of great importance. There was a wooden pier a dozen feet wide and perhaps 200 feet long extending out over the water, and we landed at a stairway at the outer end of this and climbed up. The greater part of the population in the town seemed to be gathered there to welcome us. And they welcomed us in a manner more novel than pleasant, by crowding up just as close to us as the two or three black policemen on the wharf would let them, and making remarks to each other about us. The arrival of white strangers on that hospitable shore was evidently something very uncommon. We squeezed through the narrow lane the natives left for us between two rows of darkies and made our way to solid land—none too solid, either, for the stones composing the sea wall had rolled out in places and the wall seemed in danger of caving in. We made our way up to the street that runs down to the water and adjoins the pier and set foot on the rocky soil of the island of Montserrat; made more rocky still in Plymouth by being paved, with great round stones, something like the abominations called cobblestones still to be found in some of the old streets of New-York, only much larger, much rounder, slippier, and every way harder to walk upon.

The colored ladies and gentlemen who formed the solid walls between which we walked down the pier, talked to us as if we had been old acquaintances of theirs. They made audible guesses as to whether we came from New-York or from London. They asked us how we did, begged from us, got in front of us whenever they had a chance, asked us to buy things, looked us thoroughly over from head to foot, and then, finding our appearance irresistibly comic from their standpoint of dress, (or undress), laughed in our faces, and hunted about in the crowd for their friends, for fear anybody should lose the great sight.

Some of these darkies were very nearly dressed, not more than two or three garments being wanting; and some were nearly undressed, not more than one or two garments being present. There were dandies in the crowd—wealthy young colored gentlemen, who owned black clothes and high hats of a date not to be named, and who carried canes. That some of these gentlemen were without shoes no doubt was not any fault of theirs. Indeed, shoes were the exception. A checked shirt and a pair of trousers and a straw hat for a man was the regulation dress. And for the women, how should I know, beyond seeing that they were all barefooted, and all seemed outwardly to be clad in a single calico garment, and that in bad repair and very short about the ankles.

It was no particular sight in a West Indian town such a crowd as this. They acted a little as if they might be cannibals, waiting to get a bite of us, and, indeed, their appearance indicated that a square meal of any sort, even of human flesh, would be more than acceptable to them. But I knew these West Indian colored gentlemen too well to have any hesitation about mingling with them. They are harmless as doves, if not quite as handsome. It was a new sensation to the two ladies with me to be surrounded and stared at by such a crowd, and I got them into the town as quickly as I could, expecting to find some little shops where we could buy some trinkets, and thus escape from the curiosity of the inhabitants. But escape was out of the question. We were a greater curiosity than Barnum's show going into a country town, and the crowd followed us up the street. We found ourselves in a street about as long from one end to the other as one of our shortest blocks in New-York and as wide as the driveway in Nassau-street, without any sidewalks, and running up a hill, and with low dark-colored stone houses with small windows on the side of it, and a high stone wall on the other side.

There were no shops in this first block in Plymouth, (or none visible to the naked eye), but one of the buildings was a small hotel, which did not look inviting enough for us to go in. We went to the end of that block, followed by at least 50 of the inhabitants of Plymouth, men, women, and children. Then, finding ourselves at one side of a very small stone-paved square, not more than 50 feet each way, we turned to the left and went into the only store we saw. This was no easy matter, for the doorsill was a little too high to step to from the ground, and a rough stone had been put in front of it, and it was necessary to scramble over this to get in. The crowd of natives following us waited admiringly outside while we went in to look at the goods. Of course, we pretended all the time to be as unconcerned as possible; and, of course, we felt, with this procession of half-clad darkies following through the town, very much as one of the "curiosities" in a museum might feel to find itself suddenly walking down the Bowery.

When we looked out through the store door and saw the crowd waiting for us outside we knew that we were "in for it" as long as we remained in the beautiful, attractive, lively town of Plymouth. But fortunately both the ladies were New-York Ladies, quite used to the constant stare of Sixth-avenue and Fourteenth-street, and as for me, I leave you to imagine an old New-York reporter being stared out of countenance by a crowd of Caribbean Island darkies. So we resigned ourselves to our fate, and I inquired of the clerk whether they kept cigars.

"We have some very nice cigars, Sir," said he; "just from New-York in the last steamer."

This, I thought, was rather like kicking a man after knocking him down with a brick. I could stand the crowd of darkies; I could stand, for a very brief time, the wretchedly uneven streets and the hills; but to travel down into the Lesser Antilles, the very home and hearthstone of tobacco, and be offered cigars "just from New-York in the last steamer," was too much. The clerk brought them out, and I saw at once that they were old friends. Every New-Yorker is acquainted with the kind, neatly pressed in round molds, made somewhere about Avenue B, in tenement houses, of which to smoke one would be worse than rashness, to smoke two would be suicide. Had they any native cigars? No, they had no native cigars; no native cigarettes; no native tobacco. Had they pipes? Yes, they had pipes. And the clerk led me to a case and showed me a small stock of brier root pipes that evidently came from New-York in the same steamer with the cigars. He had some pretty novelties, he said, that he would like to show us. I thought that if he had anything pretty it would be a novelty, but did not say so. He showed us some fancy boxes, covered on the outside with small shells. Were they made on the island? Oh, no! They came from Paris. He brought out several cheap and showy little things, such as one sometimes buys from a sidewalk vender in Fourteenth-street. Were any of them made on the island? Oh, no, indeed! (disdainfully) they were all imported. Had he anything for sale that was made on the island? At first he did not think he had; but another clerk came to the rescue, and reminded him of some books of pressed ferns. So he brought out two large scrap books, with ferns and sea grasses and leaves and flowers pasted to the leaves. They were very nicely put in, but the books had been handled and thumbed till they were in bad order. They were made, the clerk told us, by a lady on the island, who was compelled to do something for a living, and making these books enabled her to earn a livelihood without letting her friends know that she did anything! So even here in Montserrat, where a steamer touches once a month if it has any cargo to leave, where the people are half clad and a trifle more than semi-civilized, it is a disgrace to work! I wonder whether Robinson Crusoe didn't consider it a disgrace to have to make his own goatskin coats?

After leaving the shop we went one block further up the hill, and this brought us suddenly to the end of navigation, for the town ends abruptly at the foot of a steep hill. We were still followed by our crowd of admirers, and when we turned down to the right they turned down to the right. This cross street was evidently one of the second-rate streets of the city, for the buildings in it were smaller than the first we had seen and more out of repair. There were very few people in any of the streets, except those who were following us. But in this street there were several who had little smoldering fires built, as if they were about to cook their suppers. We went down here one block, and then turned to the right again, so as to go completely around one block. It was the same story of cobblestones, dark stone houses, and darker people. We had then been over, I think, every street of any importance in the town and had seen nothing to cause us to change our first impression—that we would hardly care to buy a residence in Plymouth and settle down there. In a minute or two we brought up in the street we had just left—the one leading down to the wooden pier. The stone wall on one side of it, we found, enclosed in an open market place. And as it was Saturday the market was in operation, and we went in, through a gate, followed by all our crowd of admirers; and when "our crowd" got in, the market would have been pretty well filled up if it had not been a large one. But it was very large, covering, I should think, about an acre, with two small wooden sheds at one end half filled up with old lumber. We saw, when we got inside, that what we had mistaken for a row of cannon balls on top of the wall facing the sea were the heads of colored inhabitants watching the steamer. When they saw us they immediately abandoned the steamer and joined our followers. And our party made a very respectable showing (in point of numbers) as they surrounded us in the market place. There could not have been less than 100 of them grinning at us, crowding up around us, and talking to us. Somehow they got it into their heads that we went into the market to buy chickens.

"Boss, does you want to buy any nice fowls?" one man came up and asked us. Then somebody else, fearing to lose a customer, told us that he had some fine fat ones. Women pushed up through the crowd and assured us, in a language very difficult to understand, that their fowls were better than anybody else's fowls in the market, and that we would be cheated if we bought anybody else's fowls. Two or three half-grown boys made their way up to us and begged us not to buy any fowls till they could run and fetch theirs, which they would present in just a minute—and then off they ran, paying no heed to our solemn assertions that we had no idea of buying any fowls.

One old woman, with a curious eye (she turned out afterwards to be a crazy or imbecile woman), pushed up and gave us some valuable information about Montserrat fowls in general. Trays of fowls, with their legs tied together, and carried on the heads of talkative colored women, were brought up for us to look at. And the fowl subject hardly quieted down before the market people developed a mania to sell us eggs. Did we want nice fresh eggs? Nice fowl eggs? "Very nice biled, boss; or you kin fry 'em in de pan wid di fat meat!" Evidently these favored people imagined that barbarians from foreign lands were not acquainted with the uses of eggs! We had taken our stand in the market in the shade of a big tree, and no opportunity to move about, on account of the crowd that surrounded us. As they gradually satisfied their curiosity and dropped back a little we looked at the trays of fruits and vegetables offered for sale—all either carried on women's heads, or laid down on the rocky ground at their feet. There was the usual assortment of tropical fruits and vegetables—oranges, bananas, plantains, sweet potatoes, pawpaws, mangoes, okras, cassava; but all in very small quantities. We were on the lookout for some alligator pears, they being then just in season, but we did not see any. I incautiously asked one of the women whether they did not have any.

"Peers! Alligator peers? Yes, boss, right away. Here, you George, run right off boy, an' fetch dem peers! You hear wat I tell you, boy? Don' you see de gemman wants to buy some peers? Git along, now, boy!"

George quickly appearing in the person of a very black boy with no hat and few other clothes to speak of, I stopped him in his rush for the gate, and made some inquiries. He was going, I found, to pick the "peers" which were still on the tree. And he would bring me—oh, any number I wanted; as many as 20, boss, if I wanted them. So I told him to bring me a sixpence worth, and left the number entirely to his honesty of purpose. Then I had to make a bulwark of myself to stand the encroachments of a sea of offers of "nice ripe peers." There were none in the market, but everybody had trees loaded with them at home, and everybody would have them picked for me "in jes' no time, boss." But I stood by my contract with George, and waited for him.

The crazy woman, meanwhile, kept herself posted resolutely in front of the ladies, and eyed them intently from head to foot with such a queer look in her face that they were half afraid of her. George was gone a long time—so long that I concluded at last he must have tumbled out of the "peer" tree and broken his neck. Meanwhile two young darkies in the crowd got up a sham fight, and sprang at each other as if they intended to pound one another to jelly—(to blackberry jam, perhaps.) They kept it up for some minutes, with many expressions of anger and defiance, evidently to "show off" before the strangers, till one of the market women stopped them, with:

"You stop yo' foolin' there, yo' boys. Didn' yo' never see no white folks before?"

The hour had almost arrived when we were to return to the ship, and none of us felt inclined to run any risk of letting the Trinidad sail off and leave us on Montserrat. I should very much dislike to experience the sensation of standing on the wooden pier at Plymouth and seeing the steamer go off. So we gave up any further notion of seeing George and his "peers" and started for the landing. We were about half way down the pier when he arrived, breathless and still hatless, bringing a basket containing about a dozen very nice pears. They were the first we had had any chance to buy, and they lasted us for many days; longer, perhaps, because when we got back to the ship we found the table well stocked with them, for the steward had been on shore, and had been a better customer in the market than we had.

I do not think we saw three white people in the town. But that evening (the ship having been delayed) a number of young white men came on board, and we heard of parties of a dozen or fifteen ladies and gentlemen sometimes coming out to see her. Here, as in many of the other West Indian islands, most of the white people live on their own plantations and do not often visit the town. And therein, I think, they show their taste. But, although Plymouth is not a place where one would want to spend much time, it is an interesting place to visit, and I should not want to lose my recollection of spending an afternoon at the head of a procession. I could not make out any Irish brogue in the talk of the natives. But I could understand so little they said that they might have had brogues in five or six different languages.[35]

35. Ibid.

Lafcadio Hearn made a similar trip down through the West Indies two years later, in 1887, on commission for *Harper's* magazine. In reading his account it is easy to see why he is remembered as a major literary stylist of the nineteenth century, while Drysdale's eye and pen belong more obviously to that of a newsman. Hearn had sailed and steamed south from St. Kitts and Nevis toward Redonda and Montserrat. He wrote in beautiful prose, if some of his descriptions may trouble readers of a later century:

> Then a high white shape like a cloud appears before us,—on the purplish dark edge of the sea. The cloud-shape enlarges, heightens, without changing contour. It is not a cloud, but an island! Its outlines begin to sharpen,—with faintest pencillings of color. Shadow valleys appear, spectral hollows, phantom slopes of pallid blue or green. The apparition is so like a mirage that it is difficult to persuade one's self one is looking at real land,—that it is not a dream. It seems to have shaped itself all suddenly out of the glowing haze. We pass many miles beyond it, and it vanishes into mist again.
>
> Another and a larger ghost; but we steam straight upon it, until it materializes into an unmistakable reality—Montserrat. It bears a family likeness to the islands we have already passed—one dominant height, with massing of bright crater shapes about it, and ranges of green hills linked together by low valleys. About its highest summit also hovers a flock of clouds. At the foot of the vast hill spreads out the little white and red town of Plymouth. The single salute of our gun is answered by a stupendous broadside of echoes.
>
> Plymouth is more than half hidden in the rich foliage that fringes the wonderfully wrinkled green of the hills at their base;—it has a curtain of palms before it. Approaching, you discern only one or two facades above the sea-wall, and the long wharf projecting through an opening in the masonry, over which young palms stand thick as canes on a sugar plantation. But on reaching the street that descends towards the heavily bowldered shore you find yourself in a delightfully drowsy little burgh,—a miniature tropical town,—with very narrow paved ways,—steep, irregular, full of odd curves and angles,—and likewise of tiny courts everywhere sending up jets of palm-plumes, or displaying above their stone enclosures great candelabra-shapes of cacti. All is old-fashioned and quiet and queer and small. Even the palms are diminutive,—slim and delicate; there is something in their pose a slenderness like the charm of young girls who have not yet ceased to be children, though soon to become women . . .

> There is a glorious sunset,—a fervid orange splendor, shading starward into delicate roses and greens. Then black boatmen come astern and quarrel furiously for the privilege of carrying one passenger ashore; and as they scream and gesticulate, half naked, their silhouettes against the sunset seem forms of great black apes.
>
> Under steam and sail we are making south again, with a warm wind blowing south-east—a wind very moist, very powerful, and soporific. Facing it, one feels almost cool, but the moment one is sheltered from it, profuse perspiration burst outs. The ship rocks over immense swells; night falls very blackly; and there are surprising displays of phosphorescence.[36]

The Shiell home, washed in these winds and sunsets, was apparently called "English House." It was described on a photograph of it by John Gawsworth as "Shiel's house of childhood haunts" and appears to be on a street steeply sloping into a mountain. On a trip to Montserrat in 1979, Reynolds Morse was told the Shiell store had been located at the southwest corner of Parliament at George Street, right in the central business district, where the Royal Bank of Canada building had replaced it. That description and the early photograph available of the home suggest that the viewpoint was east up George Street toward the rapidly rising St. George's Mountain. The recent volcanic destruction of Plymouth left only photographs and business records to prove that anything ever existed on the site.[37]

Priscilla Shiell reminded Phipps twenty years after he left Montserrat that his father had "bought over" the home in the names of him and his sisters Ada, Sall, and Harrie (Augusta had apparently already married at the time this was done). She wrote Phipps on 25 June 1905 (from Gingerland, Nevis), asking if he would sign over his claim as security so that Sallie could make business arrangements to reopen the store on Mont-

36. Hearn, *Two Years in the French West Indies.*

37. Morse, *The Quest for Redonda* [29]. On the basis of the memory of the son (John C. Kelsick) of Harriet Shiell's attorney, Morse identifies this as the location of MDS's store. MDS mentions two locations for the store in his letter to MPS of 13 May 1887—one at O'Glaria House where he had been before MPS left, and his present location, not identified (holograph original located in HRC). Photograph of Shiell home in HRC. It appears that the Shiell home was not the location of the first store, although MDs probably relocated the store to the family home after his strokes. The "Lease" is located in HRC.

serrat. Her husband, the Rev. Killikelly, had been "superannuated," and he would no longer have the salary on which she and Sall depended. Sall might pay Phipps a nominal sum for giving up his claim, his mother wrote him, in what appears to be Sallie's handwriting.[38] A response does not exist, but he obviously did not do as she requested. It is not known how Sallie's family survived her husband's retirement.

A lease between the Royal Bank of Canada and the Shiell family (managed by Harriet Shiell on behalf of herself, Spinster, Phipps [of "The Forge," Church Hill, Midhurst, Sussex, England], Carlton Killikelly, Toronto, "Printer," and Ada Catherine Manchester, Sandy Point, St. Christopher, "married woman with separate estate") dated 10 June 1922, for a term of twenty-five years at an annual rental of £82, describes the property as it was at the time:

> . . . that portion of the lower storey or shop (being part of the messuage hereditments and premises situate at the corner of George Street and Parliament Street in the town of Plymouth in the said island of Montserrat) the floor space measuring 29 feet along the side facing Parliament Street and 28 feet along the side facing George Street together with a piece of land on the South side of the said ground floor measuring 28 feet along the South side and being 6 feet wide the whole of the said premises hereby demised being bound and measured as follows that is to say: On the north by George Street 30 feet on the South by other lands of the Lessors 30 feet on the East by Parliament Street 43 feet On the West by a portion of the said messuage being the property of the Lessors 43 feet, TOGETHER with all rights, members, easements . . .

When Harriet was unable to pay for repairs accruing from hurricanes ("tempests" in the lease) to the property in 1936 that made the property "unfit" for its purpose, the bank suspended the lease.

An interesting point is almost hidden away in the lengthy letter that Phipps wrote to the Horsfords shortly after his final move to London. In his reference to Grace Wheatland's placing him in a dark closet whenever his sisters were ill, he says this was at "Corkhill." Whether he might have been sent to stay with this woman when the sisters were ill, or whether his family lived for a time at this location just north of Plymouth, is not known.

38. Holograph letter (in the hand of Sallie Shiell Killikelly?) from Priscilla Shiell to MPS, 26 June 1905 (HRC).

Parliament Street (looking south), Plymouth, Montserrat

Launching of new schooner, Montserrat

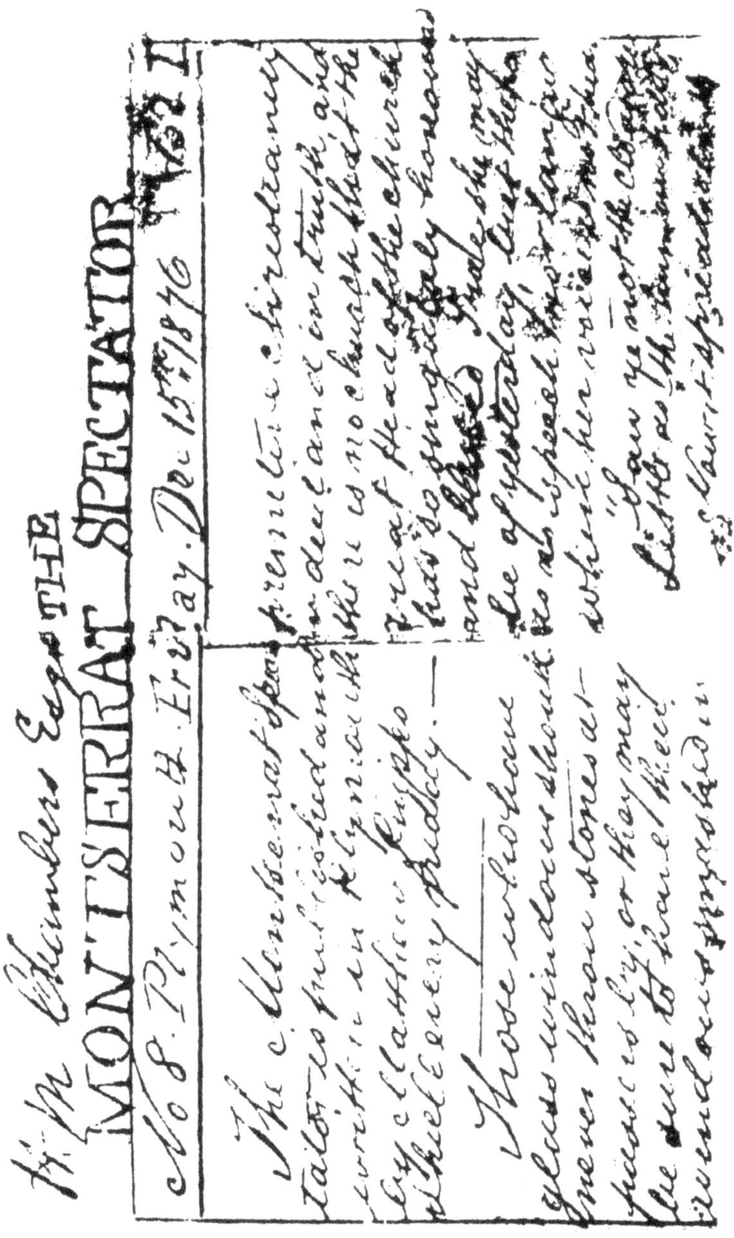

THE MONTSERRAT SPECTATOR

No 8. Plymouth Friday. Dec 15th 1876

The Montserrat Spectator, Friday, 15 December 1876
Courtesy of the Harry Ransom Humanities Research Center
The University of Texas at Austin

Henry Dyett, Percy Trott, Paddy Burke, Harry Dyett—
Montserrat friends of Phipps, ca. 1885
Courtesy of the Harry Ransom Humanities Research Center
The University of Texas at Austin

Harriet moved into the old family home when she returned from London about 1903 and had it renovated after damage from several hurricanes, but her insurance was eventually overrun by damage after damage. She remained there, living on the upper story, until her health required that she move to St. Kitts in the late 1930s. She rented the property in Plymouth, after the bank's termination of its lease, to John Eid, a merchant, for $40 per month, reduced to $30 in early 1944. Phipps received a share of the rent as he had during the term of the bank's lease. The house was sold to Eid in November 1944.[39] The bank eventually acquired ownership and constructed a new building on the property.

There seems to have been more culture in the Shiell home than what one might have expected on a tiny island like Montserrat, and especially given the description of its population by William Drysdale. Phipps's sisters played the piano ("I have known more cosmic blisses during ten minutes in meditating upon the melancholy melody of a piano being tuned above me on a tempestuous day than many men in many months").[40] They evidently read current fiction, though Shiel later confessed to laughing at the grave way his sister—"a Methodist saint"—read *Pickwick.*[41] Though he too read Dickens for a time, in later years he claimed Dickens was a clown who "hopped jog-trotting through paragraphs in bad iambics."

To young Phipps the only true literature was Greek and Hebrew tragedy, but at seventeen he discovered Poe, "just when I had begun to smoke, and the two smokes transported me to Nephelocougia, where I sojourned many days . . ." But Poe, too, he later devalued, "finding a lack of significance, his kite not 'hitched to any star.'"[42]

He recounted how at thirteen he once warned a tutor who was bent on flogging him not to touch him or he would jump from a first-floor window, "higher than ours." When the tutor brashly dared to accept Phipps's challenge, the boy jumped!—to the teacher's "everlast-

39. Holograph letter from Harriet Shiell to MPS, Basseterre, St. Kitts, 12 November 1944 (HRC). The firm of J. G. Eid was still in business in Plymouth in 1973.

40. MPS, *This Knot of Life* 68.

41. Ibid. Chapter 2, footnote 6.

42. MPS, "About Myself" (1948) 4.

ing heartshock."[43] Shiel also said in a newspaper interview in 1937 that he returned to Montserrat in 1880 after having been sent to England for an education. "Then, after my window-jump, to Harrison College in Barbados."[44] (One can wonder whether Phipps's sisters also were sent away for an education. Their reading and musical tastes suggest they received a better education than was probably available on Montserrat.)

It was during this boyhood period that Phipps began to fancy himself a writer. Excerpts from several sources indicate this:

> . . . at twelve I had written a novel, the MS. of which was long preserved in my family (never published); at thirteen I was issuing a penny-periodical, seven copies a week for seven "subscribers," written by hand—a labour of Hercules; and at fifteen I had a serial in a newspaper. But then I was hypnotized into being interested in writing Latin asclepiads, Greek Sapphic—grotesque thing: irrelevant thing!—changing into a Chinese mind a European stripling.[45]

He was more specific about this early novel in the original version of "About Myself" (1901):

> Some such impulse drove me, about the age of twelve, to my first book; but, instead of writing English, I soon found myself caring for nothing on the earth but the imbroglio of phantasms in which my fancy involved me. Ah, that book! I remember it was all about a queen in Central Africa, wonderfully like Mr. Rider Haggard's "She," only of course, more restrained. They go out hunting, and come to a chasm, over which the horses can leap, but not the dogs. I might very well have made the chasm passable to everybody, but no, my fancy must forge obstacles in its own way. And how do you think the dogs go over? They jumped upon the horses' hindquarters, and then the horses leapt with them. [46]

The "penny-periodical" actually was issued when Shiel was only eleven as an incomplete surviving copy in the Ransom Center of The University of Texas at Austin proves. Titled *The Montserrat Spectator*, it was issued "every Friday." The surviving four-page fragment—"No.

---

43. Ibid. 3.
44. Ibid.
45. Ibid.
46. MPS, "About Myself" (1901) 630.

8. Plymouth. Friday. Dec 15th 1876"—is addressed to "H. M. Chambers Esq." It includes an obituary: "A most lamentable occurrence took place in this town. Samuel Dyett died suddenly who seem to bid fair for a long life." A discussion of Methodist theology is in itself an interesting commentary on boyhood influences. He states, for example: "Some ministers only have the outward qualifications to take charge of a congregation and know nothing about conversion therefore can't teach it."[47]

The date of this "publication" pretty much sets one end of the boundary within which he was on Montserrat and when he attended boarding school in Devonshire. The year of his return to Montserrat sets the other limit, a likely enrollment at school in England in the fall term of 1877 and departure after the spring term in 1880.

An important event in Shiel's life occurred during this boyhood period: 25 January 1876. On this date a nephew was born on St. Kitts. Cyril Horsford was the second son of Samuel L. Horsford (a merchant and sugar agent who was later important in the political affairs of the West Indies) and Shiel's sister Augusta ("Gussie"). Cyril was very close to Phipps during his youth, and Phipps "coached" Cyril during his school years in England.[48]

Cyril became a distinguished throat specialist, specializing in the treatment of professional singers and speakers. In 1901, age twenty-five, he was boarding at 39 Dorset Square, W. Marylebone and identified his occupation for the 1901 census as "Medical Practitioner surg." Interestingly, Alberta Horsford, age sixty-four, born ca. 1837 in the West Indies, was boarding at the same address, "on her own means." It is possible that she was either an aunt or older sister of Samuel Horsford, possibly just visiting Cyril. *Might* she have been Sammie's mother? He was born in 1849. Just a couple of years' difference in the accuracy of the census record, on either the taker's part or her acknowledgment of age, could have placed her within the period of West Indian child-bearing . . . especially if Sammie were illegitimate, as it appears. Given the presumed illegitimacy, it also seems unusual that there would be a family unit that included Sammie and an older sister or aunt. That argument would help promote the notion that Alberta was actually Cyril's grandmother. It is interesting that her

47. MPS, "The Montserrat Spectator," mutilated text.

48. MPS, "About Myself" (1948) 4.

name was the first of the full surname, Alberta Augusta, which Gussie never used.

In his late years, Cyril's practice fared poorly, and he ultimately begged Phipps in his own old age to leave his small estate to Cyril's wife and son. Cyril claimed that his recent ill health, depression, too much medical competition, and major expenses in maintaining a home and office had broken him financially. (Of course, it was also costly, he granted, even with three poor doctors as tenants, to retain the five servants required to maintain the quarters.)[49] Phipps grumbled that Cyril's son should long ago have gone through Oxford and be providing help.

Augusta married Samuel L. Horsford in 1872. Samuel ("Sammie") appears to have been a natural son of one of the wealthy Horsford family members of Antigua, where he was born. (He is not included in the extensive "Pedigree of Horsford" listed in Oliver's *The History of Antigua*. Sir Robert Marsh Horsford was Chief Justice of Antigua at the time of Samuel Horsford's birth, having taken this office following the death of John Shiell, son of Queely Shiell, in 1847. Whether he had any relationship to Sammie is not known.)[50] The children of Gussie and Sammie were Reginald Shiell Horsford (b. 1 May 1873), Cyril Arthur Bennett (1876–1953), Samuel Leonard ("Leo," b. 1877), Olive (b. 1879?), and Muriel ("Nonnie"? b. 1881?).[51] Matthew Dowdy Shiell referred to the fancy wedding of Gus and Sammie on Nevis when he wrote Phipps about Sallie's more modest wedding ceremony when she married the Rev. C. Killikelly in 1887.[52]

All three sons of Augusta and Sammie attended Bedford Modern School according to school records, residing at "Matson House." Information about the two elder sons is also included in the 1891 Census

49. Holograph letter dated 21 November 1946 from Cyril Horsford to MPS (HRC).

50. Oliver, *The History of the Island of Antigua*.

51. The birth dates (years) of the two Horsford daughters have been estimated from those of their brothers, who appear to be older than the girls.

52. Holograph letter from MDS to his son, 29 April 1887 (HRC), No information can be found regarding Rev. Killikelly's background. The Killikelly family was one of long historical record and importance on Barbados, and one would think that he was a member of this family, although perhaps not from a legitimate line, as was so frequently still the case for many of the persons in this book.

of England, where both brothers are listed as boarders at 2 Clapham Road, St. Paul, Bedford, Bedfordshire. Each was also identified as a "scholar," as are seven other boys listed at this address, obviously also attendees at Bedford Modern School. The head of the household is identified as Leonard Matson, single, thirty-eight, "Teacher 'English' & Clerk in [*illegible*] Order." Lightly penciled above the word "Teacher" is written "Clergy." Leonard Matson's sister, Lucy, follows his entry, also single, twenty-nine, and "Teacher Music." Two servants are also listed.[53]

Reginald, age seventeen, was born on Antigua, according to the census. Cyril, age fifteen, was born on St. Kitts. (Cyril's obituary in the *Lancet* in 1953 noted that he had attended Bedford Modern School and the University of Edinburgh.)

The Archives of Bedford Modern School provides enrollment information and birthdates for all three of Augusta's sons: Reginald Shiell Horsford attended Bedford from 1889 (autumn term) to 1891 (spring term). He was born 1 May 1873. Cyril attended from 1889 (autumn term) to 1893 (autumn term). He was born, as we know, 25 January 1876. (His address in 1900 was 11 Mayfield Road, Edinburgh, when he would have been enrolled at the University of Edinburgh.) Samuel Leonard Horsford attended from 1892 (spring term) to 1893 (autumn term). He was born 28 November 1877. During Leonard's attendance at the school, Augusta lived at 9 Keppel Street, Russell Square, London, according to school records.[54] By 1900, both

53. Census of England, 1891.

54. I am extremely grateful to Richard Wildman, School Archivist of Bedford Modern School, England, for sharing information by email on 5 November 2004 about the Horsford sons' attendance at the school. In response to my query as to whether racial prejudice or color might have affected admission to the school in the 1890s, Mr. Wildman responded by email on 8 November 2004: "As far as I know, there wasn't any racial prejudice at that time (or later) as far as the Harpur Trust schools were concerned. From the 1880s, Bedford was a favourite retirement town for 'Anglo-Indians', which meant former (British) Indian Army and Indian Civil Service officers who had married relatively late (to younger wives) and came to Bedford because new houses (with servants) could be rented cheaply, and Harpur Trust school fees (and the infant mortality rate) were low. In the case of families with a long tradition of service in India, especially, there would have been a likelihood of mixed race ancestry. There were also similar links with South Africa, and on a smaller scale with the West Indies and South America."

It is also interesting to note that Augusta was staying at 9 Keppel Street

Reginald and Leo had returned to St. Kitts, according to school records, and it is likely that Augusta had also returned home by then. (When Phipps died in 1947, neither Reginald nor Leo was mentioned in his obituary, as were Cyril, Olive, and Muriel, so it is likely that they were deceased by that time. One of the two had died by the time their family firm was sold in early 1929.)[55]

When Samuel Horsford died in 1913, the *Times* (20 December 1913): 11c provided a major obituary for him:

The Hon. Samuel L. Horsford, of St. Kitts, died in London recently, aged 64.

> Mr. Horsford, who was born in Antigua in 1849, received his commercial training in that island and migrated to St. Kitts, where he succeeded to the mercantile business of the late Captain J. H. H. Berkeley, and became the agent of many of the principal sugar estates in the island. His ability and public spirit were recognized by his appointment to be a member of the Legislative Council of St. Kitts–Nevis and the Federal Council of the Leeward Islands in 1894, and in 1911 he was nominated a member of the Executive Council of the Federal Establishment, on which he sat until his death. He proved a keen debater, and a strong advocate of economy in public affairs and of representative government. A staunch Freemason, he had filled all the offices in the Mount Olive Lodge of St. Kitts, and he was for many years a member of the West India Committee and the West Indian Club in London. The Canadian Government appointed Mr. Horsford Commercial Agent for the Dominion of Canada, and he represented St. Kitts–Nevis at the conference at Ottawa in 1912, which resulted in the reciprocal trade agreement between the Dominion of Canada and a majority of the British West Indian Colonies. He was married to Miss Sheil [*sic*], of Montserrat, who, with five children, one of whom has attained distinction as a throat specialist, survive him. Mr. Horsford will be greatly missed not only in St. Kitts, where he was a general favourite, but also in this country.
>
> The funeral service will be held at College Chapel, Swiss Cottage,

---

during a period when Leonard was in school. MPS, his wife Carolina, daughter Dolores Katherine (Lola), and sister Harriet were living at 11 Keppel Street at the time of the 1901 Census. MPS had earlier lived at no. 7.

55. The history of the S. L. Horsford Co. is detailed under footnote no. 12.

at 2 o'clock on Monday, and the interment will be at Kensal Green.[56]

The SL Horsford & Co. Ltd. (the "Horsford's" companies) on St. Kitts has grown in the twenty-first century into one of the major corporations in the West Indies. While located on St. Kitts, it handles a major series of business enterprises throughout the West Indies and supports soccer teams and various cultural and civic activities. The Shiell family interests in the firm were sold in 1929.

Phipps's boarding school experience was probably much like that of his nephews, although the school he attended in Devonshire has never been identified. In 1937 Shiel told a reporter, who had gone to interview him regarding a strange story that had surfaced regarding Shiel's "kingship" of a small island in the West Indies, that he had been sent to London for an education and returned home in 1880.[57] The following event is then said to have occurred.

On Phipps's fifteenth birthday, 21 July 1880, a "coronation" event took place, he said, that was to color his entire life and writings. In "a day of carousal, of a meeting of ships . . . and of people," Phipps says he was crowned "King of Rodundo." He first recounted this story in a revised version of "About Myself" prepared for a 1929 Victor Gollancz advertising brochure. It then surfaced in the popular press in 1937. He told another reporter in 1937 that the crown, made of wood and gold, was still lying around in his little Horsham home somewhere.[58]

Redonda (the more usually accepted spelling) was a tiny rock-island north of Montserrat that reared slick and dripping from the sea like some prehistoric monster, uninhabited save for the wide-winged sea birds that nested on its cloud-pierced crest. But phosphate had

---

56. The precise date of Samuel Horsford's death in 1913 is unknown. It must be presumed that he was in London at the time of his death, as would have been Augusta, Cyril, Olive, Muriel, and probably Leonard, who wrote his Uncle Phipps in 1916 suggesting a firm, The Hepworth Co., to which MPS might offer a screenplay. This was the "White Wedding" synopsis according to a note written by JG on the letter (HRC). There are references to another niece of MPS's in London, Nella, but it is not likely that she was a sister of Olive and Muriel, but more likely a daughter of Leonard, but there is no proof of this.

57. *Star* (26 October 1937). Available at the Javier Marías web site www.javiermarias.es/REDONDIANA/redondaarticles.html.

58. *Sunday Referee* (24 October 1937). Available at the Javier Marías web site www. javiermarias.es/REDONDIANA/redondaarticles.html.

been discovered there in the year of Shiel's birth, so it was not without value. The entrancing conceit to the elder Shiell, however (if we are to accept this story of his birthday gift to his son), was the idea that a member of the Shiell family, descendants of long-dead Irish rulers, would become one of the earth's nobility. (It is also possible that Matthew saw the guano mining underway on Redonda and made an effort to claim ownership of the island to gain that opportunity for himself.) When the "Rev. Dr. Semper, of Antigua," anointed Phipps's head as King of Redonda, the boy accepted it in all seriousness. But this event worked out as neither Shiell could then have foreseen. Years later, Shiel admitted that

> . . . this notion that I am somehow the King, King of Kings, and the Kaiser of imperial Caesar, was so inveterately suggested to me, that I became incapable of expelling it. But to believe fantasies is what causes half our sorrows, as not believing realities causes half, and it would have been better for me if my people had been more reasonable here; nor can I forgive myself now for the solemnity and dignity with which I figured in that show. For what is a king without subjects? Certainly if I am a king, my kingdom is "not of this world": Redonda is a rock-island of scarcely nine square miles, and my subjects swoop with sudden steepness into the sea like streams of meteors streaming, together with eleven poor men who gathered the boobies' excrement to make "guano" (manure). And these were American people! Moreover, not long after my coronation the British Government, apprehensive that America might "annex" the rock, "annexed" it itself, i.e., stuck a little flagstaff on it; and though my parent irked heaven and earth with his claim of "priority," there the flagstaff remains, if it has not now gone to heaven on some gale's gallop; there it may ever remain. I have scaled to that rock's very top, and looked abroad at blue-eyed Beauty . . .[59]

---

59. MPS, "About Myself" (1948) 2. There may be a kernel of truth to some of this. The US Guano Islands Act of 1856 (amended 1872) provided that Americans who discovered guano deposits upon unclaimed islands could petition the US government for protection of their claims from third parties or foreign governments. In 1863 the US and British governments had debated this very issue regarding American claims on the island of Sombrero at the northern end of the Leewards, but let the matter rest for later resolution. MDS might have tried to exercise a claim to Redonda in order to gain guano-mining rights. Though Redonda is not mentioned, a history of this issue

Questions have been raised regarding the identity of the individual who might have "crowned" him. In the original version of "About Myself" (1901) Shiel does not mention this event at all. In the last version (1948) he says "the Rev. Dr. Semper, of Antigua" anointed him. In a variant of the story, in *Twentieth Century Authors* (1932), he says the individual was Bishop Mitchinson. Both names would have been familiar to him when Phipps recalled them some forty-five years after 1880.

Sources on Montserrat in 1979 suggested to Reynolds Morse that Mr. Hugh Semper was a Methodist minister "of color" related to the famous Semper family of the area. Actual records on Antigua validate the ordination of Rev. Hugh Semper on 8 January 1873 and his death on 9 August 1918. Bishop Mitchinson of Barbados was acting headmaster of Harrison College from March 1880 to December 1880, and also served as chairman of the Building Committee. This was just prior to Phipps's first year of attendance. Phipps told the *Star* reporter who interviewed him in 1937 that it was "Bishop Mitchinson of the Antilles" who officiated at the event.[60]

The most likely scenario for this "coronation" is that shortly after his return from England following the years of school in Devonshire, Phipps's family had a party for his fifteenth birthday in July 1880. This was most likely at Gussie's home on St. Kitts. His father's ship routinely passed Redonda on its brief trip to St. Kitts and back, providing the opportunity for this coronation gesture to have been made either on shipboard or at a party on St. Kitts. Several ships of friends from Montserrat and neighboring islands could have attended the party, including the Rev. Semper. He might even have sailed with the Shiells from Montserrat or have been on St. Kitts with other "tipsy" partygoers, as Phipps described them. Since Phipps's own family members were fervent teetotalers, they would certainly not have been among the wild revelers that legend now holds about attendees at the alleged ceremony.

I simply place this whole episode among the same type of story

---

is described in Skaggs's *The Great Guano Rush*. (Redonda was formally annexed by Britain to Antigua in 1872.)

60. *Star* (26 October 1937). Bishop Mitchinson was most active with events relating to Harrison College in 1880, just before MPS's first attendance at the school on 1 January 1881, so this is most likely the only contact that MPS ever had with him.

that Shiel dreamed up from time to time to amuse him at their easy acceptance by the English press. He would do just the same with the biography he gave the press in 1895. The event is never mentioned in any family correspondence. Matthew Dowdy Shiell does not appear to have had the imagination to create this "kingdom." Phipps did. Nonetheless, the story has achieved legend and the literary Kingdom of Redonda exists.

In any event, six months later (January 1881) the young "king" was sent into exile—to Harrison College, Bridgetown, Barbados: "A good school, as schools go," Shiel described it, "but I do not seem to have had any more skepticism than my teachers—any more perception that the two hours a week of chemistry and the four of Greek was a crazy state of things."[61]

He was placed under the guardianship of J. H. Shannon, Swan Street, a merchant with whom the senior Shiell conducted business. Shannon's son was a doctor who later prescribed medication for Matthew Dowdy Shiell. What the boy's activities were beyond school is unknown. We can assume from better documented times that the boy was never idle, and if the devil found a way to use those busy hands and feet and eyes, that would not be surprising either.

The school was recognized as one of the finest in the islands. Established in 1729, it opened on 2 March 1733 with the particular intent at that time to ensure that indigent boys might have an opportunity to achieve an education. It rapidly moved past that mission and became an important facility for boys throughout the Lesser Antilles. Older buildings were renovated the year before Shiel entered, and a new wing for boarders was added to the Headmaster's House. A new two-story main building with additional classrooms, a science laboratory, and a library were completed late in 1880. Possibly 150 boys were in attendance. Those who could not afford the tuition could apply for about forty scholarships available, including the ten "Foundation Scholars" funded from the original endowment established to ensure a good education for indigent youths. The regular "Oppidans or Commoners," paying full fees—£5 per session in advance—numbered about a hundred.[62]

---

61. MPS, "About Myself" (1948) 3.

62. H. N. Haskell, "Notes on the Foundation and History of Harrison College," *Journal of the Barbados Museum and Historical Society* 9, no. 2 (February

It can be assumed that Phipps paid the full fee. Many of the "boys" sported manly moustaches and beards. The new building and additions were formally opened on the night of 4 December 1880 "in the presence of a large gathering." Bishop Mitchinson was surely involved in the ceremonies. It would not be surprising if the Shiell family attended the dedication, leaving Phipps behind as they made the three-day journey home.[63]

Chemical experimentation proved to be one of Shiel's main interests throughout his life, so the importance of those years spent in Harrison's new laboratory goes without saying. (Mr. J. B. Harrison, later Sir John, was Island Professor of Chemistry and Agricultural Science.) Although Phipps later disparaged the time spent on Classics, this field too made a great impression on his thought and style. (Mr. Horace Deighton was headmaster and mathematics master, and became one of the most important figures in the history of the school. Mr. G. F. Franks was classical master.) It was probably here that Phipps made his discovery of tobacco; and in Harrison's new library he found an appreciation for Edgar Allan Poe and (strangely) Henry Wadsworth Longfellow.[64]

The general content of the school's curriculum was to follow the English Elementary Education Act of 1870 whose avowed object was to provide every child throughout the kingdom a "sound education." Some credit the establishment of this act, providing that every British child should have a compulsory elementary education, with the rapid growth in reading that followed this generation of students. The Education Commission for Harrison College, under the chairmanship of Bishop Mitchinson, responded to this act in 1874 with the statement: "Opinion may fairly vary as to the quality, extent and nature of the education given, and as to whether mental culture or purely industrial training should preponderate." Also, the school would be annually tested by comparison with "English Schools of similar standing" through the Cambridge School Examiners.[65]

1942): 64–68.

63. Ibid.

64. It is difficult to imagine that when MPS wrote the lengthy letter to the Horsfords from his early days in London in 1885 that he would list the works he was reading as Dickens, Longfellow, "and then" the Bible!

65. Haskell, "Notes," loc. cit.

That Phipps did not agree with the balance of instruction in the Classics and that in the sciences has already been remarked. And fifty years later he was still arguing against education based on memorizing rather than on "scientific" reasoning.

Three times Phipps took the matriculation examination for the University of London.[66] Finally, in December 1883 he left Harrison College, the most concrete evidence of his studies the following document dated 20 July 1884.[67]

> I hereby certify that Matthew Phipps Shiell was a pupil of Harrison College, Barbados, from January 1881 till December 1883. He possesses industry and considerable ability. He could wish for no better certificate of the variety and exactness of his knowledge, than he has gained by obtaining Honours in the Matriculate Examination of the University of London.
>
> (Signed) H. Deighton MA.–FRA
> Late Scholar of Queens'
> (M: Cambridge)
> Ho. Master of Harrison
> College, Barbados

Phipps had probably been gathering records for some time in preparation for enrollment at college in England. On 26 December 1883, Henry Dyett, Notary Public, Montserrat (and an old family friend), prepared a formal document certifying that the signature of Thomas Henry Bailey, who had certified the Registration of Baptism of Matthew Phipps Shiell [at some unspecified date] was authentic. (Reynolds Morse mistakenly believed that this document indicated that Phipps had been baptized in 1883, but that was not the case.)[68]

How Shiel spent the fifteen months following his tenure at Harrison is uncertain, but he must have been preparing for his matriculation exams while also considering a vocation in the islands. The date of the birth certificate and statement from Headmaster Horace Deighton of Harrison College suggest that Phipps was not ready to attend London University until 1885. There were probably several

66. Per a note by JG in HRC.

67. This document is in HRC.

68. This document is in HRC. The text is reprinted in Morse, *The Quest for Redonda*. Mr. Dyett went to considerable effort in making this notarized document look official, including the attachment of a red ribbon to it.

unsuccessful attempts to find a "position" for him somewhere in the West Indies. But economic conditions had become rather miserable with the decline in the sugar business, loss of land value, and this already frail economy failed rapidly in the years following the American Civil War. It may well be that Phipps spent time on St. Kitts as well as Montserrat during this period, pursuing a vocation. But his family's economic decline made the expense of much travel unlikely.

There was very little work for a young man of his inclinations in the West Indies. Precious little work for anyone, in fact. He considered apprenticing to Montserrat's "chemist," but it was clear there was need for but one pharmacist on the island. He could not assist his father, for the declining finances of the family offered no useful opportunity.[69]

All these factors no doubt contributed to indecision on the part of Phipps. Finally, the inevitable conclusion was reached. He would go to London and make an attempt to obtain a position with the Colonial Office. If that failed, he would find a teaching position and in his spare time read for the B.A. degree.

On 25 April 1885 Phipps and his father saw each other for the last time. Phipps either sailed for England from Montserrat's deep waters (a quarter of a mile out from its small wooden jetty) or perhaps from St. Kitts.[70] He was almost twenty years old, full of enthusiasm and optimism, but with little money or understanding of what was ahead. With thoughts of a new world to explore, he can perhaps be excused for the possibly negligible concern he gave to leaving his lovely islands, his placid, superstitious companions, his father and mother

69. It may be that the seriousness of the family's financial circumstances did not become clear until MPS found himself in London virtually penniless, and his father paralyzed from two strokes. If speculations about his life before he left Montserrat for a final time are true, MPS would have been rather sheltered at home during the time until he was 11 or 12, then at school in Devonshire, then at Harrison College. He would not have had to manage his own finances until he was in London at age 19.

70. Holograph letter from MDS to MPS, 15 April 1887 (HRC). "The 25th instant will be two years since I saw you last." It is possible, of course, that MDS saw his son elsewhere, on some occasion after he had already left Montserrat; but this seems highly unlikely given the difficulties and expenses in travel described in the Shiell correspondence. If there is an alternative to MDS seeing his son depart from elsewhere than Montserrat, it might be St. Kitts whence a ship might have sailed or steamed for England.

and sisters. Did he stop to wonder whether he would ever see any of them again? "Try not to be strange," his father would beg him again and again.[71]

71. Although MDS did not make this comment to MPS until a letter in 1887, he probably told him the same thing in person. It appears to represent a concern that he voiced in different ways to MPS on a rather regular basis. In another letter, he says not to "make strange." What type of possible "strange" behavior by MPS he anticipated, or what the basis of it was, is not clear. But there must have been a history of behavior that concerned the father.

Chapter 3

"I shall have to be content with becoming a teacher"

Phipps found an immediate world of excitement in London, that lodestone of all the Empire, whose gas-lit streets were flooded with emigrant colonials and continentals in those years of worldwide economic depression. Prophetic of the easy flow of words that was to come from his pen were the lengthy letters he wrote home. There is a remarkable account of these early days in London in one of the first letters he wrote his sister Augusta Horsford and her family on St. Kitts. (Like others of Shiel's letters, John Gawsworth transcribed this from an original whose location is unknown, although I suspect these personal letters of Phipps to the Horsford family were in the possession of Olive Horsford, who remained close to her uncle throughout their lives, and who appears to have been the family member most likely to have preserved her mother's correspondence).[1]

> [*At head of first page of letter*] P. S. Can I manage to make you rich W. Indian people pay the postage on the letters I write. If so, how?
>
> My business affairs are in a tangle: when I get them clear I shall tell you all about them. Tell Mrs. T plenty of howdies for me. Don't forget.
>
> Wednesday Evening
> 18 Culford Road
> Southgate Road
> Kingsland N.

---

1. There are no specific birth or death dates available for Olive Horsford, who was still corresponding with her uncle in 1944. (Based on her brothers' birth dates, it is estimated that she was born about 1879.) Shortly after 1900 she was studying art and was producing "miniatures"—probably small paintings based on photographs. She visited Jerusalem and Bethlehem among many other sites, and her Uncle Phipps envied her this particular trip, since he would have liked to search for the tomb of Lazarus. During the German bombing of London one of her feet was badly injured, and MPS repeatedly cautioned her, "Don't let them amputate!" Her sister Muriel was also in a building that was bombed twice, supposedly against the odds. There are also hints that one of the sisters (probably Muriel) managed property in London. (From correspondence between MPS and Olive in HRC.)

Ye very dear Horsfords:—*Is* tomorrow Mail-day? Everything is changed now, and one must post his letters on every "other" Thursday. Ah,—but *which* Thursday. For what magnetic will can call back yon Mail Steamer ploughing mercilessly over dingy seas, when one has posted on the wrong Thursday? She will ever plough *on,* unconscious of unpractical mistakes.

I planned to write you a long letter this time: two difficulties, however, meet me—the first is as to specially *what* I shall write; the next is as to how many words your relentless Postal Company, Governmental dignitaries, official and non-official busybodies in my affairs, and what, as to how many words these Nether-world men will consent to my writing for the sum of 4[d]. You must know. Do write and tell me.

Then again, consider the temptations that your philosophical biped who walks the streets of busy London-town has of becoming Egotistical when he writes others who walk on tiniest West Indies, emphatically *not* philosophy engendering. Or, to put it shortly, one is tempted to write of one's self overmuch, I was even now thinking, whether I might not give you a sketch of any one day in my London-town-life—of this day, for instance.

Well, I live in such a sweet little castle, so thoroughly all-my-own that you could not possibly imagine it. A little bedroom with a little sitting-room with sloping-roof looking out on a back-garden; in which former is bed, & presses, washstand, fire-place, & utensil or pot, or as we say po or poe; in which latter is table, trunks, chair and easy-chair in which may I not sit perfectly secure all the evening smoking philosophical pipe? In this latter, too, I now write you: it is my palace, or as was said, my castle, home, "ain fireside," or whatever comfortable name you choose to give it. Had it some little, bright, good, loving creature of female persuasion in it to welcome me home, or still better, had it my dear old father in it, you might even name it "earthly paradise."

In this, then, I sat me last night till late, (I can read without light of lamp till about nine o'clock) and at last went to bed without hope of sleep, my light burning, on into the small hours of morning. (By the way, if any-body else that I know in the W. I. dies, any ordinary person I mean, you need not bother to mention it in your letters. A woman called Grace Wheatland used to lock me up in a dark room of Corkhill in Montserrat when I was a boy and my sisters were sick with sore-throat and I am suffering the consequences of that woman's idiotcy [*sic*] & cruelty today.) Consequently, I sleep late in the morning and am roused by a great knocking at my door: it is the old lady who has brought up my breakfast in a tea-tray, has placed it on a stand just outside my door and has knocked to give me warning of it. Stand quickly on terra firma, thou laziest one, heedless of half-opened eyes, cast around thy form thy blood-red gown, intrude thy feet into hose whose cleanness is doubtful, pray unto thy Father in secret whose hearing of thee is not doubtful—now mayest thou eat heartily frugal philosophic breakfast composed of limited bacon, & unlimited bread, coffee, Devonshire butter, and W. Indian jelly!

Whither now wilt thou tend? First, sit down all-radiant in thy blood-red and read Dickens, then Longfellow, then the Bible. Has thou done this? Then envelop thee in clothes—not of the dandy kind today in high silk hat, maroon gloves, & choking masher—but in humblest pepper-&-salt, ordinary felt & gloves too doubtful to be put on. But whither wilt thou tend? "Take us thoughts": a pleasant day is always to be spent in London if you know how. I walk for 5 mins, to the Haggerston Ry. Station, pay my 1½, and fly thro' air to Broad Street; for I never feel that I have spent a day unless I go into the City. Broad St: is so called from its extreme narrowness and is about the same in breadth as the Broad St: in Bridgetown, B/dos, exemplifying an instinct in the English people to call things by their wrong names: what they call the Opera Comique is a theatre—not an opera, what they call Covent Garden Theatre is an opera, not a theatre; what they call "pavement" is not a "pavement" but the very opposite—the only part that is a pavement (the middle of the street) they don't call so—and so on. Well, we come into "Broad St:" (not the one down Seven Dials: the one near Thread-needle) pouch & pipe in breast pocket, Longfellow in hand. What now? Why, stroll leisurely down towards thy street—the Strand, having, (before you have gone three paces) a man who leans against a wall looking into thy face & saying with all coolness—"*You* look well, you do." As thou passeth under it, Bennett's clock with endless hammering and fuss strikes 1. Bathe today. Stop before your New Law Courts (thy frequent place of resort by day) ascend a stair in which thou mayest behold thy form with several hats on, and take solacing warm-bath. Be honest, pay thy shilling, & depart. Now for dinner. By dint of observation and London-town-experience hast thou not discovered a retreat in the very heart of the City, even down Essex Street before New Law Courts, whither thou mayest go—and get roast beef, potatoes (all *new* & excellent) bread, half-bitter, apple-pie—all, all for one shilling. What though the spoon with which thou eatest thy pie be *not* silver! Thou philosophic Uncle!—is *not* the pie itself excellent—that which stands upon the torn cloth *good?* What carest thou for the outside of a thing, the appearance of it? Thou thyself art a reality—is it not then thy duty when thou meetest a reality to open thy arms and embrace it in very friendliness?

What now? Go and spend thy day at Aquarium, Invention Exhibition at South Kensington, Crystal Palace? Nay—thou hast done this often enough and art quite tired and sick of them. But canst thou tire of *God's sky?* Canst thou not stroll down to thy St. James Park, thy Green Park, and lie thee down flat upon the grass & extend thy arms like Him who was crucified for thee, looking upward into Heaven with philosophic pipe in mouth? There, peeping through the umbrageous trees is a tower of St. Stephens, there too the Abbey, & St. Margaret's; down yonder thou canst just see the walls of Buckingham Palace & perhaps of Marlborough House, & at thy back is Carlton Terrace. Art thou not *perfectly,* perfectly happy? What more canst thou desire: does not thy God give thee meat & water, nay, even cause thee to gulp down tea, coffee, guk-guk (or beer), and envelop thee in clouds of tobacco smoke? Better still, does He not make thy conscience light, causing thee to feel like a free and brave man, making thee satisfied with his works—*thyself* inclusive? Consider, too, how thou in returning from this same park, passeth the very door (with the "To Let" printed on it) behind which that unaccountablest Jones sits with long struggling legs stuck crookedly beneath prosiest writing-desk all the day long beholding bare walls, gazing into the face of his fellow-prisoners (called "fellow-clerks"). While thou thyself art free and singing

"Oh Light and Love! Oh throng
Of thoughts whose only speech is song;
O Heart of Man! Canst thou not be
As light as air is & as free!"

And so walking back looking into girls' faces & smiling with them, stopping at a shop window to gaze at a particularly wicked picture of Mrs. Langtry that by this time I regard (?) as my own, buying ½ lb of Strawberries which I eat as I go along, I reach (by train) my "ain fireside," or house, or castle & sit to write you—utterly uncertain if tomorrow be Mail day or not.

There. I hope I have given you such a pill of a letter that you shall never be over-anxious to hear from me again. I am sure that one of the H's will never get thro' this stuff: I mean the busy one. Don't think, however, that I have got used to London without meeting some strange things: I remember the first morning I woke up at Wild's (by the way, tell Druett Wild remembers him) Hotel. I had not become quite an Englishman yet, consequently I was not so dirty as I am now—so I wanted a bath. Call pretty little servant-maid.

Servant-maid (teeth chattering terribly) Yes sir, sir, sir, sir. Please sir, yes sir, sir, sir.

Half-green W. Indian: I want a bath—is there one on the premises.

Servant-maid (chattering): Oh yes, sir, sir—many.

Half-green Will you shew me to one, please?

S. M. Oh, sir—I will bring it in to you, sir, please, sir.

Half-green (nearly fainting with astonishment) Bring it to me! Oh-ho-oo—in the W. I. we usually go to ours, but here they seem to bring 'em to you. Very well, don't strain yourself.

S. M. Hot or Cold sir, sir, sir etc.

H. G. (in an evil moment) Cold!

What was my surprise instead of seeing her bring up a large stone bath like yours in your yard (not knowing what to expect, I half-expected that) to see her bring in a beastly little tin baisin with a tea-spoonful of ice-cold water in it, put it on the floor of my bedroom, close the door, and leave me in my horror! Shall I ever forget the miseries of that bath? Echo answers "Shall I," but *I* answer "No, never!" They charged me sixpence for it in the bill, tho'!

So too when my old lady first sent me in a plate of shrimps. "Now what on earth are these things!" thought I; "if they are cock-roaches (as they seem to be) I am not going to eat 'em." I was perplexed. I tried one. Liked it. It was not a cockroach for it had a shell: but now the question arose in my mind "do you eat the shell?" If you *do, this* stomach won't manage the digestion of 'em: if you *don't* it will take you some days to pick one out of the shell, & then you will get a piece of flesh approaching in size a pin's head. So I determined to leave them till I had acquired more experience on the subject of shrimps.

Why did neither of you write me last time? I shall write an individual letter to you yourself soon, Madame 'Gus. How are you getting on? Behaving like a good-girl, I hope. Write me a long letter. I have been thinking of you lately: I would that even now I had a pen that could teach you the mystery and wonder of your life—teach you why thou art, and whence thou art, and, oh Heaven, whither thou tendest. Be earnest, woman!—be earnest. If thou be *that,* thou mayest see light yet & "learn to live." The unpardonable sin in such a life as we men live is even this,—we flit thro' it like [*incomplete*]

I, now and forever more, apply myself with what vigour, with what *force,* is in me. Wisdom, I tell thee, thou shalt learn—under penalties! I will try to teach thee by loving caress, sweetest midnight huggings, tenderest words-of-affection. I will try to teach thee by *this,* first. Or, that failing, by severe stern-browed frownings, peremptory comments or even utmost extreme "cat-o'-nine-tails!"

And *thou,* too, must do thy part, the chief part in fact. The heaven-given command to all men, my dear 'Gus, is even this: "Thou shalt *think,* thou shalt be *earnest.*" There is work for you to do here, most certainly there is;—or why were you *put* here? And yet you waste away your precious life composed of only a very few minutes (or years: much the same to the philosophic earnest eye!) Doing what? Kicking against the bars which the Eternal God hath set for thee! Oh I am deeply terribly earnest when I tell thee that this *must* not be, at most, cannot be for very long! For hast thou not heard it said, "Nature abhors a vacuum." It is verily true. Create a vacuum, and I can promise thee that, in time, there will be an explosion—of some kind!

Now, I know that except you are really much worse than I think you, you will be nothing else than pleased with me for telling you what I *think,* for giving you what extremely poor advice lies in me. If you do [*are?*], I shall be sorry; but myself is nothing, is not to be considered as anything, only [*illegible*] of myself; what myself *owe* [*illegible*] *ought* to do.

Your prophecy with respect to my living in England will, I am afraid, be true. The C. O. [*Colonial Office*] has given me a practical refusal—"They regret etc. etc." So for the present I shall have to be content with becoming a teacher in some part of the country. I have employed a couple of teaching Agencies (one in Piccadilly, one in C. Garden) who send me to the names of people wanting teachers, & I have sent heaps of applications flying all over England. It will be easy to get a place for about £30 or £40 a year beside board & lodging. Of course, I wont settle down to that.

I have not seen your friend Mr. Jones since I first came nor Mrs. Leach (at all). They live up Willesden: the Regents' Park Way, you know.

I must stop now. When is that wondrous She-She [*nephew Cyril Horsford*] coming? Tell them all howdie.

You would like to hear about all the theatres etc. I suppose; but I really can't—not today. The best thing on now is "The Mikado" by Sullivan & Gilbert—better than Iolanthe. The bands play it at the Exhibition. But I don't go to the theatres now. First of all, I really can't afford it, and then I don't (from principle) like to give my money to the beastly class of English people who play on stages. Oh my dear England—the England I love so much! What *art* thou coming to? Or as Carlyle says, "Oh my bewildered brothers! What foul infernal Circe has come over you changing you from men once rather noble of their kind to asses, hogs, and beasts of the field or the slum! I declare I should rather die." . . . You should [*illegible*] sentiments on the Opera! [*Illegible*] goodbye. God bless you. Love [*illegible*] yrs affectionately,

Phipps

[*Illegible*] teachership, Why not send She-She to [*illegible*] so that I can have him under my eye.

This remarkable letter[2] reflects Shiel as he may never be captured in any other record or account. Here is boyish excitement in the adventure that was London at possibly its most exciting pinnacle of culture, science, and power. Here is evidence of the ease with which Phipps was to dash off his future prose. Here is the young "preacher," instructing his sister toward some ill-formed religio-philosophical theory he was trying to grasp. Indeed, here are hints of the color, the skillful description, style, and excitement with which he would imbue his fiction, including this urge to bring the Divine somehow into his work.

Here are also hints of looming financial crises, overly optimistic expectations about the ease of finding a job, and unrealistic notions regarding income and the expenses of living.

A teaching position was indeed found. On 18 November 1885, Phipps writes Gussie from Bideford Grammar School, on the far southwestern edge of Devon. This was just inland, east from the Atlantic, north of Plymouth on the southern coast. He has found employment, he tells her, but also acknowledges that he owes her "much besides letters"; and, unfortunately, he is just recovering from a case

2. JG's holograph copy of MPS's lengthy letter of ca. June 1885 to Horsford family (HRC).

of measles, measles that threaten to leave him "puddingless." Mr. Brook, the headmaster, had just sat and discussed the situation at length with him, when he "was just able to crawl out of bed." The doctors thought it too "dangerous" for him to return to his pupils for the rest of the term. If Mr. Brook let him teach again and even one student came down with measles, it would be poor Mr. Brook! he told Phipps. If he let him back in the classroom, it "would have the whole town out him," since they "hate him already." He simply had to hire a new master, so Phipps must lose his recently acquired position.[3]

Shiel retained until his death a photograph of fellow teacher Max Fredericks and an unidentified woman at Bideford, so he must have held some degree of affection for his first teaching post at this school in Devon. (This might also have been in the vicinity of where he attended school as a boy, close to Plymouth and more accessible by ship to the Indies than other English ports, and remindful of the location of Gussie's portrait, made at Tiverton in Devonshire. Why, and when, was she there?)

His mind is not just on the school situation, however.

> Much as I would like to live among the stars, and talk of the stars and write for the stars—this indubitable fact remains: that I, M. P. Shiell, am an inhabitant of this (in some aspects) extremely commonplace Earth, and do daily eat commonplace beef and (with the assistance of certain "mild aperient pills") even visit a laystall or "W.C." Strange enough! But a reduction to which every august philosopher and "Man of Genius" is subject—this same (at least) weekly resort to said "W.C.!" Nay, even Christ himself—Christ! Christ the beautiful, the all-lovely, your supreme "philosopher" & "Man of Genius," must not even *he,*—were it but with the assistance of "mild (Jewish) aperient-pills!"

This obsession of Phipps with the man Jesus would continue to dominate his thinking over the years. He continually frustrates readers by insisting that his characters seek some form of Christ-like immolation rather than a "happy" conclusion to his novels. He devoted the last ten years of his life to his study, *Jesus*—a "truer" translation of the Book of Luke with commentary.

One of the things that probably most appealed to Shiel about his

3. MPS to his sister Augusta in a letter dated 18 November 1885 (typescript transcription by JG) located in HRC.

second wife, Lydia Furley, was her own interest in Jesus the man. At an early point in their romance in 1909, Lydia told Phipps that she was reading Ernest Rénan's *Life of Jesus*. "I feel no artist—whose pictures of Him I have seen—has ever presented Him anything like He was . . . fierce eyed—(at times a dark hairy type) . . . I wish I could paint Him."[4]

Lydia, dark herself, tried to explain to Shiel her interest in the darkness of "Hungarian music—or see a swarthy neck & the shine of gold worn in ear. I do not know whether my mother gloated over gipsy doings or whether the cells have memories that sleep or wake in us."[5] Lydia inadvertently, perhaps, made her own contribution towards the issue of Shiel's possible ancestral roots: "I dreamed my mouth was pressed to your brown cheek."[6]

Phipps had been ready to go up from this little Devonshire town to London before now, he tells Gussie, but it is not just a matter of finances: "the old doctor won't let me go." He does not think Phipps healthy enough just yet. Whether Phipps went to London at this point is unclear, but he reported early the next year (that black 1886) that he was most happily and comfortably situated at Hunt Bridge House in Matlock, Derbyshire, in the Vale of Derwent, a region of woods and bathing spots, northwest of Nottingham.[7]

Phipps loved these small out-of-the-way country spots, but he loved London as well. Too, he intended (or so he said in the enthusiasm of the moment) to read for his B.A. degree. His responsibilities as a teacher were probably very similar to those of his instructors at Harrison College, specializing in mathematics, so he would have been familiar with the duties of an instructor. Several early photos reveal a handsome young Phipps at Hunt Bridge House. It appears that he was happy here, but something moved him on. For late in 1886 he left

4. Holograph letter from Lydia Furley to MPS, Ardingly, Hayward's Heath, n.d. [1909?] (HRC).

5. Holograph letter from Lydia Furley to MPS, [London, November? 1908] (HRC).

6. Holograph letter from Lydia Furley to MPS [London] Tuesday—13th [April 1909] (HRC).

7. Holograph letters from MDS to MPS, 4 February 1887 and 5 March 1887 referring to how happy MPS had been with Mr. Leaf at Matlock. MDS says he had advised MPS not to leave. (With contemporary photographs of MPS at Hunt Bridge House, Matlock. All located in HRC.)

Mr. Leaf, his employer at Matlock, against the advice of his father (who later reminded him of this), to return to London. Exactly why, we do not know. To study medicine? Several months of his life are unaccounted for during this period.[8]

Then the winds of God thundered about him.

Of the first blow, there is only one historical remnant: a funeral card edged in black.[9] On 10 October 1886, his sister Ada died, at age thirty-one. How he must have had a special affection for her, this sister whose name was bestowed on so many of his fictional heroines, whose name not so oddly turned up on a daughter and a niece. There were only two of the multitudes of dead in *The Purple Cloud* that the future Adam of a new race buried: his mother and his sister, "black-haired Ada." The cause of Ada's death is unknown, but there was a constant, routine flurry of typhoid and other "fevers" and outbreaks of cholera throughout the West Indies. Why Ada was still unmarried poses an interesting question. Was it because her father had been so insistent that the elder daughters not look at a man, as Harriet said?

Various other misfortunes arose to plague the Shiell family. Fire destroyed trading goods on Nevis as well as Matthew's ship, *Dreadnaught*.[10] Then the elder Shiell had a stroke. It was not overly serious initially, but was severe enough to affect his speech and limit his activity. He gave up all his business activities except for the operation of

8. Since MPS was so adamant about studying medicine at St. Bart's, it is quite possible that he gave up the teaching position at Hunt Bridge House to go to London for this purpose. Based on his father's comments to him about the good situation he had with Mr. Leaf, and evidence of a pleasant time that he had at this Derbyshire school, one would think it must have been a powerful motive that led him from Hunt Bridge House to London at this time in 1886.

9. There is no contemporary correspondence relating to Ada's death other than the funeral card. MDS could easily speak of her with reference to what he thought was inadequate medical attention following his own stroke early in 1887, and MPS referred to her—"How silent was Ada!"—when lecturing his father in 1887. One can only wonder whether this was a personality trait of Ada, or whether a physical condition might have been involved. The fact that she was still unmarried at 31 seems unusual, except that Harriet told Olive Horsford that their father did not even want the two elder daughters to look at a man.

10. MDS's letters at this time suggest that he owned two vessels in 1887 prior to the loss of the *Dreadnaught*—that vessel and possibly the *Gold Hunter*, which he would have been unable to master following his stroke.

his small store in Plymouth. As though to further torment him, new shopkeepers offered additional competition on the impoverished island.[11]

Phipps, of course, was busily teaching school in Bideford and Matlock during this period, until he returned to London late in the fall of 1886.

Then, on the day following Christmas, 1886, Matthew Dowdy Shiell had a second stroke. He was left dumb and immobile. Not until February of 1887 was he able to write again, and even then his left side was almost completely paralyzed. Phipps had written him on 11 January, and his father was able to answer him on 4 February 1887.[12]

He is sorry Phipps is so despondent. (Might it have been because of his sister's death?) "I wish that you may soon be settled in another place, as one of the masters, and be as comfortable as with Mr. Leaf," he writes. He says that Gussie had been dispatched earlier to London to look into the situation of her brother, and her letters to Montserrat had led the old man to think his son had secured another position.

But on 5 March 1887, the father writes, "My own dear boy, your last letter dated 10th February has almost killed me. The fact of your being in London without money, and without employment . . ."[13] (Gussie had not yet arrived.)

There is no money to send him. There is no good news at all. The father sits and writes, he describes, with "the wind blowing me away, at the table in the hall where I am writing, although my sash and gealousy [*jalousie*] is closed . . . I am suffering misery enough to kill any being,

11. What common goods these stores carried is not known. Based on the clothing and materials that MDS sent MPS from the shop, and given that Sallie was able to select goods from the shop for her dowry, it appears that the emphasis was on basic mercantile items, but there is just not sufficient information to be certain.

12. It is unclear why there is no extant correspondence from MDS to his son prior to this time. It is especially puzzling as to what MPS was doing between the period he left Hunt Bridge House at the end of the summer in 1886 and these early months in 1887. One can speculate that he might actually have been sitting through lectures at St. Bart's. In any event, Gussie was on her way to check on him, and he would soon start a teaching position at Hornsey.

13. MPS's address during this period is unknown. Whether Gussie found him in living quarters preparing to go to the Anglo-French High School in Hornsey, or whether he was already at Hornsey, is not clear.

the last tooth I had is gone, put your finger into my mouth from one side to the other and you will not feel a bit of one. I have no teeth, no eyes, no feet and no hand." Everyone has left or is leaving him, he says. Sallie has been a help in the store, but she has become engaged to Mr. Killikelly, a Methodist minister from St. Vincent. At least, "both Sallie and Hagga are very sincere in their profession, and making progress toward Heaven."

"Have you given up your drawing, and Music, and how are you progressing with reference to your examn?" he asks his son. "I hope you may make out this. Take time and try."[14]

Matthew and Mr. Killikelly performed their formal dance around the engagement of the minister to Sallie two weeks later. Killikelly wrote from Chateau Bellair, St. Vincent, on 19 March 1887, asking permission to marry Matthew's daughter "Sall" and thus become also his son.[15] "Please make my affectionate regards to Mrs. Shiell," he added, and concluded, "Yours in hope, C. Killekelly." Since both Mr. Killikelly's letter and the response from Matthew are (it appears) contemporary copies on the recto and verso of the same sheet of paper, the spelling of "Killekelly" was probably a transcription error. It may be that Matthew had these letters copied to send to Phipps. [16]

Matthew responded to Killikelly, probably with great relief and muted enthusiasm, on 1 April 1887: ". . . therefore I willingly consent to your union with her in marriage." He notes that he has nothing to give but her, but she will be a good helpmeet. He also advises Killikelly to procure life insurance immediately, if he does not already have a policy. Barbados Mutual was as good as any. In between the asking and the giving of Sallie's hand in marriage, both men appear to try to outshine the other in affirming his beliefs in the principles of the West Indian Wesleyan Church.[17]

Perhaps energized by this exchange, there was slightly better news in the letter Matthew wrote Phipps on the same day (1 April 1887).

14. Ibid.

15. Holograph transcription in a contemporary hand of both the request from Rev. C. Killikelly and the response by MDS, front and back of same sheet (HRC).

16. MPS never commented about the Rev. C. Killikelly in any letter read to date.

17. This correspondence represents all that is known of Rev. C. Killikelly. If his were a forced retirement, after 18 years of marriage to Sallie, he would have been considerably older than she when they married.

Gus had written him that she found Phipps teaching at the Anglo-French High School, Ferme Park Road, Hornsey N. Matthew is sending him a money order for £2 in care of Charles Allan, Esq., a friend of Phipps from whom he can always receive mail. One pound is from his father; the other from Harriet, the daughter Matthew called "Hagga"—a compounding of her forenames, Harriet Garry—although others in the family always called her "Harrie." "Hagga" had given piano lessons to earn the money. "I am glad to tell you that she is not going to become the concubind [*sic*] of Mr. Llewellyn, or any body else. You should not write in that style even in a joke."[18] Phipps enjoyed aggravating his parents.

As for his health, Matthew has nothing but noise of misery. There is still no circulation through his left side, he says, and he is troubled by cramps. He had been treating himself with rum and ginger and bird peppers without benefit, "and sometimes with kerosene oil." He had gone to bathe in the ocean, taking a boy to assist him, but these baths brought no relief either. "Poor me," he says. He has even lost his dog Nello, who had gone aboard ship and drowned trying to swim ashore.[19]

On 15 April 1887, he writes Phipps: "I can't say that I am well pleased at your conduct towards me. I have often told you when the Mails come and I don't get a letter from you that it makes me miserable, but it appears to be of very little importance to you whether I suffer or not, as you allow so many Mails to come from time to time without a line."[20]

He did not really intend to write this mail, he says, because Phipps had not written him recently, but Phipps's mother said, "You really love revenge." "I put my hand on my heart, and said: me, I love revenge out of Phipps, you ought to be ashamed of yourself to have such a thought." So, he had written.

"The 25th instant will be two years since I saw you last," he writes, marking the date that Phipps apparently had left Montserrat

---

18. This is an interesting comment because it suggests that the practice of concubinage was still on the minds of Montserrat's inhabitants, and it further underscores MDS's lecturing MPS every time he uses language that the father disapproves.

19. Ibid. "Nello," the name of MDS's dog, sounds like a plantation name.

20. Holograph letter from MDS to MPS 15 April 1887 (HRC).

for England, on 25 April 1885.[21]

There was no relief from his suffering. Dr. Johnson had charged £15 for "dear Ada and myself" and the only benefit Matthew can see is that "may be he has helped to send her to heaven." As for himself, the doctor had prescribed a bottle of Bromide of Potassium and two small bottles of some substance with which to rub. In addition, he is taking "3 times a day Easton's Syrup, which I imported from St. Kitts, the medicine that Doctors Shannon & Rogers prescribed . . . The store will be closed as soon as I can sell off." Why does not Gus think of her children and husband and come home, he asks.[22]

Phipps, with worries of his own, no doubt tired of this deluge of complaints. "Cher Père," he answered his father; he is sorry to hear of his sufferings, but why does he not read his Bible more and not complain so much. "I am afraid you don't read your Bible, man, and have forgotten about it . . . Do you walk about the house complaining? . . . It is most ignoble, childish, *ungodly* this constant talking. I am sure it is the root of most of your trouble . . . Become a Silent man, and that means a true earnest man. How silent was Ada! How silent is God! *His* way is the sea . . ." Phipps suggests that his father go one day without speaking and see how much better he will feel as a consequence.[23]

"Love to little Harrie, poor child," he says. "I hope the day will come when I shall be able to have her with me." (The 1901 British Census indicates that Harriet was four years or so older than Phipps.)

On 24 April, his father writes Phipps that Gus had arrived home, but had only a few minutes at the jetty to speak with him before her ship sailed on to St. Kitts, so she had little time to tell him about Phipps in detail. As a result, her father wrote her these questions that he sends on to his son:[24]

---

21. The issue of when MDS last saw MPS is discussed under Chapter 2, n. 70.

22. Bromide of potassium was used as a sedative, while Easton's Syrup was prescribed as a restorative, containing quinine and strychnine in addition to iron (Holograph letter from MDS to MPS, 15 April 1887, HRC). Dr. Richard Shiell comments that the £15 fee charged by Dr. Johnson was "enormous," possibly the equivalent of several thousand dollars today.

23. Holograph transcription by JG of letter from MPS to his father, [April/May] 1887, from Anglo-French High School, Ferme Park Rd., Hornsey N. (HRC).

24. Holograph letter from MDS to MPS, 24 April 1887 (HRC).

> How does he look, describe him to me? How does he seem to behave himself? Has he a good supply of clothes, and does he look decent at all times? Do you think he has improved, and is he happy? Do you think it is better for him to live in England, not because it is England, if it be so. That he could get anything to do this way? What do you think of his pretended religion, is it real? Does he attend the house of God, and Keep the Sabbath? Has he had any thing to pay for entrance fee at the University, and has it been paid? When is the examn to take place? What are his prospects for a place after the Easter vacation? How was he off for money when you left, and was he much in debt? How much money have you given him that I have to return?

Matthew apologizes for the tone of his last letter. "I hate life but dread death." Worst of all, "Even in my family I am not happy, for some who ought to please annoy and vex me, however, I won't say more on this subject, but I am the most miserable man living."

He gives Phipps details of Sallie's wedding, which is to take place on 7 June. It will be rather quiet, with cakes, lemonade, and such; no luncheon or "nine." What a difference between this wedding and Gussie's, he said. Did Phipps remember the earlier one, the large party and many carriages at Nevis?[25] "How is the mighty fallen."

---

25. Ibid. It is unclear why Augusta and Sammie were married on Nevis. Sammie must have been working for Geo. W. Bennett & Co. of St. John's on Antigua (where he was born) at the time. Their first child, Reginald Shiell Horsford, was born on Antigua, and it does not appear that the family moved to St. Kitts until Horsford's firm opened a branch on that island in 1875.

Chapter 4

"I have begun writing, writing, writing"

The next eight months of Phipps's life are mirrored in the letters from his father, who probably did not let a mail go by without a letter for the son.

On 13 May 1887, Matthew writes Phipps that Gus has replied to his questions regarding him. She wrote:

> He looks well and has a good colour, but has some brownish marks about his temple & forehead. He has a good many clothes but they are not all in good condition. I attended to them as well as I could when he was leaving London. [This must have been in late February 1887, as Gussie found Phipps leaving the City to teach at Hornsey, a northern suburb of London.] He has some surge & tweed not made up. I don't think he is what you call happy, but he bears his position very well and is mostly cheerful. I think it better for him to live in England except very exceptional circumstances than out here—I mean unless something very extraordinary turned up for him[;] there he prefers doing a little than in the West Indies, and besides with a cultivated mind like his, he has there too a chance of something turning up in a place like England to his advantage. He also attends service but mostly church, and he has strong religious feelings. I can't tell how far they influence him; he also lives a very pure life and is proud of doing so.

He only owed a small amount to Mr. Allan, she finished.[1]

Matthew pushes a suggestion at his son: why not go "into the Wesleyan Ministry—the best church under the sun"? He would continue to urge this.

As for Matthew's personal finances, he owes Durrant £300 that he does not see how he will ever be able to pay, particularly since he has so much competition. Mrs. Henry Dyett is keeping open the store where Mrs. William Chambers had kept hers; and Collins and Hannan are opening a store at O'Glaria House "where I was when you left here."[2] He notes that Sallie and Mr. Killikelly will honeymoon at Bethel (an estate on the eastern slopes of Centre Hills), then on to St.

---

1. Holograph letter from MDS to MPS, 13 May 1887 (HRC).

2. Ibid.

Vincent's, which was rather distant, south into the Windward Islands, just west of Barbados.[3]

Phipps had written his father on 4 May 1887, and on 27 May his father answered him.[4] He cannot understand why Phipps does not know his own address and why he speaks of the former school where he had been located by saying "I have not definitely fixed on another but shall in a day or two." (The reason was that the term was coming to an end and Phipps did not know where he would be during the holidays. He had been teaching for room and board only.)

Soon, Matthew says, he will have to make a payment on his annual premium of £24 for life assurance, the only thing he will be able to leave his family when he dies, and he does not know how he will be able to pay it. He has no cash or credit, nothing to give Sallie as a dowry for her wedding except what little she can take from the store.

Earlier, Matthew had lamented his vexation with a member of the family. He writes Phipps unhappily on 10 June 1887:

> I am very sorry to know as I learnt from your letter of 18th ulto that I have been the cause of giving you any pain, or any unhappiness. You were right in supposing it was not Sall, or Hagga—your mother's tongue has been the cause of making me unhappy from time to time. She pharisees like prides herself on her religion, and if I say a word that may not be strictly right taunts and annoys me, that nothing escapes her lips but what is right. If I make a remark that no body else in the world would notice, she takes it up, till all the neighbours hear it, then when I know that every body know it, then I say what I have to say at the top of my voice, and every body know every

---

3. Bethel plantation had been the property of Queely Shiell, of William Shiell, and later of the Joseph Sturge family, and the Sturge Montserrat Company that followed, as it bought up property all over Montserrat for virtually nothing after 1865, when Montserrat enacted the Encumbered Estates Act. This authorized sale of distressed property was enacted as many sugar estates were going bankrupt. Much of this land became lime orchards. It is not clear why Bethel would be an appropriate place to honeymoon, although it had a Methodist church and a lovely setting. While Rev. Killikelly evidently was a minister on St. Vincent at this point, it also appears that by 1900 he was ministering on Nevis, considerably closer to Priscilla Shiell, and it was to Nevis that Priscilla moved to live with Sallie in 1900. While we know that Rev. Killikelly was retired by the church in 1905, there is no record of what became of him.

4. Holograph letter from MDS to MPS, 27 May 1887 (HRC).

> thing that happens in my house. The paralysis has added to my bad temper and peevishness and Priscilla provokes me beyond what it is possible for Man to bear and I had to lay everything before Gus a week after her arrival, and she wrote her on the subject. My life is the most miserable life to be found in existence . . . My dear boy, I must love your mother, not only for her own sake which I do, but I love her for all of your sakes for I love all of you.[5]

Sall is now married, he says. "All the respectable people in the island were there."[6] Who Matthew thought the "respectable people" on Montserrat were in 1887 is unknown, although they must have been a mixture of different shades of black and white, all of modest means since there was no other, perhaps the "professional class" of Montserrat, and, in the eyes of the Shiell family, good churchgoers of the Wesleyan faith.

He is sending a piece of wedding cake, as good a cake as baked in England! On 24 June he writes that he has given the cake to Mr. Watt, "who you wanted to practice Chemistry" with, for he is going to England and can mail the cake in London.

He is also sending Phipps a pound he has borrowed from Lizzie Chambers and advises him to have his "Surge & Tweed" made up. Also sending a *Montserrat Watchman* in which Phipps can see something of the wedding. When Phipps writes he does not recognize a certain lady in the wedding picture, his father informs him it is Phipps's old sweetheart, Miss Florrie Wall.[7]

---

5. Holograph letter from MDS to MPS, 10 June 1887 (HRC).

6. Ibid.

7. Ibid. At least one of the picture postcards sold at the Jas. Wall store in Plymouth in the early 20th century shows a sign hanging over a prominent building that says Llewellyn Wall Co. (A similar photograph does not show the sign.) This reminds one not only of the Florrie Wall mentioned in this letter, but of the "Mr. Llewellyn" for whom MPS had jokingly suggested to his father that Harriet could become a concubine. Whether this firm was of MPS's generation or later is not known.

Howard A. Fergus, the author of a number of volumes about Montserrat, includes a sketch of John Clifford Llewellyn Wall in his *Gallery Montserrat*. J. C. L. Wall was a prominent businessman and politician on Montserrat (b. 1903) who succeeded his grandfather, James J. Wall, and father, William Llewellyn Wall, as a leading merchant and promoter of educational reforms. Harriet named him one of her executors in 1945. It is not clear if the Llewellyn Wall store related to the Llewellyn and Wall families, or if this was just the

On 6 July 1887, Matthew writes that he is leaving that night on Mr. George Irish's vessel, *Georgenianna* (a very fine ship with every imaginable convenience and piece of equipment), to spend two days on St. Kitts. On the 8th he writes (in a note included in his letter of 6 July) that he will "call on Calle" (if that's the name) for the papers Phipps desires. Gus and family are all well. Sallie is on Barbados.[8]

Phipps's birthday arrived as usual on 21 July 1887, and his father wrote him that day with apologies for not having mentioned it in advance.[9] He sends a "P-O-D." for £2 as a gift and suggests yet again that Phipps have his "Surge & Tweed" made up. Has he given up his B.A. completely? He is very sorry to have received Phipps's letter dated 29 June in which Phipps had written that "your poor son is in a very miserable condition . . . ragged clothes . . . some weeks before I came here I was almost dying of starvation and was forced to borrow money so I am in debt £5." His situation had been so bad, he went on, that his communion with God had been interrupted.

Matthew could not help but reminisce. "I remember that of all the young men in this island, from Mr. George Irish, your pecuniary prospects for ease and comforts were better than any body I know when you were born. Could I have believed that my son would have had to put some of his books into a hat box and walking in the street of a strange country to try to sell them . . ."[10]

Further, he is outraged at what he learns of the "wages" that Phipps has received: "Fine thing for my boy to be working for what I can't get a negro here to do for me."

He'll pay the £5 for Phipps if it has not been paid in five months. "Have you given up the idea of the Colonial examination, and appointment? You must try." Or, better yet, why not go into the ministry? He cannot advise him to come home, but if Phipps so wants he will do the best he can to arrange passage.

In the meantime, he is sending Phipps some clothing from the store: four white shirts, three undershirts like the ones he wears himself (not the best "red" that he had sent before), brown socks, hand-

---

name of W. L. Wall on the shop's sign. (The general historical work of Fergus regarding Plymouth and Montserrat underlies much of this biography.)

8. Holograph letter from MDS to MPS, 6 July 1887 (HRC).

9. Holograph letter from MDS to MPS, 21 July 1887 (HRC).

10. Ibid.

kerchiefs with colored borders, towels, two nightshirts of cotton, the pair of boots he had worn at the time of his stroke, a broad cloth vest and two white ones; but he has no marine drawers to send.[11]

Phipps wrote on 19 August 1887 that he needed employment. Again, his father mentions coming home, "but I know how prejudiced the people in the West Indies are."[12] Has the memory of that wild coronation on Redonda come back to haunt him? Or does this suggest a racial or social matter, perhaps discomfort that Phipps has such lighter skin than the majority of the islanders? Or would his return home simply have indicated failure?

Matthew's health remains the same: mustard plasters have done no good. "I bought 2 leeches, and Moro Shiell put them on one of my legs. I bled much, but there has been not the slightest improvement." (Moro Shiell's relationship to Matthew is unknown.)[13]

Augusta, knowing Phipps better than his father, has suggested a new tactic: she has encouraged him to commence writing. Responding to her from Guildhall Library, 13 Southampton St., Pentonville N., on 24 August 1887, Phipps notes changes in his address.[14]

> You see from the top that I have changed my address again; so constantly am I shuffled hither and thither, seemingly without aim or purpose. Now it is at Kingsland—presently it is at Holborn—then it is at Pentonville—then it is at West Kensington. Ah, do you remember our West Kensington domicile, selected by G's own discrimination? And what the devil was the name of that woman I lived with who used to speak as if her windpipe was a mile up in the air?—Giles, Grimes, was it? I for*git* (as Allan would say) the damned woman's name. [*"Allan" is probably Charles Allan, to whom MDS directs his letters to Phipps.*]
>
> She was very good to me tho' I must say, and used to get me apricot jam in plenty. Ah, I was a gentleman in those days!
>
> Do you remember how I used to go over to Miss Bellot's, on my way to the City to get my dinner (!!!) at a certain restaurant, with that damned (excuse all these 'damned's': I am in a peculiar mood,

11. Ibid. It is likely that it was more the wish of MDS that MPS come home than any real interest of MPS.

12. Holograph letter from MDS to MPS, 19 August 1887 (HRC).

13. Ibid. "Moro" does not sound like an English or Irish name.

14. Typed copy by JG of letter from MPS to his sister Augusta, Guildhall Library, 13, Southampton St., Pentonville N., 24 August 1887 (HRC).

> and it seems to relieve me) that damned silk hat stuck on the top of my head? "Uncle is quite a swell today," they would say, at which Uncle would smile blandly, feeling not displeased. Ah, it is a foolish little goose's life, this of ours. We are a lot of little pigs. I tell you truly, Gussie, sometimes I get beastly sick of you, and myself, and all the rest of us. We are such little pigs! Consider it well and tell me, *are* we not?
>
> That cursed "Madame" has got launched. I copied it out, and they took it at the Family Herald office, but goodness knows what they are going to give me for it. [*It is not clear whether this was a new work, or the earlier story he had written in the West Indies.*] Now let me tell you something that you don't know: the way that all such things are done now, it is not selling direct to the people who want to buy: but by joining, becoming a member of some 'Literary Agency' of which there are several; or better still by employing some Private Literary Agent to sell it for you: but this requires in the former case a sov [*sovereign*], and in the latter some three sovs. It is in this way that all these great pots seem to sell their things. Later on, I, too—! Meanwhile, you have kindled a most strange fire in me; I have begun writing, writing, writing. Most strange! Writing ever—for its own sake, as if I couldn't stop. Most unaccountable, dangerous!

As far as social London goes, Mary Anderson will arrive in a week or so; there is a new photo of Mrs. Langtry and the Princess of Wales; there was a great fire in Gray's Inn Road the evening before, at which he had been present "in a great crush and crowd"; and

> Rider Haggard is the great pot as a novelist now, and you cannot live without hearing & seeing his name. "Two lovely black eyes, oh what a surprise!" is the song you will hear from all men, women and children in the streets at present. And, lastly,—I have no more room, and, bowing with my hand on my heart, must therefore retire for this time.

The song, "Two Lovely Black Eyes," was a favorite of the English music halls and an indication, too, of how seriously the Englishman took his politics.[15] Phipps's mention of the song is another indication

15. The Conservative–Liberal party disagreements were as vigorous as they have always been. MPS had written Horsford in 1895 that he was afraid the Conservatives were going to get in next time since they were winning all the bye-elections. MPS probably began paying a great deal more attention to

of his frequent attendance at such venues, his attention to what was occurring in the popular cultural scene, and his willingness to share news of it all with his relatives on islands far away.

TWO LOVELY BLACK EYES
By Charles Coburn

Strolling so happy down Bethnal Green
This gay youth you might have seen,
Tompkins and I, with his girl between,
Oh! what a surprise!
I prais'd the Conservatives frank and free,
Tompkins got angry so speedilee,
All in a moment he handed to me,
Two lovely black eyes!

Next time, I argued I thought it best,
To give the conservative side a rest.
The merits of Gladstone I freely pressed, when
Oh! what a surprise!
The chap I had met was a Tory true,
Nothing the Liberals right could do,
This was my share of that argument too,
Two lovely black eyes!

The moral you've caught I can hardly doubt
Never on politics rave and shout,
Leave it to others to fight it out, if
You would be wise
Better, far better, it is to let,
Lib'rals and Tories alone, you bet,
Unless you're willing and anxious to get,
Two lovely black eyes!

---

politics after socialistic theory grew in influence in the late 1880s, with his own attention strongly drawn to the theories of Henry George. Shortly after the turn of the century he attended (briefly) meetings of the Fabian Society and became more aggressively involved as the suffrage movement for women strengthened. This may have been to influence a favorable opinion of him by Lydia Furley. A song such as "Two Lovely Black Eyes" could be equally popular in the music halls, since it easily called to emotions on any party line.

CHORUS:

Two lovely black eyes!
Oh! what a surprise!
Only for telling a man he was wrong,
Two lovely black eyes!

In September 1887, Phipps's father is still considering arrangements for the boy to come home.[16] He really cannot afford it, he writes, even though Phipps evidently had expressed a half-wish to return to Montserrat. Matthew says he will write Sammie (Horsford) and see if passage can be arranged on one of the Hoult Steamers.

He chastises Phipps for using "profane and sinful" language; that must not be in his letters again. (Phipps had called someone named "Larsen" a "damned person.") He is having a "likeness" made for his son (10 September), but Priscilla will not consent to sit for a picture, because of an eye problem. "She has her hand on it from morning till night," Matthew says, and she cannot give up rubbing it. His miserable health is the same; the doctor has suggested electricity, sea baths, and massage, but "I can't find what massage is."[17]

He is sending, besides the clothing mentioned above, the pair of "gold sleeves buttons that dear Ada left for you." And he suggests again that Phipps go to his own creditors, Durrant and Company, 30 Great St. Helens, for assistance if necessary.

Matthew will turn sixty-three on 18 September 1887, he reminds his son.[18] Later in the month he goes to Gingerland on Nevis, hoping the warm baths there will help his "circulation." On 28 September, he writes Phipps that he had been glad to hear that his son again had employment.[19] Phipps's tenure at Anglo-French School evidently had come to an end, although on 1 August 1887 the headmaster had written out the following document for Shiel:[20]

---

16. Holograph letter from MDS to MPS, 10 September 1887 (HRC).

17. Ibid.

18. Ibid. This is the only reference that has been located that identifies the birth date of MDS.

19. Holograph letter from MDS to MPS, 28 September 1887, Nevis (HRC).

20. This document is located in HRC.

The Anglo-French
High School
Ferme Park Rd.
Hornsey, N.
Aug 1st 1887

I, the undersigned Principal of the above hereby certify that Mr. M. P. Shiell has been Junior Assistant Master here since March last and is still with me having charge of the Holiday Class. He is conscientious in the dispatch of his duties and is well educated. His knowledge of English History and Language, of Mathematics & Classics is especially good.

(Signed) L. W. Lennard

Although Phipps again had employment, his father was "sorry to hear that you have degenerated so much, as you said in your last, as to board with that woman and to have such companions." Do better, he said; be economical; pinch each penny. Try to get books to read for his B.A., perhaps from a library. Try not to be stuck up and proud.[21]

On 28 October, Matthew sends Phipps a pound in yet another attempt for him to have a suite of Blue surge and a suite of Tweed & Black pant made up; the money was for this purpose only, he specified. In addition, he is sending all the necessary material: broad cloth for pant, four yards of Tweed for a jacket; also, two used towels, handkerchiefs, and undershirts. (This preoccupation with having a suit sewn and sending Phipps the necessary material may relate to what appears to have been the early apprenticeship of Matthew as a tailor.)

Nowadays he opens the store in the morning and closes in the evening without taking in a penny, he writes. "I never expect to see you again." Strokes come in threes, he believes, and he awaits his third.[22]

11 November: nothing to write about except the old story of theology; he is very poor, without money for postage; he must pay £5. 14. 9 on his life assurance or lose it, but he has thirty days grace. He has been drinking rum with gin and half a tumbler of milk. A number of people have been poisoned from the fish they have eaten. "Have you ever fell in with any West Indians?" he asks Phipps. "Try to make friends." Above all, "*Dread* a bed of sickness."[23]

---

21. Holograph letter from MDS to MPS, 28 September 1887, Nevis (HRC).
22. Holograph letter from MDS to MPS, 28 October 1887 (HRC).
23. Holograph letter from MDS to MPS, 11 November 1887 (HRC).

Augusta Shiell Horsford, Devonshire, ca. 1880
Courtesy of the Harry Ransom Humanities Research Center
The University of Texas at Austin

Cyril Horsford, London, ca. 1891 [ca. 1890], age 15
Courtesy of the Harry Ransom Humanities Research Center
The University of Texas at Austin

Isle of Redonda

Harrison College, Bridgetown, Barbados, ca. 1880

Sarah Ann ("Sallie") Shiell, possibly Barbados, ca. 1887
Courtesy of the Harry Ransom Humanities Research Center
The University of Texas at Austin

As though forewarned, the elder Shiell learns in Phipps's next letter that the boy had been ill with fever. He was not surprised, he tells Phipps, because an old woman had dreamed she had seen Phipps out in the cold London streets without a coat.[24]

On 25 November 1887, Matthew writes, "I was more than sorry to see the piece of paper that you enclosed from the Editor of the Family Herald. He said that the style and plot are not suited for the F. H. What does he mean? You would not write any thing that the most modest lady would blush to read."[25]

He is glad to hear that Phipps intends to read for his B.A., but he wishes that he would give more thought to becoming a Methodist "Parson." Also, he will pay the £3 to Mr. Irish that Phipps owes him. Sall is "in the way," he reports, good news that, but this will be the poorest Christmas since long before he owned the *Gold Hunter*.[26]

Matthew's letter dated 9 December 1887 is the last that MPS had in his personal archives. It is quite dismal. He is afraid to ride his friend Blake's mare and is too poor to buy his own; he has been in the sea only once in three weeks and his business is a mockery. There is a heavy Northerly blowing. He is sorry for Phipps's "unfortunate 'Madam' and 'Day.'" He has no money to send, but has sent his "likeness."[27]

The church record book for "Burials in the Parish of St. Anthony in the island of Montserrat" notes the burial of Matthew D. Shield [*sic*] on 7 January 1888.[28]

Harriet Shiell wrote her niece Olive a stark picture of the final years and days of the life of her father.

> Some of your questions re my ancestors are beyond me, and cannot be answered, but my Dad's illness and death are indelibly fixed in

---

24. Holograph letter from MDS to MPS, 25 November 1887 (HRC). Superstition was obviously still a strong legacy of the slave days.

25. Ibid.

26. Ibid. It is uncertain whether the *Gold Hunter* was currently owned by MDS or whether his reference was to a schooner owned at a previous time. Dr. Richard Shiell suggests still another explanation for MDS's reference to the *Gold Hunter*. A favorite pocket-watch of many years ago was a "gold Hunter," a British term for "a valuable gold pocket-watch some 2–3 inches in diameter, kept on a chain and very popular with pick-pockets."

27. Holograph letter from MDS to MPS, 9 December 1887 (HRC).

28. Burial record copied by A. Reynolds Morse on his trip to Montserrat (*The Quest for Redonda* n.p.).

> my memory. For several years before his death he suffered from partial paralysis. I was his nurse. For he used to think that no one massaged his arm like Hagga. His death was rather sudden in the end, not more than a few days serious illness. But what a death! It nearly killed me because I was the only one left with him and I would not leave him even for a minute. He had fits all the time, fit after fit for several days with only half an hour between each one till the end came on my birthday the 7th.

The identity of Sallie's child, born in 1888, following her father's death, is uncertain. What little evidence there is suggests that she had a son, Carlton, and a daughter, Ada Catherine. Carlton was probably the elder of the two.

Carlton's address in the 1922 lease of the Plymouth property was listed as Toronto and his occupation as "Printer." Harriet's 1944 will lists him at 448 W. 40 Street, New York City, but the codicils to Harriet's will of 1945 omit his name.

Ada Catherine Killikelly (later Manchester) sent a photo of herself and "Miss Blake" to her Uncle Phipps from Montserrat, but her note is undated and the photo has disappeared. In the lease of the Plymouth property to the Royal Bank of Canada in 1922, Ada Catherine Manchester of Sandy Point, St. Kitts is identified as a "married woman with a separate estate." The date that Ada married and when her daughter Kathleen was born is not known. In 1927, Harriet wrote Olive that Ada "is quite well," but she soon wrote Phipps that Ada was extremely ill and sent him a copy of a prescription to be filled for her. She told Olive that "Kathleen is a nice little girlie, only she does not speak prettily—I used to tell her of her three *little* cousins in England who spoke very nicely and she got very interested in those little cousins, Olive and Muriel and Nella."

In a long letter to Olive from Montserrat on 2 February 1932, Harriet said to her:

> Now about Kathleen, remember will you, that it is about eighteen months since I last saw her, and that would make a world of difference in a growing child, but Alice Manchester (her new mother) passed here last week on her way to Barbados to get her passport to New York for an operation told me that Kathleen is growing, a sharp sensible little girl and is Ada re-produced—unfortunately the little thing is very delicate and by the doctor's order must not be rushed [*into school*] . . . Her father is simply devoted to her—he is rather tall,

> very slim and fair with blue eyes—yet not good-looking, his hair is what *you* would call "wicked," but out here call it *bad*. He is a reading man and intellectual and speaks in public some times—(not such an orator though as his brother Jim, whose speech your Ma never forgot—) and though he is an Anglican he is sometimes honored by being asked to be chairman of our missionary meetings. I must have told you that he was here with me for over twelve months, sent by the Bishop to restore the Church destroyed by the hurricane and the Church now finished is considered a master-piece of work . . .

Ada Killikelly Manchester has apparently died, and her husband has remarried. Harriet told Phipps in 1941 that the Honourable Tom Manchester was an executor of her estate, so he must have been Kathleen's father. His brother Jim appears to have been in the islands longer than Tom who came to work on restoring the church.

Kathleen sent a Christmas card (neither dated nor franked) to her Uncle Phipps from Toronto, and her slender-faced features are known from a photograph she sent him at some unknown date, although probably during the war. Her photo suggests a brown-skinned West Indian heritage; her greeting to her Uncle Phipps is written in French: "Toujours à toi! Kathleen."

Harriet wrote Phipps on 19 June 1942 (from Sandy Point, St. Kitts) that Kathleen was still in the Government service. (Probably in Toronto?) She says that Kathleen's "Dad is not yet better, he has been very ill indeed."[29]

Harriet added codicils to her will in 1945 so as to leave parts of her estate to Kathleen and to Olive Josephine Horsford, as well as Phipps. Miss Winifred Manchester ("Spinster"), of St. Kitts (possibly Kathleen's aunt) and J. C. L. Wall of Plymouth were named Trustees on 29 September 1945. (Wall was a relative of Phipps's "sweetheart" of years ago, Miss Florrie Wall.) Harriet also named Winifred as her attorney. Kathleen's father probably died during his illness of 1942, since he was no longer mentioned in Harriet's affairs.

This is all we know of Sallie Shiell Killikelly's family, her husband, son Carlton, daughter Ada, and granddaughter Kathleen. They join Augusta's family in a faded past, sister Ada in an earlier tomb, and Harriet most certainly "a Methodist saint" as Phipps named her long ago.

---

29. Note from Ada Killikelly is undated and photograph is not present (HRC). Photo of Kathleen Manchester and Christmas card are in HRC. Holograph letter, HRC.

Chapter 5

". . . an island in the sea of London"

M. P. Shiel's own account of these years is typically brief, undoubtedly inaccurate in many respects, and varies a bit in his several short autobiographical retellings.

> Then after my coronation I was translated to King's College, London: now matriculation and "intermediate"; about the time of my degree my father dying; and during all that alumnus-period I seem to have quite abandoned writing English . . . But when I had taught for a year what was called "mathematics" in a Derbyshire school, I thought of following my namesake James Phipps Shiel, and becoming a doctor; this thought kept me at St. Bart's six months, where upon, coming directly, every day, in contact with science, I was done with writing—or reading!—Greek poetry, except the old Homer, to whom one may so easily get addicted. But the very first operation which I saw was for strabismus—on the eyeball—and this so sickened and hypnotized me into a dislike for knifing, that I gave it up.[1]

Although Phipps had passed the matriculation examination with honors, after three tries, for the University of London in January 1884, there is no evidence that he ever paid an admission fee or attended classes on a formal basis. However, his presumed exaggeration concerning a degree and attendance at King's College might have more truth in it than has always been assumed. The following account is somewhat reinforced by a signed contemporary portrait of Phipps in the Shiel Archives at Texas marked "King's College, Strand."

Mike Barrett wrote Reynolds Morse on 4 July 1979 that he had interviewed the Archivist at King's College (text revised by Morse):

> I got to see Mr. H. A. Harvey, the Archivist at King's College today. He let me have a Photostat of Shiel's article, "'Long Tots' and Languages" from *The King's College Review*, Vol. 30, No. 4, 1929 Centenary Issue, p. 18. (This was referred to by Charlesworth Ross

1. MPS, "About Myself" (1948) 3–4. Morse adds a footnote citing a letter that MPS wrote the World Publishing Company for its 1946 edition of *The Purple Cloud*, printed on its dust jacket, in which MPS says he taught mathematics for two years in Derbyshire.

who was chief editor of the magazine at the time, in his article "The First West Indian Novelist" (*Caribbean Quarterly,* University of the West Indies, Mona, Kingston 7, Jamaica, December, 1968. p. 56) where he said: "The second shortest contribution—it was ruthlessly pruned by one of my co-editors—was on 'Long Tots' and Languages by M. P. Shiel. 'Long Tots' turned out to be columns of figures which one adds up in a mechanical way by force of habit.") The article is very short, but it does go a little way toward solving what is something of a mystery.

Archivist Harvey could find no trace at all of Shiel ever having attended the College, let alone obtaining a degree there. However in 'Long Tots' mention is made of an examination for a 'Student Interpreter.' This set bells ringing in the noted archivist's mind. A bit of digging unearthed that at one time—for about ten years—a body called King's College Civil Service Department was attached to the college and located in the basement there. Originally this was an independent college situated at Waterloo. In order to gain credibility and respectability, they asked to be affiliated and to share their premises in a more prestigious part of London. At that time King's was imposing and collecting a levy of 5% of salaries paid, and so it was delighted at the idea of the extra revenue. Hence King's College Civil Service Department came into being.

This part of the College dealt with Student Interpreterships, normally for Government posts in China and the Far East. This ties in with what Shiel says in the article. We uncovered some frail calendars detailing some examination results, but alas there was no mention of Shiel. This department eventually became an independent college again in the 1900s. It is now defunct these many decades, and Mr. Harvey thought that any records which might have been kept are now destroyed.

In Shiel's time, an education at King's tended to be something of a status symbol. Thus archivist Harvey felt that the author might have claimed a King's College education, even though the Civil Service Department was only peripherally associated with the college proper, and for a short time. Thus the fact could be (as it was in other cases) that Shiel DID go to King's College, but that is only part of the story. Mr. Harvey also felt that the records just might be in error—unlikely, but possible. But the simple fact is that so far there is no record whatsoever of any matriculation or exams.

In substantiation of this marginal association with King's College, Mr. Harvey told me that some years ago in doing some research that Arnold Bennett had always been looked upon as one of the many distinguished ex-students of the college. Yet Mr. Harvey found that the venerable Mr. Bennett had in fact attended only one lecture a week (in French) and for less than two terms! This case may be indicative of what happened with our Mr. Shiel.[2]

The text of this brief essay by Shiel, "'Long Tots' and Languages," written in 1929 for the centenary issue of *King's College Review,* provides in his own words the most forthright story that he was ever to tell about his college education:

> My last experience of "that schoolboy spot we ne'er forget, though there we are forgot," ("the tenderest thing ever said," Robert Louis Stevenson said to me one night at Roche's in Soho) was in connection with the examination for a government appointment as a "Student Interpreter" (in the East for which I seem to have considered myself the right kind of person. One had to "know"—was it seven languages? or five? And I suppose I must have "known" these languages, whose very names I have now forgotten, for my King's coach told me that I was certain of being appointed. But there is (or was) an elementary examination preliminary to the pièce de résistance: and some days beforehand my coach said to me: "I suppose you are all right in regard to long tots?" I asked him "What are long tots?" On which he looked reproachfully at me: "You don't know? Then it is no good—you won't pass the preliminary: no one can do them without practice." He explained that "long tots" are columns of figures which one adds up in a mechanical way by force of habit. So I did not go in for the exam: "long tots" had rescued me, and I can remember a feeling of relief that was mixed with my dismay.
>
> I do not consider that my education had then commenced—except the education of my memory. Five languages! perhaps seven: I had been made into a remembering machine, untrained to think a thought. It was afterward that I turned to study science; and I hear rumours of King's acquiring a fame in science. This is heartening, for the others will follow.[3]

Phipps had already alluded to his difficulty with "long tots" when he ventured the answers (in his voice as O'Malley Phipps) in the

2. Morse, *The Works of M. P. Shiel,* 3.423–24 (text of Barrett letter).

3. Ibid.

"Premier and Maker" conversation in *Shapes in the Fire:*

> "What can you not do?"
> "I cannot spin a top."
> "Proceed."
> "I cannot add up rows of figures, nor comprehend the money columns in newspapers."

To this one can add a fictional episode that echoes life in *The Invisible Voices,* where Shiel describes how a character, Whip, "one evening had an impulse to step aside from the Strand into King's College, where he was guided down to an underground room, and there Ransom sat undergoing coaching [*reading for Student Interpreterships*]. Whip suggested dining . . . but Ransom, no diner-out, smiled, answering 'Perhaps you don't know what long tots are?—rectangles of figures to be added up: one can't, if not in practice; they are in my preliminary exam.'"[4]

There is a question as to not only when but also where Phipps's participation in this program of the King's Civil Service Department occurred. In 1875 the government extended the range of entry examinations to the Civil Service, and an agreement was reached with King's College to use rooms for the programs. Among training for "boy clerkships" and "boy copyistships" in a Civil Service Department was established to offer preparation for excise and customs appointments among others. As more programs were added, additional room was needed for these "commercial" activities and premises were added at 4 Albion Place, Blackfriar's Bridge, and then 91A Waterloo Road. It was not until 1897 when King's College School moved to Wimbledon that the commercial school moved into the basement of King's College and became known as the Strand School. It seems apparent from Phipps's reference in "Premier and Maker" that his fortunes with long tots occurred sometime earlier than 1896—as one would expect from the other tracks of his career. Thus, he could have "attended" King's College at the original location of the Civil Service Department within the college, possibly at one of the subsequent expansion locations, but never at the basement level off the Strand.[5]

Charlesworth Ross, the "co-editor" of the centenary issue of the

4. MPS, *The Invisible Voices* 16–17.

5. Cf. website for King's College London Archives www.kcl.ac.uk/library/collections/archives.

King's College Review in which Shiel's essay on long tots appeared, later noted how his duties included soliciting contributions for it from alumni and others. Shiel, he said, seemed uncertain of what was wanted and invited Ross to come visit him to explain. Ross says he found Shiel living on a Civil List pension in an "almshouse" near Horsham, "old and feeble." After a lengthy visit, Ross was surprised, he said, to discover that one of Shiel's sisters had married his grandfather, and Shiel was thus his great-uncle. By 1968, when Ross wrote this essay on "The First West Indian Novelist," he had become a prominent political figure in the West Indies, having served in public office in Antigua and as commissioner of Montserrat. Most of his essay is about himself, with what he briefly wrote about Shiel being chiefly an error-prone rehash of what had already been written about him.[6]

Either Ross or Shiel could have been mistaken, or correct, in Ross's understanding of a relationship to Shiel. Samuel Horsford would have had to be the grandfather who married Phipps's sister Augusta, and Muriel is the only Shiel niece whose age and unknown state of matrimony might have allowed for marriage to a Ross. But it seems impossible—as do so many things in Shiel's life!—that Ross (who was born in 1910) could have gone twenty years without his mother telling him that Shiel, with whom she had been close since childhood, was her uncle.

There is something fishy about Ross's account of his visit with Phipps, who was neither elderly nor feeble at the time, had just moved into L'Abri, a nice little cottage, not an almshouse, and did not receive a pension until 1935. There is no evidence of Muriel having married. She was still alive into the World War, when her building was twice bombed, so it seems impossible that she would have had a son in 1910 to whom she never revealed his relationship to her uncle, a prominent author. If Ross had any relationship to the family, it is more likely that it developed from his grandfather's marriage to some other Shiell family relative on St. Kitts or Antigua, not a sister of Phipps.

Phipps's "rescue" by long tots is probably as close to an examination at King's College as he ever got. But it appears to be the most accurate representation of his college experience than has ever been documented elsewhere. Similarly, observing an operation at St. Bart's

---

6. Charlesworth Ross, "The First West Indian Novelist."

may have been as close as Phipps got to medical training, although he might have been able to spend time on an informal basis sitting in on lectures for the six-month period he claimed. (As will be noted later, the credibility of Shiel's dining with Stevenson seems highly questionable given that there simply seems no time when this could have happened before Stevenson left England for good in 1887.)

In following Phipps's calendar from late 1887 into the early years of his regular literary production, about 1891, only a few events are on record. In August 1887 he wrote Gussie that "Madame" had been submitted to the *Family Herald.*[7] In December his father wrote him that he was sorry about the fate of his "Madam" and "Day."[8] These undoubtedly allude to stories sent out and rejected. There are the additional specific references to "Madame" and its rejection by the *Family Herald.* However, "Day" must be added to other stories by Phipps whose fate is unknown.

He never explained why he began to use the briefer spelling of his name. The name of Richard Lalor Shiel, an author and supporter of Ireland's laboring class, was familiar to editors of the day and might have played a part in the choice of this spelling by Phipps. Suggestions that he changed the spelling because of some scandal or legal problem make little sense. The shortened spelling does little to hide the old.

His first published story, "The Doctor's Bee," was winner of a twenty-shilling prize and appeared in *Rare Bits* on 18 December 1889.[9] It is an inane tale of an unusual doctor (with a West Indian background) who shoots at Negroes, builds a college to teach science, and accidentally poisons himself with a deadly gas. Phipps was living at 98, De Beauvoir Road, Southgate Road, Kingsland on the day this story was published. He must surely have had some source of income during the period 1888–90, but there is virtually no documentation to suggest what it might have been. Probably the Horsfords.

He possibly attended the interpreter program at King's College,

7. Cf. MPS's letter to Augusta, 24 August 1887.

8. Cf. MDS's letter to MPS, 9 December 1887.

9. While this story published in *Rare Bits* is the first known work of fiction published by MPS in England, there may have been previous unrecorded efforts. JG revised this story somewhat and reprinted it as "The Master" in his *Crimes, Creeps and Thrills* (London, 1936) under the authorship of MPS and himself (Fytton Armstrong).

and may have sat through lectures at St. Bart's, during this period to 1890. This could have helped ease him into his role as interpreter to the International Congress of Hygiene and Demography in 1891. This seventh such congress, 10–17 August, was the first to be held in London.[10]

It is likely that he began to scratch away in several ways to find an entree into the publishing world. The editorial position that he held with the *Messenger,* as described below, must have occurred during the period 1891–92.

Shiel himself, in that all too brief autobiographical sketch, "About Myself," describes how he gave up the study of medicine after watching that first operation and

> . . . lying idle one day, gazing at the sky was given the idea to write my "Prince Zaleski" . . . Then, on writing more, I decided that writing English—my first love—was what was given me to do. I soon had no lack of interests. Through Sir Ernest Clarke, of the Royal Agricultural Society, whom I had known, I was appointed interpreter to the Congress; through Sir William Robinson and my brother-in-law, the Hon. S.L Horsford, I was brought in contact with Earl Gray and with Sir Alexander Harris, of the Colonial Office (later Governor of Newfoundland), through whom again I came into relation with Mrs. Gladstone, a very gracious lady, connected with the West Indies, who at that time took no little interest in my writing, and profoundly influenced my goings and comings; through this again W. T. Stead got to know me, conceived that I "had an imagination," and would write to me invitingly when one of his rapturous ideas in journalism attacked and urged him—he and I even writing a wild little "book" in collaboration; at the same time I was coaching my nephew, Cyril Horsford.[11]

Shiel soon discovered that editors were not necessarily interested in the original work of a creative literary stylist. Instead, he found that if one wanted to be published it was easier to sell hackwork to the hungry penny papers than the most brilliant, sharp, and scintillating results of one's imagination to more resplendent publications. So he

10. The publication that resulted from the Congress is 12 volumes in length, with papers having been presented in a number of languages, but there is no indication of the part that MPS played in the publication of the papers of the various sessions in English translation.

11. MPS, "About Myself" (1948) 5.

soon put his knowledge of several languages to work. In February of 1891 the *Strand* published, without credit, his translation of Jules Claretie's now famous little story "Slap Bang." In June, the same magazine published Phipps's translation, again without credit, of "A Torture by Hope" by a writer much more akin to his own nature—Villiers de l'Isle-Adam, another follower of Poe, best known for his *Contes Cruels,* short stories almost heartless in their sardonic horror.

There is no indication whether Shiel proposed the translation of the story or whether an editor of the *Strand* suggested it. Although Villiers de l'Isle-Adam had been dead for two years, the notes about him that accompany the story indicate that he was still alive. So it is likely that Shiel translated the story before Villiers died in 1889. Unless there were copyright problems, more of his stories would seem to have been of interest to *Strand* readers and to Shiel for additional translation duties. It is likely that in addition to his known translations there are other unrecorded translations by Shiel scattered among the penny papers and literary magazines of the early 1890s.

The translation of this story may well have turned Phipps toward darker work than the more family-oriented stories that characterized much of his output, aimed at the available markets. Elements of the supernatural would begin to show up in his stories, beginning with "Huguenin's Wife."

Shiel's appointment as interpreter to the aforementioned congress in 1891 probably made it financially possible for him to continue his writing, for after another year his feet were fairly solidly planted down a professional path of literary pursuit. The only other significant thing, other than pay, that could be said for his experience as interpreter to the Congress was that it gave him an opportunity to associate with Florence Nightingale.[12]

Sometime during this period Phipps worked for a while assisting the editor of the *Messenger,* a weekly paper devoted to financial and racing news, with an office in the Hotel Victoria (constructed 1890). This episode is described briefly in fictional form in his novel *The Weird o' It,* the most autobiographical of his novels. Here the paper is called the *Gadfly* and the proprietor is K——. Almost half a century later, Shiel places this person in *The Invisible Voices* and gives him his

12. JG indicates in a note that MPS had an opportunity to work with Florence Nightingale in the Congress. There is no record of what that activity was.

correct name, Coward: "olive—dark-elfin face, hair black, with some silver in—horsey," much the same description as in *The Weird o' It*. He includes also the fictional description of the character Jack Hay's responsibilities that so closely matches some of the actual work that Shiel had done for the *Strand* in 1891. Jack Hay, in the novel, describes himself as "secretary" to K——, going to work in the hotel at ten every morning, returning home between five and ten P.M.[13] From the novel:

> Sometimes he could not but smile a sad smile penciling his articles. One feature of *The Gadfly* was a series called "Jolly Good Fellows"—biographies with a portrait—and these he "did," having first to hunt for an old biography in little back-street rooms of Fleet Street. Dusty queer places piled with paper rags, and by hook or crook procure a portrait somewhere, evading copyrights. Then, in the tones of an old chum, he would write of names never before heard—lord mayors, lawyers, ship-owners: and once, when K—— and Lady M—— were spending the week at Monte Carlo, Jack in a memorable issue compared the owner of *Tit-Bits* [*Sir George Newnes*] with Napoleon.[14]

John Gawsworth added a brief note on the verso of the letter of 17 April 1892 referenced below, about Coward and the *Messenger* in such a way that suggests that Phipps's contribution to the paper was "no stories / biography / Sir George Newnes." Whether this sketch of Newnes, like those he produced for the *Strand,* was the total of what Phipps actually wrote for the paper is not clear. He could have simply been an editorial assistant and not have written more than racing news (dictated by Coward) and faked-up financial advice on business investments, twenty little articles a week, he said, "all beginning with the same old phrase: 'This company was formed in order to . . .'"[15]

It was apparent that he admired Newnes, who had created a revolution and accumulated a fortune in the English popular press, introducing *Tit-Bits* in 1881, following it with the *Million.* Aimed at the lower middle-class of the English reading public, the 500,000 weekly sales of the one-penny *Tit-Bits* led to the rapid introduction of rivals such as *Answers* and *Pearson's Weekly.* Then Newnes moved competi-

13. MPS, *Weird o' It* 198; *The Invisible Voices* 16–17.

14. MPS, *Weird o' It* 198.

15. Ibid.

tion up a major notch by creating the *Strand* in 1891 for a wealthier, higher class of reader.[16]

Phipps translated all the jokes for the 26 March 1892 issue of the *Million.* On 17 April 1892, he offered a short story (probably to Morris Colles, who became his literary agent) entitled "Two Fogs." There were "5500 words—which I think should sell. For all my stories I will take 30 shillings per 1000 words—for the present at least." In the same letter he inquired: "I suppose there is no news of 'Maddelena's Lover' yet?"[17] (The story never turned up.) In June 1892 the *Strand* published another brief sketch by Shiel, "Miss Lily Hanbury," in its series on people of interest in the news.

On 21 September 1892 Shiel wrote Colles (from 41 Coldbath Chambers, Roseberry Avenue, E.C.): "I herewith send you another story called '3 Men & a Girl,' which I think will hit the mark. I notice that you did not acknowledge receipt of 'The Eagle's Rock' according to your wont, but I suppose you got it all right. Is it likely to sell?"[18]

During much of 1892 Shiel lived at Coldbath Chambers and here (according to John Gawsworth) he wrote the Zaleski stories and, as noted above, "Eagle's Rock," "Three Men and a Girl," "Two Fogs," and possibly other short stories. He then moved to Rugby Chambers in Bedford Road late in the year; he lived there until sometime in 1896.[19]

Just as Shiel recorded in fictional fashion his work at the *Messenger* in his novel *The Weird o' It,* a number of readers and Ernest Dowson scholars have observed his reference to Dowson in the book. "This B——was a poet in a small, but very select, way, well known in certain so-called 'literary' circles: a fellow who, with his like at the time,

---

16. That MPS was able to have several of his works published in Newnes periodicals suggests an editorial link to someone in the firm. The connection might well have been Herbert Greenhough Smith, the editor of the *Strand* from 1891 to 1896. A copy of *The Lord of the Sea,* for sale through the Internet, bears the inscription: "H. Grenhough [*sic*] Smith, / From the Author. / July 10th, 1901." This reflected, perhaps, an earlier close relationship with Smith.

17. Copy by JG of a note, that while lacking a salutation, was obviously written by MPS to Morris Colles, 17 April 1892 (HRC).

18. Holograph copy by JG of a note from MPS to Morris Colles, 21 September 1892, 41 Coldbath Chambers, Roseberry Avenue, E.C. (HRC).

19. Note by JG (HRC).

kept night-hours, awoke at 7 p.m., drank deep, died young, and associated as comrades with the commonest people." The character B—— had been jilted by a fifteen-year-old waitress, "and had written to the girl a poem, more exquisite, in our opinion, than anything done by Horace." The poem, of course, was "Non sum qualis eram bonae sub regno Cynarae," or more briefly, just "Cynara":

> I have forgot much, Cynara! gone with the wind,
> Flung roses, roses riotously with the throng,
> Dancing, to put thy pale, lost lilies out of mind;
> But I was desolate and sick of an old passion,
> Yea, all the time, because the dance was long;
> I have been faithful to thee, Cynara! in my fashion.

The two characters drink "bovee" (a strong coffee with the taste of bovril) in a green cabmen's shelter, and B—— took Jack Hay to an upstairs room "in a mean house in Rosomon Street, Clerkenwell" where he can spend the night with friends of B—— to avoid the police.[20]

This fictional episode occurred in the general vicinity of Gray's Inn Road. Too much, however, can be made of fiction. Dowson's famous poem "Cynara" was written in 1891, when his object of virginal love was only eleven. Dowson scholars tend to agree that Shiel and Dowson shared quarters in a boarding house briefly, not in the early 1890s, but in early 1898 at 1 Guilford Place. The editors of Dowson's collected letters say, "He made one new friend at this time, M. P. Shiel. Having been an interpreter at the International Congress of Hygiene and Demography, Shiel was beginning to make a name as a writer. He stayed with Dowson in his lodgings in Guilford Place . . . and they used to dine together frequently at the Dîner Français."[21]

This sharing of quarters by Dowson and Shiel continues to puzzle. Shiel was in France almost constantly during the early part of that year, while Dowson was at Guilford Street. Perhaps this is another instance of presumed fact proceeding from fiction.

When we read further in the "London" chapter of *The Weird o' It,* we find that the section featuring Dowson is so vivid with its description of the "mean house in Rosomon Street, Clerkenwell," where Dowson's character took Jack Hay for a place to sleep, that one can

20. MPS, *The Weird o' It* 185f.

21. Dowson 279.

believe the rooms and characters were once real to Shiel: the Great Northern Goods-porter, "Fred," on his way to work in the early shift, and "in the bed a cat, and a girl of nineteen—Mary, Fred's wife, an Irish Cockney, black-haired, gray-eyed—who flippantly lifted her head, said 'Hello,' and went to sleep again."

Jack Hay is alerted that "a new acquaintance is the delight of Fred, for in such is the prospect of Beer. He who gives 2d. for beer may freely take Fred's ox, ass, wife, and everything that is Fred's . . . Not that he has no affection for Mary: but Mary he hath alway with him, beer he hath not alway."

The characters and setting are so distinctive that one is reminded of the remark that Phipps's father made to him in October 1887, hoping that he will not have to room again with "such companions." Since the letter that Phipps wrote his father describing these circumstances is lost, there is no way of knowing whether what he described to his father was ever included in his fiction or not. But I am sure that in some London somewhere, Fred still cleans the fire-irons dutifully every week, sighs ostentatiously, and curries Mary's favor so that she will tip him 2d. from his weekly salary so he can have his beer.

Shiel was still anxious about the fate of "The Eagle's Rock" after he moved from Coldbath. He wrote Colles on 20 March 1893 (from Rugby Chambers): "Among the stories you have one called 'The Eagle's Rock' which I think I can sell directly in a quarter in which I seem to be rather favored. If you have the story with you, will you be so kind as to send it to me? If not, it doesn't matter at all, but you might send it to me when it returns to you, if it does return."[22]

That the fate of "The Eagle's Rock" was still not settled several months later is evidenced by the fact that he wrote Colles again about this title on 31 July 1893: "If you have with you a little story of mine called 'The Eagle's Rock,' will you kindly return it to me. If not, when it comes back again to you will do."[23] Apparently, Colles had just sent the story out (again?), since his firm had written at the head of Shiel's letter of 20 March the following note: "This was sent to P.M. Mag on 7/2/93." This probably refers to the *Pall Mall Magazine,* although it

22. Holograph copy by JG of letter from MPS to Morris Colles, 20 March 1893, Rugby Chambers (HRC).

23. Holograph copy by JG of letter from MPS to Morris Colles, 31 July 1893, Rugby Chambers (HRC).

did not publish the story. The *Strand* did, in September 1894.

In late 1893 W. T. Stead conceived the idea for his *Daily Paper,* which he planned as a more frequent version of his prestigious weekly *Review of Reviews.* He hoped to make a feature of the new paper an ongoing serial, "The Romance of the World." This would incorporate the leading historical events of the world into fictional form. Shiel made an aborted stab at providing a novella for it, *The Rajah's Sapphire,* apparently at the invitation of Stead (who went down with the *Titanic*). The story was not used in the paper, only one trial issue of which appeared. The novella remained unpublished until it appeared, extensively revised, as a book in early 1896. This followed *Prince Zaleski* and predated *Shapes in the Fire,* making it Phipps's second book publication. Shiel acknowledged on the title page of the book that the story derived from a plot provided him "*viva voce*" from Stead. This could have been a straightforward acknowledgment, or it could have been used as a means to benefit from Stead's name and stature. Since Stead mentioned the book in his *Review of Reviews,* with his name attached to it, but not Shiel's, it must not have embarrassed him. The novel is much more interesting when it is read within a knowledge of the events of the day and Shiel's relationship to the fictional details.

John D. Squires has written in detail about Phipps's collaboration with Stead and the background of *The Rajah's Sapphire.*[24] Although Shiel states that his relationship with Stead was considerably greater than merely the collaboration on the "Sapphire" novella, there is no evidence of it other than ongoing favorable reviews of Shiel's books by Stead. Shiel used the appearance of a book review of *The Lord of the Sea* as an opportunity to write to Stead, thanking him for the review but also offering to work for the *Review of Reviews* if a position became available.

In October 1893, "Guy Harkaway's Substitute" was published by the *Strand,* and in November 1893 another brief, non-credited biographical sketch, "Rev. Augustus Stopford Brooke," appeared there.

Sometime in 1894, Phipps managed to interest a reader for John Lane in *Prince Zaleski,* possibly because of its bizarre protagonist, its "decadent" story plots, and sensuous prose, but also perhaps because

24. John D. Squires and Steve Eng, *Shiel and His Collaborators: Three Essays on William Thomas Stead, Louis Tracy and John Gawsworth* (Kettering, OH: Vainglory Press [2004]), alangullette.com/lit/shiel/essays/shiel_stead.htm.

Conan Doyle had killed Sherlock Holmes at the Reichenbach Falls in Switzerland in 1893. There developed a demand for detective stories to fill the public's taste, and a number of new sleuths appeared as writers responded. Shiel had already written the Zaleski stories, so there was a case to be made for a collection of the three stories of detection in a book.

With whom Phipps developed this connection to John Lane's Bodley House publishing firm on Vigo Street is not known. Richard Le Gallienne was a major reader for Lane at the time, as were John Buchan, John Davidson, and Grant Richards. But Richards, who would become Shiel's publisher, and Shiel did not even meet until after Richards had established his own publishing firm in 1898. So this is another mystery that may never be solved.

One wonders also whether there was any effort made by Shiel to interest the editors of the *Yellow Book,* Henry Harland and Aubrey Beardsley, in one of his stories. It seems rather strange why he, as a John Lane author, would not have had access to the pages of the new literary magazine—but then, neither did Arthur Machen. Perhaps exclusion from the magazine might help explain the critical comments that he made about John Lane's "young men" to Gus in future months. Those "damned little scribblers" he called them, although there are indications that he had at least a small degree of social life with several of them. Truth be told, Phipps just did not have the level of social standing, or family connections, or social skills, that so many of the authors in the John Lane/Bodley Head circle held. Neither was he the dedicated *littérateur* who was willing to be gone so soon with the wind and wine.

Nevertheless, Shiel describes too many social forays and feminine liaisons in his letters to have ever stayed too cloistered in his lodgings. Later letters suggest that in his hiking about the countryside, along the River Wye, and in his mountain climbing, he developed a number of geographically convenient feminine contacts.[25]

None of the stories in *Prince Zaleski* was first published separately, but Phipps wrote later of one of them, the "The S. S.," that "A slightly variant draft was accepted by 'Grand Mag,' but never appeared."[26]

---

25. See, for example, Chapter 2, footnote 11.

26. "Short Story Sources," holograph ms. list of short stories and their original place of publication in the hand of MPS responding to questions by JG,

(If this was indeed the *Grand Magazine*, as Shiel stated, this variant would have had to have been prepared after publication of the book, since that magazine did not commence publication until 1905.)

In September 1894, the *Strand* published Shiel's long-mislaid "The Eagle's Crag," a story placed in Italy but full of the feel of Redondan precipices. It is obvious why Phipps had such a personal interest in the fate of the manuscript. It is also a fine story.

Prince Zaleski had been scheduled for November 1894 publication, then announced in the papers for "early January," but Shiel was still waiting for it in mid-January.

"There is no book to send," Phipps disgustedly wrote Gussie on 14 January 1895, from Rugby Chambers, Bedford Row, W.C.[27] He had been offered a lump sum for it, he told her, but refused, insisting instead on royalties to be paid him quarterly "preferring to have an interest in the sale, as I know that publishers are crafty, and when they volunteer to pay down in that way, it is clear that they have faith in the future of the book, and in their out-look they depend, of course, on the judgment of highly skilled readers."[28]

He cannot see why Lane keeps postponing publication. As for him, he thinks the book will be published right when the public is intent on the gathering of Parliament and the book will lose much of its impact. Since royalties are paid quarterly, the next payments will be on Ladyday next (late March), and "unless it has a very extraordinary sale, I shall get now very little on Ladyday, and no more for 3 months, so that, as I was looking for funds to bring Harrie over, it cannot be done now—not at least till Autumn, especially as I have stopped writing short stories for the present."[29]

---

12 April 1935 (HRC).

27. Typescript copy by JG of letter by MPS to his sister, Augusta, Rugby Chambers, Bedford Road, W.C., 14 January 1895 (HRC). JG notes that this letter was written on embossed dove gray paper, probably suggesting improved finances and better housing.

28. Ibid.

29. Ibid. MPS kept referring to bringing Harriet "over." Harriet finally went to stay with MPS in 1900, basically to help him look after his wife Lina and the soon-arrived baby daughter Dolores Katherine (26 July 1900). His mother Priscilla Shiell wrote him: "My love to Lina. I hope the Good Lord will bring her safely through her trouble." She hopes too, that he and Harriet will get on well. The shop is closed. She is going to stay with Sall, although she is un-

"I am not very busy at the moment," he tells Gussie. He has just finished a good long story "and feel[s] like an empty bag." It may well be that this was a story for *Shapes in the Fire,* none of which, like those in *Zaleski,* was published prior to the book.[30]

The very announcement of the publication of *Prince Zaleski* in John Lane's "Keynote Series" (with Aubrey Beardsley decorations) has brought him a certain amount of attention, he tells Gussie. "I am beginning to be—well, notorious." Journalists have been after "autobiographical information" and he has provided it. "I have said that I was born in the West Indies, in the very room where the Empress Josephine first 'saw the light,' or as I put it in one case, 'first felt the heat,' (Leonard tenderly calls it 'the warmth'). If I can find one of the letters I will enclose it to shew you how fatuous a thing an English newspaper is." It is my opinion that it was out of this attitude that the legend of Redonda grew.

Gussie evidently prodded him about some matter that she thought required his attention: "I have read your last letter very carefully," he tells her, "and I think there is something in it. But it is *unnecessary,* on account of what I say above about the book. I shan't now have the money, even if I would."

Perhaps this has to do with a later comment in his letter: "What you say about the house I note: and as soon as I get some superfluous cash will see to it. At present I am rather hard up." One might presume that the old home in Plymouth required attention.

Recently, visiting a friend, he has seen on the wall a picture from the *Illustrated London News* of Blacks loading coconuts on a ship in Jamaica. He had been overcome with homesickness for the islands seeing the picture. He missed the ever-happy natives there, who were laughing, always laughing, knowing that God would fill the rivers, move the clouds, and care for them. And he suddenly realizes that he is "no Englishman!" but a stranger in the land, who is lonesome for his West Indian home and the blacks that he loved. "The negro women had the figure of Venus," he tells Gussie. "I greatly love the simple negro race. It is only the half-breeds that I think hateful and despicable, yet Dumas was one."

---

happy about it since she will not be able to "attend service." (Holograph letter Priscilla Shiell to MPS, 23 May 1900, HRC.)

30. Ibid.

In reading this, one is reminded of a comment made by Lafcadio Hearn after his trip to the West Indies in 1887: "Occasionally you observe a fine half-breed type—some tall brown girl walking by with a swaying grace like that of a sloop at sea."[31]

Phipps has developed a taste for the Englishwoman's figure, it also seems, for he tells Gussie matter-of-factly:

> Mary is in the family way. She says she feels the child jumping about in her belly. "Jumping about" is good. She has got deliciously fat: you would hardly believe. I have told her that so long as she keeps fat like that she need have no fear of my throwing her over, because I have little desire for anybody else. And isn't she proud of it, too! Knowing that I like it. When she thinks I am in danger of forgetting how fat she is, she will catch hold of a great gross lump on her legs and say: "But just look at that! Oh I don't like to be getting so fat!" Woman is all beast below the navel: above, all peri: and thus you get a very decent blend: but Man is pure human throughout. (Study this last sentence: it is one of my Aphorisms with a big A, and will appear in print some day.)

There is no indication who this Mary is, or what became of her and the baby that would have been born in mid-1895. She takes up little space in Phipps's lengthy letter, although the letter implies that Gussie knows her. He chides Gussie on another matter: "Yes, I have read Geo. Meredith, but hardly expect to hear his praises sung by my own family. Some people's family think there is nobody in the world like them, but with mine it is not so." As for London, Irving produced Saturday last a new play, *King Arthur,* and "Oh, the rage!" Also, he is learning Hebrew: "It is easy and pleasant," and he suggests that Gussie take up a similar hobby, to avoid dullness.

On 12 February 1895, he writes Gussie again with news of a more imminent appearance of the book. But it is a letter that reveals even more interestingly something of the deeper nature of his personality, a growing interest in social responsibility (if not at a personal level), a clear-cut statement of his attitude towards women and an interest in his roots![32]

---

31. *Two Years in the French West Indies* 30.

32. Typescript copy by JG of this letter from MPS to his sister Augusta Horsford, 12 February 1895, Rugby Chambers (HRC).

Feb'y 12.95

Darling Gussie—

Them that write me, I will write, but them that despises me shall be lightly esteemed. Well, you write me pretty well, and so I you: but as to my sister Harriet, she may go to the devil, if the task of sending me news of my dear mother is too much trouble for her once in two weeks. I don't, let her understand, want to hear about *her,* if she doesn't want to write me; but I do care to have an occasional report about the womb that bare me, and lent my brain its sap, and taught songs to my tongue, and exaltations to my soul. Do you know what has been wrong with her dear old leg? I hope it was no disease of the skin. By the way, I want to know the name of my father's mother, and also the maiden name of our old Granny. Will you write and let me know, and if you yourself don't know, try and find out for me. It is from these old folk, darling, that we get all we are; they fiz in our blood, and beat in our brain; it is they who stand at my shoulder and dictate to me the very words I am now writing.

But oh! What weather. Thur-r-r! it is cold. There hasn't been such weather in England for the last hundred years they say. Oh, "the parching air burns frore" (isn't that a *sweet* collection of words: not my own). You remember last Winter when we had to clean our teeth with ginger-beer? Well, it's worse now. Everything freezes, freezes. It is Arctic. The sea, the open sea, freezes. People die of it. All you have to do is to lie down in it—and you die. The distress is very great; a million men are out of work; think of that! a million: and every one of them a soul, immortal, divine, a God-Man like Jesus, the very hairs of his head all numbered, and the lice among the hairs. Ah, the world is governed foolishly! till the very apes and asses must laugh at us; and what provokes me is my feeling that I, Phipps Shiel, could manage it better: more kindly, more wisely, more humanly: and am not allowed to try! However, as I say, it is Arctic, the cold; and the poor pay the piper; and such queer, uncanny variations! Think of a thunder-storm in February! It is like the weather described by that inspired Yankee—

First it hailed, and then it blew, and then it friz and then it snew;
And then there was a shower of rain, and then it friz and snew again.

Well, my pet, I wanted to send you out my booklet this time, and wrote to John Lane to ask him if they had come from the binder's yet: but they haven't. It is positively to be published on Saturday morning next.

> The companion book to it is by Grant Allen called "The Woman Who Did"; and it is making the devil of a sensation. It is to "Prince Zaleski" what a bone button is to a diamond, or, at any rate, a pearl: but for all that, it will, I think, make a great deal more noise than "Prince Zaleski": as it has to do with the relations of the sexes; and anything on that subject *now* is bought-up by the "New Woman" like hot loaves. Damn the "New Woman"! she is fast becoming a bore, and is, if possible, even More vulgar than the old. I always say, with Ruskin, that there are no ladies in England—no hlaf-loaf, *hlaf-ords*, "bread-givers" (that is the real meaning of the word)—and in this saying I know that there is a genuine truth. [*Letter incomplete, bottom half of page torn away*]

Phipps could only have wished that his "diamond" could have competed with Grant Allen's "bone button" in the marketplace. Allen's *The Woman Who Did* went through twenty editions during its first year of publication.[33]

Shiel was fortunate to have *Prince Zaleski* published in the extremely handsome Keynotes Series. Its royal purple binding, its title page borders designed by Aubrey Beardsley, the distinctive key design interlaced with MPS's initials on the rear cover, all reflected the best of *art nouveau* book making. It is unfortunate that such a pretty book tends to have had its spine fade so badly over the years.

The letter to Gussie also confirms the terrible winter of 1894–95 that is described in John Squires's biographical information about Louis Tracy and his collaborations with Shiel. ("The parching air . . ." quoted by Shiel is Milton's description of the landscape of Hell in Book II of *Paradise Lost.*) Tracy funded twenty-three soup kitchens that fed three and one-half million starving, jobless men during this time. According to contemporary accounts, Tracy spent some $45,000 on this effort.[34]

Phipps used almost literally his description to Gussie of this Arctic England in *The Rajah's Sapphire:* "'The parched air burned frore.' People were dying of it. All you had to do was to lie down in it, and you died." And, again from the novel: "And, oh, Stefan, just think, a million of them out of work! Workless workers, we call them . . ." The closeness of the text of his letter and that of his fiction suggests

---

33. Mix, *A Study in Yellow* 41.

34. "Mr. Louis Tracy," *Bookman* (New York) 20 (September 1904): 4.

that Shiel was probably at work on the novel at this time, expanding it with contemporary detail that he could not have included in the version he drafted in 1894 for Stead's paper. John Squires has pointed out that incidences from the Sino-Japanese War of 1894–95 were also introduced in the revised novel.[35] The book was not published until the next spring, 7 March 1896 in Ward, Lock & Bowden's attractive small-format "Nautilus Series."

Meanwhile, he was staying busy in other ways, as he wrote Gussie.

Rugby Chambers W.C.
Apr.30.95

My darling Gussie—

I am writing you, but I have not the remotest idea whether this is the right Tuesday or not. If I miss one mail, I am done for. It is horribly absurd that they don't contrive some scheme by which one may know when the right day comes: the line should either run on a certain day *every* week, or else on a certain day or days every month. As it is, one can't possibly know. You should speak to Horsford about it.

This is partly why you have not heard from me. Also, I have had a little influenza.

How are you getting on? I heard from the girls. Oh, I say! Ain't they "new," ain't they stylish? ain't they got the graces, and the blandishments, and eccentricities altogether and entirely? Have you observed those "M's" of Nonnie's? Those M's, my dear! To what shall I liken them, and whereto shall they be compared? They are like three young roes that are thrins; or say, like the three Graces, fondly twined; or say again, like three juicy tendrils of the budding vine that droop from a garland on the brow of Dionysius. Nonnie's M's have twined around my heart with triple potency (is it not written that "a three-fold cord is not easily broken"?), and I wrote her a longish letter, but I said nothing of the m's, for if she finds that her small achievements do not hew an impression upon the world deep enough to cause remark, she will be led to hew harder until there is remark enough and to spare. I believe the girl has it in her, if she be properly trained and put to something. There is that little Cyril, too; I hear from Leonard he is doing wonders. Only why *did* you make them so ugly? I believe the truth is you don't lie on the right side. You should

35. John D. Squires, web.archive.org/web/20200804030751/http://www.alangullette. com/lit/shiel/essays/RediscoveringMPShiel.htm

also put a pillow under you.

Of course, by this time you have heard all about the Big Thing—Oscar Wilde. He will be sentenced this afternoon. Poor chap! I am sorry for him. It is not his fault: he is not well made: he is a moral idiot: he was born so: his mother made him so. *God will straighten him out*. It is ordained that he shall yet be perfect—without spot or blemish—perfect as a sphere of the heavens. Ah, Gussie! Gussie! The thing is too sweet to think of! The world is WELL MADE!

But what do you think—I too have had an offer of marriage, my dear! Think of me in the capacity of a wife! I who am so intensely a husband. Not a regular offer, be it said; and perhaps, after all, it was only my fancy. This is how it happened. I became friends some time ago with one of the big wigs, a chap who dines with Lord Salisbury, and has hobnobbed with the Prince of Wales: a nephew of Sir John Wilson, M. P., the "great railway King." His name is Hope Johnston. Well, a short time ago I was introduced to him by one of John Lane's "young men," and, on mutual liking, we became friends. He lives in chambers in St. James's St., and nearly every night I was there. Talk, talk; jabber, jabber, jabber. He *never* sleeps at night. He goes to bed at ten in the morning. And he is a great man for morphia. Very well, I used to stay with him till about six o'clock a.m. when I would come home through the quiet streets and toddle in to bed. But what I have to say is this: that his whole talk (sometimes) is about *buggery;* of course, he not only knows everybody, but the private life, the very thoughts of everybody. Long before this affair of Oscar Wilde became public, he foreshadowed it to me; and the names he mentioned, the picture he gave of the corruption of English society, was *awful*. Very well. Now, I was rather awkward in inserting the syringe into myself to inject the morphia, so he used to do it for me. And one night, when I had drawn up my shirt-sleeve, he stopped, and began to stroke my arm with his hand. "Ah, you *have* got a nice arm!" he said. I didn't like his *tone*. The stroking was *too* affectionate, the tone *too* effeminate. He saw me frown, and went on with the syringe. And so it passed. That, you say, wasn't much; but it was enough for me. If he had been opener, I should certainly have knocked him down. I like playing Adam, but I draw the line at Eve. My Gussie may go to sleep with the calm assurance that her brother will never get in the family way by any man.

Well, I have little news to give. Zaleski has been met with quite a crow of praise by the intelligent portion of the press; but, so far, I don't think the public has responded in proportion. They will, when one or two more of my books come out. The first, *by itself*, hardly ever does very much. The *Times* was *very* complimentary, and said I write like Æschylus! Think of *that,* my dear! Æschylus! Thanks for your praise. But why do you insist on comparing me with Conan Doyle? Conan Doyle does not pretend to be a poet. I do.

Well, I get a lot of invitations to go out to evening parties, "smokes," and the rest of it. Sometimes I wish little Reg was here: I would make him go and pretend to be me. I *never* go. Sometimes I am hard put to find an excuse, but I do find it. They come mostly from John Lane, and his many young men, and their wives. These damned little scribblers think I am one of them, and I am not. "Dining-out" helps no man to write greatly—which is hard work, and not as easy, as they think.

By the way, would you like to see the pretty evolution of a correspondence? I enclose you it. They are written by the 'newest' of new women; and she really does write very sweet stories. The papers are always talking about her.

Are you coming over in the Summer? I shan't be surprised to see you, inveterate old turner-up that you are! Or is it turner-over? You know what the man said to his wife at midnight: "P. T. O."

Horsford promised to write me, but did not. Tell him I am afraid the Conservatives will get in next time: we are losing nearly all the bye-elections.

Will you send this note to my darlings in Montserrat. Love to Sal & Reg. By the way, Leo is getting on nicely with short-hand.

Yours,
Phipps[36]

He adds a separate sheet to this letter, as a postscript, evidently written after midnight, which would date it 1 May 1895:

The rest I wrote y'day, a day before the time and now I want to add a P.S. It is late, & I can't get any more stamps, so please send rest of enclosed to my mother, as I have not written her lately, & she must be looking and to hear. *Don't forget*. Send it as quickly as you can: the old darling has had something wrong with her leg: but reticent Harrie does not say what. / M. P. S.

Richard Le Gallienne, again, may have been the John Lane "young

36. Typescript copy by JG of this letter from MPS to his sister Augusta Horsford, 30 April 1895 (HRC).

man" who introduced Shiel to Hope Johnston. Or it could have been Lane's business manager, Frederick Chapman, who introduced Shiel to members of the Lane circle from time to time. Shiel's literary acquaintances at this time seem generally to have been grounded on that tight little island within John Lane's boundaries—although John Gawsworth has indicated that Shiel dined once with Oscar Wilde at Roche's at Charing Cross Road and Old Compton Street in Soho, and once with Robert Louis Stevenson at the same location.[37]

Despite this assertion, it is difficult to identify a time when Shiel could have had an opportunity to dine with Stevenson, since Stevenson went to America in August 1887 and from there to the South Seas, where he died in 1894. Why would Stevenson have dined with a struggling young schoolmaster at Roche's in the last few months of 1886 or early 1887?

And Wilde, who was said to despise Bohemia? Dining with Phipps at Roche's? It hardly seems likely. Wilde was pretty well ensconced at the uptown Royal, where he held regular luncheon court with a routine coterie of those amused or amusing.

Regarding the crow of praise he told Gussie that he was receiving for *Zaleski*, it would have taken a very loose reading for Phipps to find in the *Times* review a true comparison with Æschylus, but the review was lengthy, and he could have found satisfaction in its comment:

> To Mr. Shiel, indeed, one might apply in part his description of Prince Zaleski:—
>
> He was nothing if not superlative; his diatribes, now culminating in a very extravaganza of hyperbole—now sailing with loose wing through the downy, witched, Dutch cloud-heaps of some quaintest tramontane Nephelococcugia of thought . . .

It seems likely that the "pretty evolution of a correspondence" that Phipps mentions to Gussie was with Ella D'Arcy (1857–1937), who was becoming a highly respected short story writer among the so-called "New Women" group. D'Arcy also was an important assistant to John Lane and Henry Harland in editing the *Yellow Book*. While Phipps may have had no great affection for John Lane's "young men," he seemed always to find a place in his heart for Lane's or anyone else's women.

37. Morse, *The Works of M. P. Shiel* 3.422n13.

Phipps as Junior Master, Matlock, 1886
Courtesy of the Harry Ransom Humanities Research Center
The University of Texas at Austin

Shiel at King's College, Strand, interpreters school, ca. 1891
Courtesy of the Harry Ransom Humanities Research Center
The University of Texas at Austin

PRINCE ZALESKI

BY M. P. SHIEL

Come now, and let us reason together.
ISAIAH

Of the strange things that befell the valiant Knight in the Sable Mountain; and how he imitated the penance of Beltenebros.
CERVANTES

'Αλλ' ἔστ' ἐκείνῳ πάντα λεκτά, πάντα δὲ τολμητά;
SOPHOCLES

LONDON: JOHN LANE, VIGO ST
BOSTON: ROBERTS BROS., 1895

Prince Zaleski title page, 1895

Ella D'Arcy, ca. 1895

Ella was born in 1857, the daughter of an Irish grain merchant. Raised in the Channel Islands, she spoke French fluently and had hoped to be a painter. But after initial study and plans to attend art school in Paris, she developed eye problems and began to write instead. She became the most frequent contributor to the *Yellow Book,* and soon an employee. She complained about a John Lane author, Frederick Rolfe ("Baron Corvo"), who, she said, left lice on the office chairs after every visit. The chairs were routinely sprayed. Corvo retaliated by calling her a "mouse-mannered piece of sex." Penelope Fitzgerald, in her biography of Charlotte Mew, however, described Ella as a "dark, handsome, untidy-looking, witty woman." Fitzgerald notes that D'Arcy was constantly hard up, flitting from one boarding house to another. Charlotte Mew developed a passionate crush on her, only to be rejected. Ella had a pity for men, Fitzgerald says, and "took lovers as she chose."[38]

In his introduction to a small collection of letters from D'Arcy to John Lane, Alan Anderson writes: "Ella D'Arcy very soon became an indispensable assistant to Harland, and although she disclaimed the title in late years, she was in fact the *Yellow Book's* sub-editor, and was paid as such by Harland out of his own pocket . . ."[39]

Anderson adds: "She now had accommodations close to the Harlands' flat at 144 Cromwell Road, and acted to some extent as Harland's secretary, bringing a degree of order to his rather chaotic lifestyle and organizing his Saturday afternoon soirées and the more imposing evening receptions."

"She never married," Anderson writes, "apparently harbouring a strong prejudice against that institution. She had no particular dislike of men, however, and in the mid 1880's she had an affair with the writer M. P. Shiel." Anderson gives Ian Fletcher as his source for this statement, based on information given Fletcher by John Gawsworth.[40]

38. Penelope Fitzgerald, *Charlotte Mew and Her Friends* 64–66, 84–86.

39. Ella D'Arcy, *Some Letters to John Lane* 6, 9.

40. JG named Ian Fletcher and Jon Wynne-Tyson as joint executors of his estate. Fletcher was professor of English at the University of Reading and held several visiting professorships in the United States. He died while at Arizona State University in 1988. JG stayed with Fletcher's young family for eighteen months in the early 1950s and shared numerous stories with him regarding the several British authors with whom JG had made friends in the 1930s. Jon Wynne-Tyson, a first-rate novelist in his own right, was designated

There apparently exists a letter from D'Arcy to Phipps that is even more indicative of a liaison between the two, although Anderson does not cite the source or location of the document. Anderson says that D'Arcy died on 5 September 1937 in the St. Pancras Institution, "thereby fulfilling the prophecy she had made in a letter to M. P. Shiel some forty years earlier." Her family had moved her to St. Pancras from Paris because of advancing dementia. Does one presume she forecast madness?[41]

"George Egerton" (Mary Chavelita Dunne Bright) also worked as an editor for Lane, and was achieving a reputation like Ella D'Arcy as one of the best of the "New Women" group of writers. It was her short story collection, *Keynotes,* for which the series had been named. George Egerton also had a major interest in genealogy, and it may have been her enthusiasm for this interest, perhaps expressed at Lane socials, that in early 1895 pushed Phipps toward a pursuit of his own family roots, as he subsequently inquired of them from Gussie.[42]

Ella D'Arcy described the Harland socials: "Never were there such evenings as those long-ago evenings in Cromwell Road! . . . The large drawing room, lighted by lamps and candles only—in those days electricity had not yet become general—would begin to fill up about nine o'clock. Two or three would have dined there. Others dropped in to coffee and cigarettes . . ."[43]

Shiel's lack of interest in literary society, except for the women, may well have been due to the fact that he was in the midst of writing

---

as JG's heir to the "Kingdom of Redonda" as King Juan II, and was given possession of numerous boxes of JG detritus following his death. Wynne-Tyson retired from his "office" as king in 1997, and the noted Spanish novelist Javier Marías assumed the "kingship." Wynne-Tyson has published his memoirs, *Finding the Words: A Publishing Life* (2004).

41. D'Arcy, *Letters* 9.

42. When George Egerton acknowledged MPS's thank-you note to her in 1935 for supporting his Civil List Pension application, she could not restrain herself from commenting, as she probably had years before, on the particular origin of the "Shiel" name, and suggested that he complete a form to submit to a genealogical society to learn more about the family! She remarked how particularly important it was to supply maternal information. She forgot to enclose the form, she acknowledged in a second letter. (Holograph letter from Egerton to MPS, 31 July 1935, HRC.)

43. J. Lewis May, *John Lane and the Nineties* 78.

and simply preferred to write rather than spend time at the Harland "Saturdays," or at the Sunday at-homes or the regular social "smokes." "Huguenin's Wife" (his first truly supernatural story) was published in *Pall Mall Magazine* for April 1895; "The Case of Euphemia Raphash" in *Chapman's Magazine of Fiction* for Christmas 1895; "Wayward Love" was published in *Cassell's Family Magazine* in its April 1896 issue; "The Spectre-Ship," in *Cassell's Family Magazine* for September 1896; and "The Secret Panel" in the *Strand* for December 1896, among others.

The stories, poem, and essay that would appear in *Shapes in the Fire*—"Xélucha," "Maria in the Rose Bush," "Vaila," "Premier and Maker," "Tulsah," "The Serpent Ship," and "Phorfor"—must have been written in this general period, apparently all prepared for the book. It is unusual that none was published in a periodical first, as Shiel himself confirmed at a later time.[44] Whether on purpose, he did not say. In any case, Phipps must have been very busy writing these short stories during the past several years.

It also appears that he was developing a group of personal acquaintances with whom to spend time, although the morphia adventure he described to Gussie (which would have occurred in early 1895) apparently was an anomaly. There are no indications elsewhere that this became a practice that he pursued beyond the episodes described here.

The "Sal" referenced in this letter is obviously Phipps's sister Sallie; "Reg" is the elder nephew, and "Leo" is Leonard, the youngest nephew. Sallie may have been on Nevis at the time; Reg on St. Kitts; and Leo studying in London. Phipps's mother and Harriet were on Montserrat.

Existing correspondence with his family does not pick up again until a year later. He had clearly been busy writing, but had not overlooked the music halls or feminine company. (He had moved from Rugby Chambers sometime during the year.)[45]

24 Percy Circus,
W.C.
Nov. 3. 96

Darling Gussie:

What has become of you? I wrote you some time ago and I hope

44. "Short Story Sources" list by MPS (see Chapter 2, footnote 28).

45. Typescript copy by JG of this letter from MPS to his sister Augusta Horsford, 3 November 1896, 24 Percy Circus, W.C. (HRC).

you got it. I have just received a most *sweet* letter from Cici, which has brought you vividly to my mind, though you must not think that you are ever really out of it. Yes, a most sweet letter: I think he is one of the nicest boys in the world: a perfectly free, and manly, and simple letter, without a trace of "St. Kitts" in it. I do hope that his face will get better of its ugly marks, because that, of course, makes him quite impossible. But that will come, when he is old enough to know the importance of it, and is prepared to take some trouble to get rid of it.

As for the other children, I know simply nothing of them. I have often thought of taking train to go to see them—but have forgotten the name of the school! However, I am writing to ask Cici.

Of myself, sweetheart, I have little to tell. I have gone into Society (of all things) and every Sunday afternoon, go to an "at-home" where I meet crowds of literary people, all Bohemianly-inclined: ladies and gentlemen: the place full of cigarette-smoke, and an odour of mixed chartreuse and noyau, the ladies *all* smoking. The hostess and I are great chums, and write to each other every week. She is very charming. But you must not suppose I go there for the sake of the Society! Oh, no! But because the prettiest woman in all London goes there—a young filly, just married to a young doctor—said to be very rich. I just lie back and gaze at them, mortally bitten and green. Meantime, I am engaged to be married to another one, one of the singers at the Sunday evenings you know so well at Queen's Hall. She knows your friend Sibley well, and calls him a cross brute.

Well, I was thinking of you the other night, thinking how happy you are and have been—everything found you—and your work in the world, that of bearing children, successfully accomplished. Would, ah would, that I could say the same! I and poor Harrie are the unlucky ones of the family: nobody to sleep with at night. The luckiest was Ada!

Poor little Reg! I have been thinking of him. Some nights ago I went to Oxford, and heard his friend Stratton of Love a Lovely Girl fame sing a nice song. He must be quite a man, with a beard, and I remember when he was born. Alas! Alas!

My love to Sammy.

But oh! What has become of little Leonard?

Yours, my darling,
Phipps

The book isn't out yet!

Cici wrote to tell me of poor Henry. How very sad. And yet I know that it is well.

Given Phipps's concern about "Henry," it is likely that this remark concerned the death of Henry Dyett, the longtime family friend who had served as notary public and held other offices on Montserrat, and whose kin "of color" had been close friends of the young Phipps. Henry's wife had maintained a store, replacing Mrs. William Chambers in that role, as a friendly competitor of Phipps's father in 1887.[46]

Phipps is out in society again, he tells Gussie, after his stated lack of enthusiasm for that activity the year before. With *Shapes in the Fire,* the second book of his that John Lane would publish in the Keynote Series, due at any time, it is likely that Phipps was now more interested in seeking social company, since there would be the new book and his writing to discuss. There was probably also the need to help promote the book and accommodate those involved in its production and sales. It is also clear that he had a specific interest in these social literary gatherings because of the women who were attending. Apparently, his affair, whatever it was, with Ella D'Arcy was over, although she would have been very involved and visible in helping manage the Saturday socials at Cromwell Street. But Phipps appears to be interested in yet another series of literary socials, apart from the Lane and Harland events, as suggested in the letter above.[47]

The hostess may have been Mrs. Shakespear (Olivia Shakespear, 1863–1938), who was prominent for hosting regular literary gatherings, these Sunday "smokes," and who, it was said, relieved W. B. Yeats of his virginity at "the advanced age of twenty-nine." Her daughter Dorothy (1886–1973) married Ezra Pound. Recognized for her beauty, Olivia may be the lovely young woman admired by Phipps at these events. But Olivia had been married to a solicitor (Hope Shakespear) for many years and was two years older than Phipps, as well as mother of a ten-year-old daughter. This does not fit the "young filly" recently married to a rich young doctor whom Shiel describes. Phipps mentions Mrs. Shakespear's attendance at later social events, at Arthur Machen's apartment in 1897, perhaps tending to confirm her presence as hostess in this series of socials that he de-

46. "Lizzie" Chambers had lent MDS £1 to send to MPS in 1887.

47. "Afternoons at home, evenings in the drawing-room were features of social life in London. Only the shyest and most diffident young artist could avoid inclusions in some such circle. Jerome K. Jerome said that the 'At Homes' were so numerous it made his brain reel to remember them and that he usually turned up on the wrong day." Mix 31.

scribes to Gussie.[48] Or the hostess could have been Ella D'Arcy and the "young filly" either Mrs. Shakespear or simply another pretty target in Phipps's eye.

The identity of the singer, mentioned in this letter, to whom Phipps says he was "engaged," is unknown, although Gussie knew others from the music hall circles. There may be a clue in *Shapes in the Fire*. He dedicates the book to "Mistress Beatrice Laws." There seems no reason to dedicate a book to a woman unless there is a very special reason for doing so.[49]

Phipps describes the content of *Shapes in the Fire* to Beatrice in his lengthy dedicatory letter and suggests that she treat the stories as a concert, taking a break at the intermission, since "Premier and Maker" is better suited for men. He advises her to take the intermission in highly romantic, very personalized, and extravagant prose, almost incomprehensible in its extreme Decadent aesthetic: "Go out on the verandah, pig's-eye, and there heave, the open secret of that torse my soul remembers to the chaste down-look of Dian's astonished eye glass, and the *schwärmerei* of the winking stars."

This lifting of a wreath in moonlight and a swarm of stars might have had a special meaning for Phipps and Mistress Law. The simile that Phipps offers in his dedication to her, to consider the stories as parts of a concert, suggests strongly that the young woman was a singer at Queen's Hall, probably in the chorus. There is no way to establish today the name of this yet another passing fancy, of which Phipps seems never bereft.

Shiel composed virtually all the stories, the poem, and the intermezzo statement on art and letters, "Premier and Maker," in the farthest artistic reach that he would make toward an overly rich, Decadent style. There are several fascinating biographical points within "Premier and Maker" that have never quite caught the attention of Shiel scholars. There are comments included that he had shared with Gussie in his 12 February 1895 letter to her. These were women as loaf-givers, for one, in this essay, and wording he was building into the short novel. It may be that the letter writing and composing the essay and novel were going on at the same time.

48. Typescript copy of letter from MPS to his sister, Augusta, 3 November 1896, 24 Percy Circus, W.C. (HRC).

49. MPS, *Shapes in the Fire* iii.

An even richer piece in "Premier and Maker" becomes a Nordic song for his father:

> My father was a ship-owner. We dwelt on the summit of an island. He went often down from us. Nothing restrained him to the land. When he rarely returned, we said: He is come! One meeting another a-crag or a-field, said: How droll! He is here and you did not know it. Simple he was, sensuous, too, passionate enough. Ocean heaved and bellowed in his brain. If it lightened, he was sublime. If thunder cracked brittling through the heaven of heavens, battle-joy it was to drink the rich brool of his challenging cry. God was his turbulent friend. The full hurricane made him Prometheus.[50]

This passage presaged by five years the description of his father that would become a central feature in Shiel's "About Myself."

The Wilde scandal sent the London literary scene into disarray. British writers of a serious literary bent turned toward a more naturalistic, softer direction in their writing. Critics began replacing the word "decadent" with "symbolist." Aubrey Beardsley, of the gracefully curved erotic figure, was dismissed as art editor of the *Yellow Book* when a number of its major contributors threatened to boycott the magazine otherwise. The word "yellow," which had virtually painted the publishing and marketing environment after the first volume of the magazine appeared in 1894, became almost a dirty word. The *Yellow Book* itself ceased publication in 1897 after only thirteen issues. After all, Victoria was still queen.[51]

Actually, Beardsley's dismissal may have had an effect on the physical design of Shiel's *Shapes in the Fire.* A replacement for Beardsley was important for the Bodley Head and the *Yellow Book.* Ella D'Arcy, Henry Harland, and John Lane all thought they were qualified to pass on the illustrations for the *Yellow Book,* but they realized they needed someone with stronger technical expertise than they for the overall art program. So Patten Wilson, who had worked for a wallpaper firm and had contributed in a minor way to several of Lane's publications, was hired to assist with artwork. This is the "P. W." who designed the title page and key motif for *Shapes in the Fire.*[52]

Phipps became involved in yet another social group soon after the

---

50. Ibid. 134.

51. Mix, *A Study in Yellow* 143–44, 160–61.

52. Ibid. 165.

book was published, when he moved to 3 Gray's Inn Place. This was just "a passage leading north out of Gray's Inn Square to the north gate of the inn."[53] Gray's Inn Place was quite close to Machen's residence at No. 4 Verulam Buildings. Shiel wrote a remembrance of Arthur Machen for John Gawsworth on 22 June 1933:

> He was near the gate on the ground floor; very noisy there. He who I think was his best friend then, Paul England, a musician, who sometimes slept there, said one morning that one day, if he slept there, he would be found "feebly but persistently beating on a drum," which was what someone came to in my "House of Sounds." But the drawing-room was remote from the street (Gray's Inn Road), and looked out charmingly on "Gray's Inn Gardens." I too looked on them from my windows high up in 3 Gray's Inn Place some way off the adjacent side of the gardens-square. There Machen and Mrs. often came to visit me—she taller than he, thin, pale, amiable, fond of me. To me, beginning housekeeping, she gave council: "don't let her (my old housekeeper) sweep the carpet with a hard broom, make her (secretly) pick up the bits," etc. The Inn then was quite a haunt of artists, Lionel Johnson (just before), James Welch (if it was the name—the actor who starred in "When Knights were Bold," brother-in-law of Richard Le Gallienne, who would come to see a friend of mine and Machen's named Egan Mew, whose "oak" faced mine; and on Sunday afternoons quite a crowd of more or less literary people would fill Machen's large drawing-room, filling it with smoke and sipping Benedictine which Machen presented with a certain unction and ceremony; "George Egerton" for one was often among them, Mrs. Shakespear (pretty! dark), who wrote novels and was in with me, and a family of reviewers who still review—Sergeant—one of whom Mrs. Machen meant me to marry, though I did not quite see eye-to-eye with her on that. Sometimes she'd take me about from guest to guest to exhibit the extra-ordinary length of my fingers—artistic, she said—I shrinking at the consciousness that the nails weren't clean. And through the smoke Machen before the fireplace, standing in his brown-velvet jacket, preaching something to someone, quite a learned

53. MPS, "The Good Machen," in *The Good Machen: A Centenary Tribute Recalled.* Certainly his description of Olivia Shakespear, mentioned specifically by name in this piece, matches every detail of beauty that MPS admired in a woman. She and Yeats had their run at romance during 1894–96, with its consummation in early, cold 1896. It is unlikely that she and MPS were ever more than minor acquaintances. See Harwood, *Olivia Shakespear and W. B. Yeats.*

> person, full of memories of impressions, quite a talker, his opinions fixed as nickel, anything in his favour wholly good, anything in his bad books wholly bad, and if there were constellations of which he approved, and constellations of which he disapproved, that would not be astonishing to me . . . He had a nice wine like champagne from a vineyard in Touraine which he let out on the metayer system, getting half the produce, and whenever I dined with him I got some. That was fairly often, for he seemed to have a fancy for me and my things; when my "Shapes in the Fire" appeared he wrote me that I had "done what he always aspired to do." He liked anything touched with mysticism, was fond of talking about secret societies, of hinting that he belonged to one or more—talk which resulted in what I say about them in my little "Primate of the Rose": and some of his friends were markedly mystic like Waite who wrote learned mysticism, "The Targum on the Babylonish Talmud," and so on. We lived in an island in the sea of London, rather touched with enchantment, and the tender grace of that day that is dead will never come back to me . . . but, then, other days with other graces have come and come, and there's as good a fish in the sea as ever was fished!![54]

The "Sergeant" urged at him was probably a daughter of Lewis Sergeant, an early mentor of Machen and longtime friend of Amelia (Amy) Hogg Machen, Machen's first wife. She patently bore none of the known feminine qualities that would have drawn Shiel to her. Shiel would complete his life with references to "the Good Machen," while Machen would finish his days referring to Shiel as an "inveterate liar."

Phipps would turn from this circle of the bizarre and the literary sophisticates, of which he had never been a major figure, toward new personal interests, a somewhat tamer writing style and a new literary market, as he would soon write his mother.

Comments to the effect that Phipps appeared to ignore his mother in print are just not accurate. He dedicated *Prince Zaleski* to her. His letters to her, and to Gussie about her over the years, attest to his concern for her. The "Spanish" influence of her complexion, as we know, was repeated often in Phipps's public admission of his attraction, throughout his life, to women who resembled her. One of his most significant literary credos—"our mothers make us most"—was embodied in much of his writing. The loaf-giver, the life-giver. It was the dominating influence of the lisping young mother figure in *The*

54. Ibid.

Purple Cloud that led to the prospect of a new beginning for the human race. Despite Phipps's many importunities to his mother, she was never to send him the "likeness" he requested.[55]

Nov. 3rd '97
3, Gray's Inn Place. W.C.

My darling Mumsie:

I haven't been writing to you lately, chiefly on account of the fact that Gussie is here, and, I presume, writes to you fairly regularly, as she has a mania for writing, and nothing to do.

She told me the other day that you had written to her, which made me feel rather jealous, as nobody writes to *me*. I understand, by the way, that Harriet for some queer and secret reason of her own does not write to Gussie now. This is very absurd. Harrie, surely, is quite old enough to know better. I want her to write and tell Sal that I have received her message, and will write her soon, and should also be glad, meanwhile, to hear from her.

Well, darling mama, I often think of you with the old love in all its freshness. I have been thinking seriously of going out to you this winter, but I'm afraid it isn't quite convenient yet, though that I hope, will come, too. Would you be glad to see me, your own, your very own, once more? Do you love me still, I wonder? Can a mother forget. . . . She *may!* Yet will not I forget thee!

Of myself, I haven't really very much news to write. I took over little Cyril to Paris in the Autumn to shew him about, and since I have come back I have been writing a novel. Novel-writing, and smoking, and riding the bicycle, and paying and receiving visits—that is my life, more or less.

I am sending you £5 to buy yourself a little *wine* and snuff, and you must try & write to say whether you have received it. I haven't got that photograph of yours *yet*. I *wish* you would take it & send it. Don't forget that a little *wine* will be good for you.

Yours till I die,

Phipps.

The novel that he was writing was possibly *The Man-Stealers* or *The Last Miracle*. He would soon be persuaded to start *The Empress of the Earth* (*The Yellow Danger*), begun, as John D. Squires has noted,

---

55. Typescript copy by JG of letter from MPS to his mother, Priscilla Shiell, 3 November 1897, 3 Gray's Inn Place, W.C. (HRC).

"in the closing days of 1897," as trouble broke out between Germany and China.[56] The success of this serial would set his feet firmly in this new format. Novel writing for serial publication would soon consume Phipps's time, and the short story writing that had been his staple for so long would generally be laid aside for the next few years. The serials, written by formula to meet publication deadlines and requested word counts, and then revised for book publication, would command his time. As income makers, however, the serials would far exceed the earning capacity of short stories.

The following year, 1898, would prove to be the most productive in Phipps's career and mark a personal turning point. He would achieve a level of book-selling success that he could only have dreamed of a few years earlier. He was already planning and beginning to write the major novels that would survive him—*The Last Miracle,* the towering and madly, magnificently written "The Second Adam" (*The Purple Cloud*), and that great adventure *The Lord of the Sea.* He would marry Carolina Garcia Gomez, the lovely Parisian-Spaniard he met while ice-skating in Paris, on 3 November 1898—in the presence of Arthur Machen, with the wedding breakfast planned by Amy Machen.

Within weeks, his love child, Ada Phipps Seward Shiel, would be born in London to Nellie Seward, of Cheltenham, the model for the heroine of *The Yellow Danger.* Lina would bear him a daughter, Dolores Katherine, in July 1900, prior to their separation and Lina's death, apparently in 1903. Contrary to historical tradition regarding the fate of Lola, Shiel was still visiting a little "seven-year-old" in Paris at Christmas in 1908. Nellie Seward moved to South Africa and left Ada in the care of her mother. In the late spring of 1908, Phipps began a love affair with Lydia Furley, a brilliant intellectual, an activist in the "woman's movement" who shared his enthusiasm for educational reform, Jesus, and the wind. They would marry in January 1919, five years after the death of her common-law husband, William Arthur Jewson. A love of women and writing would sustain Shiel until his death on 14 February 1947.

The fuller story of those additional successes and tragedies that lay ahead of Shiel, on his island in the sea of London, before he became just another shape in the fire, is still to tell.

---

56. Anyone interested in an excellent overall presentation of the life and work of MPS should explore the works of John D. Squires listed in the References.

M. P. Shiel
From *The Bookman*, 1927

The Middle Years
1897–1923

This one is for Saul and Salome

Chapter 6

". . . as a bud for the sunshine"

By the fall of 1897 M. P. Shiel was well equipped to begin a relatively brief but successful career writing serial novels for the English popular press. He had struggled through an apprenticeship of school teaching, clerking, translating, writing short stories, and seeing two collections published as major books in the decadent style of the literary aesthete before its collapse following the trial of Oscar Wilde. While Shiel did not abandon short stories, most of his energy became directed at opportunities to write for the serial novel market.

When Shiel arrived in England in April 1885 (as Matthew Phipps Shiell), he had passed the matriculation requirements for King's College, London, after graduating in 1884 from Harrison College, Barbados (a high school). His first plan was to gain employment as a schoolmaster; failing that, to seek a position with the Colonial Office . . . while he studied for exams that would lead to a degree and a prospective career as a physician. After a summer enjoying himself in the excitement of London life, he obtained a position in the fall of 1885 teaching at Bideford Grammar School, Devonshire. But a case of measles in November made him *persona non grata,* and he was dismissed to avoid *"endangering"* the students. His doctor also told him that he was not healthy enough to leave for London as quickly as he would have liked, so it was early 1886 before he again had employment.[1]

By the spring of 1886, he was happily teaching at Hunt Bridge House at Matlock, Derbyshire. He included the location in fiction that he wrote, so his experience there, working for "Mr. Leaf," had a lasting impact. But for some reason (against his father's advice) he left this position late in 1886 to return to London—possibly to spend the six months he later claimed studying medicine at Bart's. Shiel stated, in later autobiographical notes, that an observation of eye surgery was a major reason for giving up any thought of medicine as a career.

He disappears from our records until January 1887, when he wrote his father, greatly despondent over his circumstances—selling his books in the cold London streets, with no money or employment.

1. For a fuller description of these biographical details see *The Early Years.*

It may be that the death of the sister he loved so deeply, "black haired Ada," in October, and two strokes of his father, who besieged his son with descriptions of his suffering, helped feed what appears to have been a major depression. Shiel's father (who suffered his second stroke just before Christmas 1886), moneyless himself, dispatched Phipps's elder sister, Augusta Shiell Horsford, to England to see how he was faring. (It was most likely cholera that killed Ada Shiell. Her father was ill at the same time, and the West Indies was continually battling the disease.)

As the wife of the highly successful St. Kitts businessman, Samuel L. Horsford, Gussie had access to financial resources and transportation to England. Several of her children were also enrolled in English schools.[2] She found her brother entering another teaching position, this one at the Anglo-French High School, Ferme Park Road, Hornsey, a northern suburb of London. It appears he held this position from March into August of 1887, "having charge of the Holiday Class" at that time, as the schoolmaster, Mr. Lennard, wrote in a letter of recommendation for him.

Then he was absent a job again, and when he wrote his sister Gussie in late August 1887 of his frustrations, the wise sister who knew him so well suggested he take up writing. And he soon responded: ". . . you have kindled a strange fire in me; I have begun writing, writing, writing. Most strange!" A story that had been lying around for years, "Madame," was resurrected and sent off to the *Family Herald*—which turned it down. His father wrote in December, expressing disappointment over the fate of Phipps's stories, "Madame" and "Day." What Shiel produced as a result of this period of writing is not known, although he may have laid out plots and early texts that later became published stories. These two particular stories have disappeared, unless their titles and content were modified for some later appearance.

It is also likely that from 1888 to 1890 he relied on the Horsford family for financial assistance. His father died in January 1888, but Phipps apparently did not benefit from that death in any significant way. His father had gone to great lengths to try and maintain his life

---

2. The Horsford family was extremely important to MPS. The children are described in *The Early Years:* Reginald Shiell Horsford, Cyril, Samuel Leonard, Olive, Muriel, and Nella, who has been established as a member of the family since publication of the first volume of this biography.

"assurance" account, the only inheritance he expected to leave his children. He had also signed over property rights to what had become the family home on Parliament Street in Plymouth. By late 1889 or 1890, Shiel apparently spent time in a translator-training program at King's College, but he became engaged in "real" employment in 1891—as interpreter to the International Congress of Hygiene and Demography, which was holding its annual meeting in London for the first time that summer. He hinted that his brother-in-law and Mrs. Gladstone helped him gain work for this important enterprise.

He also appears to have been working in the spring of 1891 as a "secretary" in the office of James M. Coward's *The Messenger,* a weekly publication, located in "a narrow room overlooking the street" in the Hotel Victoria, reporting racing and financial news. In the novel *The Weird o' It,* where he described in fiction this episode in his life, he says he earned £2 a week. Shiel later told John Gawsworth that he wrote brief sketches of well-known people for the small paper, digging through files in the dark back rooms of Fleet Street newspapers for details, then finding a photograph to use with the sketch—a practice that he soon turned into similar work sold to the new, prestigious *Strand* magazine. These works would be unknown were it not for the fact that Shiel inscribed copies of some of these contributions for John Gawsworth.

And he published a story! "The Doctor's Bee," winner of a twenty-shilling prize, was published in *Rare Bits* on 18 December 1889. Shiel was then living at 98 de Beauvoir Road, Southgate Road, Kingsland. By the time of the 1891 census (April 1), he was a lodger (as "Phipps Shield") at #41 Coldbath Buildings (Coldbath Chambers, Roseberry Avenue, E.C.). He was a roomer with Fred Thaxter and his wife, Mary Sullivan, the real people on whom were based the fictional characters of Fred and Mary in *The Weird o' It*. "In the top front-room," he described the quarters, "a low light burned on a shaky table, giving a smell; there was a fire, and an old easy-chair with decadent bottom . . ."

It was at this address that he began translating pieces for the penny press as well as odds and ends for more substantial journals. His uncredited translation of the story "Slap Bang," by Jules Claretie, was published in the February 1891 issue of the *Strand*. He translated "A Torture by Hope," by Villiers de l'Isle-Adam, for the June 1891 issue of the *Strand*. (It is also from this address that he worked in 1891 for the small racing and financial paper, the *Messenger,* and also as a translator for the Seventh International Congress of Hygiene and Demography.)

In addition to translating the jokes in the 26 March 1892 issue of the *Million,* Shiel continued composing "portraits of celebrities" that appeared anonymously in the *Strand* (sketches like those he said he had written for the *Messenger*). At least two of these are known (tear-sheets that he signed), and it is highly likely that there were more. Gawsworth claimed that Shiel wrote the Zaleski stories, "The Eagle's Rock," "Three Men and a Girl," and "Two Fogs," among others at Coldbath Chambers. Shiel engaged Morris Colles (William Morris Colles, 1855–1926), of the Authors' Syndicate, as a literary agent, and commenced sending him stories to place where he could. It is highly unlikely that the Zaleski stories were written until after his next move—to Rugby Chambers on Bedford Row toward the end of 1892, where he lived until sometime in the fall of 1896.

Stories that he had written at Coldbath began to appear in a wide range of periodicals in 1893–95: "Guy Harkaway's Substitute" and "The Eagle's Crag" in the *Strand,* "Huguenin's Wife" in the *Pall Mall Magazine,* "A Puzzling Case" in the *Argosy,* "The Case of Euphemia Raphash" in *Chapman's,* and "Orazio Calvo" in *Belgravia Annual*—with others ready to appear in 1896.

As the earliest known examples of his writing skills, these stories are unusually well written and in some cases quite powerful. Even so, Shiel must have left this kind of work behind for at least a while, as he devoted a great deal of energy in his early months at Rugby Chambers to begin the arabesque stories that would *not* appear in periodicals, but as the complete fictional content of *Prince Zaleski* and, in the next year, *Shapes in the Fire*—those titles in John Lane's "Keynotes Series," whose initial full-blown decadent book designs by Aubrey Beardsley helped distinguish this series of avant-garde prose as much as their powerful content.

It is still uncertain what drove Shiel to compose these two books as he did, to write the stories, and to submit them each as a unified book. Conan Doyle's decision to "kill" Sherlock Holmes at the Reichenbach Falls in the *Strand* in December 1893 may have encouraged Shiel to write the three Zaleski stories (with Poe's Dupin also in mind) to fill the gap of mystery stories that the reading public was demanding. Or someone may have suggested the idea to him. But Zaleski exaggerated anything that Poe had written, filled with as much decadent surroundings and story detail and as much ornate language as Shiel could then muster.

For whatever impact the work of Doyle or Poe may have had on his decision to write these "detective" stories, Shiel wrote Gussie in exasperation: "But why do you insist on comparing me with Conan Doyle? Conan Doyle does not pretend to be a poet. I do."[3]

In fact, it is likely that Shiel saw the Zaleski stories as a subtle means of exploring (with himself, as much as any) some of the thinking that was beginning to appear relating to eugenics, the works of Lombroso, and Max Nordau.[4]

The stories could have been written from the late winter of 1893 to the spring of 1894. The establishment of John Lane's publishing program, embodied in the "Keynotes Series," encouraging the submission of experimental writing by young writers, might have become a target for Shiel's pursuit of artistic success. Someone must have urged him toward Lane. (Brian Stableford, in his introduction to a reissue of *Prince Zaleski* in 2006, states that it was Mrs. Gladstone, but there is no documentation to support that other than Shiel's comment that she "at that time took no little interest in my writing, and profoundly influenced my goings and comings."[5])

In any event, Shiel sent *Zaleski* to John Lane in the late spring of 1894. Lane asked a reader, James A. Noble, to comment on the book. Noble wrote to a Lane contact (probably Frederick Chapman, Lane's business manager) on 28 May 1894.

> With regard to the "Prince Zaleski" stories I feel less at ease. My own estimate of them is very high, and by this time experience might have taught me to trust my own judgment of a book by a new writer, but the responsibility of recommending business men to back my verdict by a possible large expenditure is greater than I like to bear alone, so I would rather you had another opinion before committing yourself though I personally have no doubt.
>
> I should like very much like your Mr. Lane to read the story entitled "Prince Zaleski and the S. S." and form his own opinion. It can be read in less than two hours.[6]

---

3. MPS to Augusta, 30 April 1895 Rugby Chambers (JG transcription, HRC).

4. Benjamin Hervey, "Prince Zaleski," *Wormwood* No. 4 (Spring 2005): 57–73.

5. MPS, "About Myself" (1948).

6. James Noble, holograph letter, 28 May 1894, in John Lane Archives (HRC).

James Ashcroft Noble (1842–1896) was a poet and critic who wrote an essay in 1895 on sexuality in contemporary British fiction. He asserted that the decadent movement was not spontaneously artistic, but was essentially writing to appeal to the "baser or vulgar" taste of the public for financial reward. He is still cited as scholars increasingly study the furor that developed over decadence in the literature of the period, with special attention to the work of the "New Woman"—a debate that became extremely heated in 1895. Lane's publications became the most visible target of the argument over whether aesthetics or commercialization was behind this new wave of writing. As Noble said, "A publisher is not likely to buy what he cannot sell." With his understanding of both the literary quality of a work and how it would sell, it is understandable why Lane would consider Noble's judgment whether to publish a book or not.

When a positive response came to Shiel saying the firm would publish *Zaleski,* he immediately leaped into correspondence with Lane. On 2 July 1894, Shiel wrote Lane: "'Prince Zaleski' is ready and waits for you as a bud for the sunshine. I hope, however, you will not be in a hurry to publish until the best part—whatever part that is—of the Autumn season comes."[7]

He would be disappointed to find that the book was not to be published in the fall, not in fact until the next year, and he became fretful after he saw delay after delay, as he would complain to Gussie in January and February of 1895. Throughout his long career, Shiel kept a close eye on the business aspects of the publication of his works, just as he did the actual formats and their physical aspects.

James Noble added a postscript to another letter to Lane regarding *Zaleski,* this one dated 8 August 1894:

> P.S. Should you determine to consider Mr. Shiel's stories there is one little point, omitted from my report, which you might submit to him that the pictorial pun "Lassie-daemon" in the cipher manifesto of the Society of Sparta is a purely English play upon words, and therefore out of place in a document intended to be intelligible to the initiated of all nationalities. This may seem a trivial point, but the workmanship of this story is so good that a single little flaw stands out.[8]

---

7. MPS holograph letter to John Lane, 2 July 1894, Rugby Chambers (HRC).

8. Noble, holograph letter to John Lane, 7 August 1894 (HRC).

Shiel was anxious to include the pun. When the story, "The S. S." was published in *Prince Zaleski*, the section referred to by Noble read: "... the society was necessarily in the main an *English,* or at least an English-speaking one—for of this, the word 'lassie' was plainly indicative." It is likely that Shiel sidestepped Noble's cautionary note concerning the pun by simply adding this "English" reference to the society's chief base of operations, although without the original manuscript there is no way to know whether he changed the text or not. In any case, this entire story—about an international flood of "suicides"—utilizes a most extravagant set of code signs, the use of Greek and Latin phrases, and other linguistic gymnastics of which Shiel must have been proud, but that should have sent Noble and Lane away with headaches.

"The S. S." is "to some extent spoilt by a rather stupid pun," said the reviewer for the *Athenaeum,* while the *Bookman* (perhaps alerted by the earlier review) called the puzzle "a hideous pun." Unfortunately, this story, with the use of the initials "S. S.," has led many unthinking genre critics to the presumption that Shiel was somehow forecasting a relationship with the Nazi regime that would spring up in the twentieth century. Obviously, there was no way that readers of the story in the nineteenth century could have possibly connected the story with events that did not occur until the next century. This tie of Shiel to Nazi Germany at this early date is absolute nonsense. Eugenics, however, was very much on his mind.

In fact, Shiel was writing about a topic of much discussion during that 1895 period—suicide, and epidemics of it. Robert Louis Stevenson had already written his now-famous cycle of stories, "The Suicide Club," in 1887.[9] And Stevenson was much admired and emulated by

9. Barbara T. Gates, *Victorian Suicide: Mad Crimes and Sad Histories* (Princeton: Princeton University Press, 1988), included in *The Victorian Web.* MPS would have been exposed to much of this discussion, including especially a rash of suicides and discussions of them in the summer of 1893. John Stokes discusses this in *In the Nineties* and mentions "The S. S." (130–31), but never mentions the short story by name, just the book title *Prince Zaleski*. Thus, there was no relationship made of this story with the Nazis until World War II. There was no reason for readers in 1895 to make such a connection. What caught the attention of critics of this story in its day was MPS's poor play on words, "Lassie-daemon," used in the manifesto of the crime club.

John D. Squires, in an email to the author of 28 June 2009, provides additional insight into MPS's writing based on this story. In determining

both the literary aesthetes and popular writers of the period. John Stokes has written extensively about this phenomenon.[10]

On 9 August 1894, Shiel wrote Lane (from Rugby Chambers):

> My dear Sir—
>
> I am leaving the M.S. of Prince Zaleski at your chambers in accordance with your directions received this morning. You will see I have mauled it about a good deal, & it is now about as perfect as I can make it.
>
> I thought of saying to you that if you ever have any books to be

---

whether MPS's writing is "science fiction" by today's standards, some theorists insist that to be science fiction a story would need to include important hard science elements.

Squires points out that it seems to him that MPS often asked the classic question of science fiction: "What if?" Instead of asking about changes in technology, or how technological change might impact the future, he was raising sociological questions often rooted in headline issues of his times. Viewed from that perspective "The S. S." may be viewed as sociological science fiction as easily as a mystery or detective story. Underneath the decadent trappings that Brian Stableford discusses so well (leaving aside his conclusion that Zaleski or MPS must have been gay), MPS combined two headline issues of the times and asked, "What if this current rash of suicides are actually murders? Who might have a motive to murder such a group of people? What if the growing eugenics movement attracted a powerful group of people willing to put their theories into practice? How might they go about it?" Dress the two "what if" questions in decadent trappings, with more than a little Poe, and you get "The S. S."

But the criticism of MPS as a proto-Nazi based on this story has nothing to do with contemporary suicides. It is focused on the eugenics philosophy of the secret society, which Zaleski and MPS shared, disagreeing only over details. The eugenics movement had a lot of support, Shaw and Wells included. There were eugenics-based laws passed in Europe and in many American states, which often stayed on the books until long after World War II. That might be the source of the eugenic planks in Prince Teddy's program outlined in the final chapter of *The Dragon*. The 1912 London conference certainly brought those theories back into the news. MPS's reiteration of them was part of the ammunition that Sam Moskowitz railed about in describing him as a Nazi. From around 1961 to 1978, when A. Reynolds Morse got involved again, Moskowitz's opinions on MPS were the only ones being published and they still echo today. The Nazi eugenics program obviously took the steam out of the movement and continues to color postwar readers' impressions of MPS.

10. John Stokes, *In the Nineties*.

translated from either the French or German I shall be very glad if you will remember to give me the job. I know both languages well, & you could depend on the high literary quality of the translations.

Would you care to publish a volume of already published magazine stories of mine at some early date—say in the Spring of next year by which time about eight new ones of mine will have appeared? All my old stories are of the "tea-cup" realistic sort of which I have grown to feel a little bit ashamed.

Yours very truly,

M. P. Shiel

John Lane Esq.

P.S. I read Ella D'Arcy's "Elegie." & do not think I ever came across any thing (in English) more impressive. Had it been 500 words shorter it would have been dead perfection—no light matter.[11]

"Elegie" was the lead story in D'Arcy's collection of short stories, *Monochromes,* published in the Keynotes Series in 1895. It had been published in *Blackwood's Magazine* in November 1891. This story about a musical composition written as a response to the tragic ending of a young "green love," is strong only in the ease with which the young composer is able to walk so quickly away from the tragedy once his composing was done.

In a letter of 2 July 1894, Shiel had asked Lane: "Will you be so kind as to tell me the number of Blackwood's in which appeared the story *'Elegie'* to which you directed my attention some little time ago? I shall be much obliged."[12]

Shiel exaggerates in his praise of the story. But his flattery of it to Lane, and doubtless his eventual flattery of it to Ella, as well as his flattery of her, must have led to an affair between the two that has been mentioned in several sources. He later wrote Gussie: "By the way, would you like to see the pretty evolution of a correspondence? I enclose you it. They are written by the 'newest' of the new women, and she really does write very sweet stories. The papers are always talking about her."[13]

11. MPS holograph letter to Lane, 9 August 1894, Rugby Chambers (HRC).
12. MPS holograph letter, 24 July 1894, Rugby Chambers, to Lane (HRC).
13. MPS to Augusta, 30 April 1895, Rugby Chambers (JG transcription, HRC).

This was patently Ella D'Arcy. One of her responsibilities as an employee of Lane was to make arrangements for the "smokes" that Lane and Henry Harland hosted for Bodley Head authors and the *Yellow Book* groups. She could have known Shiel from both his publications for Lane and for his occasional appearances at their offices and social events.

D'Arcy remembered the Lane socials fondly: "Never were there such evenings as those long-ago evenings in Cromwell Road! . . . The large drawing room, lighted by lamps and candles only—those days electricity had not yet become general—would begin to fill up about nine o'clock. Two or three would have dined there. Others dropped in for coffee and cigarettes . . ."[14]

Shiel's affair with D'Arcy must have been a brief one. Penelope Fitzgerald in her biography of Charlotte Mew says of D'Arcy, "She had a hard enough struggle to support herself, and took lovers as she chose, without drawing any particular attention to it. Frederick Rolfe, who could not stand her (it was Ella who complained about his lice), called her 'a mouse-mannered piece of sex.'" Mew says this hardly described Ella, who was a "dark, handsome, untidy-looking, witty woman."[15] Rumor included John Lane and Henry Harland, editor of the *Yellow Book,* among those reputed lovers. Heavily involved as she was in Lane's enterprises, Ella might have been helpful in getting *Shapes in the Fire* into print.

Years later, probably about 1904, Shiel apparently tried to reestablish a relationship with D'Arcy. He seems to have badgered her with letters requesting responses and seems to have gotten so peeved with her silences that he called her few responses "curt" and "frosty"—as she mentions in the following letter to him.[16]

144 Cromwell Road / S.W. / May 18. [ca. 1904?]

Dear Phipps Shiel,

I am moving to-day to 57 Marlow Road. Digs which enjoy an excellent view of the gloomy red-brick palace where I shall perchance end my days.

---

14. J. Lewis, *John Lane and the Nineties* 78.

15. Fitzgerald, *Charlotte Mew and Her Friends* 66.

16. D'Arcy holograph letter to MPS, 18 April [1904?], in the collection of Barry Humphries.

Some day next week, you must invite me to have tea with you, and then I might go and see the rooms you tell me about. But didn't we decide, anyway, the Row would be too far from my work?

Ah! if I had the making of the world . . . I would have made it better. I would have built it nearer to the heart's desire, as dear Omar expresses it; yes, even although I might have had to spend a whole fortnight over it. But after all, what is a fortnight in comparison with the results I would have achieved? By the way you write such capital letters yourself, I can't think why you should pine [~~for~~] to receive any from me: especially as mine are so "curt" so "frosty" so "hypercritical"? But you remember how different I was ten years ago[?]

Sincerely yours, / Ella D'Arcy

Only a reader or two have had access to this letter, but it helped serve as the basis for a widely published assumption that Shiel and D'Arcy were intimate in 1895, and that D'Arcy forecast her demise in "the gloomy red-brick palace" that was St. Pancras mental institution. Sadly, when reality and health deserted her in the mid-1930s, after years of living in Paris, her hair dyed orange, Ella was committed to the hospital and died there in 1939.

Lane would have had little interest in the "tea-cup" stories that Shiel had produced up to that time—as Shiel described them to Lane to see whether he might want to publish a collection. It is difficult to characterize those magazine stories, as we know them, that Shiel had written prior to this date as "tea-cup," although he might have been thinking of them as straightforwardly written stories, not "decadent" or experimental in the sense of what John Lane was looking for in the Keynotes Series.

But perhaps Shiel obtained enough encouragement from Lane and his associates regarding *Zaleski,* and as a result of his romance with D'Arcy, that he plunged vigorously into writing the elaborately languaged stories that became *Shapes in the Fire,* published in the same Keynotes Series in 1896.

In the meantime, production of *Zaleski* proceeded. In an undated "Sunday" letter (probably 18 November 1894) Shiel wrote Lane that "I returned from Matlock y'day, after some days absence, but did not find proofs of 'Prince Zaleski'; I had left instruction here to send on any letters &c., and therefore suppose you have not sent it. At least, I hope not. Here, however, I now am."[17]

He wrote Lane a few days later, [Thursday] 22 November 1894, that he was reading proofs and wondering about the financial arrangements to be made for the book:

> I have received partial proofs of "Prince Zaleski," which [*struck through*] I have corrected and sent to printer in Edinboro', which I presume, is what you intend.
>
> Perhaps I need not remind you that you have not yet sent an agreement; and I do not even know what the terms are to be precisely. This for form's sake you will doubtless see to. I quite hope that our relation may be a long one, and I dare say you will fill in agreement as liberally as you usually do.
>
> I hope I am right in sending proofs to Edinboro': if not, send me a postcard.[18]

It would be interesting to know what drew him to Matlock, where he had taught school, a location that appears to have been important to him over the years and drew him back again and again. Perhaps it was "Mary," whose pregnancy he described to Gussie in January 1895. Or it may have been the sheer attractiveness of the area, lying as it did at the southern edge of the Peak District, with mountain climbing and rugged hiking—the kind of place for wilderness wandering that he had loved as a boy on Montserrat.

While Shiel was preparing *Zaleski* for publication, other short stories that he had written in Coldbath Chambers continued to appear. One of the best and most interesting was "The Eagle's Crag," which Shiel had pestered Colles about for months because for a while it appeared that it had been mislaid. It is a story with a fugitive hidden on an ocean peak in Italy, but it has very much the feel of the precipices of Montserrat and the rock Redonda. It appeared in the September 1894 issue of the *Strand*.

Zaleski was advertised for November 1894 publication, then announced in the papers for early January; but Shiel wrote Gussie on 14 January 1895, "There is no book to send." Lane had offered him a lump sum for it, but he had refused, asking instead to have royalties

17. MPS holograph letter to Lane, 18 November 1894, Rugby Chambers (HRC).

18. MPS holograph letter to Lane, 22 November 1894, Rugby Chambers (HRC).

paid him quarterly—"preferring to have an interest in the sale, as I know that publishers are crafty, and when they volunteer to pay down in that way, it is clear that they have faith in the future of the book, and in their out-look they depend, of course, on the judgment of highly skilled readers."

Later, Shiel made a decision that directly opposed this in the future arrangements for *The Purple Cloud,* taking a lump sum in desperation and, as events played out, losing any future income from perhaps his finest work and excellent sales.

He cannot understand why Lane keeps postponing publication of *Zaleski*. As for him, he thinks the book will be published right when the public is intent on the gathering of Parliament and the book will lose much of its impact. Since royalties are paid quarterly, the next payment will be on Ladyday next (late March), and "unless it has a very extraordinary sale, I shall get now very little on Ladyday, and no more for 3 months, so that, as I was looking for funds to bring Harrie over, it cannot be done now—not at least until Autumn, especially as I have stopped writing short stories for the present."

"I am not very busy at the moment," he tells Gussie on 14 January 1895. He has just finished a good long story "and feel[s] like an empty bag." It is possible that he had begun the stories that would appear in *Shapes in the Fire* in 1896, that richly extravagant collection published in the Keynotes Series, although it is more likely that he did not begin that book until he received encouragement following the reception of *Prince Zaleski*. It is possible that the story he mentioned to Gussie was "Huguenin's Wife," "The Case of Euphemia Raphash," or "Orazio Calvo," all published later in 1895, although Gawsworth said these titles had been written earlier. Shiel continued to write stories that were more appropriate for publication in the general magazines of fiction, but only slightly removed in tone from the works of more decadent style that he wrote for John Lane. The supernatural is very much present. These are some of his strongest stories.

On the other hand, as we shall see, he was also pushed into dashing off the rather poor novelette in February 1895, *The Rajah's Sapphire,* published as his second book in March 1896.

He told Gussie that the very announcement of a book to be published in the Keynotes Series had brought him a certain amount of attention. "I am beginning to be—well, notorious." Journalists have been after "autobiographical information" and he has provided it. "I have said that I was born in the West Indies, in the very room where the Empress Josephine first 'saw the light.' Or as I put it in one case, 'first felt the heat, (Leonard [*his nephew*] tenderly calls it 'the warmth.') If I can find one of the letters I will enclose it to shew you how fatuous a thing an English newspaper is."[19]

He was smart enough to stay in touch with Lane, despite the fact that he was irritated over the delay in producing *Prince Zaleski*. Two days after he wrote the lengthy letter to Gussie, he wrote Lane (16 January 1895).

> Dear Mr. Lane—
>
> Many thanks for the Bodley Life, which I have just read and liked. I consider the little piece in italics "To the Reader" a charming bit of home-made mother-tongue English. But the name of the writer is not given.

---

19. MPS to Augusta, 14 January 1895, Rugby Chambers (JG transcription, HRC). Examples of these "fatuous" things turned up as the present volume was ready for press. In searching a new database of Australian newspapers, Jay Cruikshank found a reference to "A Popular Novelist M. P. Shiel" in a small outback newspaper, *Camperdown Chronicle* (Victoria, Australia) (29 December 1903): 7. Cruikshank sent the reference to John D. Squires. This profile appeared to be written by someone who knew or had interviewed MPS. It described his physical appearance, commented on his quality as a writer, and referred to his latest novel, *Unto the Third Generation* (1903).

It also included a paragraph of "Adventures": "In the course of his travels Mr. Shiel has met with some strange adventures. On one occasion he and his father were swimming off the Spanish coast when they were pursued by a shark. That was just about the most exciting race he ever took part in. Then, on another occasion, he was captured by an attaman of Zingari—i.e., a captain of gipsies—among the Sierra Morena mountains in Spain, and held a prisoner. But by the connivance of the brigand's daughter he was able to make his escape."

The profile was signed "M.A.P." In attempting to determine the author, John D. Squires asked the "Fiction Mags" discussion group for assistance. Mike Ashley suggested that "M.A.P." was not the author but the initials of a periodical. The likely source was "M.A.P." (*Mainly about People*), a popular penny weekly of pleasant gossip, personal portraits, and social news. Kirsten MacLeod followed up with a Google search that showed the original appearance of this piece had been in the penny periodical on 17 October 1903. M.A.P. was edited by T. P. O'Connor, who had established the *Sun* with Louis Tracy. MacLeod noted that the piece had been in a footnote discussion of MPS in *Writers, Readers, and Reputation: Literary Life in Britain, 1870–1918*, by Philip Waller (2006), 392n. It seems likely that O'Connor wrote this piece.

> *Of course,* the writing of a great book is the finest thing in the world. What is finer? Only there are so few of them—not ten altogether, since the world began. And of those few, the Great God Pan & Prince Zaleski are not, *not*, two! Nor yet Bleak House and Pendennis! Not even the Ballad of that hot young woman who couldn't do without a man. Oh, why don't nuns run about the streets of London with those dear petitions? If I had been that "grave youth nobly dressed," I should have been rapidly a gay one ignobly *un*dressed. But the whole thing is not true to life: she could have got a priest.
>
> Yours truly, / M. P. Shiel[20]

John Lane had published *The Life of Sir Thomas Bodley* as a Christmas 1894 keepsake—"Privately Printed for John Lane and His Friends"—in which he explained in an introduction why he had adopted Bodley as the patron saint of The Bodley Head firm: "Bodley, the most pious of founders! Who could so fittingly be enshrined as a patron? Besides, Bodley was one of the most notable worthies of Devon, my native county." It was this small pamphlet to which Shiel was referring.

"The Ballad of that hot young woman" refers to John Davidson's poem "A Ballad of a Nun," which appeared in the October 1894 issue of the *Yellow Book*. In a medieval-imaged poem, a young nun leaves her convent for the city and gives her virginity to a youth in a long night of love; she returns to her monastery the following morning welcomed by a bloody and flagellated image of the Virgin Mary. Interestingly, the same issue of the *Yellow Book* contained works by other writers with whom Shiel held some degree of friendship, or admired: Ernest Dowson, Nora Hopper, Theodore Wratislaw, Ella D'Arcy, and William Watson.

One of the most startling lines that a Shiel reader may recognize in the Davidson poem is the following:

> "Strange lady, what would you with me?"
> "Your love, your love, sweet Lord," she said;
> "I bring you my virginity."

Years later, in 1933, John Gawsworth asked Shiel for a brief piece for a planned tribute to Machen. Shiel wrote "The Good Machen" at Horsham on 22 June 1933. When he sent this to Gawsworth the next day, he appended a brief note:

---

20. MPS holograph letter to Lane, 16 January 1895, Rugby Chambers (HRC).

> I sent you last night some notes on Machen, all that I remember, but I think you know it all already. One of my cameo memories of that time is of a servant of his—about twenty old—French, I think in parentage. Once upon a midnight dreary . . . suddenly there came a . . . rapping at my oak, and it was not a raven but a canary: *she,* wishing to be kissed. . . . "Your love, your love, sweet Sir," she said. "I bring you my virginity"—having stolen out while the good Machen and Mrs Machen slept, probably leaving their flat-door open . . .

When Gawsworth shared this with Machen, Machen immediately sent a strong response to him, 23 August 1933: "'The Machens' Little French Maid': Let me beg you not to make Shiel the authority for any statement about me or my life. The man is an inveterate liar."

Although it has never been pointed out before, Shiel had obviously filched those final lines from John Davidson's widely admired poem. Since Shiel had told Gawsworth "I think you know it all already," he may have felt that he owed Gawsworth another Machen story, and simply combined lines from the poem, whether expecting a reader to recognize them or not in this "cameo."

Shiel followed his letter of 16 January 1895 to Lane with another lengthy, important letter to Gussie (12 February 1895). *Zaleski* is finally due, but there are other matters that relate to Shiel's attitude toward the New Woman (and the old), as well as a description of the weather that was repeated almost verbatim in *The Rajah's Sapphire,* a project that W. T. Stead had mysteriously introduced as a responsibility for Shiel's work-time.

> But oh! What weather. Thur-r-r! it is cold. There hasn't been such weather in England for the last hundred years they say. Oh, "the parching air burns frore" (isn't that a *sweet* collection of words: not my own). You remember last Winter when we had to clean our teeth with ginger-beer? Well, it's worse now. Everything freezes, freezes. It is Arctic. The sea, the open sea, freezes. People die of it. All you have to do is to lie down in it—and you die. The distress is very great; a million men are out of work; think of that! a million: and every one of them a soul, immortal, divine, a God-Man like Jesus, the very hairs of his head all numbered, and the lice among the hairs. Ah, the world is governed foolishly! till the very apes and asses must laugh at us; and what provokes me is my feeling that I, Phipps Shiel, could manage it better: more kindly, more wisely, more humanly: and am not allowed to try! However, as I say, it is Arctic, the cold; and the poor

pay the piper; and such queer, uncanny variations! Think of a thunder-storm in February! It is like the weather described by that inspired Yankee—

First it hailed, and then it blew, and then it friz and then it snew;
And then there was a shower of rain, and then it friz and snew again.

Well, my pet, I wanted to send you out my booklet this time, and wrote to John Lane to ask him if they had come from the binder's yet: but they haven't. It is positively to be published on Saturday morning next.

The companion book to it is by Grant Allen called "The Woman Who Did"; and it is making the devil of a sensation. It is to "Prince Zaleski" what a bone button is to a diamond, or, at any rate, a pearl: but for all that, it will, I think, make a great deal more noise than "Prince Zaleski": as it has to do with the relations of the sexes; and anything on that subject *now* is bought-up by the "New Woman" like hot loaves. Damn the "New Woman"! she is fast becoming a bore, and is, if possible, even More vulgar than the old. I always say, with Ruskin, that there are no ladies in England—no hlaf-loaf, *hlaf-ords,* "bread-givers" (that is the real meaning of the word)—and in this saying I know that there is a genuine truth. [*Letter incomplete, bottom half of page torn away*]

Shiel wrote Lane on 21 February 1895, declining an invitation to a lecture by Francis Elgar, explaining that he was working on a "vile" novelette (*The Rajah's Sapphire*)—"for Mr. Stead of all people." He commended the lovely production of *Prince Zaleski,* although a century later its royal purple binding has tended to fade badly, the spine invariably crisp and colorless.

Rugby Chambers. / Bedford Row. / W.C. / Feby 21st 95.

Dear Mr. Lane,

I waited till now to reply to your kind invitation to meet that twisted whisp of life, that squint of the sum-of-things, Francis Elgar, LL.D, in the hope that I might be able to have the pleasure. But I am afraid I cannot. I am under engagement to finish by next Monday a vile melodramatic kind of novelette (for Mr. Stead of all people), and as I have neglected to set about, I am now working all day & far into the night to get it done. I am so made that I cannot do even vile things altogether vilely, and every minute is therefore precious to me. I am especially sorry, as I wanted to make the acquaintance of your

Other Young Men. Will you excuse me? And don't forget to invite me to the next.

Yours truly / M. P. Shiel

P.S. Thanks for "Prince Zaleski": I rather like his dress.[21]

This was another instance in which Lane appears to have sent Shiel a finely printed invitation, illustrated by Aubrey Beardsley: "John Lane requests the pleasure of the company of . . . to meet his Oddship Francis Elgar, LL.D., President of the Sette of Odd Volumes, at a 'Smoke' on Friday, February 22nd, 1895." Elgar was a naval architect, well known for his design of several major vessels and an active role with the Royal Navy. Why Shiel characterized him as he did—to Lane!—is not clear. The Sette of Odd Volumes was an exclusive dining and literary social group.

Shiel continued writing intense, lengthy letters to Gussie, regarding this and other current personal and writing matters. By the time he wrote her again, the literary and social world would be shaken as a result of the unsuccessful suit that Oscar Wilde brought against the Marquess of Queensberry for criminal libel, and the two criminal trials of Wilde referred against him from evidence presented in the suit that he had filed. The first trial began on 26 April, in which the jury could not return a verdict, but after the second trial at the end of May, Wilde was convicted of gross indecency and sentenced on 25 May 1895 to two years' hard labor. Shiel wrote Gussie on 30 April 1895 from Rugby Chambers, expecting a verdict, but actually before the jury failed to reach a verdict.

Of course, by this time you have heard all about the Big Thing—Oscar Wilde. He will be sentenced this afternoon. Poor chap! I am sorry for him. It is not his fault: he is not well made: he is a *moral idiot*: he was born so: his mother made him so. *God will straighten him out*. It is ordained that he shall yet be perfect—without spot or blemish—perfect as a sphere of the heavens. Ah, Gussie! Gussie! The thing is too sweet to think of! The world is WELL MADE!

But what do you think—I too have had an offer of marriage, my dear! Think of *me* in the capacity of a wife! I who am so intensely a husband. Not a regular offer, be it said; and perhaps, after all, it was only my fancy. This is how it happened. I became friends some time

21. MPS holograph letter to Lane, 21 February 1895, Rugby Chambers (HRC).

ago with one of the big wigs, a chap who dines with Lord Salisbury, and has hobnobbed with the Prince of Wales: a nephew of Sir John Wilson, M. P., the "great railway King." His name is Hope Johnston. Well, a short time ago I was introduced to him by one of John Lane's "young men," and, on mutual liking, we became friends. He lives in chambers in St. James's St., and nearly every night I was there. Talk, talk; jabber, jabber, jabber. He *never* sleeps at night. He goes to bed at ten in the morning. And he is a great man for morphia. Very well, I used to stay with him till about six o'clock a. m. when I would come home through the quiet streets and toddle in to bed. But what I have to say is this: that his whole talk (sometimes) is about *buggery;* of course, he not only knows everybody, but the private life, the very thoughts of everybody. Long before this affair of Oscar Wilde became public, he foreshadowed it to me; and the names he mentioned, the picture he gave of the corruption of English society, was *awful*. Very well. Now, I was rather awkward in inserting the syringe into myself to inject the morphia, so he used to do it for me. And one night, when I had drawn up my shirt-sleeve, he stopped, and began to stroke my arm with his hand. "Ah, you *have* got a nice arm!" he said. I didn't like his *tone*. The stroking was *too* affectionate, the tone *too* effeminate. He saw me frown, and went on with the syringe. And so it passed. That, you say, wasn't much; but it was enough for me. If he had been opener, I should certainly have knocked him down. I like playing Adam, but I draw the line at Eve. My Gussie may go to sleep with the calm assurance that her brother will never get in the family way by any man.

Well, I have little news to give. Zaleski has been met with quite a crow of praise by the intelligent portion of the press; but, so far, I don't think the public has responded in proportion. They will, when one or two more of my books come out. The first, *by itself,* hardly ever does very much. The *Times* was *very* complimentary, and said I write like Æschylus! Think of *that*, my dear! Æschylus! Thanks for your praise. But why do you insist on comparing me with Conan Doyle? Conan Doyle does not pretend to be a poet. I do.

Well, I get a lot of invitations to go out to evening parties, "smokes," and the rest of it. Sometimes I wish little Reg [*his nephew*] was here: I would make him go and pretend to be me. I *never* go. Sometimes I am hard put to find an excuse, but I do find it. They come mostly from John Lane, and his many young men, and their wives. These damned little scribblers think I am one of them, and I am not. "Dining-out" helps no man to write greatly—which is hard work, and not an easy, as they think. By the way, would you like to see the pretty evolution of a correspondence? I enclose you it. They are written by the 'newest' of new women; and she really does write very sweet stories. The papers are always talking about her.

This letter appears to pin down the general time period in which Shiel was involved with Ella D'Arcy, as discussed above. It also has the feeling of "protesting too much" regarding the possibility of a homosexual relationship—like one of the exaggerations that Shiel would create in other instances to flatter or protect himself.

Arthur Machen, who would soon become a neighbor of Shiel on Gray's Inn Road, admired the book and wrote Lane in March asking him to congratulate Shiel. "I think that his 'Prince Zaleski' is very admirable—a most curious and charming work."

Other reviewers of the book were not unlike the one in the *Review of Reviews* who said, "The book contains three short stories, reminding one now of Poe and now of Stevenson's 'New Arabian Nights' all told with convincing art and a power of uncommon invention which few writers have equalled." The *Athenaeum* picked up a similar comparison: "Mr. M. P. Shiel seems to have aimed at a combination of the mysterious terror inspired by Poe's tales and of the sensational amazement which Mr. Sherlock Holmes's extraordinary perspicacity provokes." The *Bookman* thought his "mysteries are very good if a trifle laboured, and he has put them into literary form," but it is doubtful that any comment could have been worse than that from the *Saturday Review:* "This, we sincerely hope, is the low water-mark in 'Keynotes,' We doubt if Mr. John Lane in his short but brilliant career has ever published anything half so bad before . . . there is no doubt of its being Sherlock——demented." (This was H. G. Wells!)

All in all, Shiel could not have wished for a wider and more positive reception to *Zaleski* than it received.

By the time *Shapes in the Fire* appeared, late in 1896, Lane had dismissed Beardsley from the staff of the *Yellow Book,* and Patten Wilson—who had worked for a wallpaper firm—designed Shiel's second book in the Keynotes Series.

The stories in *Shapes in the Fire* have been characterized as the most extravagant work written by Shiel in the decadent style. By any standard applied to his work, they represent some of his strongest and most creative work in the short story form. (Only "The Dark Lot of

One Saul," twenty years hence, would match it in style.) It is remarkable that Shiel was able to create this body of work in the year between the appearance of *Prince Zaleski* (works poorer by far than the stories in *Shapes in the Fire*) and that book's publication in 1896. His story "Vaila," reworked later as "The House of Sounds," continues to be recognized as a masterpiece of horror. And the entire body of writing in this book is at once imaginative and elaborately empurpled, with a strong undercurrent of eroticism running through it.

After the discovery on Shiel's marriage certificate that Theodore Wratislaw—a decadent poet and passionate lover of music halls—was a witness at Shiel's marriage to Lina Garcia Gomez in 1898, it is easy to imagine that Shiel immersed himself in the works of D'Arcy, Wratislaw, and others in the John Lane circle between the publication of *Prince Zaleski* and *Shapes in the Fire*. That might explain the rapid development of Shiel's decadent literary voice.

Shiel wrote Gussie on 3 November 1896 (from 24 Percy Circus)[22] that he had gone into "society," spending every Sunday afternoon at an "at-home" where he was "in" with the hostess; he was engaged to a singer in Queen's Hall, but *Shapes in the Fire* had not yet been published. A case could be made that this singer was "Mistress Beatrice Laws," to whom this collection of stories was dedicated. In any case, the book's publication followed swiftly, although Mistress Laws continues unidentified.

But *Shapes in the Fire* was to be the last of Shiel's concentrated forays into this exotic medium, the last of his works for Lane, and perhaps a signal of the end of the Decadent movement just ahead—the work of social and literary forces far larger than he—and a marker of new directions ahead in his career.

Decadence was being forced out of sight. John Lane altered his publishing program as Wilde's trial broke, allowing the *Yellow Book* to fade into silence in the spring of 1897, after thirteen issues, and initiating a more subdued publishing venue. Shiel moved from Rugby Chambers to 3 Gray's Inn Place late in 1896, where Arthur Machen, his wife, and a new social circle would soon join him . . . and he would move from his heady decadent writing phase on into "the fictional serial trade."

---

22. MPS to Augusta, 3 November 1896, 24 Percy Circus, W.C. (JG transcription HRC).

Chapter 7

"the fictional serial trade"

Shiel was well prepared for new writing challenges as the effects of the trials of Oscar Wilde shook the publishing world. He had been writing for a decade, chiefly the short stories, translations, and miscellanea that had appeared in every kind of outlet that he, or his literary agent Morris Colles, could find—as well as the publication of those major books, *Prince Zaleski* and *Shapes in the Fire* (with *The Rajah's Sapphire* slipped in between).

But the short stories in both *Prince Zaleski* and *Shapes in the Fire* appear to have been written specifically for the books themselves, while *The Rajah's Sapphire* is important in that it provides a link to a new period of Shiel's career that would leave John Lane and the literary elitism associated with his decadent book publications behind. New influences and opportunities were developing for Shiel beyond his short stories.

William T. Stead, who had established the extremely successful *Review of Reviews* in 1890, apparently urged Shiel to write the brief novella, *The Rajah's Sapphire*. Shiel said of this: "W. T. Stead got to know me, conceived that I 'had an imagination,' and would write to me invitingly when one of his rapturous ideas in journalism attacked and urged him—he and I even writing a wild little book in collaboration . . ."[1] This was published as Shiel's second book in March 1896, written from a plot, he said on its title page,—given him—*viva voce*—by Stead.

It had been Stead's intention to establish a companion publication to the *Review of Reviews* with a *Daily Paper* that was intended to reach a wider audience than the 200,000 total readers of the *Review*. It would carry not only brief news of the day but would emphasize his most personal philosophical messages. Its title page was to bear the legend "For the Union of all who Love, in the service of all who Suffer." It would also include in each issue a continuing serial, "The Romance of the World," a fictional embodiment of the news of the day. Stead imagined that if 100,000 readers would invest £1 each in the new publication, they could recover their investment after a year,

1. "About Myself" (1947) 4.

while the contributed funds would become an invested income source for Stead's organization. Readers did not bite on the offer.[2]

A specimen issue was distributed in the *Review of Reviews* in November 1893. It immediately failed in its effort to attract investors or to gain a more general readership by including the continuing serial as a hook for readers.[3]

It has long been assumed that Shiel commenced *The Rajah's Sapphire* as a prospective contribution to this series of "novels." It is possible that Shiel was not involved in this early effort at all. While the work may have been commissioned in 1893, there is no evidence establishing that any of it was actually written then. Facts indicate that the writing of it was not taken up seriously until February 1895, although Shiel acknowledged that he was late getting to the task.

Grant Richards recalled in his memoirs that Shiel had an early "shot" at meeting the initial interest of Stead in the "Romance of the World" feature, but the idea never materialized. (Richards worked for Stead and his *Review of Reviews* for almost eight years; he opened his own firm in January 1897.) Richards may simply have recalled the book that Shiel wrote in 1895, *The Rajah's Sapphire,* in which Shiel acknowledged Stead's contribution. Stead tried the *Daily Paper* venture again after the turn of the century and almost went bankrupt in doing so, developing a severe depression as well—similar to an episode of exhaustion in early 1895.[4]

The first and only issue of the *Daily Paper* (Wednesday, 4 October 1893) includes as its "The Romance of the World from Day to Day, Our Serial" a story that begins in the African bush. "Chapter I—A Bronze Andromeda" concerns a young settler, Fort Victoria, Dr. Jameson, Mr. Rhodes, and the murder of women and children by Matabele tribesmen. A map of Mashonaland is included with the story. These brief action chapters reflected the initial events that would lead to the "First Matabele War" that lasted from November of 1893 until January 1894. It was this kind of story, tied to current events, that Stead envisioned for his new paper.[5]

---

2. Grace Eckley, *Maiden Tribute* 208–9.

3. Eckley 283–84.

4. Eckley 209.

5. *Daily Paper,* Wednesday, 4 October 1893. (From photocopy provided by Dr. Eckley.)

There is no evidence of Shiel's hand in this brief beginning of the "romance." Grace Eckley, W. T. Stead's biographer, suspects that Stead may have written this installment himself.[6] There are other brief articles in the issue that range from "The Church Congress at Birmingham" to "Yesterdays Long Ago: The Battle of Salamis." Stead, obviously, would have had his immediate staff or others provide this material for the paper. It is conceivable that here, as in other Stead enterprises of this period, Shiel might have contributed brief articles for Stead. But the conception of Shiel's developing the "Sapphire" plot into a short novel would have had to have occurred in June or July 1893, before Stead went to Chicago in October, spending several months on the American continent before returning to England in March 1894. The chronology does not seem to fit.

Another very subtle hint at writing that Shiel may have done for Stead comes from reading the novel that Stead wrote as the 1894 "Christmas Novel" for the *Review of Reviews: The Splendid Paupers: A Tale of the Coming Plutocracy.* As busy as he was, Stead could have used ghostwriting or editorial assistance on this long novel.

In any event, apparently from the *Sapphire* plot verbally suggested by Stead, Shiel completed at least an initial version of *The Rajah's Sapphire* in February 1895, although the small, decorative book itself was not published until January 1896. Shiel described to John Lane on Thursday, 21 February, the urgency with which he was working, night and day, to complete this novelette—"as I have neglected to set about"—by the next Monday (25 February 1895), apparently a deadline imposed by Stead.[7] (Shiel had not mentioned this to Lane in January.) There is no explanation why Stead was anxious to have the work in hand, or what use he intended to make of it. It is possible that Stead had paid Shiel an advance for the story as he began to gather material for the *Daily Paper* in the summer of 1893, and that he eventually wanted Shiel to complete the work for which Stead had paid him. Ward, Lock & Bowden published the book in January 1896.

Grant Richards, who worked on the first issue of the *Paper,* writes in his memoir:

> I find in my diary a note to the effect that on October 7th, 1893, I remained at Clowes Printing Office till midnight subediting Daily

---

6. Eckley 209.

7. Holograph letter from MPS to Lane, Thursday, 21 February 1895 (HRC).

Paper specimen numbers. That was the name Stead had chosen for his daily. It came out, that specimen, as a supplement to the Review, and no one paid much attention to it. A first installment of the serial story that he had planned was included. I cannot remember who was responsible for that installment, but I do remember that M. P. Shiel had a shot at the kind of thing that Stead wanted. Shiel's effort came to nothing as far as Mowbray House was concerned. But he made use of it as a short novel *The Rajah's Sapphire,* which he published in a series which Ward Lock put out.[8]

Despite Shiel's acknowledgment to Stead on the title page of that work, it is difficult to see what Stead gained from Shiel's completion of the book and its publication, or why he pressured Shiel to write the story (on deadline in February 1895) in the first place. A brief note in the *Review of Reviews,* reporting publication of the book, does not even mention Shiel as its author, only comments that it had been written from a plot by Stead and "has a lot of go and incident in it."[9]

In publishing a new edition of *The Rajah's Sapphire* in 1980, John D. Squires has provided a detailed background behind the development of a Shiel/Stead collaboration and recited Stead's telling a friend, Dr. E. J. Dillon, on 12 February 1912, a "thrilling story" about the "sudden appearance of a talisman from Poland which brought ill-luck to everyone who possessed it."[10]

This could just as easily be the "plot" that Stead provided Shiel, since there is very little else to the novella. A selfish British countess (Ada Macdonald) persuades a German diplomat (Markgraf Stefan von Reutlingen) to acquire for her the "Rajah's Sapphire," a beautiful gem, but with a reputation of bringing ill luck to whoever owns or is around it. Stefan and the "High-flyer," the millionaire Ralph Ralloner, are both after the hand of Ada. Ralloner is manic for speed, madly driving a ship into another and killing four hundred passengers, also skating into a crowd and injuring Ada—hiding behind his fortune and unknown for his misdeeds until the rapid conclusion of the story. It is presumed that the jewel has somehow facilitated murder, accident, tragedy. After the High-flyer's death, found out finally for revenge by

8. Grant Richards, *Memoirs of a Misspent Youth* 282.

9. *Review of Reviews* 13 (March 1896): 375.

10. John D. Squires, Afterword to *Great Strike* (Kettering, OH: Vainglory Press, 2005) and rev. www.alangullette.com/lit/shiel/essay/shiel_tracy.htm

a victim of the shipwreck, Ada and Stefan are united and the enormous jewel is cut into dozens of smaller stones.

As noted earlier, regarding the personal record that exists of the writing of this little book, there are these letters. Phipps wrote Gussie on 14 January 1895: "I am not very busy at the moment." Similarly, he wrote John Lane rather quietly on 16 January, thanking him for the "Bodley." On 12 February 1895, Shiel wrote Gussie about the pitiless cold of the winter season and the terrible state of the national economy, forcing a million men out of work. And by 21 February he wrote Lane, "I am under engagement to finish by next Monday a vile melodramatic kind of novelette (for Mr. Stead of all people), and as I have neglected to set about, I am now working all day & far into the night to get it done."[11]

Thus, by the end of January 1895 and the first week in February, Shiel had commenced *The Rajah's Sapphire*. And when he wrote Gussie on 12 February, he was halfway through the book, writing to her the precise words he was writing in the novella about the pitiless cold, the million men out of work. He has the selfish Ada step out of character in the book and deplore the working conditions for these million men, freezing, workless. As a change, she said she would "rather like the Socialism."[12]

This little novel is interesting for other reasons. The story begins on "the 27th of January, in this year of grace 1895, and so, of course, the birthday of Wilhelm." (Perhaps this was the actual day when Shiel began the story.) Early in the book, the German ambassador Stefan discusses the Sino-Japanese war with a Chinese diplomat, the siege of Wei-Hei-Wei, and forecasts a Japanese victory in the war. This approach is very much like that of keeping the story close to actual events, as Shiel would in *Empress of the Earth*. But *The Rajah's Sapphire* quickly deserts actuality and moves rapidly to conclusion.

This strategy of storytelling may also owe much to the conception that W. T. Stead introduced for the ill-fated *Daily Paper*'s continuing serial, "The Romance of the World from Day to Day." Stead may have established in Shiel's mind a pattern of tying daily events to fiction, as he would undertake in several serials to come.

---

11. These letters are in original holograph (to Lane) or in transcription by JG (to Gussie HRC).

12. *The Rajah's Sapphire* (1981) 75.

Interestingly enough, one of the succors of the hungry, jobless men described in *The Rajah's Sapphire* was Louis Tracy, who helped introduce Shiel into the fictional serial trade.

Louis Tracy was born in Liverpool on 18 March 1863. After early military training, he began a career in journalism in 1884, moving from place to place, including India, until he assisted T. P. O'Connor in starting the *Sun* in 1892. While there, he convinced Arthur Harmsworth (later Lord, then Viscount Northcliffe, 1865–1922) to join him in the purchase of the *Evening News and Post*. Tracy edited the paper, renamed the *Evening News,* for a short time, and then sold his shares to Harmsworth in the winter of 1894. He really wanted to pursue a writing career. Had he delayed his sale of the shares, he would have made a fortune. Nevertheless, he apparently did well.[13]

Through these fortunate business financial moves, Tracy obtained sufficient money to allow him to establish soup kitchens during the winter of 1894–95 that fed thousands of the hungry, while he also began to write adventure novels in penny papers for the amusement of the hungry. Tracy shared Shiel's concern for the jobless, and such commonly shared feelings may have contributed to what became their lengthy collaboration in following years in writing collaborative serial novels.

Tracy's highly successful *The Final War*—a novel in which a conspiracy of the European powers set out to destroy England and steal her colonies—was published in *Pearson's Weekly* from 28 December 1895 to 1 August 1896. America came to England's fictional aid in trouncing Europe.

"After finishing this romance I went to America," Tracy said, "to get local colour for *An American Emperor,*" his next novel, passing through customs in New York on 18 July 1896. The novel was serialized in *Pearson's Weekly* from 26 December 1896 to 26 June 1897. Tracy's practice was to develop an outline of the serial, but to write its episodes from week to week. Tracy fell ill from a recurrent "fever" while the serial was in progress, and Shiel was asked to step in for him, writing chapters 29–39, which appeared beginning 17 April 1897 and continuing into the early summer.[14]

The willingness of Tracy and Peter Keary, the managing editor of *Pearson's,* to let Shiel assume this responsibility suggests that they were

13. Squires, op. cit.

14. Ibid.

already familiar with his work—possibly based on *The Rajah's Sapphire* or the still mysterious *The Man-Stealers,* which may have existed in some form at the time. Otherwise, in 1897 Shiel had only his short stories and *The Rajah's Sapphire* to provide any evidence that he was capable of picking up the serial for Tracy. Whether Tracy even knew Shiel at this point is unknown, but it seems unlikely that he would let a writer unknown to him pick up his work.

Shiel had written his mother on 3 November 1897: "I took little Cyril to Paris in the Autumn to shew him about, and since I have come back, I have been writing a novel." Earlier in the letter, he asked her: "I often think of you with the old love in all its freshness . . . Do you love me still, I wonder?"[15] In the first twenty pages of *The Man-Stealers,* Verdier asks Lise: "Do you love me still with the old flame, jade?"[16] Shiel had earlier lifted lines from letters that he wrote Gussie to incorporate into *The Rajah's Sapphire*. The same words seem just as likely to flow into his letters as into his serials, or from the fiction into his letters.

Given the specific words that he wrote his mother—that in the late fall of 1897 he was novel writing—one must speculate as to what the novels were. He had not yet started work on *The Empress of the Earth*, and there are only memories from forty years later as to what he had started working on after his contributions to Tracy's *An American Emperor*. *The Man-Stealers* appears a likely candidate for a novel he was then completing, based on the similarities in the sentence noted above. It seems likely that whatever the novel, or novels, he was working on in early November 1897, he laid them aside—with Peter Keary's urging—to seize the immediate income from the more timely serial.

The Man-Stealers, a novel regarding a French plot to kidnap the Duke of Wellington, was listed as a published work on captions above the stories when his serial, *The Empress of the Earth,* began publication in *Short Stories* on 5 February 1898. It may be that this work had appeared in one of Pearson's stable of cheap penny papers during 1896–97, not in *Short Stories,* but possibly in a companion paper. Evidence above suggests that he began working on it in the fall of 1897, and as he later told John Gawsworth, also on "Yellow Danger, Contraband

---

15. MPS to his mother, 3 November 1897, 2 Gray's Inn Place, W.C., transcribed by JG (HRC). MPS had moved to this address sometime in the fall of 1897.

16. *The Man-Stealers* 19.

of War, Cold Steel. And the first chapters of 'Isle of Lies.'" Files of the fragile publications in which so much of his early work was published have disappeared, as have so many of the other cheap papers of the time, so it has been impossible to identify a serial publication of the novel. The story may have been in composition, queued for publication in a Pearson paper, but simply pushed aside by the two Shiel serials tied to contemporary events. Another possibility, however, may be that Shiel was writing episodes of *The Man-Stealers* in an obscure Pearson publication as the issues containing the serial appeared. This was Louis Tracy's practice. That would explain why this title was listed in the captions of *Empress,* appearing in a Pearson publication. At this point, there are simply not enough available facts, so one can only speculate. I believe that Shiel jumped at a more lucrative opportunity for the Chinese war serial and left *The Man-Stealers* waiting with Pearson for publication along with drafts of other novels that would show up in the future.

With respect to Shiel's personal life, he told his mother that he had taken his nephew Cyril to France in the fall. Since he later said that he had spotted his first wife Lina skating in Paris when she was sixteen, it seems likely that it was on this or a similar trip that he had prayed for her and "got her"—although it would not be until 1898 that they were married. There were likely many skating trips to Paris before their engagement, while he was pursuing with equal fervor the English maid, "Ada Seward," who would become the heroine of *The Empress of the Earth.*

The two future-war novels established a trend for Tracy's future success in both England and America. As John D. Squires has noted, Tracy's fiction frequently featured American characters, which made it much easier to sell his novels on both sides of the Atlantic. While Shiel's early serial novels would echo Tracy's plots in some ways, he never emulated Tracy's successful ploys of using American heroes. This may help explain his problem in attracting American publishers for many of his early novels. Shiel's stories often appealed to the jingoistic feelings of his English audience, as full as they were of the still ascendant sun of the British Empire. But he also included his very personal feelings about religion, land ownership, the class system—in a manner that Tracy never would, nor even consider. In some later books, the weight of Shiel's ideas overwhelmed their popular appeal and they failed as sellers. In time, he was financially devastated as the appeal of his serials waned and his books no longer interested the reading public.[17]

Shiel said of Tracy's attitude toward his own work: ". . . my old friend, Mr. Louis Tracy, C.B.E., has said to me 'Strange fellow, Shiel: you could make as much money as Bernard Shaw and Edgar Wallace put together, but you persist in casting your pearls before swineherds, who know not pearls.'"[18]

Shiel was now working from 3 Gray's Inn Place, where he had moved sometime in the fall of 1896. This was just across a large garden area—full of elm trees and cawing rooks, Jerome K. Jerome said—where Arthur Machen lived at 4 Verulam Buildings. Shiel described Machen's quarters:

> . . . the drawing-room was remote from the street (Gray's Inn Road), and looked out charmingly on "Gray's Inn Gardens". I too looked on them from my windows high up in 3 Gray's Inn Place some way off on the adjacent side of the gardens-square. There, Machen and Mrs. often came to visit me—she taller than he, thin, pale, amiable, fond of me. To me, beginning housekeeping, she gave council: "don't let her (my old housekeeper) sweep the carpet with a hard broom, make her (secretly) pick up the bits", etc.[19]

Machen and Amelia Hogg married in August 1887 and moved first to his quarters in Great Russell Street, then to the countryside, and finally to 4 Verulam Buildings, off Gray's Inn Road, in late 1897. Machen was twenty-four when he and Amelia married. She was thirty-seven. Although she came from a Catholic family in Sussex, she had a reputation as having been rather an unchurched hoyden among the artists and actors in London in the previous decade. Jerome K. Jerome said of her:

> Arthur Machen married a dear friend of mine, a Miss Hogg. She had been a first nighter, and one of the founders of the Playgoers' Club . . . Amy Hogg was also a pioneer. She lived by herself in diggings opposite the British Museum, frequented restaurants and aerated bread-shops, and had many men friends; all of which was considered very shocking in those days.[20]

---

17. Squires, op. cit.

18. MPS, "The Inconsistency of a Novelist," in Morse (1948) 8. Letter from Tracy to MPS, 24 January 1911.

19. MPS, "The Good Machen," in *The Good Machen: A Centenary Tribute Recalled*.

20. Jerome K. Jerome, *My Life and Times* 115.

Amy and Arthur also owned a small vineyard in Touraine, France. The Machens were pleased to offer wine from their own growth to dinner guests, and to Oscar Wilde and other friends at the Florence Restaurant in Rupert Street, where it was kept in stock.

An entirely new social circle opened for Shiel at this Gray's Inn location, including regular attendance in Machen's quarters on smoky Sunday evenings with literary folk now removed from the decadent *Yellow Book* socials of just a year before. Machen had written John Lane a letter mistakenly dated "Nov. 15. 95"—a letter obviously written before the publication of *The Three Imposters,* since Machen offers to "soften" the text (the book was already published, and Machen had removed the word "entrails"), asks Lane if he has read a story by M. R. James (that was published in the March 1895 issue of the *National Review*), asking him to congratulate Shiel for him (when Shiel's *Zaleski* had been published in February 1895)—all indications that for whatever reason, Machen had November on his mind when he meant to date his letter March, probably 15 March 1895. "I think that his 'Prince Zaleski' is a very admirable—a most curious and charming work."[21] Then Machen wrote enthusiastically about Shiel's work in the 18 February 1899 issue of *Literature:* ". . . those who revel in the creation of a bizarre and powerful imagination may perhaps find something to satisfy them in Mr. M. P. Shiel's *'Prince Zaleski,'* and *'Shapes in the Fire,'* stories which tell of a wilder wonderland than Poe dreamed of in his most fantastic moments."[22]

Thus, Machen had admired Shiel's early work, although the major push for a personal friendship for Phipps apparently came from Machen's wife, Amy, who took him under a motherly wing, introducing him to guests, showing off his "long fingers," embarrassing Shiel who was concerned that they were "not clean." Many years later (1924), after several emotional dust storms settled, Machen wrote Carl Van Vechten about Shiel in a friendly and excitingly descriptive way.[23]

> M. P. Shiel: I knew him very well once; but I have lost sight of him for years. The fact is—all this is in strict confidence, and not for

---

21. Holograph letter from Machen to Lane, 15 November 1895 (4 Verulam Bldgs., Gray's Inn, HRC).

22. *Literature* (18 February 1899): 182.

23. Holograph letter from Van Vechten to Alfred A. Knopf, 14 January 1924, in the Berg Collection, NYPL.

> the ear of Burton Rascoe!—I didn't feel worthy of knowing a man who looked like the Sultan of the Easkra Islands, and, as they tell, was not devoid of the fiery inclinations which would well become such a potentate. In fact, Shiel came from the isle of Montserrat, and was of mixed race, no doubt, though his features were not in the least negroid. I always felt that his head should not have been covered with a bowler—"Derby," in America?—but with a turban of a fiery red, fastened by a Monte Cristo emerald. I honestly think that "right" and "wrong" were words entirely without meaning to him. For Prince Zaleski and Shapes in the Fire I have the highest admiration, for the latter most of all. It is Poe, perhaps, but Poe written with an unearthly radiance about it.[24]

There is no indication that Louis Tracy ever participated in these or other literary social circles. He was apparently content to spend time with his wife, Ethel, and small son, and devote his energies to family and community interests.

One of the persons that Shiel made friends with during his bachelor days in Gray's Inn barely enters our documentation for those days. On a slip of notepaper Shiel penciled the following for John Gawsworth in 1935. (Gawsworth had just edited a selection of poems by Theodore Wratislaw.)

> I met Theodore Wratislaw at Arthur Machen's, who told me that Wratislaw was a Polish count, Machen then living in Gray's Inn, and I too. Wratislaw would often after that come to see me at 3 Gray's Inn Place; perhaps once a month he would dine with me during two years; he had a liking for ice-cream, and I had a housekeeper who knew how to make it with real cream, not with imaginary cream. He liked me to read the stuff I was writing aloud to him—I was doing my Yellow Danger, Contraband of War, Cold Steel. And the first chapters of "Isle of Lies," while he did poems—had previously done a book of poems, for he told me that instead of making love to a girl, he'd just hand her his book of poems, saying "these are my sentiments". But he had ideas of writing a novel, though that was a mystery to him how it was done, how so many words could be written by human patience, and he would frequently ferret into my modus operandi of writing a

---

24. From the Van Vechten Archives of the New York Public Library. From "additional notes" (14 January 1924) attached to a letter from Van Vechten to Alfred A. Knopf, 3 October 1923.

> book. "No imagination," he would complain, "not a trace". The reason was that he had a disdain for "melodrama", and I could never bring him to see that all the great world-stories, like Genesis, Homer, Hamlet, are melodramatic. I myself was then ultra-melodramatic, not only in matter but in manner, and once or twice he'd break into laughter as I read myself aloud, as once when a monastery on Lake Isana, Abyssinia, (in my Isle of Lies) "sweltered in a thundering blaze". He was in the Civil Service (Somerset House) and only came to me at night; once or twice we went to dine at Roche's in Soho. I think he lived in St. John's Wood. Then I got married, soon after went to live near Paris, gave up my Gray's Inn flat, and lost track of him. . . . Wratislaw was dark-skinned, slim, a rather cynical expression.[25]

What is especially interesting about this note, it not only explains why Wratislaw had such a prominent place in Shiel's wedding in 1898, but it provides specific clues as to the fiction that Shiel was drafting during the two years that he was close to Wratislaw. He would begin *The Empress of the Earth* in the late fall of 1897 and place *Contraband of War* into serial publication before mid-1898 (overlapping *Empress*), but would also begin *Cold Steel* by the end of the summer of 1898, after returning to London from Paris, and must have started work on *The Isle of Lies*. We also know that he had *The Last Miracle* in some form, as well as drafts of "The Last Adam" and *The Lord of the Sea*—in addition to the work that he and Louis Tracy shared on *The Evil That Men Do*. And somewhere in this, probably preceding *Empress* as a prospective serial was the mysterious *The Man-Stealers,* as promoted in published issues of *Empress.* An amazing mass of fiction! Little wonder that he and Louis Tracy both were looking for assistance in getting their novels into serial publication.

Shiel's association with Wratislaw may be of even more interest in what it may suggest about the possibility of Shiel's homosexual proclivities—interests that some have suggested for many years without documentation to support such a possibility.[26] Wratislaw was an acquaintance of Oscar Wilde and the Uranian circle that spent their time fluttering around his flame—as much a literary fashion show as it was

---

25. Original holograph note by MPS to JG, 10 September 1935, in the Berg Collection, NYPL.

26. Brian Stableford, "Prince Zaleski," in MPS, *Prince Zaleski* (Leyburn, UK: Tartarus Press, 2002) xx.

anything else. Wratislaw wrote several small volumes of singularly rich poetry during this period (1892–96), and it was probably *Orchids,* this fourth volume of poetry, to which Shiel referred. In its review of the book in the *Academy,* the reviewer noted: "Mr. Wratislaw belongs to those young gentlemen who yearn to be regarded as naughty."[27]

But Wratislaw had already established a reputation for himself as a poet with homoerotic leanings. At Oxford, in the late 1880s, he had been associated with "the Pembroke set," a homosexual group. "To a Sicilian Boy" (from *Caprices,* 1893) continues to be published in collections of nineteenth-century homosexual literature. Many years later, Wratislaw wrote a brief memoir of an overnight visit he made to Wilde's estate at Goring-on-Thames in 1893, during which Wratislaw listened to Wilde expound on literary theory and observed him and a son in a domestic setting, but his visit was otherwise marked by a sick cold and embarrassment because he had worn formal clothes to the country.[28] Wilde may have wanted to check out this fashionable new young poet, but Wratislaw does not suggest that he was anything other than an awkward acolyte glad to have the visit.

Shiel's description of the occasional visits he had with Wratislaw does not really suggest a more personal relationship, although Wratislaw signed Shiel's wedding certificate. Wratislaw soon gave up his writing career, except for a study of Swinburne whose verse was similar to his own. He was married three times, dying in 1933.

Despite shared social concerns for their starving fellow countrymen, it is not known when or how Shiel first met Louis Tracy, or even if Shiel was brought in by Tracy or by Pearson's staff to assist when Tracy became ill during the serialization of *An American Emperor.* But Shiel's contributions were retained in the book version, published in America in August 1897 and in England the following month, neither with mention of Shiel's contributions. Not unusual, perhaps, in that Shiel's name alone would appear a few years later on a book (*The Evil That Men Do*) to which Tracy had contributed to its serialized version, apparently with that text retained in the book—although those sections of that novel that Tracy wrote have never been identified.

27. Review of *Orchids* in the *Academy* (1 August 1896).

28. *Oscar Wilde: A Memoir* (1979).

Lina and servant Jeanne, 1898
Courtesy of the Harry Ransom Humanities Research Center
The University of Texas at Austin

Lina in Paris, 1898

Courtesy of the Harry Ransom Humanities Research Center
The University of Texas at Austin

Phipps and Lina in Paris. 1898
Courtesy of the Harry Ransom Humanities Research Center
The University of Texas at Austin

Ella D'Arcy, ca. 1896
Courtesy of the Harry Ransom Humanities Research Center
The University of Texas at Austin

The owners of the penny papers that published serial novels were not so many that it is possible that Shiel and Tracy met one another walking in and out of the same publishers' doors, just as they were to meet other fellow writers during that early, heady period . . . when the English public had become educated enough so broadly as to pursue amusement in the burgeoning press. It was certainly anxious to meet their growing reading interests. In any event, Shiel's work on *An American Emperor* would be of significant benefit in establishing his credentials as a serial novelist, although it is possible that he already had *The Man-Stealers* in publication. And the two men would engage in various forms of collaboration from 1897 to about 1912.

The opportunity to publish a serial novel based on historical events soon emerged with "the troubles in China." The success of such ventures—serials based on current events—with the English readership seems to vindicate W. T. Stead's earlier interest in providing similar entertainment in his planned supplement to the *Review of Reviews*, but too much competition was already in place, and Stead's interest in expressing strong editorial points of view was not what the general readership was looking for. His reputation as a publisher of headier reading and breaking news was already well established. A crusade to protect young women from white slavery, in which he allowed himself to be jailed, also made him a larger-than-life figure.[29]

The public purchased its printed fictional pleasure in the penny papers of the time, and Pearson's several cheap publications were developing a faithful readership that enjoyed dramatic serial tales. Peter Keary obviously recognized a good thing when he saw it, and the action novels of Tracy and Shiel reflecting contemporary headlines were public pleasers.

Events offered an opportunity for a new war serial. In November 1897 two German missionaries were murdered in a small village in China near the birthplace of Confucius. Kaiser Wilhelm II immediately went into full bluster and started what history recorded as the "Scramble for Concessions," when France, Germany, and Russia all occupied ports in China for a time. In a few years, these events would trigger the Boxer Rebellion. In 1929 in "About Myself" Shiel wrote: "When some trouble broke out in China, Keary, of Pearson's, for whom Tracy had written a very 'successful' serial [*The Final War*],

29. Eckley, op. cit.

asked me to do a 'war-serial', which became my 'successful' *Yellow Danger*."[30]

It has been suggested that Tracy had recommended Shiel for this assignment, possibly in gratitude for Shiel's picking up Tracy's serial in February 1897, when Tracy became ill, although Peter Keary surely knew Shiel well enough by then. As noted earlier, it is possible that Shiel's novel *The Man-Stealers* had already been serialized in some obscure Pearson paper, was being serialized, or was possibly accepted for publication but laid aside. It is also possible that the novel was serialized in provincial papers through a newspaper syndicate, as were several of Shiel's short stories. It was listed among Shiel's publications in the caption of the first installment of his new serial, though *The Man-Stealers* would not be issued in book form for another two years. There is no trace of a serial version.

Shiel was beginning to burst with more ideas for novels than he could find interest in publishers, or time for his pen to accommodate. That was important for buying his bread and feeding his habits . . . the trips to France and vacation hikes and climbing in the Matlock area, and then more exclusively among the vales and jagged mountains along the River Wye. It continues to amaze that Shiel could find time for his outpouring of prose—in all its richness of imagination, its tightness of plot, and in many cases its literary quality. But, as Shiel was to say, it was one thing to write the serials; it was labor to turn them into books.

What else was Shiel doing? He wrote his mother on 7 November 1897, as noted earlier, that he had taken his nephew Cyril with him to visit Paris earlier in the fall, and was writing a novel. "Gussie is here, and, I presume, writes to you fairly regularly . . . Novel-writing, and smoking, and riding the bicycle, and paying and receiving visits—that is my life, more or less." He was also finding time for escapes to Paris, to Matlock, and the western parts of England, on either side of the River Wye.

And his trips to Paris? He had this to say about Paris in his serial-to-come, *The Empress of the Earth:*

> Paris is the *fille de joie* of the cities of the earth. She alone is purely feminine. She is as queer, and treacherous, and lovely, and indescrib-

30. MPS, "About Myself" (1947) 5. Squires, op. cit.

> able as a woman. Who so truly loves woman will not escape her witchery. She is a divine sinner.[31]

Shiel apparently felt the same lure while breathing the winds along the River Wye. In both surroundings, it was the witchery of young women that would emerge to overshadow his life and color his fiction in the months ahead.

31. *The Empress of the Earth*, *Short Stories* (12 March 1898). *The Yellow Danger* 93.

Chapter 8

"The Empress of the Earth"

The Empress of the Earth was published in Pearson's weekly, *Short Stories,* from 5 February to 18 June 1898. The story was quite a success. Shiel cleverly wove incidents from previous week's headlines into each successive installment as the opportunity presented itself, so as wild as it reads today, the serial can almost be used to trace contemporary events for several weeks of real time during February 1898. Shiel's primary source was most likely the *Review of Reviews,* the Stead publication with which Shiel had had a long relationship. The actual historical events were reported in the *Review,* but there was also considerable technical detail published there—regarding battleships, weaponry, and naval war maneuvers, much of which Shiel was able to work into the details of his novel.[1]

Shiel later acknowledged that he had started the serial with no idea how the story would proceed after the first few chapters he had written. History helped write it for him! . . . with the assistance of historical and technical details from each issue of the *Review of Reviews.*

So he wrote it literally as each weekly installment was due at the paper, incorporating headline events as the crisis unfolded. (There actually was speculation in the London papers that a general European war might break out over the frenzy to carve up China, with England fighting a united Europe to protect her paramount position in the China trade.) The serial was so popular that Keary ordered Shiel to stretch it out from the originally contracted 70,000 words to 100,000, and finally 150,000 words.[2]

By the April 9 installment, Shiel's English hero, John Hardy, was captured by the Sino-Japanese mastermind, Dr. Yen How (who appears to have been at least partially modeled on Sun Yat Sen), and

1. The most comprehensive studies of this novel have been written by John D. Squires and are included in the following essays.

2. John D. Squires, "Rediscovering M. P. Shiel (1865–1947)."

undergoes gruesome torture in Peking because he had dared kiss Ada Seward, with whom Yen How was madly infatuated.[3]

John D. Squires points out that the "torture" Shiel described bears a striking resemblance to the description that Villiers de l'Isle-Adam had written in his short story "A Torture by Hope," which Shiel had translated from the French for the *Strand* (June 1891).[4] It may not be the first and certainly was not the last instance in which Shiel borrowed more than liberally or directly plagiarized the work of another author. Shiel, in this instance, would probably simply have claimed to have written the first version of this in English.

It was through the benefit of his vacations—or by hook and crook in London—that by the fall of 1897 Shiel had already established a romantic relationship with Nellie Seward of Cheltenham, the model for the "Ada Seward" of the serial. She would also bear his love-child, Ada Phipps Shiel, in November 1898—only weeks after his marriage to Carolina Garcia Gomez, whom he had affianced during his frequent trips to France. From January to March 1898, Shiel was in France, probably courting Lina and writing *The Empress of the Earth,* while Nellie became pregnant immediately after Phipps returned to England at the end of March or in early April 1898.[5]

This period is important for other reasons, for it is in early 1898 that biographers of Ernest Dowson have speculated that Shiel and Dowson briefly shared a room at 1 Guilford Place. Shiel would help feed this legend in his novel *The Weird o' It,* written in 1902, after Dowson's death, when he included a Dowson-like character in the story. But Shiel never claimed to have roomed with Dowson in real life—as he actually did live, in the early 1890s, with the characters Fred and Mary in the novel. But they will be dealt with later. Shiel appears to

---

3. John D. Squires, "Some Contemporary Themes in Shiel's Early Novels," in Morse, ed., *Shiel in Diverse Hands* 249–326.

4. John D. Squires, email to the author, 10 August 2009.

5. One can only guess that MPS either met Ada/Nellie/Kate Seward in 1897 during a trip to the Cheltenham area or at a music-hall event (more likely), although he became friendly with Nellie's parents. A group of photographs of their love-child daughter, Ada, in HRC along with a letter from Grandmother Seward to MPS are the most legitimate documents that establish their relationship. Census records, as noted, are also important, but it appears obvious that MPS was pursuing Lina while he had already established a relationship with Nellie.

have been in France during the months speculated for his sharing quarters with Dowson, so that theory simply lacks any facts that would have brought them together for some brief period during this time. Other than the novel, there is no actual evidence that Shiel and Dowson ever spent time together, although both probably were frequent visitors to the shabbier eating and drinking places in the darker side of London.[6]

"Ada Seward" is introduced in the first chapter of the story—in the issue of *Pearson's Weekly* for 5 February 1898. "Ada Seward is the presiding deity in the nursery of Mrs. Pattison, of Fulham," the story reads. In the novel, John Hardy says to her at their first meeting (in a music hall where the American entertainer Lottie Collins is to perform), "I shall call you 'Nell.' I like that better."

"It is my second name," she says in the story. "They call me 'Ada.'"

The 1901 Census indicates that Ada Seward Shiel, the daughter of Nellie and Phipps, was born in London. Nellie had probably been living in London for some time, as a maid in Fulham, before the birth of Ada, so that Phipps would not have had to make trips to Cheltenham to see her. The census records provide, at times, more confusion than assistance, but in this instance they identify for us, finally, the identity of both the fictional and real-life "Ada Seward."

Nellie Seward's parents were John and Annie Seward of 23 Elm Street, Cheltenham, the address from which Grandmother Annie wrote Shiel requesting financial assistance for his love-child Ada in a later year. But Nellie does not appear with her parents and brother or sister on either the 1881, the 1891, or the 1901 English Census. However, there is a daughter, "Kate," whose age appears to mirror that of "Nellie." In *The Empress of the Earth,* the heroine, Ada Seward, is identified as a Fulham nursemaid, in the home of "Mrs. Pattison." The 1901 English Census lists Kate Seward as a twenty-three-year-old servant in the household of Edward S. Pattison of Fulham! In 1903, Kate ("Nellie") married, leaving Ada with her parents and departing for South Africa. For Phipps, she left photographs of their baby daughter, but she would disappear from his life, if not from his fiction.

However, in the case of Ada Seward, the character in the story, Shiel never hesitated in identifying her with "Nellie" Seward of Chel-

6. For the undocumented Dowson link to MPS, see Ernest Dowson, *Letters of Ernest Dowson*.

tenham.[7] "She was a small creature," Shiel describes her,

> with skin of a warm yellowish colour, and little quaint Chinese eyes, and light hair with the faintest tinge of red in it; not perhaps pretty, but with some unspeakable attraction of piquancy about her queer, saucy little face, which had caused her to receive no less than twelve offers of marriage before she was twenty. Her friends declared that she was the living image of Miss Marie Tempest, the "Geisha" prima donna. Her figure was typically English.[8]

We can follow, with more specificity, Nellie's family in the English census records. Her mother, Annie Seward, lived in Cheltenham at 23 Elm Street. In the 1901 census, her husband is John Albert, a retired painter, a son Walter F., 13, a painter decorator (worker), and granddaughter, Ada Shiel, age 2. "Kate" is listed as living in London with the Pattison family.

In the 1891 census, John A. (a painter and grainer) and Annie Seward (both 48) are listed at the same Elm Street address in Cheltenham, with their children listed in the Census as Willie G., age 22, a plumber, Kate, 13, John A., 11, and Walter, 8. Ten years earlier still, in 1881, their children had been Arthur, 14, Willie Geo., 12, Alice Maud, 9, Helen, 6, and Kate, 3. In 1871, their children had been Arthur and George. Birth records indicate that Kate was born in either 1877 or 1878.

The evidence in fact and in fiction overwhelmingly indicates that Kate Seward was both the real-life "Nellie" and the "Ada" of *The Empress of the Earth,* who had "twelve offers of marriage" before she was twenty. How she came by the nickname Nellie, which was also used for her by her mother, is just not evident from these sources.

While it was infatuation for Ada Seward that drove Dr. Yen How to torture Hardy, it is the "artist" Bosey Jay whom Hardy loves, though he loves not the art that Bosey embodies. And Yen How is

---

7. As noted on the backs of photos of baby Ada Seward Shiel, in the photographic archives in HRC, and also noted by MPS on a copy of *The Yellow Danger* offered for sale in Bertram Rota Ltd catalog No. 114, Winter, 1958 described thus: "The 'heroine's' copy, inscribed 'Nellie with the Author's Love,' and 'Nellie Seward of Cheltenham is the Ada Seward of this book. F. A.—M. P. Shiel.'" (Item 512, p. 35.) The present location of this book is unknown.

8. *The Yellow Danger* 86.

smitten with Ada and will have England to have her. Of Bosey, Shiel says, "She was a lady of many accomplishments. She sang like a bird; she had written two novels of the 'problem' kind; she was a sociologist; she had painted one knows not how many pictures; she was not yet nineteen; and she was rather pretty."[9]

"Bosey had a fairly substantial body," he described her, "with a waist that struck one as being quite as large as that of Eve or Venus. She wore her red-gold hair in coil upon coil of *négligé* richness about her head; her eyes were a bright green."

Given that Phipps tended to base his fictional characters upon people he knew, it is impossible to ascribe this list of qualities to any single person of whom we are aware. Shiel never made an effort to attach Bosey to anyone known to us in his personal life, although it is certain he had a wide choice of female acquaintances to whom the general physical attributes might be ascribed. It may be that Bosey was a composite of the traits then associated with the "New Woman," and that Phipps was describing her, tongue in cheek, as though he were making an obeisance to the new order of Woman.[10] This is unlike his usual development of a character, however, but there is no one, like Ada, who is known in real life that matches the characteristics of Bosey.

Shiel's imagination takes over the serial after March 1898 and leaves history behind. He had already included events relating to the ongoing Dreyfus Affair that he had invested in the novel, because he was in Paris during the disruptions in the streets of Paris that followed the trial of Émile Zola for "treasonous" comments about the military.

Shiel might well have been in Paris as early as 13 January 1898 when Zola's scathing editorial "J'Accuse" ("I Accuse") was published on the front page of the daily *L'Aurore*. Zola attacked the acquittal of Major Walsin Esterhazy for spying (after only three minutes of consideration by a military court), while he also attacked the 1894 conviction of the Jewish captain Alfred Dreyfus and his confinement in an iron cage on Devil's Island. Zola accused the French military of a cover-up, based on anti-Semitism aimed at Dreyfus, a charge that would lead to Zola's own conviction for libel against the military.

Zola was brought to trial on 8 February and convicted on 23 Feb-

9. Ibid. 80.

10. Surmised by John D. Squires.

ruary. Sentenced to imprisonment, he fled to England. But his vigorous ongoing efforts helped lead to the ultimate release of Dreyfus from Devil's Island. Shiel used the February uproar following the conviction of Zola in his serial—describing vividly the commotion in the Chamber of Deputies and the firing of arms and the clash of swords in the streets.

Shiel's writing about these events had all the immediacy of a physical presence, an energy and excitement, the rudeness of crowds, a "being there" that the contemporary reader must have been caught up in, just as Shiel might have been. Much of the novel is just as exciting today as when it was published on a weekly basis.

Shiel had enough of the novel already written for serial publication—and at least one if not two issues of the story had been published—when he approached Grant Richards from France (45 Rue de Maubeuge, Paris), probably in mid-February 1898:

> There is a serial of mine now appearing in 'Short Stories,'—one of those absurd 'future stories'—all about China and War, and the rest of it. It is said to be very exciting, and I fancy from certain indications (though they may not have told me so), that it is doing well. It is called 'The Empress of the Earth: A Tale of the Yellow War.' And the political plot is this: that China deliberately sets the nations of Europe at war with each other by giving to the great Continental Powers vast tracts of Chinese land—and so on, of course, these three are fought over by England. The object of China is to produce a decimated and exhausted Europe, so that she may overrun Europe and destroy the white race. (The Yellow Danger!!!) This she does. She sweeps in locust swarms over Europe, and then only England is left. England saves the world. Then, of course, she is 'Empress of the Earth.' For only America is left and America in view of England's vast power, has now to acknowledge England as her suzerain. It is not finished yet, but will be in three weeks or so. I believe that if published in book form soon, while the China bother is on the tapis, it might be widely successful: though its interest is not altogether temporary. Do you care to undertake the Publication. They have not been polite enough to send me the numbers that have appeared, but I dare say you could get proofs of it as far as it has been printed. Would you let me know?[11]

---

11. MPS to Richards, n.d., probably February 1898, 45 Rue de Maubeuge,

Shiel offered the story to Richards for book publication, although he had sold "all serial rights" to Pearson, who believed that he had purchased book rights as well. Not surprisingly, this resulted in a legal squabble between the two publishers. While the firms were arguing this out, Shiel began sending proofs of the serial to Richards as he received them from Pearson with the expectation that the story could be published as both a serial and as a book.

On 26 February 1898, Shiel wrote Grant Richards (from 11 Avenue de la Grande Armée, Paris), sending him proofs of those parts of the serial that had thus far been published, and described the planned length of a book:

> Dear Mr. Grant Richards / I now at last send you proofs of my story in "Short Stories" which I have got from England. I have *written* more of it, but they have not sent the proofs. / If you will do me the favour of reading it quickly—as the matter is more or less pressing—and giving me your decision, I shall be much obliged. / I originally undertook to make it 70,000 words in length; then Pearson writes to ask if I will make it 100,000 words; then comes a telegram: can I make it 150,000 Words? What I intend to do is this: I shall make it 150,000 words for them, but 50,000 of this will be merely for the sake of the money. The *book* will consist of 100,000 words which is quite enough. Of these I have already written about 80,000 and send you about 60,000. (I think) / The proofs have not been corrected that I send you, & there are many absurdities in it. This you will understand.
>
> / Yours very truly / M. P. Shiel.[12]

Richards responded on 9 March. His reader thinks highly of the work, and Richards said that he was going to take the story home to read himself that night. He says that Shiel is writing from France; when does he plan to return? His reader believes the love interest should be cut. Perhaps the book might be published as *The Yellow Terror*.[13]

Gare du Nord, Paris, holograph transcription by JG (HRC).

12. MPS to Richards, 26 February 1898, 11 Avenue de la Grande Armée, Paris, holograph transcription by JG (HRC).

13. Richards to MPS, 14 March 1898 (Richards' Archives, microfilm edition, Univ. Michigan).

In the 12 March 1898 issue of *Short Stories,* Shiel's novel described the riots that ensued following Zola's conviction:

> Paris, in her rages, as in all else, is like a woman. She tears her finery and ribbons to shreds; she foams at the mouth; her hair is all over the place.
>
> Her last exuberance had taken the shape of the Dreyfus riots, half Anti-Semitic in its *objectif,* partly Anti-Zolaesque, and partly only rowdy. At all events, Monsieur Zola, in the people's plight for an object for their wrath, had been the scapegoat. The Government has triumphed. Monsieur Zola had been declared a *"degenere"* by the University; he had been regarded as *"cas"* by the scientific *alienistes;* he had been hopelessly lampooned and caricatured by the press; the sale of his books had ceased; he was regarded as a man over and done for.

Shiel's descriptions of the heated debates in the Chamber of Deputies are so vivid that it is possible that he was in attendance during the events, while he also experienced the efforts of the French army to maintain order in the streets. Just as innocently as his hero John Hardy did in the novel, Shiel may have "found himself in front of the Chambre de Députée, and dropped in with a stream of the public," and quickly found himself among the riot, everybody "rushing everywhere."

Shiel and Richards continued their discussion of a possible book to be drawn from the serial in subsequent letters over the next several weeks. Shiel was writing the novel in Paris, living at 11 Avenue de la Grande Armée, sending it part by part to Richards as the proofs of the serial came to him from Pearson. He must have been busily pursuing, as well, the young Spanish girl who would become his wife.

Chapter 9

"a lovely Spanish girl of sixteen"

During the exchange of letters with Richards over the possible publication of the serial-in-progress as a book, Shiel is also busily considering several other projects that he hoped to have published in various Pearson publications after the completions of *The Empress of the Earth.*

In addition to his serial writing and negotiating book publication with Grant Richards, Shiel certainly sought pleasure in Paris, a city with which he was quite familiar. Probably a year or more earlier, skating in the Palais de Glace, he had spied Carolina Garcia Gomez, a pretty Spanish girl of sixteen. She was most likely still in convent school, skating in the company of her older sisters Salvadore and Micaela and their friends. Out of the "grasp and drag" of some twenty other young men taken with Lina's beauty, Shiel later says he prayed to God for her. Then he "grabbed her, got her"—as he always succeeded, he said, when he prayed for a young woman. As his lead character, John Hardy, says in *The Empress of the Earth:* "If you only knew how much I like girls!" Shiel must have been on his knees a lot.[1]

Lina's family had been in mourning following the death of her father, Miguel Garcia Gomez, of Seville, probably sometime in 1896 or 1897. Traditionally, the mourning period would have been at least a year, and possibly as long as two and a half years. The short story "The Death-Dance" (1935),[2] which appears to include a number of facts about the family, identifies the character Lina's father as a lead-mine engineer who died of consumption in Spain. One would expect that the mourning period must have been completed by sometime in 1898, and probably earlier if the girls were allowed to skate. And Lina's family was not the traditional Spanish family.

What part Shiel actually played, by the way, in the writing of this short story and another that described personal details of his family life in the mid-1930s ("The Falls Scandal") has been cleared considerably

1. MPS, "About Myself" (1947) 5, and *The Yellow Danger* 81.

2. *Thrills, Crimes, and Mysteries*, ed. JG (London: Associated Newspapers, [1935]), 163–200. A copy of this in ms. shows 165 pages by MPS, 4 by JG. Morse, *Works* (1948) 132. Present location of Ms. unknown.

by the discovery of an offer for sale of the ms. of "The Death-Dance" some years ago by the London bookseller Bertram Rota. This makes it clear that Shiel wrote this particular story in its entirety. Its details appear to fit closely with what is known about Lina's family and events described in contemporary letters and factual sources. (This was probably the copy of the story as listed in Gawsworth's inventory of Shiel's archives with 165 pages of ms. by Shiel and four pages ms. by JG.)[3]

It is not so clear what portion of "The Falls Scandal" Shiel wrote and what Gawsworth contributed. The inventory in Morse (1948) lists this title with ten pages of ms. by Shiel and ten pages by Gawsworth. Gawsworth apparently sold it, and the present location of these fragments is unknown.[4]

Lina's sisters, Salvadore and Micaela, were very close to her, as evidenced by the family photographs, letters, and her frequent visits with them after her marriage. Family photographs suggest that the girls—Salva probably some four or more years older than Lina, and Mica—younger—lived a rather free, cosmopolitan lifestyle. Early photographs of the girls, taken apparently in Spain and Paris, are sweetly innocent in appearance. Later photos show them smoking cigarettes, boating, and lounging in an artist's atelier—photos that may have driven Shiel to the anger he directed at Lina in their last year together. Shiel consistently urged Lina never to smoke, and the photo that she sent him in an aggressive pose smoking with Mica and a servant must have felt like a slap to his face.

Whether the sisters—especially Salva, the elder—were married or not is not known, but group pictures of the family include a number of girls in the company of young men. These suggesting that there must have been an extended family or a number of friends with whom they spent time. The girls had sometime recently given up life in a convent school, based on their dress in the photographs.

The short story "The Death-Dance" describes the young, domineering mother of the girls, after whom Phipps and Lina's baby would be named (Dolores):

> At an early age the Princess Dolores had quarrelled with her husband, and being a girl of quite a grim will and hard head, had struck

3. The story was published in *Crimes, Creeps and Thrills,* ed. JG (London: E. H. Samuel, 1936), 273–85. Morse, *Works* (1948) 132.

4. Op. cit. 133, 117.

> out against returning to him. *Shamais! Shamais!*—never! never! were perhaps the words oftenest on her lips. She had thus found herself a lonely wife, with three daughters on her hands. If now she had settled down in her rustic little castle, doing her small best, and going to Mass on Sundays, that might have been a good thing for Europe and America: but no, she adventures to Paris. Here we all at once find her transformed from a countess into a princess—a transformation which (an investigator would be told) was *"all in order,"* though how it came to be "in order" must always remain a thing impenetrable to the British brain. Anyway, she is now the Princess, the girls are put into convent-school, the world becomes the hotel of mama. At that convent there arrived picture-postcards from the Andes, from Naples, from Cuba, from Monte Carlo. Perhaps at one time mama even showed herself on the New York stage; for she danced like daffodils and Ariel: but this was a secret spoken of in hints.
>
> To the girls, meantime, their mother's life was all a meteor wonder. Anon she would make a descent upon the convent, trailing clouds of glory—angel's-visits, rare and flying, that left precious presents behind, and a perfume of the large heyday and bazaar of the world. Now, the impressions of childhood last long and deep; and for this reason alone her mother remained enthroned in Lina's dream as the queen of all the queens and fairies.[5]

It is strange that among the pictures that Shiel retained of Lina and her sisters and friends throughout his life, no photograph of the mother, "Lola," appears to have been saved. There are several photographs of Lina and her sisters in photographs left in Shiel's archives, and a woman who might have been Lola is pictured in at least two photographs, but she is not so identified on the back of the photos as were others. It is hard to believe that Lina would not have had a photo of her. There was no reason for Phipps to have discarded any of the photos when he had saved the others so long.

"The Death-Dance" may well have described Shiel *himself* (as the character Matthew Burke) as he visualized himself as a young man.

Lord Hugh Beaumont, in the story, is asked by Lina what his friend "Mattieu" is like, and he tells her:

> dark—quite a contrast to me altogether—shorter—his hair a fleece of black curls curling round his forehead; slightly bow-legged, with ra-

5. *Thrills, Crimes and Mysteries.*

> ther a droop of the right shoulder, which gives him an air of listening a little with the right ear—like Dr. Johnson. Small-face, Lina; hardly very weighty in personal presence; short Roman nose, moustache, grey eyes—drooping and small—very touching somehow—certainly, one must say that—rather touching to the heart—making a man feel a father to him. Gifted, you know! Creative! Every week he invents something, from a bicycle-brake to a new theory of the nebula, though none of his inventions ever materialise—there are too many of them! Fond of his ease and pipe—lazy often—vain, Lina—yes, a little vain and dependent upon approbation—but a soul so nobly erected, so related to truth—oh a heart so good—[6]

The full circumstances of the building of a marriage between Phipps and Lina are unknown, but there is scattered information available about their life after marriage. In his "About Myself," written in 1929, Shiel says Lina was sixteen when he was struck with her beauty as she skated in the Palais de Glace in Paris, her name initially unknown to him. Their marriage record indicates that she was eighteen at the time of the wedding, and this is consistent with her age as it is listed in the 1901 census. Quite possibly, Phipps's courtship might have extended over several years, beginning perhaps in 1896, before or in that fruitful fall that he spent with his nephew Cyril in Paris in 1897. In some ways it seems unlikely that the daughter of what initially appears to have been a rather patrician family would have allowed the exceedingly rapid development from courtship to marriage of Lina and Phipps, but the mother appears far from conventional. Later, Phipps may have had little to show for himself—except for his skills at persuasion—but at the time he initially courted Lina he had the appearance of a successful young author, with a steady income from his serial work and three books behind him. Of course, that financial success would not last.

In any event, Phipps was not only wooing "Lina" in Paris, but al-

---

6. Ibid. Also *Mainly about People* (17 October 1903) described MPS thus: "Figure to yourself a powerfully built man, standing five feet eight or so, very broad and deep of chest, with crisp, curling hair, dark like his short spiky moustache, a plump, brownish face, and aquiline nose, light grey eyes in which lurks a smouldering fire, and a certain foreign air, and you will have some idea of the appearance of Mr. Matthew Phipps Shiel, B.A., the most haunting writer of the day. For the rest, a citizen of the world, he is a man of easy, dignified manners, slow, but convincing of speech, and an apostle of an unusual form of physical culture, to which I shall refer again."

so bedding Nellie Seward in England . . . and probably others of whom we do not know, but it can be reasonably certain that they existed somewhere.

Shiel's headquarters in the early spring of 1898 continued to be at 11 Avenue de Grande Armée, Paris. It was from here that he must have pursued Parisian pleasures and romance, while he poured out the words for *The Empress of the Earth* and developed ideas for other novels to come. He later claimed to have met Jules Claretie and Pierre Louÿs in Paris, and if in fact that occurred, it was probably during the extensive time he spent in Paris during 1898 and 1899. Phipps most likely would have encountered them in some popular dining spot for French littérateurs. There is no indication that such meetings had any influence on his work.

The fact that a French translator sought him out to translate the stories in *Prince Zaleski* suggests that he was in touch with the literary establishment in Paris. He became acquainted with Henry-D. Davray, the distinguished French journalist who translated *The Purple Cloud,* reviewed his work, and was very active in translating the books of H. G. Wells and numerous other authors around the turn of the century. Davray was the foreign editor of *Le Mercure de France,* probably the most respected French literary magazine of the day.

On 9 March, a Tuesday in 1898, Shiel wrote Richards that he is sending him another 10,000 words of proofs from the serial, and says that he will be able to send the rest of the story in about ten days. He is almost finished, but will not be returning to England for at least a month. He requests Richards to make an offer as to terms for the proposed book to be developed from the serial. He assures him that copyright for a prospective book belongs to him.[7]

Richards responded at length on 11 March 1898.[8]

> Dear Mr. Shiel,
>
> When an author writes as you do, one is both satisfied and put on one's honour to do the best one can. Well, frankly, I am in rather a difficult position. Such books have been published, and have had considerable success. On the other hand, for no apparent reason that would make them inferior to their more successful brethren, there

---

7. MPS to Richards, Saturday, 26 February 1898, 11 Ave du Grande Armée, holograph transcription by JG (HRC).

8. Richards Archives.

have been failures. I might say I would give you fifty pounds; you might take it, and then it might be a huge success, and naturally you would feel, although you had sold the copyright, that you had still a certain right to expect more, which, on precedent, I suppose I should give, if I was making a fortune out of the book. If I start you with a ten percent royalty, it will take something like sixteen hundred copies, I believe, to make this fifty pounds for you. Here are my offers: I will give you fifty pounds down for *all* rights with the stipulation that if it sells over fifteen hundred copies I give you another twenty-five pounds. Or I will give you a royalty calculated on this basis: ten per cent of the first fifteen hundred copies, fifteen per cent afterwards; and in this case the profits derived from the American edition, if I can arrange one, would be divided between us equally. If, as I hope, one or other of these terms will suit you, let me know by return, so that I should be free to announce the book.

You say, I see, that I can have the complete manuscript in my hands in ten days from now. This would enable me to bring it out some week or so before the end of April, and I should hurry it forward all I possibly could.

I haven't finished reading what you sent me, but there are one or two things that I hope you will be able to do. Perhaps the most important is to follow up my reader's suggestion, and in revising for the final appearance, do what you can to take out the love interest, which I presume you put in rather with the intention of pleasing its serial reader. Your fight between the ships is magnificent, but I notice that the word [*unclear*] occurs three or four times. In chapter five you speak of the windows of the *Daily Mail*. The *Daily Mail* offices are now, and for the rest of the year, certainly in a little street in Whitefriars whose window could [*unclear*] no kind of [crest]. Hadn't you better alter it to the *Daily Chronicle*? I am told by an authority on the House of Commons history that the House of Commons [*unclear phrase*] although vivid—in one or two respects. Thus, there are always questions in the House whether there are people to answer them or not, and there are no such things these days as tramway bills.

At the bottom of this galley (98) there is a paragraph in which a sentence commences "Frenzy of the _____" It goes on: "There ensued one of those whirlwind 'scenes' which have occurred at intervals." This seems to be a little lame, and the lines that follow are surely extravagant. In a story of this kind it is so important to do what you have done elsewhere—cultivate an absolute verisimilitude and a likelihood, and a scene like this only puts off the reader. In the next galley you speak of the Kingdoms of Russia, France and Germany in the same paragraph. I cannot imagine Sir William Harcourt referring to a party as the Healeyites, but I may possibly be wrong here. And the following paragraph has the same note of extravagance. The War fever would not make leopards change their spots.

But, although I make these suggestions, you must understand that I am immensely interested in the book and I believe in it.

How about the title? I waver between the Yellow Terror and the Yellow Peril. In some ways the latter is best, but the clash of "l"s makes a rather unpleasant sound.

Very sincerely yours, Grant Richards

The following Tuesday Shiel sent additional proofs to Richards, but said that having the completed text ready to send in ten days, as he had earlier believed possible, would be too rash. Pearson's has 30,000 additional words in hand, but is slow with the proofs. Yes, Egan Mew is a very good friend, Phipps answered Richards.[9] He has the "oak" across from Shiel at his Gray's Inn Place address in London. Mew had written works concerning the history of ceramics, and John Lane had published several of his books. Mew was certainly a member of the smoky "Sunday" evenings group that met at Arthur Machen's quarters across the inner court from Shiel—to chat, smoke, drink Machen's special wine or Benedictine, listen to his opinions ("fixed in nickel," Shiel said), admire his bulldog, and enjoy visiting with Machen's wife, Amy Hogg Machen (who died of the effects of breast cancer in 1899), and their friends, Jerome K. Jerome, W. W. Jacobs, James Welch, Olivia Shakespear, George Egerton, Lewis Sergeant, and others possibly more drawn to the events by Amy than by her husband.

On 13 March 1898 Shiel presented a counter-proposal to the terms Richards had offered. Phipps reminds him that the proofs from *Short Stories* are uncorrected, with "many absurdities." He disagrees with Richards's reader about cutting the love interest. Does one presume that the reader meant the inclusion of Ada in the story? "Sudden action in a story always needs a sudden motive," Shiel answers Richards. He must mean that Yen How has to have a reason for his hatred for John Hardy. Shiel adds that he has always intended the title for the book to be *The Yellow Danger*.

---

9. MPS to Richards, Tuesday, 16 (?) March 1898, 11 Ave du Grande Armée, holograph transcription by JG (HRC).

Salvadore, Micaela, and Carolina Gomez in Convent School
Courtesy of the Harry Ransom Humanities Research Center
The University of Texas at Austin

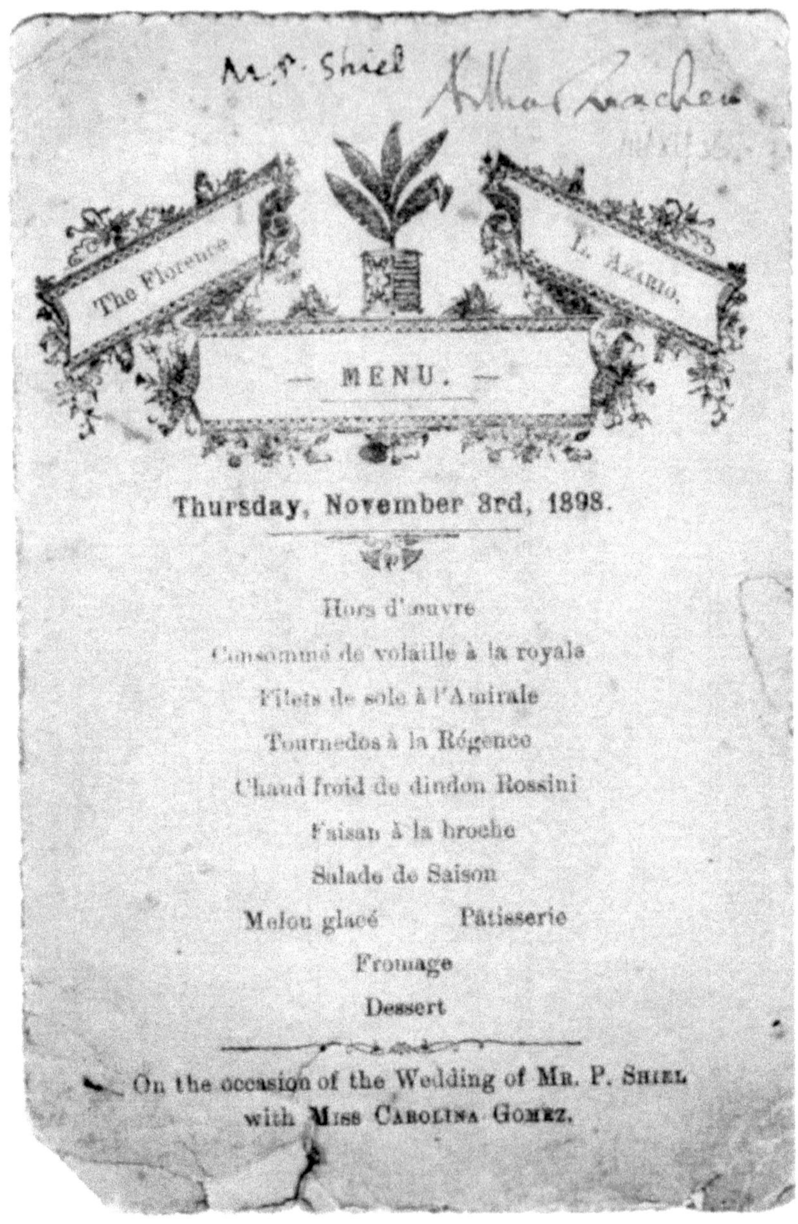

M. P. Shiel

The Florence

L. Azario.

— MENU. —

Thursday, November 3rd, 1898.

Hors d'œuvre

Consommé de volaille à la royale

Filets de sole à l'Amirale

Tournedos à la Régence

Chaud froid de dindon Rossini

Faisan à la broche

Salade de Saison

Melon glacé Pâtisserie

Fromage

Dessert

On the occasion of the Wedding of Mr. P. Shiel
with Miss Carolina Gomez.

Wedding Menu for Phipps and Lina, 1898
Courtesy of the Harry Ransom Humanities Research Center
The University of Texas at Austin

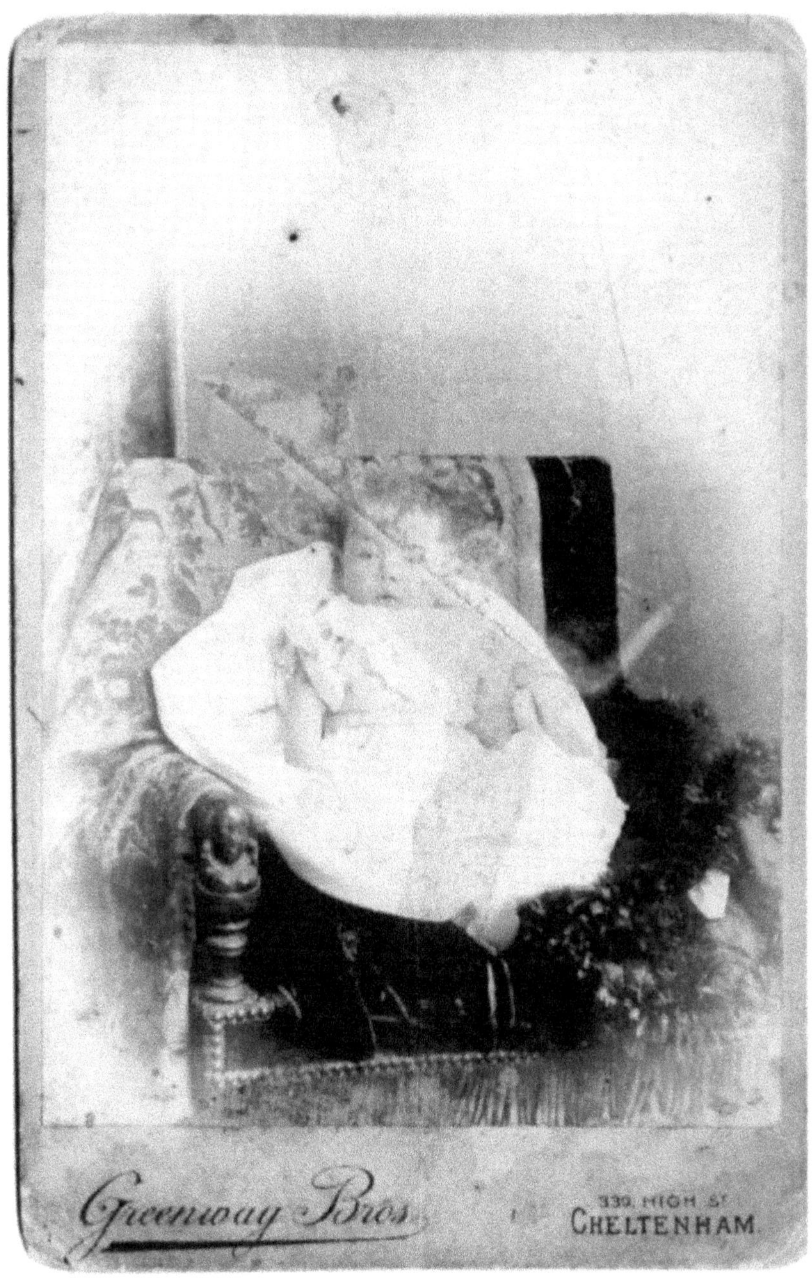

Love child Ada Phipps Seward Shiel in Cheltenham, 1899
Courtesy of the Harry Ransom Humanities Research Center
The University of Texas at Austin

Lina and Baby Lola Shiel on Keppel St., 1901.
Courtesy of the Harry Ransom Humanities Research Center
The University of Texas at Austin

Baby Lola Shiel on Keppel St., 1901
Courtesy of the Harry Ransom Humanities Research Center
The University of Texas at Austin

Lina with cigarette, dog, seated Mica, servant Louise, 1903
Courtesy of the Harry Ransom Humanities Research Center
The University of Texas at Austin

Ada Phipps Shiel on chair in Cheltenham, 1904
Courtesy of the Harry Ransom Humanities Research Center
The University of Texas at Austin

Ada Phipps Shiel with dog in Cheltenham, 1904
Courtesy of the Harry Ransom Humanities Research Center
The University of Texas at Austin

Pearson's consent is not necessary to proceed with the book, Shiel (still at 11 Avenue de la Grande Armée, Paris) wrote Richards on 25 March. He had wanted to bring out the story as a book while the Chinese issue was hot; two different classes of people buy books and magazines, he said. It is best to tap both markets. He still intends to write another 50,000 words extra for Pearson, which are not to appear in the book. Only the "side interest"—the European war—is topical.

Richards responded on 28 March 1898. He is concerned about a disagreement with Pearson, who claims the book rights to *The Yellow Danger*. Rather petulantly, Shiel answered Richards on 31 March 1898. "It looks as if my second attempt at publishing with you is again going to be a fiasco."

What was the first attempt? Possibly a book version of *The Man-Stealers*? With the references to this title in the leading captions of *The Empress of the Earth* and *Contraband of War* in their serial appearances, it appears possible that this work had been (or was being) published in one of the several Pearson penny papers, but evidence of serial publication of that work has not turned up. Nor does correspondence with Richards or anyone else exist regarding that title.

Shiel was probably referring to the need to establish his rights to book publication, and establishing another set of agreements—a "second attempt"—regarding the book publication of *The Yellow Danger* in his comment to Richards about a "second attempt." But this is speculation.

While Pearson (through the person of Peter Keary) was claiming book rights to *The Yellow Danger,* Shiel was sure he had sold Pearson serial rights only. In early April a literary agent agreed with Shiel that "complete serial rights" would not include book rights. Will Richards finance a lawsuit with Pearson if necessary, Shiel asked? Fortunately, it became unnecessary even to discuss such action further, as the situation was settled in Shiel's favor; Pearson gave up the argument.[10]

By the end of March Shiel had completed the serial, so that its dependence on real history was over. The story continued in *Short Stories* until the middle of June, but the later episodes were built on fiction rather than current events. Shiel was even casting about for names familiar to him to place as characters in the serial: "Paddy Burke," the

10. MPS to Richards, n.d., [early April?, apparently still from France] JG translation (HRC).

young black friend from his boyhood, the name Machen, and other names of real people were inserted in the story as crew members of a battleship.

John D. Squires points out that John Hardy's own "torture of hope" by Yen How bears many resemblances to the story "A Torture by Hope" by Villiers de l'Isle-Adam that Shiel had translated in 1891. Though the language in the serial is Shiel's, many of the incidents in that chapter clearly originated from plot elements in Villiers's story. One can only wonder whether Shiel was intentionally lifting the ideas or subconsciously "remembering" incidents he had "written" earlier in the translation. Not likely. Shiel must have known what he was doing and felt right to do so. Anyway, Villiers was dead, and no one else was likely to spot the similarities. Following Chapter XVIII of *The Empress of the Earth*—"The Chinese Iron," with its torture scenes—the story becomes pure, powerful Shiel fiction, with a fecundity of imagination and detail.

By mid-May 1898, Shiel had returned to 3 Gray's Inn Place, (W.C.) from France. The serial was complete; he was working on the book version of it; and *Contraband of War* had begun its appearance in *Pearson's Weekly* on 7 May. Shiel was always a hard worker. He wrote Richards that he had considered and acted on all the comments of Richards's reader that he could, but "Because a thing is 'not important' to a story, that is no reason why it should be cut out of a literary work."[11] He also agreed to terms for book sales—£50 for 1500 copies and £50 for copies sold beyond that.[12] He then follows in this letter, saying: "I have altered the wording as much as I thought necessary . . . One must do one's work in one's own way." Since Richards's reader had earlier suggested cutting the "love" interest, he may have been referring to Ada, but Shiel rightly felt he needed a strong motive for Yen How's hatred. While John Hardy's affections were centered on "Bosey Jay," who plays a generally small part in the novel, it is also possible that this is the element that Richards's reader suggested deleting. In retrospect, this character appears to embody all the most criticized traits of the "new woman," as Shiel saw them, and he most likely

11. MPS to Richards, n.d. [May?], 3 Gray's Inn Place, W.C., transcribed by JG (HRC).

12. Morse, *Works* 2.63.

wanted to retain his reference to that group in the novel. Bosey also provided the moral avenue through which Hardy might "save his soul" (from the unrepentant depths to which it had sunk), although this is a subtle point (but important in Shiel's belief in Christ-like repentance) that Richards's reader probably did not understand.

> Oh, Mr. Hardy, I am glad!" she cried, springing up vivaciously as John entered the studio. "Ah, and I have heard! I have heard!"
>
> "About the battle, and all that?"
>
> "What else, if 'all that' means Mr. John Hardy? Do sit down. How very brave you must be!"
>
> "All Englishmen are brave."
>
> "Are they? A good many of them are detestable cowards, to my certain knowledge. Men do live in regions of fantasy! Women are more prosaic —and clearer. Did you not see an average English girl in the sovereign presence of a mouse, Mr. Hardy?"
>
> "Girls are different," said John.
>
> Bosey's lips tightened with pressure. This was precisely the kind of ancient point of view, purely male, to which she had the most touchy antipathy. John was hopelessly "old," she actively "new."
>
> "Oh, different, of course," she said, "in pose of nervous structure, and so on, and so on. But is it not rather cheap to say it? And substitute for the mouse the broker's man, and you get at once a measure of the average Englishman's courage."
>
> "Somebody has been telling you wrong," said John. "All Englishmen are brave. Only foreign people are afraid of things."
>
> She looked at him in absolute pity, for his narrowness, his insularism, his unintelligence.[13]

Bosey urges him simply to tell her of the events that so twisted his soul and achieve "redemption," but Hardy refuses. That Shiel included such a subtle moral dilemma in an adventure serial says a great deal about his artistic impulses and principles.

Shiel proceeded to adopt as many of the changes recommended for the story as he could. He wrote Richards on a "Friday Night" in May, agreeing that the novel could be cut further, but telling him: "I am feeling very queer tonight after a week of abnormal work & fancy shall want to stay in bed all day tomorrow. Please let me off."[14]

---

13. *The Yellow Danger* 281–82.

14. MPS to Richards, Friday, May ?, 3 Gray's Inn Place, W.C., transcribed

In the meantime, as the serial version was proceeding through *Short Stories,* his short story "The Awful Voyage of Ralphie Hamilton" (about an unplanned balloon ride) appeared in the 9 April 1898 issue of the *Boy's Friend,* while his new serial, *Contraband of War,* had already commenced publication on 7 May, in *Pearson's Weekly*—before the completion of *Empress.* This new serial, too, retained the reference to *The Man-Stealers* in its captions, just as had *The Empress of the Earth.*

One cannot leave the *Empress* serial without recognizing that Shiel managed to insert in spots a richness of writing that added quality to an otherwise non-stop novel of action.

> At this hour the moon was westering far down the steep slope of her setting course, and all the smooth sea was branded with trails of tremulous silver. The old and drowsing Night, heavy with vigil, was all enkindled now and aglow, instinct with the glamour of the moonbeams absorbed through many a long hour . . .[15]

A decadent purple had not fully abandoned his writing.

Grant Richards finally published *The Empress of the Earth* as *The Yellow Danger* in July 1898. The book was on bestseller lists for several weeks in August and September. Shiel not only trimmed the serial for the book as promised, but had to excise some anti-American comments and rewrite the last chapter at the insistence of Fenno, the American publisher, before the book was published on 30 September 1899.

In a memoir written in the 1930s, *Author Hunting,* Richards says that he made £90 from his publication of *The Yellow Danger*. After all the time that he spent with Shiel over many years, publishing his books, encouraging him, providing financial support, and expressing concern when Shiel was in prison, it is strange that Richards mentions Shiel only once in each of the two volumes he wrote about his publishing life: *Memories of a Misspent Youth 1872–1896* (1933) and *Author Hunting by an Old Literary Sportsman: Memories of Years Spent Mainly in Publishing 1897–1925* (1934). It may have been because Shiel was alive when both those books were published, and Richards may have wanted to stay away from some issues that might have damaged Shiel's reputation. He had obviously enjoyed Shiel's fiction himself and had provided support

---

by JG (HRC).

15. *The Empress of the Earth, Short Stories* (30 April 1898).

for Shiel when other publishers would likely have cast him aside.

The Empress of the Earth had shown Shiel at his most energetic, displaying his thoroughness in developing facts respecting the technical details of ships and battles, and his skill in developing a storyline that closely followed actual events and incorporated popular daily culture of English life into his fiction.

With respect to his accuracy in describing warships and their battles in the novel, Phipps explained to his friend W. H. Chesson that he had acquaintances in the Admiralty who helped with this kind of detail. Even the popular music hall became a factor in the story, where the favorite American performer, high-kicking young Lottie Collins, recognizes the naval success of Hardy in song and captures her audience with the favorite "Ta-ra-ra-boom-der-ay!" dance routine . . . while popular English poets celebrated the exploits of Hardy in their published verse.

Interestingly, there are significant character issues in *The Empress of the Earth* that can easily escape readers. One can get caught up in the action of the story and the personal battle between naval officer John Hardy and Dr. Yen How and look no deeper. Because John Hardy had been kissed by the Ada whom Yen How so desperately desired, he had Hardy imprisoned in China and tortured to a point where he was made to "scream" like a cat.

Thus, vengeance against Yen How and the destruction of the vast Chinese army and navy was a driving vindictive force for Hardy, but it also became a terrible thorn of moral guilt for which he refused the self-redemption that "Bosey" offered. The war was ultimately won, England became the Empress of the Earth, but Hardy's redemption remained elusive.

Bosey had begged him to tell her "all your trouble" that drove his passion for vengeance, and "He had the impulse to tell it all out, and save his soul." But he "sprung up" and away to pursue his "pitiless heart."

In closing the novel, Shiel included poems by real but "rather minor poets"—William Watson, John Davidson, and Francis Thompson—to "sing for the nation its august present, and suggest its future." Shiel concluded, as he would throughout his career: "We bet on Man."

At a level above action, there is style, there is moral subtlety, there are characters richly portrayed—the story is a classic literary tragedy. "So wild a pity is in the world, and so bitter a sob."

Chapter 10

"Will you come to the wedding, will you come?"

The Empress of the Earth was so successful that it immediately earned Shiel another commission for a serial to capitalize on the outbreak of the Spanish-American War. Peter Keary of *Pearson's* must have spotted an opportunity to build on the success of *The Empress of the Earth* with a serial tied to this new war. The American battleship the *USS Maine* was blown up on 15 February 1898, and war was declared on 15 April. This story would allow Shiel to use the knowledge that he had gained about the battle of ships in *Empress,* and to place the battles in his old home waters of the Caribbean.

The writing of *The Empress of the Earth* was in hand, and while it ran on in serial publication, Shiel had the time to work on other ideas. The new serial would be one; there is at least one short story to show for the period; and there are probably other works composed during this time—as well as the initial development of idea for his major works that would not appear for several years—*The Last Miracle,* "The Last Adam," *The Lord of the Sea.*

Contraband of War ran in *Pearson's Weekly,* 7 May–9 July 1898, overlapping *The Empress of the Earth* for some two months. Even while he was depending on the new serial to entertain readers in *Pearson's,* the book publication of *The Yellow Danger* in July earned praise from a reviewer for helping take the minds of English readers away from the Spanish-American fray! *The Yellow Danger* was on bestseller lists in August and September of 1898, and over the next couple of years it would go into more than ten printings or editions, with a variety of subtitles to help promote it. Yet Grant Richards would say later in life that it earned his firm only £90. The number of copies sold of the book, based on records of Richards's firm, does not suggest a level of true bestsellerdom.

George Locke, bookseller and bibliophile, had an opportunity to examine the badly deteriorated ledgers of Grant Richards in the 1970s, and was able to determine that 1,728 copies of *The Yellow Danger* were sold between its publication in July and the end of 1898.

It appeared from the records that 1,596 copies constituted the first printing, while 843 copies of a second printing soon followed.[1]

As he had in *The Empress of the Earth,* Shiel incorporated ongoing war news into successive weekly installments of *Contraband of War,* lending verisimilitude to the first half of the serial. Ensuing events in the war, including the overwhelming nature of the final American naval victory off Santiago, Cuba, outstripped Shiel's imagination at the end, and he would desert that war for a more personal contest and series of battles between two characters in the novel. He would later have the same problem with his novelization of the Russo-Japanese War, *The Yellow Wave* (1905), which was soon dated by his failure to anticipate Japan's crushing victory over the Russian fleet at Tsushima.

Candidly, *Contraband of War* is a boring novel—unless a reader can find much interest in a long-standing feud between an American businessman, Dick Hocking, and a Spanish financier, Immanuel Appaddaca, who chase each other about the Caribbean in endless battles of wits and ships. There was nothing in the story to engage the British reader's jingoistic imagination as had *The Empress of the Earth,* no British hero or heroine, no heroine at all . . . and the climax is the unlikely joining of the two contestants in a business partnership, with the doggedness of the American and the shrewdness of the Spaniard set to balance each other in their "wedding"—that is, a merging of their firms.

For one interested in Shiel's personal life inserted in the serial, the chief energy and excitement of the story involve a running battle between ships of Hocking and Appaddaca in the Caribbean, with the island of Redonda a foil that the slower ship of the American, with lesser draught, could cling to more tightly in endless circles while the Spanish ship, on an outer circle, could not achieve an angle from which to fire upon the other. In the end each ship goes its separate, frustrated way.

Redonda was "a mere rock, rising with craggy sides from the water, conical in shape, and uninhabited, save by boobies, and three men who live on its summit for the purpose of collecting the guano of the innumerable sea-fowl which haunt its shrubless seawall," Shiel described it in the novel, and continued: "From the summit a view (which the present writer has twice enjoyed) is obtained for many a

---

1. George Locke, "'Danger's' Yellowed Accounts," in Morse, *Works* 2.58.

mile over the sea as far as the coasts of Nevis to the north and Montserrat to the south."[2]

Not a word is said of the alleged kingship of that island Redonda, a "kingship" that the author would not mention or claim until thirty years later! But from that later mouse, a literary mountain of courtly fancy grew.

Shiel quickly had the manuscript of *Contraband of War* in the hands of Grant Richards for book publication, and he had already written a draft of *The Last Miracle*.

Louis Tracy wrote a sequel to *An American Emperor*, "The Lost Provinces," that ran from 1 January to 11 June 1898 in *Pearson's Weekly* and was published in book form that November—with no apparent involvement of Shiel, who was immersed in his own writing.

The balance of 1898 was one of Shiel's most creative periods—in writing and in romance. He could not stop writing. He could not stop his love affairs with Nellie Seward in London or Lina Gomez in Paris.

During this time he published two serial novels, *The Empress of the Earth* and *Contraband of War*, and also conceived the three novels that would make his lasting reputation—*The Last Miracle*, *The Purple Cloud*, and *The Lord of the Sea*. Shiel had actually managed to draft *The Last Miracle* during the publication of his two serials. And by late summer of 1898 he had moved on with work on the historical novel *Cold Steel*, which would begin serialization late in the year. He must have been back and forth between London and Paris as he wound down his work on the serials in actual publication.

Since these major novels were on Shiel's mind in 1898–99, it is worth considering the issue of whether he had initially conceived them as part of a larger whole. In their book publication format, each of the three major novels would be linked loosely in a prefatory text format that purports to show that each is the transcription of a medium's accounts of successively distant future events, notebooks numbered I, II, III and IV.

The first of the "notebooks" published was *The Lord of the Sea* (notebook no. II), the second was *The Purple Cloud* (no. III), and *The Last Miracle* was identified as notebook no. I—although it was the last

2. *Contraband of War* 205.

to see any form of publication. It was deemed, according to the fictional "author" who transcribed the notebooks, that no. IV was unworthy of publication. The framing device may have been suggested to Shiel by W. T. Stead, as John D. Squires has surmised, but when Shiel decided to add this prefatory material to each of the novels is unknown. It first appears at the time of the book publication of each title, since there is no serial that carried it. (Only *The Purple Cloud* was serialized, but only in an abridged version.) The device might also have been devised to further the potential of the sales of each, by building on the popularity of each for the other. At least the novels in their book format were publicized as being derived from the same medium's "notebooks." Since the earliest versions of each novel no longer exist, and only *The Purple Cloud* was published in a greatly abbreviated serial version without reference to the medium, there is no means by which it can be known whether this device was included in their original manuscript versions or not.

Shiel's need for money had been further sharpened with his wedding on 3 November 1898 to the pretty young Parisian-Spaniard Carolina Garcia Gomez in Saint Peter's Italian Church in Holborn. Legend (apparently John Gawsworth's tale, although Gawsworth never mentioned Shiel in the 1933 draft of his biography of Machen) has it that his London neighbor and friend Arthur Machen was among the witnesses for the ceremony that day, but his name is not listed on the wedding certificate.[3] It was Lina's mother, Dolores "Lola" Garcia Gomez, who signed the certificate as one of two witnesses. Theodore William Graf Wratislaw, a contributor of poetry to the *Yellow Book,* who might be called one of John Lane's "Young Men," was the other formal witness. Shiel has described Wratislaw's interest in his writing in 1897/98. Lina's father was identified as Miguel Garcia Gomez of Seville, deceased; Phipps's father, a West Indian merchant, also deceased. Lina, a "spinster," listed her address as the Hotel Victoria, where she would have been staying with her mother and sisters. It was here that Phipps had worked in 1891 on the sporting journal described in *The Weird o' It*. Shiel would have taken Lina as his wife home to his quarters at Gray's Inn after their marriage.

Phipps appears to have been enthusiastic about the coming wedding.

---

3. Book 17, p. 21, Register Book of Marriages, District of Holborn, County of London.

He wrote Frederic Chapman, of John Lane's firm, on 18 October 1898, asking for copies of his two books in the Keynotes Series:

> My dear Chapman,
>
> I want to trouble you again, by asking if you could be so very good as to send [*inserted:* tomorrow (Saturday)] me a copy of each of my Two, though I am afraid I am getting in John Lane's debt.
>
> I am going to get married next week to a little Spanish girl, with mantilla, dagger, and everything complete. Will you come to the wedding, will you come? If so I will send you further particulars—when I know them.
>
> Yours very truly,
> M. P. Shiel.

There is no indication how many guests attended either the wedding or the wedding dinner. Shiel probably mentioned the coming wedding to Chapman as a means of persuading him to send copies of *Prince Zaleski* and *Shapes in the Fire,* books that he intended to give to prospective supporters. The attendance of Wratislaw, however, does suggest that there may have been more of the John Lane circle, and others involved in Shiel's varied literary activities, who attended the wedding.

Shiel and Wratislaw shared a mutual passion for music halls, and undoubtedly also for the dancers and singers who traversed their stage. The music hall was a cultural high spot for the middle-class with whom Shiel identified, whose performers were frequent occupants of his life and stories. "The Music-Hall," a poem by Wratislaw (from *Caprices,* 1893) should have stirred Shiel as much as anything by Ernest Dowson.

> The curtain on the grouping dancers falls,
> The heaven of color has vanished from our eyes;
> Stirred in our seats we wait with vague surmise
> What haply comes that pleases or that palls.
> Touched on the stand the thrice-struck baton calls,
> Once more I watch the unfolding curtain rise,
> I hear the exultant violins premise
> The well-known tune that thrills me and enthralls.
> Then trembling in my joy I see you flash
> Before the footlights to the cymbals' clash,
> With laughing lips, swift feet, and brilliant glance,

You, fair as heaven and as a rainbow bright,
You, queen of song and empress of the dance,
Flower of mine eyes, my love, my heart's delight!

Consider Shiel's dedicatory letter to the music-hall singer in *Shapes in the Fire*—inviting her outdoors, under "the chaste down-look of Dian's astonished eye glass, and the *schwärmerei* of the winking stars." Finding Wratislaw's name at the wedding throws a completely fresh perspective on *Shapes in the Fire,* whose posture and language was more decadently rich than had been that of *Prince Zaleski. Zaleski* had been baroque, exaggerated Greek opulence. One could listen to the poetry by Wratislaw and the stories in *Shapes in the Fire* and feel they were in the same aesthetic room. Shiel must have immersed himself in the decadent literature of the period, from Ella D'Arcy to Wratislaw, to have so rapidly developed the voice behind the stories in *Shapes in the Fire.* Poe was certainly there, and John Lane's circle, though not for long, as the decadents fled. Next came Machen's group, and then the opportunities for serial writing and different influences.

The copies of his two John Lane books that Shiel requested from Chapman were probably to be used for the purpose that he would suggest to Richards—to give copies of his books to persons who might help promote his newer works. For instance, he wrote Richards on 26 October 1898, suggesting that copies of *The Yellow Danger* be sent "to Sir Charles Dilke and Lord Sal. [i.e., Salisbury] and one or two to one or two other people of that sort."[4] Salisbury was Prime Minister; Dilke was supportive of women's rights, trade unions, and universal schooling; both were "imperialists" to a degree. Shiel had also left a copy of the manuscript of *Contraband of War* at Richards's office late that same day in October, having missed Richards in person. Richards already had in hand the manuscript of *The Last Miracle,* and on the 28th Phipps thanked him for returning it, since he did not have a copy. He expressed disappointment that there was no interest in periodical publication of the title, but was encouraged by Richards's own interest in the novel and promised to complete it soon.[5]

Even on his wedding day Phipps was chasing money. He wrote

4. MPS to Richards, 26 October 1898, 3 Gray's Inn Place, transcribed by JG (HRC).

5. MPS to Richards, 28 October 1898, 3 Gray's Inn Place, transcribed by JG (HRC).

Richards that very day, saying he was being married, is "short," and can Richards provide him an advance against the pending reissue of *The Yellow Danger* in a cheap edition? Keary owes him money, he says, but is away.[6] Richards came through, and Shiel sent him a piece of the wedding cake.

Machen's wife, Amy, who was fond of Shiel, probably arranged the wedding luncheon on 3 November 1898. She may very well have paid for the event as well. The luncheon menu has survived, signed by both Shiel and Machen, probably not contemporaneously, since a pencil note on the menu is dated 14/XI/06. The meal was held at "The Florence," a restaurant managed by L. Azario on Rupert Street. The Machens ate there regularly, and Azario had a business relationship with Machen, perhaps dating since 1895.[7]

Azario had an arrangement to sell the wine that came from grapes grown on Machen's leasehold vinery in Touraine. Machen was so proud of the wine that he served it at his own meals and at his "Sundays," the social gatherings where Phipps had become acquainted with Amy. Again, the point should be made that there is no verifiable evidence as to who was at the dinner other than Phipps, Lina, her mother, probably the other named witness at the wedding, Theodore William Graf Wratislaw, and probably Amy and Arthur Machen. Those others at the wedding would most likely have also attended the luncheon.

Shiel later blamed Lina's mother, Lola Gomez, for the meddling that was a major cause of the failure of the marriage. She repeatedly urged Lina to leave Phipps behind in London to return to her in France, harping constantly over Shiel's persistent precarious finances. Many of Shiel's letters to Grant Richards over the period of the marriage contained pleas for advances against royalties, or loans against work to be delivered, because of his and family needs.

The birth of Shiel's love-child, Ada Phipps Seward Shiel, in November 1898, only a few weeks after his marriage to Lina, immediately caused a crisis with Lina. The longer-term impact must have produced enormous personal and financial pressure on Shiel, to sustain himself and a wife, and to balance these personal conflicts that he

---

6. MPS to Richards, 3 November 1898, 3 Gray's Inn Place, transcribed by JG (HRC).

7. JG, *The Life of Arthur Machen* (Leyburn, UK: Tartarus Press, 2007).

had inflicted on himself and these two young women.

Census records indicate that Ada was born in London, not in Cheltenham. It is possible that Nellie was living with the Pattisons at the time of Ada's birth, although the baby and her mother probably soon moved to her parents' home in Cheltenham, where Ada lived until probably her late teens.

She made an effort to reach her father by writing Richards's firm in 1921 (when she was twenty-two), but Richards had to respond that he did not know Shiel's whereabouts. Richards was subsequently able to reach Shiel, informed him that "Aida" had inquired about him and, after a temporary loss of her letter, forwarded it to Shiel on 16 December 1921.[8] There is no record of what might have developed in the relationship of father and daughter, except that Shiel had in his effects four prescriptions, on a single sheet, written by an unidentified doctor for "Miss Shiel / 44 Porchester Sq." on 19 April 1930. The four prescriptions are undecipherable. "Ada Seward" has been interposed above her name in the same hand, but it appears that Gawsworth added pencil notes to the sheet. "Expensive" below the address; "Worthington"; "now lives Kensington / not with daughter Mrs. Nimmo." One must presume that Gawsworth provided these scribbles after Shiel's death. But this was long after Shiel's dealings with Richards in 1898.

Richards was not able to attend Shiel's wedding. He wrote on 15 November 1898 to apologize and thanked him for the wedding cake, which was more than he was able to eat all at once. He says that *Contraband of War* is not as good as the first title, but he offers £70 for it and wants to see the remainder of it in January.[9] On 17 November 1898, Phipps wrote Richards (from 3 Gray's Inn Place, W.C., his old home near the Machen family, where he would have taken Lina after their marriage), enclosing the whole of *Contraband of War*. He also thanked Richards for a cheque.

Then Richards quickly wrote again, on 18 November 1898, saying the book is only 68,000 words; he offers £50 for it plus £20 more if sales reach 3,000 copies.

Richards went so far as to write Phipps in November that he hoped "Mrs. Shiel will make you go on with The Last Miracle. That is where

8. Richards to MPS (HRC).

9. Richards to MPS, 15 November 1898 (HRC).

all our hopes lie." Despite the best efforts of Richards and Shiel's regular literary agent, Morris Colles, of agent J. B. Pinker, and the initial interest of Richards, no serial or book publisher could be found for *The Last Miracle,* presumably due to its "agnostic tone," as Phipps himself allowed. The focus of the letters between Shiel and Richards would shift to other books, the most immediate being a new serial novel ready for publication—*Cold Steel*.

Lina probably felt adrift in London. Shiel may have early promenaded her through London's streets to show her off, but Lina did not speak English and would have had no interest in the "lectures" and similar activities that Shiel was used to pursuing in the city. He later said that Lina did not think London pretty. Did he take her to the music halls? Theodore Wratislaw was among the decadents who were passionate about them and "glorified the music hall in their work."[10]

Amy Machen, kind woman that she appeared to be, reached out to Lina. She sent her a brief note (in French) on November 12, apologizing because she will be unable to attend church with her the next day, since someone is coming to dine with them, but she will see her (being neighbors at Gray's Inn) while visiting their common friend Egan Mew—who lived in the flat across the hall from Phipps and Lina. On 12 December, Amy asked Lina if she would like to accompany her to Whiteley's, London's first department store. Amy's health had been in serious decline after struggling with cancer for six years, and she died in the summer of 1899.[11]

4 Verulam Bdgs / Gray's Inn / 12 Nov [1898]

Dear Madam,

I am very sorry that I will not be able to accompany you to church tomorrow morning; but someone is coming to dine with us, and I will be obliged to occupy myself with that a little.

After noon I will have the pleasure to see you again at Mister Mew's.

We will go at 4:30.

Goodbye. I hope that you are well today.

Your sincere friend / A. Machen

---

10. MacLeod, *Fictions of British Decadence* 32.

11. Notes in French, tr. Kirsten MacLeod; originals in the HRC. Both notes are on small folded blue sheets, written in a bold hand, probably carried by Amy's servant to Lina.

It is unlikely that Amy was a regular attendee at church.

4 Verulam Bdgs / Gray's Inn / 12 Dec [1898]

Dear Madam,

Would you like to go with me to Whiteley's? Good: come get me at 2 o'clock—precisely.

Your sincere friend / A. Machen.

Lina probably never attended a "Sunday" at the Machens'. These socials probably ceased after the winter. Amy's health had been in serious decline after her struggle with cancer, and she most likely became soporific under opiates for pain. Her friend, Jerome, wrote of her last days:

> The memory lingers with me of when I last saw his wife. It was a Sunday afternoon . . . The windows looked out into a great garden, and the rooks were cawing in the elms. She was dying, and Machen, with two cats under his arm, was moving softly about, waiting on her. We did not talk much. I stayed there until the sunset filled the room with a strange purple light.[12]

With the death of Amy in August 1899, Machen sealed the image of Amy away in some corner of his being and refused to talk again of her. By many accounts, he developed a severe depression and is said to have wandered the streets of London alone and despondent. It would not have been unusual for him to react to Shiel with personal dislike after Amy died and Shiel wrote about the two of them in rather intimate detail, even though he had admired Shiel's early Keynotes titles. Writing of Amy was an invasion of privacy.

By December 1898 Phipps's *Cold Steel* was being serialized in *Pearson's Weekly*—a story that he hoped would bring financial reward in the new year. His immediate financial hopes shifted to the anticipated success of this swashbuckling historical romance about Henry VIII. The serial began in *Pearson's Weekly* on 31 December 1898 and concluded with the 6 May 1899 issue. Years later, Shiel said that the physical characteristics of the heroine of this adventure novel, Laura—"a creature of simply gorgeous loveliness, Spanish in type"—were based on Lina.

On 25 January 1899, Phipps sent the corrected proofs of *Contra-*

---

12. Jerome K. Jerome, *My Life and Times* 115.

band of War to Richards, while noting that he had no suggestion as to how best to price the Colonial Edition of *The Yellow Danger*. In March, Richards published *Contraband of War*—to better critical reviews, it appears, than the serial had received—although the book would not sell well.

Early in the new year, Phipps received a letter from his mother. She had written him, in a letter dated 4 January 1899, expressing surprise that he had not told her that he planned to be married, and stating that she was shocked that he had been married in a Roman Catholic church! She thanked him for the piece of wedding cake he had sent her and told him that she had enjoyed *The Yellow Danger*. She is sorry that he "is hard up." Harriet was busy, she said, making "an order."[13] So the old store was still in business, a dozen years after the death of Shiel's father. It apparently would remain so until Harriet left for England in 1900 to help attend Lina in her pregnancy.

In March or April of 1899, Phipps wrote Richards that he hoped the *Morning Leader* would take the "religion story" as a serial, and that *Contraband of War* would do well as a book, but acknowledged that initial reviews of the serial had been unfavorable.[14] Reviewers of the book publication of the title have mentioned the abruptness of its conclusion. It may be that Shiel saw that it was not being well received and simply disposed of the serial more quickly than he might have otherwise. After his personal absorption in the avalanche of action and drama of *The Empress of the Earth,* he probably found very little to get excited about in the events and personalities of *Contraband of War.* It is not a very good story, and the writing lacks the fire of the previous work.

He planned to get the manuscript of the book version of *Cold Steel* to Richards soon. But he wrote Richards again, quickly, asking him not to mention to Pearson that he has shown him the manuscript of *Cold Steel.*[15] He apparently was concerned that there would be confusion over rights to the novel; or he may simply have been working

---

13. Holograph letter from Priscilla Shiell to MPS, 4 January 1899, Montserrat (HRC).

14. Holograph transcription by JG of undated, unaddressed letter from MPS to Richards (HRC).

15. Holograph transcription by JG of undated, unaddressed letter from MPS to Richards (HRC).

Pearson on other story angles. (The address from which he wrote these letters is uncertain, although he noted that he was in the process of moving to other quarters. It may well be that Lina was in France during this period.)

On a card postmarked 9 May 1899, from Cooper's Hill House, Brockworth, near Gloucester, Shiel wrote Richards that he would be at this address until Saturday, and requested that the manuscript of *Cold Steel* be sent to him here.[16] Shortly thereafter, he wrote that he was at The Royal George, Birdlip, Gloucester, where he would be for a week. Richards can send him the proofs of *Cold Steel* there, and he will make corrections.[17] Apparently, Shiel had gone up to Gloucester to see Nellie's baby, Ada. Lina had either gone to France as a result, or Shiel had seized her absence for the visit north. The small Cotswold village of Birdlip is only a short distance from Cheltenham and Gloucester, all in the rugged, picturesque hills above the rivers Wye and Severn. It appears that Shiel maintained regular visits to see Nellie and the baby for more than two years after Ada's birth. Nellie sent Shiel a photograph of the baby in February 1900, signing the photo on its verso, "Your Valentine."[18] It appears that Lina would dash away to her mother several times during her five years of marriage to Phipps. After the arrival of Shiel's sister, Harriet, in May 1900 to help Lina in her pregnancy, and with the birth of Dolores Katherine Shiel in July 1900, things remained more settled for a year or two. From all appearances Lina and Harriet got along quite well.

Meantime, on a Thursday, apparently 16 May 1899, Shiel wrote Richards from 27 Montague Place, W.C. (across the street from the British Museum), noting that this was a temporary address. He thinks a 6d edition of *The Yellow Danger* would do well. On a Monday, apparently in the same month, he wrote again, asking if there was news regarding negotiations about additional publications of *The Yellow Danger* and asking what Richards's views are of *Cold Steel.* "The strike story is going famously," he said, "& I dare say will begin to appear soon."[19]

---

16. Postcard, postmarked 9 March 1899, MPS to Richards (HRC).

17. Holograph transcription by JG of undated letter from MPS to Richards (HRC).

18. Photograph in HRC.

19. Transcription by JG of undated, unaddressed letter from MPS to Rich-

There is no record of when Shiel first mentioned this "strike story" to Richards, or how he described it to him.

Shiel followed this by writing Richards again in early June, saying he was well into the "strike story" for *Pearson's,* where he expected the serialization to begin soon. On 15 June 1899, he added that Pearson was looking into copyrighting the strike story in America. Then in a letter probably written in July, Shiel confessed that he had been told to halt work on the story for now, but he reassured Richards that all remained well. Nothing else is said about this story until a serial appeared under Louis Tracy's name late in early 1900, as described below.

Shiel had also written Lina from the Montague address, also on a Thursday, perhaps the same day in May, the 16th, that he wrote Richards. Lina had been in France with her mother and sisters, whether in anger at Phipps or just for a family visit is unclear, but he was willing to adjust his life to accommodate their relationship. John Gawsworth transcribed and translated from the French this and following letters from Phipps to Lina. Their correspondence was all in French. (The originals and transcripts by Gawsworth are all in the Ransom Center, Austin.)

[27 Montague Place 16 May 1899?]

My darling,

Just a line to remember me to you. I hope you too have dropped me a line today. You will have done so if you love me. Do you *really* love me? You don't very often tell me so, my dear. But I leave that to you, having confidence in the future, in your soft heart, in my little self.

Now I'm going to do something big for you—cut myself off from my country: to have always to speak a foreign tongue, never to make an epigram, or to say anything witty or remarkable (because I can't do so in French) and to be always surrounded by an alien atmosphere, all that, you know, is not exactly easy.

But I do it believing in you, your self-respect, your integrity, and your love for me. Also I hope that you will never make me regret it. If you do make me regret it, I will love you just the same, always, always just the same!

Now I don't count on coming until Tuesday, Tuesday night I hope. I will kiss you with the holy strength of my love, Carolina

ards (HRC). It may be that MPS was still in Gloucester at this time or had moved to London.

Shiel. Prepare well thy couch, O Woman.

Until I see you again I commit you to God's good care, my dearest.

Regards to your mother and sisters.

Your best Friend.

P.S. No word in your last letter regarding your health. I suppose all's well. Write soon. When you write don't forget to remind me about the *ticket*, the *books* and all the things I should do.

This is a very friendly and loving letter, and extremely cordial toward Lina's family. Shiel is apparently going to great lengths to be on good terms with Lina and her family. This hint at a question regarding Lina's health may portend an early illness that would take her life so soon. Again, from the same Montague address, Shiel wrote Lina—on a Wednesday, probably 22 May 1899. It appears that he is promising to forsake England to live with Lina in France—or at least, so his letters suggested to her.

My Darling,

Thank you for your little note which I received this morning. Last evening I wrote to you.

In reply to your question *when,* all I can tell you at the moment is that it won't be much longer now: Tomorrow perhaps, Saturday perhaps, or perhaps Tuesday. I don't know. As soon as I can: if you get bored without me just think *how* bored I get without you! My hearth, my warmth, my theme that you are.

I love you.

I am on the point of selling my furniture, rather of giving it away. The prices that are offered for things one sells like that in London are ridiculous—not a tenth of the original price. But it doesn't matter: it is only for once.

But it is vital that I don't lose a lot of time just when I'm going to France, just at the moment when I'm beginning to work and you know that I can't work if I'm not in my own place with all my stuff around me. Consequently I implore you to decide on a house and do all that you can before my arrival. You ought also to book a room in a *pension* for us where we could stay a week or a few days.

Do you remember M. Gaude's *pension*? And our heavenly orgies there? I implore you not to eat meanwhile any fragrant sauces like you did before, and no *pickles*. Afterwards, yes, yes. We will write over the head of bed these two words "Venus Genetrix."

I am enclosing a little note from Olive. It amused me a lot. She is a simple little girl with a tendency, I think, to "guignolisme."

I won't forget, I hope, the books you told me to bring (autographed). Is there anything else that you want me to do? I'll expect a letter from you tomorrow, or the day after, eh? To please me!

So long. I kiss you, my life!

Your husband

By the first week in June 1899, Shiel was at 31 Rue Ballu in Paris, apparently with Lina. He had written Richards that he was going to France and wanted to resolve issues regarding *Cold Steel* first. Mr. Kirk has been helpful, Shiel tells Richards, but he needs his agreement.[20] On 7 June 1899, he accepts the terms offered on *Cold Steel,* but for the amount of £120 as per their oral agreement! He needs the money as soon as possible.[21] On 13 June Richards writes Shiel that "Ours is a partnership I thoroughly believe in, and you can depend on me doing all that I can to that end." On 15 June Shiel thanks Richards for the bill and notes, "With regards to copyright of the Strike story in America, I am writing Pearson's and shall let you know as soon as I receive his answer."[22] He will send the completed manuscript of *Cold Steel* soon, but tells Richards that he had forgotten to send Shiel half of the copy to correct. (This is prior to Shiel's telling Richards that *Pearson's* had told him to leave the strike story.)

Still in Paris on a Sunday in June 1899, Shiel wrote Richards that there was a problem with the bill that required immediate changes to satisfy Shiel's bankers. The manuscript of *Cold Steel* will reach Richards soon. If there is any income due on *The Yellow Danger* Shiel would like to have it, since he is "short" and setting up a new house.

Shiel had also written the literary agent J. B. Pinker on 24 June 1899 from 31 rue Ballu: "I presume that you have not been able to place serially my story *The Last Miracle*, as I have not heard from you. If you despair, would you be so kind as to send it to the above address for me at your convenience . . . P.S. Do you know of any literary agent in Paris of whom you could tell me? Some one has translated

20. Transcription by JG of letter from MPS to Richards, undated but probably last week in May 1899 (HRC).

21. Transcription by JG of letter from MPS to Richards, 7 June 1899, 31 rue Ballu, Paris (HRC).

22. Transcription by JG of letter from MPS to Richards, 15 June 1899, rue Ballu, Paris (HRC).

into French one of my books and wants to place it, but I am all at sea . . ."[23]

On 30 June, he wrote Pinker again: "Many thanks for sending me M.S. of my story *The Last Miracle*. Unfortunately you have sent only half. There is another lot about the same size, type-written, ending with the words—'not so bad though—not so bad—' or something similar. Might I ask you if you will do me the favour to hunt it up, and send it as soon as you can? It is of importance to me as I have no copy."[24]

By 2 July, Shiel was writing from 36 Avenue du Chemin de Fer, Colombes, Paris. On that date, he wrote Richards:

> I now send you a full copy of "Cold Steel" carefully gone through. I would have sent it before, but two chapters got lost, and I had the greatest trouble to get them from London, as NO copies were left at Pearson's except one. Moreover, I have sent it to a friend of mine (Wheeler) who is an expert in the age concerned & he has read it and suggested some alterations. It turns out Calvo's hot air contrivance was done before his age by a Persian man; so I have put that in and left the incident . . . Someone is translating my Zaleski into French so I shall be crowned by the Academy & be famous![25]

From notes made by A. Reynolds Morse for his Shiel bibliography in 1947, John Gawsworth indicated that "Wheeler" was a friend of Arthur Machen.

Shiel was exceedingly fond of working various gadgets into his stories, and his use of balloons and other early aircraft turned up in several of his novels as means of assisting escapes (as here) or committing murder (in *By Force of Circumstances*, by "Gordon Holmes"). It is also apparent from this letter to Richards that he was quite particular in being accurate with his use of such devices and made a special attempt to do so—such as his consultations with his admiralty friends for the use of battleships in *The Empress of the Earth*, and in this instance verifying that his use of a "hot air contrivance" was possible.

On 7 July 1899 he tells Richards he is glad that Richards is rushing out *Cold Steel* and hopes he "will see fit to boom it a bit." Shiel rewrote the last chapter of *The Yellow Danger* for American publica-

23. Morse, 2.158.

24. Ibid.

25. Morse *Works* 2.78–79.

tion, and he asked Richards to send him what is due from that sale when Richards gets the amount.[26]

Later in July, Phipps tells Richards that the proofs for *Cold Steel* are finished and will be sent on Wednesday. He now urges quick publication. But he needs help again with his bankers. He is "expecting every week my next Pearson's story set up in print. As soon as I get it you shall have it." He apparently is referring to the "strike story," but within a week he completely changed his story of what had happened with respect to that work.[27]

He followed this letter with another (on a Sunday), saying he would send the proofs of *Cold Steel* on Wednesday. He tells Richards angrily that the printers have altered his copy, with ridiculous changes in paragraphing and punctuation. He urges Richards to write them with directions to follow the original copy. He has had to mark up the proofs extensively in order to restore the text to its original state. Perhaps of more interest, however, he noted that "Pearson has interrupted me in writing the *Strike Story,* but is only temporary—and *for the best* for you & me." He will be sending something new soon—"The Second Adam"! Thus, he had been writing in the summer of 1899, in France, the novel that would become his most famous and most enduring.

One might wonder whether Shiel was actually ever deep into the strike story, or whether he was spending time on "The Second Adam" and other ideas—leaving the strike-based serial to Tracy—as events may prove. But Tracy had begun another project, "The Adventures of Sirdar Mohammed Khan," a series of six related short stories published monthly in *Pearson's Magazine* in issues 43 to 48, from July to December 1899. (The New York edition of *Pearson's* ran the stories at the same time.)

During the July–early August period, when Shiel sent Richards several undated letters conveying this information, a devastating hurricane struck Montserrat—on 7 August, a storm of such magnitude that it would be referred to for years as one of historic nature. Shiel must have been in correspondence with his family about the storm, which caused the deaths of seventy-four islanders. "The Lord Mayor

26. Morse *Works* 2.64.

27. Ibid.

. . . [opened] a public subscription for the relief of the survivors."[28]

Throughout the summer and fall of 1899, while he was still in France, Shiel urged Richards to hurry *Cold Steel*. Things did not go as either man hoped. Shiel's initial popular success with *The Empress of the Earth* and *Contraband of War* was based, in large measure, on Shiel's skill at incorporating actual headline events from each crisis into the successive weekly installments of those serials. It is ironic then (as John D. Squires has noted) that his hopes for the success of the book version of the swashbuckling *Cold Steel* were crushed by another international crisis.

As Shiel was correcting proofs for Richards and urging him to hurry the book to print, England was reinforcing her South African colonies in anticipation of trouble with the Boer Republics. On 13 October 1899 the Boers invaded Natal, and by the end of the month Kimberley, Mafeking, and Ladysmith were besieged. Richards released *Cold Steel* on 14 November 1899, but the public's attention was on the war. Though generally favorable reviews appeared, *Cold Steel* had dismal sales. This left Shiel in a funk. He had talked Grant Richards into a large advance against anticipated royalties that would now have to be repaid.

Shiel blamed the war for other personal disasters as well. He had first mentioned *The Purple Cloud* to Richards in July 1899 as "The Second Adam." Shiel was not above offering manuscripts to several publishers seeking the best terms, and it is unclear if he ever formally offered the book to Richards at all. He claimed never to have sent Richards the manuscript of the novel. Chatto & Windus eventually published the book version of *The Purple Cloud* in September 1901, while Richards had brought out *The Lord of the Sea* in May of that year, as stories were swapped between publishers to reconcile Shiel's manipulations.

Shiel was playing a balancing act among his various publishers with these several books. C. Arthur Pearson, Ltd. had initially agreed to publish serial versions of the two books, but its managing director, Peter Keary, insisted that book versions not be published sooner than four months after completion of the serials. The respective book publishers were equally concerned that the anticipated books not compete with one another, and expected a six-month delay between them.

---

28. *Review of Reviews* (London) 20 (September 1899): 235.

Shiel was now desperate for money with the failure of *Cold Steel,* and anxious to get the serials into print so the books could proceed on time.

By late December 1899, Phipps had returned to London alone. He wrote Lina regarding his search for new quarters for them. She was still in France and must have known that she was pregnant. The great sacrifice that Shiel had promised Lina, to give up his country and live in France with her, was soon forgotten. The quarters described in the following undated letter are not where they would eventually set up house, which would be at an Addison Road location. In the meantime, however, Shiel had moved into a Keppel Street lodging, and Lina would share this brief address for several months after she returned to London. Gawsworth estimated in a scribbled note on his translation of the following letter from Phipps to Lina that it was written probably in early February 1900.[29]

> 5 Keppel St. / Russell Square / London W.C. [? February 1900]
>
> My Shishi: I received your letter today and kissed it twenty times. Already, already I begin to sigh!! And until Saturday seems to me a whole eternity. But of course I'll wait, as arranged.
>
> Today I saw a flat that I liked a lot. It is opposite the British Museum, in Bloomsbury—a very smart house. It has got electric light and consists of seven rooms and a kitchen: only it's a bit dark being below street level. The rent is 2000 francs. If it were for myself alone I would have taken it, but I am determined not to take a house without you seeing it. Therefore you must stay here with me for a few days after you come over.
>
> Until now I have done nothing important as I had a terrible journey. We couldn't get off at Calais, we had to go on to Folkestone. But I went to see how "Cold Steel" was getting on: They told me it is beginning to sell well but like all books at present, the war is affecting it terribly.
>
> As for the lawyers and all that. Don't worry as it is not worth it. I'll send you another hundred francs for your things tomorrow or the day after. I don't want you to come by the Dieppe–Newhaven route because the sea voyage would be too much for you at present. You'll come via Calais–Dover, Second Class, which is absolutely comfortable. So that's settled. You take a ticket for Charing Cross.

29. Translation by JG of original in HRC.

> I hope you won't accept any money from your Mama, whatever the reason. Anything you need you have already, or you will have by asking your little Banker and Agent. We are not beggars.
>
> My sister and the three little negresses were overjoyed to see me, and the thought of seeing you makes them silly with enthusiasm. But just on the day when you will be coming one or two of them will be going. Don't forget the *turons*. (Les devoured the bit I brought with his big mouth.) I hope [*remainder missing*]

The date of Lina's return is not clear. A letter to Richards dated 11 January 1900 bears Shiel's return address as 98 Addison Rd., W., although Shiel may have so addressed the letter in anticipation of a move from 5 Keppel Street to that address. Not surprisingly, Shiel requests modification of royalty terms on an amended *Yellow Danger* agreement.

Shiel's reference to his sister and the "three little negresses" is the only reference that can be found in his family correspondence that acknowledges any "color" in the family, although other historical sources refer to their father, Samuel Horsford, as a black merchant and prominent politician from St. Kitts. His ancestry continues to be a mystery, and a contemporary photograph of Cyril indicates an obvious West Indian mixture of color that came from his mother, Augusta, and his father.

The "three little negresses" were obviously his nieces, Muriel (21), Olive (19), and Nella (also about 19)—hardly "little." At least two of them would be departing for spring school as Lina returned from France. Nella (as "Netta" in census records) had been attending Claremont College in the village of Corsham, Wiltshire, while Muriel attended a private school in Penarth, Wales. Olive was studying art in London. The girl's ages are inferred from records of the time, but there is no reason to believe any were twins, simply close in birth. Despite later confusion regarding the lives of the Horsford children, Olive and Muriel were both alive in World War II, and in 1946 Shiel apologized to Olive that he had just not been up to a visit by her and Nella.

For all the noise that circulated in literary circles for years concerning Shiel's race, it is amazing that neither Reynolds Morse nor Gawsworth picked up Shiel's throwaway references to his nieces as "negresses" or made some reference to it. After all, each had access to this correspondence. It is clear that for whatever motive, each chose to ignore what it signaled. Of course, Augusta could have had mixed-blood children by virtue of her marriage to Sammie, in which case Phipps would have been out of the racial loop, but it is clear he knew of the cross-racial links. And with what Phipps and Augusta knew of their grandmother's color, their father's illegitimacy, and their mother's dark skin, they would have known good and well of the touch of the "negro" in their own blood.

Shiel's reference to "lawyers" in the letter to Lina is unclear. He seemed to be in constant debate with his publishers, so there may be a dispute that was strong enough that legal threats were made. It is not obvious if that were the case. Neither is there a personal matter that would appear to involve lawyers. Rather amusing, but leaving a question as to who "Les" was, he was a close enough friend or relative to Shiel that Lina would know who he was when he ate up both pastry and cake as Phipps recites!

Confusing the matter of when residence was set up on Addison Road, Shiel's old address at 5 Keppel Street on Russell Square was still the address on a letter he wrote Richards on 11 February 1900. He noted that he had received a copy of the 6d reprint of *The Yellow Danger* and wondered whether Richards had any word of a possible American edition of *The Purple Cloud*.[30]

When he wrote Richards again, on 28 February, the address he used was 98 Addison Road, where his daughter Lola would be born in July. Since Shiel apparently wrote on whatever stationery was at hand, any letter with a pre-printed address might not represent at all where he was living at the time he wrote a letter. When Gawsworth copied Shiel's letters, he simply wrote down the address that was on the letter.

In the letter received by Richards on 28 February 1900 Shiel said: "I now have a chance to finish a story of which you have read part—the Church one—called 'The Last Miracle'. . . . I think it is a pity to abandon it, but if I can't get it accepted serially, you know why—no paper dares on account of the agnostic tone . . ."

Shiel could expect to make at least £380 from a serial, he said; will Richards pay him £120 for all other rights? "As to 'The Lord of the Sea,' that will be appearing in *Pearson's* after completion of a story by Louis Tracy, as to the putting in of which before mine I have a grievance. Mine will run quite four to five months, so it will be about eight months before it can be published in book. From what they tell

30. From original in the Grant Richards Archives (microfilm in HRC).

me, however, it will repay waiting."

In letters of 6 and 28 March 1900, he was requesting a response regarding Richard's interest in *The Last Miracle,* which he obviously would like to sell for book publication if no one would accept it for periodical publication. He also complained over the many typographical errors in the reprint of *The Yellow Danger*.

Tracy's serial, *The Invaders,* began its run in *Pearson's Weekly* from 10 March to 11 August 1900, thus bumping *The Lord of the Sea* from the serial queue. *The Invaders* was a tie to the Boer War in which Germany and France take advantage of the diversion of the English Army to South Africa to launch a sneak attack on England.

Shiel was furious with Keary for delaying the serial publication of *The Lord of the Sea.* He wrote Richards (from 98 Addison Rd., W., apparently in February) enclosing a copy of *Shapes in the Fire,* probably for some promotional effort, and asked for a decision on the new book as soon as possible.

"After leaving you today I gave it pretty hard to Keary, as I said I would—but without the bamboo, after all—with the hand. He took it rather well, so that now I am, if anything, sorry. However, he really deserves it." Is Shiel actually referring to a physical encounter with Keary?

Shiel wrote Richards (from Ivy House, Halberton, Tiverton, Devon) on 29 May 1900, saying that he wants to get a book out by autumn. He intends to work hard on *The Last Miracle* and notes that his two serials have been delayed "by the wretched war." It is likely that Shiel was on one of his vacation hikes . . . although Lina was home awaiting a child due in July. His sister Harriet had arrived from Montserrat and was with Lina, but the specific date of her arrival is not documented.

Phipps's mother had written him on 23 May, hoping the two would get along. She was going to live with her daughter Sallie Killikelly on Nevis, unhappily, since she will not be able to attend "services." The store is closed. "My love to Lina. I hope the Good Lord will bring her safely through her trouble." Phipps had written his family as early as 1895, wishing that he could soon bring Harriet "over." Her presence in 1900 would probably help him in several ways.

It is not being cynical, but only realistic in knowing Shiel's nature, to suspect that with Lina in her last months of pregnancy he was out along his waysides where other romances had been established. His occasional trips to Devon over the years, however, raise a somewhat different question. It was at Tiverton that his sisters, Augusta and Sallie, both had their portraits made at some uncertain (but different) dates, and Tiverton was quite close to Bideford, where Phipps held his first teaching position in the fall of 1885. It is also likely that he attended school in that area in the late 1870s. There is no physical evidence in the way of correspondence or other record to tie him to a possible relationship with a specific woman in that area. He may simply have had friends or family to draw him back to Devon—or its physical attractiveness that brought tourists for holidays. But it seems there must have been a particular reason for his sisters to have had photographs made in Tiverton, probably sometime before 1880.

The anticipated serial that Shiel had written Richards about in the preceding summer of 1899, the "strike story," disappeared from his correspondence and, as suggested earlier, could well have become the similar-sounding story that was published under Tracy's name early in 1901. It remains uncertain why Shiel dropped the story—or was asked to drop it—and how a work so similar could become a serial by Tracy.

Given the similarity of the title in Shiel's letters to Richards to the published serial, it seems hard to believe that Tracy, with whom Shiel had already collaborated in *An American Emperor,* just happened to write another strike story to submit to Pearson on speculation. Pearson may have rejected Shiel's version of the story and turned the project over to Tracy, although Shiel had written Richards that Pearson had requested that he delay his writing, but that he expected to pick it up again soon.

I suspect that Shiel and Tracy had planned to write the serial collaboratively and that Shiel had outlined a plot, but events prevented him and Tracy from actually beginning the work. As noted above, Tracy had begun a series of six short stories for *Pearson's* in July 1899 that ran through December, so he may have had to delay work on the serial as well. And Pearson may have had another serial that they felt was more appropriate than the strike story in the early spring and summer of 1899.

In any event, 1900 seems the watershed year for Shiel and Tracy's future relationship. Shiel had counted on *The Lord of the Sea* as a real moneymaker for him, anticipating success for both the serial and book to follow. When Peter Keary pulled *The Lord of the Sea* from the serialization queue at *Pearson's Weekly,* it was a major financial blow to Shiel. But Keary's action does not appear to have interfered with the ongoing personal and collaborative relationship of Shiel and Tracy.

On 2 July 1900 *The Man-Stealers* was published in London by Hutchinson & Co., but only after a dispute between Richards and Hutchinson over publication rights to this and succeeding novels. (Shiel had never mentioned this title to Richards, and any prior publication as a serial continues unlocated.) Richards believed that first refusal for book rights for new novels from Shiel belonged to him. On the 13th, a new edition of *The Yellow Danger* was published, and in the same month *Cold Steel* was reprinted. A new serialization of *The Yellow Danger* was also appearing. And Phipps had high hopes for *The Lord of the Sea.*

During this flurry of publishing activity, Dolores Katherine Shiel was born at Addison Road, 21 July 1900, possibly with Harriet Shiell helping as midwife. Augusta Horsford may well have assisted her sister, Harriet, who moved from Montserrat to London preceding the birth of Lola. Augusta had been frequently in England during the years preceding and immediately after the turn of the century, keeping an eye on her three daughters and three sons who were attending school at various spots around the country. The census of 1901 shows that she was living in the same apartment building as her son, Cyril, who was just beginning his medical career. The census lists her under her actual first name, "Alberta" Horsford, but stumbles over her age, listing her as being sixty-four years old.[31]

On 3 September 1900 Shiel wrote Richards disputing Richards's claims to publishing rights over *The Lord of the Sea* or "The Second Adam," while begging for a modification of their terms over *Cold Steel* so the whole loss suffered from that book should not fall on him. He also complained again over the scheduling, since Pearson had Shiel's promise that the book would not come out until four months after the serial. Pearson was cutting the serial seriously, leaving half of the first part out. Shiel was still offering *The Last Miracle* with specific royalties: "I say 20% because I don't see why the Boer war should fall more on my shoulders than on yours—in fact, I am against the whole damned thing . . ."

He added: "The last time on the subject of 'The Lord of the Sea' you say you have a right over it, though I confess I can't see that you

31. General Register Office England & Wales, Death Index: 1916–2005 Record for England & Wales, Death Index: 1916–2005. Augusta A. Horsford, Q2 1927.

returned the manuscript and so on: (The manuscript of 'The Second Adam' you did not have from me at all)."

Richards responded on 6 September: "In reference to *The Lord of the Sea* I suggest this as a basis of compromise between you, Hutchinson and myself. I should propose to release you from the agreement with you for the book [*The Purple Cloud*] on the condition that within six weeks of today you deliver to me *The Last Miracle* ready for the printers, in length not falling short of 60,000 words."

Shiel answered 13 September. He provided Richards a receipt, signed by him over a penny stamp, for £70 in full payment for the book copyright and all interests in a story entitled *The Purple Cloud*. A handwritten note initialed by Shiel states: "In the event of Chatto & Windus being able to dispose of the United States rights, two thirds of the net sum received from this source is to belong to the Author." A separate note, apparently by Richards's staff, states: "vide LB 39 17/1/01 Our interest in the American Sales relinquished." No American edition would be published until twenty years later, despite Shiel's hopes for it in 1901.

Shiel had been too desperate for immediate money to gamble on the uncertainty of future royalties of *The Purple Cloud*. Thus, since he had sold his rights to the book, its publication in the fall of 1901 by Chatto & Windus would bring him no additional income.

Correspondence and negotiations with Richards continued. Sir Robert Hart had written an article warning of "the yellow peril" in the *Fortnightly*, and Phipps suggested to Richards on 25 October 1900 that he quote from the article in the Richards ads for the publisher's new books that would appear in Friday's edition of the *Westminster Gazette*.

On 3 November 1900 Shiel requested a £40 advance from Richards against the publication of *The Lord of the Sea*, which he now fears may be too "serious." He is again in "dire" financial straits. He has found the missing leaf (apparently of the proofs) and wants to add four to five thousand additional words to the novel. Richards can publish it by spring, since Chatto is not bringing out the "other one" (*The Purple Cloud*) until the autumn of 1901. It is to appear first, he says, in a monthly paper, starting around Christmas.

During this period, the "strike story" that had so strangely involved Shiel and Louis Tracy in 1899 commenced publication as "The Great Strike" in *Pearson's Weekly* on 29 December 1900 and ran to 13

April 1901. It is a novel of industrial unrest in Northern England. No author was listed on the first episode, but Tracy was identified as the author in the second and later segments. It does not appear that Shiel's relationship with this work will ever be determined, although the fact that the author was not immediately identified leaves open the idea that a collaboration had been planned.

John D. Squires notes:

> In the chapters Shiel contributed to *An American Emperor* and to the four subsequent books he later acknowledged as full collaborations with Tracy, it is fairly easy to spot Shiel's stylistic touches. They are much harder to find in *The Great Strike*. The characters, plotting and style seem much closer to Tracy's normal work than Shiel's. Particularly the character of the villain, Black Sam, "a good-for-nothing man and a virulent Socialist" seems alien to Shiel. He thought himself a socialist, though a proponent of Henry George rather than Marx. Shiel would have been more inclined to write a novel espousing socialism, as indeed he did explicitly in *The Lord of the Sea,* and again in the closing chapters of *The Yellow Wave* (1905). Socialist notions frequently pop up throughout his opus, though generally just in passing. If his initial draft followed Shiel's heart on this point, that may well be why Pearson rejected it. And an outright rejection by Pearson on such political grounds may help explain why his pro-socialist messages were just inserted as asides in most later novels rather than made central to the plot. Even in *The Lord of the Sea* there are so many elements of the story that some readers failed to note the essence of the novel was an attack on private ownership of land based on Henry George's theory.

The Purple Cloud began serialization in the *Royal Magazine* in January 1901, where it ran until June in a highly abridged version. Even Shiel's brother-in-law, Samuel Horsford, wrote Lina saying he liked the story. This short version of the novel is the tale that first caught the attention of many young Edwardians, the story that would remain in the memories of many budding young authors to surface in their stated admiration for Shiel's writing in later years. In many cases, it was this interest that would eventually help secure Shiel a pension, and it was the book that would lead to ongoing recognition for Shiel as an author at least into another century. By the fall of 1897 he was ready for a serial assignment of his own, but he had obviously been working on other novels.

The publication process for *The Lord of the Sea* also continued. On 6 January 1901 Shiel informed Richards (from the Addison Road address) that "Your people have written me saying send the proofs of 'Lord of the Sea' sent you on December 13. I have sent in ALL—proofs and first revise" to Mr. Lyons, Richards's assistant, except for the middle chapter, which he does not have. If the firm cannot find it, Shiel says that he will reread it if they will send another copy. Again he suggests that Richards use a quotation from Sir Robert Hart's *Fortnightly* article in publicizing the new edition of *The Yellow Danger* to counteract a public impression that the book is "wild."

In the meantime, Phipps and Lina were so desperate for money that Shiel made arrangements in early 1901 to move Lina, Harriet, and the baby from their large three-room apartment on Addison Road into less expensive quarters, first to 9 Keppel Street and then to the country, while Phipps would find cheaper housing in the city in which to work. The expectation was that he could write his way out of their immediate difficulties.

A professional photo taken of Lola as a baby documents early 1901 as the period in which the Shiel family lived at 9 Keppel Street. A note on the back indicates that it was taken at this address, while a lovely photo of Lina, hair down and angelic, with baby Lola notes that it too was taken at Keppel Street. The family was living at this address when the census was taken the night of 31 March 1901.

The row of one-room flats on Keppel Street (since destroyed) would house Phipps and his family at several different addresses there over time, as it also would Gussie. It is likely that one could get in and out of these shabby quarters as quickly as one liked.

Lina, Harriet, and the baby were then sent to live at The Pheasant, Chalfont St. Giles, probably in early April 1901. Phipps wrote Richards on 27 March from 9 Keppel Street giving a new address for himself, 45 Acton Street—an address that appeared on his letters until the summer of 1901. The Acton Street address might have been printed on the stationery Shiel used, but without the originals in hand it is not possible to say. Similarly, one can only guess at the dates of most of the letters that Phipps and Lina exchanged during this period of separation, except for Lina's letter that says "tomorrow" will be Lola's birthday. (Shiel's letters consulted are copies by Gawsworth; Lina's are original documents, received by Shiel.)

The family's new addresses would be significant.

Chapter 11

45 Acton Street

Shiel's marriage with Lina would have its ups and downs over the next five years, not helped at all by his ongoing financial desperation. Yet these years would see some of his very best writing. Theirs was an unlikely relationship from the start. Phipps's "love" appears to have been chiefly lust, some affection, and initially a tie to "Baby." Lina appears to have made the best of her marriage to this inconstant and constantly penurious author. And it is amazing that with his repeated efforts to find the money on which to live, to maintain Lina and Lola, and, for awhile, his sister, Harriet, who was caring for them—and possibly some bit of support for his love daughter, Ada—Shiel wrote his most respected fiction: *The Last Miracle, The Lord of the Sea, The Purple Cloud,* and *The Weird o' It*. And more. Where did he find the time?

As he had for years, Shiel made an effort to maintain financial security while writing, writing, writing—now with a family to care for—and it appears that he tried to be as creative as he could in relocating them from the greater expense of London while he found cheaper lodgings for himself until he could work through the most immediate fiscal crisis. It should have been clear that such efforts could only forestall the inevitable ahead. But Shiel seems sincere, hot with passion, as he wriggled through the next year.

A modern description of the country place to which Shiel moved his family notes: "Chalfont St. Giles, with its duck pond, 18th century cottages and ancient High Street is a picturesque village on the edge of the Chilterns, 25 miles from London. The Pheasant Inn dates from the 16th century; Milton lived there while composing 'Paradise Lost.'"

Fortunately, the four months or so that Shiel's family lived in the country are well documented in letters between them. Shiel constantly promises to visit but does not always manage; he sends baby food and powder for Lola and magazines for Lina, forwards mail to his sister Harriet, and occasionally tells Lina how his writing is going. There is family concern over the manner in which Lola's legs are developing, and Phipps constantly advises Lina regarding "Baby's" exercises, clothing, and other health issues.

45 Acton St. / Gray's Inn Rd. / W.C. / Thursday [? March 1901]
My Darling

Just a brief note, as I have been so taken up today with looking for a room, and with other things, that my tiredness prevents me lifting pen. Anyway, I am far from well.

Tomorrow you will receive the Chapman's and other things.

Write and tell me at once how you are liking it over there, the food, etc.

I hope that you won't feel uprooted, and don't forget that you are not in your own house. Those country people are very proud and don't put up with much. I hope that you will like it. Baby ought to be outdoors for most of the day. Here are the letters for Harriet. You ought to write to your mother.

Your dear

The letters between Lina and Phipps that John Gawsworth translated offer an intimate view of their relationship during the spring of 1901 and the burden that Shiel carried with his writing, his struggle for money, and the early interest he had that Lina maintain contact with her family in France. His apparent closeness with Lina's mother and sisters would change dramatically over the next few years, as his financial straits did not improve and as the ties that bound Lina and Phipps weakened.

Queen Victoria died on 22 January 1901, and authors probably had to scramble to ensure that their texts reflected a change in the monarchy. On 27 February Shiel wrote Richards that he had received copies of the newly released edition of *The Yellow Danger* and asked whether there had been any news from America regarding *The Purple Cloud;* on 3 March he expressed disappointment at all the typographical errors in the new *Yellow Danger*. On 7 March he asked Richards whether he might have an advance of £25–30: he is down with the flu, he offers to correct proofs of *The Lord of the Sea* for the Stokes edition, if he likes, but otherwise "let him alter about the Queen to suit the present."

On 9 March Shiel wrote Richards, sorry that he could not send the money but hopes he can soon. He is setting up a new house. Shiel wonders how a 6d edition of *Cold Steel* would do. "It is not a book intended for the literary hundreds, but for the thousands; and what with its coincidence with Ladysmith and other things, I don't fancy it had a fair chance. Personally, I consider it much the most adapted to the reading populace of the things I have done."

Lina wrote him, soon after they moved in April, "Mon cher Phipps"; their baby was described by neighbors as "the prettiest child in Bucks." She was cutting a tooth. Harriet was not sending family letters along to Phipps but would share them with him when he next came to visit. Phipps responded:

45 Acton St. W.C. / Monday [March? 1901]

My dearly beloved

I do ask you humbly to pardon me for not having written before; I have been far from well, and also busy. That doesn't mean that all my thoughts haven't been for you. I received your letter this morning and was agreeably surprised at the improvement in your style. I couldn't help kissing your declarations. One is "crazy" with joy over something sudden and transient, but one is "full" of joy over something lasting, like the possession of a daughter so that expression isn't quite sincere and sincerity is essential to good style. Thank you a thousand times all the same for all the pretty consoling things you tell me. If you love me, multiply your love a million times and you will have mine.

I'll do all I can to be with you on Thursday. It won't be long, darling, before my body is sunk and buried in the flesh of my love: but I try to think of all that lest my brain weaken: and I hope I won't think of it either until I can be beside you: and then we will ride to the stars.

I am very glad that Baby looks blooming. Today I met in the street our friend the mad Doctor who talks of killing off everybody with microbes. I told him that she has bow legs and he thinks it will disappear *so long as* she is not allowed to walk too soon. Therefore, he agrees with Cyril, and it is up to you to look after her.

You'll soon have the journals, and soon after, I hope, the books. Be patient! Remember me to Harriet, and for you and the Baby a thousand kisses.

Your All

Have you written to your mother?

45 Acton St. Gray's Inn Rd. W.C.
Saturday [March? 1901]

My dearly beloved

I received your little note and kissed it a lot. I am afraid that I won't be able to come over tomorrow because at the moment I daren't lose an hour since we have got to have money at once. So console yourself the best way you can until one day next week. I hope you received the Chapman's. I haven't yet sent the gloves or books, but they'll follow soon.

It gave me a little thrill around my heart to hear that you were thinking of me all the time. I wonder if it is true. Needless to say it is true on my part.

A thousand kisses for you, and a few for the Baby and Harriet. I am very glad that Baby is better. You ought to bend her legs from time to time even though she cries. Write again quickly. I love to see your handwriting. Don't forget to write to your mother.

Your Love

I won't forget the money to pay your rent Tuesday.

45 Acton St. W.C. Friday [? April 1901]

My beloved,

I had hopes of seeing you today but it now looks as if there'll be a delay. I received your note and I see that you have made some friends which makes me think "Why doesn't she wait until she has some decent clothes before going to see people?" It hurts me very much to see all the Women in the West End of London in their smart summer frocks and to think that you haven't got any. What makes it worse is that I simply can't make out quite how this comes about. It's damnable luck.

Yesterday I went to fetch Harriet's letters and the girl told me that Les had collected them. Can you imagine the stupidity of that idiot! He collected the letters without knowing your address. I went to get them from him and he wasn't there so all I could do was leave your address and I hope that Harriet has received them by now.

No more this evening, as I am feeling sad. Keep your chin up and expect me soon.

Your "always faithful"
Phipp

P.S. You ought to ask Candida to stay a day or to with you.

Lina responded, Saturday, Two o'clock [April? 1901] with her usual patience.

> My dearly beloved / I have received your letter . . . Harrie has been disappointed in not receiving the money as she hoped. . . As for me, don't be sad that I haven't a dress to my name at the moment. I haven't seen anybody better dressed, and anyway, when one is young and not too ugly one has no need of adornment[.]
>
> Your wife who loves you / Lina / . . .

> 45 Acton St. W.C. Saturday [April? 1901]
>
> My Darling,
>
> I haven't had the *time* to write you yesterday and oddly enough I've even forgotten the Chapman's for Baby. But you'll get it Monday or Tuesday. Monday I hope to write to you to come at once: but don't be too sure! The Three Weird Sisters are fickle, my poor Lili. Meanwhile, if I were you, I would not go about at all until I were dressed up like a bird, and you will be, too.
>
> I hope that Harrie has received her letters which I sent off Thursday evening (a letter and a photograph).
>
> They weren't awfully enthusiastic over the umbrella at the pawnshop though I sang its praises and preached it like a religion. They even asked me, with ill-concealed suspicion: "Is it yours?" I replied: "Yes—or rather it belongs to *Her,* and She and I are One."
>
> I'm waiting for a letter to tell me how things are going, but don't put yourself out to write me too often, except when I send you money or something. It's got hotter lately, and it has occurred to me to tell you to keep an eye on the weather from day to day and to modify Baby's clothing accordingly.
>
> So long, my darling
> Think of me Your Fifi

Shiel had not only been selling the furniture from their former dwelling, he was even pawning personal items like Lina's umbrella.

> 45 Acton St. W.C. Tuesday [? April 1901]
>
> My dearest,
>
> I didn't write to you yesterday as I had to wait two hours at the station down there and I didn't get here till after seven. Today I am sending you the Chapman's, *The Royal, Le Petit Journal* and *Le Petit Parisien*. I was very sad to leave you yesterday. I don't know why: I

hope it wasn't an omen of a long separation. At the moment things are a little odd with us, but perhaps it will all work out in time.

Don't forget to write from time to time. Your letters are always a great comfort to me, especially when you tell me that you love me. As for me, you are the only thing on earth that I love, that I have, and that I want. You must really be my "always faithful," as you said to me. Supposing I get myself up as a woman and we both become nuns? What do you think about that? During the night I'd change my sex and come and sleep beside you. But supposing you swelled? What a scandal!

Think of me. I think of you

Your Love

Love to Harrie Don't forget to *vary* baby's diet!!!

45 Acton St. W.C. / Friday [April? 1901]

My 'Shishi'

I hope you will forgive me for having disappointed you in not going yesterday. I could not, and will not be able to any day next week. While waiting, I send herewith enclosed the money to pay for your week.

We must cultivate our patience while the clouds around us disperse a little: which will I think be soon.

"The Lord of the Sea" is about to be published, and it is quite possible that it will be a success.

Harriet will shortly receive her letters. I kiss you most tenderly, my second soul. Write me news of Baby soon. I hope you don't let her swallow pins and things. You mustn't let her touch anything she can swallow: and don't forget to vary her nourishment as much as possible.

Your Beloved

Lina was generous, as always, with her response. "My darling / . . . We are quite happy here . . . My dear, you know very well that I am not upset with you, for you are The King of Upsetters! . . . I expect you on Sunday without fail. / Harrie sends you regards."

Shiel had been desperately pursuing money from Richards—as well as pawning or selling everything from the umbrella to furniture. On 26 March 1901 he wrote Richards providing a new address (from 9 Keppel St., W.C., but advising of 45 Acton Street) and requests an update on royalties. "I never dreamt of the cumulative efficacy of ha'pennies till now!" [A halfpenny was the standard royalty on a 6d novel.]

On 7 April, he wrote Richards's assistant, James Lyons, regarding his agreements with the firm, his accounts due, and requesting a check. He followed this with a letter on 16 April to Lyons, saying he will stop by for the check. Does Lyons know when *The Lord of Sea* will appear? (These letters all still on stationery with the Keppel St. address.)

That Shiel was not idle at this time with relatively strange literary pursuits was the publication on 18 April 1901 of a poem, "The Cat," in the *Westminster Gazette*. He was also peeved with Lina.

[Postcard] [2 May 1901]

My darling,

I would think it very nice if you had the goodness to answer me when I write, particularly when I send you money.

Have you received the letter I sent on Friday?

Love,

Phipps

[______________________]

Mrs. Shiel
The Pheasant
Chalfont St. Giles
Bucks.

Richards proceeded with plans for book publication in May of *The Lord of the Sea*. On 3 May, Shiel wrote Richards (letterhead 9 Keppel St. W.C., although he may have moved from his Acton St. address to 1 Guilford Place, W.C.) urging him to publish *The Lord of the Sea* as soon as possible, "as otherwise it will kill the other one which is to appear in the Autumn." He was referring, of course, to *The Purple Cloud,* which Keary ran in an abbreviated serial version in another of the Pearson magazine stable—the more upscale *Royal Magazine*—monthly from January to June 1901 with illustrations by J. J. Cameron. Shiel also asked Richards whether he had been in touch with Stokes in America about *The Purple Cloud* as they had discussed earlier. Keary, of Pearson's, had written Shiel that the serial in the *Royal Magazine* had been quite a success, with many complimentary letters received.

Within weeks, Richards published *The Lord of the Sea*. Shiel did not let up. He shortly wrote Richards enclosing *The Purple Cloud*. It is to appear in England in August, he says, so if the American edition of it publishes at the same time, copyright will be assured. Richards, who was not the publisher of *The Purple Cloud,* obviously had no obligation to help Shiel find a publisher for the American edition of that title.

Shiel then wrote Lyons (Acton St. address) on 3 July 1901 disputing liability for the cost of printers' corrections to proofs of *The Lord of the Sea,* and requests full royalties due. On the 4th he wrote again, haggling over the terms of the contract and the pitiful royalties due. "Never you take to writing books," he tells Lyons, "it is a cause of sighing."

One can only wonder at the patience of Grant Richards through these ongoing dealings with Shiel. Lina continued her own level of patience, and would so for another year.

Thursday [25 July 1901]

My beloved Phipps / I received your letter this morning together with the journals and the Chapman's food thank you greatly. / Tomorrow is baby's birthday . . . I expect you Saturday without fail. Think of Baby tomorrow. I kiss you thousands of times. / Your wife / Lina / Love from Harrie

Unfortunately, most of the correspondence during this period is undated.

45 Acton St. W.C. [? August 1901]

My darling,

No letter from you today. It is very possible that you will see me over there tomorrow, but I am not sure. It depends whether I see somebody who ought to be there. Otherwise, I'll write to you immediately afterwards.

I hope that all goes well.
A whole shipload of kisses
Phippie

[45 Acton St. or 1 Guilford Place?] Sunday [? August 1901]

My dearly beloved

A thousand thanks for your letter, and for what you say in it, which made me cry. How nice you are, and good, and altogether adorable. I agree with you that the best thing you could wish me is that we shall always be as we are at present. I also received Harriet's cake and tell her that it's "something like a cake", very good, and that I have almost finished it already.

God grant that I can come over there and fetch you Wednesday and bring you all to London. There are four people who owe me money but I'm not sure if I'll have it in time or shall have enough. O how annoying these constant absurdities are. Always the same stupid story: but one has to put up with it as long as God wishes, I suppose.

Have you heard about the two actresses who committed suicide in Bloomsbury? Two young sisters together, poor girls. My heart bled for them.

I am very glad that all goes well with Baby. In this heat it is essential to look after her bowels because that's their weak spot in Summer.

So long, my darling
Your Fifi

The cake is making me very vicious. They are going to publish your photograph in another paper, and also in America. I have sent them both off.

This was probably a birthday cake that Harriet had prepared for Lola's birthday. Earlier, on 13 July 1901, a review of *The Lord of the Sea* and a photo of Phipps and Lina were published in the *Candid Friend*. It was also in this issue that the first significant comments were raised about Shiel's national or racial origin. The *Candid Friend* was a weekly, established and edited by Frank Harris, that lasted for just over a year. Harris probably wrote the paper's comment:

> The most mysterious of British authors, M. P. Shiel, is fast becoming the central figure of a cycle of legends. It is said that his birthplace has never been revealed to mortal man—I do not know about mortal woman: he is married to a Spanish lady—and his race is as great a mystery as his birthplace. His friends are agreed that he is a blend of two or three of the great races, but they differ utterly as to which two or three of the great races culminate in him. He is a man of disappearances. He will have left his chambers for months, and is believed to be in Ecuador or Teheran, when, at five o'clock on a summer's morning, his neighbors are roused by a furious knocking, and a pale and flurried man is crying at their doors, "I've brought Mr. Shiel's horse! I've brought Mr. Shiel's horse!" Or he has been lost for a year, and a friend, meeting a dusky brood of gipsies on the Great North Road, is driven by a sudden and inexplicable impulse to say to them, "Can you tell me M. P. Shiel's address?" And the swarthy crew cry, in one sing-song, "The Paradise, Brondesbury," or "49, the Chiltern Hundred."

> His books are in keeping with this man of legend. He is a genuine stylist in that his writing is the expression of a personality. Sometimes he writes with extraordinary power, almost with the violence of an inspired madman, and the roaring phrase jostles the violent image: sometimes he writes with a horrible crudity. His imagination is chiefly busied with great happenings that change the destiny of the human race, and shake the world. In "The Lord of the Sea" (Grant Richards), his hero, Richard Hogarth, really Raphael Spinoza, is a young English farmer who realizes, actually realizes as an inspired enthusiast, that the land is the common property of mankind as is the air or sea. Persecuted by a wealthy Jew, he is wrongfully convicted of murder, and condemned to prison for life. He makes one of the most ingenious escapes in all fiction from prison; becomes the possessor of immense wealth; and sets about forcing his land theory on the world by making himself lord of the sea. You can revel in breathless excitement from beginning to end of this rushing book. There is in it a wealth of plot, and an almost luxuriance of incident: Mr. Shiel literally flings his panting reader from astounding event to astounding event, shaving impossibility with a most dexterous skill. Yet, for all its extravagance, the book gives one to think; and Mr. Shiel's amazing madmen are persons of the most ingenious invention.

Shiel responded to the *Candid Friend* with the first version of "About Myself," published in the 17 August 1901 issue. (Revisions appeared in 1929 and 1947.)

> My birthplace, as has been remarked in THE CANDID FRIEND, is, like the burial-place of Moses, wrapped in mystery. To myself the arcanum has been revealed; but it is too sacred for every ear. Let it suffice that it is an island, a small island, set in far, high regions of sunlight and the palm, remote enough from Europe. "Knowest thou the land where the orange-blossom blooms? It is there! It is there!" I was born at the moment of an earthquake and a storm, or, rather, these were born at the moment of me. Nature sneezed at my coming. The sheet-lightning, like a sheeted ghost, came peering into the chamber, winking a million to the second. And, with lullaby rough enough, this mixture of Heaven and Earth and Hell which I call "I," and sometimes "We," came out, and began to cry.
>
> I have spoken of a storm and an earthquake: feeble words to ears in Europe, where such things are amateur. There, however, they are

more literal. That little island (it is called Montserrat) is a very great and holy place, full of passionate woes, the very apex and hub, it seems to me, of the world. God cannot let it be, but is ever at it, it would appear, to destroy it: indeed, it is foredoomed, like Delos (birthplace of Apollo!) sooner or later to disappear (. . .). I have an idea that at the moment of my death it will sink: I do not know if it is true. I have passed on the calm sea some vast, blazing day, like an Eternity of light (whether in the body I know not), close under its piled augustness of crags, and my eyes have filled with tears of love and pity for it, and all its despondent manias, and wayward Orestian frenzies, and coming doom. It has souffraires (hot sulfur-springs), and sometimes, after one of its tantrums, passing invisible ships many a mile out at sea can smell that fume of Hell it sends.

OF SUCH RED EARTH WAS I KNEADED. No one born in such a place can be quite sane, especially if his father, like mine, happens to be a great poet; nor, from boyhood, have I ever set up any pretence of being responsible for my actions. When there was a storm, and all men cowered awestruck, and the bounds of Heaven and Earth were lost, ah, then was my father's heyday! His heart alone was strong: for the storm was his brother, and own father's son with him. I, though then very young, can remember him stalking in a loose robe up and down the travailing house, in the very mood of that bellowing throat without, like Lear himself, with "That's right! How grand! Crack your cheeks, then—rage! blow!" while we others, and my poor mother, had our hands on our mouths, and our mouths in the dust.

NEVER CAN BE EFFACED FROM MY MEMORY that red, heroic figure, as of Prometheus, those outcries of his, those mutterings, and, I should like to add, cursings; but, to tell the truth, my poor father would not curse, though he could not but have wanted to, having the extraordinary taste to be a Methodist preacher, not by profession, be it said, but of that kind they call "local preachers", his trade being that of ship-owner, and many ships he had on the sea, and knew them all by name.

HIS CHILDREN, TOO, he knew by name, though it was something of a feat, for there were nine girls, and then, lastly, I. At each birth of a girl, a prayer-meeting gathered in the house, attended by everybody, for my father was the local "boss", with the sobriquet of "the Governor", the meeting being intended to thank God for the child, but with a mental reservation, a "but" of disaffection, and a hint to Heaven that it would be graceful to make the next a boy. For many years, no boy would come for I was ever stubborn; but my father, a true Irishman, kept plodding on, like the present Czar of Russia, and by a last effort I was evolved, taken to the lamplight, and discovered to be male. Then, while the earth shivered, the storm raved, and Heaven's lightning blinked to see me, there was an added grand racket of prayer and thanksgiving: though why they should have been so very thankful, I, "in the light of maturer experience," cannot tell, cannot tell. But God knows best.

Phipps was just about ready to have Lina, Harriet, and the baby return to London, although dates are uncertain:

45 Acton St. [*i.e.*, 1 Guilford Place?] Wednesday [? August 1901]
My Chichi:

Your letter received informing me that you have arranged to remain until Saturday. Very well, on Saturday I hope to see you. This is to tell you to ask Mrs. Luff to send me immediately bill up to today.

Saturday! It appears to me very, very far away, because I am to have you in my arms. I seem to drowse a letter, as if I were weary, in the dusk, and I dream that I embrace you, clasp you violently, with the plunging ferocious kisses you love, and that you tease me saying another has loved you, but I do not believe it.

I am very busy at the moment.

A thousand kisses for my darling and one on the c—t; and a thousand also for the little one and Harrie.

Hope you received the Chapman's and the journals?

Your Fifi

The maid and I have finished the cake; it has ruined my character.

W. T. Stead reviewed *The Lord of the Sea* as a "Book of the Month" in the August 1901 issue of the *Review of Reviews,* featuring not only Shiel's book but George Moore's *Sister Teresa* as well. On 15 August 1901 Shiel wrote to Stead from 31, Torrington Sqr. W.C. (Any significance of this address is unknown.)

My Dear Mr. Stead:

I was surprised to see today that you had made my *Lord of the Sea one of* the "Books of the Month:" surprised, for you had told me that you had made arrangements for Moore's book, and I did not expect that you would resort to the device of this *two*. As I cannot help thinking that this was done out of favour to me, I am writing to say how kind and good I think that. But it is nothing strange for you to act in that way, is it?

Yours very truly,
M. P. Shiel

P.S. I don't believe that land nationalization would mean the millennium: but that every act of private or public justice is a step in that direction: and that so great an act of justice would be a great stride in that direction. For such as you and me, isn't the question thus: "Is it just?"

P.P.S. If one of the men who help you to run the *Review of Reviews* die, or take to drink, or otherwise fail you, I shall be always glad, if you will offer it me, to take his place. I am at present reviewing and doing *causeries* for the *Daily News:* but have heaps of time.

Chatto & Windus published *The Purple Cloud* that fall. To compound Shiel's financial woes, however, no American publisher could be found, so the 1901 text actually went into the public domain in America six months later. Though he was entitled to royalties on *The Lord of the Sea,* Grant Richards duly applied them first to the royalties previously advanced to Shiel on *Cold Steel.* In short, by this time Shiel had written the books by which he is best remembered today, but was receiving almost no money for his best work.

Recognition came from another direction. On 16 February 1902 young Arthur Ransome wrote his mother that Grant Richards had agreed to see him about a position with his firm. Ransome was hired as an office boy the following week and worked for Richards for six months. When refused a raise, he left for a similar position with the Unicorn Press. Ransome resigned after a year in which he began to sell stories and articles to the magazines. During the time he worked for Richards he was sent to pick up a manuscript from Shiel. According to John Gawsworth, Shiel wrote a letter from Guilford Place in May, but it appears more likely that Shiel stayed at Acton Street until he brought his family to live at 1 Guilford Place from early August 1901 until their separation in 1903. Shiel autographed a copy of *The Weird o' It* with the Guilford address on 1 December 1902. Thus, Ransome's errand would have taken him to the Guilford address.

Ransome's visit to the Shiel apartment, which he described in a faintly disguised manner in his book *Bohemia in London* (dedicated to

Shiel), most likely occurred in May or early June 1902, just prior to Ransome's terminating his job with Richards. He was more specific with his comments about Shiel as he wrote about him in his autobiography many years later—although one might wonder as to the accuracy of memories obscured by time.

> Office-boy and errand-boy alike, I soon knew quite a number of authors by sight. I was sometimes sent to collect a manuscript. It was thus that I met M. P. Shiel for the first time, in a lodging in Guilford Street, where he was sitting on a chair in the middle of a bedroom, writing on a pad and throwing down the sheets as he wrote them to be picked up and put into order by a young woman who was sitting on the floor keeping a baby quiet. I joined her on the floor and waited, watching Shiel and thinking of Balzac. Shiel stopped at last and gave me the bundle of manuscript for which the printers were waiting. Incredibly he said, 'No time to talk now (I had not said a word), but you can come and see me again.' In this way began an odd acquaintanceship that lasted many years, not without its surprises, as when he invited me to supper on a prosperous day when he had about a dozen guests and was living in a handsome flat. Without preamble of any kind he said, 'I want to introduce you to my sister.' I turned to see beside me a smiling negress. I sat next to her at the supper-table and while Shiel was, as usual, discoursing on philosophy, she painted for me a delightful picture of Shiel and herself, small children sitting on an island under a palm-tree, hidden among the leaves of which, in a tin box, he kept his precious manuscripts. I do not to this day know the truth of Shiel's ancestry, but he had in him something of the flamboyant turbulence of the elder Dumas and, like Dumas, he may have owed something to Africa. At the time I met him he had outgrown the period when he had been one of John Lane's young men writing stories in elaborate prose such as *Prince Zaleski* or *Shapes in the Fire;* he was writing serial stories at great length for *Pearson's, Tit-Bits* and such magazines, each chapter ending with a crisis 'to be continued in our next', so that when he prepared them for publication as books he had to disguise as best he could the concessions he had made to please his editors. The best of his books have a queer, flickering light in them, occasional volcanic power and an originality that lifts them high out of the morass of popular melodrama. . . .
>
> I always liked him, even when, after I had presented a letter of introduction from him to a friend of his in Paris, who must have

passed the news on, other friends came rattling at the door of my hotel bedroom, asked for him, said how much they would like to wring his neck, and peered eagerly all around my room as if they half-hoped I might have him there, hidden under the bed . . .[1]

The details of that first visit with Shiel in late May or early June 1902, as he recounted them in *Bohemia in London,* are so fascinating in their detail, disguised though they may be, that they are worth including here.

> It is a joyous day for a young man when one of his articles wins him a letter from a well-known writer. I walked though Bloomsbury with elation, feeling, square in my pocket, the note that invited me to call on a novelist whose work had given me a paragraph in one of my diminutive essays. He was so well known that it was a little surprising to find him in Bloomsbury at all. Why not in St. John's Wood? I asked. Why not in the real country? At least, I pictured a very sumptuous flat. Through the old streets I walked, through the squares of tall old houses once fashionable but now infested by landladies, expecting all the time, as I neared the street he had mentioned, to find more signs of opulence. I found it at last, and it was dingy, miserable, more depressing than the rest. The novelist lived at No. 7. I rang the bell and waited with a fluttering heart.
>
> Presently the door opened a suspicious six inches, and the tousled head of an elderly woman in curl-papers showed itself in the opening. On asking for my novelist, I was told to come in, and driven into the usual lodging-house dining-room. A huge gilt mirror hung over the mantelpiece, faded rhododendrons upside down made a grisly pattern on the wall-paper, the table was covered with a purple tasselled cloth with holes in it, and the furniture was upholstered in a material that had once been pink. The curtains drawn across the windows were yellow and grey with age and dust, and I could not bear to look at the carpet. There were four pictures on the walls, portraits of Queen Victoria and Mr. Gladstone, and two enlarged photographs, coloured, and magnificently framed, that showed the curl-papered lady who had opened the door, dressed in a low-necked evening gown, with jewels about her fat, creased neck, and flowers in her hair.
>
> The door had been left open, and presently she shouted, "Go upstairs! First on the left." The door of "first on the left" was ajar, and a

1. *The Autobiography of Arthur Ransome* 71ff.

baby was squalling inside. I knocked, and went into the most dishevelled room it is possible to imagine. There was a big bed in it, unmade, the bed-clothes tumbled anyhow, several broken chairs, and a washing-stand with a basin out of which someone had taken a bite. The novelist, in a dressing-gown open at the neck, and showing plainly that there was nothing but skin beneath it, was writing at a desk, throwing off his sheets as fast as he covered them. A very pretty little Irish girl, of about nineteen or twenty, picked them up as they fell, and sorted them, at the same time doing her best to quiet the baby who sprawled all over her, as she sat on the floor. They stood up when I came in, and the novelist tried to apologise for the disorder, but the baby howled so loudly that it was impossible to hear him.

"Take it out!" he shouted to the girl, and she obediently picked it up and carried it out of the room.

"That was a very good essay of yours, young man, and I thank you for it. I scarcely thought you would be as young as you are. How young are you?"

I told him.

"Fortunate fellow. Old enough for wine, and too young for liqueurs. The best of all ages. I hope you thank Jupiter every morning for your youth. Ah me, what it is to be young! I was a strapping fellow when I was as young as you. And now! Oh, you fortunate young dog!" He thumped his broad chest, that was covered with thick black hair, as I could see, for the dressing gown had fallen partly open. His big eyes twinkled under their strong dark brows, and he suddenly buried a huge unwashen hand in his curly black hair.

"Aha! You are thinking that it is not worth while to be a success, if this is all it leads to. Eh! What? Yes. I am right. I can always tell. That is the curse of it. Look at my wife, for example. She loves me. Yes. But she does not guess that I know she looks upon me as a big bull baby, very queer and mad, but so strong that it has to be humoured. In fact, when she carried off that vociferous little Victor Hugo, she was only looking upon you as a lamb offered providentially for sacrifice in place of Isaac. She is always afraid I shall throw Victor Hugo out of the window. It is very annoying to know that she feels like that. Funny woman. Pretty, don't you think? But what about that wine? If you go and shout 'Mrs. Gatch!' at the top of that staircase, the she-dragon who runs this place will come and bring up a bottle of something or other. I would shout myself, but you are younger than I."

I crossed the landing and shouted for Mrs. Gatch. Presently she stood below me in the narrow hall.

"Well, and what is it?" she asked crossly.

I was just going to reply, when the voice of the novelist bellowed from his room, like the voice of one of the winds of God.

"Mrs. Gatch, you are a bad-tempered woman. Don't deny it. Bring me a bottle of the best bad burgundy you have in the filthy cellar."

It was clear that Mrs. Gatch was frightened of him, for she brought the bottle at once, wiping it on her apron as she came into the room. We drank out of a couple of glasses my great man brought from a box in the corner. Then he talked of literature, and so well that the untidy bed, the unclean room, the wife and the baby were as if they never had been. In spite of his unwashen hands, in spite of the dressing-gown, he won his way back to greatness. He lifted the tumbler magnificently to watch the ruby of the wine, while he talked of Edgar Allan Poe, and of his methods, and of that wonderful article on the principles of composition. Poe was profound, he said, to have imagined that article, but the article represented him profounder than he really was. From Poe we came to detective and mystery tales, Gaboriau, Sherlock Holmes, and the analytical attitude, and so to the relations between criticism and art. It was a most opulent conversation.

I sat on a three-legged chair where I could see out of the window, and presently noticed the novelist's wife walking up and down on the opposite pavement, carrying the child and a blue parasol. She had not troubled to put on a hat, and she was evidently waiting till we had done our talk. It was clear that they had no other room. And so, regretfully, calculating a time that would leave her at the top of the street, while I escaped at the bottom, not wishing to put her to confusion, I told the novelist of an appointment with my editor, shook hands with him, was pressed to come again, ran downstairs, and walked away up the street. I walked quickly away, but not so quickly that I did not see the little woman hurry back into the house with Victor Hugo, to resume, doubtless, her occupation of sorting the pages of deathless prose that her "big bull baby" dropped from his desk.

I saw him more than once there later, and always the room was in the same condition, the child howling, the wife pretty, untidy as ever, the great man unwashed but working. How he could work! Sheet after sheet used to drop from his desk. Sometimes when I called upon him he would be in the middle of a chapter, and then he would ask me to sit down and smoke, while his pen whirled imperturbably to the end. He could write in any noise, and he could throw off his work completely as soon as the pen was out of his hand. He was quite contented in the lodging-house, living with wife and child in a single room. He seemed more amused than annoyed by its inconveniences. "After all," he would say, "I have to pretend to superb intellect, and the pretence would be exposed at once if I let such things worry me."

One day I had a post-card from him, saying he was going abroad. I did not hear from him again for several years, when a letter that came in a crested envelope told me he was settled in a flat. Would I come to dinner?

He was in Bloomsbury again, but the flat was more comfortable than the room. It was very decently furnished, and quite clean. A book of his, that had had a great success in America, was the explanation of his magnificence. The door was opened by an elderly housekeeper, and I was ushered into his study with considerable ceremony.

He rose to greet me, but sat down again at once, and said that he was very ill.

I said I was sorry to hear it.

"Damn you, young man! You can afford to be. Look at you, you young bullock, and then look at me—a miserable wreck"

He lay back in his chair, with his black hair crisp and curly, his cheeks red and healthy, and his heavy black eyebrows stiff and strong over his active eyes. He was dressed, except that he had not a collar, and the muscles of his throat were as fine and beautiful as those of a statue. I could not think of him as ill.

But from time to time he reached languidly to the table, and took a tumbler of yellow opaque liquid, from which he drank a little, and then, after making a wry face, put the tumbler back.

Presently he explained. "Have you heard," he said, "that a great doctor, a man called Verkerrsen, has been investigating the long life of the Hungarians, and attributes it to the quantities of sour milk that they drink?"

I had not heard.

"Yes," he went on, "The whole matter is explained in an article in the *Medical Journal*. You had better read it." He took a sip from the tumbler, and made a horrible grimace. "Ugh!" he said, "but I think the Hungarian sour milk must be nicer than the sour milk of London. Ugh! Disgusting. But I *must* take it, I suppose."

He loved theories above everything else, and went on sipping heroically till he finished the glass. Then he jumped to his feet, and arched his biceps, and smote proudly on his chest. "Ah!" he cried, "it was worth it. I feel better already. Let's have supper."

Supper was brought in, admirably cooked, and laid on the study table. We sat down to it with the elderly housekeeper. The novelist, restored by sour milk to ebullient health, was as happy as could be, joking now with her, now with me, talking most joyfully. Something crossed his mind, when he was half way through his soup, but it was no more than the shadow of a bird flying over a flower-bed in the sunlight. He bent towards me. "I say," he said, "my wife is dying in Dublin this week. Pass the toast."

I did not know what to reply. But there was no need, for he had passed on instantaneously to a new ingenious notion of his, that everything was a brain, that molecules were brains, that we were aggregations of tiny brains, that the world was a huge brain with us as parasites upon it, and that the universe, made up of brains, was nothing but a mighty brain itself. He could think of nothing else till supper was done.

Then, when the housekeeper had cleared away the supper things, he went to the cupboard and pulled out two long narrow stands, each holding a dozen liqueur glasses. "My own idea," he explained, and proceeded to place upon the table one by one a dozen different bottles of liqueurs—Chartreuse, Benedictine, crème de menthe, anisette, cherry brandy, and several with fantastic names of his own invention. "Let us drink each liqueur to a different genius," he said. "Chartreuse for Alexandre mon cher Dumas, Benedictine for the noble Balzac, cherry brandy for Fielding, anisette for Sterne, crème de menthe—dull stuff, crème de menthe; we'll drink crème de menthe; to—to—to Samuel Richardson. He'd have thought it so naughty."

There was a curious point about this man. He loved the bravery and show of conviviality, but he was not a Hans Breitmann to "solfe der infinide in von edernal shpree." He never got "dipsy," and he hated drunkenness above all other vices. The only time we quarrelled was when, hearing that I was going to see him, another man whom I scarcely knew forced himself upon me, and had to be introduced. The great man plied him with liqueurs till he fell on the floor, and quarrelled with me for six months because he had to help to carry the fellow to his lodgings.

I should like to see him again, but Bloomsbury has been the poorer for some time, being without him. I think he is in France. I never dared ask if the wife lived or died. It would have been so difficult to find the correct manner. Something like this, I suppose: "By the way, that wife of yours; underground or not? Pass the cigarettes."[2]

In his autobiography Ransome described some initial concern he had that while he had dedicated the book to Shiel, the content of his essay might not be well received. He indicated Shiel's reaction:

> I finished it before the summer ended and went up to London with it, a little worried because in one of its chapters I had written of M. P. Shiel in a manner that, though friendly, I feared he might not approve. I told him what I had done and asked if I might dedicate the book to him. Shiel, not hoodwinked in the least, replied, "Dedicate the book to me and libel me as much as you please."

Ransome had another, final, word to say about Shiel in his autobiography:

> . . . The last time I saw him was many years later, in St Martin's Lane. He passed me, panting, a stout elderly man in a velvet jacket, running along the edge of the pavement, in and out of the gutter, elbows well tucked in. 'Wait!' he gasped. 'Back in a minute. I turn at St Martin's Church.' I waited for him and he came back. He had long given up his early belief in sour milk as an elixir of life, at least in English sour milk, but now made a point of running each day from his lodging to St Martin's Church, and strongly advised me to do the same. If a man were to run a mile or two every day, he was sure, there was nothing to prevent his living for ever.

In 1902 Shiel's fiction took a new direction. *In Love's Whirlpool* was serialized in *Cassell's Saturday Journal* from 14 May 1902 to 3 September 1902, and published by Grant Richards as *The Weird o' It* that December. This was the first of a series of novels published between 1902 and 1909 that are sometimes described as his middle period romantics. Unlike the majority of his prior novels, they were set in contemporary England and concerned with something closer to everyday life. In a broad sense they were more like the traditional romantic mystery stories that Louis Tracy typically wrote. But unlike a typical Tracy romance or adventure novel, *The Weird o' It* includes multiple layers of story and philosophical thought. While the serial would be heavy enough with Shiel's promotion of his lifelong person-

2. Ransome, "A Novelist," *Bohemia in London* 255–64.

al agenda, the final version of it, published as a book, is rather overwhelming—graphically realistic in some instances. Thomas Hardy had just recently given up writing novels because of public reaction to his *Jude the Obscure*. Shiel's novel reminds me of Hardy's realism.

The Weird o' It is Shiel's most autobiographical novel—or the one with the most autobiographical hints—including as it does references to his lodgings in 1891, to the much-cited fictional encounters with Ernest Dowson, references to his work as an assistant to Mr. K— of the *Messenger,* and the inclusion of his sisters as (rather untypical of them in real life) characters in the novel. He probably enjoyed their reactions to the manner he used their names over the actions of the women in the story.

There are other references to real-life events in the novel. Jack Hay's flower festival—bringing flowers from the country into the slums of London for the enjoyment of children and adults alike—is probably modeled on the Pearson's "Fresh Air Fund." This program, however, broadly promoted by Pearson's in all its publications, was aimed at taking poor children from their bleak surroundings in the city to the countryside for time in its "fresh air." Started in 1892 for children of London, it was expanded in 1894 to children in the provinces with a total of 74,074 participants. For ninepence each, children were enabled to spend a Saturday in the country with costs paying for "a large beef pie and cake and tea and jam and bread and butter and a good supply of sweet new milk."[3] Under another name, this program continues into the twenty-first century.

As records have become available for the 1891 census, it is now possible to identify James M. Coward, "newspaper proprietor," age thirty-eight, as Shiel's employer on the *Messenger*. Coward was born in Islington, London, ca. 1853; his wife, "Ellen Louisa," was age thirty-two, and a sister, Mary A. B. Cox [*probably sister of Ellen*], was ten, the latter two both also indicated as working on "news." They lived at 11 Clifton Hill in St. Marylebone, London. In the 1901 census, James Munro Coward, "Editor & Mentor [*word?*] to Author," was a boarder at 40–43 Gt. Marlborough St. Chambers, Westminster. He was apparently living by himself. There is no record of the fate of his little newspaper, or for whom Coward was working in 1901, or when he died. That Coward had been important to Phipps was more firmly

3. *Pearson's*, April 6, 1895.

suggested when Phipps included him as a character in a short story written several dozen years later.

An even more exciting discovery in the 1891 census confirms the speculation in part 1 of this biography that the characters Fred and Mary were based on actual people. In fact, "Phipps Shield" is listed in the census as a "lodger" at No. 41, Coldbath Buildings, with Frederick Thaxter (a "railway porter," age twenty-seven) and Mary Sullivan (his wife, age also twenty-seven). Phipps is identified as a "clerk," age twenty-six, born in the West Indies.

It is likely that when Shiel wrote *The Weird o' It* he took his recollections of Fred and Mary, and his lodging with them, included them in his novel, and simply placed the story of an encounter with Dowson within that memory frame. Dowson had died the year before Shiel wrote this novel, and while Shiel may have known Dowson during the concurrent years they spent in untidy parts of London, there is a feel to the story that he simply made use of Dowson's image as a fictional device for the plot. There is no real evidence to support this episode as fact or invention in one way or another—although it is entirely possible that the two could have shared quarters at some time, or that Dowson had introduced him to Fred and Mary at their lodgings where he could stay. How long he shared lodgings with the couple is not known, but probably until he moved to Rugby Chambers late in 1892.

It is from this Coldbath address that Phipps probably worked on the *Messenger* with Coward and probably worked for the International Congress of Hygiene and Demography, meeting as it did in London in the summer of 1891. He may have worked as an interpreter for some unknown period of time—probably helping produce pre-conference and daily translations for the participants and contributing to the twelve-volume set of papers from the Congress that followed. (His name, however, does not appear in that publication in any capacity.)

It was also from Coldbath Chambers that he began to have small contributions appear in cheap magazines. He began to use W. Morris Colles (who was head of the Authors' Syndicate) as his literary agent—writing a large batch of short stories at this address before he moved to Rugby Chambers in late 1892. Thus, one can see why *In Love's Whirlpool* and its subsequent publication as *The Weird o' It* contain clues—if somewhat uneasy ones—regarding Shiel's personal life in the London of 1891.

As a lead-up to the publication of the serial, *Cassell's Saturday Journal* ran a lengthy promotion of the story in its 30 April 1902 issue (p. 688, "Everybody's Business"):

> Our readers will doubtless participate in the satisfaction with which we are able to announce that we have arranged for the appearance in our columns shortly of a new, brilliant story entitled *In Love's Whirlpool,* specially written for the Saturday Journal by the so-gifted writer, M. P. Shiel, author of *The Yellow Danger* and other weird and fascinating novels.
>
> Vivid descriptions, daring flights of imagination, startling and original development of plot, and an almost Oriental richness of colouring are the notable features of Mr. SHIEL'S fiction. But the story now in preparation for our pages, while it is marked by the distinctive quality of Mr. SHIEL'S work, will also, we hint, reveal some new aspects of his genius as a writer.
>
> The work will in short mark something of a new departure, and to the surprises of the story itself there will be added the novelty of a fresh feature in the style of the author. The period of the tale is the present day; it is worked out with dramatic intensity and all the linguistic play of an audacious imagination, and it is moreover pervaded with a powerful love interest. Modern as the period is, the atmosphere of the story is charged with the glamour of romance, and the varied fortunes of the characters introduced will enchain the readers's [*sic*?] attention from the first page to the last. The opening chapters of *In Love's Whirlpool* will appear in Number 972 of the Saturday Journal, published on Wednesday, the fourteenth of next month.

When the serial commenced, *Cassell's* took another unusual step, featuring an interview with Shiel (14 May 1902, p. 727, "*In Love's Whirlpool,* Mr. M. P. Shiel has Something to Say").

> The editor says that he called on M. P. Shiel and asked if elements of *The Purple Cloud, The Lord of the Sea* and *The Yellow Danger* were going to appear in *In Love's Whirlpool,* adding that Shiel was known as the "master of the strange and mysterious." "Yes", was the reply, "but the interest of *In Love's Whirlpool* depends mainly on the simple human emotions. Its chief feature is the passion of love, and that is where I am making to some extent a new departure. The scenes are laid in the mountains of Cumberland—a region with which I am very familiar—and London and Australia."
>
> Shiel says that the book deals with a poison used in everyday life,

and the interviewer asked Mr. Shiel if he was familiar with chemistry. "Well I have spent several terms in a London Hospital, have written on medical subjects, and have made a study of poisons—toxicology as it is termed."

The reporter then asked Shiel where he got his inspirations for his plots. Shiel replied, "It is an odd confession, although my experience is not altogether an unheard of one—but I *dream* some of my plots. I have indeed written three stories which have been dreams from beginning to end. In other cases dreams have given me some hints and ideas. But in every instance my plots come to me. I never have to sit down and laboriously invent them. Having obtained my plot, however, the construction of the novel entails a good deal of earnest work. I commence by elaborating the whole thing in writing, putting down every incident to be described in each chapter, the heads of which I fill in. Even when the story is written, I do not regard it as finished, but go over it again and again, occasionally rewriting it entirely. In some cases I have rewritten a tale three times before I was satisfied with it. Writing a novel is a more serious business than many people suppose. Too much facility in producing a work does not as a rule argue much for the quality of it.

"You remember the quotation about easy writing being very hard reading." The reporter then asked, "Do you impose on yourself any rule as to the daily quantity of work you produce?" Shiel replied: "Yes, I endeavor to produce a fixed number of words a day, or rather every night, for I may mention that I cannot work at all while the sun is shining. I do all my work at night." "I have heard, Mr. Shiel, that your story telling talent is largely of your tropical origin?"

"Well yes, that may be," said Mr. Shiel with a smile. "I was born in the West Indies and I have a dash of Spanish blood. But as an author I have found my abilities as a linguist helpful. I have a passion for languages and speak and write several. This has given me a verbal fluency as well as an insight into the literature of other races.

"Harking back, however, to what I have said about plots, I may mention that in the case of *The Yellow Danger,* I wrote the first chapter without the faintest idea of what was to follow. Yet it has so far been my most successful book—I won't say my best."

"That distinction, perhaps is reserved for *In Love's Whirlpool*?" "Well, although it is in another vein than my previous tales, it is as strong a piece of work as I have ever done. The interest centers mainly on the heroine. There is tragedy and some smart detective work."

Even before the serial version of *The Weird o' It* had commenced publication, Shiel was busily working with Richards on arrangements for its book publication. For all the hard work that Shiel put into his writing, he placed a major amount of time looking after the financial aspects of his work, even if it meant trying to work one publisher against another, to achieve whatever financial advantage he could from his publications.

On 27 April 1902, Shiel agreed with Richards regarding copyrighting *The Weird o' It* in the U.S. Shiel would bear half the cost, presumably against the earnings of the book. Serial publication was planned for about the middle of May. Also on 27 April (receipt marked), Shiel wrote to his longtime agent Morris Colles: "I have brought you my last serial '*The Weird o' It*' with the hope that you will be able to sell it for me *serially* in America. It is already copyrighted over there. The English and American book rights have been taken by Grant Richards." How the book was copyrighted in the U.S. is unknown, since there is no record that shows the necessary publication. Even printing a small selection from it would have sufficed.

Immediately responding to a question from Colles, also on 27 April, Shiel said, "In answer to yours, the book will appear here sometime in the Autumn. The last half of it will be different in book-form, and I am still some way from finishing it. I agree to your commission of 15%."

Phipps wrote Lina in late July that there had been an inquiry from America regarding the book—one must assume this was for serial publication—and that he had asked £100. The title would never be published in the U.S., either as a book or as a serial . . . another blow to Shiel's financial expectations.

Almost two years later, when Shiel and Richards were haggling in January 1904 over the rights to *The Evil That Men Do,* Richards reminded Shiel of a reference that he had made about Louis Tracy in 1902: ". . . the only reference to Mr. Tracy that I can find is in a sentence of yours in a letter of April 27th 1902 in which you say, 'I have just received a letter from my friend Tracy', and asking me as a result of this if I can lend you £20." The specifics of what Shiel anticipated from the contact by Tracy are not known, but they obviously suggest the basis for a comment that Phipps made to Lina in a July letter regarding a "tale" that he and Tracy had presented to *Tit-Bits* magazine.

Shiel's inscriptions in his books are frequently revealing, interesting, and useful to locate him at a particular time. A good example is an inscription in a copy of *The Weird o' It* that appeared on the book market a century after its publication.

> Horace J. Smith / from the Author, 1 Guilford Place, W.C.
> 1st Dec. 1902
> With letter laid in
>
> Excuse me for not answering your very entertaining and witty letter of the 22nd before, as I am troubled about many things. I am sending you a copy of my last book just published, which has one or two things in it with which you will not agree, but which may entertain you. Did you read Wells' Anticipations? You have much the same sort of minds, you and he. But please do not be over-modern: that's horrid. The world will have to unlearn over half of modern science as it has had to unlearn the Ptolemaic System of sun and earth. I sometimes read scientific books just to laugh: the writers know everything.
>
> Yours in haste, M. P. Shiel

Of special significance is his reference to being "troubled about many things." This could be a reference to what had been occurring with his family during the summer, as well as problems that developed over two of his books. Difficulties in Shiel's family life were revealed in his correspondence with Lina, who was apparently drawn to France by the "illness" of her mother. Initially, her sister Micaela had written her on Tuesday, 3 June, regarding a parcel that had been mailed to Lina, commenting, also: "When Mama is better, Mama will send you a summer frock. Mama's health gets worse and worse." Subsequently, in an undated letter, Micaela wrote again, saying, "I send you seventy-five francs in haste so that you may take the train immediately as Mama is very ill. Send us a telegram to inform us of the day, the hour and by which station you will arrive, so that we can meet you. I kiss you warmly. Micaëla. Regards to your husband and kiss baby for me."

Mama's "illness" was never disclosed.

So Lina had gone to her mother—Lola was ill in Dieppe—"Mama is mad about baby," she wrote Phipps on 17 June 1902. Her visit must have done a great deal to improve her mother's health, and her description of the family's activities must soon have begun to sound like a family vacation.

Shiel responded:

[n.p.] Wednesday [? 25 June 1902]

My Darling

Many thanks for your note. I have been waiting for the photographs, but they haven't come. You ought to be very happy with all your family around you, and I fear to be forgotten. I can't come to Paris at present, and I don't know when I can manage it—in a short while anyway, me and you, but meanwhile you must come back immediately.

Here's the week gone since you left and I have truly become amorous all over again.

I won't expect you later than Friday.

Your stories of Baby's little absurdities amuse me hugely. I have a kind of wish to see her again. I hope that you don't let her eat all kinds of extraordinary things.

As to your Mama, tell her that I won't forgive her. She and you have plotted together to make me a widower. The next time she summons you in this fashion I will reply: "Yes, send me Mica, and you will have Lina—but not for long."

Think of me. You are always in my heart; and when I think of you my breast softens, my loins harden—little brute!

Kiss everyone for me, and also the newcomer. I hope she is well.

You haven't said a single word about *Cigarettes*. Do you now smoke? I hope not. I would be terribly disgusted.

I pray to God that he will save and protect you, my truly well-beloved.

Fifi

The book is not yet finished: but it moves on.

Harrie sends you her love.

The photographs that Lina had apparently promised him of her family were soon received. They appear to be photos taken of the girls at school. Phipps's striking reference to Lina's resemblance to a pretty "Spanish boy" would immediately rouse those several Shiel observers who over the years have insisted that he had homosexual tendencies. But Lina was Spanish, and she probably accepted his compliment, "beautiful," without a second thought to her resembling a boy, especially since all three sisters have bangs in the photo. It is likely that this photo was taken when the girls were young teens in convent school. Lina was the closest person to Phipps's sexual life and would have been immediately distressed had she gathered some other meaning from what he said about her good looks.

[Friday 4 July 1902?]

My dear wife:

I write to tell you that I am absolutely and admirably delighted with the photographs. Nothing is more amazing for me than to think that the little being with the "fringe," correct and regular, is my wife. It is very surprising. But she much resembles you as you now are, and also Salva and Mica. Mica has truly the air of a little angel, blissful and ridiculous, and as for you, if I wasn't a Christian, I would certainly have improprieties in my thoughts of this little image of a Spanish boy. You are the most beautiful of all, Mica, the most celestial, and Salva the liveliest.

Write me soon to tell me the date of your arrival. This shall be Friday. You can return there after.

I have had an enquiry from America as to the price of "The Weird o' It" and I have asked £100; but as for the tale that *Tit-Bits* has for me and Tracy I have heard nothing. For the moment I'm broke, but that will stop shortly. I send lots of kisses for Baby and everyone.

Affectionately

Write to Harriet

These two letters in the summer of 1902 are quite informative for their references to Shiel's literary work. The book that he was not quite through with was possibly his revision of *In Love's Whirlpool* to create the book version, which was strikingly different from the serial. But his reference to "the tale that *Tit-Bits* has for me and Tracy" could also have been the book he told Lina he was working on—possibly *The Evil That Men Do*, "partly written" in that summer of 1902, as Shiel's agent A. P. Watt would report to Ward, Lock the next year. John D. Squires has suggested that collaborative serials and books by "Gordon Holmes," and at least one (*Three Men and a Maid*) by "Robert Fraser"—could have appeared in obscure penny papers before their publication as books in 1903 and later. Squires makes clear that we are still far from knowing the full extent to which the men worked with each other, Shiel and Tracy—works that sometimes were published under the pen name, or which part of such works was written by one or the other. The "Gordon Holmes" pseudonym was used on three of them, "Robert Fraser" on another, but it now appears that books under each of their names could have included writing by the other—especially, it appears, those which were originally serialized.

Also, it should be noted that in his July 1902 letter to Lina, Phipps simply says the name "Tracy"—suggesting that Lina would know who Tracy was, and probably knew him in person.

Lina and her family were in fairly regular touch throughout the summer of 1902. Lina must have returned to London sometime in July, and her mother wrote her immediately. "My dear child [Gawsworth translated], it is a week since you left for London, and indeed, it seems to me a century since I have been so long without seeing you and without having news of you, but today I believe that you will not do the same as in the past . . . I expect to leave on the last of the month and I will write to you before, and after, I go . . . Without anything further, you know already how much your mother loves you. [*Signed*] Lola. Salva is writing to you tomorrow."

Lola thanked Lina for the music and cloth she sent, much more material than she could handle. She also urged her to be candid in her correspondence—suggesting that she was not getting a full story of the relationship between Lina and Phipps.

Where Mama Lola was going away is never explained, possibly Spain, but obviously the sisters were glad to take advantage of her absence. Salva wrote Lina:

> I write you this short letter to thank you first of all for the music of The Toreador which you had the kindness to send me, and also to tell you how empty the house is without you and Baby. If I have not written to you before, it is not forgetfulness but I am very busy with my singing and dancing lessons. I am longing for Christmas for then I shall be going to work in London and shall have the pleasure of being among you for some time. In expectation of this pleasure I give you and Baby a big hug. Your sister, Salva. Remember me to your husband.

Immediately their mother was away, Salva wrote to Lina, "sending you 100 francs which Nadine lent me while Mama is away. As soon as you receive this, set off and come. Above all, send me a telegram telling me if you have received the money and also telling me the time of your arrival. I expect you without fail tomorrow. I expect you with impatience. Your sister, Salva. Above all send a telegram.

Nadine kisses you warmly. 17 rue de Madrid Paris."

How long Lina stayed, if she actually made this trip, is unknown, but Micaela wrote Lina on 13 August from Le Tréport, a holiday resort on the Channel coast at the mouth of the river Bresle, at the foot of the highest cliffs in France. (Gawsworth translated her letter from the French.)

> Forgive me, Lina my dear, if I have not written to you before now. I can prove to you that it really isn't my fault. I did not know that all the letters that you wrote to me at the Convent Mama read before me. When I left the Convent I tore up the letters so that Mama should not see them; therefore I could not write to you, not knowing your address. I asked Candida for it and she said she couldn't remember it and that she would send it me. / I wrote to her in London and got no answer. It was only by looking through letters that Mama had that I found your address and as you see, I have made haste to write to you. I am once again at Mama's and have rented a little house to spend the summer, on the bank of the river. We bathe almost every day. Mama is very kind to me now, since I was away she has realized how things are, for she is no longer the same towards Salva. / Write to me soon to let me know if you have received my letter. / I kiss you affectionately / Micaëla / Regards to your husband / Here is my address / Mlle Micaëla Gomez / Poste Restante / Place del la Poste / Le Tréport / Seine Inferieure

"Candida" was apparently a friend of the Gomez sisters who lived in London. Earlier, when Lina, Harriet, and the baby were at Chalfont, Shiel had suggested that Candida should visit Lina. At some point, prior to Micaela's letter to Lina, she had written Candida, asked if she knew Lina's address, and told her: "I have left the Convent and that she can write me at the Poste Restante and should give me her address. Thank you a thousand times. Happy memories . . . Mademoiselle Micaëla Gomez, Poste Restante, Avenue de la Grande Armée, Paris. I have written this letter without saying a word to anyone."

The sisters apparently had to do their best to establish some measure of independence from their "Mama," whom Shiel would soon call "the Spanish Squall." Photographs that Lina had of her sisters wrapped in towels, of Salva sitting on a boat, were probably taken at Le Tréport.

Shiel had also been busy in 1902 with short stories, although several probably were written in 1901 or earlier. In January, his story

"Ben" (a Skin-the-Goat story extracted from *Unto the Third Generation*) was published in the *English Illustrated Magazine*. In February, "The Cashmere Shawl" appeared in the *Penny Pictorial Magazine,* and an "adaptation" from the Norwegian, "The Battle of Waterloo," was published on 24 March in *Cassell's Magazine* (the volume for December 1901 to May 1902). "The Bride" was published in May in the *English Illustrated Magazine*. And in America, "What Happened Behind the Locked Door" appeared by "M. J. Shiel" in August in the *Chicago Tribune,* probably as a result of wide distribution by the National Press Association among now-perished newspapers. (This story appeared under the title "The Tale of Henry and Rowena" in the collection *Here Comes the Lady* [1928], but it had been first published much earlier than either 1902 or 1928—possibly in the 1890s.) This spate of short stories concluded on 6 December 1902 when "Family Pride" was published in the *Pictorial Magazine*.

As previously described, Arthur Ransome visited the Shiel family in Guilford Place during May or early June of this period in 1902, just before Lina went to France. Since *In Love's Whirlpool* apparently was ready for publication in April, it is unlikely that this was the novel that Shiel was writing when Ransome stopped by Shiel's flat either to pick up a manuscript or to visit. The timing is such that he might have picked up Shiel's revisions of the serial for book publication by Richards and then visited Shiel again, a short time later, when Shiel might have been writing *The Evil That Men Do*.

These stories were all wrapped around the serialization of *In Love's Whirlpool* and the collaborative work with Tracy (for *Tit-Bits*) that he mentioned to Lina in July 1902. When proofs arrived for *The Weird o' It,* Shiel was so angry with the changes that he found from what he had submitted in manuscript that he insisted to Richards that his name not even be printed on the book.

Richards answered on 1 October 1902:

> My dear Mr. Shiel / Our letters crossed, I think. I am afraid it is quite impossible to take your name off the book: in the first place my travellers have been offering it to the booksellers since I first arranged for its publication: it is appearing, and has appeared, in all my catalogues under your name; and further, the covers have already been prepared for it. You tell me that as it stands the book is not fit to appear. I have not, of course, read it all, but if it comes up to the promise of the earlier chapters, which I did read in manuscript, I do not

> doubt that it will be as successful as your other books; you yourself told me about a fortnight ago that you thought it would go into several thousands; was the number you said? You must remember that I have made no alterations except to cut 2 paragraphs whose elimination in no way influences the story.

Shiel and Richards met to discuss the issue, unsatisfactorily it appears, and Shiel wrote Richards again with his displeasure with the changes in his text while also offering Richards the opportunity to publish his newest work after its completion as a serial, obviously *The Evil That Men Do*. Richards wrote again on 15 October:

> My dear Shiel / Since I saw you and had your letter yesterday I have been going through the accounts for your books, and I am surprised to find that with the exception of *The Yellow Danger* there has been a loss on each one of them. Under the circumstances, and taking into consideration the fact I cannot see any part of the manuscript of this new novel, I am afraid I cannot sign an agreement now, although I certainly hope you won't make an arrangement with any other publisher yet but that you will be able to submit me proofs as you get them from the paper and that we shall then be able to come to terms. I should be sorry for anyone else to publish this book after all these years, although on the recent cases the result has been so unsatisfactory for both of us.

Shiel continued his complaints about changes made to the text of *The Weird o' It*. Richards responded yet again, saying on 19 November 1902 that he had altered only two paragraphs "to prevent the fear of possible circumstances" to both of them. But he wrote immediately the next day, 20 November, to say, "My dear Shiel / I am very mortified to find that you are right and that the printers have taken liberties with your text without any references at all to me." These had made not much effect, however, and the book simply could not be postponed.

It would be fascinating to know what the two paragraphs were that Richards believed might be troublesome to him and Shiel—libelous? And was this material included in the serial version?

Shiel closed the year's business in December with an agreement regarding the settlement of the issues regarding *The Weird o' It* and the publication by Richards of Shiel's "next" book, that would cause a serious breach with Richards in the future. Richards had written him regarding compensation for *The Weird o' It* and his rights to publish *The Evil That Men Do* "or" Shiel's "next" novel.

17 December 1902

My dear Shiel / I am glad to make the arrangements you wish: that is to say, I will pay you seventy pounds by bill at four months, twenty pounds of which sum with the thirty pounds already paid to you purchases for me all the English, Continental and Colonial rights of *The Weird o' It,* and the remaining fifty pounds of which ranks as an advance against royalties for the novel, *The Evil That Men Do*, that you are now writing or the novel which you can next have ready, such royalties being the same as those originally arranged for *The Weird o' It,* the conditions of the first agreement for which, including the clause dealing with author's corrections, shall govern the agreement of this book. / Believe me, my dear Shiel / Sincerely yours / Grant Richards

17 December 1902 to Grant Richards from Shiel
handwritten on preprinted Richards stationery,
signed by Shiel over a 6 pence tax stamp

My dear Richards: / With regards to your letter of today concerning The Weird o' It and the next novel I may write, I agree to the terms therein set forth & acknowledge the receipt of your acceptance for £70. / Yours / *M. P. Shiel*

A great deal of financial success would accompany Shiel into 1903, but this agreement remained an albatross during the year, and his personal life would undergo a dramatic change as a result.

Chapter 12

"... on account of the Spanish Squall"

After another year of struggling with Lina to keep her with him and away from her mother, any warmth that might still have existed in 1902 would turn bitter by 1903. Their personal ties had been weak from the beginning—Lina a lovely object of lust, a higher degree of affection for her by Phipps than for some, and the child that they shared. It is also likely that the presence of Harriet was a moderating effect on what otherwise might have been a relationship broken much sooner than that coming schism in the summer of 1903.

Two serial novels consumed Shiel's literary work in 1903. The literary agent A. P. Watt sold Shiel's novel *Unto the Third Generation* to the *Morning Leader* early in 1903 for serial publication, while Watt sold (apparently all rights) to *The Evil That Men Do* to Ward, Lock in the summer of 1903—despite the fact that Shiel had *already* sold book rights to that title to Grant Richards for £50 in December 1902—"the next novel that I may write." *Unto the Third Generation* moved first.[1]

24 February 1903 on letterhead of A. P. Watt & Sons Hastings House / Norfolk Street Strand / London, W.C.
to *The Morning Leader*
(copy)

> W. A. Ebbutt Esq., / "The Morning Leader" / Stonecutter Street, E.C. / Dear Mr. Eb[b]utt, / Referring to our conversation of this morning, I now have the pleasure of informing you that I am authorized by Mr. M. P. Sheil [*sic*] to accept the offer which you have been good enough to make for a new serial story from his pen. Under these circumstances, I take this opportunity of putting formally on record the terms of the agreement between us. They are, as I understand, them, as follows:— / (1) / That you agree to purchase the British serial rights for use once in "The Morning Leader" only (after which all rights are to revert to the author) of a new serial story to be written by Mr. M. P. Sheil. / (2). That the serial publication of the

1. This exchange of letters is in the A. P. Watt Archive, University of North Carolina–Chapel Hill. The Watt letters, as might be expected, are copies, while the correspondence from Ward, Lock and MPS are originals.

said new story is to commence in "The Morning Leader" on the thirtieth day of March 1903. / (3). That the said new story is to be of one hundred thousand (100,000) words in length and is to be divided into instalments as follows:— / 2 instalments of 5000 words each / 4 instalments of 4000 words each / 2 instalments of 3000 words each / and the remaining 34 instalments are to be of 2000 words each. 42 instalments in all. / (4). That Mr. M. P. Sheil is to submit an outline of the Plot of the said new story for your approval within the next three or four days and before going on with the writing of the remainder of the manuscript. / (5). That Mr. Sheil is, after you have approved of the [*second sheet*] above mentioned outline, to deliver the first two instalments of the said new story on or before the seventh of March next and the remaining instalments in ample time to enable you to publish at the rate of one instalment daily commencing as provided above on the thirtieth of March 1903. / (6). That for the above mentioned rights in the said new story you are to pay us, on the receipt by you of the complete "copy" or manuscript, the sum of two hundred and fifth [*sic*] pounds (£250). / One line from you confirming the above will oblige. / I am, dear Mr. Ebbutt, / Yours sincerely, [*signed*] A. P. Watt

25 February 1903 from the *Morning Leader* to A. P. Watt

Dear Mr. Watt, / Regarding Mr Shiel's story, I have to confirm the terms set forth in your letter of yesterday's date with the modifications as below: / Clause three. / The story is to consist of two instalments of 5,000 words each, five instalments of 4,000 words each, and thirty five of 2,000 words each. / Clause five to read that after approval of the out-line of the story / 2 instalments shall be delivered 7 March. / 3 more 14 March. / 4 more 21 March. / 4 more 28 March. / and thereafter that we be left with not less than twelve instalments in hand at any date. / Faithfully Yours, / [signed] W. A. Ebbutt / News Editor

10 March 1903 from the *Morning Leader* to A. P. Watt

Dear Mr. Watt, / We received, yesterday, from Mr. Shiel the first instalment of the new story. Its title is to be "Unto the Third Generation" and we have received a synopsis and have come to an understanding as to the general outline of the plot. / Yours faithfully, / [*signed*] W. A. Ebbutt

Unto the Third Generation was published in the *Morning Leader*

from 30 March to 20 May 1903. Apparently some business issue arose, because it was not until 24 May 1903 that Ebbutt wrote Watt that he had "submitted the correspondence in the matter of Mr. Shiel's story [*inserted:* to the proprietors] that have decided to waive any further Question. A cheque due on account of the story will be sent you." The *Morning Leader* management probably wanted to clarify what rights in that title it had purchased.

By 22 July 1903, Shiel was in communication with A. P. Watt regarding Ward, Lock's offer of £160 for book publication of *The Evil That Men Do.* By this time, he was using 64 Frederick St., W., as his address, so he had apparently returned from France.

Chatto & Windus published *Unto the Third Generation* in September 1903. Shiel inscribed a copy "From the author" to Grant Richards on 27 October, indicating the book was signed at and evidently sent to Richards from 7 Medina Mansions, Gt. Titchfield St., London W., where Shiel had evidently relocated from a brief residence at 64 Frederick St. Harriet had probably moved in with Olive or another of the Horsford family—possibly Gussie, if she was in England at the time—until Harriet returned to the West Indies probably in 1904.

While there is no physical evidence that Tracy contributed to *Unto the Third Generation,* much of it seems stylistically very similar to *The Evil That Men Do* in which it was understood that Tracy made significant contributions. Perhaps coincidentally, Tracy's output that year increased from one or two serials or books in previous years to five books published in 1903. It is difficult to judge when some of these were actually written. Most were probably serialized, though none of those five books under Tracy's name in 1903 have been confirmed as having had serial publication. Some of the 1903 books might have been written in 1902 or even earlier. But Tracy's output remained at four or five books a year through 1907. He may have wanted help from Shiel just to keep up with the volume. 1903 was also the year that Edward J. Clode (1868–1941) left Brentano's to start his own publishing firm in New York, and Tracy and Clode became quite close.

Clode's first bestseller was probably Tracy's *Wings of the Morning,* published in September 1903. A great adventure story of survivors of a shipwreck, a desert island, pirates, and a tension-driven romance, this was probably Tracy's most successful work. It went through multiple editions in America, England, and Canada, was placed on reading lists for American public schools, and remains entertaining to the present day. That success sparked a personal and business relationship between Tracy and Clode that continued throughout Tracy's life. This was certainly to Shiel's benefit.

While *Unto the Third Generation* was being published in the *Morning Leader,* Shiel began working on the sale of various other literary properties. He must have handled most of the arrangements from France, where he set up lodgings for himself, corresponding with Lina and his literary agents from various addresses there. He had obviously been unhappy with Lina's ties to her family and was prepared to break away. Shiel's letter of 12 June suggests that Lina had left him for a visit to her sister and then failed to return to England, providing Shiel a reason for breaking their relationship at last.

42 rue de Moscou [near the coast, just south of Calais]
12 June 1903

My little hen,

On the point of my departure from Paris for the country perhaps I can write you once more.

I had nearly come to the decision to tell you what I have decided to do for you in this sad situation, but on account of the Spanish Squall (feeble and sonorous) that your Mama is, I could not.

Naturally the thought of having you with me as my wife as before never entered my head, and it will never enter, but I wanted to tell you, that since you were not in a respectable house, and that such a thing sooner or later would prove fatal in the little story of your life, I wanted you to live elsewhere in Paris, with your Baby, until such a time as you could have lived your own life apart from your excellent Mama and my dear little Mica. I would have done this with pleasure and I would have settled all your little debts with your good, even though eccentric, Mama.

It so happens by a series of windfalls that I am richer (or, rather, less poor) at present than you have ever known me, and that would not have been too great a sacrifice.

So, when your Mama went off the deep end, I was stung for the moment with the idea of snatching you and your baby from her clutches in accordance with International law, but I did not take a single step in that direction.

My poor darling, it would have meant great trouble, expense, and time for me. I can't, and I won't. There are, perhaps, men who would have done it for certain women, to prove their power, their love and so on, but that would not be my cup of tea.

You must remember, darling, that I have my own little life to live, which is no longer than any other, and it would be silly for me to spend it messing around with a group of amusing little women from Seville; in any case it might get into the papers, it might get as far as London, and that I wouldn't like. It is not my fault that you find yourself in the fix you're in: for a day's fun, a sea voyage, and to see poor Mica in her "casa", you threw overboard everything decent, precious, and the real happiness that life can hold, as Esau sold his birthright for a mess of pottage, and it wouldn't be fair for me go to the wall and smirch my honourable name to save you. If you had wanted to break with your Mama while I was here by promising to pay her what you owed her, you could have done. But no it seems to me that you prefer squalor and misery rather than cleanliness and comfort and I must admit that I am not interested enough to drag you away from your Mama by force. I am still very fond of you, but it would be a bit silly, and I absolutely won't.

Another thing, your baby would have to stay with you, at least for several years. What can I do about it? I'm very fond of her too, not because 'it's my daughter', as you seem to think, but because she is a human being I have known who hasn't done any harm to anybody and who has been exposed, defenceless, to the most terrible dangers that human imagination can conceive. But what's to be done? I've done all I can for the moment to have her with me and have not been able to, and, I repeat, I have my own life, which interests me very much, to live.

If you ever want to write to me, send your letter to the above address and it will be forwarded.

Affectionately
M. P. Shiel

I send you my sincere love and I commend you and your baby to God who, so they say, likes to look after children and drunkards.

This is a precipitous end to the marriage of Phipps and Lina, leaving us in factual limbo as to the fate of Lina and Lola. It appears from comments made later in Shiel's life that Lina did not live long after this separation (perhaps dying from tuberculosis), while there is a suggestion in his correspondence with Lydia Furley Jewson, his second wife, that Lola might still have been in France in 1909. What caused this particular shout from Shiel about Lina's lifestyle in France? Possibly a photo she sent him, lounging rather flauntingly, smoking a cigarette, in front of Salva and a servant. Phipps had already told her how disgusting it would be if she were to smoke. Shiel's reference to "drunkards" is quite specific. From Lina's expression in this photograph, she might well have been intoxicated. But this is pure conjecture.

Shiel was not quite so speedily gone from France, however. On an autograph postcard signed, mailed in June 1903 from Shiel to Morris Colles, he said ". . . I am sorry now that I sent you 'Cold Steel' as I have a more suitable for 6d called 'The Manstealers,' a story of the Duke of Wellington, 90,000 words. It is out of print & sold well. I shall be back in England, & then will let you have it. Yours very truly, M.P. Shiel."[2]

In a 27 June 1903 [receipt stamp] letter to Colles, Shiel noted that his return to England, now addressed from Villa des Lilas, St. Pierre les-Elbeuf, Normandie, had been delayed. He was undoubtedly caught up in his separation from Lina and Lola. He enclosed for Colles a copy of *The Man-Stealers* for a possible 6d edition. (A revised edition did not appear until 1908.)

Shiel then moved right ahead with allowing Watt to sell *The Evil That Men Do* to Ward, Lock, despite his sale of that title to Grant Richards—at least, as Richards was to understand it. Preliminary discussions must already have begun, because Shiel wrote to Watt on 22 July 1903 from 64 Frederick St., W.C. (date not photocopied but stamped in by Watt 22 JUL 1903):

> Dear Mr. Watt, / Yours to hand. I have decided to accept Mr. Lock's offer of £160 for the story 'The Evil that Men Do.' I assume that the arrangement will be private between us three, and not a precedent for as to my prices; also, I assume from your letter that my acceptance now makes the contract formal. / I should like to know and shall be obliged if you will find out for me whether, if the story happens to come to 100,000 words Mr. Lock will care (no more money being asked for; also whether he has any preferences as to the length of the instalments; also if he minds letting me know what paper or papers it will probably go into, as that is a guide to me in writing. / Yours very truly, /

2. From ABE listing by James Pepper Rare Books, Inc. of TS of "He Wakes an Echo," with enclosure, as noted 10 July 2002.

[signed] M. P. Shiel

Shiel obviously had no intention of letting Grant Richards hear of the sale of this title to Ward, Lock—"private between us three." Watt immediately passed Shiel's decision on to Ward, Lock.

23 July 1903 from A. P. Watt firm to Ward, Lock (copy)

Dear Mr. Lock, / Referring to our conversation of yesterday morning, I now have the pleasure of informing you that I am authorized by Mr. M. P. Shiel to accept the offer which you have been good enough to make for the new novel he is now writing and which is, at present entitled "THE EVIL THAT MEN DO". The terms of the agreement at which we have arrived are, as I understand them as follow:— / (1). That you purchase the British serial rights of "THE EVIL THAT MEN DO", a new novel partly written and to be completed by Mr. M. P. Shiel. / That the new novel is when complete to be of not less than eighty thousand words in length. / (3). That for the above mentioned serial rights you are to pay us the sum of one hundred and sixty pounds (£160) on the receipt by you of the complete 'copy' or manuscript of the said new novel. / (4). That you are to let us know within the next few days what length you would wish Mr. Shiel to make the various instalments of the story and Mr. Shiel is to deliver the remainder of the "copy" or manuscript at as early a date as possible. / (5). We are at liberty to publish the said new novel in book form on the conclusion of your first serial publication and in any case not later than one year after the date upon which the complete 'copy' or manuscript of the said new novel is delivered to you. / One line from you confirming this arrangement will [*second sheet*] oblige. / Believe me, dear Mr. Lock, / Yours sincerely, / P.S. / I am advising Mr. Shiel that you are desirous of having the first refusal of the British and Colonial book rights of "THE EVIL THAT MEN DO."

23 July 1903 from A. P. Watt to Shiel (copy)

M. P. Shiel, Esq., / 64, Frederick Street, W.C. / Dear Mr. Shiel, / I forgot when writing to you yesterday to say that Mr. Lock expects us, in consideration of his buying the serial rights of "THE EVIL THAT MEN DO", to give him—of course on terms hereafter to be fixed by us—the first refusal of the British and Colonial book rights of the story. To this I take it there is no objection. / I am, / Yours sincerely, (signed)

A. P. Watt.

Something must have begun to make Grant Richards nervous, since he had not heard from Shiel, as promised, so he wrote him on 3 September 1903 (carbon copy, stamped with signature).

> Dear Shiel, / Some time ago, in June I think, you saw Mr. Lyons and made a suggestion to him about the holding over of your new book until next Spring, and you said you would be willing to enter into any arrangement for the repayment of the advance I made you that I liked to propose. You wrote on July 1st from St. Pierre les-Elbeuf acknowledging the receipt of your statements and saying that you expected to be back in England in the course of a week or so and that you would then call with reference to the matter of the new novel. You did not do so, however, and I understand that Mr. Lyons has written to you more than once but has had no reply. Is this treating me quite fairly? / Sincerely yours, / Grant Richards [stamped]

> 11 September 1903 From Ward, Lock to A. P. Watt Esq.
>
> Dear Sir, / We have pleasure in agreeing to the arrangement outlined in your letter of the 23rd July in regard to M P Shiel's new story THE EVIL THAT MEN DO. By British rights mentioned in paragraph 1, we of course understand 'British and Colonial rights.' / We are still waiting, we may remind you, to hear in regard to the book rights. / We are Yours faithfully / For WARD, LOCK & CO., LIMITED / [initialed]

> 14 September 1903 from A. S. Watt to Shiel (copy)
>
> M. P. Shiel, Esq., / 64. Frederick Street, W.C. / Dear Mr. Shiel, / Messrs. Ward, Lock & Co., would now like to know on what terms we can offer them the British and Colonial book rights of your new novel in which they have already purchased certain serial rights. Kindly let me know your views as to terms and I will then see them in the matter and endeavour to bring it to a satisfactory conclusion without delay. / I have only just received Mr. Lock's formal confirmation of my letter covering the terms upon which we have sold the serial rights in your new story and I now enclose copies of the two letters ours of the 23rd July to Mr. Lock and his of the 11th of September to us which form the agreement between you and him. / Believe me, dear Mr. Shiel, / Yours sincerely, (SIGNED) A. S. WATT. / P.S. By the bye, I take this opportunity of saying that we usually expect when we sell the serial rights of a story to have the sale of the book rights also. I mention this as I see you have arranged yourself

with Messrs. Chatto & Windus to publish "THE EVIL THAT MEN DO" in book form. I think there is little doubt if you had asked us to negotiate this sale we should have been able to get you better terms than you have got yourself. / 2 letters encl.

Shiel met with Lyons on behalf of Richards in the middle of October 1903, but Richards and Lyons were not satisfied with Shiel's explanation regarding the status of a new work, which Richards understood would be his to publish. Richards had also noticed that Shiel's novel *Unto the Third Generation* had been published by Chatto & Windus in September.

Richards to Shiel on 19 October 1903 (copy)

My dear Shiel, / Mr. Lyons seems to have carried away a different impression of the interview from what you have. But when you come in, and if I am out perhaps you will see him, you can see how the matter stands. If you can arrange that your call shall be early in this week I shall be obliged. / What is this new book of yours that Chatto has just published? / Sincerely yours, [unsigned]

Meantime, on 24 October 1903, Shiel's intriguing short story "A Shot at the Sun" was published in the *Pictorial Magazine*. Although based on plantations in the American South, this story is redolent with images of slavery, superstition, and the culture of the West Indies, as Shiel might have heard such tales told on darkened porches in his youth.

Shiel may have held back from finalizing the sale of book rights to *The Evil That Men Do* to Ward, Lock even before Richards's inquiry. Ward, Lock kept pressing Watt with reference to these rights, while Shiel had been haggling with Richards over *The Weird o' It* and the rights to his "next" book. He probably also had on his mind the potential sales and publication dates of others of his works, or titles that he had worked on collaboratively with Tracy.

8 December 1903 from A. S. Watt to Ward, Lock (copy)

Dear Sirs, / I shall be greatly obliged if you will kindly let me know, if possible by return, when you propose to begin and end serial publication of Mr. M. P. Shiel's new story "THE EVIL THAT MEN DO". / Thanking you in anticipation. / I am, / Yours sincerely, / (SIGNED) A. S. WATT.

15 December 1903 From Ward, Lock to A. P. Watt Esq.

Dear Sir, / Replying to your letter of the 8th inst regarding Mr M. P. Shiel's new story THE EVIL THAT MEN DO, we should say that though the date is not definitely settled it will probably be early in the new year, and it will be advisable for you to take immediate steps regarding the American copyright, for which purpose we will formally publish here at any time you may suggest. / We understood that Mr Shiel accepted our offer for the book rights of this tale. We have not received a written confirmation from you on the subject, and would be glad of an answer by return 'yes' or 'no'. / Yours faithfully, / WARD, LOCK & CO., LIMITED / [*initialed unknown*]
[*In holograph at top of page:*] Got copy and offer / Appleton / advise Shiel—[*presumably by A. S. Watt*]

Neither A. P. Watt nor Ward, Lock seemed to understand what arrangement had been made for book rights, although it appears that Watt finally felt he had been authorized by Shiel to sell all rights to the novel to Ward, Lock on 22 July 1903 for £160. By following the dates of the correspondence of the various parties involved, it is possible to see how the circumstances developed.

Chapter 13

Re-Enter Louis Tracy

The dispute with Richards over *The Evil That Men Do* dominated the early months of 1904, but Shiel was, if anything, resilient and hardworking. There are records that suggest what he was doing, but they continue to raise more questions than they answer.

Shiel had foreseen the problem he was going to have with Richards and finally advised him on 5 January 1904 that Louis Tracy had collaborated on the serial. Using this detail provided a means to escape his 1902 agreement with Richards. He would not have to tell Richards when all rights to the title were sold to Ward, Lock. The novel had been referred to as "partly written" (by Tracy) by Watt in July 1903 (perhaps referring only to the status of the novel as it existed in 1903). By sometime in 1903 (or 1902!), Tracy undoubtedly helped write some part of the serial version of *The Evil That Men Do* so that it would be ready for publication early in 1904. He may not have known of the manipulation of the publishers by Shiel, but it is obvious that Shiel used Tracy's assistance to his own advantage. In fairness to Shiel, he may have started the sale to Ward, Lock believing that it was only for the serial rights, but that was not the way the business arrangement concluded.

When Shiel wrote to Richards on 5 January 1904 telling him that Tracy had collaborated in the writing of *The Evil That Men Do* and that they could make more money from another publisher, Richards wrote Tracy to ask him about the circumstances before he responded to Shiel. (Shiel had included a check for £50, intending that to be a refund of the "advance" for his "next book" that Richards had paid him on 17 December 1902.) Richards wrote Tracy before he responded to Shiel.

Grant Richards to Louis Tracy, 6 January 1904
(file copy)

Dear Mr. Tracy, / I have just received a letter from Mr. M. P. Shiel, written under what seems to be a misapprehension. He refers to you for the first time as part author with him of a book for the publication of which I arranged, and for which I paid him, some time ago. He now says that you and he have had a better offer for the book which you cannot help accepting. I should be sorry to stand in Mr. Shiel's way or in yours, but it is not, of course, possible for me to allow the matter to be dismissed thus summarily, and I am writing to him to this effect; but at the same time, as he refers to you, I thought it best to write to you also. / Sincerely yours, / Grant Richards [unsigned]

Then Richards answered Shiel on 8 January (letter is a file copy).

My dear Shiel, / Your letter of January 5th staggers me and I am afraid that I must warn you immediately that I shall take what legal steps are open to me to prevent the book which I purchased from you by the agreement between us of December 17th, 1902 being published elsewhere. You now mention Mr. Tracy's name for the first time as having been with you part author of the book, so that I wrote to Mr. Tracy on receiving your letter; and now return your cheque for fifty pounds.

One point: you say "Tracy knows of your letter asking me to pay back the fifty pounds." I do not understand this at all. I have never asked you to pay back the fifty pounds. You yourself suggested to Mr. Lyons that if I would assent to the book being postponed over a season you would be willing to return the sum you had had in advance of royalties for it until it could be published, and I believe in writing to you were reminded of this. This was the only possible basis in which you could have returned the fifty pounds.

I hope this matter may be cleared up immediately and without recourse to law, as the obtaining of an injunction is a worrying business. / Believe me, my dear Shiel, / Sincerely yours, / Grant Richards

Grant Richards to Shiel, 12 January 1904 (file copy)

My dear Shiel, / I am afraid your memory is playing you false and you will find that my legal right to this novel we are discussing is undoubted. On December 17th 1902 I paid you by bill fifty pounds, which was to rank as "an advance against royalties for the novel, 'The Evil that Men Do', that you are now writing", which as I have read part of it is easy for me to identify without this title "or the novel that you can next have ready". To this arrangement I have your written and stamped assent. Some time in the following June you came in to see Mr. Lyons and regretted that you had not been able to deliver the manuscript of the novel, said that you were anxious to publish it serially, and suggested that as its serial publication would delay my book publication and would mean my having to stand out of the money I had advanced a longer time than had been contemplated, you should immediately repay out of the money you would receive for the serial publication the fifty pounds I had advanced, although our agreement should stand and I should, of course, repay the money to you when at a future date, the serial publication being completed, I should be able to make my book issue; or you would agree to any reasonable proposal I might make. To the definite proposal Mr. Lyons on my behalf tentatively agreed; and on August 25th, when he had been expecting you to come in for some time and you had not done so, he wrote you the letter to which, no doubt, you refer, and of which you ask for a copy. Here is that copy:—

"I have been expecting you to look in ere this.

"On looking into your account I find that you owe £26 5s. 2d, and this is apart from the £50 which was advanced on your new book.

"If you can let me have a cheque for the £50 and also as much of the other as possible before the end of this week I shall be very much obliged."

We received no reply to this letter.

Ultimately on October 15th you did write saying that as you understood the arrangement you were to be permitted to bring the book out serially and that I should bring it out as a book in the Spring: that is to say, this Spring. And you go on to say: "What has happened to upset this arrangement? Or nothing has happened, but you think that I may sell the book rights to some firm without letting you know after having already received an advance from you?"

You assure me again that you had told me that Mr. Tracy was part author with you of this book, and you quote my opinion of the collaboration. I cannot remember having ever heard that Mr. Tracy was to collaborate with you in any book, but if you did tell me I could not have understood that it was for the book I had bought; and indeed the only reference to Mr. Tracy that I can find is in a sentence of yours in a letter of April 27th 1902 in which you say, "I have just received a letter from my friend Tracy", and asking me as a result of this if I can lend you £20 [? *unclear on source copy*]. It might be as well, as you tell me it is so Tracy who is responsible for your present suggestion that the book should go elsewhere, if I send a copy of this letter to him, and I shall propose to do so to-morrow unless we can settle the matter satisfactorily in the meantime.

As I judge from your last letter that you are wanting me to take temporary possession of the £50 you have sent me, I am doing so, but you must understand that it is at your disposal at any time, and that I have in deference to your wishes cashed the cheque without any abdication of the legal rights which the agreement gives me. / Believe me, my dear Shiel, / Sincerely yours, [*stamped signature*]

Of course, Shiel had already agreed to let Ward, Lock publish the title, and he and Tracy were ready to free the serial version for publication.

Grant Richards to Shiel, 14 January 1904 (file copy)

Dear Shiel, / It seems to me impossible that you could have misread my letter in the way that your note of the 13th implied. We do not agree as to the facts, nor do we agree in opinion either. I shall be extremely sorry to have to avail myself of my legal rights but it is well to make you clearly understand that I shall do so rather than allow any other publisher to issue the story which I bought of you on December 17th, 1902.

Another point: I was not proposing to send any letter of yours to Mr. Tracy, but as you seem to regard him as your partner in the matter of this novel and as the fountain of the trouble that has arisen, I told you that it was possible I should send a copy of the letter I was myself writing—my letter to you of the 12th—to him that he might be fully aware of the process of the negotiation. I have not, however, done this.

I am glad to hear of a successor to 'The Yellow Danger' and hope that it may have the same success both for your sake and for the sake of your publisher. I shall be very pleased to discuss the matter with your agent. / Sincerely yours, [*unsigned*]

Grant Richards to Shiel, 25 February 1904 (file copy)

My dear Shiel, / If you will come in tomorrow at 4 o'clock I think we shall be able to settle this vexed question between us on the lines of your letter of February 14th but with, naturally, some modifications.

By the way, I have before me a recent letter of Mr. Tracy's in which he says that although he collaborated with you in "The Evil that Men Do", he left all the arrangements, financial and otherwise, in your hands. / Sincerely yours / Grant Richards [*stamped signature*]

While the dispute with Richards was being resolved, other events began to claim attention. Especially interesting is a letter that Shiel wrote to Peter Keary indicating that he had begun a novel based on the Russo-Japanese fray—with an indication that Lina was *still alive* in February 1904.

> 7 Medina Mansion Gt. Titchfield St. W 7th Feby 1904
>
> Dear Mr. Keary
>
> This is to let you know, in view of the "Declaration" that the story is pretty well on, and you can have what's done as soon as you require it (at present with typewriter.)
>
> I have an offer to go out to the seat of war to do graphic descriptive articles à la Stevens, but I haven't accepted it yet, as they offer very little pay. Why don't you send me? I could still do the story; and, if you boomed my name as the author of The Yellow Danger, and would undertake to give my wife £200 in case of my death, I should not want much in money, and should undertake you something with booming. I can get some very special letters to officials in Japan from my friend Yoshio Markino, who is a son of one of the Choshu Samurai; and might even get on one of the battleships, if they are not all blown to the deuce by the time I get there.
>
> If this appeals to you, please send me a wire.
>
> Yours truly,
>
> M. P. Shiel

Yoshio Markino (1874–1956) was a Japanese artist and writer born into an impoverished branch of the Choshu, one of the principal Samurai clans. After four years in America, he moved to London in December 1897; it became his primary residence to 1942. His best-known book was *A Japanese Artist in London* (London: Chatto & Windus, 1910). He was the probable model for the Yoshio character in Shiel's *The Yellow Wave*. He may have met Shiel through Arthur Ransome, who mentions Markino several times in his autobiography. Ransome also collaborated with Markino on one of his earliest published articles, "The Class System of Japan," in *Week's Survey* (21 November 1903): 85–86. Shiel never made another reference to Markino as far as is known.[1]

This reference to Shiel's offer to go to the war site, if £200 were paid to his wife were he to die on assignment, is rather startling given

1. John D. Squires has so identified Markino in correspondence with the author.

the events of the summer before. Shiel and Lina must not have fully separated as of February 1904; at least, Shiel must have felt that the marriage was still in effect, and that he bore some responsibility to Lina as her husband. Unfortunately, there is no specific record that confirms the actual death of Lina.

In *Bohemia in London,* written during the summer of 1907, Arthur Ransome mentioned Shiel's comment at dinner that his wife was dying; but Ransome did not date the event at which Shiel made this statement. In 1906, Shiel wrote W. H. Chesson that he had suffered the same kind of loss as had Chesson, the death of a wife. In any event, it appears that Lina lived longer than has been presumed in the past, at least into 1904. From correspondence with Shiel's second wife, Lydia, it can be inferred that Lola was probably not taken off to Spain until 1909.

Finally!—on 2 March 1904 Shiel wrote a letter agreement to Richards offering first refusal for his next book in exchange for Richards's agreement to relinquish his claims to *The Evil That Men Do*. On that basis, publication of the serial began two weeks later, appearing in *People* from 13 March to 7 August. A new serial was also already planned for *Pearson's Weekly—The Yellow Wave*—parts of which were already in Keary's hands.

Shiel to Grant Richards, 2 March 1904

Dear Mr. Richards, / In consideration of your releasing me from that part of the contract between us contained in your letter to me of December 17th 1902 that applies to the publication of the novel that you refer to in that letter as the one that I shall next have ready, but which, Mr. Tracy having collaborated with me in the completion, I am now anxious that Messrs. Ward and Lock should publish, I agree to give you the refusal of the novel that I am now writing for "Pearson's Weekly", part of which is now in Mr. Keary's hands, entitled provisionally "The Yellow Wave", on the following terms:—A royalty of ten per cent on the published price of the first fifteen hundred copies sold and then of twenty per cent on the published price, thirteen copies counting as twelve, the royalty on the Colonial edition being two pence a copy, and the profits from any American book publication being divided equally between us, you paying me on publication the sum of fifty pounds in advance and on account of royalties that may accrue to me. I undertake further in the event of my corrections of the proofs exceeding an average of seven shillings and sixpence per sheet of thirty-two pages that the amount of that excess can be deducted from any sums due to me. / Believe me, dear Mr. Richards, / Very faithfully yours, / M. P. Shiel [*signed over a 6d tax stamp on Richards stationery*]

James Lyons to Shiel, 27 April 1904 (file copy)

Dear Mr. Shiel, / I have to inform you that your acceptance for £28 14s. due April 26th has been dishonoured. Mr. Grant Richards is at present away from the office through illness and I am not proposing to take any steps until his return. / Very faithfully yours, / James Lyons [*stamped*]

Grant Richards to Shiel, 22 September 1904 (file copy)

My dear Shiel, / A few days ago you came in to see me and finding me out left word that you would come in the next day at twelve o'clock; but you did not do so. I am sorry you did not come because it was really necessary that I should see you, among other things with reference to the little financial difficulty between us. I have prevented the solicitors proceeding in the matter but I cannot allow it to stand over indefinitely. / Sincerely yours, Grant Richards [*stamp*]

"Tuesday" (probably early October 1904) from Shiel
at 7 Medina Mansions, Gt Titchfield St. W.
to Grant Richards (transcription by JG)

My dear Richards, / Excuse me for not answering your letter before. I have been away.

I only called in to see you about that war-story that I began for Keary, but as you were out, and what I had to say was not of much importance I did not return. Keary did not *like* the story, and has not published it, nor did I finish it, except in a very perfunctory manner, and as you were to publish it, I called to ask what you thought of the matter. Perhaps I might get a few pounds for it from some fifth-rate man, but I doubt whether you would be over-keen about it in its present form. This being so, will you tell me whether by my agreement with you I shall *have* to give you my next, or whether I can claim the right to have this one published by you (*if* I choose). With regard to the other matter between us, I think that we must agree to differ, as it seems to me that the second contract annuls the first, and, if this is so, a bill accepted on your representation that the second does not annul the first would not stand in law—i.e. as far as I can make out. / Yours very truly / *M. P. Shiel*

Shiel wrote Richards that Keary did not like the war story, so he had only finished it in a perfunctory manner, that it cannot be taken serially, and that he is not sure that Richards would like it as it stands—will it count as his obligatory next book per his contract with Richards? Richards reacted angrily to what he perceived as another effort by Shiel to find a way out of his obligation to Richards.

> Grant Richards to Shiel, 7 October 1904 (file copy)
>
> My dear Shiel, / I have looked at the letter of agreement from you dated March 2nd, 1904, and I find that it only gives me a right over the book provisionally entitled 'The Yellow Wave', and then it is only the right of refusal on certain terms; you cannot force me to publish it. Please let me hear from you immediately about this. / Sincerely yours, / Grant Richards [stamp?]

Richards eventually was a complete loser in this affair. He had to declare bankruptcy in late 1904; Alexander Moring acquired his assets—and his liabilities. The receivership demanded £75 from Shiel, including the £50 that Richards had advanced Shiel in December 1902 for *The Evil That Men Do*. It is unlikely that Shiel returned any money.

The Evil That Men Do was finally serialized in *People* from 13 March to 7 August 1904 and published as a book by Ward, Lock in September 1904. Shiel inscribed a copy of the book to K. Price on 21 September 1904—an inscription only weeks after publication and one that raises an important question. Shiel was very likely in the Chepstow vicinity when he inscribed the book. He had begun a relationship with the John Price family of Woolaston as early as spring 1903, as suggested by his reference to their address, "Woodside," in *The Lost Viol*. This relationship would leave a major mark on his life. It seems reasonable, given the date of the inscription and the likely location where Phipps was at the time, that the book was inscribed to a member of this Price family, but which member of the Price family was it? Most likely an older sister, Kate, age twenty-eight.

Since *The Evil That Men Do* appears to have been conceived and written within the same time frame as *Unto the Third Generation,* and *The Evil That Men Do* was acknowledged to have been written in collaboration with Tracy, there appears to be the need for a completely new inspection of the texts of those works and Shiel's possible relationship with Tracy in writing them. There has always been a feeling of kinship between those two novels. As a pair, they have much of the feeling of the "Gordon Holmes" collaborations by Shiel and Tracy. The two men may well have collaborated on both serials, while Shiel tightened the titles for book publication.

Clode published Tracy's novel *The Pillar of Light* in June 1904. Shiel told Gawsworth that he revised the last half of the novel, although it is hard to find his hand in it. The first half of the story, with its rescue at a lighthouse of a ship lost off the southwestern British coast, is much more gripping than its latter parts. The convoluted identities, and the circumstances that bring romantic conclusions, almost feel like a Shiel plot, even if his style of writing is not visible.

After Peter Keary told Shiel that he did not think very highly of *The Yellow Wave,* Shiel realized the title was not going to be published as a serial by *Pearson's,* so he set Watt on the trail to effect book publication. The sales price finally garnered demonstrates how little revenue was expected from book publication as compared to serial publication. It was late fall 1904 before Watt arranged with Ward, Lock for that firm's publication of *The Yellow Wave.* Shiel was paid £40 for it.

In the meantime, Shiel had begun another novel, *The Lost Viol,* in early 1903. That novel, like others, bore his hallmark references to known geography and persons' names. "Woodside," where his heroine, Hannah, lived, was also the name of the address of the John Price family, although the novel is set on the heights of Norfolk, where homes crumbled from eroding cliffs into the sea; and "Horsford" is named as the lighthouse-keeper. This is the earliest known reference, tenuous though it be, of Shiel to this family near Woolaston, to whom he had letters forwarded during the early months of 1905.

Ward, Lock began the purchase of the new title while arrangements were still being made to complete their purchase of *The Yellow Wave.* They would be sorry to have gotten involved with either one!

Shiel to A. P. Watt

7 Medina Mansions / 4 Nov. '04

> With regard to Yellow Wave your telegram gave £50 not £40 as Mr. Lock's last offer—a mistake of the P.O. no doubt. But I suppose that I must accept the £40. Please do so for me at once. / Yours truly, / M. P. Shiel.

[Note: This holograph letter concludes with the worst scrawl of a signature that I have ever observed in a Shiel letter.]

A. P. Watt to Shiel at 7 Medina Mansions, 8 November 1904 (copy)

Dear Mr. Shiel, / Am I correct in supposing that we are at liberty to authorize Mr. Lock to publish "THE YELLOW WAVE" in book form on or after the 31st of March next? Please let me have a line from you on this point, if possible by return, and / Believe me, / Yours sincerely, / [*unsigned*] /
P.S. / In accordance with your authorization I have now written to Mr. Lock accepting his offer of the sum of forty pounds (£40) for the book rights of the above story.

A. P. Watt firm to G. E. Lock Esq., 8 November 1904 (copy)

Dear Mr. Lock, / I have the pleasure of informing you that I am now authorized by Mr. M. P. Shiel to accept your offer of the sum of forty pounds (£40), payable now, for the British and Colonial book rights for his new novel at present entitled "THE YELLOW WAVE." / I understand from Mr. Shiel that you would be at liberty to publish the story in book form on or after the thirty-first day of March next. / I shall be glad to have your cheque for the above mentioned amount at your early convenience. / Thanking you in anticipation, / I am, Yours sincerely, /[*unsigned*]

Ward, Lock to A. P. Watt Esq., 10 November 1904

Dear Sir, / We beg to confirm our offer for Mr. Shiel's book "The Yellow Wave", and to say that your letter of the 8th correctly expresses the arrangement. Cheque shall be passed in due course. / Yours faithfully, / WARD, LOCK & CO., LIMITED / [*Initialed*]

Holograph receipt to Ward, Lock, 12 November 1904
for payment a/c "The Yellow Wave" presumably
for Shiel or Watt signature (copy)

Memorandum _________ In consideration of the sum of Forty Pounds __(£40)__ receipt of which I hereby acknowledged, I sell and assign to Ward Lock & Co. Ltd. Of Warwick House Salisbury Square London & Publishers the British & Colonial book rights of story entitled '*The Yellow Wave*' by M. P. Shiel / signed / Witness / Address

A. P. Watt to G. M. Lock Esq., 1 December 1904 (copy)

Dear Mr. Lock, / You will be interested to know that I am in receipt of a letter from Mr M. P. Shiel in which he writes:— / "Yours to hand re Mr. Lock's message about 'Yellow Wave'. He can publish any time he likes after January and he can have the MS. as soon as he writes me to say that he is ready for it." / I am, / Yours sincerely, / (sgd) A. P. WATT

Ward, Lock to A. P. Watt Esq., 2 December 1904

Dear Sir, / We are obliged by yours of the 1st inst regarding Mr Shiel's message re 'The Yellow Wave'. We think it very advisable to publish the book as early in the New Year as possible, and shall be glad if Mr Shiel will return the MS to me immediately so that we may get along with the composition. / We are Yours faithfully, / WARD, LOCK & CO., LIMITED / [*initialed*]

The following week Ward, Lock offered to purchase *The Lost Viol* through Watt while their arrangement for the publication of *The Yellow Wave* was just concluding.

Ward, Lock to A. P. Watt Esq., 6 December 1904

Dear Sir, / Mr Shiel has shown us a synopsis of a story entitled "The Lost Viol" which we have read with interest, and we have pleasure in offering Two Hundred Pounds for the complete copyright of a story containing not less than 80,000 words on the lines of the said synopsis, copy to be delivered within six months if possible. / We shall be glad if you will submit this proposal to Mr Shiel, and let us hear if he is agreeable to accept it. / Awaiting the favor of your reply / We are Yours faithfully, / WARD, LOCK & CO., LIMITED / [*initialed*]

A. S. Watt to Shiel at 7 Medina Mansions, 8 December 1904 (copy)

Dear Mr. Shiel, / As the result of our recent negotiations with Messrs. Lock and of your having shown them a new synopsis, they write to me to-day as follows:— "Mr. Shiel has shown us a synopsis of a story entitled 'THE LOST VIOL' which we have read with interest, and we have pleasure in offering Two Hundred Pounds for the complete copyright of a story containing not less than 80,000 words, on the lines of the said synopsis, copy to be delivered within six months if possible" / Will you kindly let me know if this is an offer which you care to accept and / Believe me, dear Mr. Shiel, / Yours Sincerely, / A. S. WATT.

Holograph letter from Shiel to A. S. Watt, 11 December 1904

7 Medina Mansions / Gt. Titchfield St. / Dec. 11th. '04 / Dear Mr. Watt: / Yours to hand, communicating offer by Mr. Lock of £200 for copyright of a story 'The Lost Viol.' / You might say that I will accept that, though it is much less than I am in the habit of getting, provided Mr. Lock will make me an advance of £60 in which case I [*over*] undertake to have the story finished in three months. / It might be a convenience if Mr. Lock will return me the synopsis. / Yours truly / M. P. Shiel / A. S. Watt Esq.

Shiel could not help but make one more try at working out a better deal for the new novel before accepting Lock's offer. Shiel wrote Peter Keary on 12 December 1904 to gauge his interest.

I am sending you herewith a detailed synopsis of a story called for the moment The Lost Viol. I may mention, in confidence, that I sent it first to Ward & Lock who are buying serials to sell, and they write offering me £200 for 80,000 words of it, including book-rights. As this seems very little, and as it would be very convenient to me to get one or two advances, as you have given me before, I am sending it to you to see if you will have it. It is strongly melodramatic, and I think should suit you. I should have sent it to you first, but I have been bothering you too much lately with synopses. However, I have written it out already, and if you will run your eye through it and let me know promptly, I shall be much obliged. I wish too, to write to remind you about your promise to think of me with regard to The Evening Standard & St. James Gazette changes . . . [Ferret Fantasy *Catalogue Q*, November 1981, item 531]

While he had sent a synopsis of *The Lost Viol* to Keary, he pushed on Watt to help retrieve another copy that he had provided Ward, Lock for its consideration.

Holograph letter from Shiel to A.S. Watt, 19 December 1904

7 Medina Mansions / Gt. Titchfield St. / 19th. Dec. 04. / Dear Mr. Watt: / Did you ask Mr. Lock for synopsis of a story 'The Lost Viol', which I asked you to get from him for me some time ago? It will be a convenience if you will send this for me as soon as you can. Mr. Lock wrote to ask if I wanted it but I did not answer him directly. / Yours truly, / M. P. Shiel / A.S. Watt Esq.

Ward, Lock to A. P. Watt, 19 December 1904

Dear Sir, / We shall be glad if you will let us know at your earliest convenience if Mr Shiel accepts the offer made in ours of the 6th inst. / Awaiting your reply / We are Yours faithfully, / WARD, LOCK & CO., LIMITED [*initialed*]

A. P. Watt firm to Ward, Lock, 20 December 1904 (copy)

Dear Sirs, / Referring to yours of the 19th [*inserted in holograph: requiring decision*] I now write to say that I understand Mr. Shiel is willing to accept your offer of the sum of £200, (two hundred pounds) for the copyright of a new novel—although that is much less than he is in the habit of getting in other quarters—provided that you will pay down on the signing of the agreement £60. of the above mentioned amount, Mr. Shiel on his part undertaking to have the story finished and to deliver the complete MS. within three months. / I shall be glad to know that you are willing to meet Mr. Shiel in this matter and will ask you when next you write kindly to return the synopsis of the story. Mr. Shiel would be glad to have it before him when he begins to write the MS. / We are looking forward to hearing from you regarding Mr. Gallon's story to-morrow or on Friday at the latest. / I am, Yours sincerely, / [*unsigned*]

Ward, Lock to A. P. Watt Esq., 21 December 1904

Dear Sir, / We are obliged by your letter of the 20th inst, and note Mr Shiel is willing to accept our offer for his new story THE LOST VIOL synopsis of which is returned herewith in accordance with your request. / Regarding the request for an immediate cash payment, we think this is a somewhat unusual demand, and we cannot quite see our way to acceed [*sic*] to it, unless Mr Shiel is willing to allow discount in regard to the cash payment. We will meet Mr Shiel, and make him payment if the MS meets with our approval. / Please let us hear from you in regard to this, and oblige. / Yours faithfully, / WARD, LOCK & CO., LIMITED. / [*initialed*]

Ward, Lock to A. P. Watt, 5 January 1905

Receipt form, signed and countersigned, indicating payment of £57 on a/c of copyright for "new story" *The Lost Viol*, with note "Sent M.P.S. / J 6" 5 January 1905 receipt from "Shiel" to A. P. Watt marked "(copy) / No. 1129"

Note: This holograph instrument does not appear to be written by or signed by Shiel. It probably represents an in-house document sent to Shiel for him to sign and return as per note on receipt from Ward, Lock to Watt dated 5 January 1905.

Received from Ward, Lock & Co., Limited, the sum of Fifty-seven Pounds in payment on a/c of copyright of new story by M. P. Shiel (to be delivered) at present entitled 'The Lost Viol.' / (signed) M. P. Shiel

Ward, Lock to A. P. Watt Esq., 1 April 1905

Receipt form, signed and countersigned, indicating payment of £100 on a/c of *The Lost Viol*.

Ward, Lock to A. P. Watt Esq., 6 April 1905

Dear Sir, / Regarding M Shiel's story "The Lost Viol." We have had this most carefully counted word for word, and find that it only contains 70,431 words. The story was of course contracted for as an 80,000 word tale, and we shall be glad to learn whether Mr. Shiel can see any way in which he could work in the additional number of words required, or if he is agreeable that we should make a pro rata reduction i.e. Twenty [*inserted five*] Pounds from the account to cover this shortage. / Awaiting your reply, / we are Yours faithfully, / WARD, LOCK & CO., LIMITED. / [*initialed*]

The following letter from Leslie MacDonald, a woman whom John Gawsworth indicated was separated from her husband, shows that Shiel had moved on with his personal life. He must have returned from the Chepstow countryside to London by April 1905.

82 Delancey Street Regents Park N.W.
Wednesday 27th April 1904

Dearest

. . . Come & see me *at once,* as soon as you get this or I shall die —

Leslie

There are no further indications of how this affair proceeded, but the rewards of an earlier romance arrived. On 2 May 1904, Shiel had a letter from Annie Seward, the grandmother of his love-child, Ada Phipps Seward Shiel.

May 2 [1904] 23, Elm Street Cheltenham

Dear Mr. Shiel

You told me to write to you again and you would think about a piano for Ada . . . but I do wish you could see your way to send me something towards her keep. She is getting very expensive and no one to help it is rather hard, if the boss had not been so ill I should not have ask you, but he is still in bed, not had his clothes on yet this year, so it depends upon me. Well, I am glad to tell you she is very well and getting on nice at school. You can just almost see her grow, only she grows to[o] fast for her clothes . . . her mother do not send, one thing she do not say so, but I think only hard times out there . . . I always have been with Nellie in the dark . . .

I hope Mrs. Shiel and your other little girl are well, you yourself. I am reading your tale in paper, you I see have not forgot name or place round Cheltenham, but I can't say I care a lot about the tale, there seem so much wickedness in it. Well dear Mr. Shiel you must excuse bad writing, With kind regard from self and love to you from Ada. Believe me I remain yours very truly

[Annie] Seward

Ada [says?] she will write to you next time bless her.[2]

A note on this letter in the hand of John Gawsworth states: "Mother of Nellie grandmother of Ada. Nellie in South Africa." The prior summer, "Kate" Seward had married another Cheltenham native and apparently quickly departed for the gold or diamond fields of South Africa. Mrs. Seward included photos for Phipps of Ada at age five. There are no records to reveal how Shiel reacted to this or what his relationship was with this daughter over the years, although Ada attempted to write him in 1921 through Grant Richards. It is strange to find Mrs. Seward writing such a friendly letter to Shiel, but she was after assistance . . . and Shiel had probably charmed her during his romance with Nellie. She could also see that he was being published and probably thought it a good time to approach him for financial assistance. Her comment regarding Shiel's "other little girl" in May 1904 helps establish the ongoing presence of Lola past formerly assumed years.

Mrs. Seward's comment about Shiel's familiarity with the Cheltenham area, as it was described in *The Evil That Men Do* (which she was reading as it appeared as a serial), is another indication of the use Shiel made in his stories of the geography he knew so well—and quite frequently that area around the River Wye and south of the Severn is described with great accuracy—just as he now was incorporating fa-

2. Original holograph letter in HRC with notes by JG.

miliar names into *The Lost Viol.*

Shiel would develop several other romantic relationships in this Chepstow area in the years to come, and its geography also figures heavily in the novel that he wrote with Louis Tracy, *By Force of Circumstances,* published in 1909 by Clode under the "Gordon Holmes" pseudonym.

A. Reynolds Morse and bibliographer Norman Lamb developed a great deal of information about the collaborations of Shiel and Tracy that was included in Morse's first bibliography of Shiel's work. However, John D. Squires carried their initial work a great deal further, using information that came to light following their work to establish a much more complete record of the writers' association. This includes works that appeared under the pseudonym "Gordon Holmes" as well as the name "Robert Fraser." Thus, most of the information regarding their work together owes much to Squires's ongoing detective work. As of this writing, fresh details are gradually coming to light concerning these works, but many more questions are generated with these fresh details. Basically, it appears that Tracy did not want to offer Tracy and "Holmes" novels all to Clode in the same year.

In "About Myself" (1929), Shiel remarked on his work with Tracy: ". . . and simultaneously [I] was in with Louis Tracy, with whom I wrote several 'books' under a pen-name, he having 'the idea,' I concocting 'the plot,' writing the first half, he the second—in a wildly different style! I can't think now with what motive I so wasted myself."

The motive was quite clear. It was a means to improve Shiel's income (as well as extend Tracy's own production), while making use of ties that Tracy had with both Ward, Lock in England and Clode in America.

It appears that after Shiel and Tracy discovered they could work so satisfactorily in tandem in producing serial fiction and subsequent book publications from these works, they purposely used such a method to extend the sales of their production capability—and, perhaps, also fill in for each other as demands on the use of their time might develop. There is no information available as to how they shared the revenue from these efforts.

The novel, *The Pillar of Light,* represents an example of the puzzles surrounding how one writer might have helped the other. This title has a complicated publishing history. Clode published Tracy's *The Pillar of Light* in New York in June 1904. It did not appear in England until it was serialized in Pearson's *Lady's Home Magazine* from December 1904 through March 1905. But this left the story incomplete. The name of the magazine was changed to the *Lady's Home Magazine of Fiction* with the January 1905 issue, and the magazine was terminated with the March issue. The serial was not completed until Pearson launched still another magazine, the *Novel Magazine,* in April 1905 that carried the story to its conclusion. It was published by Ward, Lock in England in 1905.

This is actually one of Tracy's better novels, involving intertwining romances, an exciting shipwreck, and a dramatic rescue. The chapters describing those events are very well done, occurring in the initial two-thirds of the novel, presumably untouched by Shiel's revisions. After the rescue from the lighthouse, the novel degenerates into a maudlin resolution of several romances, with no significant changes in style.

Tracy was living at this time (1904) on the North Sea coast at Whitby, where he was a volunteer member of the Coast Guard. Reportedly, he actively assisted when shipwrecks occurred, so those chapters of accidents, survival, and rescue may well have been based on experience. They certainly reflect his love of the sea.

There is no stylistic evidence that Shiel touched the text of the book. However, a reader looking for Shiel in it might be brought to a halt at the beginning of Chapter XIX: "A week passed. In the fickle memory of the outer world the story of the Gulf Rock lighthouse was becoming mellow with age. Men now talked of war in Africa, of the Yellow Peril, of some baccarat squabble in a Westend club . . ."[3]

A. Reynolds Morse, in the original edition of his "Shielography," mentions that Shiel had provided a note in John Gawsworth's copy of the Clode edition of *The Pillar of Light:* "I revised last part of this for its appearance in September, 1905." But he did not identify specific details of the text he revised. In his update of his bibliography, Morse said that he had subsequently been able to compare both book editions of the title, and their texts were identical. Since the title was published as a serial between the two editions of the book, it is possible that Shiel might have modified that text for its book appearance, but the serial text is unavailable to compare with the book. Shiel's contributions to this title may simply never be determined.

---

3. *The Pillar of Light* (Clode edition, 1904) 319.

Finding a lack of interest by Keary in *The Lost Viol* as a Pearson serial, Shiel approved a response by Watt to Ward, Lock. On 10 December 1904, Watt wrote the firm that Shiel had agreed to their terms. "I understand Mr. Shiel is willing to accept your offer of the sum of £200 (two hundred pounds) for the copyright of a new novel. . . . provided that you will pay down on the signing of the agreement £60 of the above mentioned amount." Ward, Lock refused to make an immediate cash payment unless Shiel was willing to accept a discount. Shiel agreed and signed a receipt on 5 January 1905: "Received from Ward, Lock & Co, Limited, the sum of fifty-seven pounds in payment on account of copyright of new story by M. P. Shiel (to be delivered) at present entitled 'The Lost Viol.'"

During these negotiations, the receiver for Grant Richards's bankruptcy was still making attempts to recover monies paid by Richards to Shiel.

From Receiver via Richards to Shiel, 25 January 1905

M. P. Shiel, Esq. / Dear Sir, / With reference to your call here yesterday, I find that by the terms of the agreement you are bound to offer your book, "The Yellow Wave" first to Mr. Grant Richards, so that this is now a matter for the Official Receiver to deal with. / Faithfully yours, / Grant Richards [*stamped*] / [*unclear second signature, apparently for the Receiver appointed out of Richards bankruptcy proceedings*]

Another appeal was made a month later. Regardless of what the receiver was able to say to Shiel, he obviously had no means of retrieving the funds that Richards had advanced Shiel.

Grant Richards to Shiel via the Receiver, 23 February 1905
(file copy)

M. P. Shiel, Esq. / Dear Sir, / I have to-day seen Mr. M. A. Moncrieff, the Trustee, with reference to the topic of our conversation yesterday. I have looked at the books and find that you were paid *£50* in advance on account of royalties on a book to be submitted with a view to publication—which apparently you have not done in that the manuscript has been sold to Mssers Ward, Lock & Co. I must, therefore, ask you to refund the *£50*.

There is also an amount of £26. 14s. 0 due from you on account of a dishonoured bill, judgment for which has been obtained. I should like to know what you propose to do in regard to this bill and the costs incurred in obtaining the judgment thereon. / Faithfully yours, / Grant Richards [*stamped signature*] / H. C. K. Stileman [Stiteman?] / Receiver & Manager [*stamped signature*]

A complete typewritten copy of *The Lost Viol* was delivered to Ward, Lock on 23 March 1905. On 1 April 1905, Ward, Lock paid a further £100 to Mr. Watt (as Shiel's agent), but subsequently alleged that the story contained only 70,000 words rather than the 80,000 contracted for, and withheld £40, the balance of the amount it had agreed to pay, pending some arrangement with regard to the alleged deficiency.

After negotiations, Shiel regarded his contract to have been voided by Ward, Lock's failure to pay the agreed amount and subsequently resold, through Watt, the "volume" (book) rights to John Long, another London publisher. Long was the publisher of the "Dick Donovan" stories, some early science fiction novels, and various publications of a serious nature. Apparently, Watt had worked with John Long previously, but Shiel is not on record for having ever dealt with the firm.

On 11 August 1905, Ward, Lock published *The Lost Viol* (for copyright purposes only, in a few copies not for public sale) and on the next day applied for copyright. The firm subsequently sued John Long to prevent that firm from proceeding with its intended publication of the book. Ward, Lock was granted an injunction in a court decision issued by Judge J. Kekewich in August 1906.[4]

Whether John Long ever recovered whatever money it had paid Shiel for *The Lost Viol* is unknown. The judge stated, "But I must not be understood as indicating the slightest opinion as to the rights between the plaintiffs [*Ward, Lock*] and the author on the one hand or between the defendant [*Long*] and the author on the other." It is likely that John Long never recovered its investment in the book or the costs of the lawsuit.

As a result of the delays brought about by the court case, a serial version of *The Lost Viol* was never published. In the meantime, however, Clode proceeded with its plan to publish the novel in America and announced in *Publisher's Weekly* a publication date of 8 September 1905.

---

4. *Ward, Lock & Co. Limited v. Long* [1905 W. 2720].

In a rather strange move in the early stages of this fracas, since it picks up on the idea that W. T. Stead had attempted to put in motion years earlier, Shiel suggested the creation of a new publication to Peter Keary. He wrote from 7 Medina Mansions, on 19 February 1905.

> I have been thinking that a penny *Review of Reviews* might be a fine success, and I thought I'd submit the idea to you. I think it should make it a Sunday paper, of that quite new type, then it might contain the big news of the week, if any, but no more, and the rest of the copy would be cribbed and gratis. Will you kindly let me know what you think of it? 6d seems too much even for monthly. I, for instance, like to get it for my own reading, but think hard to pay 6d. Mightn't there be a monthly one at 3d, which would then bear the same relation to the *Rapid Review* that the *Royal* bears to *Pearson's Mag*? But I think I prefer the 1d idea.[5]

There are no records of any further discussion of this idea. In the summer Phipps heard from his mother. She wrote him on 26 June 1905, from Gingerland on the island of Nevis. She was brief.

"It is a long time since we communicated with each other." Mr. Killikelly has been superannuated, she said. She and Sal have depended on his salary. Sal wants to go to Montserrat, to open the old business again. Dowdy had had the house bought over in the names of Sallie, Harriet, Ada and Phipps. "Would you kindly give up your claim to me as security to assist Sall's business transaction?" Sall might pay a nominal sum for his giving up his share, she said.[6]

There is no record of Shiel's response, but he apparently did not do as his mother requested. She died in 1910. Several family losses quickly followed. Reginald Horsford died of unknown causes in London in the spring of 1912. Sallie Shiell Killikelly died in February 1913 in the West Indies, leaving a son, Carlton, and a daughter Ada Catherine, while the fate of her husband is unknown. Shiel's brother-in-law, Samuel Horsford, died 18 December 1913 in London—survived by his wife and five children. Horsford had just arrived from St. Kitts the month before (12 October). There were four children left when the Horsford firm was sold in 1929, apparently the three daughters and

---

5. Ferret Fantasy *Catalogue Q* (November 1981), item 532.

6. Original holograph letter is in HRC. This could not be in her hand. It was probably written out by Sallie.

Cyril. Leonard died in 1921.[7] He maintained a London telephone until the early twenties; and was in touch with Phipps in 1919. It is likely that after Samuel died, Gussie stayed on to live in London, probably with Muriel who owned a number of properties at Brunswick Square. Harriet rented out the lower floor of the family property in Plymouth, Montserrat, until it was eventually sold to the surviving family members' benefit. But those events lie ahead.

Shiel published two books under his own name in 1905. Ward, Lock issued his novelization of the Russo-Japanese War in June, *The Yellow Wave*—a story that Keary and Richards had both passed on as either a serial or a book. It is unlikely that Tracy was involved with this title. Since Ward, Lock had planned the publication of this novel for the summer of 1905—undoubtedly to take advantage of the war—it is understandable why it wanted to delay *The Lost Viol,* regardless of the dispute with Shiel over the number of words he had written for that title. As noted, Clode released Shiel's *The Lost Viol* in America in September. Ward, Lock finally published the book in 1908, although that firm had produced a few copies for copyright purposes in 1905. This middle-period romantic novel was stronger than others, several of which Tracy obviously had a hand in.

A major friendship developed when Shiel wrote a letter to Wilfred[8] Hugh Chesson, the husband of the successful poet and critic, Nora Hopper Chesson, who died on 14 April 1906. (She was born 2 January 1871 and married Chesson in 1901. It was said that she had been an influence on Yeats.)[9]

---

7. General Register Office England & Wales, Death Index: 1916–2005. Samuel L. Horsford Q3 1921.

8. Chesson's name is spelled "Wilfrid" and "Wilfred" in various sources; the latter is correct.

9. The guide to the W. H. Chesson Papers at Georgetown University (prepared by Ted L. Jackson) provides a succinct but comprehensive biography of both W. H. Chesson and his wife Norah Hopper Chesson.

> "Wilfred Hugh Chesson (1870–1953), a son of the famous secretary of the Aborigines Protection Society, Frederick William Chesson (1833–1888), was an author, publisher's reader, critic, book collector and freelance literary journalist best known for his biography of the graphic artist George Cruikshank, his acknowledged discovery of Joseph Conrad's first novel *Almayer's Folly,* and his marriage in 1901 to the prominent poet Eleanor Jane 'Nora' Hopper. During the 1890's Chesson's career began in

Elmdale / Chepstow / April 1906 /

Dear Sir: / Though personally unknown to you, I venture to write to express my great sympathy with you for what has happened. I, too, have felt it, for though I have never seen her, her mind and personality have been known to me through her writings, and by report. And now one says "so young and so fair." I am very sorry for you. / Yours very sincerely / M. P. Shiel

The resulting correspondence between Shiel and Chesson (1870–1953) would last until Shiel died, and provides a record of much of Shiel's activities (and addresses) over the years. Chesson was a pub-

---

the office of T. Fisher Unwin, where he worked as a publisher's reader, passing along promising manuscripts to his colleague Edward Garnett, and helped to introduce another colleague, G. K. Chesterton, into the publishing business. Chesson was also the author of two novels, *Name This Child* and *A Great Lie,* as well as other works including children's versions of Shakespeare's stories co-authored by E. Nesbit. From the early years of the 20th century, Chesson worked as a literary freelancer, writing reviews, obituaries, prefaces, and performing editorial work; living still at Childwall, it was necessary for him to take in lodgers to supplement the meager income this provided. Chesson was personally acquainted with many of the most noted literary figures and other luminaries of his day, including Richard Garnett, Oscar Wilde, Joseph Conrad, H. G. Wells, and M. P. Shiel, and contributed to newspapers and magazines such as the *Athenaeum, G. K's Weekly, The Daily Chronicle,* and *The Occult Review*.

"Eleanor Jane 'Nora' Hopper (1871–1906) was a writer who achieved some renown in the 1890s for books of poetry and prose, the first being *Ballads in Prose* (1894), which was praised by W. B. Yeats, followed by *Under Quicken Boughs* (1896), both of which placed her securely in the center of the Irish Literary Revival. The daughter of an Irish military officer and a Welsh mother, she studied folklore at the British Museum with the encouragement of Richard Garnett before embarking on her vocation; it is remarkable that she had no first-hand knowledge of Ireland until 1905, given the thorough, if imagined, Irishness of her work. Nora Hopper continued to write poetry, children's verse, reviews, and drama through her career and contributed prolifically to magazines and journals such as *The Lyceum, Household Words,* and *Yellow Book*. She married W. H. Chesson in 1901 and purchased the house known locally as Childwall in the Kew Gardens district of Richmond outside of London. Chesson complained once that his wife had become so well known as Nora Hopper that 'the press refused her the privilege of being equally well known' as Nora Chesson. She died in 1906 following the birth of their third child, Dagmar, and her last work, the historical novel *Father Felix's Chronicles,* was published posthumously, edited by her husband in 1907."

lisher's reader, editor, critic, and author of a book about the caricaturist George Cruikshank. He became a frequent reviewer of Shiel's work and proposed a book about Shiel in the 1920s, which was rejected. A visit by Chesson to Phipps and Lydia in 1923 offers an engaging look at a meeting between these men who had written each other for seventeen years without ever meeting. Nora's death left a young daughter and son for Chesson to rear. Shiel's letter above obviously refers to his own loss of a wife.

Shiel's only book published in 1906 was not really new. *The Last Miracle* had existed in draft at least since 1898. Tracy's output for the year was also down, but it included the first of the Gordon Holmes titles to which Shiel admitted to contributing. *The Late Tenant* was serialized both in England and America and first published in book form by Clode in October. The serial ran in *Pearson's Weekly* under the title "The Whiff of Violets," from 9 August to 1 November 1906. The serial began a few weeks earlier in America, in the *Sunday Magazine* of the *New York Tribune* from 15 July to 23 September 1906. The "Sunday Magazine" supplement also appeared in a number of other newspapers, including the *Boston Post,* the *Buffalo Courier,* the *Baltimore Sun,* the *Chicago Record Herald,* and many others in the syndicate, reaching by 1912 more than 1,400,000 readers. Gawsworth said that Shiel told him that he had revised pages 1–26 and wrote pages 27–168 and 176–96 in the Clode edition—a substantial part of the story's 285 pages. (Cassell published the book in England the following year, 1907.)

Shiel must have spent much of his time writing his contribution to the serial—from perhaps June until August 1906. Given the collaboration that immediately followed, he must have spent a considerable amount of time in late 1906 on *Three Men and a Maid,* published early in 1907 by Clode under the Robert Fraser pseudonym. We do not know why this appeared as by Fraser in the Clode edition. On 16 April 1907, Richards wrote Clode about publishing the English edition, but he was advised by return mail that Fraser was an English author and Ward, Lock would issue the book in London. When the British edition was finally released in October 1908 it was published under Tracy's name with the title changed to *Fennell's Tower,* though the first printing retained the American title in the running heads. Shiel has not been linked to Tracy's three other novels published in 1907, none published under the Holmes pseudonym.

In November 1906 Grant Richards visited New York and dropped in on Clode, who gave him a copy of *The Lost Viol* as a present. On his return to London Richards wrote Clode thanking him for the book, which he had read on the voyage home. Richards said he had enjoyed it, as he did all Shiel's books. He also warned Clode that it was the sort of book that in England would probably draw the praise of intelligent reviewers, but no matter how much he promoted it, it would be unlikely to attract a wide audience. Though the Clode edition is one of the most common early Shiel titles to be found in the used book market today, it was the last Shiel novel to be published in America until Clode agreed to take 500 sheets from the 1913 Richards edition of *The Dragon* to publish under its imprint.

In many ways, the collaborations of Shiel and Tracy were truly lifesavers for Shiel. It is not unfair to say that the quality of Tracy's stories degenerated without the influence of Shiel's occasional hand, but in fairness to Tracy it must also be said that he helped provide a market for Shiel's work—not only Clode in America but Ward, Lock in England. Tracy's attention became quickly focused on the establishment of a strong political relationship between Britain and the United States with the advent of the war. And, ironically, he began to find success in the movie industry—an interest that Shiel had pursued with such little success a dozen years before!

Chapter 14

Mary Price and Elizabeth Price Sircar

Reading "Mary" of Lydney's plaintive letter to M. P. Shiel of 25 June 1908—printed below—with its comment "Kiss the Dear Children for me hoping both you & Lizzie & they are well," one wonders who these persons were and what their possible relationship to Mary and Shiel could have been, given the circumstances inherent in Mary's letter. (Based on her scrawled address, census records establish "Mary"—long unidentified—as Mary Jane Price, probably born in late 1890.)

That question now seems quite reasonably resolved. "Lizzie" is probably Mary Jane Price's older sister, Elizabeth, born in 1880 to John and Martha Price of The Common, Lydney, in the civil parish of Woolaston, Gloucestershire. Another sister, Kate, was four years older than Elizabeth. Lydney lies some six miles northeast of Chepstow, where the River Wye enters the massive Severn, which empties southwest into the Bristol Channel of the Atlantic. It was along the River Wye and its wooded steeps that Shiel had vacationed for years, and where he took up residence in Chepstow for many months at a time. He urged the journalist W. H. Chesson to visit him there in March 1907, extolling the beauty of the region. Edward Thomas—the nature writer who later gained prominence as a poet—planned to visit Shiel for several days at the same time. Chesson was unable to visit (he had children to care for), but Thomas did spend the planned time with Shiel.

Elizabeth was born in 1880 to John and Martha Price, John a general laborer, age thirty-one in the 1881 Census of England, Martha age thirty—parents of Kate, age five, and Elizabeth, age less than one year. By the 1891 census, John and Martha were parents of Thomas, nine, George, six, and Mary Jane, six months old, all living at Woodside, Lydney, Woolaston. Kate was now fifteen, a housemaid with the Henry Piggott family who maintained the St. Chloe School (a small music school) at Chloe Green. Elizabeth, age eleven, was living near her parents with the farming family of Harry Biddle, working as a nursemaid.

By the 1901 census, Mary was a schoolgirl, age ten, with her brother George, the only son left at home, age sixteen. He was working now, too, as a laborer, as was his father. Kate and Elizabeth were no longer listed in the census, but we now know that by late 1901 Elizabeth had somehow gotten involved with Surja Kumar Sircar (born ca. 1874 in Calenterr, India), who was listed in the 1901 census as a student, living as a boarder in Kensington, London.[1] Why Sircar came to Chepstow in 1901 (after being a student in London early the same year) is unknown, but Elizabeth ("Lizzie") became the mother of Dorothy Violet M. Sircar, born July–September 1902, in Chepstow, and Eileen Phyllis L. Sircar, born April–June 1904 in Chepstow. Sircar could well have been involved in shipping interests that heavily plied the waters into the Bristol Channel of the Atlantic Ocean. There is no record of a marriage between Lizzie and Sircar.

Shiel's relationship with the John Price family of Lydney, Woolaston, Glos., was of long standing. Woolaston was "lower down the mountain" from steep Woodside, with the Severn "trailing itself away through a vale of haze," as he described in one of his own favorite stories, "Many a Tear," published in 1908. He had probably initially arranged to board with the family at Woodside while he was vacationing in the area as early as 1902. In fact, he inscribed a copy of *The Evil That Men Do* to K. Price on 21 September 1904 in the same month the novel was published. This was probably "Kate," who was twenty-eight, the eldest of the three Price daughters who entered Shiel's life in one manner or another. Shiel probably soon established a residence at Elmdale, Chepstow, where he would stay for lengthy periods of time. It was here that he had first written W. H. Chesson about the death of Nora Chesson in April 1906. John was a laborer, as noted above, who probably had been glad to have Shiel as a boarder from time to time, and to whom Shiel could have mail forwarded. When a postcard arrived at Shiel's address in Medina Mansions, London, in January 1905, it was forwarded in care of John Price at Woodside.

---

1. Per census records as noted. On the verso of a letter from Kenneth Shiel to his father in 1946, JG added a penciled inscription: "MPS told me that Kenneth was not his son, though 'Dolly' *was* his daughter. Their mother was named 'Sircar.'" JG would have added this note after MPS's death, and thus apparently never knew the actual status of the three children that Elizabeth Price "Sircar" mothered: Dorothy and Elaine by Sircar, Caesar Kenneth by MPS.

Carte Postale [postmarked] 12—1 / 05 Algere
Mr. M. P. Shiel / Medina Mansions [*struck through*] ℅ John Price / Woodside Woolaston / Gloucester/
[*On colorful postcard face*] Algiers / weather splendid / here / Hope to see / you soon / George

It has never been determined who "George" was. While there is more to tell about the Price daughters, John Price apparently died on 11 August 1927, age seventy-six, as a memorial inscription in St. Andrew's Churchyard, Woolaston, indicates. There is no record for his wife, Martha. Among the effects left in the Kenneth Shiel family by his mother are photographs of a handsome young Indian graduate (probably Sircar), several photos of an attractive woman (probably Elizabeth) and one of a grieving woman standing by a graveside in St. Andrew's Churchyard, again likely Elizabeth.[2]

In April 1905 Phipps had been "on the River Wye" and was still in Chepstow in June. Kate's whereabouts are unknown. Elizabeth would have been twenty-five, the mother of the two young Sircar daughters, and apparently also living in Chepstow. Mary Price was then about fourteen and probably already more than a gleam in Phipps's eyes. Thus, Mary could very easily have envisioned Phipps as a personal romantic interest as well as a neighbor and friend of her sisters, Kate and Elizabeth Price Sircar.

From early 1905 through the spring of 1906 it appears that Shiel spent much of his time in the Chepstow area. After the postcard from "George," in January 1905, addressed to Shiel at Medina Mansions, was forwarded to the Price residence in Woodside, Shiel soon began to address letters from Elmdale, Chepstow. He wrote Peter Keary on 19 February (on letterhead for 7 Medina Mansions) suggesting that a penny version of the *Review of Reviews* might be a success—but he could have been in Elmdale when he wrote Keary. He reported that he had been "on the River Wye" on 5 April 1905. He inscribed a copy of *The Yellow Wave* to Keary, dated 27 June 1905 at Elmdale.

On 21 December 1905, he invited the French translator and editor Henry Davray to "pass some days with me" and provided direc-

2. Kenneth Shiel's daughter, Margaret Parry, has made copies of these photographs available. Only Kenneth Shiel was specifically identified on a photo.

tions for travel by rail from Paddington Station. On 8 March 1906, he wrote Davray from Elmdale concerning the translation of *Unto the Third Generation* into Spanish and French. And he wrote W. H. Chesson on 18 April 1906, from Elmdale, expressing his sympathy over the death of Nora Hopper Chesson.

Shiel's writing energies during this period must have been spent to some large extent on *The White Wedding* and *The Isle of Lies,* both of which are suspected to have been serialized in the *Daily Chronicle* in early 1907 and 1908, but neither has been confirmed. In a note from Shiel to John Gawsworth in the 1930s, Shiel indicated that he had done at least some writing on *The Isle of Lies* in 1899! Shiel's time was also at least partially consumed by novels in which he collaborated with Louis Tracy. *The Late Tenant,* by "Gordon Holmes," was serialized first in America by the Associated Sunday Magazines (e.g., *Sunday Magazine* of the *New York Tribune*) from 15 July to 23 September 1906. Then, within weeks, it appeared in England as "The Whiff of Violets," still under the Gordon Holmes pseudonym, in *Pearson's Weekly,* from 9 August to 1 November 1906. This is the Gordon Holmes novel that feels as much Shiel—in style and content—as *The Evil That Men Do* and *Unto the Third Generation*.

Thus, there is a long trail of correspondence indicating that Shiel may very well have spent over two years resident in Elmdale, Chepstow—probably from February 1905 to the summer of 1907, with occasional breaks for travel to London or brief stays there to attend to business. In fact, he probably was spending time in the area as early as 1902, or even earlier, starting a courtship with the Price daughters . . . and others not identified.

Elmdale is still a small village south of Woolaston and must have been so tiny in the early 1900s that a letter addressed to Shiel at Elmdale got to him easily. Based on his lengthy stay there, and the invitations that he sent to friends inviting their visit, it is possible that he rented or maintained some control of this residence for several years.

That there were breaks is indicated in a letter dated 17 January 1907 to Peter Keary (from 1 Guilford Place, or on letterhead with this address):

> Dear Mr. Keary, I send you enclosed 2000 words on my book for Mr. A. P. [*Pearson*] and thank you very much for the opportunity.

> The book was published today. I haven't read yet, "Get On or Get Out" by Peter Keary, since I am very much "out" for the moment and cherish the shilling, but I shall soon be getting and, I am sure, enjoying it. But think of you breaking out in this way! Yours very truly, M. P. Shiel.

The "book" was *The Last Miracle,* published on 7 January 1907 by T. Werner Laurie, although the book is dated 1906 on its title page. A Colonial edition was published at the same time.

What the "enclosed 2000 words on my book for Mr. A. P." represent is unknown, unless they were part of a serialization of *The White Wedding,* whose publication in the *Daily Chronicle* beginning in March has long been suspected but never verified.

Get On or Get Out was a self-help book, apparently one of a series that Keary wrote in his spare time and published by Pearson.

Chesson reviewed *The Last Miracle* in the *Daily Chronicle,* 4 February 1907. Shiel wrote Chesson on 10 March 1907 (from Elmdale), inviting him to visit and commenting: "I read your articles on me and on my friend Mr. Keary with much pleasure and amusement. Are **YOU** a lobster? *I* am."

Chesson was unable to visit, and Shiel followed with another letter, dated 21 March 1907: "I was sorry that you could not come. But will you when you can & care to? I won't write again, but at any time that you feel like writing to say that you will, here I am ready to be joyful. I gave Mr. Thomas your description of his peaceful *and* public browsing on Parnassus & he thought it rich."

The relationship between Lizzie Price and Surja Sircar was broken, presumably by divorce (if they were actually married), by 1907. Marriage records indicate that sometime between April and June 1907 Surja Kumar Sircar married Nellie Moore in London. A first child, Sushil Kumar Sircar, was born early in 1910, most certainly a child of this union. The birth of a second child, Liela E. Sircar, was registered in July–August–September 1914—the mother listed as Moore. The specific date Surja married in London, whether he and Lizzie had actually been married, and when Lizzie and her two daughters moved from Chepstow to London, are all unknown. But the move would certainly have had to occur after the birth of Eileen in 1904.

Poster for *The Evil That Men Do* serial, 1904
J. R. Hamilton, ed. *My Life with Sherlock Holmes* (1968)
Bell St. N.W. 1, 1904. Archives Dept.
City of Westminster Libraries

Surja Kumar Sircar, common-law husband of Elizabeth Price
Courtesy of the Maggie Parry Family

Elizabeth Price Sircar, mother of Caesar Kenneth Shiel
Courtesy of the Maggie Parry Family

Caesar Kenneth Price Shiel (born 1914), ca. 1950
Son of Shiel and Elizabeth Price Sircar
Courtesy of the Maggie Parry Family

The name S. K. Sircar appears in the London telephone directory from 1912 (when his telephone service was first listed) until the mid-1930s. He was living at Pearl, Precious Stones, 118 Holborn, E.C. In 1982, the name S. Sircar appears in the telephone directory, with an address of 50 Frederick St., W1—an address that will become quite important as Shiel's relationship with the Price family continued as described below. It is possible that this S. Sircar was the child Sushil born in 1910.

Mary Price had written Phipps in June 1908, possibly referring to an attempted suicide or abortion by ingesting some dangerous substance:

> Woodside / Woolaston / Lydney / Glos.—June 25.08
>
> My Dear Mr. Shiel, / I was so pleased to get your letter for I thought you had turned against me since I done the foolish act. I am glad to say I am getting better fast, but the Doctor says it is not all out of my system yet. I am grieved to tell you Father & Mother will not allow me to write to you & say they will put a stop to you writing to me. But we will see about that wont we. When you write on a Friday so that I may get the letter on the Sat[urday] [*lost text*] when they are not [lost text] Chepstow on Thur[sday] [*rest of page torn off*] / [*recto*] over the Chase I passed our dear old spot there, & shall ever remember it as long as I live how I long for those days to come back again but I don't suppose they ever will. I am sorry we did not go up there when you were down. Kiss the Dear Children for me hoping both you & Lizzie & they are well. I remain / Yours with love / Mary

So Phipps was well known to the family, and when Mary wrote him in June 1908 to "Kiss the Dear Children," she was obviously writing to him in London, not in Chepstow where he had so frequently set up residence. Mary would have lived only a few miles from her sister when Lizzie had been living in Chepstow. It appears, however, that between 1904 and 1907 Sircar had moved Lizzie and his two daughters to London, and Mary naively could have believed that Phipps simply had some means of seeing them in London—as a family friend, not as competition for Mary's affection.

In any event, Lizzie and Sircar were separated or divorced by 1907 or 1908, and Lizzie was apparently located in a flat at 50 Frederick Street, most likely where she had lived with Sircar. Then, at some point before 1914, probably in December 1913, Phipps moved into the same address with Lizzie at 50 Frederick Street. He obviously had known Elizabeth, perhaps in the old biblical way, for some time before that. She became pregnant by him in the summer of 1913. There is no record of what became of the younger Price daughter, Mary, who had been so infatuated with Phipps.

Lizzie must have offered shelter to a virtually destitute and broken Shiel in early December 1913. She was already six months pregnant with his son. Whether she had employment and who was looking after her young daughters are unknown. They may have been spending much of their time with their grandparents Price in Woolaston. Sircar had moved to Holborn with his new wife.

Lizzie bore Shiel's son, Caesar Kenneth Shiel, on 13 March 1914, as she claimed on a birth certificate. After Phipps moved into the same address as Lizzie, her daughter, Dorothy Sircar (age thirteen), like her aunt Mary and mother Lizzie before her, became a sexual target for Shiel, who, he said later, had been taught to love as a boy of five in the West Indies by a girl who was eight. He argued later that such early relationships were perfectly natural. In his eyes, Dorothy, at (almost) thirteen, was a mature young woman, a "Hindoo," anyway, he said, and he leaped at sexual play with her—"carnal knowledge," rape in the eyes of the law.

But before those events played out, Shiel had already met the woman who would become the most companionable, as well as the strongest intellectual challenge for him, of any woman in his life—Lydia Furley. It is necessary to fall back to the late spring of 1908 to find her and to introduce Lizzie Price once again.

Chapter 15

"Love's language . . ."

In the 1947 version of "About Myself," Shiel wrote about his second marriage: ". . . it was some fifteen years before I married again, when I met at a lecture, Lydia, who resembles Lina and my mother." While there is no evidence of what the lecture was and how Phipps and Lydia were introduced at that time, there are letters that Lydia began to write Phipps in the early summer of 1908 that pretty well establish the time when Phipps mounted a vigorous intellectual and physical seduction of this bright, pretty, darksome woman. She reminded him of the beginning of this early summer love affair on its second anniversary in 1910.

He had not yet freed himself from several other romantic entanglements in 1908, but Lydia became the woman he pursued more vigorously than any other in his life. In time, in her own way, Lydia became a match for Phipps in her range of interests, her fertile mind, and her activism in social causes, especially those affecting women's rights. She was not the narcissist that he was. She cared for others in ways that he did not. She was honest where he was not. But she loved the inner—almost boyish—gypsy Shiel that he covered with an increasingly thicker, selfish public persona over the years. They remained virtual "other selves" throughout their lives.

Esther Lydia Furley was born 16 August 1872, in Shoreditch, London. Her father was a goldbeater—one of three generations of these artisans. They used hammers to beat gold strips into gold leaf for use in decorating books, furniture, signs, and other objects. The Furley family lived at the end of the street, in a neighborhood long since destroyed, among others with various lines of handiwork—bootmakers, lithographers, and other types of artisans.

Lydia was one of fourteen children, not all of whom survived birth or lived very long. Her mother was Esther, her father Philip Charles Furley. There were four sisters and a brother (or two) in the family for whom records exist. Lydia stayed affectionately close to her sisters and their children throughout her life and theirs. During the early years in which she became involved with Phipps, she brought him into the circle of family with whom she was most closely involved.

Lydia's mother Esther Furley was a widow of fifty-four in the census of 1901, with two of her children still living with her that March evening. Ethel (nineteen) was a waitress, and Horace (eighteen) was an apprentice compositor. A granddaughter, also a "Lydia," less than eight months of age, was also living with her father, Horace, at the same address—with no indication of who her mother was. Widow Furley is listed as head of the household. What is known about our Lydia's other family members follows.

- Phoebe Furley (b. 1865, Shoreditch) married George Alfred Bentley (b. 1860). They had daughters Dorothy (b. 1888) and Olive Mortlock (b. 1889). Phoebe's sister, Matilda Marion Furley, apparently lived with them from ca. 1890 to 1900. (It is likely that one of the daughters also shared her mother's name, "Phoebe.") George had a ribbon and silk business.
- Florence Eliza Furley was born in the December quarter, 1875, in Shoreditch. She married Joseph Ritson (a self-employed lithographer's agent) in the March quarter, 1895. They had daughters Florence Margherita (b. 1896), Victoria Lydia (b. 1898) and another unidentified child born later. "Flo" was Lydia's favorite sister.
- Matilda Marion Furley was born in 1878. Matilda Marion, age thirteen, nicknamed "Jack," was living with her sister Phoebe Bentley's family in 1891. She married Thomas Clare, a sausage maker, in the June quarter, 1900. In 1901, the couple was living with Thomas's uncle Arthur J. Cusack. By 1914, their address was 62 Woodstock Road, Bedford Park.
- Ethel Grace Furley, born September 1881, Shoreditch, married Ernest Charles Harsant in January 1905.
- Horace Alfred Furley was born in the March quarter, 1883, at the same Shoreditch location. Another son apparently survived to adulthood, but his name is not known. Neither brother appears to have played a significant part in Lydia's life. Horace had a daughter, also named Lydia, born in 1900.
- Ethel Florence Furley died at age two in the June quarter, 1895, London. She was apparently a very late-born sister.

The sisters Phoebe Bentley (and apparently her own daughter, Phoebe Miln) and Florence Ritson were especially close to Lydia, based on what Lydia would say about them to Phipps in her letters. According to Lydia's granddaughter, Mrs. Barbara Brennan (1928–2009),[1] Lydia went to stay with Phoebe and her husband "Milne" when she was twelve years old (at 2 Balmes Road, Beauvoir Town, West Hackney). Barbara was probably confused in thinking Phoebe Bentley was a Milne. She was a Bentley. One of Lydia's nieces (probably another "Phoebe," daughter of Phoebe Bentley) was married to Chrichton Miln, for whom Phipps helped find employment in early 1909.[2]

As William Arthur Jewson indicated in his diary of the first four months of 1914 before he died, Lydia and her family met socially several times a week. Friday, 2 January 1914: "Lyd out with Jack." Saturday, 3 January 1914: "Ethel called." Sunday, 4 January: "Jack called also Tom." Monday, 5 January: "Lyd to Ethel's for day." Wednesday, 7 January: "Harsants, Ritsons, Phoebe Doris [?] & others spent the day with us. Gerald and children to a Cinema. I had tea & dinner at Popular, visited club & went to Alhambra." And so the family visits continued during the months as Jewson recorded until he died in May.[3]

Lydia turned out to be a rebel. She learned to be a seamstress, worked as a waitress in a London teahouse, and became engaged in the early efforts to promote women's rights; she became increasingly active in socialist and theosophical circles, as she grew older. Those circles would include the Pankhurst family as well as Nellie Limousin, the militant socialist and suffragette aunt of Eric Blair ("George Orwell") and Nellie's friends. It was apparently at the teahouse where she worked that Lydia met William Arthur Jewson, "a gentleman of independent means," with whom she had a son, Gerald Arthur Jewson Furley, born 4 July 1897 at her home in Clerkenwell. (Birth certificate identified Lydia as a dressmaker, did not identify father, listed Gerald's name with Furley surname. It was never corrected although

1. Autobiographical notes by Barbara Brennan provided to John D. Squires by Tim Brennan, 6 January 2003.

2. Most of this family history has been developed from research in the census records of the time as well as details from Lydia's letters to MPS. There are also family recollections passed along from Lydia's granddaughter Barbara Brennan to her son Tim Brennan, and from his own research.

3. Jewson, "Diary."

Gerald used Jewson throughout his life.[4]

What attracted Lydia to Jewson is unknown. His cultured background? The opportunity he offered for security and an opportunity to better herself? What was there about Lydia that attracted Jewson? He was born in 1856, sixteen years older than Lydia. His father Frederick Bowen Jewson was "a successful musician & composer & a professor of pianoforte at the Royal Academy of Music, London," according to notes from Barbara Brennan, Gerald's daughter. William Arthur had married his cousin Blanche in his early twenties, but they eventually separated, with no children. After the birth of Gerald in 1897, William Arthur Jewson and Lydia established a home at 54 St. Charles Square, in Kensington. Lydia was fond of the trees around them and the nearby parks in which she walked.

As Lydia was to inform Phipps, she did not hold a lot out for marriage, and she and Jewson simply lived in a common-law arrangement. Jewson and his wife Blanche never divorced, and Blanche did not remarry until after Jewson died in 1914. Although Lydia and Shiel began living together in 1916, they were not married until 1919. And probably then only because they had set out to establish some type of alternative "school" that required a more proper marital appearance to pursue a socialist-oriented enterprise! At least, this has been speculated by Lydia's granddaughter, Barbara Brennan.[5]

It was apparently in late spring or early summer in 1908 when Lydia and Phipps became engaged in a conversation following a lecture in London. Phipps immediately set out to establish a relationship with this darkly attractive, bright young woman. There is something of a voyeuristic feeling in following so closely Shiel's intellectual and sexual pursuit of Lydia . . . and her response, in her letters to him. Her letters provide a record of their romance, while also establishing the quality and depth of her own personality.

Shiel was just extricating himself from the relationship with Mary Price, in Woolaston, Lydney (near Chepstow), where she had written him on 25 June 1908 . . . hoping to maintain an affair with him, but asking that he "Kiss the Dear Children for me hoping both you & Lizzie & they are well." The likely relationship between Mary Price and Elizabeth Price has been discussed earlier.

---

4. Tim Brennan, "History, family, history."

5. Barbara Brennan notes to John D. Squires, 6 January 2003.

Lydia immediately recognized Phipps as someone she could "learn" from, or so he made her think. She made arrangements to visit further with him, in more intimate circumstances—although with second thoughts, as she wrote him on a Saturday, probably in very early June 1908, on the embossed letterhead for 54 St. Charles Sq., W., in Kensington.

> Dear Mr. Shiel / May I retract my half given promise to spend the day on the river. / My tramp's mood lasted until five oclock this morning—when to the twittering of the sparrows—& the light of the strong still morning I fell asleep— / Deep down so truly a tramp that I feel it safer to return my world lest I am caught & carried on, as an irresponsible vagabond, which is too delightful to be dwelt on—& having assumed the position of Kensington housewife—I cannot consistently combine the two. / Thank you for having asked me—& maybe you can understand my changed mood better than I do myself— / Yours Lydia Jewson / P.S. Wednesday afternoon I can go to Kensington Gardens to tea—are you willing.

In a letter with the corner bearing the address and date torn off, but probably written in June 1908, Lydia, her husband, and Shiel had obviously met again at some event, and Lydia invited him to join them at a play. She was intrigued by Shiel's apparent reference to a Medium he knew. He was shaping himself, in her eyes, as a fellow rebel.

> Dear Mr. Shiel— / I am sending you a notice of the play I spoke of—(we have booked ~~two~~ pit seats.) I went to the last play written by Margaret M [?]—"The Hour" & enjoyed it immensely—The Medium you spoke of I hope to hear more about at some future time—as it would be really worth sitting if we could get in touch with those we meant so much by—& are now so vague & doubtful. Before filling this sheet entirely I must thank you for an enjoyable time—last night—healthy & good to remember. Yrs. Lydia Jewson

On a Wednesday, probably still in late June, she tells Shiel about social arrangements made for the evening—Miss Campbell (a medium and musician?) and friends were coming, to enjoy music rather than pursue the spiritual world or make plans to further the Woman Question. Her "husband" ("Gel" or "Gell") is likely to perform, although she does not directly say so. It was simply his habit to play for guests. Shiel may come if he likes; he has obviously threatened to drown himself unless she provides him company. It would not provide her any gratification were he to do so, she wrote him—just leave her without his friendship and help. There are chores that have to be done, Wednesday laundry, and regular visits with her mother and sister. So, come visit her at home with others; she will come see him next week!

> Dear Mr. Shiel— / I am hurriedly answering yours of this morning's post as Wednesdays are always spent by me—with my mother & sister . . . I have written to a niece to take her to the Academy & she may come back home with us—as Miss Campbell & some of her friends are coming in the evening—not for the Woman's question—but some music, do not know whether you are attracted if so, come—I am grateful for the book you are sending me & will try to get to the wisdom . . . I think you kind to trouble so much—& you have gone so far ahead of me—that it is not easy for me to understand what to you is so simple. I am pleased to come to you—when I can—apart from cost & neighborliness for you are interesting—& for that reason—do not think that your death by drowning—would afford me any gratification. It would leave me—without your help—& friendship. / I will write again one day next week—& ask you to be at home when I call—but—will give you due notice. / Yrs. Lydia Jewson

Shiel wrote, suggesting that she read H. G. Wells and his own *Purple Cloud*. He appears also to have sent her a copy of *The Last Miracle* with its lengthy philosophical afterword and suggestions for breathing properly. It is interesting to see that she had already started visiting Shiel at his home, to "learn" from him. She answered his in a letter dated [Thursday] 25 June [1908]. The real news, however, is her acknowledgment that she had written to support an activity frowned on by the police, and is somewhat concerned that she may be called to testify if her letter turns up. This concern did not keep her from participating in a march for women's rights the following Saturday.

> Dear Mr. Shiel / I have read Wells & am going to reread. Can you spare me time next week—to help me to understand it better— / I enjoyed my talk with you so much—& if it is not too much task on your time. I shall be glad to try and follow your ideas further. / When I come I will bring books and papers—& would be pleased to read

your Purple Cloud if you will lend me a copy—(will take it when I call). / The real object of my letter is to tell you to see Daily Telegraph Police News of today's date. Alas—how the Mighty have fallen—I am not the only one with an evil in their minds— / I am wondering whether my letter will be discovered among the papers & I shall accordingly be called up as a witness—I am silent—if so. / Anticipating your announcement [?] [*two illegible words on letter fold*] Lydia Jewson

This did not faze Shiel. He soon wrote, asking about her generally and also about how she was growing in wisdom. (It is interesting that his father asked him virtually the same question every day during his youth.) Shiel had apparently been in France, while she and many of her friends—"the ugly and unloved"—had marched on 27 June in a demonstration for women's rights. A series of such protests had started two weeks earlier, with heavy participation. She wrote him on a Thursday, probably 2 July 1908 from St. Charles Square.

Dear Mr. Shiel— / I am well—many thanks for your kind inquiry—as to growing in wisdom—at the moment I am some what bewildered—indeed I am *very* seriously wondering if the only wise-ones are not they who make no search for wisdom—but are content to live on, for this eternal searching need a strong, strong mind. / You were not correct in your address to Miss Campbell—do you not remember we left her in Westbourne Grove, the night we came from the theatre—not Ladbroke Grove—that is our address. 64 Westbourne Grove will find Miss Campbell. / We marched side by side in last Saturday's march of the ugly & unloved ones (according to the expressed view of many onlookers) You were not in London, I suppose—or you would have seen something of the enormous crowds, who idly watched us marching for freedom. / I could not wait for your return from Paris to pay my visit to the Mahatma—I went last Monday—& am to attend his class for discussion Saturday next— / I have been to Bern Shaw's play & am looking forward to the séance. I think I have received all the shocks during my career in the material world, the spiritual shocks are all that can affect me now—Yrs Lydia Jewson[6]

---

6. This may have been Gandhi who was in London from July to November 1908. "Miss Campbell" was active in the suffrage movement, hosting musical events and teas to help promote the activity in London.

The background of Lydia's actions at that time was a result of the organization of massive demonstrations in London in favor of women's suffrage. Three such demonstrations were carried out in June 1908, the first on 13 June. Elizabeth Robins described the events in her book *Way Stations*.

> On June 21st an impressive historical and symbolical pageant, organised by the National Union of Suffrage Societies, marched through crowded, cheering streets from the Embankment to the Albert Hall. Under the chairmanship of the President, Mrs. Fawcett, a mass meeting was held of such size and enthusiasm as men of long political experience declared had seldom been equalled . . . A week later came the monster demonstration in Hyde Park, under the auspices of the Women's Social and Political Union. . . . "The Times" said of it: "Its organisers had counted on an audience of 250,000. That expectation was certainly fulfilled, and probably it was doubled, and it would be difficult to contradict anyone who asserted that it was trebled" . . . The "Daily Chronicle" said: "Never, on the admission of the most experienced observers, has so vast a throng gathered in London to witness an outlay of political force."

More aggressive feminist activities would follow in November, when Lydia and others were locked to the surrounding fences for their assault against the grounds. In the meantime, Lydia kept busy with her wide-ranging pursuit of interests. Despite Shiel's gradually successful seduction, Lydia continued to care for her common-law husband with affection throughout his life and tended to her son Gerald as well as any mother might. Her mother and sisters got lots of attention, but Lydia also pursued her intellectual curiosity vigorously. She had not waited for Phipps to return from France before she visited the "Mahatma," as she noted in the letter above.

On a Monday, probably in the middle of July, Lydia had been to an annual fair at Chelsea, where Shiel planned to take a balloon ride. (The Chelsea Historical Pageant, with its depiction of events in British history especially related to the Chelsea area, with music, exhibits, and flourish of banners and flags, had completed its programs in July and August. Lydia must have caught the exhibits and pageantry just prior to the family's departure to the Isle of Sheppey for the summer.)

> [2 *sheets*] Dear Mr. Shiel— / You are too kind in sending the books I asked for so soon— / I presume this is before the balloon as-

cent. I trust I may see you safe & sane again after it— / I have been at Chelsea—to witness the pageant—& while trying to follow the various once clearest & now forgotten events I saw a fair white balloon sail by—& I tried to recognize you as an occupant, but—alas—but still I wondered if it was your party—sailing over the treetops—& how much more like ants on a [*word?*] hill we must look like from that height. / In reply to your last letter. I have only thanks for your kindness in giving me the address of our frail fat brother (morally frail) & I do not think him very evil—but his attentions are tiresome—I am truly sorry for him—& I hope him safely thro. with it—someone should tell him he is likely to be misunderstood by the British miss & matron. / I spent Saturday afternoon in Kew Gardens with the dear old Lucas & read Wells to him (he is ever kind to my moods—& madnesses) You speak of Wells not being literary—as to such merits I am quite unable to form an opinion—so you must have seen by my too outspoken remarks at your last book. Style—I do not understand—& shall ask you about the absence of adjectives when I see you. /

From what Mr. Lucas tells—I believe—a Miss McWall—a lady friend of his—lives in your building. She is a keen investigator of spiritual phenomena, a suffragetter, & a little bit of a writer—also—I believe. / I feel after reading Wells that my hopes are more selfish than yours. / I cannot but wonder what part I shall play in those beings who will laugh & reach out their hands among the class. My small self that looms as large on my outlook, distorted no doubt by my closeness to it—Will it be no more a Something that stands so near to me that its shadow—always—comes between me—& every object I see—If to lose that sense of Self is to attain Nirvana then truly I am a long way from it. / Dead old Carlyle says that is always a dark spot on our Selves & I do not feel I can bear to blot it out. / May I call—about five oclk [*i.e., o'clock*] Thursday—do not reply if at home. / Mrs. L.J.

Lydia maintained her ties to Phipps by writing him on 27 July, a Monday, to provide an address for a speaker whom he wanted to write. Her family was obviously preparing for departure to Jewson's property at Sheppey where they spent a few months each summer.

Dear Mr. Shiel. / It occurred to me in the small hours of this morning—that you had not Mr. Lucas's address in case you may want to write him direct—so am enclosing same. I expected him—to

> have called before we left but, he has not done so—& we leave Thursday *early*—so shall not see him until after our return. / But—that is only one reason why I write, the other is—will you please send me—a copy of Goethe's poems—that is if you have a small volume—also, one you do not set great store by—as I should like to take it with me—to try to understand it—(in English of course) / I have just read your appendix to The Last Miracle—& it is strange—very strange— / That gift of youth you set such store by—I feel very [*illegible word*]—like Faust I almost wish my lost—last ten years back again—although it cannot really be lost I suppose—but I might have pursued something more attainable—maybe less attractive on that account., / But I will try & make better use of my remaining four years now. I see a lifetime counts for little in such a search. / We return near the 15th Sept. When Gerald returns to school—as far as at present arranged. / If you have not what I asked for—or if you think it better for me not to try—to fathom any further for a time—I will be grateful to you for your interest. The breathing exercise is not very good so far—I have for my *text*— / Fill all the stops of life with truthful breath—I hope you will have a good time with the Fabians. I should think it a charmed circle. / Mrs. Lydia Jewson

There is no indication other than this mention by Lydia that Shiel had ever been involved with the Fabians—that group that promoted socialist intellectual causes, whose members included George Bernard Shaw, Annie Besant, H. G. Wells, Hubert Bland, Emmeline Pankhurst . . . and Shiel's friend from the Keynote Series days, the poet John Davidson. It is possible that Shiel might have attended a meeting with Davidson. The group's promotion of the nationalization of land was certainly a major thesis of Shiel's political beliefs, fed by the ideas of Henry George. But that group seemed to function (frankly) as an intellectual society beyond the time and means of Shiel. It is likely that Shiel was continuing to puff himself in the eyes of Lydia.

Shiel determined that he would find and give Lydia a copy of Goethe's poems before she left. The Jewson family routinely moved during the late summer to a rustic country home called The Coppice, at Eastchurch on the Isle of Sheppey. They generally spent July and August there, returning for the beginning of the school term for Gerald in September. In 1908, they apparently did not leave for Sheppey until late July or early August. As Lydia wrote Shiel from The Coppice, probably early in August 1908, she received the book as they were leaving for their summer holiday off England's mid-east coast.

> Dear Mr. Shiel— / I want to write to thank you for the book I received just as we were driving from the house—Thursday morning on the first stage of our journey here . . . last night at 8 oclock I was struggling across the fields with a big basket—of potatoes, beans & plums—until Gell saw me looming out of the evening light—& came to share a load . . . I hope we sell this place this year—I think now I am used to it—I want something fresh—a walking tour—but—why trouble about next year while today is here . . . Now to the real cause of this letter—the book you so generously sent me . . . I salute your kindness but only asked for a book—& not a gift . . . / How much you have to enlarge your Consciousness—German, French—etc.—& please forgive my humble endeavors . . . One more— / Thank you— / Yours Lydia Jewson

Shiel was busy with his writing during this period from September 1908 into the early months of 1909. Pearson published a 6d edition of *The Yellow Danger* in August. "Many a Tear," one of his very best short stories, was published in the September 1908 issue of *Pearson's Magazine* (New York) and again in the January 1909 issue of the *Novel Magazine*.

Although it has not been confirmed, there has been some thought that *The Isle of Lies* (published as a book in 1909) was serialized in the *Daily Chronicle* in 1908. (Reynolds Morse observed that Shiel had written notes on the back of a typescript of "The Return of Cummings Monk" that mentioned the book several times, and specifically Shiel had written "I still had to complete the last installment of my *Isle of Lies,* then appearing as a serial.")

The Message, a serial by Louis Tracy, began publication in *Pearson's Magazine* (New York) with the October 1908 issue and concluded in the March 1909 issue. *Pearson's Magazine Illustrated* reprinted the story during the same general time period but ran it in a more piecemeal fashion. It has long been suspected that Shiel contributed to this serial, but I fail to spot his hand in it.

He certainly had to keep busy writing regardless of his chase of Lydia. But the cheap papers in which so much of his work was published simply no longer exist. *The Message* begins as a social romance that turns into a rather intense African adventure novel. There is no stylistic evidence of Shiel's hand in the work, but he might well have written pieces of the novel in a straightforward manner. There is just no way to know.

Lydia continued her correspondence from The Coppice. In a letter dated Sunday, 22 August 1908, she not only tells more about herself but also indicates what Shiel has been doing—writing to her son Gerald and probably, as he would on a regular basis during this period, sending Gerald chocolates. Gerald liked this attention while he was young, but as he grew older he developed a strong dislike for Shiel and proved to be an obstacle to the marriage of Phipps and Lydia until 1919. It is also of interest to note that Lydia refers in the following undated letter to the death of a friend of Shiel, and tells him straightforwardly that she has no interest in marriage as an institution. Who Shiel's friend was is unknown. (One might just imagine that Shiel used the death to engender sympathy from Lydia.)

> Dear Mr. Shiel. / I was glad to receive your letter—but was content to wait—when I learnt from yours to Gerald that you were both busy & depressed—so—first I want to express my sorrow for your sorrow at the death of your friend. We love but few—so to lose one leaves a dark gap—
>
> In your dark wakeful hours—maybe some thought of him has not helped to quiet you—but would marriage do this for you—& if so is such a reason to marry for— / My views of marriage is so opposed to that of most of my fellows—that perhaps it is better unwritten—anyway—it is too lengthy for pen & ink . . . You ask me to tell you some more of myself. I can do this easily—like the man in Bernard Shaw's play . . .
>
> To begin—since I came here I have completed my thirty sixth year—& have decided to try and realise the remaining four years of youth before I turn the corner behind which it forever lies out of sight— / My mother has been staying here—she leaves next Monday—& I feel age is unlovely—(it is brutal but true) My vanity forbids it. / . . . a lovely walk here along the top of the cliffs . . . & we walk home at low tide through the water—that is Gerald & I do so. Gel does not care to dry himself by wind and sun as we do . . . I am not longing for Kensington Gardens but I love all places with trees . . . your shilling & chocolates has given you an abiding place in Gerald's [*two illegible words*] . . . Sincerely Yrs. Lydia Jewson

Mica Garcia Gomez in Artist Atelier Paris, ca. 1903 [?]
Courtesy of the Harry Ransom Humanities Research Center
The University of Texas at Austin

Esther Lydia Furley at age 12
Courtesy of the Harry Ransom Humanities Research Center
The University of Texas at Austin

Lydia Furley (age 18), ca. 1890 in London
Courtesy of the Harry Ransom Humanities Research Center
The University of Texas at Austin

William Arthur Jewson in his late teens, ca. 1870
Courtesy of his great-grandson Tim Brennan

Lydia maintained a regular correspondence with Shiel during the Jewson family summer stay at The Coppice at Eastchurch. She wrote him in an undated letter probably in late summer of 1908. "My Friend / I shall be glad to receive the book on Friendship which I have not read— / Thanks for form letter and correct [*cost?*] / Yrs Lydia J—" The acquisition of a book served as an excuse for their letters. But probably late in August, a weather event on the Isle of Sheppey brought a rich letter to Shiel, with evidence that Lydia now knew of Shiel's love of the wind and storm. Her letter is warmly personal, and a photograph is included for Shiel. Would that it had been preserved in his archives!

> [*incomplete*] You who love it—would fit your words to it very well—Two things have happened—first—the top of my tallest elm blew down that night . . . & I have fallen from the swing . . . please do not laugh . . . I am enclosing a copy of a photo taken by the village school masters son—it is in my "tramps" robes— / Have you walked much with bare feet they as <are? are as?> sensitive as hands—it is lovely . . . I shall hardly dare to use the word friend—altho—it means more than any other word—to me—when I address you as Dear Mr. Shiel—I always picture you with a bowler hat—do you ever wear one. Must leave off—but not nearly finished. L.J.

The family was still at The Coppice when Lydia wrote Shiel on Thursday, 3 September 1908. *The Lost Viol* was finally being published in a British edition in October, after its initial publication in the United States by Clode in 1905. Ward, Lock had purchased the novel in late 1904 and had paid Shiel some £157 for it in the spring of 1905, but decided to publish his *The Yellow Wave* instead, since it could be linked to the ongoing Russo-Japanese war. Shiel undoubtedly had a copy of the American edition to give to Lydia, although the British edition was probably not yet in his hands. She immediately identified Hannah as a strong feminist figure in the novel.

> Dear Mr. Shiel— / Books welcomed to read—that is—first the preface to Montaigne / secondly—essay on friendship—then—your book. / Your Hannah what a woman—you have made—what gladness. What grit. I read right on until finished. That was bedtime—but was too excited to sleep / dozed off & on—thinking of all I would say of her to you—waking right up at about five oclk. I held her close—then I could stay inactive no longer—dressed, & was off to Leysdown—four miles distant by carriers cart—at 6.30 a long

> shadow walked beside me across the fields—(there is no road) & I just bounded along—Gerald & his father I left behind me—(they had not read of Hannah) A grand walk along the sands. A little wait in a great silence & then home again. / Most lovely of all the mornings here. I shall never forget it—May I thank you for giving me such happiness. Shall read the letters many times— / Montaigne is rather above me—at first reading—being literature—but am reaching out—growth does not allow stretching—so must go slowly—will persevere to understand. / This letter is going to be a long affair, so if you are still on your book just pigeon hole it (this letter) for a bit as the rest will keep. / The weather is very rough as you see by newspaper accounts—& at night the wind is tremendous. I cannot sleep through it. I like better to be out bathing with it— / indoors—not at all— / Once in the night I found myself wondering how if I had to describe it in words—how I should do so—& I thought a ship with great loose flappy sails—& a crew wailing—was the most like. Wind is very difficult to put in a book I should think but [*incomplete*]

Writing on a Sunday, most likely in September 1908, Lydia refers to his kite flying as a potential release of the grief over his friend's death. Probably as a result of Lydia's enthusiasm for Hannah in *The Lost Viol,* it appears that Shiel has asked her if she would like to be a heroine in one of his fictions.

> My Dear Friend— / Your report received—now for mine—a strange mixture of deadly dullness & elation extreme . . . Saturday so "wild & wayward" that on the way to the bank at Regent Street with the "boys" (the old boy & the small boy) I accidentally rushed them both off to Hal [?] Woods & tawny oak leaves . . . Yes, I would like to be a heroine—but one of my own making . . . I hope all traces of newness will leave you—& the kite flying of your childhood's second spell—is the very remedy . . . just a line when you move out & you wish to hear from me will bring a quick reply from Yrs Lydia Jewson

Lydia seemed careful to bring Shiel into family activities, while he looked for every opportunity to spend time with her, as this undated letter, probably from early October 1908, shows.

> Dear—Gladly I will go to Faust if you are able to get seats—other—than stalls or box—which I rather doubt— / If not—we will go to hear the music—& walk home—if a good night. / Until tomorrow / Yrs Lydia Jewson

Lydia wrote on Friday, 9 October 1908:

> Friend of mine / The enclosed explains itself—I have reread your last to me—& see now—that maybe you are a bird on the wing—& I cannot catch up—You say in your letter you quite hope we shall meet before you go to France. / Let the hope be strong—& its fulfillment certain / . . . The fullness of life is yours now you have returned to your father—Yours, Lydia Jewson [*no enclosure present*]

Quite what she meant by his having "returned" to his father is unclear, unless she meant a new dedication on his part to a study of Jesus. She wrote again, immediately, the next day, Tuesday, 10 October 1908, sharing very personal thoughts with him. Shiel's preparations for a visit to France had perhaps stung her—this bird on the wing.

> Dear—morning is here without anger—from two oclock until five, awake—with thoughts—my hands hard pressed—& a soft shining felt—as a bright back ground unseen. At five I went to sleep—& the grey morning when I again awoke had displaced the warm radiance. / Do not go away until I have again seen you—come back to me Saturday & I will gladly go to the promenade if you wish to take me—or any where else you like better. / Gerald & I will be here—for tea—as he is home from school—that day—Come any time after four. / Gel is playing at the house of Dr. [D? Grant?] in the evening . . . / I go today to the Tate gallery with Eva Barr. / Send me *one* line to tell me if you will be here as I ask—if you have not already arranged to go away— / More I will not write— / Lydia Jewson

Three days later, Tuesday, 13 October 1908, she was already preparing to meet him at his flat, although still signing her letter with a formal name.

> My Dear Friend / I can come to you tomorrow Wednesday 14th . . . Forgive my haste today is my "washing day"—& am just off to my mother's—shall look forward to tomorrow while at the tub—Mrs. Lydia Jewson

She followed with a postcard, postmarked North Kensington / 12:15 AM / 19 [October?] / 08 [*addressed to*] M. P. Shiel Esq. / 3 Grafton Mansions / Dukes Road / W.C. She obviously preferred that he not send her a response, as she began to construct various means for him to communicate with her with a series of coded messages, obviously now beginning to hide the closeness of their relationship.

> [*mutilated*] . . . All passing to public worship. I in secret. "The strong pleasure is [*illegible pencil*] nerves unto pain." . . . I wonder how it is with you this morning—The sun streams between the trees—in streaks as through church windows. Single leaves fall. If that is the law of attraction—which draws them down to the earth—from whence they came—what a law. I almost hate it . . . Come. Do not write. I will be at Queen's Rd. Tube Station at 4.30 anyway, walking a while, returning to new work later. Come only if compelled. / Lydia Jewson

Sometime during this period, October and November 1908, the simmering romance between Lydia and Phipps became a full-blown storm and resulted in occasional playfulness while more serious circumstances lay ahead. There were only so many occasions when Lydia could sit by Shiel's fireside, absorbing his "instructions," and avoid the gypsy attraction of this "man among men."

Shiel was clearly pushing for a closer physical relationship than the one of distant affection that Lydia played for awhile, even after she began expressions of endearment in her letters. A loose, brief page wandering by itself among Shiel's file of Lydia's correspondence is obviously a reflection of this . . . kisses were too dangerous, but also an obstacle that was quickly removed.

> I sought God & found you. / You suspect—why I write this much—yet say so little. When my mouth never seeks yours—dear heart. / I am old & cunning—with a wisdom, sadly learned—or rather—well learnt. / This paper is a passive medium—& your eyes are alight when I look far into them. You suspect all this, I know.

On a "Sunday / for Monday" Lydia wrote Shiel quite a romantic letter—strong enough to make a letter-reading voyeur curious as to what had occurred the night before.

> Dear— / Not on the door step this morning, only a line or so to ask how you are—but unable to hear the answer—no matter it is good to be able to write. / What a long day Sunday must have been for you—after my early raid. / What you miss by sleeping so late. / Little child, why not see me Tuesday afternoon—let me mother you—a little. / Come—& be coached to be good—& not to cry because the moon is in the sky—& we cannot reach it— / Maybe we should grow wings one day & then the wonder of it all—will pass for us— / Take heart of grace—dear—& send me a Postcard only to say

> you received your book sent by post—that I shall understand to mean you will be at Queen's Road Tube Station at 4.30 Tuesday / do not write—at all if you cannot come. I leave here early Tuesday morning so the card must come by the first post—We will walk to go to tea—& behave like men—you & I— / Laugh while you read this & be glad we are doing the right thing. & "music" in your ears, your beating heart shall quake / Yours Lydia Jewson

On a Monday, possibly the following day in October, Lydia wrote Phipps.

> Dear— / We were each writing—to each other last night—what a disease this is—its symptoms are funny—if one is in a condition for fate [?] to be good & not pathetic . . . Gell goes to play at a concert. I take Gerald to the Kings Theatre . . . Can you get a seat next to ours . . . My cold is not much . . . Yours, Lydia Jewson

Lydia's romantic relationship with Shiel had gotten to the point that she felt she had to meet him more clandestinely, and her letters indicate the system of hiding their intent. "I will be at Queen's Rd Tube Station at 4 oclk if you will be there / do not write further / Yrs Lydia Jewson."

Her letters become more lengthy and descriptive, more carefully composed, perhaps conscious efforts to show Shiel that she was able to converse with him, write to him, on a level higher than she had tried to previously. Among the scraps of Lydia's letter are two pages of thoughts about Jesus and religion—undated, but perhaps the attachment intended to go with her letter of 9 October. This may have been intended as a response to one of her "lessons" with Shiel, the demonstration of a lift in her learning.

> [*Incomplete*] Hell is the evil that [*illegible*] also & the countenance of that evil in the world is the measure of their hell . . . [*with two pages of notes*]

She shared a brief vivid Sunday morning scene and acknowledged what must have been a declaration of love from Shiel.

> The other sheet was written during the night—I being in my favorite job—nursing (a man—not one of my own) in a boarding house . . . It is Sunday morning with the cheeky chirping sparrows, rattle of milk jars—& early mournful church bell . . . In the beginning of our brief time of seeing each other I spoke of us as fellow

creations with no regard to sex—but we were man & woman from the first—& all that followed was contained therein . . . Your salute I accept & in response send you my love. Lydia Jewson.

Lydia continued to work at being a socialist disciple. On a Friday she referred to her involvement with what appears to have been a woman's labor group, the Vestal Workers—perhaps representative of the concept of a "vestal sisterhood" that became popular in the late Victorian era—and apparently apologized for not having better understood whatever topic she and Shiel had just discussed. Her family activities continued.

> Another letter supplement to my wail of yesterday. / The fresh wind & rain splashes—last evening—on my way to the Vestal Workers—blew the cobwebs from my brain—& a more clear headed creature I became as I walked. / This morning the "Boys" & I went to the Skating Rink—where one or two falls shook me up & greatly improved the mad mixture—of which I am made . . . / The question—Do we make or mar our lives interests me very greatly. We will talk of this—if you will—when I see you next. / I give you the subject so you will be prepared to teach me. / Be tolerant to me dear. As knowledge must ever be to ignorance. / Goodbye dear. / Lydia

Shiel wrote W. H. Chesson on 18 October 1908, (from 3, Grafton Mans. / Dukes Rd W.C.) to say that he had not answered his letter since he had "been away." Shiel and Chesson had both been awaiting the publication of *The Isle of Lies.*

On 3 November, a Tuesday in 1908, Lydia turned down Shiel's proposal of marriage and made an effort to break away from what had become such an intense relationship. It obviously followed a quarrel. Shiel wanted a more permanent relationship with Lydia, while she had her own long-held feelings against marriage and a strong feeling of loyalty to her common-law husband, William Jewson, the father of her son. As might be expected, the heat that had been generated between Phipps and Lydia could not be so easily put aside, although Lydia must have earnestly tried to turn the relationship back into something a bit more platonic over the winter.

> Dear / My choice is made & I remain here— / The crisis comes—the fever passes & life goes on once more— / You have said—that I am womanly—may some touch of that womanliness—reach you—beyond these hard words—some tenderness—some sorrow—& very

human weakness—resentment towards this power that catches & whirls us—then throws us giddily down—half fearful. / I chose to write as my nerve has gone for fighting—& much would be said—& much has already been said—since I saw you last— / Count Sunday morning—as my last visit—to you—bright & free—our meeting is finished. / The honour you have paid me—by asking me to marry you—will be remembered & maybe—in a very short time—all rebel impulses & "tramps" moods will leave me—to a calmness I have never yet known being always so unlike my fellows—as to be never understood least of all by myself. / Little child—goodbye, I am not very strong—maybe—I shall hear that music—you wrote of—one day. / I will make all excuses for tomorrow evening. Goodbye.

Reconciliation of this rejection occurred quickly. Shiel must have spent time during early November on one of his hikes in Devon or along the River Wye. Lydia wrote him, saying more perhaps about their attraction to one another, a shared "gipsy" darkness of feature, than what one can ever otherwise find in their correspondence. These comments regarding the influence of "cells," genetic memory, suggest a level of sophistication, a level of intellectual companionship, that would help bind these two for more than thirty years.

> Drink deep of your surroundings . . . Your entry into my life is the central event from & towards which I count my days . . . I also experience this & and a sound long forgotten seems to struggle—for remembrance when I hear Hungarian music—or see a swarthy neck & the shine of gold worn in ear. I do not know whether my mother gloated over gipsy doings or whether the cells have memories that sleep or wake in us . . . / Dear heart. I know I am close beside you—in your wanderings . . . Yours Lydia

The long November was probably filled with Lydia's visits with Shiel. She wrote on Wednesday, 30 November 1908:

> The last day of the month—my dear friend & it shall be reason enough for me to write you—I will make it so anyhow—& your letter contained two questions—which I answer— / I am as lenient as your mother—& do not think you force yourself [?] my notice. I thank you for my honoured place near her—& your generosity. / I do haunt the gardens—sometimes—very ghost like my hauntings have been—Friday last I crossed [*illegible word*] with my sister & saw & loved the sky—through the trees (just as clear—dark & bare—as in

summer.) The colours were a glory & may be a promise. / Today I went to the Marble Arch on my way to a lecture & was less ghost like—had indeed a little of my old swing as I went—& felt a little younger than I have been—for every hour—of every day—of my six & thirty years—seemed in a heap on my back—but today I had my back less bent—& the weight slipped into a more bearable position. / Yes, even my vanity had to pay its share. / I came on this register of my thoughts (enclosed) written the summer before last—& I thought recorded for my own reading. I send them to you. When I wrote them the Purpose of God lay like a fair open road before me—I had only to walk to reach the goal in far perspective. I have——doubts & now—I know what a long way forward I must go to get back to where I stood then—as doubt—back turnings each—if we will learn. / I will take heart of grace & go on. / I also enclose the lines from your book (have made another copy to read often) They are dear. They aim high—you will remember these.

You go to Paris, I presume—& will perhaps see that little seven year old—full of Christmas— / I am very busy—it is a good, good time & work is good, too. / You write God loveth a cheerful giver. To give is easy. You told me *all* is of God—then the power to love & the strength to withhold is also of Him. This little letter will not require any answer—but it will be nice to know when you are once more in London. My kindly thought—will be with you. Nearness is not seeing or touching. There is but one will in the Universe & all will be well at Last. Lydia

On a Thursday, soon after she learned of Phipps's plans to go to Paris over Christmas, she asked Shiel to write Gerald a letter explaining why he would be absent.

Dear— / Your midnight greeting—was mine this morning—sent I presume after your guests had left you—I too was present sometime despite your disbelief in the Spirit . . . have been to Gray's Inn to look at rooms . . . yesterday I went walking, walking with one of my sisters . . . I stop now—will you send Gerald a line—telling him of your going—he is asking me—his news will serve also for Yours Lydia Jewson

Shiel wrote Chesson on 1 December to say "I have just got your p.c. / The reason you have not received book [*The Isle of Lies*] is that I have been away, and only home a couple of days ago. It will be sent you tomorrow. But I did not correct the proofs, and in some respects am not satisfied with it as it stands." The novel was not to be formally published until January 1909.

Toward the end of 1908, Lydia's niece (probably Phoebe Bentley Miln, but perhaps the daughter of another sister) became ill and Lydia went to stay with her for a time. The niece's illness was never explained, although she apparently faced surgery. When Lydia wrote Shiel, on a Wednesday, she struck through the St. Charles address, apparently staying at her niece's home on High Street in Harlesden N.W. Her remark that Chrichton Miln has "good works" must refer to the contents of the young man's bookshelves.

The habit that Lydia developed about the turn of the year in referring to Shiel as a "dear chum," or "little child," may either be a somewhat innocently intended expression of endearment or a means of distancing herself from a stronger romantic expression.

> My Dear Chum—first thank you for the book—I skimmed some of the conversational parts Monday evening when I returned home & hear echos [*sic*] of our "talks" by your fireside. / Sunday last a consultation was held by the doctors here—the result being when the "white one" is strong enough & recovered from the attack she will have to undergo an operation—much slighter than was at first supposed. She is much better—but low & whimpering—poor little thing . . . I am wondering whether the effect of the Hampstead walk has left you . . . If I can manage, I may come to you some where near your breakfast time (tomorrow Thursday) but everything is very uncertain when illness is claiming one's time. / Between whiles I am reading a book of A. C. Benson's Memoirs of Arthur Hamilton much of interest in it, I find having finished Tristan & Iseult such like intoxications. I will put aside such sweets & take to something safe & calm. Chrichton Milne has some good works—so it will be nice to have them sometimes. I sew most of the time, like aunts in general & nursing females in particular but thought comes and goes with the needle & thread & I long for action of some kind . . . Strongly hoping to see you tomorrow—your chum Lydia.

Shiel did not go to France as soon as Lydia expected, and she wrote him on another undated Thursday.

> Dear—you have been ill—sad am I—you are better—glad am I— / I passed & repassed your window—& my thoughts flew off after you to Paris—& all the time you were within. I salute you—my

> lord—little knowing— / I hear we are to tea together Friday at Luke's. / Things have been happening fast & furious—I have much to tell you when we meet. I wait for Saturday—try & keep it for me—(about 7). / Dear little child, I send my love tender as a mother's—Dear little chum, my love strong as a brother's. L.

What is especially interesting about what Lydia reveals in her letters to Shiel at this time late in 1908, is that he will be in Paris at Christmas spending time with "that little seven-year old." The obvious implication is that Lola was still in Paris with her aunts and grandmother, or even that Lina might still have been alive. The latter seems very unlikely, since Shiel was pushing Lydia to marry him and would not have done so had Lina still been alive . . . although he did not see that the common-law marriage that had resulted from Lydia's ten-year arrangement with William Arthur Jewson, and a commonly shared son, was an obstacle at all.

It had been five years since the 1903 date of Shiel's separation from Lina and Lola, and the generally held conclusion among Shiel scholars has been that Lina died soon after and her sister Salva had taken Lola to Spain. Lydia's comment implies that such an event had not yet occurred, but there is no correspondence or other record to indicate what the actual circumstances were. A postcard of condolence that Lydia sent to Shiel on 25 February 1909 may suggest a loss to him by either a death or separation—and this might represent the date at which Lola (or someone else dear to him) left his life forever.

The known deaths of members of Shiel's family that occurred during this period are those of his mother in 1910, his nephew Reginald in London in the spring of 1912, his sister Sallie in the West Indies in 1913, his brother-in-law Samuel Horsford in London in 1913, his sister Gussie in London in 1927. Lydia mentions in her letters despondent correspondence from Phipps referring to the death of a male friend in 1908 and the loss of someone dear to Shiel in February 1909. But neither is identified in her letters, and there is no record left by Shiel as to who or what it was that caused him to write her about these losses in such tragic terms. We only know that a close male friend died in 1908, and Lola was probably taken to Spain in 1909.

Plain old domestic issues, and a hint at the basic playfulness and adventurous spirit that were such strong attributes of Lydia, are made clear in a note written on a Wednesday evening, probably in January 1909.

William Arthur Jewson (age 48), 1904
Courtesy of his great-grandson Tim Brennan

Gerald Arthur Jewson Furley, January 1918
Courtesy of his grandson Tim Brennan

Gerald Arthur Jewson Furley, December 1918
Courtesy of his grandson Tim Brennan

Lydia Furley Jewson, Winter 1907/08
Courtesy of her great-grandson Tim Brennan

> Dear little child— / do not say swear words when you receive this—but—owing to my only domestic's wanting to go to a party tomorrow—also burst pipes & a small flood I must be here tomorrow—as Gell is going out—& someone must be here to see workmen etc. / I have in fact just come in through the second floor window after climbing in the out building in the snow & diving into the cistern—so you see all my plight. I shall do my shopping in the morning—as far as I can say—anything is a chance & will call near twelve—do not alter your arrangements for me dear—I am quite content & fully understand. / Gerald & I have had a glorious time in the snow this morning—Hope to see you when I call. Can stay an hour or so—Lydia

On 21 January Lydia wrote Shiel to thank him for his assistance in finding employment for the husband of her niece and what an improvement that had made in her health.

> A hurried & delighted letter to thank you for the post—my nephew is to begin Monday. / The delight when he wired the result was splendidly healing to the poor little girl his wife. I am writing from her bedside now—so young & ill—but good news is a grand restorative. / I shall spend all my spare time here—until she is well . . . I took my work up this morning. I do hope it will be accepted—if not try again—it is a safety valve. / I do not know when I shall see you again—My love to you—male among men [*no closing*]

Chrichton Miln, the husband of Phoebe, wrote Shiel to thank him for his help (from 168 High Street / Harlesden N.W.) on 21 January 1909. (What Shiel could have done to help this young man with employment cannot be imagined. Formal UK passenger lists identify Chrichton J. Miln as a journalist, born in Canada on 31 August 1887, who spent a great deal of time traveling back and forth between England and various ports in Africa during World War II. He and Phoebe Bentley were parents of Chrichton G. W. Miln, born in Middlesex in 1912.)

> Dear Mr. Shiel: / Without wishing to "stop over" I just say—thank you! Your kind letter got me work in five minutes & took a great burden from off my shoulders. If ever a time comes that I can be of any assistance to You I hope that you will not have forgotten me, & if God sees fit to [*m*—?] some of my young ambitions I shall never forget one who was kind to a rather desperate young man. /

Thank you a thousand times, & if you have an half hour to waste some Evening, or on a Sunday, I wish you would allow me to thank you in person. With all good wishes, / Yours sincerely / Chrichton Miln

Phipps had returned from Paris in late January 1909, but he wrote his friend W. H. Chesson on 1 February that he was returning to Paris for "a little time" on Tuesday. Shiel's literary life was continuing as well as his romantic life. Chesson had written a review of *The Isle of Lies* in the 27 January 1909 issue of the *Daily Chronicle*. He questioned how Jeanne Auvache, an uneducated and evilly jealous woman, who "tells" part of the story in the novel, could have spoken so literarily.

Shiel responded to Chesson's review.

Dear Chesson / I have been reading the article, and have been struck by the thought that you must be an uncommonly plucky sort; probably a bit obstinate and dogged, too, persisting in your dogma, not merely because, but partly because, the mass of people do not agree with it. Under Nero you would have died, my friend, at a very tender age. But I think that I am the same kind myself, and that makes two of us—a host! How well Horatius kept the bridge . . ! etc. Anyway, you certainly do me a service that cannot be measured, and my many thanks.

I am going to France for a little time on Tuesday; when I come back we will see each other, sans faute. / Very sincerely yours, / M. P. Shiel / P.S. My answer to your criticism on Jeanne's literary abilities is (1) that a French girl of that class is vastly more intelligent and read than an English girl of that class; (2) that her words are *translated* into *my* own words, she having written in French.

Lydia wrote Phipps on Sunday, 7 February.

To greet you on your return—London or Paris here or there—still an ever present one. / What is this "something" in me which loves that "something" in you—a Knowledge of which is not of sense—which knows of its sweetness without taste—its softness & bright shining without touch or sight—also a singing & a deep hush without hearing . . . My love has an abiding place. Soft & strong the bonds which bind—Surespace [*illegible*] is the web of fate. / Lydia

On 8 February 1909 young Gerald Jewson wrote a note to Shiel.

> [*In a childish hand*] "Dear Mr. Shiel / Thanks very, very much for those lovely sweets . . . / From your little friend Gerald"
>
> [*Followed in an adult hand*] "P.S. If you have no engagement Saturday evening you may expect the mother of the above."

Lydia sent Phipps a postcard, postmarked Kensington, W.C. / 8:30 PM / FE 25 / 09 [Thursday, 25 February 1909], addressed to M. P. Shiel Esq. / 3 Grafton Mansions / Dukes Road / W.C. with a brief note: "Comfort. I send you dear—from my full heart—" This is obviously a response to an emotional note from Phipps describing a major loss to him on that or a recent day. However, with Phipps's several recent visits to Paris, it is likely that it related to the little girl that Lydia expected him to see at Christmas. Lola was probably finally taken to Spain by Salvadore, as John Gawsworth later said.

With news in February that her sister "Flo" Ritson was returning to London soon (from where is unknown), Lydia is faced with sharing the news of her affair with Phipps. She was too close to this sister not to do so; and she needed someone with whom to share her secret. Even her niece, whose husband Shiel has somehow helped gain employment, apparently only thought of Shiel as a close friend of her aunt.

On Monday 8 March, Lydia wrote Phipps that her sister Flo had arrived, but she had been so busy seeing other relatives that Lydia had not yet had a chance to visit with her. Despite Jewson's "independent means," Lydia appears to have been making an effort to provide an income for herself, sewing and attempting to sell her work, and sitting with ill people. She had photos made and sent them to Phipps.

> My dear little Pal—after many days—the photo's arrive . . . I hope you will find in them some semblance—of the Lydia you know—so well. I must have a little "talk" in sending them. You will be glad to hear my sister Flo—(Mrs. Ritson) arrived in London—Saturday. I have not yet had any near talk with her—as they—(she & her three children) went to various relatives . . . [has supported] her career—to that end I have secured some sittings from an R.A. & shall try & turn my hobby into money . . . My good old head, still goes on trying to solve things & it seems to me—that it can be only one will—in the vast concern of Creation—& all the lesser ills are subservient to the Greater End . . . [*no closing*]

Lydia had apparently sewn something for Shiel, as she indicated in this undated note. She had hoped to send it with those photos of herself.

> This little bit of work I have done for you was not finished in time to send with photos. I hope you will receive it safely—I not knowing if you are in Paris or whether good old London holds us both— / Lydia

By Friday, 12 March, Lydia had spent time with Florence and had learned about all the personal problems that Florence had to deal with—chiefly concerning, it appears, managing three children and an apparent ne'er-do-well husband, Joseph Ritson, a self-employed lithographer's agent. Shiel must have immediately asked Lydia if there was some means by which he could help with Flo's difficulties.

> No, dear, I have not anything to write you about. This concern I have left to her own management. I gave her your address for her to write direct. She was here Wednesday—& we decided the only permanent way out of their constantly recurring difficulties is for her husband to get regular employment—but—he is a born rover . . . a good mother such as Flo is, is a rare & beautiful thing—& her children should have the full benefit of her sweetness & love. So—a letter of introduction for Mr. Ritson would be the best thing—& the only way. / This need not keep you longer in town . . . the month will have passed, & the beauty you find in it will have passed . . . I have been to one or two lectures—one—"I. Zangwill's God" very interesting—I must read him—& I have been reading Well's "Food of the Gods" feeling quite dwarfed. I thought of your future race—how great—& good. / I hope you will hear soon from my sister . . . I am going to post this & tramp a while. My love, dear.

It appears that in his letter to Lydia of Friday, 12 March, when Phipps had indicated to Lydia that he might somehow be able to help Flo, he appeared also to have been so angry with Jewson—probably as an obstacle—that he had cursed him to Lydia. If he cannot pull Lydia away from Jewson, Phipps wanted to go to France (he apparently told her) to escape the friction that had developed with Lydia over the issue.

Somewhere in the flow of correspondence at that time, Lydia wrote Shiel a lengthy letter that expanded beyond the immediate issue of Flo's problems, but did not yet indicate that she had told Flo of the actual relationship between herself and Phipps. She defended Jewson, who had done so much for her, and continued to do so—while probably well aware that he was being cuckolded.

[Two sheets, folded to make 8 pages]

[*Incomplete*] Love's language—is wildly extravagant—but dear & delicious remembered & repeated many times. My pen is a poor servant—to me—eyes & hands are more. / Little dear—your help for my sister is a great blessedness to think of & I will see her tomorrow evening I hope—(not yet having seen her alone) & we'll then arrange for her to come to you Monday morning about 12.30. If she cannot do so you shall hear by the first post of that day. Make her talk to you. She is shy rather compared to her elder & reprobate sister Lyd. My pedestal is a lofty affair & I am poised thereon by her without possibilities of fall—for all I do must be right to her. Indeed my heart is all motherly towards her & her's. Also for you dear. I agree with you—for I know we are one. I carry you—like an unborn thing—a sweet load of love—a sharp pang occasionally telling me how alive & vital my burden is—but without deliverance any desire for the same. I will bear it—& try not to bend my back. I will be worthy—the honour—you have engendered. /

I cannot explain why we do as we do—except by saying it is the necessity that compels & the place is perfect—which can keep me to a course which is right—& against the power of my love for you. The greatest pull I have ever known—in an opposite direction. / I heard of your visit to the boy & girl—but it was Olive who was kept from going to the concert with me—by the weather—not I who was kept from her—the weather is never insurmountable to me—in truth the sharpening wind & rainy snow of the last two weeks have cut & lashed my face, as I have gone through & soothed me—as Wagner's maddest music is a sweet slumber song to me—& understood & felt in some unexplainable manner— /

As to your going last spoken of—go dear. I think it wise & Paris or St. Pancras will mean no increase of distance for me & you will find some relief from the sharpness of this tearing apart—of two tenderest halves—all quivering & slow to heal. / Be more than half happy—if you can—dear—for your misery is worse to think of than the misery anyone else can possibly be—& yet in a way I know how lusty & strong you are like a little lion—& can bear—what would embitter & wither some less strong. / When the big pangs simmer down—I shall be gay as you wish—not quite yet. But I am mad to learn. I will

> go on—you are always my silent judge—nodding in approval or otherwise at all my acts—none shall displease you, dear. I will try my level best. Do not damn anybody—least of all a man who kindly places in my hands the means I ask of him—it is not like you, all my time of sitting for him—will be with you looking on—dear dear love. / Lydia.

By the following Sunday, Lydia wrote Phipps that she has told her "little human tale" to her sister. Flo is going to meet Phipps the following day, Monday, not only for the two to become acquainted, but also to determine how Phipps might "help" Flo—which probably means help her husband with employment, as Phipps had recently done for the husband of Lydia's niece. Where did Phipps manage to chase up jobs for these men?

> Dearest—the heart to heart talk is over & my sister knows my little human tale. She comes to you tomorrow—12.30. I do not see quite how you can help her—nor she either—but I want you to meet. She the dearest apart—from me—& you the dearest part of me. Lyd.

As it turned out, Phipps and Flo did not meet the next day, but he made plans to dine with her and her husband later in March. The actual employment situation of Ritson is never made clear.

Shiel must have had a fairly steady income during this period in order to have time even to consider assisting someone else. It is likely that he was involved with Louis Tracy on serial work, while he was also beginning to write more short stories than he had for several years. "Many a Tear," one of his best short stories, set in the mountainous Woolaston area, was published in the January 1909 issue of the *Novel Magazine*. On 13 March 1909, his story "Dickie" was published in the *Saturday Evening Mail* (Fiction Supplement). "A Night in Venice" was published in *Gunter's Magazine* in the June 1909 issue. It is also likely that his novel *This Knot of Life* was serialized during the year, prior to its book publication by Everett & Co. in November 1910, but there is no evidence to support this. It is this book that contains Shiel's lengthy essay "On Reading" (subsequently broken into "On Reading" and "On Writing" by anthologists), an important statement regarding his theory of literary construction. While foolish in many ways, it is always interesting and, in many aspects, of significant biographical importance. How the publisher, Everett & Co., could have been convinced to publish a novel of popular fiction with this long essay at its beginning is difficult to fathom.

Why Shiel seems to have never shared information with Lydia about his writing efforts is strange. It was only after a book's publication that he appeared to share it with her and debate his ideas. Perhaps it was because he was so intensely involved in writing Grant Richards and others in the literary world about what appears to have been, at the time, of more financial concern to him than their literary merits—which argues against his long-expressed view that he wrote for God! Nevertheless, it is apparent that he wrote Lina more about his work than he did Lydia. Lina would have been more concerned with the business of his writing, Lydia with the ideas. Also, there may have been concern regarding the privacy both he and Tracy may have wanted for their collaborations. Later, after their marriage in 1919, Lydia helped write out the texts of Shiel's novels until their separation in 1929.

On Sunday, 28 March 1909, Florence Ritson (writing from 166 Valetta Road, Acton Vale, W.) acknowledged a letter from Shiel that offered friendship and inquired about Lydia. Lydia appears to have been making an effort to stay away from Phipps because of the pressure that he had placed on her to separate from Jewson. Florence wrote (with apparent understanding of the situation with Phipps and Lydia):

> Dear Mr. Shiel / I have received your letter this morning. Offers of friendship are too valuable to be lightly cast aside and in order to reciprocate I shall have great pleasure in accepting your kind invitation for my husband & myself to lunch with you on Friday next, if that day will be convenient to you. Now for news of Lydia. I saw her last Thursday, at my sister's, she seemed fairly bright, on Saturday she paid me a visit, and I am afraid I cannot give you a very bright account of her. It seems so very strange to see her always so sad and miserable. I felt very sorry for her. It is so unlike her. I am hoping she will not have to as she evidently is doing for so long. I shall have a letter from her during the week as I expect she may pay me a visit on Saturday. I will not mention that you were inquiring about her, / Yours Sincerely / Florence Ritson

How Shiel's meeting with Flo and her husband went is unrecorded, and what he might have been able to do to help her is also unknown. Lydia appeared to have been going through a severe amount of distress regarding her affair with Shiel and tried to avoid him for several weeks.

Their apparent separation was broken by a chance meeting, upsetting Lydia as she wrote to Phipps on "Tuesday–13" of April 1909. If there had been any question of what their relationship had become, it is dispelled in this letter.

> Little pal—My sister has had news of you—I learned today when I called—Dear old girl—she is sounding the depths—The Good Friday venture was a dreary business—but—she is a wonder / brick. / The remembrance of you—at our chance meeting, has stuck in my side & hurts with every turn—O my dear, why has it been my part to do this bitter, bitter thing. O why could I not have given you your happiness—& seized my own at the same time—What a barrenness for such a wretch. / Little love, many times each day I bless you (wondering if our blessings are as important & as our curses.) I speak your name softly to my listening self—& bless you—with all that is tenderest—& most womanly in me. You—who are the background of my life—all else starts & fades, you remain—filling all—constant in all my waking hours—and more—for a few nights back—I dreamed my mouth was pressed to your brown cheek—& I held tightly your strong arms—& pressed close to your side as you remember was my way—but—to dream we sleep—& to know we have dreamed—we must awake— / I had told myself I would not make any move—towards you not even so much as a letter but just this—lest you think me hard—You said I was grim, think me gentle, dear, in my love for you if only I might have served you in some way—still without that privilege—just loving you—Lydia.

That Lydia was continually torn between her relationship with Shiel and her obligation to her family, and how she knew she appeared to be so inconsistent toward him, is reflected in another undated Thursday letter.

> My dear—Sadness Saturday, Sadness is mine today. What a complexity is this thing called life . . . Little child my glaring inconsistencies must puzzle & annoy you—forgive me . . . I come Monday.

In 1909 both Shiel and Tracy published two novels under their own names, and their collaboration *By Force of Circumstances* was released by Clode in March 1909 as by "Gordon Holmes." Shiel wrote pages 44–192 of the 342-page Clode edition, beginning with chapter III to the end of chapter X, according to information Shiel provided John Gawsworth. This story must have been serialized, but under what title, when and where, and under what author's name is unknown.

It is impossible to miss Shiel's contributions in *By Force of Circumstances*. One could simply print the section that Shiel wrote in a different color from the passages written by Tracy. Phipps's style is all over those pages. A reader cannot imagine anyone else writing a passage like this: "They walked under trees through which the moonlight, peeping, dappled the path with a pattern of leaves . . ." (G&D ed., 177).

Far more interesting in tying the story directly to Shiel is the geography of this novel—located in the general area of Bridgewater, at the head of the River Parrett ("Parret" in the book), southwest of Bristol. The full force of this location strikes one in the final chapters, when Inspector Furneaux asks Elinor to direct the yacht up to ". . . Lydney, a town on the other side of the channel . . . A three hours' run at full speed brought them to a pier from which Lydney is distant a couple of miles. There an inspector of police met them, and they walked to the railway station, which is much nearer the coast than the town."

A hundred years later, the railway continues in the same location. This area of England, south of the River Wye, that spilled into the mighty Severn was a favorite haunt of Phipps for his "hikes" and lovemaking. It is obvious that he followed that familiar pattern of laying out a plot with as close a relationship as possible to the geography and other facts with which he was familiar. While Tracy apparently wrote this section of the novel, he must have been following notes made by Shiel.

Why Shiel retained letters from women with whom he had had brief relationships during his wanderings in those vales and hills about the river Wye is hard to understand. Perhaps he saved them with their addresses for future need. It could not have been for affectionate recollection. But the following telegram from an unidentified woman at an inn ("Nr Oxford") arrived and was tucked away in his files during the end of this episode with Lydia and the Ritson family. Perhaps Shiel visited this "friend" again in the spring of 1909. It is unlikely that the inn, some ten miles south of Oxford, was the home address of this woman. How frequently he was seeing Lydia we do not know, since there is not another letter from her until June.

> [*printed*] Telegram / Sanford-on-Thames Heyford Hill / Littlemore / Nr Oxford 2.5.09
>
> Dear Mr. Shiel / What has become of you? Have you been jaunting again? I am up to my eyes in spring cleaning & my husband away! What have you been doing with yourself. Twice we saw you in the summer. / Now write in a few days. As I am shortly going to Worcester to fetch my hubby home. How very cold the winds are & what a lot of rain we got. Anything sensational to tell me. Any more conquests in the [*illegible*] Already [*illegible*] last night. Tread through Shakespeare's Venus & Adonis. I say a lively young lady! / Have you a nice book to send me. Something lively & write soon, mind. / Best love & wishes from Yours ever [*remainder of page torn off*]

On a Tuesday, probably 8 June 1909, Lydia recounted Shiel news about the Jewson family activities and indicated that she had been with Shiel the night before. Lydia's visits to Shiel for "instruction" had long since turned into visits for another purpose, and despite her best efforts she does not appear to have been able to maintain their separations for long. (Gerald is away at a boarding school in Ardingly, Sussex.)

> This morning brought me a letter from the boy—He is—better but still finding the heat very trying. / After my flight from you last night—before sleeping——I lay long—with my hands one upon the other—& between my breasts—& thought & remembered. / O my love—my dear love—nothing more can be written. / Goodnight. Lydia

Another letter followed on Sunday 14 June, indicating that Shiel had apparently sent her a portrait, but she prefers him face to face.

> Little Pal—thanks many times for venturing to send—I have waited long & am at length in possession of the pictured face—but—memory serves well. / What fine fingering a woman's words. What a delight to be able to turn out such—the neat work—in the Vestal furnace too is enviable. I prize it truly . . . I ask you if you will be at Queen's Road Tube Station—Friday next that I may have a face to face talk—I will be there at half past three—do not answer if you come— / Thanks again—dear generous little love. Lydia.

She wrote again on 7 July. Shiel was away on one of his treks into the countryside, and the Jewson family was soon leaving for Sheppey.

> Dear. I am glad to know you're away from the smoke cloud—&

> where winds sound loud among the trees . . . There is one which sounds like a rush of water—where the wind shakes it—as it did yesterday & my thoughts of you were mixed with its movement . . . We went to see Gerald Tuesday—for his birthday treat. Dear old chap is much subdued—not miserable however. He is at present going thro a tussle with the head master—over the question of being baptised—his airs were very like his mother . . . He comes home—on the 28th, a few days later we leave London. I long for bare feet—treading cold grass—in the early morning . . . I have been reading the Church-of-the-Overman—(The Last Miracle). I dwell on the words . . . [*No closing*]

Lydia wrote from The Coppice, Eastchurch, Sheppey, "Aug. 1st. 09." Gerald has been ill and commands her attention. Lydia suggests that Phipps seek solace in the winds he loves. (Any reader of these pages thus far must believe that Shiel was probably seeking "solace" from someone else along his trail.)

> Distance overrides clemency. We left London some little while since—as my boy has developed a nervous affection & is under treatment. / The Doctor tells me—my firmness must correct it as little faith in himself apparently—as I hold in such medicine well— / Dear—Why not go to the good little Mother—Seawinds—shattering sick fancies—leaving behind all such—as the ship speeds on. / About myself—nothing—the Tale is told—beggared of all—but remembrance—bitter sweet. / Lydia

Then, on Saturday, 18 September 1909, back from the family vacation on Sheppey, it appears from Lydia's letter that their affair has resumed but is now especially clandestine. She longs for the day when it will not need to be so, but it is difficult to see how she can so wish as long as Jewson is alive.

> Seeking you again for another moment of time—catching at a star— / your written words so dear—the blessings of this love of ours. How would one live through the consummation in thought, it is a deluge—and we—drowned. / Our rare meetings so guarded—restraint so right—but suggest the joy of our other oneness . . . High is my hope—sometimes—that I shall some time be able to come to you & offer myself for your having—openly avowing you, my male—long waited for—. . . & chance may yet—be kind to me—as in—bringing me to you, that day [*no closing*]

This letter may suggest an important distinction in Lydia's mind between their physical relationship and "our other oneness," a relationship based on her ability to associate fully with Phipps at his level of thinking, something that she had been trying to accomplish since she first met him.

In her letter dated 26 October (but probably written on Monday, 25 October 1909) Lydia invited him to attend a lecture with the family, and added a very affectionate farewell:

> Dear / Gell has asked me to send you this list of lectures—we have missed the first three—but are going to the last tomorrow Tuesday at five—he also says if you are inclined to go—we shall be outside the Bleuhevill Café at four oclock for tea. Gell will be pleased if you will join us . . . I actually fought—against the desire to even write you. How futile it seems. My hand is shaking with the strong emotions I feel—this task I have set myself is all too great—But frightening fit I must be. And—you dear—how are you—not in the depths I hope . . . Enough of this . . . My love dear to you.

How could Gell not recognize that there was more than friendship and "learning" at work between his wife and Shiel? Perhaps he preferred not to know.

The letter above was dated 26 October [1909], although at the foot of the letter is a notation: "W. L. Courtney / 11 Oct 09." W. L. Courtney (1850–1928) was an influential journalist, editor of the *Fortnightly Review* and chief dramatic critic and literary editor of the *Daily Telegraph*. The note may simply indicate who was the first in this particular series of speakers. It would make more sense if it had indicated who the next speaker would be.

On a Thursday, sometime late in 1909, Lydia was arranging to visit Shiel after not having encountered him on her walk through the park in the morning.

> No sign of you today—so as promised I write you. / I walked for half an hour until 4.50 the Gardens closing at that time—instead of tramping I returned to my sister's & joined the children's party—where I had left Gerald & small & sundry. / I hope is well with your, dear. / Little child how cheap—we become sometimes. I will call Saturday night about eight oclock. Will you leave a letter for me if you are not at home—such short notice is not fair to you & I am not fair to myself either. / No more tonight. / The "push" that is behind

the show of things uses me roughly, but to perfect ends no doubt— Yours, Lydia.

She evidently began to try and establish some separation from their intense relationship. Lydia urged Shiel to consider the wind as a replacement for her during his tramps along the Wye, as she wrote him on 14 November, a Saturday, undoubtedly in 1909.

> Little child—there is indeed no harm in your telling me where you are—yet I *ask* you not to write me. O the pity of it that a letter can have such power—or that I have so little—the old quiet must come back to me—if I am not to whine & play the cur generally—One's part must be played without howling, in fairness to others . . . / I wonder if your thinking during your walk by the Wye is all unknown to me—not, if it is with a man—as with a woman. If I were with you on such wanderings I wonder whether I could understand what the voices of the wind say to you, a little I think. / Dear turn the two corners of your mouth up—a "flapper" will flap your way—& solace she will bring—& all bitterness will be lost in her sweetness which will cover where I stood for a space. L.J.

There are increasing gaps in the letters from Lydia in Shiel's archive. What these gaps represent in their relationship is unclear. Another letter does not appear until almost a year later, when Lydia writes Phipps in a more reflective than romantic mood. Thus, on "June 16th. 10" (i.e., Thursday, 16 June 1910):

> Missing you this morning to re-read you. On reading—seemed fit. Twice carefully thro. I have been & peeped in it—at odd moments. Although you give me not only the key to learning to read—but also to writing. This will testify—how little it can do towards making a silk purse from a sow's ear. / However I am privileged to make you chuckle—a bit. / You were—ten years of age—blissfully [*illegible word*] it. May be you never were a grub, you lively one. / I have enjoyed your Science of Bliss. That is—enjoyed your enjoyment second-hand, a pint pot, trying to hold a pint full. / You say "any deep need in a people breeds of itself the means whereby to meet it." / I find hope there. Love of God is the greatest need of life—. . . Your write "Personality is a sham or pure illusion." I am no more I than I am you. You know this to be true. This thought churns round my brain. / It must be so—for what is—is a Unity—our way of parcelling it out leads to confusion. [*Incomplete; no closing*]

Lydia follows this with a letter on Wednesday, 6 July 1910, remembering the anniversary of their initial meeting two years earlier.

> Dear little Pal. This morning's awakening—was grey & your letter means maybe all—mine to you do. . . . Dear if fortune favours I will come to you tomorrow because your abiding place is my consciousness. / It is the return of the season which brought our first meeting—& the Spring to the earth, & in my tramps around my heart beat strong & as full—but, I cannot express more— / I go on—just loving You. / Lydia.

Chapter 16

"My dear Chesson"

Shiel had no books released in 1910. Louis Tracy had three, including another by Holmes, titled in America *The de Bercy Affair* (Clode, 1910) and, in England, serialized under the title *The Feldisham Mystery* in the *Red Magazine* from 1 June to 1 August 1910. Shiel denied any part in this title. Since he admitted writing a significant portion of *The House of Silence,* published under the Gordon Holmes pseudonym by Clode in 1911, Shiel undoubtedly spent time on that work late in 1910 or early 1911. Eveleigh Nash published this last Holmes novel, to which he said he contributed, under the title *The Silent House* in 1911. His writing energies appear to have become consumed by short stories, an effort especially strong in 1911.

Shiel's "Miche: The Story of a Child's Tragedy" (a girl and a circus lion's friendship) was published in the May 1910 issue of the *Royal Magazine*. An unidentified story is referred to in a letter to Peter Keary (from Grafton Mansions, 23 March, apparently 1910): "Here is the story—'The Dear Ones'—which I have spent a night in making as readable to you as I could recopying most of the pages. I will call about Tuesday to see."[1]

The several stories that would be published in 1911 (all in the *Red Magazine*) have a fresh, strong touch: "A Good Thing" in the 1 May 1911 issue; "The Tale of Adam and Hannah" in the 15 June 1911 issue; and "The Bell of St. Sépulcre" in the 1 November 1911 issue. A similar group of strong stories would be published the next year. It appears that Phipps had found a ready publisher for his short stories in John R. Stock, the editor of the *Red Magazine* and several similar siblings in Harmsworth's Amalgamated Press group of periodicals.

It is interesting that so many of these stories are located in the countryside of Provence, France, in rugged areas that Phipps must have tramped in as he did around and above the wilds of the River Wye. Even as he was breaking up with Lina in 1903, he told her that he would be leaving "for the country" whence he was then staying, in

1. Letter for sale in a Locke catalogue.

a Paris suburb, just south of Calais. He was undoubtedly going to Provence.

An indication of an attraction that Shiel found in his travels throughout France is recorded in a letter from a cosmopolitan friend that he made during those trips. H. Seymour (whoever he was) sent Shiel a handwritten note, dated "17/6/11": "Dear Shiel, / By a strange coincidence I made the acquaintance of Miss Mary Moore . . ." He had called on her, he said, and she was pleased that Shiel remembered her. Included with his brief letter was a business card: "'Visits Patients / At Home 2 to 7 / Massage Baths daily / By Hospital Trained Nurse / Miss Mary Moore (4 certificates) / Hotel de Clermont / 40 Rue de la Rochefoucauld"—presumably in Poitiers.

An extremely important letter from Lydia, with brief thoughts on "Jesus, the man," is undated, but written at Ardingly, Hayward's Heath, where Gerald attended boarding school. This would date the letter probably to July 1910. Despite several references in Lydia's letters that mention visits to France, she never elaborates on the purposes of her trips.

> A few written lines dear—to tell you I am leaving here today & starting for France tomorrow, Sunday—. . . I am reading E. Rénan's Life of Jesus. What simplicity. How I could have loved those followers & Him. I feel no artist—whose pictures of Him I have seen—has ever presented Him anything like He was . . . fierce eyed—(at times & dark hairy type) . . . I wish I could paint Him. I would shock the saint worshippers with my present [*illegible*] of Him . . . [*no closing*]

By 1910, Jewson had apparently decided to take the family to Sheppey for a longer period of time, to oversee the construction of a larger cottage on the island. Lydia wrote Phipps about these uncertain plans on Monday 25 July, apparently 1910.

> Little Pal. We are lively once more for the boy is home sooner than expected owing to the kindly visit of chicken pox—except to the poor chaps left behind. / Also I am learning to ride a bicycle. Can go alone—but somewhat wobbly. / There is talk of our leaving London for six months—& of the year & having a bigger cottage built at Sheppey 2 [*correct*] but we talk more than we act owing to too much working—but I hope it will be as there is an old garden ready made for the site (at present two tarred wooden cottages are on it—but beyond repair) . . . I love working in the garden—but our present place

is only a hillside—& so large & rough that my two months labour is lost sight of . . . I have unearthed a book on chemistry (Stackhardt & Heaton) & will join a class when I return—as I like to work in company. / Dear I am humble & proud at the same time—as I am God in nature & a weed upon the wall. My love to you—dear & thanks for your long letter. / Lydia

There are no other letters from Lydia in Shiel's files until 1912. It is also more than a year since Shiel appears to have responded to his friend and critic, W. H. Chesson, who had finally written him in October 1910 about *This Knot of Life* and its lengthy essay "On Reading"—virtually a year after its publication. Although Chesson had written reviews of Shiel's books for years, he did not review this one.

10, Coburg Mansions, W.C. / Oct. 11. 10. /

My dear Chesson, / I am ever delighted to have a line from you and when I had once unravelled the rhyme "redden with rust his dust," I was happy. So you have bought and read "This Knot of Life." Why bought you don't explain! I have always a useless lot of my books about; and should be only too glad to send you any one of them, at any time, if you would send me a p.c. I don't send without the p.c. because I don't know if you have already; and, then, remember, you are a reviewer, and to send one's book to a reviewer may be to sue for a review, which is Mr. Hall Caine's patent, and I must not plagiarise. As to "cat and Kin," since you would not come, I have actually gone to you, but by the time I found out Sandycombe Rd. it was so late in the night that I drew back. If you will come now, I'll welcome you with both palms up. Note change of address—this being near to Brunswick Square, W.C. I don't think you are old; and it doesn't matter, anyway; drink sour milk. I myself, God forgive me, will soon be rather tainted in that way, or am already: a little languid at the thought of writing more. I would continue to write simply and solely for you; but I'm a little bit—what shall I say?—languid at it, and don't think I'll bother long. The essay, or letter, yes, is "raw," for the reason that I committed the mistake of attempting to say a great deal more than I had the space to prove, so that half of it has the look of mere opinions, instead of more value than anybody else's. What I say of Milton, for instance, must seem absurd to many: I say he had the mind of a child compared with, say, the mind of the modern man in the street. Well, I should not have said that, since I lacked the space to prove it, though I *can* prove it—to some utter demonstration as to

> compel every mind, however unwilling, to see and know it with the same clearness that I do: and what I could prove of Milton, I could prove of Dante, Shakespeare, Plato, Caesar—that they were *a lower type of life and of mind* than the modern man in the street, and that it is time for us to think of them in that way, as we think of apes. But now I weary you. I hope the two little ones are going well, and yourself, too. / Your sincere / M. P. Shiel

What is especially interesting in this letter are Shiel's reflections on comments that Chesson had made regarding his work, "On Reading," published as an introduction to the novel. Shiel admits that the essay was "raw," since he did not have enough space to present the basis for some of his arguments. And he certainly indicates that he does not have the energy to pursue these ideas any further at the time.

Shiel made an effort to get a copy of *The Yellow Danger* for Chesson to read and provided some interesting personal points in a letter of Friday, 4 November 1910.

> My dear Chesson, / I have been rather in a whirl of things for a week, and, moreover, did not happen to have a "Yellow Danger" which, in the 6/ edition is out of print; but by dint of insistence in begging, I have managed to get two . . . copies from Mudie, one for you and one for me. A lot of it is blatant journalistic stuff, but there's another named "The Yellow *Wave*" of which I think well. Perhaps it is this that you meant to ask for? If so, I can send.
>
> I shall look out, then, for the new book. I found the Cruikshank good to read. I should think you could do something on Poe—or Borrow? A little friend of mine, named Ransome, has just done one on Poe, but, as far as I can see, he has very little to say. Of making many books there is no end. / Your sincere / Shiel.

Chesson provided Shiel with a critique of *The Yellow Danger,* to which Shiel responded in a letter that was marked "received 12 Dec 1910."

> My dear Chesson, / Many thanks for your two letters. I was glad that you were able to like 'Yellow Danger,' but fully agree as to its lack of celestialness; for that is not necessarily celestial which is about the Celestials, nor golden which is Yellow. / Also I am delighted at your good opinion of "Yellow Wave." It is the one of mine that I like the best, though the worst "seller." (Written under French and Hebrew influence). / Yes, the "service-papers," or one or two of them,

took up "Yellow Danger," and I was charged with being a naval officer in disguise! The truth was that I know some military people, whom I anon pump for information. / I indiscreetly took up your Cruikshank some days since, to look at it anew, and spent hours on it. It gives me a definite sense of Time and romantic impression.

Anon, too, you fill one with sudden glee and surprise—"ladies who resembled the bowls of tobacco pipes"! I shall never forget that. When you are cynical, you say—"as little charm as a stentorian oration in a small chapel": "distract the subjects of farmer George from their shops and Bibles" etc. / The fault I find is the fault I find with Meredith, that anon one has to spend fifteen, thirty seconds of one's life wondering what on earth you mean, and when one discovers, one finds that there is nothing particularly witty or profound in the thing to justify one's time-and-labor outlay, since all your best things are quite easy to understand. Even now I am not sure that I understand what you mean by "George had not long been in the world before he played ghost on his father's copperplates." What happens, I think, is this, that when Meredith, and you, have nothing clever to say, you say it fantastically, to make it look clever. But the fantastic is only admirable when it is at bottom rational—when something is to be gained by it; otherwise give me a plain statement in commonplace words. In the case, for instance, of "Time's scythe reddening his dust with rust," something *is* to be gained; it has pith and wit and music; but let's be as lucid as possible.

My impression that you are mainly a critic and monograph-doer is due to the fact that I have not come across sight of yours but criticism. I see you have written "Name this Child," but never read. In fact, I read little, except science-books. But should like to see some more of yours. / I have done a little booklet named "The Mansteal-ers" in that same Cruikshank period, and if I can find a copy presently, will send it you with this. / That amuses me, your mention of a monograph on me. I can't think what you would find to put in it; and I don't expect you would get much meat out of it! But if ever you think of it, and can get a publisher to take it up beforehand, I would add to his contribution by £50, £30 to be paid on the commencement of the undertaking, £20 on its completion. / So here's a long letter for you. / Your very sincere / M. P. Shiel.

He did send Chesson a copy of *The Man-Stealers* with this letter (the first revised edition, 1908, with minor revisions in his hand) inscribed "W. H. Chesson / from the author / 10 Coburg Mans. W.C. /

Dec. 12. 10." Chesson subsequently wrote page references on the endpapers to events in the novel. This book is now in the collections of the Harry Ransom Center, The University of Texas at Austin.

Chesson then wrote Shiel, apparently saying that he was not yet ready to commence writing this monograph on Shiel, who responded with a postcard marked by Chesson "Received Dec 19, 1910": "Many thanks for yours. So, then, you will let me hear when about to begin? / In haste, / M. P. Shiel." Chesson submitted a proposal to James Nisbet & Co. for such a work, for inclusion in the firm's "Writers of the Day" series, but Nisbet rejected it on 27 October 1915. (Coincidentally, Shiel was then in prison!)

Shiel was in touch with Grant Richards in the spring of 1911, needing a publisher, although Richards had not published a word by Shiel since the fracas over *The Evil That Men Do* in early 1904. He suggested that Richards reissue *Cold Steel* under the title *The Two Kings* as a 6d edition. He wrote Richards on 3 April 1911 (from Coburg Mansions) enclosing an 85,000-word revision of *Cold Steel* under the title *The Two Kings*. He had done so, he said, at the suggestion of a friend, the editor of the *Red Magazine* (i.e., John Stock). He had trimmed 40,000 words and had rewritten the result twice.[2]

Also, on 24 May Shiel sent Richards a copy of a play that he had written based on *The White Wedding*, asking if he knew someone who might like to bring it to the stage. He said that Clode had told him that Richards had called him "one of the ten men in England worth reading," to which Shiel said he replied, "Where are the nine?" "It is extremely bully and good of you to have taken all that trouble with my play," Shiel wrote Richards on June 16.

Anticipating that Richards would publish *The Two Kings*, or simply wanting a loan, Shiel asked Richards on 10 June for an advance on the book, saying that he was overdue on his rent. Unfortunately, Richards disabused him of any potential market for either the play or for his own firm's publication of the revision of *Cold Steel*. On 3 July 1911, Richards told Shiel:

> I did not make any secret when I talked to you of my anxiety to do *The Two Kings*—to do anything of yours in fact—but have been making indirect inquiries and I find that the libraries would very much frown on a reissue of *Cold Steel*, even if it were considerably altered as

2. Morse, *Works* 2.79, where the letter is misdated as 3 February.

it is. . . . They would not help the book . . . and even booksellers we should have to tell of the near identity of the book with *Cold Steel*. It would not be safe as a commercial proposition.

On the same day that Richards wrote him with this unhappy news (3 July), Shiel wrote Richards that Clode had written him requesting a "real" story, but had sent no money. Obviously in desperate need of financial support, he expressed concern to Richards on 4 July at his delay in returning *The Two Kings,* which Shiel had expected him to take. Shiel also provided data to Richards on the good sales of his novels in 6d format. *Isle of Lies* sold nine thousand copies within ten days of its publication as a *Daily Mail* 6d novel.

In his letter of 4 July, Shiel told Richards that T. Werner Laurie was going to publish a collection of his stories, but asked if Richards might not like to publish a collection (he was obviously looking for the quickest pound). "It has been said to me: 'If you have no novel ready, can't you let us have a book of short stories?' and such as this was my answer. But I think that 'the short-story' has not yet been written—except perhaps in France. 'Rayba'—(House of Sounds) in this is an attempt." He was obviously referring to the "short-story" as a literary art form, appreciating, as so many authors of his time did, the strong work that French authors had been producing.

Shiel described what might form the basis for the collection, when he wrote Richards on 15 July 1911 with a list of the stories to be included: "One of them, 'Dark Lot of One Saul' has not yet been printed, but will be soon. It has lately been accepted by The English Review, but a little editor whom I know came by here and grabbed it—editor of The Grand Magazine, so will appear in that. The copyright is all mine." As it turned out, "Dark Lot of One Saul" was not published in the *Grand Magazine* until February 1912 and did not appear in a book until it was included in the collection *Here Comes the Lady* in 1928. Many consider this tale of a sailor forever trapped in a cave beneath the sea to be Shiel's finest short story.

Richards did not follow up on any of Shiel's proposals. As planned, T. Werner Laurie (who had published several of Shiel's preceding books, including *The Last Miracle*) published *The Pale Ape and Other Pulses* in October 1911. (Shiel changed the title in proofs from *The Pale Ape and Other Happenings,* he told John Gawsworth. Thus, the first issue of this book has this original title on its binding, to save costs it was said, since these bindings had already been produced. A later issue corrected the title on the binding to reflect that on the title page, with the word "Pulses.")

Having stated this, I find it strange that the binding with *Happenings* is such a more cheaply made production than that of the binding with *Pulses,* the latter in this writer's hands having heavier boards and gilt lettering—a variant whose existence Morse said was unverified. The first issue, and the immediate reissues with *Pulses* on the binding, apparently have lighter boards and the title in yellow ink. It is apparent that this matter is not resolved.

Reviewers (with the exception of W. H. Chesson in the *Daily Chronicle*) did not greet *The Pale Ape* with enthusiasm. The *Bookman* said, "Mr. Shiel can do better than this." *T.P.'s Weekly* had only a brief notice, but did observe, "The study which gives its title to the book has in it the very chuckle of ferocious madness." Chesson observed the author "has a style crowded with bright novelties of expression, and if it were a style scrupulously ordinary, we should find it much less easy to listen to his dreams . . . There are two or three masterpieces of narrative . . ."

Shiel wrote Chesson (Wednesday, 25 October 1911): ". . . in the present collection of stories the only one which I thought had any merit was that 'Many a Tear' which you praise. I only published them because requested to—written long since, except 'Tear'." In the same letter, he told Chesson that he was "inventing an air-boat with which I intend to undertake the conquest of England (pro bono p.) *If* the thing is any good, I assure you I could have England under my thumb as easily as kissing hands. Then many things will become new. But, oh, the bother of it."

Chesson later must have asked Shiel how the state of his invention was going, for Shiel responded on 5 June 1913: "As to my air-boat, that is going forward, and I have good hopes of success, but there have been long interruptions in my building, and many obstructions. There is a certain obstinacy and malice in things . . . But on this I am relying mostly on figures and known facts, and you may hear more of it some time." What Shiel probably had on his mind were the airships that he had included in the serial *To Arms!* (*The Dragon*), just completed in March—a book that would bedevil both Shiel and Grant Richards after it appeared.

Shiel's real saviors during 1911 were probably Louis Tracy and John Stock, the editor of the *Red Magazine,* who began routinely to accept Shiel's stories for publication as they were offered. The last confirmed collaboration of Shiel and Tracy was Tracy's only new book published in 1911, the novel titled *The House of Silence* (as by "Gordon Holmes") in America, and *The Silent House* (as by Tracy) in England. This mystery of murder and lost wills must also have been serialized, but information about such a publication is unknown. It may be that newspaper syndicates published these "Gordon Holmes" collaborations, as were other Tracy works, with subsequent Clode book editions.

Shiel acknowledged to Gawsworth that he wrote through page 187 of the Clode edition, and pages 7–204 of the Eveleigh Nash edition. Shiel told Gawsworth in 1935, "The dullness of the end surprises me. Tracy slept." Shiel did spot eleven lines that he had written with "that inspiration which visits often neither me nor anyone else." The lines begin: "The hearts of women—why, they ought to be ground into powder and abolished out of creation—their wayward, obscure, and fantastic hearts!"

It continues to surprise that Shiel was able to maintain the level and pace of writing that he did during this phase of his career, keeping a complete separation of the writing that he did in collaboration with Tracy and the writing he produced for his own name. It must have taken a prodigious effort, while he also stayed absolutely quiet about the collaboration. There has never been an indication, other than the debate Shiel had with Richards over the fairness he wanted for Tracy in the book publication of *The Evil That Men Do,* that each author had some degree of compensation coming for their share of the work on a book. The two authors must have made a pact to maintain an element of secrecy about their collaborations.

Shiel and Tracy retained a routine friendly relationship with each other throughout their long period of writing partnership. In 1910, Shiel urged Tracy to have some portrait miniatures made by his niece, Olive Horsford. Olive had pursued a career as an artist painting watercolors and portraits in miniature on ivory, using a special technique to achieve effective and lovely results. Her work was exhibited in a number of important venues throughout the period of roughly 1907 through the 1930s.[3]

3. Aronson and Wieseman 211–12. "Although Olive Horsford remains a shadowy figure, this miniature confirms that she was an accomplished paint-

Shiel wrote several postcards to Olive assuring her that Tracy had prospective business for her. He wrote her at 12 Hilgrove Road on 4 March 1910 that she should come soon. "When I quoted £5 to Tracy, I thought he would be having two done. You should get more for one. . . . Dress artistically." Whether this miniature was ever done for Tracy is unknown.

What Shiel was able to earn for the work that he did with Tracy, and from whom such income came, has never been determined. But it must have saved him many times over in a near ten-year period from absolute financial collapse. It appears that Tracy managed all these financial arrangements. Whether it was the succor for the overdue rent that he mentioned to Richards in June 1911, it undoubtedly helped on many other occasions.

Actually, it had been early in 1911 that Tracy procured a copy of *This Knot of Life* and wrote Shiel about his essay "On Writing."

24 Jan 1911
Fairlawn, Whitby, Yorkshire

My dear Shiel: / After writing you yesterday, I was driven forth by a damnable Steamobile, which is crushing our road into a new smoothness. Hence I strolled into the station and there picked up a book of yours, This Knot of Life, which is very very readable in as much as it contains your essay "On Writing". I devoured it, the essay, last night—read it with care and jubilation, yet not without a carking fear lest I should be found among the slain. Happily you spared me though I should have been glad of the immortality thereby conferred, since your fine pronouncement will live many a century.

Surely the time will come when people who read will think with you, and then some poker and noser in musty libraries will disinter you and say, "Here my friend, was a prophet." But what need of my

---

er with a creative approach to technique. The surface of the miniature has been methodically scratched with a fine needle after painting, giving a linen-like texture and a soft blended aspect to the work. . . ." "Olive Horsford lived in London and exhibited at the Royal Academy of Arts in London between 1907 and 1940. She also exhibited work at the Walker Art Gallery in Liverpool, the Royal Miniature Society and other venues. She was related to the London physician Dr. Cyril Horsford (b. 1876), who was descended from a prominent Antiguan family." General Register Office England & Wales, Death Index: 1916–2005 Record for England & Wales, Death Index: 1916–2005. Olive J. Horsford Q4 1954.

thin pipe of praise? You know what a great thing you have done, and therein is your reward. What though of the two earlier letters? I want to browse on them, and chew on some small stone of knowledge from them, and learn something of the art which I practice with such dim understanding.

You will yet horrify the writer who is heedless of the beauty of words. I believe I could prove in this scanty sheet the influence of your magic, but alas time and a sounding steam roll forbid. . . . Who then is Mrs. Meade? And why no mention of Ruskin? Farewell!

Yours ever, Louis Tracy.

There is no evidence of further collaboration by Shiel and Tracy following *The House of Silence*. Shiel's last comment about Tracy is in his essay "The Inconsistency of a Novelist," first published in John Gawsworth's *Ten Contemporaries* (Ernest Benn, 1932). It still reflects the tension he always felt in the relationship between writing as commerce and writing as art, but given Shiel's long desperation for income his comment in the final sentence of the following displays his self-deception at its worst.

> . . . so that when in a few years the writer fills shelves with empty books, the impression left is that his (her!) only motive was to earn a livelihood, and that he is a common workman, who works for himself and for another man, not for Man, not for a planet, not, so to say, for God. And since no one is quite unlike his environment, I too, no doubt, am of this kind. Not wholly, though I fancy—perhaps because my father had some money; so that when my old friend, Mr. Louis Tracy, C.B.E., has said to me "Strange fellow, Shiel: you could make as much money as Bernard Shaw and Edgar Wallace put together, but you persist in casting your pearls before swine-herds, who know not pearls," I have answered something like this: "It is *you*, Tracy, who are strange, if you do not conceive that different people can be pleased by different things, that Mr. Shaw may have had a liking for oranges, and I a liking, not less genuine, for pineapple. And, if I made that money, whatever would I do with it? . . ."

Tracy died on 13 August 1928 at his home, Dunholme, in Sellindge, a small village outside of Ashford, Kent.

Three of Shiel's short stories were published in the *Red Magazine* during 1911. John Stock, the editor, had become Shiel's most reliable avenue for the publication of his short fiction—increasingly important as the market for serials diminished.

Richards did not publish another Shiel title until the disastrous *The Dragon* in 1913, plans for its publication having been initiated in 1912. Since this title was reissued as *The Yellow Peril* in 1929, one of four titles published by Gollancz in an attempt to revitalize a market for Shiel, many readers have confused this work with the earlier "yellow" titles. But this story included warring airships and destruction by the use of ray artillery, an attempted jingoistic tale that was not connected to real historical events as *The Yellow Danger* and *The Yellow Wave* had been. It is likely that *The Dragon* was purposely retitled to take advantage of the success associated with *The Yellow Danger,* while it also included more modern warfare without the dated historical distractions the other novels presented.

Two years go by between letters from Lydia in Shiel's files, when she wrote on Wednesday, "March 27th [19]12." The Jewson family was moving from its longtime home at 54 St. Charles Square to a new home at 23 Blandford St., Bedford Park, farther west from Kensington. It appears that intimacy between the two had continued, but the gap in Lydia's correspondence is unexplained. These gaps may simply be the result of events in Shiel's life, his moving about, perhaps, that resulted in his inability to save letters that Lydia may well have written during these years.

> Dearest. We are leaving our old house today—Lest the strange ways of fate should need it—I am sending our new address above. / A homeless one glimpsing a dear remembered fireside & turning from the open door—into the darkening drizzle—is not as loath as I to hear & say no word. / You I bless. / You I love. / You are everywhere in everything—
>
> [She added additional text to the letter]
>
> Wednesday at 12—twelve noon, for a long glance of gladness—that is all . . . Forget my talk of volcanoes & fire—if I see you tomorrow—that is by post I speak so. The wind blows my paper—as I am on a seat in the open writing this, on my way to my mother—the poor forlorn one. I will not keep you in suspense—but will wire if possible to you—in the morning if prevented. You see, dear, how sickening all this "if" and "perhaps" . . . My love is yours dear—& tender I am to you. / Lydia

Whatever their relationship was between the date of this letter in 1912 and a resumption of Lydia's letters (in 1916) that were preserved in Shiel's archives is simply unknown. He did send her an inscribed copy ("Mrs. Jewson / From the author / July 9. 1912") of *The Pale Ape,* and probably subsequently (after their marriage) made manuscript corrections throughout the book with a holograph insert on p. 58 revising a story, "Cummings Monk." This was probably done in anticipation of a later reprinting of the story. This book is in the Ransom Center.

By mid-1913 Shiel had become involved with Lizzie Price, and there surely was a gap in his relationship with Lydia. He continued writing serials. *To Arms!,* another variation of his Yellow Peril theme, was published in the *Red Magazine,* beginning on 1 January 1913 and concluding in the 15 March 1913 issue. Grant Richards published the serial as the disastrous *The Dragon* in May 1913.

Shiel had initially proposed to Richards (on 20 January) that the book version bear a somewhat different title. Richards responded emphatically on 28 January 1913: "Thanks for the copy, but I want you to alter the title. I doubt the libraries' willingness to circulate a book called *The Dragon Anti-christ,* and even if they did, I have it in my bones that the title would stand in the book's way." As it turned out, everything stood in the book's way.

Sallie Shiel Killikelly died in the West Indies in February 1913. While there is no record of how Phipps received the news, it must have come from his sister Harriet. He had not seen Sallie in some thirty years. There is no indication that they were ever as close as he and his other sisters. After Shiel did not sell over his interest in the old store on Montserrat, as his mother had requested, so that Sallie could reopen the store there in 1905, there was probably even less of a residual warmth from the days of their youth.

On 5 March 1913, Phipps wrote Richards (from Coburg Mansions) regarding negotiations with Clode for the American edition of *The Dragon,* and he followed quickly with a letter begging for an advance. He thanks Richards for a cheque on 10 April and describes a "defeeted" argument with printers and a similar problem that Louis Tracy once had. (In the novel Eulalia says, "Before I knew anything he had me off my feet." The Queen responds, "Say crushingly defeeted.") Shiel followed with a postcard on 16 April, asking if there had been any word from Clode regarding the book. Richards was able to tell him on 30 April that "Dodd, Mead don't want *The Dragon,* so I am writing to Clode telling him I am supplying him with his 500." That is, 500 sets of sheets of the book are going to Clode in America for distribution under its imprint.

Shiel continued to have his work appear in following months. "The Torture of Fear" was published on 19 May in the *Weekly Tale Teller*. A positive note was struck in mid-May when *Le Nuage Pourpre,* a translation of *The Purple Cloud* by Shiel's longtime French friend Henry Davray (with the assistance of Gabriel de Lautrec), was published by Pierre Lafitte & Cie. in Paris. He was disappointed, however, when he had to write the literary agent, C. F. Cazenove, on 22 May 1913 that it was too late to sell *The Lord of the Sea,* since he was correcting that title in preparation for a 6d or 8d edition contemplated by Pearson. Pearson did issue it in a "lightly revised" 6d edition, also in May 1913.

On 13 June, Shiel wrote Richards to say he will be by tomorrow, happy to hear he is due money, and will pick it up. He told Richards that he was sorry to hear that Richards had been ill and commented "Modern man does not eat too much, but too often." He wrote again, the same day, with suggestions for marketing *The Dragon*—even suggesting to Richards the hire of "Sandwich men" to carry placards recommending the novel. Richards was not impressed.

> June 25th, 1913. / M. P. Shiel, Esq. /
>
> My dear Shiel: Sandwich men cost, as a matter of fact, a great deal more than eight pence a day—more than twice that sum. Perhaps they only get eight pence a day from the contractors. And I am sorry to say that I do not believe that form of advertising would move the book; indeed I am convinced it would not. When I did it with "The Yellow Danger" it was new. That book took hold better than this has done. The critics who have dealt with "The Dragon" have none of them done it justice; in fact I have yet to find the critic who has done you justice with any of your work.
>
> I really want particularly to see you. Could you make a definite appointment to come in here on Friday at 8:30? / Sincerely yours [*signed*]
>
> P.S. Since the above was dictated I have spoken to you and [you] have told me that you will come in on Friday. Please do not be late.

On 30 June, Shiel expressed disappointment over Clode's low offer of royalties for its edition of *The Dragon,* but he apparently got away for a vacation later in the summer as he wrote Chesson, in an undated letter.

> 10 Coburg Mans. W.C. / My dear Chesson, / Thanks for card, which I have only just got, having been breathing a little on the East coast. You are a fellow apparently of many sides! And are now detected in reading the Occult Review! Need I say that I don't understand what the quotation is all about? "Polarity" is a lovely word—a writer in the "Occult" can use it to mean nearly any thing that comes into his head. Of saying many things there is no end! There is a man named Bagby, or Bugbear, whose name, by some fate, if I spend a 1/2d on a paper, I come across—he is your man for vague polarities, talk, talk, and never a thought, only memories of impressions which he takes for thoughts, and as water hisses at fire, so I hiss at that man's pursuit of me. Forgive, if he's a friend: he has caught me this day, and I pour it out upon you.
>
> I am glad that you are interested in flight: it seems to me that the future is big with this thing. The man who first produces a real airboat (aeroplanes are not good) could reduce England to starvation, without fail, within two weeks—if he liked; and somebody will produce it before many years, for I'm sure that it is not difficult. It needs an electrician's undivided attention for some months, and it will be done. It would have been done before, but that the mind of mechanicians are all preoccupied with aeroplanes and airships, and haven't the liberation to turn away to something quite new. / Adieu! / Your sincere / M. P. Shiel

Of all surprising things, perhaps, was an interest that Shiel shared with Richards in the summer of 1913 (11 July). He wants to buy a farm from a friend, Hamilton Edwards of Harmsworth, to supplement his writing income, but he needs £30 for a down payment. It is difficult to imagine how he thought he could thus supplement his income. Edwards edited the *Boy's Friend* and became in time a manager of Harmsworth's Amalgamated Press.

Shiel thanked Chesson on Sunday, 31 August 1913, for sending along two papers with references to him. The publisher has told him that the book "has been something of 'a success.' Though, anyway, one does not get much meat out of the sale of books, unless one is Charles Garvice. I have had a lot of reviews of it, some of which would surprise you by their fatuity: one sneers at me for not describing world-battles in the same words as 'Mary had a little lamb.' But then most of them are not thinking of books, but, very properly of their board and lodging. Such is life in feudal England."

Shiel was still living at Coburg Mansions at the end of August, but shortly moved to 2 Harpur Street where, as he wrote Richards, he was "in lodgings"—that turned out to be for about two months.

He sent two brief postcards to Richards in September, one postmarked 8 September 1913, expecting a reply regarding Appleton's interest in publishing *The Dragon* in America. Then, on a postcard that was postmarked 11 September, he told Richards that Appleton was off, to go back to Clode. So Richards made arrangements with Clode to supply that firm 500 copies of sheets from his English edition for sale in America.

Shiel could not have imagined how things would deteriorate over the next two months, with respect to either his publishing success or to his personal life. *The Dragon* failed and markets for his fiction disappeared. Lizzie Sircar was pregnant, and it is uncertain what his relationship was with Lydia. By December, he and Lizzie shared the same address: 50 Frederick St.

After the death of Jewson of a heart attack in 1914, Lydia returned to the home at 54 St. Charles Street, in Ladbroke Grove, Kensington. Jewson had purchased property at 42 Woodstock Road in March, moving from Blandford Street. He and Lydia lived there for only six weeks before he died. Jewson left the Blandford residence and the Isle of Sheppey cottage to Lydia in his will. Gerald inherited the St. Charles Street property and his father's financial holdings and income. However, Lydia was living at St. Charles Street when a dramatic reunion with Shiel took place soon after he was released from prison in 1916. There was a great deal of distress in store for Shiel, however, before that event, two years ahead.

Chapter 17

"rather in distress . . ."

The year 1914 would completely undo Phipps, when the birth of an illegitimate son, financial collapse, the plagiarizing of a story, conviction for rape, and incarceration would engulf him. So much for this alleged "king"-to-be. But Lydia would stand by him when he most needed her, and their marriage would ultimately follow, resulting in a new period of social and political activism and successful novel writing.

Events leading up to these problems had been foreshadowed in the closing months of 1913, when *The Dragon* failed dramatically. Shiel's suggestion to Ward, Lock for a new title foundered, as he wrote Grant Richards (from Harpur Street) on 15 October: "A little while since Ward & Lock wrote asking me to send them the beginning of a book for them to order—with a view to 'serial.' I produced this bit, 'The Strangest of All' and sent it to them. This morning I got it back, they saying that it won't do because the relationship between the two men in it is decadent." Shiel asked Richards to read the brief draft and let him know if Richards would make it worth his while to finish it, ending his letter, "Let me know quickly."

This proposal appears to have led to the story that Shiel let Gawsworth complete in 1935 as "The Death-Dance." Gawsworth took the section of the original novel as Shiel had written it, then added a small final section that concludes this text as a short story. Gawsworth also copied the "Synopsis" that would extend this text to a novel "from a draft by M.P.S." with a note by Shiel: "A tale of human emotions not very easy to give an idea of in a synopsis, but probably strong." This already acknowledged the anticipated reception that his suggested novel received. Although rejected as too decadent in 1913, some aspect of it fortunately survives in the short story and synopsis.[1] The story is full of references to Lina and her mother—"the Princess de Miraflores," who had the first of her three daughters at age thirteen—that probably bring us closer to Shiel's feelings about this marital situation than any record beyond the original correspond-

1. It is fortunate that a manuscript trail can be traced in the holdings of HRC.

ence among Phipps and the "Spaniards." But the major offending element of the story is the unnaturally consuming friendship of the two principal males.

The relationship between "Beaumont" and "Burke" is so strong that when Beaumont loses his sight from an accidental dose of poison, Burke blinds himself so that he can be placed in the same institution as Beaumont just to "hear his voice"! The proposed novel reaches ridiculous heights when the two blind men unknowingly battle each other with canes in the institution.

The very fact that Shiel had developed an idea for a new novel means that he had not yet given up any thought of continuing such writing—especially if it could have serial publication. But the devastation of the failure of *The Dragon,* and this reaction by Ward, Lock to his proposed new novel, probably led to such a block that he would shortly sink to plagiarism.

Richards obviously did not think much of the proposed novel either, however gently he may have phrased it, and probably recommended that Shiel seek financial assistance from the Royal Literary Fund.

Phipps continued writing frequent letters to Richards—this from 2 Harpur Street, on 22 October 1913, regarding the proposed novel that he would abandon as such, but eventually use for "The Death-Dance" twenty years later.

> My dear Richards:
>
> Many thanks for reading my stuff & for your good opinion. On reflection, though, I have come to the conclusion that it is useless my going to the end with a book if it is not to come out serially. This one seemed to me to have so much possibility, that I was led to bother you, but I'll let it slide. Not that my books sell badly on the whole: "The Dragon" has been far the worst, except for one volume of stories. But the best of them would not have paid me, apart from serial. So send it for me. I hope 'Valentine' is doing you good.
>
> Your Sincere / M. P. Shiel

Grant Richards had published his own novel, *Valentine,* a few weeks earlier. Then, on 24 October, Shiel wrote Richards (still at 2 Harpur Street) and detailed the income that he had gained from various books. He obviously felt that an advance from *The Dragon* should have been better than he received.

My dear Richards,

I am "in lodgings" for the moment and separated from statistics but can tell exactly the amounts I received from the sale of recent books: "Evil that Men Do" . . . 100 pounds Ward Lock, "Lost Viol" 250 pounds all rights Ward Lock, "Third Generation" 75 pounds (Chatto). "Isle of Lies" 60 pounds (Laurie), "White Wedding" 70 pounds about (Laurie), "Last Miracle" church cursing book about 50 pounds (Laurie), "This Knot of Life" 60 pounds. Everett (I was a little overpaid in advance for this). "Pale Ape" 25 pounds (short stories bought before publication). These are about all I think.

Besides these sums I have got for each of these 20 to 50 pounds for 6d. editions (except "Last Miracle"—Church book unsalable). "Evi'" 6d. rights, 100 pounds, including "Pale Ape" and "Third Generation."

These facts being true, imagine the knock-down blow when I asked 5 pounds on Dragon's 25 and couldn't get it.

But don't imagine I blame you at all. I have always believed and preached that you are the ideal publisher provided you have the money; and I can quite see that subject of "Dragon" was stale.

Your sincere / M. P. Shiel

Richards was rather stung by Shiel's apparent criticism of his firm's marketing. He immediately wrote Phipps on 25 October:

> Thanks for your letter; but it does not really tell me what I want to know. In those cases in which publishers of your recent books have bought them outright, then naturally when you get back to your papers you will not be able to tell me the figures of your actual sales. But in those cases in which you have been paid a royalty I take it you have had statements of sales, and if I could know what they showed I could learn to what extent our organization on the face of it failed—if it did fail. Your suggestion that the subject of "The Dragon" was stale is of course a possible one, but it had not occurred to me. I liked the book more than ordinarily. / By the way, as some of the sums you received included serial rights they cannot be compared with the others.

Shiel provided some minor corrections to these figures when he wrote Richards again, still from Harpur St., probably at the very end of October.

My Dear Richards,

In reply to yours, the figures I have given *are* the figures of the actual sales, if you multiply them by twenty, except where I have stated that I sold outright. Of course, I don't remember the odd shillings. In the case of "White Wedding" I remember now that I got £15 with the second a/c, so the amount is £85, not £70, as I said. In the case of "Knot of Life", you must take out about £10, I think from the £60 paid me in advance on royalties.

I went in, *en passant*, a day or two ago to ask if you had sent the 500 copies to Clode, and if you knew when he publishes.

Your sincere / M. P. Shiel

He wrote Richards on 2 November 1913 (still from 2 Harpur Street), argument or not, he needed money:

My dear Richards,

If by any means you can lend us £5 on the strength of the enclosed to Clode, I shall rejoice greatly in you. The collapse of that "Dragon", so unexpected by me, both here and in America, has thrown me into shallows and miseries, until I find my feet again, with a new serial. See if you can lend me a hand. I should think that by this time the book has been published by Clode, and though he has not given me any idea when he will send me what little will be due to me (about £12, if he sells the 500 copies), I suppose that it won't be long. Then he can send to you, and you give me the overplus, if any.

Your sincere / M. P. Shiel

Of course, if anything is *on the way* from him to me, I'll send to you. I haven't heard from him for weeks.

Richards suggested that Shiel apply for financial assistance from the Royal Literary Fund, but pursued *The Dragon* argument. He wrote Shiel on 10 December saying ". . . 'The Dragon' has been in greater demand than its predecessors. I wish you would get out and show me actual statements of the previous sales. I am really nettled that, compared with what you think of other publishers, we seem to have done so badly."

Richards appeared to be the only friend—or source of funds—that Shiel could turn to at the time, and Richards had helped him frequently with money in the past. It is fortunate that his letters to Richards at this time still survive, since they help frame the events that would be so important to his literary life as well as his personal. He continued his regular letters.

Shiel followed up on the recommendation from Richards that he apply for assistance from the Royal Literary Fund. He sent letters seeking references from Lord Northcliffe and C. Arthur Pearson. Alfred Charles William Harmsworth, 1st Viscount Northcliffe, wrote from the *Times* on 12 November 1913: "Dear Mr. Shiel. Certainly you may use my name as a reference. I have not seen you for some years, but when I did know you, you were undoubtedly worthy. Yours sincerely, Northcliffe."

Pearson responded from 18 Henrietta Street, London W.C., on the same date: "Dear Mr. Shiel. Certainly use me as a reference, and I will do all I can to help you. Yours sincerely, C. Arthur Pearson Ltd." Initialed by Pearson over the firm's name.

Shiel must have gotten money from Clode, since he delayed filing a request for support until the next year. But an extremely important letter from Shiel to Richards on 18 December 1913 indicates a new address: 50 Frederick Street, W.C. He had moved in with Lizzie Sircar, who was six months pregnant with his son. Richards had been on a trip to the United States.

> My dear Richards,
>
> I am glad that you have got back safe, and thanks for your book, which, however—no, je-ne comprende pas. You ask me for the sales of my late books. I give them to you, not approximately, but exactly to within 1s, showing you that the worst of them has done at least twice as well as "Dragon", and the best considerably more than three times as well (exclusive of 6d rights); and now you write that someone says that "Dragon" has been in greater demand than the others. Now, both can't be true, and I hope you haven't the misfortune to believe the untrue! If you do, that is not a compliment to me, for I make so little from any of my books, that I can't possibly *forget,* don't you know, so if I have misled you, I have necessarily done it willfully—without motive, which would be stupid; and if this does not convince you, why not ask the publishers I have named over the telephone, mentioning that you do it at my request, and no doubt they'll satisfy you. As for looking for the accounts, I haven't the energy, for the reason that I doubt whether, if I looked, I would find.
>
> Your sincere / M. P. Shiel
>
> Note address. Did you see Clode? When does he publish that book of mine? I hope you had a good time

The week prior to this letter, Samuel Horsford, Shiel's brother-in-law, died in London. The source of his illness is unknown, but he had arrived from St. Kitts at Southampton on 13 October perhaps seeking treatment. As the husband of Gussie and father of Shiel's nieces and nephews who had been so important to him in his early years, Sammie had been a lifelong friend. The year was not beginning well for Shiel.

The bickering extended into 1914. Richards went to America just before the Christmas holidays, and did not write Phipps again until 8 January 1914.

> My dear Shiel: / I ought to have answered earlier your letter of December 18th. What with my return from America and the Christmas holidays I have been particularly busy. / I hope I did not express myself badly. There was not for a moment the slightest thought in my mind of the absolute bona fides of everything you said. But I am still running my head up against the question of where those books could have been sold, since the big buyers say they took more of "The Dragon" than they did of its predecessors. And it is a matter that annoys my travellers even more than it does me, as you may imagine. If I cannot sell your books as well as other people can sell them, then, at least as far as you are concerned, I have failed in my duty. / Yes; I saw Clode and he gave me instructions to ship his copies at the close of the year, so I suppose he will publish the book towards the end of this month. / Sincerely yours, [*signed*]

While the early months of 1914 were not good, an absolute flood of hellish events would cover the rest of the year. First, Shiel felt compelled to challenge Richards regarding sales of *The Dragon*. He wrote on 25 February 1914, from the Frederick Street address:

> My dear Richards:
>
> I should like to know just how we stand *re* "Dragon". You have not troubled to send me any statement, because of its insignificance, I suppose. But please do in a moment of opportunity.
>
> I hope you are going well.
>
> Your sincere / M. P. Shiel

Richards quickly responded, and Shiel answered on 1 March 1914.

> My dear Richards,
>
> Thanks for statement re "Dragon" I think you will agree that there is only one word for it—"ridiculous", though I have good reason to do anything but laugh. The essential popularity of the book I

give you is not a matter of *opinion:* it was bought of me by Harmsworth, who are just like mercury thermometers to the popular temperament, and it ran to its end with no little success (I was told) in a popular print like *The Red*. Then when I publish as a book I get for it just a quarter of what is paid me in advance for my most unpopular book. I don't think you will say that that's practical politics. I can't even sell it in a cheap form, as usual, without doing a lot of work on it, as it is much too long: so that, on the whole I get practically nothing. I imagined that, this being so, you would at any rate have offered me the usual king's shilling—I don't think that anyone has ever thought of *offering* me less, but I signed for less from you since I was assured of its popularity already, and you undertook verbally, you remember, that I should get more than £25, so, understanding that you would see me through, I was not careful as to what was in the contract, which was not our first. Tell me what you will do, then; or does it seem to you that I have got a fair day's wage?

Anyway, don't think that I put the blame of the collapse upon you. I don't *know* that you are to blame at all, and I am sure that, to *book*-readers, the staleness of the subject had an influence. I only say that the failure ought not to fall only on the weakest back, for that's a thing, always, that cries to heaven. If you think of it, you will say the same.

Your sincere / M. P. Shiel

Richards is more than ready to put *The Dragon* episode behind him.

March 6th, 1914. M. P. Shiel, Esq. /

My dear Shiel: / Perhaps you are right and the "staleness" of the subject of our book may have had something to do with the small sale. I do know that we are not to blame here. I always believed in the book. It attracted me. And I made my people believe in it. We spent more on advertising it than the sales of any one of your books with the exception of "The Yellow Danger" would justify from the commercial point of view. In the result we lost money over it. That is the fortune of war. I don't complain—except of the public; in fact I only tell you in order that you may see that the book's failure does not only fall on your back. / I am afraid one cannot argue from the success of a story as a serial in a magazine like the "Red" to its likely success in book form. However, I hope you may still get something out of it in cheaper form. / Sincerely yours, [*signed*]

The record of further correspondence between Shiel and Richards fails us for a number of months, but they were months in which a number of events are recorded. It is probably not surprising that Shiel was under a great deal of pressure when he pushed so hard on Richards. On 13 March 1914, Caesar Kenneth Shiel was born to Elizabeth Sircar "Shiel," formerly Price, of 50 Frederick Street, St. Pancras—as registered on 21 April by the baby's mother, listing Shiel as its father. There is no evidence that they were ever married or that she had any entitlement to his name.

The baby boy joined the two sisters, Eileen and Dorothy Sircar, who had been born in Chepstow. Shiel stayed on with the family for some eight months, but there is no indication that he and Kenneth ever met after that. But Kenneth wrote Shiel in 1946, saying he should have been in touch sooner. He provided a few details about his sisters, and his own ambition to own a dairy farm or move perhaps to Canada. There is no evidence that Shiel ever answered his son's letter.

On 11 April 1914 a new Shiel short story, "The Whirligig," was published in the *Weekly Tale Teller*. On 12 April 1914 the Clode edition of *The Dragon* was reviewed in *New York Times Book Review*.

An event of personal significance to Shiel occurred on 26 April 1914 when William Arthur Jewson died of a stroke. There is no evidence of what Shiel's immediate reaction to this event may have been, but Jewson's death would free Lydia from her feelings of obligation to, if not affection for, this man who was the father of her son, and who had been kind to her for so many years. Every bit of record indicates that Jewson let Lydia do pretty much what she wanted to do. What their spousal relations were can only be conjectured.

"The Place of Pain," one of Shiel's most praised stories, wherein a rock rolled in a river is said to produce a lens in which visions of people on a hellish moon can be seen, was published in the 1 May 1914 issue of the *Red Magazine*. On 19 June 1914 another story, "The Waif" (with that clever "Skin-the-Goat" at his gypsy thievery, extracted from its first publication in *Unto the Third Generation*), was published in the *Red Magazine,* and on 1 August 1914 "16. Brook Street" and "The Ideal Wife" (a contribution to "The Red Round Table" feature) were published in the *Red Magazine*. In September, *Contraband of War* was issued as a Pearson 6d reprint.

And on 4 August 1914 England declared war on Germany.

Shiel finally filed an application to the Royal Literary Fund on 21

September 1914. He was able to include the references that he had obtained the previous fall from Northcliffe and Pearson, and Grant Richards had written a supportive statement.

> I am applying in the enclosed for a grant from the RLF because of impecuniosity due to a falling off in popularity, to some failure of my sight, and then to the war. Some years ago I made a very fair income from the writing of serials and novels and was almost "popular"—or thought to be; but I pleased the editor more than his readers, and I have gradually been found out, and marked. The process has gone on. I have recently been "sold up," and since then have been rather in distress.
>
> In November last, too, I was very hard up, and was then recommended to apply to you; on which I got from Lord Northcliffe and Mr. C Arthur Pearson the notes which I enclose. But then I got a stroke of luck, an "order" for a story so did not apply . . .

Edwardian Fiction: An Oxford Companion adds: "He applied to the Royal Literary Fund in 1914, stating that he was going blind, had three children, the youngest four months old, and that his annual income had declined from about £2,000 at the turn of the century to about £150." Shiel said the children were living with his "wife's" parents—apparently the Price family in Lydney.[2]

Anticipating Shiel's petition to the Fund for assistance, Grant Richards wrote Llewelyn Roberts, secretary of the Fund, to support the application. He said that he had been publishing Shiel since 1897 and had known him since the early 1890s when Shiel did work for Stead. He believed that Shiel's chief source of income was not from books, but from commissions to write serial novels for the popular press, but that demand in that quarter had ceased for the present.

He went on to say:

> I have read practically everything Shiel has written, and I have never doubted that he has in him more than a dash of genius—of genius, however, of a very unpractical and not always money-bringing quality. I think one might say of him that he is extraordinarily clever and a little mad. His cleverest, and also his maddest, books were those he wrote for John Lane's Keynote series—Shapes in the Fire and Prince Zaleski; his most popular "The Yellow Danger". He has, I be-

2. Kemp, Mitchell, and Trotter 361.

> lieve, always been poor: often very poor. I also believe he has always worked hard and that if he can get no work now it is no fault of his own. Certainly from what I know of him I believe it would be difficult to find anyone who more thoroughly deserved assistance.

John Stock, editor of the *Red Magazine,* also endorsed Shiel's application strongly. W. P. Ker was lukewarm: Shiel's *White Wedding,* he said, was "absurd nonsense, but it is not illiterate. I think the author has some reputation as a practicing novelist, and although this book is very poor I do not care to vote against the author's claim for consideration."[3]

On 1 October 1914, Shiel wrote Richards, still from 50 Frederick Street, that Llewelyn Roberts of the Royal Literary Fund had interviewed him that morning and had shown him a letter from Richards that praised Shiel, for which Shiel thanked Richards warmly.

> My dear Richards:
>
> In an interview which I had this morning with Mr. Llewelyn Roberts, I got a glimpse of a long letter which you gave yourself the pains to write about me. Thanks. For this I put your name in my white book, and for these cheery words of yours to me. May you, too, see good days.
>
> Your sincere / M. P. Shiel

Just two weeks later, Shiel's supporters for assistance from the Fund must surely have been shocked by a turn of events—if they became aware of the situation. Meantime, the Fund did respond to his expression of need—with a grant of £10.

On 11 October he wrote Richards again, regarding an idea for a new novel that Richards had suggested:

> I have been looking round the rooms of my mind re your ideas for a Kaiser book, and I think that that will be all right. Only, it is the kind of thing for which you must give me a little time: when I'm once started, I'll quickly be through, but the first line is reluctant in coming. Anyway, I shall soon be off.
>
> I am writing under a sky swept by searchlights in a dim-lit London; someone was just telling me that six Zepp[e]lins are coming, and immediately afterwards I heard a thump like a bomb which made me jump—not quite nice this holy Sabbath eve. But, as I reckon, it should do us a lot of good.

3. Undated letter from Ker to Llewelyn Roberts. File 2946, Royal Literary Fund Archives. British Library.

It would be interesting to know the subject matter of this "Kaiser" book that Richards had suggested to Shiel, but those details do not exist. It may be that Richards had suggested a serial novel that might follow the pattern of Shiel's early such efforts with *The Yellow Danger* and *Contraband of War*.

Meantime, the first sign that things were probably not right with Lizzie Sircar was a form letter dated 30 September 1914 that Arthur O'Hare (153 Euston Road, King's Cross, London W.) sent to Grant Richards requesting a reference for Shiel. Shiel was looking for a new home. Blank areas on the form had been filled in so that it read:

> Dear Sir / Mr. Shiel / Has applied to me for rooms at 8/6/6 per week /
>
> He has given your name as his employer / will you kindly inform me if this is true / & would he make a suitable tenant / Yours faithfully /
>
> Arthur O'Hare / Kindly reply at your earliest convenience[4]

Shiel was apparently still living at 50 Frederick Street. It might be tempting to think that he moved in with Lydia once Jewson died, since Gerald had joined the army in August 1914, but in many ways Lydia's scruples were far superior to Shiel's. How aware Lydia was of the Sircar events never shows up in their correspondence or other records.

On 26 October 1914, Elizabeth Sircar filed charges against Shiel for having obtained "carnal knowledge" of her daughter, Dorothy Sircar, aged twelve years, five months. On Friday, 30 October, at 5 P.M., Shiel was received into custody, jailed, and remanded from a magistrate's court to an upper court's hearing on Tuesday, 3 November. There, he was "committed to trial." The informant or complainer, at the time of Shiel's arrest, was identified as E. Stephens. Shiel's occupation (and using his still legal name, "Shiell") on the warrant was listed as "clerk." There was a doctor's fee submitted for 3 shillings sixpence, probably for an examination of the victim by Dr. Michael Malone Lee. The indictment refers to "Elizabeth Sircar" as "alias Price," and there is no indication that she was married to Shiel.[5]

A jury trial was held on 16 November in the Central Criminal Court, Justice Coleridge presiding. The witnesses—all represented by deposition except for Dorothy and Dr. Lee, who appeared in per-

4. Original form in HRC.

5. The full story of these events is detailed in MacLeod, "M. P. Shiel and the Love of Pubescent Girls."

son—included P.S. [i.e., Police Sergeant] E. Dion, Eileen Sircar (Dorothy's younger sister), Dr. Michael Malone Lee, George Stephens, and Charles Meaton. Their evidence had been presented to the grand jury. Apparently serving as his own, and only, representative for the defense, Shiel probably went through his standard argument that the age of consent in English law was illogical, and that women younger than Dorothy had all been successful young mothers of major historical personages. Shiel was convicted and sentenced to sixteen months at hard labor. He submitted an appeal to the Court of Criminal Appeal on 14 December, but it was denied.

Interestingly, Elizabeth's address on the November court document was listed as 29 Argyle Street. Had she moved from the 50 Frederick Street address to get away from Shiel?

Court records identified "Shiell" as a "metal worker." Interestingly, at that time, there was a firm in London, E. Stephens & Sons Metal Working, so there could have been a confusion of Shiel's occupation with that of E. Stephens or George Stephens, both names mentioned as involved in the case as complainant and witness (possibly the same person). It does not seem likely that Shiel would have stated that his employment was either "clerk" or "metal worker," although "clerk" seems a more likely possibility. Had he begun work for the Censor's Office? Again, there is no record of this employment, although Shiel wrote his niece Olive during World War II that she was working in that office as he had in the First World War.

No sooner was Phipps incarcerated as Prisoner #2225 (under his still legal name, Shiell) at H. M. Prison Wormwood Scrubs, than Grant Richards set out to inquire about his health and general situation. There are two form-letter responses to Richards from the prison that have survived—the first, dated 24 November 1914, simply acknowledges receiving "letter of 23rd instant . . . for which I thank you and the Medical Officer has seen the letter." The second, dated 24 January 1915, notes "that the above prisoner is still in my custody." Both are signed with an undecipherable name, apparently designated as either Warden or Governor. There is no way to tell what questions Richards posed to the prison. However, the comment from the warden that the Medical Officer had seen Richards's letter, might suggest that Richards provided some type of information regarding Shiel's physical condition that should be taken into account in his serving at hard labor.

A prison term of sixteen months would probably date from the time of his incarceration to February 1916. There is an undated letter from Shiel to Richards, probably January 1916, thanking Richards for his interest and arguing against the law under which he was imprisoned.

My Dear Richards,

I have been told that you have written, and now write to say that I shall be let out of this place on the 20th, so that you may either write me here before then, or after that day write to 54 St. Charles' Square, Ladbroke Grove, W.

I had well planned, and was beginning, our book which you suggested, when I ran [a]foul of one of Booth's and Stead's smug and thoughtless emotions: and here's Old Bill Bailey.

I have written letter after letter to the Home Secretary, protesting that my innocence is as snow—supposing, I mean, that I had done all that I am charged with, though it does not even chance to be true that I did just what I was "convicted" of, viz. "carnal knowledge"—whether knowledge imparted or received I don't know—were there ever such ponderous people? making mountains out of molehills and crimes out of love-toyings?—-the lady in question being—not two days or months—but two years past her puberty, older then than was Napoleon's mother when her first-born was born, and Napoleon's mother was not a Hindoo, as this girl is, but an Italian; nor ~~is~~ was this girl much younger than Warren Hastings' mother when he was born, Hastings' mother not being a Hindoo, but an English girl; so that the fathers of those really strong-minded men would have got longer "sentences" for getting them, under the Stead and Booth régime, than I have got: and, of course, as I have been trying to cry out in my weak voice for years, the twentieth century rejects a country whose laws are the outcome of the sudden emotions and enthusiasms of such raw meat since France and Germany are not going to keep company with her. In vain have I screamed to the Home Secretary that those two young mothers brought forth their offspring without any pain (do you know Metchnikoff's "Nature of Man"? very interesting); that races brought forth without pain by child-mothers are beautiful races, such as Andalusians, Circassians, Cashmerians; that ugly races, like the English, are races brought forth in shrieking travail; that I myself am wildly non-English, that I have copulated, as a matter of course, from the age of two or three with ladies of a similar age in lands where that is not considered at all extraordinary; that my view of the matter is not a view peculiar to myself, but is a view shared by nine-tenths of the human race with the highest of European scientists; that to subject me to pain and penalties for differing from the view peculiar to Booth, a zoological freak like Booth, is a dirty piece of tyranny; and that if Englishmen elect to make themselves the laughingstock of the world, that was is no reason for putting harmless poor people into their grotesque prisons. But cui bono? "Though you bray a fool in a mortar . . ." etc. Here I still am. Though I still have my say to say; and my case is just beginning when it is supposed to end.

Meantime, here in the prison, I have been treated with the most extraordinary kindness and consideration, as unmerited as the outrage committed upon me by those who sent and kept me here. That kindness, which has made my year here pass not unpleasantly, is, wholly or partly, due to a letter which you wrote about me; and I think you will divine whether or not I thank you from a full heart for your persistent partisanship and favour toward me.

Please cut out and send for me to (54 St. Charles Sqr. W.), Mrs. Jewson, the note below. England permits us to send wicked anti-Booth people one letter per month, on a Sunday. Every Englishman is at heart a Salvationist. But it's bad luck, as I have long preached: for the Salvation Army can't permanently withstand a landing of Uhlans, nor General Booth outflank General Kluck.

Yours ever sincere, Shiel

Since there is no note attached, either the censors removed it or Richards had it sent on to Lydia Jewson. Interestingly, Shiel went back to making this same argument in his novel *How the Old Woman Got Home,* possibly his best novel once he took up novel writing again. In a number of ways, Shiel never became acclimated to the social laws of urban England, especially when they conflicted with his own personal drives. (In the novel Jessie is in labor, her "wise woman" is Mrs. Furley, and this her doctor talking.)

Not a disease—a natural function. She won't suffer much—only seventeen; and if she had had the wit to have the child four years ago in disdain of the little Lord George, she would have had no pain at all. That's the age for a first parturition . . . . Pain is the wages of sin—somebody's sin—and sin is ignorance, this poor child's pain now being the result of her sin in accepting the ignorant notions of a nation of grocers, Quakers, 'lords,' and lawyers, ugly, dull people, like beer (made of vegetables); it is the child-mother countries that produce beauties, geniuses, Jesuses, Helens, like wine (made of fruit),

Jesus's mother fourteen, Helen's twelve, Napoleon's, Hasting's—

Obviously, the address Shiel provided for forwarding his mail is Lydia's longtime address where she had lived with Jewson and their son, Gerald. After his release, apparently in February 1916, Shiel appears to have rented a flat at 62 Frederick Street, Gray's Inn Rd., W.C., the address to which Lydia responded to his letters in May. It is ironic that this address was so close to where he had lived with Lizzie—at 50 Frederick Street. This must have been a place of low rent and rapid turnover—although, amazingly, an S. Sircar was still living at 52 Frederick Street in the 1980s. Perhaps this was the Sharma Sircar who was born to S. K. Sircar and his wife in 1911.

While Shiel was in prison, another tie to a more successful past was broken when Peter Keary, managing director and co-proprietor of C. Arthur Pearson, died on 29 January 1915.

Since Shiel claimed to have worked in the Censor's Office during the war, he might have gone into that employment just before his arrest, especially since the court document indicates that his occupation in October 1914 was "clerk." It is conceivable that he returned to that employment after his release, or entered it later, although this is all passing strange, given that he would have been a felon. In an aside, he mentioned in his later versions of "About Myself" that he was in the Censor's Office during the war. As noted above, he told Olive that he had worked there.

Another scandal was attached to his name by the time he left prison. Stewart Edward White (fast becoming a popular and successful American novelist) wrote a letter to the *Bookman* (New York), included in "The Bookman's Mail Bag" in the May 1915 issue.[6] He stated that the short story "One Man in a Thousand," by Shiel, published in the *Red Magazine* in the 1 January 1915 issue, was an almost verbatim copy of White's story "The Two-Gun Man," filched from his book *Arizona Nights* (1907).

He was correct. Shiel changed the name of the cowboy and tinkered with the grammar in a few spots, but otherwise his story was a total piracy of White's work. White said the editor of the *Red Magazine,* John R. Scott [i.e., Stock], was asked by White's agent to comment, and Stock wrote White in response:

---

6. *Bookman* 41 (1915): 337–38.

> . . . I beg to inform you that naturally when I accepted the story . . . I did so on the understanding that it was an original story. Nobody had been more amazed than myself that a writer with the reputation which Mr. Shiel holds could have stooped to such a gross and wicked piece of plagiarism. I have been in communication with M. P. Shiel, but, unfortunately, cannot gain any satisfactory reply to my letters. I must express my extreme regret that such a thing should have happened, and will communicate with you again immediately I hear from him.

Stock's response to White was included with White's letter to the *Bookman*. The editor concluded, "Now, why do you suppose that a man with a fair literary reputation and somewhat of a market should do such a thing, jeopardising his reputation and his chance of selling anything in the future? It is certainly a conundrum." Shiel, of course, was in prison.

"One Man in a Thousand" was the last Shiel story published until 1922 when the *Red Magazine*'s editor, Stock, published "Three Men and a Girl" in another Harmsworth periodical, the *Yellow Magazine*. It is quite possible that Stock had acquired this story earlier and only published it after any noise about Shiel's theft from White had been forgotten. (Shiel had originally offered "Three Men and a Girl" to Colles for sale in 1892, and it might have been published around that time and reprinted in 1922.) Strangely enough, it does not appear that there was ever any additional public reference to the affair, either in the American or British press, although it surely must have come to the attention of others in the writing world as well as of Shiel's friends and family.

Meanwhile, it was Lydia to whom Shiel turned after his release from prison. Perhaps not too quickly, although correspondence between Lydia and Phipps resumed in early 1916, as it had existed prior to 1914, when whatever affair he had with Elizabeth Price Sircar must have interfered with his long friendship and intimacy with Lydia. There are simply no records to indicate whether Shiel maintained correspondence, a relationship, or silence with Lydia during the time he lived with Lizzie or was in prison.

It is not surprising that he renewed a direct relationship with Lydia using the same method that he had employed years earlier, when he had sent chocolates to ease into good relations with whomever he wanted to impress. In this case, it was gardening books he sent to

Lydia, at a time when her thoughts were on the Irish rebellion and the execution of several of its leaders—she loved them all!

Lydia is back at the old address, 54 St. Charles Square, Ladbroke Grove W. on this "Saturday morn" (Saturday, 13 May 1916), and responded to Shiel at his 62 Frederick Street address. It appears from the tone of her letter that they had already been in touch after his release. What Shiel had to "teach" her after all these years is truly a puzzle. It may be that the topic had to do with Shiel's theories of education and plans that the two soon developed for an alternative scheme of education.

> Your sweet package to hand—Thanks for the thought of me. / The garden books are tempting—in the wet green—& I long for an open place. / Shall we go tomorrow week for the healing of my soul—will you take me & teach me?—Lydia— / They have shot James Connolly & one other—so *all* who signed the proclamation of the Irish Republic have been cleared from a time & place—where such are not understood. (I love them all.)

Soon she is openly looking forward to their sexual reunion. Although Gerald was no longer at home (having joined the Army in 1914), they were meeting at places other than at the Jewson home on St. Charles Square. (Beginning in April 1915, Gerald took part in the Dardanelles campaign at Gallipoli—landing at Suvla Bay, according to his daughter.)

Lydia could not have been more explicit in the following letter, written on a Friday. "My dear—haste—I am one big ache—& you are the cure. Shall look for a card to say the place where . . ."

During this period, Lydia's letters are frequently simply notes regarding when and where they can meet. The reason is undoubtedly due to the fact that she had a job and had obligations that did not allow her the kind of freedom that she had in earlier years. On a Wednesday she wrote, "My Dearest—will you come to meet me—at 9.30 tomorrow Thursday evening—same place as last—be there when I arrive, the waiting is not pleasant. Till then Goodbye / Lydia."

On a Sunday she wrote in such a way as to suggest that Phipps had been off on one of his jaunts into the countryside. "Dear— / Hope to be able to call about five oclock Tuesday next if you are back . . . Can stay until seven / Lydia."

Lydia suggested (in a note, only dated as a Saturday) a time that they could apparently meet at her home. This is unusual since she generally wrote Phipps regarding meeting at a train station.

> My Dear— / Your card & letters to hand— / I will be here on Monday evening after 6.30. Come to me at that time to talk. Lyd of your heart. / Would that my rest had been there—

On an undated Sunday, "Dearest—I am coming tomorrow Monday evening (about 7) Will you be waiting for me if possible as our next meeting is uncertain— / Yours. Lydia." On a Monday, "A hasty note to wish you well—dear—& to tell you I hope to be able to be at the Queens Rd Tube Station Thursday next at 11 oclock & if you are free & willing we can go for a walk—& tea— . . . / Goodbye—dear— / Lydia."

On a Sunday, she is preparing to leave town. (Since this is undated, it might have been written during an early phase of their romantic relationship.)

> Just returned from my morning tramp. What a morning. I am hoping you too were out early—then the wind on its way—may have touched your cheek & mine. (dear dark face—seen by the light of the fire. strangely reminiscent of some other time & place—baffling—except it is the certainty it is not a dream—but a memory) / Dear I send this to you with love for you—& pity that we shall not meet for a while—. . . leave London soon—& revel in the country places. / Knowing I am constantly conscious of you during my waking hours—so while sense of time lasts. / Lydia

Then she returns and writes as usual from the Kensington address. "Hope to be out shopping Thursday afternoon—if so—I shall find my way to you. Arrived safely last evening / Lyd."

She wrote on a Wednesday that she will meet him to visit at a railway station the next day. "Tomorrow (Thursday) evening—9.30 I will be at Edgware Road, Met: Railway Station. Will you come to there that we may be together a while. / My dear love, / Lydia."

On another Sunday, "If you are in London—Wednesday next—I will come to you . . . / L." If Phipps was not in London, where was he? Had he time to make his hikes as he had in earlier years?

Lydia had been working at the Savoy Theatre in the spring of 1916, from which she wrote (without a date):

The sun is joyous & the road inviting at Golders Green—on Tuesday—but happy chance was not mine that time. / However I strolled along a bit & took long breaths—missing you much—tis the fortunes of love. I venture on these days. / My dear heart, how precious you are these few moments of time & one snatches at— / If you are in town send me a line or two to the Theatre. (Miss Brema's [?] Company) & I may be able to come to you Friday—about tea time or early evening. I will write again if I hear from you—that [*lost text?*] are here still—Mean while hold me close in your thoughts, dear / Lydia [*last half of this quarter-page has been torn off*]

Work, apparently at the Savoy, makes her late getting home.

What of the night? Good. / Yes, my feet have trodden your hills, & I have passed the way you have been—each without the other—Why did God make & keep apart so good a pair? / . . . I note what you write, as to sending on any postal matter (nothing to hand, so far) & I suppose you will give me notice—of any change of address. / You invite me to see you. That is gladness. I will not delay myself. Will you come to me here. Say, Wednesday. / My work is keeping me later just now. I shall, however, be home at eight oclock, & an hour or two, of our lives, may be spent in company—if you will . . . Goodnight—my dear love. / Lydia.

But on a Sunday, she writes that she is no longer employed.

This is to tell you—I scrambled into my clothes—in time to make my appearance before the great British public. / Forgive the hurried flight. / I have finished now at the Theatre—"resting" is the professional term—for out-of-work. / I would so like a tramp round Golder's Green with you. So am calling at your flat about one oclock, Wednesday morning . . . The birds were rioting—greeting the spring . . . Hoping you are rid of your cough. / Lydia

On Friday, 19 May, Lydia wrote Shiel, arranging to meet and discuss "alteration." This may refer to plans to move into a flat together.

Thank you—my dear—for your card—You may expect to see me at Baker St. Station (in the Street) at 11:25 Sunday morn: (10:25 old time). / I will come any way—any weather—& we can make any alterations there & then if necessary. / Forgive more now— / Lydia / All work & no play—make me a dull dog—

Apparently Phipps has been considering asking his nephew Cyril for financial assistance and asked Lydia to visit Cyril. Lydia responded to his letter on a Tuesday, sometime in 1916. From the tone of her letters she must have been employed during this period. There is fatigue in many of these letters. It appears the two are going to Chalfont for some occasion. What kind of employment Shiel may have gained in 1916 has never been made clear. He seems to have had more free time than Lydia had, although when, in this period, as he said he did, was he occupied with the Censor's Office? The only evidence for it is the previously noted comment that he made to his niece, Olive. There was no reason for him to have made this up thirty years after the event. Lydia had an amount coming to her from the estate of Jewson, and Shiel also had a bit of income from the rental of the property in Plymouth. They obviously were looking for a home together that their finances could afford.

> The budget to hand—read with interest—concerning the letter to Dr. Horsford—My visit to him must be after this week as I have no moment for myself so will speak of this when we meet. / Am forwarding article as wished— / Forgive terseness—dear am very tired— / The day after the outing is Sunday—not Saturday—please say what time (early on, say 11 oclock) at (outside) Baker St. Station—Let me hear soon. Lyd." [*over*] "Excuse the somewhat mixed scrawling / Will you look for a train to Chalfont near 10.30—or 11—& then write me. I love the mornings so Please get up—for my sake / My love dear. Goodnight

On a Tuesday morning, she was planning for a move that will bring Phipps and her, and her tools and his, together.

> An hour or two of sound sleep & since awake—walking with you—dear heart—beneath the trees—of Grays Inn—living with you—sharing the common things—loving you in utter abandonment—& now—as King you come to me—Sunday about 5 oclock. / Let me see if something cannot be managed—& the tools given a place & you your work shop—& me— / I think I finish here / Lydia / A line from you—dear.

Lydia wrote Phipps, on an undated Saturday, setting up a meeting, apparently to go look at the flat they were considering.

> Good— / I will be at the British Museum Tube Station—at 5.30 Monday—there we will go together & see inside the box—which is to be for us a Garden of Eden—My dear heart. / I do not ask for happiness. I want you—& will take my chance—as to results. / The "inner Kiss"—& remembered words—keep me fairly riotous—altho—sewing & working as usual. My dear devil—what fires you have lighted—& must quench— / You cannot think of me too much—it is my right & I chance it. Lydia.

By 15 August, Lydia is satisfied with a flat and writes on the letterhead of Buckland & Sons, 4 Bloomsbury Square—perhaps the agent that she has been working with to find a suitable location.

> After much thinking—I have decided to book the flat—as I think we can manage there—the thought of light—& the open space & trees is very attractive to me. So I will go to the agent again today & give him the references—(in your name) Miss Belcher for one & Mrs. Jewson for the other—& there await events. / I shall not send any furniture—until after Dave's [?] return (Sep 7th) / Will tell any more when we meet Thursday evening. / For you all my love & craving remain brave / Lydia / August—Buckland & Sons— / 4 Bloomsbury Square

That Lydia was anxious to establish a home with Shiel could not have been said any stronger than her reminder to him, "The long years dwindle . . ."

> Your card received / My dear heart, I am grateful & have thanked the God I deny—with tears in all sincerity. / Do not let anything hinder our plan— / the agent has told me we have to pay 10/6—for the agreement. Pay it, dear, for me. / I cannot wait any longer. The long years dwindle—but the days lengthen—between us now. / I will be at the approved place at 9. oclk—Thursday—half an hour earlier than usual—& you will be there also—my dear love. Until then—& for all time. Your / Lydia

And again she wrote, perhaps asking him to forego a tramp: "The book—dear heart—as promised. I hurt—think of me. Hold me close. I need you so. / Lydia / Forget Madam Moss & Madam Moon—for me / My Love."

There were things that needed to be done before they could move into the flat. Lydia wrote Shiel at 62 Frederick St., Gray's Inn Rd., W.C. Her letter was postmarked "Paddington / 3 15 PM / 29 Aug

16" (Tuesday, 29 August 1916), although her letter retained the embossed St. Charles Sq. address:

> My Dear—Will you please write to agent about the running water tap—& also we shall want another door key. *Two* spots have appeared on my face. Lyd.

A fragment completes the group of letters from Lydia that Phipps retained throughout his life. It suggests an emotional expectation from Lydia of the part that she soon expected to play in Shiel's life, although they were not married until 1919. [*fragment*] ". . . your [*illegible*] . . . I shall soon [*text lost*] the old wife. / Lydia."

Laid in with the last group of Lydia's letters in Shiel's files, indicative of their social life beyond their socialist pursuits, was a "Programme" (folded sheet, title on recto and inner doublespread, nothing on p. [4]) 40, Berkeley Square, W. Miss Grace Hazlehurst Matinee Musicale. Thursday, 2 July at 3.15. Under the patronage of H.R.H. Princess Christian of Schleswig-Holstein [et al.].

The Jewson home and other properties belonged to Gerald, and he sold them after he returned to London in 1919. In the meantime, Phipps and Lydia took up residence in the flat in London, with space and trees around them.

Chapter 18

Restoring a Career

Perhaps it is not surprising that Shiel's work on short stories and other fiction was quiescent for the five or six years following his release from prison. Instead, Shiel tried his hand at converting several of his novels into plays for the cinema, and wrote at least one new play. He approached his nephew, Leonard Horsford—Cyril's brother—asking for possible contacts. (Leonard was thirty-nine. His occupation is unknown. He had married Gertrude Hawker in 1912 and died in 1921. There is no evidence of children from their marriage. And there is no indication of why he might have had information regarding the cinema. But Phipps must have had some notion that Leonard might be able to advise him.)

Leonard answered from 11 Cambridge Place, Paddington, W., 8 September 1916.

> My dear Uncle / Sorry could not write before. / The Hepworth Co. in Dover St. Piccadilly would be the likely people for your Film play, but if you send me a copy of it I can put it before some other producer whom I know & I know it will have very careful consideration. / Why not come round on Sunday at 3 & have some dinner. Let me know— / Yours etc. / Leonard / P.S. don't come on Sunday shall be going out early. [*Gawsworth has written in pencil at head:* "White Wedding Synopsis"]

The activities of Phipps and Lydia are not well documented for the immediate years following their reunion in 1916 and the establishment of a common residence soon after. One of the things that Phipps would probably discover quickly was that Lydia had continued to expand the range of her intellectual curiosity, aggressively pursuing her social interests; she was no longer the immature if brilliant woman whom Phipps had first courted in 1908. Lydia had become as strong as Shiel and was probably not as burdened as he by ideas developed much earlier and not grown beyond, although Shiel's continued interest in science would lead him to read extensively in works by early theorists in cosmic physics in the 1920s.

They were married on 31 January 1919. The marriage certificate identified Lydia as "Esther Lydia Furley, spinster, age 46," the wedding in the Register's Office, District of Kensington, County of London, in the presence of Amy Alice Sandeman and James Sillett. Lydia's father was identified as Philip Charles Furley, deceased, a Gold Beater.

Both Phipps and Lydia had become very involved in the efforts of various socialist groups and others looking for new models of education. This was a topic close to Shiel's heart. He had been critical of standard educational practices since his early experience in Harrison College on Barbados as a boy of fifteen.

Gerald Jewson's daughter, Mrs. Barbara Brennan, has speculated that Phipps and Lydia married because they "planned with Mrs. Pankhurst to run a school on 'modern' lines. Phipps as headmaster—hence marriage was a necessity."[1] The Brennan family has in its possession a photograph of Lydia—"with Miss Limousin & the Pankhurst sisters Christabel & Sylvia all perched on one of the Sphinx at the foot of Cleopatra's needle on the Thames Embankment. There is another person—I was told it was Mrs. Pankhurst but my son Tim has researched the photograph in detail. He feels very sure it is Mrs. Teresa Greig.[2] Miss Limousin is wearing a large picture hat which obscures her face."

Gerald Jewson returned home in early 1919 to find that Phipps and his mother had married. During the summer Gerald met Elsie Lovell, a dressmaker who worked at Marshall & Snellgrove's Shop in Oxford Street. They married in December 1920. Barbara Brennan described the family situation, as she recalled hearing about it from her mother and father:

> Lydia (being a Bohemian & free thinker and not herself married) suggested to Gerald that he should live with Elsie "Why marry?" But Gerald was determined to marry—the shock of his father's sudden death when he was 16 & the revelation that he himself was a bastard remained with him. Gerald and Elsie were married Dec. 6th 1920. Gerald took Elsie on a honeymoon to the trenches in France & Flanders.
>
> They returned to the cottage in Wisboro' Green Sussex. The cottage, BADGERS, but renamed "Woodstock" by Lydia & Phipps.

1. Barbara Brennan notes to John D. Squires, 6 January 2003.

2. Teresa Billington-Greig (1877–1964) was a suffragette who created the *Women's Freedom League.*

> Gerald's father had money & investments. He left the Bedford Park House to Lydia also a cottage on the Isle of Sheppey. Lydia had sold these. She had bought a house in Hampstead Garden Suburb (or rented one).
>
> I think my father bought the house in Wisboro' Green on his mother's instigation. It consisted of 3 cottages in one building. The end cottage had a tenant an old lady called Mrs. Fielder—in her nineties—Gerald & Elsie had the center cottage & the end one was for Lydia & Phipps. Mary Davis—an old family servant & friend came with them—she had been with the Jewson family before William Arthur was married. Phipps used to sleep most of the day—He was awake at night—writing. He was a runner—& would run through the night for several miles.
>
> Family friends & relations would come and stay one after the other. Phipps would chat up the female visitors. Yvonne a niece came to stay—she was 14 years old & Aunt Flo's (Florence) daughter. However she quickly returned to London—Phipps had been showing too much interest in her.

Shiel's conviction that motion pictures were going to become the rage led him to rewrite at least five of his novels as plays and to make efforts to market them. He was probably also nervous about the short story market after plagiarizing the Stewart Edward White story that became his "One Man in a Thousand," published in the *Red Magazine* in 1914. Thus, it was a couple of years before he somehow found the courage, or gall, to approach the editor who had supported him earlier, John Stock, and persuade him to publish "Three Men and a Girl" in the 6 February 1922 issue of the *Yellow Magazine*. This story had been around since Shiel offered it to his agent Colles to sell in 1892. It is also possible that Stock had purchased the story several years earlier and finally decided to publish it, hoping that any noise about the plagiarized story had dissipated. It is very strange that there was never a public comment made about Shiel's plagiarism following the reference to it in the *Bookman*. Perhaps the war washed such news away. Shiel's new writing became focused on the plays.

In addition to their possible interest in establishing a school along "modern lines," Phipps and Lydia appear to have been involved in various socialist activities over the next few years. In 1919, Shiel translated *The Hungarian Revolution* for the Worker's Socialist Federation. This was a 56-page pamphlet that carried the subtitle: "An Eye-

Witness's Account of the first five Days by Charles Henry Schmitt / Translated by M. P. Shiel. / Price nine pence. / Worker's Socialist Federation. / [1919] / 400 Old Ford Road, London, E. 3."

A. Reynolds Morse described this rare work: "The account of the uprising is not especially explosive, and its chief claim to fame lies in its relation to Shiel as translator, not to history as it occurred." The Library of Congress identifies Schmitt as "Schmitt, Heinrich, 1894–1976," who also used the pseudonym "Frank Arnau" for a series of mystery novels. Somehow, this author seems unlikely. The original version of this work was probably published in a Communist German journal, but it cannot be located.

On 16 April 1919, *The Times* noted an event that Phipps and Lydia described in their own way to W. H. Chesson when he visited them several years later. Parliament was discussing the possibility of sending an Allied expedition to post-revolutionary Russia in support of the White troops of the Tsarist Regime.

> **"Scene" in the Strangers' Gallery**
>
> A woman sitting in the front row shouted out "You are leading the people into another war." She and a companion . . . were seized . . . and led from the Gallery. They offered no resistance, but one continued shouting "You have not settled the last war, and you are leading the workers into another. You are a gang of murderers." They had no sooner been removed than a third woman rose on the opposite side of the gallery and said in a matter-of-fact way, "We want Soviets." She did not wait to be removed, but quietly walked out.

Fresh back from the war, Gerald was all for going soldiering off to Russia, according to a story told later by W. H. Chesson, and was not aware that his mother and Shiel were so strongly opposed to such an expedition. Once Gerald found a young woman who suited him for marriage (Elsie Lovell), he gave up all thoughts of warfare and spent as much time traveling Europe with her as he could. There were ample funds left to him by his father to support this interest. For their honeymoon, Gerald took his new bride to all the battlefields in which he had a part. They spent the years immediately following their marriage in Europe (Spain and Italy) until Elsie became pregnant in 1925. Phipps and Lydia would soon join them in Italy.[3]

---

3. Barbara Brennan, op. cit.

In June 1919, Shiel received his first letter from W. H. Chesson since 1913, and eagerly responded. (His letter was on the 54 St. Charles' Square stationery, but neither he nor Lydia had lived at that address since 1916.) His letter is dated "June 3. 19."

> My dear Chesson, / I was quite delighted to see the old fist again. Some time ago I was near you, asked for Sandycombe Rd., was misdirected (apparently), and in the end never saw it. But I have often had you in good remembrance, and hoped that it was well with you. As to the cinema proposal, yes, I shall be quite glad to tackle it when the lady writes; I have already done two, one of which is to appear shortly, so I am in that way. In fact, my opinion is that it is quite a high art-form—purer drama (Schauspiel—Show-play) than the spoken drama, and in the future, when acclimatised to the world, may go far. / I am supposed to be going to Spain in a month's time—not sure. Meantime, am here and *"at home."* Anyway, I will write again later. / Your sincere / M. P. Shiel.

The two plays to which Shiel referred were probably *Herbert Spenser* and *The Yellow Deluge,* a work based on his novel *The Yellow Wave*. Shiel wrote the literary agent Cazenove (C. F. Cazenove, "Literary Agency of London") on 20 August 1919, offering a play, and on 27 August 1919 he wrote Curtis Brown Ltd. asking if that firm would undertake the placing of these works. Even by early the next year, he was still endeavoring to place the plays. On 1 February 1920 (from Laker's Lodge, Loxwood, Sussex), he wrote the literary agent J. B. Pinker sending the play *The Yellow Deluge,* hoping to get it staged. He had already sent that firm a copy of *Herbert Spenser.* For all his efforts, no one ever became interested in publishing or staging the plays. The manuscripts of both plays reside, unpublished, in the Ransom Center in Austin.

Loxwood is south of London, approximately halfway to Brighton on the coast. For whatever reason, Shiel had retreated to a cottage on the River Rother, wilder and more remote then than today. Loxwood is also quite near Wisborough Green, where Gerald Jewson purchased the cottage "Badgers," where Phipps and Lydia lived with Gerald and his wife. They renamed the cottage "Woodstock." Indeed, this dwelling is on Loxwood Road. Wisborough Green is just west of Horsham, where Shiel purchased the cottage in 1930 that he called "L'Abri," the Shelter.

Barbara Brennan and her son Tim visited the "cottage" Woodstock in 1998 and found it much the way it was when Phipps, Lydia, Gerald, and his wife lived there.

> . . . the end room had a separate door out into the garden; it also had the interior door to the hall passage with a Yale lock. This door had a letter flap cut into the base of the door. This must have been Phipps's room—he could go on his nightly runs. He could sleep during the day without being disturbed—the door locked & the letters put through the flap. There was a small cupboard room on the other side of the passage. This room had an Elsan chemical lavatory.[4]

Shiel wrote Chesson three weeks after he wrote Pinker (mid-February 1920), from the same Loxwood address—a letter that included several interesting points about what he had been doing, or not doing, or what he might do. (There is no evident reason why Shiel spent six months or more from early 1920 until later in the year at this location—unless it was simply to find some privacy away from Wisborough Green in this high, wooded retreat above a stream.) Shiel was taking notes for *Children of the Wind*.

> Laker's Lodge Cottage / Loxwood / Sussex. 17.2.20 /
> My dear Chesson, / That is quite charming to hear from you. You will see that I have banished myself from the crazy world down here—five miles from ry. station—and haven't even paper as yet to write on. So the birthday book must wait, unless you send, or *bring* it, and coming to stay some days, in which case I will tell you beforehand *how* to come. It is pretty of you to think of me and write still of me, though I haven't written anything for a longish time, as I have been captured by some mathematical studies which I want to rush through to their end. But later on I may write a novel about a wonderful jewel, like Richard Marsh and those sorts of people. I should much like to see your article on Essayists; will you buy a copy & send me, and I will then refund you. It was only by much wit and will that I induced someone to bring me a newspaper daily, I am so high and dry from the river—the muddy! Yet winding safe to sea. So write again. / Your very sincere / M. P. Shiel.

It is interesting to find this echo of Swinburne—"winding safe to sea"—in Shiel's letter. He frequently referred to the work of another author, but seldom echoed the lines quite as literally as this. For men-

---

4. Barbara Brennan, op. cit.

tal exercise Shiel enjoyed laying out mathematical puzzles to solve, and there are pages of such exercises in his archives. But he was not a slave to puzzles, as he wrote Chesson on 10 April 1920.

> Laker's Lodge Cottage / Loxwood Sussex, / Apr. 10. 20. /
> My dear Chesson, / Many thanks for yours, with the extract from your article: I should have answered before, but March is my month of flags and hurrahs, and I have been "on the tramp." It isn't bad down here, and it was unfortunate that I should have said anything about "mathematics" in the same letter in which I asked you to come. I am not such a slave of mathematics that I can't shake a friendly and kindred hand. The England of 1920 is, indeed, not rich in house-room, and I have little here, but I dare say you could accommodate yourself to this, if you would come. . . even unbeautiful receptacles for veracious contents having a merit—from the contents. / By "veracious", I think, you do mean *true* but just *sincere*—true-wishing. Of course, though, *true* is the highest—in an essay, anyway. Does actual Truth "let" the fellow, does she kiss him, lie with him, shew him her pussy, transport him with her Panic raptures? That is the question. I can't think that such a mind as the little Chesterton ever said anything that's *true:* Belloc's a higher type. ("The Servile State.") Beerbohm I don't know. / May you fare well. / M. P. Shiel. / Enc. Of name for album.

It seems only appropriate that this section conclude with the role Lydia and Phipps played in the establishment of a "new school," or the role they played in revolutionary socialist activities in 1919 and 1920. It appears that their involvement with Sylvia Pankhurst made her obligated to them. Most likely, this was payment due Phipps for his translation of *The Hungarian Revolution* (1919) for the Worker's Socialist Federation, which was headed by Pankhurst. The organization published a newspaper, and it is conceivable that Lydia or Phipps may have contributed to it. A small pamphlet written by Pankhurst, *The Schooling of the Future* (1918), published by the same firm and impossible to find, might very well have something to say about whatever Phipps and Lydia were proposing about educational systems at the time.

Another title in which Shiel may have had a hand is suggested in correspondence he had in 1938 with James Henle of Vanguard Press. "As to 'recent events in Russia'," Shiel wrote, "I don't propose to understand them—I don't *try* to, for I know that I should fail, perhaps only a Russian can. That Bukharin was one of my heroes—I once translated a book of his in my enthusiasm!"[5]

The "book" that Shiel mentioned was most likely a small, 7-page essay by Nikolai Bukharin, *Soviets or Parliament,* published by the same Worker's Socialist Federation in 1918, as it did *The Hungarian Revolution,* which is announced on this small pamphlet as "In The Press." Since no translator is credited on this piece, it is conceivable that Shiel might have done it.[6]

In November, Phipps set out to retrieve the money due him (for whatever his work) through legal demands. His solicitor did not have good news. In a letter addressed to Mr. M. P. Shiel, The Queen's Head, Petworth, Sussex, the firm of Montague, Mileham, Solomon & Meyer—Solicitors, with a printed letterhead and address of 5 & 6 Bucklesbury, London E.C., 29 November 1920, advised him:

> Dear Sir, / We are in receipt of your letter of the 27th inst., and have communicated with Miss Pankhurst demanding payment of the sum of £23:19:0 before noon on Thursday next. / From the press we gather that this lady is in prison and consequently we do not think the moment is propitious for commencing proceedings against her. She probably has no money of her own, and her imprisonment will prevent her from approaching any friend who might help her. However, we shall be glad of your instructions on this point, and if you wish us to commence proceedings, perhaps you will be good enough to remit the sum of £4.4.0 to cover preliminary expenses. / Yours faithfully / Montague [*corporate scrawled signature*][7]

Lydia remained an active member of various offshoots of this and similar organizations. She reviewed *Earth Bound* by Rosa Luxemburg in the first issue (1921) of the *Communist Review.* Where there is one such work there are probably more. Of course, she remained a lifelong friend of Nellie Limousin, her neighbor and companion of Mrs. Pankhurst and her two daughters in their early marches and arrests on behalf of women's suffrage. Nellie was also the young aunt of Eric Blair, who would adopt the pen name George Orwell.

---

5. Transcript in the Vanguard Collection, Columbia University.

6. The image of this little pamphlet is available on the Internet, digitized by Microsoft from the original in the University of Toronto Library, and made available through the Marxists Internet Archive.

7. Typescript in HRC.

Phipps may not have cared for the living arrangements at Wisborough Green or tired of it, since for whatever reason he occasionally spent time at "The Queen's Head" in nearby Petworth or in the seclusion of Laker's Lodge Cottage.

Phipps had begun to make notes regarding the Zulu tribe in Africa about 1920, in preparation for a new novel, *Children of the Wind*. One can find Shiel's notes, written in his tiny script, on the backs of letters to him or virtually anything that he could find to write on at the time. There is no indication of what steered him toward this exciting, successful story, but the energy and excitement that he experienced in the writing is visible in the novel itself. He apparently realized that his ideas for motion pictures were not coming to fruition, and his old habit of writing fiction reasserted itself.

Africa was not an entirely new topic for Shiel. He told in "About Myself" how as a boy, in making an early effort at novel writing, he had written an African adventure "all about a queen in Central Africa" with horses leaping a chasm with dogs leaping on the horses' backs to make their own way across.

By November 1921, Shiel was back in touch with Grant Richards, writing from 15 Wells St., W.C. 1. He proposed publication of a pamphlet on socialism to Richards, possibly a by-product of his work for Pankhurst. He had also kept him apprised of his work on the African novel. On 21 November he wrote Richards acknowledging the return of the pamphlet that Richards deemed too slight and unlikely to sell, but also telling Richards that the novel was finished and only needed typing up.

Old habits returned. Phipps wrote Richards on 12 May 1922 (12A Myddleton Square, E.C. 1) that he had delayed sending him the manuscript because he had submitted it to a Cassell's editor for possible serialization. Richards was undoubtedly peeved again with Shiel for his delays, as he had been in the past. Shiel responded in early June (from Cyril's address, 24 Harley Street, W.), saying that he cannot understand why Richards claims that he had always lost money on Shiel's books. They had always sold well in cheap editions, Shiel said, and had done well in serial publication. It was not until 20 June 1922 that he finally sent the manuscript on to Richards. He expects to go to Italy the following week and will send him an address there. On 27 July he wrote Richards from Tratoria Borgioli, ponte a Vingoni, Distorno di Firenze, Italy, regarding a contract for the novel.

On 18 October 1922, he was still at this address, from which he wrote Richards regarding the corrected proofs for *Children of the Wind* and asking about serial publication. On 22 October, he proposed to Richards that he update *The Yellow Danger* and asked Richards to approach Pearson regarding serial publication. On 13 November he responded to Richards about copyright issues regarding the proposed update. On 28 November he sent Richards a new address, from Albergo Roma, Syracuse, Sicily, saying he would be at that location "for some weeks." A letter followed this on 8 December, regarding drawings and corrections to proofs of *Children of the Wind* (from 13 Via San Martino, Siracusa, Sicily). On 4 January 1923, he acknowledged receiving an advance copy of the novel. However, Spicer of *Hutchinson's Adventure-Story Magazine* is considering serialization, which might delay book publication.

He wrote his friend Chesson from this address in Siracusa on 22 January 1923, saying ". . . for nearly a year I have been wandering in Italy without much fixity of address." He suggests that Chesson request a copy of *Children of the Wind,* since Richards had now released it.

Indeed, Shiel had spent eight months in the loveliest parts of Italy and the tip of Sicily, probably tagging along with Lydia and her son and Elsie, chiefly "swatting flies," he told Chesson. Somehow, during that time, he had made the acquaintance of a young Italian author, Rocco Lazazzera, who translated *The Purple Cloud. La Nuvola Porpora* was published in early 1924, with a preface by Lazazzera dated December 1923. Shiel's copy of the book is located in the Ransom Center, along with a novel by Lazazzera, *Kardugia* (1925), inscribed: "Omaggio d'amore d'allievo a maestro, l'autore, Natale 1925." The warmth of this inscription has suggested, again, to some critics that Shiel may have had homosexual leanings; rather ridiculous on this basis, it seems to me, where there is only an affectionate salute made to Shiel. There is no evidence at all that Shiel in his traipsing about Italy with Lydia, Gerald, and Elsie could have established much of a deeper friendship with this young author.

Rather, this episode appears to explain a passage in the 1948 version of "About Myself," in which Shiel says, "The war—Censor's Office—toward the end—Italy—privilege of kissing the Pope's great bit, his toe—and, meantime, no writing, but then commencing afresh, having something to say . . ." It appears that the reference to Italy had nothing to do with a wartime assignment, but merely reflects the time that he spent there with Lydia and her family as tourists. Perhaps they did meet the Pope!

Shiel had openly discussed with Richards in 1913 the relationship of the two men in the proposed serial, *The Strangest of All* (which became the story "The Death-Dance"), as considered too "decadent' by Ward, Lock, while the inclusion of a lesbian relationship in *Children of the Wind*—between the heroine, a lost heiress, Spiciewegiehotiu, and her bonded friend, Sueela—appears to be just another literary device to add sexual tension to this adventure novel. The suggestion that Lazazzera's warm inscription in a book was the basis for some kind of sexual relationship is beyond reasonable consideration.

By February 1923, Shiel and Lydia had returned to England, their address 88 Grove Park Terrace, Chiswick, W. *Children of the Wind* had just been published, and Shiel was probably at least making notes toward a new novel, *How the Old Woman Got Home*.

Reviews of *Children of the Wind* were generally positive. Especially important were comments by the well-regarded journalist Edward Shanks, who used his review of the novel to write a more extended essay about Shiel's work.[8]

Then, at long last, Phipps and W. H. Chesson actually met in person, almost twenty years after they had become close through correspondence and after the many pleas that Shiel had made for Chesson to visit. Chesson briefly described two visits that Shiel, and apparently Lydia, made to his home at Childwall on 6 June and 10 August 1923.

> On Wednesday 6 June 1923 M. P. Shiel came to Childwall and W.H.C. opened the door to him. Some slight—very slight—impression I had of what Don J might have been like in evening attire, urbane, softly spoken; with jetty hair and dark complexion in velvet jacket. He spoke of Couèism as of one of the most important prescriptions for welfare and said "I found that without knowing about it. I had written a novel which was all Couèism—'The Isle of Lies'["]; and he began to sketch the plot. He spoke of A. E. W. Mason rather appreciatively. He told me his own father was a local preacher, spoke of the dissenting religion pressure on his boyhood. "How has your soul been getting on this last week?" was a question put to him then. He spoke of the power of the imagination as distinct from will—the subconscious made beneficently active by imagi-

8. Edward Shanks, "The Work of Mr. M. P. Shiel," *Queen* (8 February 1923).

nation (retailing Coué's teaching) and when I asked how one should deal with a sharp stabbing pain he answered "The subject cries out 'Ça passe, ça passe, ça passe' as rapidly as he can."

On 10 Aug 1923 M. P. Shiel said he had been rereading Poe's Tales, and the disappointment was severe. "The Fall of the House of Usher" he particularly deprecated as "so mechanical." Poe's prose style he deemed "artificial." He had recommended his wife Lydia to read the tales and repented! As a boy he had been entranced by Poe.

I told Shiel that "He Defines Greatness of Mind" in "Cummings King Monk" reminded one of the 1st dialogue in Plato's Dialogues where Socrates discusses the meaning of temperate with Charmides. In talking of drama Shiel pressed on me the dramatic merits of the *Bacchae* by Euripides and sketched the tragedy of the imperiously insane Pentheus.

He said Sir Alfred Harmsworth had tried to entice him away from Pearson who ran his "Yellow Danger." "We are the people for the £SD you know" said the great man. "He had no delicacy," remarked Shiel. S said Harmsworth spent an hour every day exercising in front of a bust of Napoleon trying to look like Napoleon. St. John Harmsworth the younger Harmsworth thought he looked like & wanted to look like Alfred. When said Shiel I had been in his room one day and having taken my leave was descending the staircase he called back with Just a moment please. I want to ask you something. Do you think I am like Alfred? Of course I said he was. [Lydia Shiel was disgusted at his compliance.]

Shiel said Lord Rothermere was "gross, the kind of man who picks up a lady in Oxford Circus to spend the night with, quite a sultan in his way." Lord R.'s loud backing up of the French policy in the Ruhr he attributed to the wish to push the Paris edition of his "The Daily Mail."

Mrs. Shiel told of how she & Phipps [M. P. S.] were bundled out of the House of Commons for interrupting from the Strangers Gallery in or about 1918 when there was a move to send British soldiers *after* the war to a "regular death trap" in Russia to fight the Bolshies, it not being at all certain that the soldiers so sent really were anti-Bolshevik. Mrs. Shiel, dressed well, with another lady and Phipps went together. Mrs. S. interrupted Bottomley with "Shame!" The lady friend also cried "Shame!" and while officials were grappling with the 2 ladies Shiel uttered a few sentences condemning the government's use of British soldiers in Russia. "Phipps got a black eye," remarked Mrs. S. "I gave

> as good as I got" remarked S. grimly. Mrs. S. commented on the savagery of the police. "They *tore* at us; their faces were so angry and red." The protesting three were released at the end of the debates. Gerald Jewson (Mrs. S' son by her 1st husband) wanted to go soldiering to Russia & did not know that his mother was the "well-dressed woman" referred to by the Press as being interrupted.[9]

Considering all that had been said about Shiel's race, one cannot help but notice Chesson's reference to Shiel's dark complexion and his apparent handsome appearance that the reference to "Don J" suggests. The story about the Shiel couple's action in Parliament echoes the *Times* news report and reminds one of the aggressive action in which Lydia had been engaged during the marches on behalf of feminism, or her support for Irish independence in 1908 and 1909. She had always been the more aggressive in support of political and ideological movements, while Shiel confined himself for the most part to the incorporation of his ideas in his novels.

Over the next few years, Lydia would be a great help to Phipps in the development of his manuscripts for marketing, spending hours on the transcription of his stories, but she would grow increasingly closer to her theosophical friends and their ideas—and closer to her family—while Phipps drifted more deeply into novel writing and his eventual focus on the New Testament translation that became his manuscript "Jesus." The pair would begin moving gradually apart. The romance of their early years was wearing thin. They would quietly separate in 1929. Lydia had a dozen independent and interesting years ahead, before she died of a heart attack on 16 February 1942 and was buried in Wisborough Green Cemetery.[10]

Several quite popular and relatively successful novels—*How the Old Woman Got Home, Dr. Krasinski's Secret*—began to fill Shiel's time as had his writing habits early in the century, while the business arrangements to which he had always devoted so much time became just as much an obsession as they had been in earlier years. And just as he had relished tweaking the noses of journalists pursuing his private life in the previous century, so did he soon manage the largest conjuration of his West Indian life for the press and his admirers. The mythical Redonda lay just ahead.

---

9. Typescript by Chesson in HRC.

10. Barbara Brennan, op. cit.

THE FINAL YEARS
1923–1947

Dedicated to the Memory of John D. Squires

For a number of years, I and others have gathered the residual bones of Shiel and dropped them into this ossuary with the notion that in time that lead box would be opened and the remnants rebuilt into a description of the concluding years of this remarkable writer. This is that construction.

The African Tale

The launch of a history of the later years of M. P. Shiel can be derived from the concluding description in "The Middle Years" of Shiel's writing the novel *Children of the Wind* and his travels through Italy with his wife Lydia along with her son and his wife.

A retelling of that period filled out with details from biographical notes composed by Mrs. Barbara Brennan, the granddaughter of Lydia Shiel, sets the stage for the later years of Shiel's life, as he was intent that his body eventually find no corruption.

There is no source that indicates what drew Shiel's attention to the Zulu nation in the early years of the 1920s, but it became the basis for a new novel. This was especially significant in that Shiel was back at work with Grant Richards as though the scandals of just a few years before had never occurred. He assembled extensive notes about the Zulus—written in his small hand on any scrap of paper at hand.

One can recall Shiel's fascination with H. Rider Haggard as a youth and his own account of a brief adventure story he had written involving an African queen. Shiel's adventure fiction was no more like any other African adventure fiction that was being written in the 1920s (and there was a lot of it) than his popular romances had been like any others that were published during the early years of the new century. There were elements of decadence in all Shiel's work.

By 12 November 1921 he was able to write Grant Richards (from 15 Wells St., W.C. 1) that the "novel" (*Children of the Wind*) was finished and only needed typing up.

However, he does not send the novel to Richards until 20 June 1922, advising that he is going to Italy next week and will send him an address from there. Neither Richards nor other publishers had been interested in the last novel that Shiel had written before his time in prison—*The Strangest of All.* Its depiction of the close "friendship" between two men and the tension that developed because one of the men was secretly married to "Lina" and the other was secretly in love with her was considered just too "decadent." The love between the two men was so consuming that when one lost his sight by poison, the other blinded himself with fire so that he could be in the same institution as the other, just to "hear him talk." Both then, in their blindness, fence each other with their walking canes!

In the 1930s, John Gawsworth took the brief précis of this story, added a few words to it, and brought the resulting short story to a conclusion as "The Death-Dance." This is fiction with a very strong autobiographical base. Fortunately, the much longer synopsis for the story as a novel has also survived. Thus, it is possible to see that Shiel (with 165 pages of manuscript), not Gawsworth (with 4 pages of manuscript), wrote virtually the entire story.

Shiel continued to think that fiction with a quasi-homosexual or quasi-lesbian relationship presented a thematic opportunity to create a powerful story, and he picked this idea up again to include in *Children of the Wind*.

In this novel, a lost British heiress (Spiciewegiehotiu) is queen of an African tribe, attended by a lovely African girl, Sueela. Spicie's cousin, Cobby, sets out from England to find his cousin (who is heiress to millions) and bring her home. This novel is fresh, full of adventure and tribal lore, and ends on a popular note. The bond between the British heiress and her African handmaiden does not seem to have created the level of anxiety or distaste with his publisher, Grant Richards, as had the earlier *The Strangest of All*—but the level of exaggerated decadence in the newer novel does not reach the level of what Shiel had proposed in the earlier work.

The opportunity for Shiel to work on this new novel, and the impetus for it, seem to be related to the return home from war of Lydia's son Gerald. The disposition of his father's estate, his marriage, his travels with his wife and baby Marjorie throughout Europe, and their lengthy trips to Italy drew Lydia and Shiel away from their long-established ties to socialistic activities and habits in England.

As Shiel wrote W. H. Chesson on 22 January 1923, from 13 Via S. Martino, Syracusa, Sicily:

> My dear Chesson,
>
> I have meditated writing you some time, but for nearly a year have been wandering in Italy without much fixity of address, and, in fact, letters written to me have gone seeking me in vain. Here, though, where Winter is merely nominal, I intend staying some time within a stone's throw of that Fons Arethusae which was to the ancient world the symbol of all that is romantic, and seeking from my windows a sea all mixed up with colouring-matter and dyes from the vats and wine-press of Being—very great and strange, and yet near and dear. I last heard from you when I was at Loxwood in Sussex,

when you importuned me to write something fresh, and, though I was then preoccupied with other things, I have since written a story called "Children of the Wind" which, I see, is about to be published. I haven't a copy to send you, but if you would like to read, and would send a p.c. to the publisher (Grant Rich.) 8, St. Martin's Str., Leicester Squ. W.C. stating that I suggested it, he will send you a copy for me. I do hope all this time you have been, and are, going strong.

Your since / M. P. Shiel

Records at HRC indicate there are 16 pages of this novel in the handwriting of Lydia Shiel with corrections in Shiel's hand. She appears to have assisted in the preparation of the manuscript that had been left with Richards. It is not surprising that Shiel dedicated the novel to her.

Richards sent proofs of the title to Shiel in Italy, where he corrected and returned them to Richards on 8 December 1922.

Actually, the novel might have been published earlier, but a proof had been submitted to *Hutchinson's Adventure-Story Magazine,* whose editor, Spicer, declined it. Shiel continued to believe in the success of serialization.

Children of the Wind was published on 23 January 1923 and reviewed in the *Times Literary Supplement* on 15 February 1923. Edward Shanks followed with a review in the *Queen* that was so enthusiastic regarding both the novel and Shiel in general that it surely promoted the interest that Shiel's fiction quickly gained.

In March, Shiel and Lydia were again in England at 88 Grove Park Terrace, Chiswick. Shiel wrote Chesson on 18 April that he would like to visit with him as soon as he returned from a two-week visit to Sussex. He wants to discuss Coué and psychoanalysis, he says, but his real interest is probably in asking Chesson whether he could provide a copy of the 6d edition of *The Man-Stealers,* a copy of which he does not have. Shortly later, in April, he wrote Grant Richards: "Yes, I am writing another, but it is hardly half-finished yet. Most of my time in Italy was spent swatting flies."

Shiel hurried back to his old habits with the publication of his new books. He had delayed the original submission to Richards of *Children* while he sought a serial publisher for it. He complained about the many corrections he had to make in the proofs, complained about the small advance he got from Richards, and later urged him to send £25 in advance, which Richards provided.

Later in the year, after Shiel and Chesson had met in person for the first time, in June and August 1923, after twenty years of increasingly warm correspondence, Shiel wrote Chesson that he wanted to borrow the novel that he had sent Chesson in 1910.

Shiel had written Chesson on 5 April 1923: "We are now near, and I ask if you will come and see me, or, if you prefers, I will go to see you. We have never met, and yet I seem to know you fairly well."

> December 18, 1923
> My Dear Chesson,
>
> I thought you might be looking in one evening. Please do when the spirit moves, sending me a p.c.
>
> I want to borrow of you the 6d edition of my "Manstealers" which I sent you, to be returned in a few weeks.
>
> They want to bring out a new edition, and I don't seem to be able to drop upon a copy. There is the 6/- edition, but that's no good.
>
> Your sincere / M. P. Shiel

The Man-Stealers, as the subtitle describes—"an incident in the life of the Iron Duke"—was a rousing adventure novel regarding a French attempt to kidnap the Duke of Wellington. Chesson had favored the book, and Shiel felt a fresh edition could again have the success the book had had after its initial publication. It had been listed as a "Best-seller" on the list compiled in the *Bookman* in 1900. A revised edition of the book was not published until 1927.

The Barbara Brennan Memoir

We are fortunate that Mrs. Barbara Brennan, daughter of Lydia's son Gerald and his wife Elsie Lovell, made extensive notes about Shiel's presence among her family members during this period. That memoir has been shared by her son Tim Brennan for this text and provides an intimate view of the years in which Shiel traveled abroad, wrote, and eventually went another way from Lydia's family. It must be understood that Mrs. Brennan derived some of the detail of this time, and her attitude toward Phipps, from the memory and feelings of her son.

This memoir helps provide many details of this period of Shiel's life, both personal and while he was re-entering his old habits of novel writing—and dickering over their commercial fate. But it was during his travels to Italy with Lydia and her son's family that he corrected *Children of the Wind* and began *How the Old Woman Got Home*.

The memoir that she composed for her family began directly:

> My name is Barbara Brennan. I am Tim Brennan's mother. Esther Lydia Furley Jewson Shiel was my grandmother. I remember her well until her death, 16 February 1942 when I was 13 years old.
>
> She was born on 16 August 1872. Her father was a gold beater—one of a family of three generations of gold beaters. They lived in Clerkenwell, London. Her father had a workshop at the end of the yard. My grandmother told me she was one of 14 children but not all reached maturity . . .
>
> My father—Gerald Arthur Jewson—(Lydia's son) was born 4 July 1897. My grandfather William Arthur Jewson came from a musical family. He was born in 1856 . . . He met Lydia in a teashop where she was working as a waitress. She was 24 years old. My father was born on 4 July 1897 at his mother's home.
>
> William Arthur & Esther Lydia set up home together at 54 St. Charles Square in 1897/98 with baby Gerald, as Mr. & Mrs. Jewson. (They were unmarried) . . .
>
> When Gerald was 11 years he went as a day pupil to Marylebone Grammar School founded by the Philosophical Society. Then at 13 years he went as a boarder to Ardingly School Sussex. The family moved to a house in Blandford Street Bedford Park, Cheswick . . .
>
> Around 1910–1912 Lydia met Matthew Phipps Shiel. We know

from W. Arthur's 1914 diary that Lydia went to the Women's Suffrage Movement's political meetings. That she and Miss Limousin were friends. Phipps says in his "About Myself" that he met Lydia at a lecture. Lydia belonged to the Theosophical Society. She certainly went to Suffrage meetings & was a friend of the Pankhursts. My grandfather bailed her out from Bow Street Magistrates court—she had been amongst the Suffragettes who had "chained" themselves to the railings around Buckingham Palace. I think she was enamoured with Phipps & suggested breaking with William Arthur in 1912. He however did not agree—they should remain together whilst Gerald was still a child. Gerald had not been baptised as a baby. ("He should choose for himself when an adult.") Ardingly was set up for education of poor clergymen's sons. Gerald went for Confirmation preparation but he was not baptised. So he left Ardingly & entered Margate Grammar School as a boarder. He enjoyed school at Margate.

In March 1914 the Blandford Street House was sold (or let) & 42 Woodstock Road was bought. Six weeks later on 26 April 1914 William Arthur had a cerebral thrombosis & heart attack & died. He was cremated at the new Golders Green Crematorium.

Gerald sat his Senior Oxford exams. He passed well at English, History & Latin but failed in Mathematics which meant he had failed the whole examination—he had failed to matriculate.

Phipps was around for he advised Lydia that Gerald should go to a cramming school for a year so that he would qualify for entrance to college for study for a Science degree. Gerald did not like Phipps. He was not interested in Science & Math. His favorite subject was History. However 4 August 1914 was the outbreak of the Great War. Gerald had had his 17th Birthday on 4 July 1914. He enlisted at Stamford Brook, Turnham Green, London, at the local Middlesex Territorial Army barracks. He was sent to Bedford for training. In April 1915 he took part in the Dardanelles Campaign at Gallipoli—landing at Suvla Bay. He survived Gallipoli & then became part of Allenby's campaign in Palestine. He was blown up in an aeroplane attack & sent to hospital in Cairo to recuperate.

Gerald returned to England early in 1919 when the war ended. He discovered that Phipps and Lydia were together. They married in 1919. They planned with Mrs. Pankhurst to run a school on "modern" lines. Phipps as headmaster—hence marriage was a necessity.

Gerald met my mother during the Summer of 1919. Elsie Lovell, my mother, was a dress maker—she worked at Marshall & Snellgrove's

Shop in Oxford Street . . . Lydia (being a Bohemian & free thinker and not herself married) suggested to Gerald that he should live with Elsie "Why marry?" But Gerald was determined to marry—the shock of his father's sudden death when he was 16 & the revelation that he himself was a bastard remained with him. Gerald and Elsie were married Dec. 6th 1920. Gerald took Elsie on a honeymoon to the trenches in France & Flanders. . . .

I think my father bought the house in Wisboro' Green on his mother's instigation. It consisted of 3 cottages in one building. The end cottage had a tenant an old lady called Mrs. Fielder—in her nineties—Gerald & Elsie had the center cottage & the end one was for Lydia & Phipps. Mary Davis—an old family servant & friend came with them—she had been with the Jewson family before William Arthur was married. Phipps used to sleep most of the day—He was awake at night—writing. He was a runner—& would run through the night for several miles.

Family friends & relations would come and stay one after the other. Phipps would chat up the female visitors. Yvonne a niece came to stay—she was 14 years old & Aunt Flo's (Florence) daughter. However she quickly returned to London—Phipps had been showing too much interest in her.

Gerald & Elsie used the quarterly interest from his father's money (never touch the capital) & they went traveling through Germany, Austria, Italy, Roumania & Hungary . . . Gerald had a wanderlust & Elsie was happy to adventure with him.

Back in Wisboro' Green they shared the cottage (originally built for charcoal burners.) They worked at restoring the cottage walls had layer upon layer of wallpaper. Finally the paper was all stripped away & the original lath & plaster (wattle & daub) & old old beams were revealed. The cottages were 14th Century . . .

Lydia suggested that Gerald would take a post in a Berlitz English School in Sicily . . .

Apparently Phipps must have come too—though my parents never spoke about him when talking of Sicily. However in the forward to his book about "The Old Women"—he dedicates it to his little woman who copied it out for him—(a marathon task) for Lydia. At this time my grandmother decided she would be called NONA—the Italian for grandmother—she did not wish to be called "Granny."

Early in 1927 Elsie's father died in a street accident. He fell & was run over by a bus in London. Elsie, Gerald & Marjorie returned to England. Elsie was pregnant in May 1927. She decided she did not want to return to either Sicily or to Wisboro'.

Accommodation was very hard to find—they succeeded in renting a basement flat in Marylebone—a good address. The flat had an area at the front with its own entrance & steps up to the street with railings & a gate . . .

I was born on 21 February 1928 in the basement flat. It was snowing. This time my mother had a young up to date Scottish Doctor. He told her to look at the clock—I will give you a whiff of chloroform—the baby will be born & when you look at the clock again it will be just 5 minutes later . . . . I was born hale & hearty with no damage. Elsie had an excellent midwife.

Meanwhile in Wisboro' Green Nona & Phipps marriage was breaking up. When Tim & I visited "The Badgers" Loxwood Rd, Wisboro' Green in Sept. 1998 . . . the present owners . . . showed us over the house. We noticed that the end room had a separate door out into the garden; it also had the interior door to the hall passage with a Yale lock. This door had a letter flap cut into the base of the door. This must have been Phipps' room—he could go on his nightly runs. He could sleep during the day without being disturbed—the door locked & the letters put through the flap. There was a small cupboard room on the other side of the passage. This room had an Elsan chemical lavatory when the Collards first bought the property.

An elderly lady visited while we were there—she told us how her husband (now deceased) could remember the strange man from Badgers who would go running at night. He himself was only a boy of about 10 years. The strange man would stop him & ask him educational questions. Phipps.

Lydia & Phipps had a legal separation in 1929. The cottage "Woodstock" was sold by Gerald. (It reverted to the original name of Badgers.)

When the cottage Wisboro' Green was sold Lydia persuaded Gerald to buy 62 Woodstock Road (800 so that Matilda & Tom Clare could move out & buy Champions Farm in Wisboro' Green. Nona (Lydia) had found a wooden bungalow 3 miles from Wisboro' Green on Bedham Hill near Hawkhurst Court on the Petworth Road. There was a brick kiln which had been partially converted into a cottage with a living room & kitchen added. Steps led up to the upper part of the kiln which had 4 brick columns supporting a roof. The 2 properties were situated in 1½ acres of rough garden. There was no water, gas, electricity or sewage.

Rainwater was collected from the roof into a large tank. "Pure rain from heaven." But it had small wiggly insects in it. When Elsie, Gerald, myself & Marjorie visited, Elsie insisted all drinking water should be boiled. Nona thought this quite unnecessary. But Elsie was adamant. It was boiled.

We had oil lamps and candles to go to bed with. The bungalow had a verandah at one end—the tiled roof overhanging but the verandah was open to the rain on 3 sides. There was a wide room—"kitcho-dino" with a paraffin cooking stove at one side and table with dresser (constructed from orange boxes) against the wall. A passage with 2 bedrooms on the left & a wide sitting room with a brick built chimney & fire place with 2 ingle nook windows at the end. The fire burnt wood & logs cut from the woods behind the bungalow. French windows opened on to a lawn. In the evenings the rabbits & their young would play on the grass. My grandmother had an extra room built on to the right hand side making a T shape to the building. This room had its own door on to the garden.

There was an earth closet attached with bucket that Gerald had to go forth with a spade & attend to.

Lydia had met a Scot—James McKechnie—perhaps in London—maybe at the Theosophical Society. He had lived in Burma for several years & had joined a Buddhist monastery & had become a monk. He lived in the bungalow. We knew him as FRA meaning brother.

Nona had wooden steps built leading to the open upper floor of the Kiln. The open side walls were boarded in with plaster board making an upper room.

In the summer of 1930 when I was 2 years old & Marjorie was 5, we holidayed with my grandmother. My parents slept in the lower room of the Kiln which had 6 foot walls & was bitterly cold & damp.

We had a wash hand stand with large bowl & a jug of water for washing in. In the evening my parents sat with Nona & Fra in their sitting room in the bungalow while Marjorie & I were put to bed in the upper room on our own. Over the years Lydia added more rooms to the bungalow and also a small flat over the kitchen in the Kiln building.

When it was winter—November–March—Lydia would come to 62 Woodstock Rd. and spend until March living with us. Although she had money of her own she stated she would live on the old age pension 10/- a week—not that she received a government pension.

She would give money to many a "hard" case who could tell a "good" story.

She had visitors to stay at the Kiln. Her great friend Miss Limousin came to stay. I remember being told not to play near the Kiln or make a lot of noise as it would disturb Miss Limousin.

We have a photo of my grandmother with Miss Limousin & the Pankhurst sisters Christabel & Sylvia all perched on one of the Sphynxs at the foot of Cleopatra's needle on the Thames Embankment. There is another person—I was told it was Mrs. Pankhurst but my son Tim has researched the photograph in detail. He feels very sure it is Mrs. Teresa Greig. Miss Limousin is wearing a large picture hat which obscures her face . . .

Some time in 1921–1924 my parents went to Paris & stayed at the hotel where Eric Blair ["George Orwell"] was working as a waiter.

I am afraid my mother was not very impressed by him. Elsie came from working class stock. She felt that Eric could live in poor conditions as a down and out but when he wanted—at any time—he could return to the comforts & good food of Aunt Nellie's home . . .

Matthew Phipps Shiel did not visit the Kiln or our family. My father was pleased—he could not stand Phipps.

Mrs. Brennan added the following note to the previous recollection.

During the war 1941 my mother & I moved down to the Kiln . . .

Nona still came to stay from Nov to March each year until the bombing got too bad. We used to visit the Kiln Easter, Whitsun, & September for holidays. Fra stayed at the Kiln during the winters.

Lydia died in the bungalow from a stroke on 16 February 1942. FRA stayed on as caretaker till about 1946 when he moved to Petworth. My father sold the Kiln to the Langdons & the bungalow to another couple in 1947.

Lydia is buried in Wisboro' Green Church yard.

BMB

Mrs. Brennan died 27 April 2009.

The Knopf Tale

For the most part, readers and critics both received *The Children of the Wind* very enthusiastically. Many reviewers found it difficult to separate the carefully composed prose with a novel in which the "picturesque figures" were touched "with a bestiality which makes them real" (*Times Literary Supplement*). It now seems that the reviews that Mr. Edward Shanks wrote concerning this novel helped drive Shiel's immediate successes in issuing several new editions of his earlier work and some completely new work several years along.

> Mr. Shiel has long been known to amateurs of such things as one of the curiosities of literatures. He is a fantastic writer, a sort of extravagant undisciplined Poe; and when he is at his best there is a strange and, I think, an unique quality of imagination in his work . . . His gift is wild and undisciplined, and sometimes even repulsively extravagant, but it is a gift. (*Queen,* 8 February 1923)

It was one of several comments that engaged the attention of Alfred A. Knopf. Perhaps even stronger general enthusiasm for the works of Shiel developed when Knopf published *Children of the Wind* in America in August 1923.

Glowing descriptions that Hugh Walpole and Carl Van Vechten exchanged about Shiel helped promote the favorable reception that he was to achieve from Knopf and then Vanguard.

In May 1923, before Knopf issued *The Children of the Wind* in October, Van Vechten acknowledged to Walpole: "Now that I have read *The Purple Cloud* I am with you on Shiel. We are going to make *The Children of the Wind* go, so that we can revive the others. *The Purple Cloud* is immense . . . He has imagination, glamour, vitality, style."[1]

Van Vechten was even more enthusiastic as he wrote directly to Knopf on 3 October 1923: "Shiel is, to my mind, much more than a commercial proposition. He is an artist, and in his strange way an important one . . . He has glamour, imagination, and a brilliant style . . . And there is a certain grandeur about his manner, about the utterly magnificent way he permits his imagination to work, which reminds me of no one else but Herman Melville . . ."[2]

1. *Letters of Carl Van Vechten* (New Haven: Yale University Press, 1987).
2. Ibid.

Van Vechten continued on 12 November 1923: "Dear Alfred, I've received a charming letter from Shiel—who, by the way, lives in London & is a friend of Arthur Machen . . ."[3]

Meantime, Shiel maintained his contacts with other friends.

On 16 August 1923, he had written Walter Owen. He would send Owen a copy of *The Purple Cloud* but did not have a copy to do so. The title was being translated into Italian, he told him, and it was published in early 1924.

On 10 December Shiel wrote a description of *The Rajah's Sapphire* for Richards, seeking a new edition. But he had no copy to send him. It is difficult to imagine Shiel being so desperate as to promote this early and unworthy work. He also told Richards that he was not pleased with the 6/- edition of *The Man-Stealers* and would attempt to provide him a rewritten version of the novel.

When Van Vechten approached Arthur Machen about Shiel, Machen provided a significant response. On 14 January 1924, he wrote Van Vechten:

> M. P. Shiel: I knew him very well once; but I have lost sight of him for years. The fact is—all this is in strict confidence, and not for the ear of Burton Rascoe!—I didn't feel worthy of knowing a man who looked like the Sultan of the Easkra [Easter?] Islands, and, as they tell, was not devoid of the fiery inclinations which would well become such a potentate. In fact, Shiel came from the isle of Montserrat, and was of mixed race, no doubt, though his features were not in the least Negroid. I always felt that his head should not have been covered with a bowler—"Derby," in America?—but with a turban of a fiery red, fastened by a Monte Cristo emerald. I honestly think that "right" and "wrong" were words entirely without meaning to him. For *Prince Zaleski* and *Shapes in the Fire* I have the highest admiration, for the latter most of all. It is Poe, perhaps, but Poe written with an unearthly radiance about it.

One of the most frequently cited comments by Machen occurred in a letter to Philip D. Sherman on 24 March 1924. He included a photograph of himself, and said, "I doubt whether anything of Shiel's beyond *Prince Zaleski* & *Shapes in the Fire* is worth collecting."

In England, Shiel was using the potential of the republication of his books in America as an incentive for Richards's re-attention. Shiel

---

3. Ibid.

(writing from 88 Grove Park Terrace, Chiswick, to Richards on 21 January 1924) noted that Knopf planned to issue five of his old books: *The Lord of the Sea, Cold Steel, The Purple Cloud, The Isle of Lies,* and *The Dragon*.

Shiel has been rewriting the first two, their length now not more than 80,000 words. He thinks they should be brought out again in England. *The Lord of the Sea* and *Cold Steel* are much improved, he believes, but acknowledges that he has not been able to work on his new book due to this revision work.

Despite his expectation that Knopf would eventually publish these titles, only *Children of the Wind* and *The Lord of the Sea* would ever be published by Knopf. Shiel must have begun his flirtation with Gollancz to publish these titles at about the same time. It was not until 1930 that *The Purple Cloud* was finally published by Vanguard.

On 4 May 1924 Shiel wrote Chesson that he has been busy reading through five old books for American publication and invites Chesson to come pick up his copy of *The Man-Stealers* that Shiel had borrowed to revise for a new edition.

On 16 June 1924 Chesson visited Shiel at 88 Grove Park Terrace, Chiswick. Chesson said that Phipps told him that he was looking over *The Purple Cloud* for an edition of his works for Knopf. He expressed abhorrence of the adjective, he told Chesson.

"Christ says 'Thou fool, this night thy soul will be required of thee' and it sounds strong. The modern man must needs say 'You damned fool' and it sounds weak. There is a sentence of mine which I can't imagine myself writing now or hereafter." It was a sentence about sensation caused by the sound of paper in motion. "Rustling," "warily" occur in it. The load of adjectives and adverbs displeased him much. "I remarked that the only escape from the adjective was increase in number of nouns, so that a noun meaning rustling paper would save one from the aesthetic annoyance of adjectiving paper with rustling!"

On 12 August 1924, Shiel congratulated Van Vechten on his novel *The Tattooed Countess:*

> Bravo, you are among the Liberators, and of the Bretheren: That's right, slash into them, don't be afraid, kick 'em, the more you bully them, the more they'll buckle under, for the dull are all cowards *au fond*. Didn't she sneak victoriously off in the end, snapping her fingers at the crew of them, little caring what they said, though wise

> enough to care what they could do—splendid; and I fully shared in her triumph, and was only sorry that here Bibi was such a little egoist, though that, too, is true and well done. The whole thing has all the heiterkeit and allgemeinheit which Goethe demands, and I heartily congratulate you . . . I have lately received some copies of an Italian translation of my *Purple Cloud,* and it occurs to me to send you one, as you have a set of my books. But it seems to have been translated from the French translation, and not much of me remains. The amusing part is the introduction, in which I am held up as a moral teacher. If Italy reads me, she is saved; if she reads Pitigrilli, she is lost.

On 21 September 1924, he is able to inscribe a copy of Knopf's newly published *The Lord of the Sea* to Grant Richards (from 88 Grove Park Terrace, W.). And the next day, 22 September 1924, he wrote to Van Vechten.

Hugh Walpole reviewed the Knopf *The Lord of the Sea* in the *New York Herald Tribune* on 28 September 1924. James Branch Cabell wrote Van Vechten: "My dear Carl, It was good of you to send me *The Lord of the Sea,* a volume which I am sampling with huge delight. Here is a very charming romance, unmarred by timorous concessions to the merely plausible."

During the fall months of 1924, Shiel and Walpole repeatedly made efforts to meet, but constant obstacles kept the two from ever meeting in person. On 19 October 1924, Shiel wrote sister Gussie that he could not visit because of the pressure of work. It had also interrupted writing his new book "by work of altering five (to please my present taste) for America, and now I am obsessed by the new one . . ." (probably *How the Old Woman Got Home*).

Lord had been republished in America, he told her, but he did not expect much of it. There was news of a hurricane in the *Daily Herald*. "It appears that Montserrat suffered most—that wonderful little land of passions and tantrums. If I had ten lives I would have been willing to give them all to be there to see that wind and feel it in my hair. Harriet, though, was in St. Kitts, I think—happily for her perhaps . . ."

Shiel's brief version of "About Myself" was published in the *Borzoi Broadside* in September 1924 to promote his Knopf publications.

Shiel was writing all his friends at the time. On 5 September 1924 he wrote to Chesson "let us meet soon." Later in September he sent a note to Van Vechten:

> Thanks for yours which reached me a little before copies of *Lord of Sea* with its flagrant envoi from you, which has made me ask myself what I have done to be so favored, so that my thanks are warm. As to Mr. Hugh Walpole, as far as I can make out, all the "success" that has come my way of late years is directly or indirectly due to that good man, whom, however, I do not "know personally", so that I can't help being thankful—and admiring, for apart from the question whether the praise is merited or not, there is shewn in the making of it a generousness of blood above all proves men to be sons of Chrhonic Zeus.

On 23 December Shiel had written Walpole that he was going down to Sussex for Christmas, and he proposed that they meet at 90 Piccadilly on 7 January 1925. Again, this plan failed.

It was not until 1 July 1925 that Shiel wrote Walpole with sympathy over the death of Walpole's mother, "Fathers are nobodies, but a mother is one's self; or so it was with me." Shiel is working on a story about angels, he says.

By December 1924 Shiel tells Richards that the new book is finished but must be retyped before it can be submitted. It should be available in two to three weeks. However, it is 20 February 1925 before he sends Richards a postcard indicating the book is being copied; he is sorry for the delay.

Some of the delay was probably due to the Shiels' moving, since he informs Richards on 4 April 1925 of a new address: Woodstock, Wisborough Green, Sussex. As Mrs. Brennan has described, the Woodstock property had been divided into three living areas, with special arrangements made for Phipps to come and go as he liked, especially with his interest in running at night. But it also appears that at about this time Gerald and family went to Sicily. Phipps must have remained in England as he wrote Chesson on 19 April: "I have been busy writing, and partly preoccupied with coming down here in villeggiatura . . . I am in an old shanty built under the Tudors for troglodyte man, but the country round about is nice."

He wants to borrow any of Machen's books for a paper he has promised to write about Machen—for the *Borzois*. On 25 May 1925, he wrote Chesson thanking him for the loan of the two Machen books which he now returns. He is also sorry that he missed Chesson when he dropped by to visit.

He wrote Walpole again on 10 February 1926, regarding Walpole's diabetes and Shiel's belief that a positive attitude "cures." He is disappointed that Walpole had not sent him a copy of *Portrait of a Man with Red Hair* (a "shocker")

> for sometimes that sort amuses me, and I am often on the brink of trying one—have lately read one, "Trent's Last Case" by Bentley, an old friend of mine, now in *The Daily Telegraph;* but I don't consider it very tricky. . . . have written neither book, nor to friend, being deep in atoms and their ways. There is a certain man sent from God—a young Dane, named Niels Bohr—to whom I am all on my knees, a fellow who will sit down, and after listening a little to the whisperings of the Spirit, will make a guess about how atoms carry on—far down in the dark of their privacy, a guess that will afterwards be found to come truer far than holy Writ, true to the sixth decimal: he is Ivanhoe and Lancelot, hero of romance, the real thing.

He wrote Walpole on 4 May: "That blasted Grant Richards has had a M.S. of mine for eight months, and sends to say he can't publish at once through 'reorganization of business' so I have sent for it."

2 June 1926—Letter from Alan Tytheridge, Tokyo, Japan, to Carl Van Vechten (℅ A. A. Knopf): Enclosed copy of his article from *Tokyo Nichi-Nichi;* has been a Shiel fan since he read *The Purple Cloud* in 1901 in the *Royal Magazine*. Had exchanged a few letters with Shiel in 1911, had lost contact, thought him deceased, then in 1924, returning for a time to England had finally met Shiel. Praises Van Vechten for his perception in seeing more than an entertainer in Shiel, hopes to see a collected edition. [NYPL]

9 August 1926—Letter to the *Daily Herald,* "A Well-Known Novelist sees Red." Regarding the labor movement.

18 December 1926—Letter to Chesson (Woodstock). Shiel has been abroad some time and glad to be back in England. Wants to buy or borrow Chesson's copy of the 6d ed. of *The Man-Stealers* to send to Richards and a film company.

28 December 1926—Letter to Chesson (same). Thanks for sending the book.

23 January 1927—Letter to Chesson (same). Requests a statement from his review for the book. Intends to use it to promote new revised edition of the book.

9–11 February 1927—“Many a Tear” serialized in the *Daily Herald.*

27 February 1927—Letter to [Ann Chesson] Mrs. MacCormack (Woodstock). Shiel and his wife had lately been in Paris and would have called if they had known her address. Invites her to visit. “I have asked your father, but the stubborn person does not budge.” [Squires collection]

27 March 1927—Postcard to Madame MacCormack. We are pleased at your promise to come. [Squires collection]

May 1927—*How the Old Woman Got Home* published (Rocco Lazazzera appears as minor character).

25 May 1927—Letter to Chesson (same). What has become of your daughter and son-in-law? They were to visit in April and have not answered subsequent letters.

Shiel was unaware that Ann Chesson MacCormack had committed suicide.

1 June 1927—Inscription by Shiel in a copy of *How the Old Woman Got Home* (Richards Press): “Walter Owen, from M. P. Shiel, June 1, 1927.” [Squires collection]

30 June 1927—*How the Old Woman Got Home* reviewed in the *Times Literary Supplement:* “. . . plays a number of ingenious variations on the theme of the long-lost heir . . .”

July 1927—6d reprint of *The Man-Stealers* from Hutchinson & Co.

2 July 1927—Letter to the *Daily Herald* responding to a review of *How the Old Woman Got Home*.

3 July 1927—Postcard to Hugh Walpole (Woodstock): “???” Presence of card noted in collection but without contents. The heavy question marks might have been intended as the contents.

7 July 1927—Letter to the *Times Literary Supplement* from Woodstock, Wisborough Green, Sussex, responding to review of *How the Old Woman Got Home*.

8 July 1927—Letter to Shiel from Carl Van Vechten: “I followed the old

woman breathlessly home in silent wonder. I always read your books in a sort of glow, and this is no exception. You seem to write at white heat. The reader must burn too—be he a true reader." [*Works* 2.196.]

9 July 1927—Letter to Shiel from Hugh Walpole: "I'm delighted to hear from you again, and enjoyed *The Old Lady* greatly, although I don't for an instant agree with your old mathematical weeds." [*Works* 2.196.]

14 July 1927—Letter to Hugh Walpole (Woodstock): "Bravo! I am not forgotten . . ." Sorry Walpole has not been well; recommends *Digestive Economy* by Forster, glad Walpole liked parts of *Old Woman*.

30 August 1927—Letter to J. B. Pinker: "I am having typed for publication in America, a set of 25 short stories." [*Works* 2.269.]

28 September [1927?]—Letter to Hugh Walpole (Woodstock) Accepts Walpole's invitation to visit.

November 1927—Inscription in a copy of *Fair Exchange: A Novel in the First Person* (London: Heinemann, [1927]): "To M. P. Shiel, friend in need. Grant Richards, Nov: 1927."

15 November 1927 [1928?]—Inscription in a copy of *The Coast of Pleasure* (London: Cape, [1928]): "To M. P. Shiel with the Author's regard Grant Richards."

1928—Burchell Marshall buys the firm of S. L. Horsford & Co. (and eventually develops it into the largest Black Owned Enterprise in the Eastern Caribbean).

March 1928—*Prince Zaleski* reprinted by Martin Secker.

12–15 March 1928—"In 2073 (A.D.)" serialized in the *Daily Herald*.

30 March 1928—Letter from James L. Shepherd, Secretary, The Workers Theatre Movement:

> Dear Sir,
> Yes, please send any plays you may have for the W.T.M. to the above address. [41, Marcellus Road, London, N.7.] We are in urgent need of plays suitable for a WORKERS theatre.

The following is the information for which you ask:
Playroom Six. 6, New Compton Street, W.C. 2.
Telephone: Regent 3988
Gate Theatre. 16, Villiers Street, W.C. 2
Telephone: Chancery 7263
Everyman Theatre. Hampstead, N.W.3. (Opposite Hampstead Tube Station)
Telephone Hampstead 7224

I am not sure of Robert Atkins address but believe it is 54, Gloucester Gardens, W.2., Telephone: Hampstead 7224.

5 April 1928—Letter from Charles Daniels of Richards Press to George Macy of Macy-Masius re: possible name change for *Old Woman;* sends Shiel's address. [Columbia]

7 May 1928—Letter to Chesson (Woodstock). A new 6d edition of *The Man-Stealers* is out, so he can replace loaned book. Sorry to hear of Chesson's money problems.

May [?] 1928—Letter to Daniels at Richards Press, enclosing new book, *Joy's Choice* [*Here Comes the Lady*].

11 May 1928—Letter to Shiel from Arnold Bennett, apparently in response to a note of thanks from Shiel for Bennett's review of the Martin Secker reissue of *Prince Zaleski* which appeared in the *Evening Standard* on 3 May 1928. "I am very glad to hear from you. I still remember the thrills that I had from *Prince Zaleski* and *The Purple Cloud*. I have several readers who express their pleasure at seeing my references to your work. Goodness had nothing to do with my remarks. As a contributor to *The Evening Standard* I have no friends and do not want any. Friends would only be in the way. When I feel I ought to castigate a friend, I ignore him. It is the only way. . . . Sincerely, Arnold Bennett." [*Works* 2.35.]

21 May 1928—Shiel and Macy write cross letters to each other about *Old Woman*. Macy requests alternative titles. [Columbia]

6 June 1928—Shiel's (sarcastic) letter to Macy with alternative titles for *Old Woman,* a copy of the Secker reprint of *Zaleski,* and a typed list of review quotes. Concerned to see proofs of *Old Woman* before publication. [Columbia]

Shiel submitted these titles as alternatives:

> *American Money.*
> *Honey's In the Rock!*
> *"Dream-Stuff, O!"*
> *The Way of It.*
> *The Way Out.*
> *Fates and Faces.*
> *Grey and Red.*
> *This Shadow-Show.*
> *"The North-Wind Doth Blow."*
> *What Thing the Wind Sings.*

16 June 1928—Letter to Daniels at Richards, enclosing signed contract for *Joy's Choice*.

21 June 1928—Macy to Shiel letter thanking Shiel for copy of *Zaleski* and review quotes; expects proofs within two weeks. Retaining original title to *Old Woman* in hopes that "the use of the nursery rhyme may fasten some attention on the book." [Columbia]

31 July 1928—Macy to Shiel letter: "I can readily believe that you are quite busy, but we do want to get this book published and your delay in returning the proofs is rather inconveniencing us. Won't you try to get them back now?" [Columbia]

The separation of Shiel and Lydia in 1929 was a quiet one, as the few sources that mention it have noted. There is no correspondence between the two that would enlighten the event, but since they lived together until the separation there is no reason to expect any correspondence. Lydia was typing out copy for Shiel right up to their point of separation, despite the fact that Mrs. Brennan wrote in her remembrance of her aunt Lydia that she and Phipps had a stormy and emotional relationship, with a legal separation of the two in 1929.

Woodstock was sold, and property with a small cottage and kiln was purchased. Remodeling converted the kiln into additional living quarters, called in family lore simply "the Kiln." After a brief interlude of living in a hostel, Shiel purchased "L'Abri," a cottage just outside Horsham, which he decorated in West Indian fashion and where he would spend the rest of his life.

Mrs. Brennan notes that Lydia was beset by hangers-on, in one case a family being legally forced out by Gerald. Probably of the most significance was the arrival of a new friend, probably introduced through theosophical activities, the "Brother," "Fra," or "FRA." Mrs. Brennan calls him a Scot, named James McKechnie. He had lived in Burma, joined a monastery, and became a monk.

Given Lydia's long inclination toward sexual practices, one is inclined to believe that she and Fra developed a romance, a relationship built on theosophical interests and participation.

“My Dear Fytton”: The Letters of M. P. Shiel to John Gawsworth

More than any other factor, John Gawsworth described and defined the Shiel that modern-day readers, critics, and scholars portray and identify as a writer and a person. A brilliant young poet, editor, and bibliographer, Terence Ian Fytton Armstrong (Gawsworth’s legal name; 1912–1970) began around 1930 to hum around the authors lingering on from the years of nineteenth-century decadence, most specifically Arthur Machen and Shiel, with plans to compile a list of the first editions of each author.

By late 1931 or early 1932, Gawsworth had reviewed the first editions of Shiel’s publications to include in his volume, *Ten Contemporaries* (London: Ernest Benn, 1932). In the process, he apparently had been to see Phipps at his new home at L’Abri, asking him to review the list that he intended to include in his collection of descriptions of books by ten authors.

In the process, Shiel gave him a copy of the appreciative essay that Alan Tytheridge had written in the *Tokyo Nichi-Nichi* (in eight issues in July 1924) concerning him, but requested its return in a note to Gawsworth.

The earliest known letter from Shiel to Gawsworth follows, indicating that Shiel had reviewed the list of his first editions that Gawsworth had compiled and requested the return of the copy that Shiel had provided him of the Tytheridge essay—and inviting a visit. Although the Redonda myth is mentioned in this 1929 version of “About Myself,” written to help promote the Gollancz editions, it clearly did not catch Gawsworth’s attention for several years.

These letters are the only letters by Gawsworth to Shiel in the Ransom Center. It is obvious that many other letters escaped Gawsworth’s possession, perhaps through sales, but the location of others is unknown. The dates are a muddle.

Although Gawsworth penciled dates on the letters that lack them, it appears that they do not necessarily follow the pattern that Gawsworth believed when he added the dates in later years. The correspondence regarding the gathering and publication of Shiel’s *Poems* would appear to belong to a period much later than 1932.

L'Abri / New Rd., Worthing Rd / [Printed] Horsham, Sussex / [In Gawsworth's hand: "? Late '31 early '32"]

My dear Armstrong,

Yes (in reply) to what seems good as to my bibliography. You have the pamphlet "About Myself"—copy out of that whatever you wish.

I am now free, and shall be delighted to see you whenever you are moved toward me. If that is soon, please bring with you the Japanese M.S. I handed you; if not soon, will you send, as I have to write soon to the sender of it to me, and may decide to send it back.

Your sincere / M. P. Shiel

Gawsworth copied out "The Inconsistency of a Novelist," which Shiel had pointed him to from the pamphlet "About Myself," and included it as a preface to *Ten Contemporaries*.

Gawsworth's development of a project with Phipps appears to have been the gathering from Shiel's various books of the "poems" that had been included in the texts, with plans to have them published as a collection. Shiel appears to have treated the project as more of a nuisance than something to celebrate. There are several letters (from 1935 or '36) in which Shiel requests copies of the contents to proof.

By that time, Shiel had met Gawsworth's first wife, Barbara Kentish, the other half of the "duet" to whom Shiel refers in his letter. Gawsworth and Barbara were married in 1933 so any presumed "late summer 1932" letters are obviously of a later date, most likely 1935 or 1936.

Gawsworth had by then searched out the "poems" that Shiel had included in his fiction, with plans to have them published: "the Eleven" to which Shiel refers in this letter. Gawsworth had penciled a 1932 date on the letter, but a "Happy New Year" clearly suggests very late in one year or early in a following year—probably 1935 or '36. It could not be in August 1932 as Gawsworth had penciled on it.

[L'Abri] / [1935 or '36]

Herewith the Eleven, as you wish—I don't see why. When ready, send to me to read, then I'll send back.

Happy New Year to the duet.

M.P.S.

[In Gawsworth's hand: "August 1932?"]

[L'Abri] / [1935 or '36]

I shall look out for you Sunday. I can't correct poems without M.S.; please send or bring.

M.P.S.

[L'Abri] / [1935 or '36]

Bravo for three editions? Also Bravo re Sunday 18th! Herewith proofs. In haste. / M.P.sh

Armstrong has penciled an explanation of the "three editions" mentioned in Shiel's letter on its foot. "Of my *Lyrics to Kingcup*. JG"

L'Abri, / Monday / [1935 or 1936]

My dear boy,

Herewith the so-called poems. In such a case the principal thing is bigness of print: please insist upon that.

I am half-inclined to go to London to hear the lectures! Are you going to write them out? That may be desirable; in which case bring 'em & show. In any case give some little care to thinking them out.

My love to Barbara, and to you.

M.P.S.

The collection of eleven of Shiel's poems appeared in November 1936 as a publication from the Richards Press: *Richards' Shilling Selections from Edwardian Poets: M. P. Shiel.*

Of more significance in the series of letters after August 1932 and the poetry project is an indication of a rapidly developing closeness between the two men. Shiel's affection for Barbara Gawsworth is also clear and plays an important role in the divorce of Gawsworth and Barbara in later years—an act that displeased Shiel immensely. Another activity that would soon show up in the correspondence was the apparent gathering by Gawsworth of Shiel books that he would have signed and sell for the benefit of Phipps. This exercise, in turn, would in time become a practice that was of more direct benefit to Armstrong himself—the gathering of material for Shiel to sign and Gawsworth to sell for himself. It is not possible to determine when this shift occurred or what the monetary advantage to Gawsworth might be. A few years later, Gawsworth devised a bookplate that suggested it had been the property of Phipps and himself to enhance its prospective value.

However, there is evidence in the period following the publication of the Shiel poems that Gawsworth did sell newly written material by

Shiel, and also proposed that the two collaborate—a suggestion that Shiel considered with caution.

L'Abri, / New Rd., Worthing Rd., /
Horsham Sussex / Sept.18 35

My dear Fytton,

Thanks so much for "Zaleski" typescript. The reason of my eagerness is very simple: a magazine editor "is interested" in seeing, and the altered version is more likely to please. So I sent two telegrams, not knowing where you were.

Do you know whether there is in existence anywhere the M.S. of one of my 90's books? I have an offer of £30 for one, and, like a miser, am reluctant to let it slip. I know a woman in London who had the M.S. of Zaleski, but I shouldn't wonder if she has now lit a fire with it.

As to your writing more "Zaleski" stories, you are Napoleon who said "don't use to me that bête de mot". And since Napoleons have a way of succeeding, I bid you God-speed, provided you call them your stories; I could never say that yours were mine, could I? On the whole, I think you had better wait until we debate it more. The basic idea seems good, only the how of executing it is doubtful.

Come as soon as you can. My love to Barbara.

M.P.S.

[Gawsworth has questioned in the margin, re the woman with the Zaleski Ms.: "? Mrs. "Sircar"]

As it became more difficult to find sufficient books for Shiel to sign for Gawsworth to sell to their advantage, Shiel began a practice that he probably thought might be useful for new editions of his various stories as well as create more marketable results of this authorship. This involved his copying out the full texts of many of his earlier stories in holograph, creating an uncertainty as to whether these copies were actually the original holograph compositions or newly copied out (and perhaps edited somewhat) that collectors or dealers were glad to own or to market.

This probably explains why Shiel thanked Gawsworth for the "Zaleski typescript" mentioned in the letter above. It probably also explains what the "five stories" were that Shiel mentions in the following that Gawsworth had sold for £10.10 and Shiel insisted that Gawsworth had a share of.

New Rd. Worthing Rd. /
Horsham, Sussex / [*Lacks salutation*]

Right! As to Sunday.
Send a p.c. on Friday to say hour of arrival.

In great haste. / M. P. Shiel

Holograph note by Shiel with signature across two postage stamps signifying formal receipt by Shiel of £10.10 for five stories.

Gawsworth notes 25 August 1935.

"Received of John Gawsworth £10.10 for five stories. / M.P. Shiel" [*signed across postal stamps*]

It is my feeling that these "five stories" were copied out for marketing. I once owned one of these. The other possibility is that these were stories that Shiel had newly written or revised to include in the various "thrills" collections that Gawsworth was editing. Shiel was probably referring to one of these new submissions when he wrote Gawsworth the following, indicating that he deserved a portion of what he had sold on Shiel's behalf.

[L'Abri] / Monday morning [early 1936?]

I have just got yours. [*Inserted:* with cheques] and now send "I. Voices" and "Red Road."

You might mention to Wiggins that all the corrections (practically) are of departures by the printers from copy. Some of your (good) corrections I have left out, not to pile up. I had to pay Benn's printers £4 for "Say Au R'voir", though I made no corrections of my own, printers attributing their mistakes to author, and laughing while he pays. Don't make up any more corrections, except of something obviously wrong.

What about Barbara's Love-Story book? My remembrances to her. Say if you have taken "Luke" to Watts.

Yours, / M.P.S.

[*At foot of page*]
Charge the usual £10.10 for 'Red Road,' your checking is £3.3, as you deserve.

Shiel's fondness for Barbara is noted above. Barbara Kentish was society editor for the *Daily Mail* and obtained for Gawsworth (whom she had married) the job of editing his first anthology *Thrills, Crimes and Mysteries* (published by Associated Newspapers, Ltd. at Christmastime

1935). Steve Eng, a Shiel scholar, describes her assistance to Gawsworth in placing him as editor in other newspaper collections.

Eng also reported that Gawsworth had persuaded Oswell Blakeston to "complete" some of the stories that Shiel had not finished because of boredom. Thus it may be, as Blakeston describes in correspondence with John D. Squires, that those brief "conclusions" to several of these stories were not written by Gawsworth but by Blakeston, only as much as two or three pages of typescript he admits, done with reluctance but hoping their publication would benefit Shiel financially.

Candidly, Blakeston's account does not appear accurate, since the manuscripts of the portions of a story that Shiel had written and which Gawsworth completed exist in the Ransom Center at the University of Texas at Austin. One can see the amount of manuscript that Shiel contributed along with the amount from Gawsworth.

There is the possibility that Blakeston wrote the small fragments that Gawsworth added to the Shiel text and accepted them as though they were Gawsworth's own creations in the manuscripts. But the manuscripts that exist should reveal the amount of text created by each author.

The overwhelming majority of the text of several of the stories that Shiel laid aside because of his obsession with his work on *Jesus* are clearly by Shiel himself and in a few cases are strongly autobiographical.

That Shiel needed financial help and determined several schemes to avoid paying bills is described in this letter to Gawsworth shortly after the publication of his stories in the newspaper anthology and his collection *The Invisible Voices,* consisting of eleven earlier published stories linked by narrative between each story—which Gawsworth may have written. The links are not Shiel's prose at its best.

In response to a request from Gawsworth in the spring of 1933, Shiel composed a brief piece for a planned tribute to Machen (written at Horsford on 22 June 1933). He appended his story of "the Machens' Little French Maid." Gawsworth shared Shiel's text within his biography-in-progress with Machen on 23 August 1933. Machen virtually exploded, writing from Amersham: "The Machens' Little French Maid: Let me beg you not to make Shiel the authority for any statement about me or my life. He is an inveterate liar."

This piece, finally headed "The Good Machen" was published in the *Aylesford Review* in 1963 after Gawsworth produced a few copies at his Twyn Barlwm Press.

L'Abri
New R., Worthing Rd.,
Horsham, Sussex

[23 January 1936]
My dear Fytton,

I am rather anxious about you, since in your last you wrote you were not well, and I have since written unanswered. I should be anxious about myself (but am not) since two people born in the same year as I lie stiff, and do not bend the knee in prayer—the King and his Kipling. But you, write soon and reassure me. And answer my question as to my Luke book.

I want you, if well, to do something else for me: a certain typist at Hastings has a legal claim on me—only 6/6 but it is not in the public interest that it should be paid; for which reason I hereby give you the "goods and chattels" in this house: so now they are yours; and will you write to G. Catching Esq., Registrar, County Court House, Horsham, saying "You should note that the goods and chattels at 'L'Abri,' Worthing Rd., in the custody of Mr. M. P. Shiel, are my property", that's all. As to the initial "G", you must copy that, as I do.

Remind your Barbara of

Your M.P.S

In a telegram to him, Gawsworth has marked "? Feb 1937" and addressed to GAWSWORTH 33 GREAT JAMES ST WC 3 Shiel has sent a note "PLEASE COME ON FOURTEEN TOMORROW ENGAGED WRITING SHIEL"

L'Abri / Tuesday
[Gawsworth writes "? Aug 1937"]

I sent you "Phantom Man o' War" on Saturday, with synopsis of "Au R'voir" without letter, in haste to catch train. If you get a list of publishers of reprints, and pointed out that Spanish things are topical, you may dispose of "Phantom".

And you won't forget about Walpole & Baldwin for both are readers, will you?

And did you ask Howe re "This Above All"?

And are you making effort (desperate) to keep on being a publisher?

M.P.S.

[*Gawsworth has written two clarifications.* "Contraband of War" *re* "Phantom" *and* "P. P. Howe, (Bodley Head)"]

L'Abri. / New Rd., Worthing Rd., /
Horsham, Sussex

Oct.23. 37.
My dear Fellow, thanks for the cutting about the King Novelist, the main point about which for me is that you seem to be again jocund, and the appendix napoo—hurrah! I have been very afflicted in your affliction. The other thing in the cutting which touches me close is the "thousands of tons of silicate of aluminum" that comes from Redonda, the implication being that King Philip richly reaps, though in truth scents no sou from them. However, in consequence of the cutting, I have had in the last day or two two visitors, obnoxious, but promising—reporters to interview me from The Observer and The Star.

You didn't send your brother's address, from which I share the presage that you will soon be turning up smiling and well.

M.P.S.

[*Gawsworth has written in the margin* "Sunday Referee" *and has lined through* "The Observer" *and inserted* "Sunday Referee."]

L'Abri. / New Rd., Worthing Rd., /
Horsham, Sussex / "Monday"

[*Gawsworth has penciled at head of letter* "? 19 Feb' 38"]
My dear Fellow,

Herewith the typing bill: remind me when you come to pay 2/6, and now come when you please, sending a p.c. forewarning. I enclose 12 p.p. to be retyped—omissions of bits and muddles. Please tell her to send direct to me, in *duplicate,* with pages of copy which I send her to show what she has left out. Did you get from me poems, ≠c? You don't seem to have said so. I hope you go strong now. Only now my dog bite has healed.

Yours / M.P.S

[*See Barbara Gawsworth's letter to Harold Billings (12 June 1958) regarding the dog bite.*]

"L'Abri" / New Rd. / Nov. 18 '41

My dear Fytton, I got "Marlow Hill" all right, and have carefully read the letter after long silence (due on my side to uncertainty as to your address), though I have been thinking often of you, especially every time I go into Horsham and see on the tobacco-shops "No Tobacco",

"No cigarettes", as that I live more in apprehension of finding myself smokeless, wrecked. As to your "Marlow Hill", I got a good deal of enjoyment from it, it being very characteristic, yet an advance in not that I understand every line, even now; I think that, because some meaning is clear to you, you are apt to consider it clear to everyone. You—and I—know, for instance, why you call it "Marlow Hill", but not everyone will. Still, there is no doubt, you wear laurel round the brows. And, as to the letter what shall I say? This, at any rate, that you must not listen to your lawyer, who does not "countenance a reconciliation": that is the irony of lawyers, whose interest is in having a "case".

I, on the contrary, strongly countenance a reconciliation, knowing that our side is not blameless. To understand is to pardon, and I understand you; you are a poet, and you conceived that love-affairs with different petticoats furnish the subject-matters for love-poems: "To Olga"! But Barbara would hardly understand that. I expected that she would be bitter, though I am horrified that she is so bitter. On the whole, after thinking of it, I have decided to advise you to write her another letter, a penitent letter, a humble letter, a masterpiece in humility, mentioning that the others were transitory caprices, but that she is the everlasting hills, and the hereditary Queen. It won't hurt your hand or pen to write it; then see what happens, and write me again.

Thanks so much for offering to send "New Testament in Modern Speech"; I shall be quite glad to get. And if you can find and send me back my last essay "Persistence of Personality After Death", I think I see my way to getting it printed.

I rejoice to see that you are now "Aircraftsman, 1st Class", though I'm afraid that that does not convey much meaning to my mind. It is extraordinary that I still do not quite know just what your work is!

When do I see you again?

Phipps.

L'Abri. / New Rd. Worthing Rd. /
Horsham, Sussex / 5 26 '46

My dear Fytton

As to the man who wishes to sell you a M.S. of mine, I know nothing about him.

Now I have a letter from "Ellery Queen", who says not a word about my "Lend Lease" which you sent him, but through some favoritism to me, he wishes to publish in his magazine "A case for Deduction" which appeared in "*Thrills*", to publish it by "M. P. Shiel and John Gawsworth" on condition that he gets an undertaking that it shall not appear anywhere before appearing in his magazine, and that then the joint author be John, better known than Fytton. Will you therefore write and send to me that undertaking, and I will send to you a cheque for one quarter of the payment which I receive.

Yours with love, / M.P.S.

[*Gawsworth adds a note in margin* "Formerly called 'In Dark Water Whirled' before I collaborated & finished it."]

[*And finally Gawsworth's note:* "Last letter / Shiel died 2:40 pm 17/2/47 in Chichester."]

Shiel's *Book of Luke*

Where is Shiel's *Book of Luke?*

For years after Shiel's death there has been concern and interest in the fate of his completed work, *Jesus*. A. Reynolds Morse, in his bibliography *The Works of M. P. Shiel,* listed the final existing manuscripts, now in the Ransom Center, among them the "Fourth and Final Draft" among a number of other remnants of his work on the Gospel.

However, in 1935 Shiel believed that he had completed a book that was ready to be published: *The Book of Luke.* That book, ready, as he believed, for publication both in England and the United States, can only be identified by following the history of the incomplete manuscripts of *Jesus*.

Nineteen notebooks, numbered 22 to 40 of this final "fair copy" manuscript for the typist, are in the Ransom Center, the last half of the completed work. Notebooks numbered 1 to 21, the first half of the work, were missing from the surviving group of manuscripts that came to Texas from Gawsworth, apparently (as Shiel had written to Ren Morris) having been completed and sent to a typing agency. These have never been found.

However, there is another "final" version of Shiel's work on transcribing with notes, the work on this Gospel, a book that in 1935 he called *Book of Luke,* or simply *Luke.*

On a Monday, probably sometime in 1935, Shiel asked Gawsworth: "Say if you have taken 'Luke' to Watts."

He has written Annamarie Miller on 22 July 1935: "a publisher has had my Luke for two months . . ."

On 23 January 1936, he asks Gawsworth to answer his question as to whether this book had been delivered to Richards Press. Further to this, he wrote Walter Owen on 12 February 1936, "I have spent two years on doing a translation of the book of Luke, with criticism and so far can't get any London publisher bold enough to publish, though it is coming out in America."

There is no trace of this edition of the work that I have been able to locate. Wiggins at Richards Press writes Shiel on 12 October 1937 that Vanguard is developing cold feet over *Jesus,* that it has reservations about Shiel's book on hand and doubts that *Jesus* would sell.

Then on 14 December 1937, Shiel sends a postcard to Wiggins asking him to return a copy of the *Luke* manuscript.

Shiel wrote his longtime Brooklyn fan correspondent, Mrs. Annamarie V. Miller, on 21 February 1939: "I want a large sum to boom a book which I am certain will do good if boomed—the 'Jesus' as to which you ask for news. This was to have been brought out here by 'The Richards Press,' but the specimen-page that they sent me was in such small type, that I wouldn't have it, and determined to let it lie, and part-publish it myself at the right time. So at the present time I am on the job of writing film-abridgements."

He had written Mrs. Miller as early as 30 March 1937: "I am a little bothered by the fact that my book 'Jesus' which took me two years to write (more) has turned out to be 145,000 words long, instead of 100, or so, and I am wondering whether any publisher will be found willing to undertake the expense. But, having done the job, I am done with it."

But he didn't leave it done. He continued to pick it up, reworking it over the years as it consumed his writing time as *Jesus* until at least 1946, as he wrote Morse. He had described it to Mrs. Miller on 24 October 1937 as "That, it seems to me, is my top-note and magnum opus, because in reading deeply into the New Testament I have found out things, such as that Paul the Apostle was Lazarus of Bethany, who remained four days in a tomb to be 'raised from the dead' by Jesus . . ."

The gathering of manuscripts relating to this title that are assembled in the Ransom Center requires the work of a textual bibliographer to follow Shiel's line of work in developing *Jesus* over its years of composition. It may be possible to identify the work that he claimed to have completed and attempted to market as the *Book of Luke* in 1935 and 1936.

In an undated letter to Gawsworth, but based on its contents, sometime in early 1936, Shiel asked him: "Say if you have taken 'Luke' to Watts." There is a discussion of this matter among the compilation of Gawsworth letters.

For some ten years, from 1937 until 1946, W. H. Chesson sent Shiel a birthday greeting and Shiel responded, frequently with interesting biographical news. On 26 November 1937, Shiel wrote Chesson: "I don't read much—do mathematics, and am doing a book named 'Jesus', meant to deal a blow at the Christian priest."

The following year, on 24 March 1938, Shiel elaborated on the content of Jesus: "I am able to demonstrate by reading deeply into the internal evidence of the Bible that the apostle Paul was Lazarus of Bethany, that the author of the 'Matthew' gospel was Martha of Bethany, and that the author of the 'John' gospel was a boy, not over fourteen: I call him Littlejohn. Priests will object, but, as to protests, I agree with, and rejoice at, your view that a 'certain tolerance of mendacity (and enmity to truth) is implicit in the process of getting a "living."'"

By 11 August 1944, however, Shiel told Chesson ". . . in my present attempt to make an honest translation of the Book of Luke with 'Remarks' at the end of each chapter: so that whether I shall ever finish it, I doubt."

He alerted Chesson in the next birthday exchange:

L'Abri, / New Rd., / Worthing Rd., /
Horsham, Sussex

July 22 '45
My dear Chesson, very refreshing, as usual, comes the birthday remembrance of me, though of course it evokes the reflection that once—soon—by the Law of probability you will write and have no answer, or you not write, and I shall wonder and guess why: on such slippery slopes we stand and slip. However, courage! We are well made, and I, for my part, look forward without the least fear to that "dark portal, veiled, home of all mortal". Meantime I enjoy eating and the sight of the skies spread out; our sun is a bit stingy of its heat and light, and Winter in our latitude is rather disagreeable, it looks as if the good God was an under-god, and was rather beaten by Nature in His amateur efforts at creation; but I am convinced that He did His best, and since I have not murdered anyone, I have no apprehension of His vengeance on "the other side" . . . You do not tell how you are going at No. 337: strong, I hope. Some day we may meet—if we be quick about it!

Your sincere / Shiel

In his final letter to Chesson, with whom he had been in contact since 1906 when he sent condolences to Chesson concerning the death of his wife, the 1890s poet Nora Hopper (Mrs. Chesson), one finally gets a feeling for the depression that seemed to touch Shiel more and more in his final years, "I am done now, I think, with making rhymes."

L'Abri. / New Rd. / Worthing Rd., /
Horsham, Sussex.

July 24, 46

My dear Chesson, bravo for the poem: you show that you had a wife who was a rhymster, though the last line here gets to be obscurer to the reader than to the writer, that being why you "young" poets, of whom I know several, tend to neglect instant comprehension by the reader: in fact, they fancy that obscurity is poetic—unlike Milton, Dante. As for me, I am done now, I think, with making rhymes, for though I am still well apparently, there is a certain failure of poetic emotion at sight of the world—failure of the god-hormone to function, as I call it: the good God pours out his universe upon my eyes (and ears), and I receive it coldly. Also, corresponding with this, is a certain weakness of leg: I who used to run six miles every morning can hardly now run one, and a doctor-friend tells me frankly "You should not run you *are too old*": pray for me . . . . I note that like me, you spend your time mainly in reading—only what I read cannot be contradicted, being mathematics, though you, too, if you find The Daily Mail despicable can drop it.

Yours / M.P.S.

It was with the same note of sadness that he wrote his epistolary love of many years, "Nance" (Annamarie Miller), on 4 October 1946 in his last letter to her: "I for my part retain for you a large share of the old affection, though, as for the love of woman in general, I have slowed down with the years . . . With love and thanks, Phipps."

Refusing Corruption: A Shape in the Fire

Shiel to Chesson 11 August 1944: "I, at any rate, will not be eaten by worms, as all my fathers were, for I have lately joined the Cremation Society, and bought exemption from 'corruption,' whereas the claim to Jesus, 'He will not suffer his holy one to see corruption' is nonsense, for in 'three days' in the latitude of Jerusalem: 'by this time' (four days) 'he stinketh'; whereas I for my part intend to depart in the Winter."

1. Letters from Barbara Gawsworth to Harold Billings

Merrie Hollow Hill,
Seymour Court Road,
Marlow, / Bucks.

June 12th 1958
Dear Mr. Billings,
I am indeed sorry I have not replied before to your letter regarding M. P. Shiel, but I have been trying to trace his daughter. As you know, she is married to a doctor, who at least 5 years ago was living in the vicinity of Harley St. London. W. I have been trying and trying to remember his name but cannot. I suggest you write a note to the Editor of "The Lancet" explaining your problem. 'The Lancet" is the official medical journal and is read by every doctor and would undoubtedly be seen by her husband.

I knew Shiel quite well and used to visit him at his bungalow near Horsham fairly frequently with my husband. The scene was usually the same. He invariably wore a black velvet smoking jacket, old tweed trousers and slippers. I doubt whether he ever bothered to comb his mass of black hair. Without any polite formalities he would immediately talk about his latest theory of mathematics or a plot for a book. On a table was food consisting of vegetarian dishes such as nuts, prunes, oranges etc. There were usually about 18 assorted dishes on the table. These were never cleared away, and as one dish was emptied so it was refilled. As time went on quite a thick coating of dust used to cover most of the eatables, but this was a detail he never bothered about. He did not eat at any set time but took the food when he felt hungry.

He had tremendous physical courage. On one occasion he was badly bitten in the leg by a dog. He immediately poured a bottle of neat iodine on it and proceeded to run round his garden quite cheerfully until the pain abated. Neither did he bear a grudge against the dog but patted it at the next meeting without any further ill effects. He loved running and used to do a sprint of some miles daily right until his final illness.

His taste in furnishings was awful. The bungalow was cluttered up with knick knacks, tasseled velvet hung from the mantelpiece. Curtains of beads were everywhere, and so were vases etc. In fact, except for literature, he had little knowledge or appreciation of painting or music. He did like the song 'O sol o mio' [*sic*] very much, and used to say it was in the air when the world was created.

At one time he thought he had discovered the secret of perpetual motion. For months his kitchen was cluttered with wires, and all forms of gadgets, but unfortunately someone who came to help him, touched something and stopped whatever was supposed to continue working indefinitely.

He always boasted that he had quite a few illigitimate [*sic*] children scattered here and there, and that he called them all Nancy, after someone he was fond of in his youth. This of course may be one of his amusing generalizations. He said they were all girls. I believe one did turn up at his funeral.

I suppose Mrs. Miller has given you the name and address of his neighbours who could give you invaluable information. Also that of my ex-husband who is his literary executor. My husband at present might be found ℅ "The English Digest". Furnival St. London.E.C.4. There is also a woman journalist, now I believe in New York, whose name is Elliseva Sayers. She came down with me and my husband to see Shiel some time ago. She would be able to help you quite a lot.

If there is any further information you would like, please let me know and I will do my best to help.

Sincerely yours,
Barbara Gawsworth

Merrie Hollow
Seymour Court Hill,
Marlow. / Bucks.

August 8th 1958
Dear Mr. Billings,

I have not written earlier as I have been trying to contact my former husband, and at last have been able to. An article appeared in England's worst sensational newspaper, "The Daily Mirror," about my husband having been made a 'King' of an island bequeathed to him by Shiel, and I have written him a note via the newspaper reporter who has written to me and told me he has forwarded it. I told him to contact you at once. I have posted you a copy of the paper by sea mail. (Air mail for papers costs the earth here.)

Now as regards Shiel's ashes. Shiel bequeathed these to my husband and I went with him to the undertakers to collect them. Incidentally, there is rather a macabre incident connected with this. We were both rather depressed and went to a club off Leicester Square for a drink. My husband put the ashes which were in a cardboard box on the counter and turned away to speak to a friend. The barman seeing the package was getting wet from spilt drinks put the packet on a shelf at the back of the bar fairly high up, not of course knowing its contents. Some time after I happened to be watching the barman cutting a sandwich and just as he was spreading it with some salmon I noticed a tiny trickle of ash falling from the box into the sandwich. I was speechless with horror and so was my husband. We could do nothing except ask for the box back. The sandwich was duly handed to the late James Agate the most distinguished dramatic critic at the time. Of all people it would be him, who had an intense admiration for Shiel's work but disliked my husband very much indeed, a feeling heartily reciprocated. As we went out my husband could not help going up to Agate and saying "You've just eaten part of M .P. Shiel". "You're drunk" was all Agate said and proceeded to finish his sandwich, as we went out.

The ashes were put in an old West Indian brass tea caddy and these went wherever my husband went. As far as I know he still has them. I expect he would be glad for your University to have them.

As far as Shiel's attendance at King's College, London, the very imagination that made his books so vivid, also I regret to say sometimes coloured his ordinary life, and I would not be surprised if it turned out that he had never been there at all. But of course this is only my personal opinion and may be very wrong of course.

I don't know the circumstances of the funeral. My husband was there so was his daughter who married the doctor and the doctor. But beyond that I cannot remember who he said was present. I have asked my husband in my note to let you know.

The people who would give you full details about Shiel's illness are his neighbours whose address Mrs. Miller of New York will be able to give you I feel sure. I have a feeling it was a blood clot that killed him but again I am not positive.

Have you a copy of a poem written by Shiel called "Song of the Cock" which appeared in "Fifty Years of Modern" verse an anthology chosen by my husband? If not, I will type it out and send it to you with pleasure. I mention this as it was not generally know[n] that Shiel could write verse.

I will write again if and when I get anything further of interest.

I would be most interested to read your monograph of Shiel in your "Library Chronicle" if you could spare time to send it.

Yours very sincerely, / Barbara Gawsworth

2. Letter from Kate Gocher to Harold Billings

Gwalia / New Road / Worthing Road
Horsham Sussex / Eng.

Jan 9 1959
Dear Sir,
In answer to yours.

Mr. Shiel was my neighbour as I think you know. He always looked to my boys if he could not manage little things himself. He had his days when writing, no one disturbed him. Other days he would putter about in his garden, attending to his roses. He would go for long runs to keep himself fit, before going to bed. At times he stayed in bed all day. Winter months I had a key & had a nice fire going for him to come out too [*sic*]. I was sorry when the Doctor said he must go to Hospital to have proper treatment. My Son or myself went to see him most weeks. He was always looking forward to coming home. I did not see the Certificate of Death. But I thought he had a stroke. The Nephew took over & arranged the Cremation. Dr. Horsford Harley Street. Mr. Shiel told me his daughter was brought up by her Grandmother. I have not known the address.

I cannot tell you any more except to say all around missed him very much at the time.

I am Sir, / Yours Respectfully /
K Gocher

3. Letter from John Gawsworth to Harold Billings (in holograph on Air Letter "urgent")

30 Castellain Road, Maida Vale, London W.9

Nov. 4 1958
Dear Mr. Billings:

I owe you many apologies for not writing before but (1) I have been ill (2) I am still ill, confined to house, jobless, broke (3) the Shiel papers were not with me when you wrote. Now things are possible. You are prepared to buy: I am prepared to sell & collaborate. (The Shiel papers are by my side tho' mixed in many boxes.) I am quite happy to envisage a Billings "Life of Shiel" and give you every assistance. I merely want the book done, and aid you through the press with it. The first thing I must have is some money & immediately, say £150. If you will suggest some items from 1–257 (Morse pp. 125–135) [excluding Jesus (for which I want £100 pounds] they would await your cheque for departure at Rota, Hollings, or bookseller you know if I had them still. In any case I must have $50 dollars by return if I am not to be evicted. It is tragic to have to write in this way at pistol point as it were, but I cannot even sort 7 crates of mixed papers here with the landlord drumming on the door. I have yearly folders (except 1914–1923) of most of Shiel's life, and once you save mine! They will be extricated, priced, passed on etc. I am, I repeat, absolutely content to play second fiddle in your book & once I am better in the Spring, follow up clues, requirements, photos etc. this side to aid you to make it the last word on the subject. I suggest depositing MS for you with some bookseller you know in case you don't care to trust my integrity—thou' that's a poor way to start a collaboration & a friendship. I apologise!

Your / John Gawsworth

The Disposition of L'Abri

Mrs. Annamarie V. Miller wrote me on 7 April 1958:

> The cottage, L'Abri, was sold in order to settle the estate. It was left to my son, Patrick. The money was put in a bank in England until he was 21, and then was allowed to have it in two lots . . . I think that I like 'How the Old Woman Got Home,' best of all . . . During the war I sent him food packages. After his death a package I had sent arrived and Mrs Gocher wrote to me asking what should be done with it. I told her to keep it and in reply she revealed Shiel used to give her the cans of meat I sent—so that was the first I knew that he didn't eat meat . . .
>
> Sincerely and best wishes
> Annamarie V. Miller

Envoi

Tracing the life of M. P. Shiel has been a geographic adventure, from the first days of a son of ex-slaves and Irish plantation managers on a tumultuous sea-bound island of ferrite beaches and forested volcanoes to those last days of an elderly man puttering in his rose garden on an English countryside. He had been a writer of richly imaginative ecstatic fiction, a stylist this author has followed through his "Early Years," the "Middle Years," and now these "Final Years," filching what it has been possible to glean from these sources like his bones deposited in an ossuary which have turned, as he wished, into fire-wasted ashes lost somewhere in a brass tea caddy, if it still exists. His words are incorruptible.

References

Akenson, Donald Harman. *If the Irish Ran the World: Montserrat, 1630–1730.* Montreal: McGill-Queen's University Press, 1997.

Anderson, Dorothy, and Richard Shiell. *Montserrat to Melbourne: The Story of a Shiell Family.* [Melbourne, 1985.] See also entries under Richard Shiell.

Aronson, Julie, and Marjorie E. Wieseman. *Perfect Likeness: European and American Portrait Miniatures from the Cincinnati Art Museum.* New Haven: Yale University Press, 2006.

Beckson, Karl. *London in the 1890s: A Cultural History.* New York: W. W. Norton, 1992.

Berleant-Schiller, Riva. "The White Minority and the Emancipation Process in Montserrat, 1807–32." *New West Indian Guide/Nieuwe West-Indische Gids* 70, Nos. 3–4 (1996): 255–81.

Billings, Harold. "Mrs Machen and Mrs Shiel." *Faunus: The Journal of the Friends of Arthur Machen* No. 19 (Spring 2009): 6–14.

Brennan, Barbara. Autobiographical notes sent by email to John D. Squires by her son Tim Brennan, 6 January 2003.

Brennan, Tim. "History, Family, History." In Hilda Kean, P. Martin, and S. J. Morgan, ed. *Seeing History: Public History in Britain Now.* London: Francis Boutle, 2000. 37–50.

[Coleridge, Henry Nelson.] *Six Months in the West Indies in 1825.* New York: Negro Universities Press, 1970.

D'Arcy, Ella. *Some Letters to John Lane.* Ed. Alan Anderson. Edinburgh: Tragara Press, 1990.

David, Hugh. *The Fitzrovians: A Portrait of Bohemian Society, 1900–55.* London: Michael Joseph, 1988. An entertaining and useful guide

N.B. At the time of publication, www.alangulette.com/lit/Shiel, where many of the papers cited herein once could be found, seems no longer to support the various author pages. However, many still may be found by searching for the urls using the Wayback Machine at archive.org.

to the eating and drinking places of an older London.

Demers, Antoine. *The Catholic Church in Montserrat, West Indies, 1756–1980.* [Plymouth, Montserrat,] 1980.

Dowson, Ernest. *The Letters of Ernest Dowson.* Ed. Desmond Flower and Henry Maas. Rutherford, NJ: Fairleigh Dickinson University Press, 1967.

Drysdale, William, "A Visit to Montserrat: Two Hours in Plymouth, Its Capital Town. Where Steamers Do Not Often Land and Strangers Are as Good as a Circus—A Reception in The Market Place." *New York Times* (29 December 1885): 4.

English, T. Savage. *Records of Montserrat.* Plymouth, 1930. Typescript. Two copies are known to exist, one in the Public Library on Montserrat and another in the Institute of Commonwealth Studies, London. In 2003, the UT Austin General Libraries obtained a copy of the typescript from Montserrat, scanned it, and made it available via the Internet. www.lib.utexas.edu/books/records-of-montserrat/.

Fergus, Howard A. *Gallery Montserrat: Some Prominent People in Our History.* Jamaica: Canoe Press University of the West Indies, 1996.

———. *History of Alliouagana: A Short History of Montserrat.* Plymouth: Montserrat: University Centre, 1975.

———. *Montserrat: A History of a Caribbean Colony.* London: Macmillan Caribbean, 1994.

Fitzgerald, Penelope. *Charlotte Mew and Her Friends.* London: Collins, 1984.

Gullette, Alan. *M. P. Shiel (1865–1947): The Lord of Language.* web.archive.org/web/20191221020026/alangullette.com/lit/shiel/

Hall, Douglas. *Five of the Leewards 1834–1870: The Major Problems of the Post-Emancipation Period in Antigua, Barbuda, Montserrat, Nevis and St. Kitts.* [Barbados]: Caribbean Universities Press, 1971.

Harwood, John. *Olivia Shakespear and W. B. Yeats: After Long Silence.* New York: St. Martin's Press, 1989.

Haskell, H. N. "Some Notes on the Foundation and History of Harrison College." *Journal of the Barbados Museum and Historical Society* 8, No. 4 (August 1941) 186–93; 9, No. 1 (November 1941): 3–16; 9, No. 2 (February 1942): 59–81.

Hearn, Lafcadio. *Two Years in the French West Indies.* New York: Harper, 1890.

Hervey, Benjamin. "Prince Zaleski." *Wormwood* No. 4 (Spring 2005): 57–72.

Horsford, John. *A Voice from the West Indies: Being a Review of the Character and Results of Missionary Reports in the British and Other Colonies in the Charibbean Sea.* London: Alexander Heylin, 1856.

Jerome, Jerome K. *My Life and Times*. London: Hodder & Stoughton, 1926.

Jewson, William Arthur. "The Diary of William Arthur Jewson." 1 January–23 May 1914. TLC, 21 pp. Transcribed 1996 from the original MS by Tim Brennan.

MacLeod, Kirsten. *Fictions of British Decadence: High Art, Popular Writing, and the* Fin de Siècle. London: Palgrave Macmillan, 2006.

———. "M. P. Shiel and the Love of Pubescent Girls: The Other Love That Dare Not Speak Its Name." *English Literature in Transition 1880–1920* 51, No. 4 (2008): 335–80.

May, J. Lewis. *John Lane and the Nineties.* London: John Lane/The Bodley Head, 1936.

Mead, Margaret. *Letters from the Field 1925–1975.* New York: Harper & Row, 1977. 284–91.

Mix, Katherine Lyon. *A Study in Yellow:* The Yellow Book *and Its Contributors.* Lawrence: University of Kansas Press, 1960.

Morse, Albert Reynolds. *The Works of M. P. Shiel.* Cleveland: Reynolds Morse Foundation:

I. *Writings* (1979).

II. *The Shielography Updated,* part 1 (1980).

III. *The Shielography Updated,* part 2 (1980).

IV. *M. P. Shiel in Diverse Hands: A Collection of Essays* (1983).

Morse, Albert Reynolds. *The Quest for M. P. Shiel's Realm of Redonda.* Cleveland: Reynolds Morse Foundation, 1979.

Oliver, Vere Langford. *The History of the Island of Antigua, One of the Leeward Caribbees in the West Indies, from the First Settlement in 1635 to the Present Time.* London: Mitchell & Hughes, 1894–99. 3 vols.

Ransome, Arthur. *The Autobiography of Arthur Ransome*. London: Jonathan Cape, 1976.

———. *Bohemia in London*. London: Chapman & Hall, 1907. While Ransome's essay about Shiel, "The Novelist," is just beyond the date line of the present book, its importance as a description of

Shiel's life "at home" must be recognized.

Richards, Grant. *Memories of a Misspent Youth, 1872–1896.* New York: Harper, 1933.

———. *Author Hunting by an Old Literary Sports Man: Memories of Years Spent Mainly in Publishing, 1897–1925.* New York: Coward-McCann, 1934.

Ross, Charlesworth. "The First West Indian Novelist," *Caribbean Quarterly* 14, No. 4 (December 1968): 56–60.

Semper, Dudley. "This is the Last Will and Testament of Mr. Dudley Semper of the Island of Montserrat . . . this fourteenth day of March in the year of our Lord one thousand eight hundred and thirty three . . ." PRO Prob 11/1836. Transcribed 2004 by Claudia Semper, to whom a great debt is owed for sharing this work and clarifying the relationship between Dudley Semper and William Shiell.

Shiel, M. P. "About Myself." *Candid Friend* (17 August 1901): 630–31. Rev. ed. in A. Reynolds Morse. *The Works of M. P. Shiel: A Study in Bibliography.* Los Angeles: Fantasy Publishing Co., 1948. 1–6. Revised in 1947 for publication in this work, per Morse. Reprinted also in Morse, *The Works of M. P. Shiel.* Cleveland: Reynolds Morse Foundation, 1980. 3.417–22.

———. "The Good Machen." In *The Good Machen: A Centenary Tribute Recalled.* With a Foreword by Brocard Sewell and an Afterword by Hilery Machen. London: Aylesford Press, 1993.

———. "'Long Tots' and Languages." *King's College Review* 30, No. 4 (1929 Centenary Issue): 18.

———. "The Montserrat Spectator." No. 8. Plymouth. Friday. Dec 15th 1876. Holograph Ms. newspaper (mutilated) in the hand of MPS in the Ransom Center, University of Texas–Austin.

———. "Myself." *Borzoi Broadside* (September 1924). "About Myself" revised for this advertising text, the first reference to the Redonda legend appears here.

———. *Science, Life and Literature.* London: Williams & Norgate, 1950.

———. *This Knot of Life.* London: Everett, [1909].

———. *The Weird o' It.* London: Grant Richards, 1902.

———. *The Yellow Wave.* London: Ward, Lock, 1905.

Shiell, Richard, and Dorothy Anderson. *Shiell Genealogy: Essays:* The

Possible Origins of Matthew Phipps Shiell; A Family Tree of Matthew Phipps Shiell; II_William.htm" William Shiell (1785–1853); John Shiell (1788–1847); James Phipps Shiell (1790–1834); Henry Shiell (1826–1889); Mary Ann Shiell (1829–1896); Queely Shiell (1755–1847) web.archive.org/web/20191221020026/alangullette.com/lit/shiel/ See also entry under Dorothy Anderson.

———. *The Shiell Family of the Caribbean Island of Montserrat.* Foreword by Harold Billings. Melbourne: MBE Business Service Center, 2005.

Skaggs, Jimmy M. *The Great Guano Rush: Entrepreneurs and American Overseas Expansion.* New York: St. Martin's Press, 1994.

Squires, John D. [*Essays*] web.archive.org/web/20191221020026/alangullette.com/lit/shiel/

———. "Rediscovering M. P. Shiel (1865–1947)." *New York Review of Science Fiction* 13, No. 9 (May 2001): 12–15. web.archive.org/web/20200804030751/http://www.alangullette.com/lit/shiel/essays/RediscoveringMPShiel.htm Squires has been the most intrepid and scholarly student of M. P. Shiel and his works since the late 1970s. He has written voluminously about Shiel, his life, his works, his literary sources, his collaborations—all with respect for Shiel's literary efforts, but also with sound scholarly integrity and thorough research principles. The whole of Shiel's life and his publications are pretty much laid out in the many publications that Squires has prepared about him. While there are other pieces by Squires available at this Shiel web site, this particular essay is one of the farthest ranging summations of Shiel and his work that is available online. An excellent printed source is Squires's entry for Shiel in *The Penguin Encyclopedia of Horror and the Supernatural,* ed. Jack Sullivan (New York: Viking, 1986), 382–84, as well as the major essay, "Some Contemporary Themes in Shiel's Early Novels."

———. "Some Contemporary Themes in Shiel's Early Novels," in Morse, *Diverse Hands* 249–326.

———, and Steve Eng. *Shiel and His Collaborators: Three Essays on William Thomas Stead, Louis Tracy and John Gawsworth.* Kettering, OH: Vainglory Press, 2004; www.alangullette.com/lit/shiel/essays/shiel_stead.htm

Stokes, John. *In the Nineties.* Chicago: University of Chicago Press, 1989.

Sturge, Joseph, and Thomas Harvey. *The West Indies in 1837: Being the Journal of a Visit to Antigua, Montserrat, Dominica, St. Lucia, Barbados, and Jamaica Undertaken for the Purpose of Ascertaining the Actual Condition of the Negro Population of these Islands.* London: Frank Cass, 1968. 80–89.

Wheeler, Marion M. *Montserrat, West Indies: A Chronological History.* [Plymouth]: Montserrat National Trust, 1988.

Wratislaw, Theodore. *Oscar Wilde: A Memoir.* Foreword by Sir John Betjeman. Introduction and Notes by Karl Beckson. London: Eighteen Nineties Society, 1979.

THE WORKS OF M. P. SHIEL

Books

Original publication dates only

Prince Zaleski. London: John Lane, 1895. Short stories.

The Rajah's Sapphire (with W. T. Stead). London: Ward, Lock & Bowden, 1896.

Shapes in the Fire. London: John Lane, 1896. Short stories.

The Yellow Danger. London: Grant Richards, 1898.

Contraband of War. London: Grant Richards, 1899.

Cold Steel. London: Grant Richards, 1899.

The Man-Stealers. London: Hutchinson, 1900.

The Lord of the Sea. London: Grant Richards, 1901.

The Purple Cloud. London: Chatto & Windus, 1901.

The Weird o' It. London: Grant Richards, 1902.

Unto the Third Generation. London: Chatto & Windus, 1903.

The Evil That Men Do. London: Ward, Lock, 1904.

The Lost Viol. New York: Edward J. Clode, 1905.

The Yellow Wave. London: Ward, Lock, 1905.

The Last Miracle. London: T. Werner Laurie, 1906.

The White Wedding. London: T. Werner Laurie, 1908.

The Isle of Lies. London: T. Werner Laurie, 1909.

This Knot of Life. London: Everett & Co., 1909.

The Pale Ape and Other Pulses. London: T. Werner Laurie, 1911. Short stories.

The Dragon. London: Grant Richards, 1913. Reissued as *The Yellow Peril* (1929).

Children of the Wind. London: Grant Richards, 1923.

How the Old Woman Got Home. London: Richards Press, 1927.

Here Comes the Lady. London: Richards Press, 1928. Short stories.

Dr. Krasinski's Secret. New York: Vanguard Press, 1929.

The Black Box. New York: Vanguard Press, 1930.

Say Au R'voir But Not Goodbye. London: Ernest Benn, 1933.

This Above All. New York: Vanguard Press, 1933. Reissued as *Above All Else* (1943).

The Invisible Voices. London: Richards Press, 1935. Short stories.

Richards' Shilling Selections from Edwardian Poets—M. P. Shiel. London: Richards Press, 1936.

The Young Men Are Coming! London: Allen & Unwin, 1937.

The Best Short Stories of M. P. Shiel. Ed. John Gawsworth. London: Victor Gollancz, 1948.

Science, Life and Literature. Ed. John Gawsworth. London: Williams and Norgate, 1950. Essays.

Xélucha and Others. Sauk City, WI: Arkham House, 1975. Short stories.

Prince Zaleski and Cummings King Monk. Sauk City, WI: Mycroft & Moran, 1977. Short stories.

The Empress of the Earth 1898; The Purple Cloud 1901. "Some Short Stories" Offprints of the Original Editions. Cleveland: Reynolds Morse Foundation, 1979.

The New King. Cleveland: Reynolds Morse Foundation, [1980].

Known Periodical Appearances

All magazines are published in UK except where noted.
Compiled by John D. Squires.

"The Doctor's Bee." *Rare Bits* (14 December 1889): 57–58. [One pound prizewinner in short story contest and Shiel's first professional publication. Later revised by John Gawsworth as "The Master."]

"Slap Bang" by Jules Claretie, ill. W. Rainey. *Strand Magazine* 1 (February 1891): 150–53. [Uncredited translation from the French by M. P. Shiel.]

"A Torture by Hope" by Villiers de l'Isle-Adam, ill. Paul Hardy. *Strand Magazine* 1 (June 1891): 559–62. [Uncredited translation from the French by M. P. Shiel.]

"Portraits of Celebrities: Miss Lily Hanbury." *Strand Magazine* 3 (June 1892): 600. [Short, uncredited biographical note by M. P. Shiel.]

"Guy Harkaway's Substitute," ill. J. Finnemore. *Strand Magazine* 6 (October 1893): 379–87.

"Portraits of Celebrities: The Rev. Augustus Stopford Brooke." *Strand Magazine* 6 (November 1893): 497. [Short, uncredited biographical note by M. P. Shiel.]

"The Eagle's Crag," ill. A. Pearse. *Strand Magazine* 8 (September 1894): 308–16.

"Huguenin's Wife," ill. F. O. H. *Pall Mall Magazine* 5, No. 24 (April 1895): 568–76.

"A Puzzling Case!" *Argosy* 59 (May 1895): 634–39.

"Orazio Calvo." *Belgravia Annual* (December 1895): 97–112.

"The Case of Euphemia Raphash." *Chapman's Magazine of Fiction* 2 (Christmas 1895): 422–36.

"Wayward Love," ill. S. Paget. *Cassell's Family Magazine* 22 (April 1896): 355–62.

"The Spectre Ship," ill. Gordon Browne. *Cassell's Family Magazine* (September 1896): 755–64.

"The Secret Panel," ill. A. J. Johnson. *Strand Magazine* 12 (December 1896): 712–19.

An American Emperor by Louis Tracy, serialized in *Pearson's Weekly* Nos. 336–362 (26 December 1896–26 June 1897). [Shiel stepped in for Tracy to write Chapters 29–39 per John Gawsworth to Reynolds Morse.]

"A Night in Venice." *Cornhill Magazine* New Series 3, No. 16 (October 1897): 500–14. [See also "The Torture of Fear" (1897) and "The Venetian Day" in *The Invisible Voices* (1935).]

"The Torture of Fear." *Washington Post* (14 November 1897): 21. Also *Rochester Democrat and Chronicle* (14 November 1897): 16. [See also "Night in Venice" (1897) and "The Venetian Day" in *The Invisible Voices* (1935).]

The Man-Stealers. [Details unverified, but it was listed among Shiel's prior publications in *Short Stories* No. 475 (5 February 1898 et seq.). It is unlikely that it actually appeared.]

The Empress of the Earth, ill. Lawson Wood. Serialized in *Short Stories* Nos. 475–494 (5 February 1898–18 June 1898).

"The Awful Voyage of Ralphie Hamilton." *Boy's Friend* No. 167 (9 April 1898): 89–90.

Contraband of War. Serialized in *Pearson's Weekly* Nos. 407–416 (7 May 1898–9 July 1898).

Cold Steel. Serialized in *Pearson's Weekly* Nos. 441–459 (31 December 1898–6 May 1899).

Ad in *Pearson's Weekly* No. 520 (7 July 1900) for *The Yellow Peril* by M. P. Shiel being serialized in the *Illustrated Weekly News.* [Re-serialization of *The Yellow Danger*, which ran 30 June 1900–1 September 1900, then continuing 8 September–13 October 1900 in *The Curiosity Shop*.]

Half-page advertisement for *The Yellow Peril* also appeared on the back covers of *Pick-Me-Up* for 18 and 25 August and 1 September 1900, announcing the serialization in the *Illustrated Weekly News* with chapter headings and puffs for the story.

The Purple Cloud, ill. J. J. Cameron. Serialized in the *Royal Magazine* Nos. 27–32 (January–June, 1901).

"The Cat." *Westminster Gazette* (18 April 1901): 2. Poem.

"About Myself." *Candid Friend* (17 August 1901): 630–31.

"Ben." *English Illustrated Magazine* No. 220 (January 1902): 321–28.

"The Cashmere Shawl." *Penny Pictorial Magazine* No. 141 (15 February 1902): 452–55.

The Battle of Waterloo, a comedy adapted from the Norwegian of Kielland by M. P. Shiel, ill. G. Nicolet. *Cassell's Magazine* (December 1901–24 March 1902): 560–66.

"The Bride," ill. Frank Chesworth. *English Illustrated Magazine* No. 224 (May 1902): 159–68.

In Love's Whirlpool. Serialized in *Cassell's Saturday Journal* Nos. 972–988 (14 May–3 September 1902). [Published in book form as *The Weird o' It* (1902).]

"What Happened Behind the Locked Door" by M. J. [*sic*] Shiel. *Chicago Daily Tribune* (31 August 1902): 7. ["The Tale of Henry and Rowena" in *Here Comes the Lady* (1928.)]

"Family Pride." *Pictorial Magazine* No. 183 (Christmas Number, week ending 6 December 1902): 42–47.

Unto the Third Generation, ill. W. H. Serialized in the *Morning Leader* Nos. 3389–3433 (30 March 1903–20 May 1903).

"A Shot at the Sun." One illustration by unknown. *Pictorial Magazine* No. 230 (24 October 1903): 402–4.

The Evil That Men Do. Serialized in *People* Nos. 170–191 (13 March–7 August 1904).

The Pillar of Light by Louis Tracy. Serialized in the *Lady's Home Magazine* Nos. 48–51 (December 1904–March 1905). (The name changed to the *Lady's Home Magazine of Fiction* with the January 1905 issue and the magazine was terminated with the March issue. Pearson launched *The Novel Magazine* in April 1905 that continued the serial to its end.) [Shiel contributed to this novel.]

The Whiff of Violets by Gordon Holmes. Serialized in *Pearson's Weekly*, Nos. 838–850 (9 August–1 November 1906). [First serialized in America as *The Late Tenant* in the *Sunday Magazine of the New York Tribune* (15 July 1906–23 September 1906). Shiel contributed to this novel.]

The White Wedding. Serialized in the *Daily Chronicle,* perhaps beginning 12 March 1907?

"Many a Tear," ill. Bayard Jones. *Pearson's Magazine* (New York) 20, No. 3 (September 1908): 283–90. [A photo of Louis Tracy with a blurb for *The Message*, a new serial to commence in the October issue, is included in the front advertising section of this issue on the reverse of the contents page. Shiel may have contributed to *The Message*.]

The Isle of Lies. Serialized in the *Daily Chronicle,* possibly in 1908?

The Message by Louis Tracy. Serialized in *Pearson's Magazine* (New York) 20, No. 4–21, No. 3 (October 1908–March 1909). Reprinted in *Pearson's Magazine Illustrated* [London], 20 [with parts 1–3, Chapters I–IX, October, November, and December 1908?] and 21, No. 1 (January 1909) [with part 4: Chapters X–XII], No. 2 (February 1909) [with part 5: Chapters XIII–XV], and No. 3 (March 1909) [with part 6: chapters XVI–XVII (Conclusion). Shiel may have contributed to this novel.]

"Many a Tear." *Novel Magazine* (London) No. 46 (January 1909): 468–73.

"Dickie." *Saturday Evening Mail* Fiction Supplement (New York) (13 March 1909).

"A Night in Venice." *Gunter Magazine* (June 1909).

"Michie: The Story of a Child's Tragedy." *Royal Magazine* No. 139 (May 1910): 86–91.

"A Good Thing," ill. Wilmot Lunt. *Red Magazine* No. 50 (1 May 1911): 197–217.

"The Tale of Adam and Hannah," ill. E. F. Sherie. *Red Magazine* No. 53 (15 June 1911): 625–37.

"The Bell of St. Sépulcre," ill. René Bull. *Red Magazine* No. 62 (1 November 1911): 247–53.

"The Tale of Gaston and Mathilde," ill. G. Henry Evison. *Red Magazine* No. 68 (1 November 1912): 220–28.

"Dark Lot of One Saul." *Grand Magazine* No. 84 (February 1912): 843–59.

To Arms!, ill. Christopher Clark, R. I. Serialized in the *Red Magazine* Nos. 90–95 (1 January–15 March 1913).

"The Torture of Fear." *Weekly Tale Teller* No. 210 (10 May 1913): 1–7.

"The Whirligig." *Weekly Tale Teller* No. 258 (11 April 1914); 1–11.

"The Place of Pain," ill. Arthur Twidle. *Red Magazine* No. 122 (1 May 1914): 181–87.

"The Waif," ill. Louis Smythe. *Red Magazine* No. 125 (15 June 1914): 576–81.

"16, Brook Street," ill. Fred Holmes. *Red Magazine* No. 128 (1 August 1914): 272+. (This issue also contains at p. 220 Shiel's contribution to "The Red Round Table" regarding "The Ideal Wife.")

"One Man in a Thousand." *Red Magazine* No. 138 (1 January 1915): 774–80.

"Three Men and a Girl." *Yellow Magazine* No. 50 (6 February 1922).

"Many a Tear." Serialized in the *Daily Herald,* London (9, 10, and 11 February 1927).

"In 2073 A.D." Serialized in the *Daily Herald,* London (12, 13, 14, and 15 March 1928).

"Things that Frighten Me." *Daily Chronicle* (18 April 1929).

"How to Be Happy." *Plain Dealer* 1, No. 1 (September 1933): 28–29.

"Many a Tear." *Argosy Magazine* No. 101 (October 1934): 95–100.

"Time-Travelling." *Tomorrow* 2, No. 3 (Autumn 1938): 12.

"Travelling While You Dream." *English Digest* 2, No. 2 (December 1939): 41–43.

"The S. S." *Encore Magazine* No. 47 (January 1946): 1–11; No. 48 (February 1946): 224–38.

"Cummings Monk." *Ellery Queen's Mystery Magazine* (New York) No. 27 (February 1946): 66–78. [A lightly edited version of "He Wakes an Echo."]

"Writing and Myself." *Literary Digest* 2, No. 3 (Autumn 1947): 14–16.

"A Case for Deduction" by M. P. Shiel and John Gawsworth. *Ellery Queen's Mystery Magazine* (New York) No. 60 (November 1948): 84–107.

The Purple Cloud, ill. Lawrence. *Famous Fantastic Mysteries* (New York) 10, No. 5 (June 1949): 10–112. [Abridged by the editor from the 1930 Vanguard text.]

"The Persistence of Personality After Death." *Enquiry* 2, No. 2 (August 1949).

"The Place of Pain." *Avon Fantasy Reader* (New York) No. 16 (1951): 76–84.

"The Return of Prince Zaleski" by M. P. Shiel [and John Gawsworth]. *Ellery Queen's Mystery Magazine* (New York) 25, No. 1 (January 1955): 82–88.

"The Secret Panel." *Saint Mystery Magazine* 10, No. 1 (March 1964): 64–74.

"Of Myself" and "An Address to the Horsham Rotary Club." *Aylesford Review* 7, No. 3 (Autumn 1965): 139–45.

"Tulsah." *Incredible Adventures* No. 1 (1977): 88–95.

"The Pale Ape," tr. into Japanese by Takukomeya. *New Series of Horror and the Supernatural,* Tokyo, Vol. 5 (June 1977).

Index

"About Myself" 78, 83–85, 128, 201, 215, 268, 317, 337, 411, 427, 428, 442, 450, 458, 459
Academy 196
Agnes (ship) 36
Allan, Charles 103, 110
Allen, Eleanor 24
Allen, Grant 140, 179
American Emperor, An (Tracy–Shiel) 189, 190, 196, 201, 234, 254, 257
Anderson, Alan 149–50
Anderson, Dorothy 12, 21, 26, 30, 32, 35
Anderson, Mary 111
Argosy 166
Arizona Nights (White) 411
Armstrong, Terence Ian Fytton. *See* Gawsworth, John
Athenaeum 169, 182
"Au R'voir" 462, 464
Aurore, L' 208
Author Hunting (Richards) 230
"Awful Voyage of Ralphie Hamilton, The" 230
Aylesford Review 463
Azario, L. 238

Bacchae (Euripides) 430
Bailey, Thomas Henry 88
"Ballad of a Nun, A" (Davidson) 177
Ballads in Prose (Hopper) 323n9
Balzac, Honoré de 272
Barrett, Mike 122
"Battle of Waterloo, The" 289
Baynes, Edward Dacre 25, 26–28
Beardsley, Aubrey 13, 135, 137, 140, 155, 166
Belgravia Annual 166
"Bell of St. Sépulcre, The" 381
"Ben" 289
Bennett, Arnold 455
Benson, A. C. 361
Bentley, E. C. 452
Bentley, Phoebe 338–39, 361, 367
Berkeley, J. H. H. 82
Berleant-Schiller, Riva 33, 35
Bible 62, 63, 93, 104
Blackwood's Magazine 171
Blake, Priscilla Ann. *See* Shiell, Priscilla Ann (Blake)
Blake, Sarah Harman 45
Blake, William 36–37
Blakeston, Oswell 463
Bohemia in London (Ransome) 271–72, 273, 307
Bohr, Niels 452
Book of Luke, The 468–71
Bookman (London) 169, 182, 388, 440
Bookman (New York) 411–12, 421
Booth, William 409, 410
Borrow, George 384
Boy's Friend 230, 395
Breitmann, Hans 277
Brennan, Barbara 339, 340, 420, 424, 437, 441–46, 451, 456–57
Brennan, Tim 424, 444, 446
"Bride, The" 289
Brook, Mr. 98
Bukharin, Nikolai 426
Burke, Paddy 60–61, 62, 76
By Force of Circumstances (Shiel–Tracy) 247, 317, 374–75

Cabell, James Branch 450
Caine, Hall 383
Campbell, Miss 341–43
Candid Friend 267–68
Caprices (Wratislaw) 196, 236
Carlyle, Thomas 97

"Case for Deduction, A" 466–67
"Case of Euphemia Raphash, The" 151, 166, 175
"Cashmere Shawl, The" 289
Cassell's (publisher) 324, 427
Cassell's Family Magazine 151
Cassell's Magazine 289
Cassell's Saturday Journal 278, 281
"Cat, The" 265
Chapman, Frederick 144, 167, 236, 237
Chapman's Magazine of Fiction 151, 166
Chatto & Windus 249, 256, 271, 294, 300
Chesson, Nora Hopper 322, 323n9, 324, 327, 329, 470
Chesson, Wilfred Hugh 231, 307, 322–24, 326, 327, 329, 330, 358, 360, 368, 383–86, 388, 395, 422–25, 428, 429, 431, 438, 439, 440, 449, 451, 452, 455, 469–72
Chesterton, G. K. 323n9
Chicago Tribune 289
Children of the Wind 424, 427, 428, 429, 437–39, 441, 447
Clare, Tom 444
Claretie, Jules 129, 165, 216
Clarke, Sir Ernest 128
"Class System of Japan, The" (Markino–Ransome) 306
Clode, Edward J. 294–95, 317, 318, 320, 322, 324–25, 353, 374, 386, 387, 389, 393–96, 400–402, 404
Cold Steel 195, 234, 241, 242, 243, 246, 247, 248, 249, 250, 255, 260, 386–87, 449
Coleridge, Henry 20
Coburn, Charles 112
Colles, William Morris 131, 133, 166, 174, 184, 240, 280, 283, 297, 412, 421
Columbus, Christopher 17
Communist Review 426
Contraband of War 195, 227, 228, 230, 232, 233–34, 237, 239, 241–42, 249, 404, 407
Corvo, Baron 149, 172
Courtney, W. L. 378
Coward, Ellen Louisa 279
Coward, James M. 165, 279–80
Cox, Mary A. B. 279
Cruikshank, George 324, 384, 385
"Cynara" (Dowson) 132

Daily Chronicle (London) 217, 329, 330, 344, 347, 368, 388
Daily Herald (London) 450, 452, 453, 454
Daily Mail (London) 217, 387, 430, 462
Daily Mirror (London) 473–74
Daily Paper 134, 184, 185, 186–87, 188
Daily Telegraph (London) 378, 452
D'Arcy, Ella 144, 148–50, 153, 154, 155, 171–73, 182, 183, 200, 237
"Dark Lot of One Saul, The" 182–83, 387
Dasher (ship) 31, 32
Davidson, John 177, 178, 346
Davis, Mary 421, 443
Davray, Henry-D. 216, 328–29, 394
"Day" 127, 164
de Bercy Affair, The (Tracy) 381
"Death-Dance, The" (Shiel–Gawsworth) 212–15, 397–98, 429, 438
Deighton, Horace 87, 88
Dickens, Charles 77, 93
"Dickie" 372
Dilke, Sir Charles 237
Dillon, E. J. 187
"Doctor's Bee, The" 127, 165
Dowdy, Sarah 30, 31, 33, 35, 36
Dowson, Ernest 131–32, 205–6, 236, 279, 280
Doyle, Sir Arthur Conan 135, 143, 166, 167
Dr. Krasinski's Secret 431
Dragon, The 325, 392, 393–96, 397, 398, 399, 401–3, 404
Dreyfus, Alfred 208–9, 211
Drysdale, William 63–69, 70, 77
Dumas, Alexandre 137
Dyett, Harry 61, 76
Dyett, Henry 61, 76, 88, 153
Dyett, Mrs. Henry 106
Dyett, Samuel 79

"Eagle's Crag, The" [formerly "The Eagle's Rock"] 131, 133, 136, 166, 174
Earth Bound (Luxemburg) 426
Ebbutt, W. A. 292–93
Eckley, Grace 186
Edwardian Fiction: An Oxford Companion (Kemp et al.) 405
Edwards, Hamilton 395
Egerton, George 150, 156
Eid, John 77
"Elegie" (D'Arcy) 171
Elgar, Francis 179–80
Empress of the Earth, The 158, 190, 191, 195, 202–3, 204–12, 216–18, 227, 228, 230–32, 233, 234, 242, 247, 249
Eng, Steve 463
English, T. Savage 19
English Illustrated Magazine 289
English Review 387
Esterhazy, Walsin 208
Euripides 430
Evening News and Post (London) 189
Evening Standard (London) 455
Everett & Co. 372
Evil That Men Do, The (Shiel–Tracy) 195, 196, 283, 286, 289, 290, 291, 292, 294, 297–305, 307, 309, 316, 327, 329, 331, 386, 389, 399

Fair Exchange (Richards) 454
"Fall of the House of Usher, The" (Poe) 430
"Falls Scandal, The" 212, 213
Family Herald 111, 119, 127, 164
"Family Pride" 289
Father Felix's Chronicles (Hopper) 323n9
Feldisham Mystery, The (Tracy) 381
Fennel's Tower 324
Fergus, Howard A. 108n7
Final War, The (Tracy) 189, 201
"First West Indian Novelist, The" (Ross) 123, 126
Fitzgerald, Penelope 149, 172
Fletcher, Ian 149
Fortnightly Review 256, 258, 378
Franks, G. H. 87
Fredericks, Max 98
Furley, Esther 337–38
Furley, Esther Grace 338
Furley, Ethel Florence 338
Furley, Florence Eliza. *See* Ritson, Florence Eliza
Furley, Gerald Arthur Jewson 339–40, 346, 348, 354, 355, 357, 360, 364–65, 367, 368–69, 375, 377, 382, 396, 410, 413, 418, 420–21, 422, 423, 441–43, 457
Furley, Horace Alfred 338
Furley, Lydia. *See* Jewson, Lydia Furley
Furley, Matilda Marion 338, 444
Furley, Philip Charles 337
Furley, Phoebe. *See* Bentley, Phoebe

Gadfly 129, 130
Gandhi, Mahatma 343n6
Garcia Gomez, Carolina. *See* Shiel, Carolina
Garcia Gomez, Dolores 235, 238, 284, 287, 288, 296
Garcia Gomez, Micaela 212, 213, 219, 224, 284, 286, 288, 296, 349
Garcia Gomez, Miguel 212, 235
Garcia Gomez, Salvadore 212, 213, 219, 287, 297, 362, 369
Garvice, Charles 395
Gatch, Mrs. 274–75
Gawsworth, Barbara 459, 460, 462, 465, 466, 472–75
Gawsworth, John 12, 42, 61, 71, 91, 127n9, 143, 149, 165, 177–78, 190, 194, 213, 235, 247, 250, 251, 252, 260, 288, 310, 315, 316, 318, 324, 369, 374, 387, 389, 391, 397, 428, 458–67, 468, 469, 475–76
George, Henry 112n15, 257, 346
Georgenianna (ship) 109
Get On or Get Out (Keary) 330
Gilbert, W. S. 97
Gocher, Kate 475, 477
Gold Hunter (ship) 119
Goldwater, Walter 47
Gollancz, Victor 83
"Good Machen, The" 177, 463

"Good Thing, A" 381
Grand Magazine 135–36, 387
Great Lie, A (Chesson) 323n9
"Great Strike, The" (Shiel–Tracy) 256–57
Greig, Teresa 446
Gullette, Alan 13
Gunter's Magazine 372
"Guy Harkaway's Substitute" 134, 166

Haggard, H. Rider 78, 111, 431
Hall, Douglas 25–26
Hamilton, Arthur 361
Hardy, Thomas 279
Harland, Henry 135, 144, 149, 151, 155, 172
Harmsworth, Arthur 189, 430
Harper's 70
Harris, Sir Alexander 128
Harrison, J. B. 87
Hart, Sir Robert 256, 258
Harvey, H. A. 122–24
Harvey, Thomas 24
Hastings, Warren 409
Hawker, Gertrude 419
"He Defines Greatness of Mind" 430
Herbert Spenser 423
Hearn, Lafcadio 70–71, 138
Henle, James 425
Here Comes the Lady 289, 387
History of the Island of Antigua, The (Oliver) 80
Homer 122
Hopper, Eleanor Jane "Nora." *See* Chesson, Nora Hopper
Horsford, Alberta 79–80
Horsford, Augusta. *See* Shiell, Alberta Augusta
Horsford, Cyril 79–80, 81, 97, 116, 128, 191, 202, 215, 251, 322, 416, 427
Horsford, John 22–23, 49
Horsford, Muriel 80, 126, 251, 322
Horsford, Nella 251
Horsford, Olive 18n2, 43, 44, 80, 91, 120, 121, 251, 389–90, 411, 416
Horsford, Reginald 41, 80, 81–82, 151, 152, 181, 321, 362
Horsford, Samuel L. 23, 41, 79, 82–83, 126, 164, 251, 257, 321, 362, 401–2
Horsford, Samuel Leonard 80, 81–82, 128, 151, 176, 419
House of Silence, The (Tracy–Shiel) 381, 389, 391
"House of Sounds, The" 156, 183, 387
How the Old Woman Got Home 61n28, 410, 429, 431, 441, 450, 453–54, 455, 456, 477
Hugo, Victor 274
"Huguenin's Wife" 129, 151, 166, 175
Hungarian Revolution, The (Schmitt [tr. Shiel]) 421–22, 425–26
Hutchinson & Co. 255
Hutchinson's Adventure-Story Magazine 428, 439

"Ideal Wife, The" 404
Illustrated London News 137
In Love's Whirlpool 278, 280–82, 286, 289. *See also Weird o' It, The*
"In 2073 (A.D.)" 454
"Inconsistency of a Novelist, The" 391, 459
Invaders, The (Tracy) 253
Invisible Voices, The 125, 129, 462, 463
Iolanthe (Gilbert & Sullivan) 97
Irish, George 109
Irish, Peter 35, 36
Irving, Henry 138
Isle of Lies, The 195, 329, 347, 358, 360–61, 368, 387, 399, 429

"J'Accuse" (Zola) 208
James, M. R. 193
Jane (ship) 35
Japanese Artist in London, A (Markino) 306
Jerome, Jerome K. 192, 241
Jesus 98, 431, 463, 468–69
Jesus Christ 98, 178, 357, 382
Jewson, Blanche 340
Jewson, Frederick Bowen 340
Jewson, Lydia Furley 99, 159, 296, 307, 324, 336–37, 339–48, 350–

51, 353–62, 366–80, 382–83, 392–93, 396–97, 404, 407, 410–11, 412–25, 426, 429–31, 437, 439, 441–44, 445, 446, 456–57
Jewson, William Arthur 159, 339–41, 352, 358, 362, 363, 369, 373, 396, 404, 421, 441–42, 443
Johnson, Lionel 156
Johnston, Hope 142, 143, 181
Joy's Choice 456
Jude the Obscure (Hardy) 279

Kardugia (Lazazzera) 428
Keary, Peter 189, 201, 202, 227, 232, 238, 249, 253, 254, 265, 306, 307, 308–9, 310, 313, 319, 321, 322, 328, 329–30, 381, 411
Kentish, Barbara. *See* Gawsworth, Barbara
Ker, W. P. 406
Keynotes (D'Arcy) 150
Killikelly, Ada Catherine 120–21, 321
Killikelly, Carlton 72, 80, 102, 106, 321
Killikelly, Kathleen 120–21
Killikelly, Sallie 253, 321
King's College Review 122, 124, 126
Kipling, Rudyard 464
Knopf, Alfred A. 447–57

Lady's Home Magazine [of Fiction] 318
Lamb, Norman 317
Lancet 472
Lane, John 135, 136, 137, 139, 142, 143, 144, 149, 150, 153, 155, 166, 167–68, 170–72, 173–77, 179–80, 182, 183, 184, 188, 193, 218, 236, 237
Langtry, Lillie 94, 111
Last Miracle, The 61, 158, 159, 195, 234–35, 237, 239–40, 246–47, 252, 253, 255–56, 324, 330, 342, 346, 377, 387, 399
Late Tenant, The 324, 329
Lautrec, Gabriel de 394
Lawrie, T. Werner 330, 387
Laws, Beatrice 154, 183
Lazazzera, Rocco 428, 453
Le Gallienne, Richard 135, 143–44, 156
Lee, Michael Malone 407–8
"Lend Lease" 466
Lennard, L. W. 114
Life of Jesus (Renan) 99, 382
Life of Sir Thomas Bodley, The (Bodley) 177
Limousin, Nellie 339, 420, 426, 442, 446
Literature 193
Locke, George 232
Long, John 320
"'Long Tots' and Languages" 122–23, 124, 126
Longfellow, Henry Wadsworth 87, 93
Lord of the Sea, The 11, 131n16, 134, 159, 195, 234, 249, 252, 254, 255–56, 257, 258, 260, 264–66, 267, 268, 270–71, 394, 449, 450–51
"Lost Provinces, The" (Tracy) 234
Lost Viol, The 309, 310, 312–15, 317, 319–20, 322, 325, 353, 354, 399
Louÿs, Pierre 216
Lovell, Elsie 422, 441, 442–44, 446
Luckock, Benjamin 20
Luxemburg, Rosa 426
Lyons, James 265, 266, 299, 300, 304, 308

MacCormack, Ann Chesson 453
MacDonald, Leslie 315
Machen, Arthur 135, 153, 156–57, 159, 177–78, 182, 183, 192–94, 218, 235, 237, 238, 241, 247, 448, 451, 458, 463
Machen, Amelia (Amy) Hogg 156–57, 159, 183, 192–93, 218, 238, 240–41
McKechnie, James 445, 457
McNamara, Lucy 21
McNamara, Mary 21, 35
Macy-Masius 455–56
"Madame" 111, 127, 164
"Maddelena's Lover" 131
Man-Stealers, The 158, 190, 191, 195, 201, 202, 227, 230, 255,

297, 385, 439, 440, 448, 449, 452, 453
Manchester, Tim 121
Manchester, Winifred 121
"Many a Tear" 61n28, 327, 347, 372, 388, 453
"Maria in the Rose Bush" 151
Markino, Yoshio 306
Marsh, Richard 424
Marshall, Burchell 454
Mason, A. E. W. 429
"Master, The" (Shiel–Gawsworth) 127n9
Matson, Leonard 81
Matson, Lucy 81
Mead, Margaret 39
Meade, Anthony 35
Meaton, Charles 408
Melville, Herman 447
Mercure de France 216
Meredith, George 138, 385
Message, The (Tracy) 347–48
Messenger 128, 129, 131, 165, 166, 279, 280
Metchnikoff, Élie 409
Methodism 22, 34, 46, 49, 62, 79, 106
Mew, Charlotte 149, 172
Mew, Egan 156, 218, 240
"Miche: The Story of a Child's Tragedy" 381
Mikado, The (Gilbert & Sullivan) 97
Miller, Annamarie V. 468, 469, 471, 473, 474, 477
Million 131, 166
Miln, Chrichton J. 361, 367–68
Miln, Phoebe Bentley. *See* Bentley, Phoebe
Milton, John 140, 383–84
Mitchinson, Bishop 85, 87
Moncrieff, M. A. 319
Monochromes (D'Arcy) 171
Montaigne, Michel de 353, 354
Montserrat 17, 19–20, 21–22, 24–29, 32, 35–36, 39, 46, 47–48, 51–54, 59, 62, 63–72, 74, 78–79, 89, 108n7, 248–49, 450
Montserrat Spectator 75, 78–79
Montserrat Watchman 108
Moore, George 270
Moore, Mary 382
Moore, Nellie 330
Moring, Alexander 309
Morning Leader (London) 242, 292–94, 295
Morse, A. Reynolds 12, 13, 19, 71, 85, 122, 213, 247, 251, 317, 318, 347, 388, 422, 468, 469
"Music-Hall, The" (Wratislaw) 236–37

Name This Child (Chesson) 323, 385
Napoleon Bonaparte 409, 430
Nash, Eveleigh 381
National Review 193
Nature of Man, The (Metchnikoff) 409
Nesbit, E. 323n9
New Arabian Nights (Stevenson) 182
New York, N.Y. 66
New York Herald Tribune 450
New York Times 63–69
New York Times Book Review 404
New York Tribune 324, 329
Newnes, Sir George 130–31
"Night in Venice, A" 372
Nightingale, Florence 129
Nisbet, James 386
Noble, James Ashcroft 167–69
Northcliffe, Lord 401, 405
Novel Magazine 318, 347, 372

Occult Review 395
O'Connor, T. P. 189
O'Hare, Arthur 407
Oliver, Vere Langford 80
"On Reading" 372, 383, 384
"On Writing" 372, 390
"One Man in a Thousand" 411–12, 421
"Orazio Calvo" 166, 175
Orchids (Wratislaw) 196
Orwell, George 339, 426, 446
Owen, Walter 448, 453, 468

Pale Ape and Other Pulses, The 387–88, 393, 399
Pall Mall Magazine 133–34, 151, 166
Pankhurst, E. Sylvia 425, 426, 427, 446
Paradise Lost (Milton) 140

Pattison, Edward S. 206
Pearson, C. Arthur 190–91, 201, 210, 211, 218, 227, 242–43, 244, 248, 249, 254, 257, 279, 319, 329, 347, 394, 401, 405, 411, 428, 430
Pearson's Magazine 248, 252, 254, 310, 347
Pearson's Weekly 189, 206, 230, 232, 234, 241, 244, 246, 254, 256, 307, 324, 329
Penny Pictorial Magazine 289
People 307, 309
"Phantom Man o' War" 464
"Phorfor" 151
Pictorial Magazine 49, 289, 300
Pillar of Light, The (Tracy) 310, 317–18
Pinker, J. B. 240, 246–47, 423, 424, 454
"Place of Pain, The" 404
Plato 430
Plymouth, Montserrat 17, 19–20, 28, 52, 63, 65–66, 67, 69, 70, 71–73, 322, 416
Poe, Edgar Allan 77, 87, 166, 167, 182, 237, 275, 384, 430, 448
Poems 458–61
Portrait of a Man with Red Hair (Walpole) 451
Pound, Ezra 153
"Premier and Maker" 125, 151, 154–55
Price, Elizabeth. *See* Sircar, Elizabeth Price
Price, John 309, 326, 327–28
Price, Kate 309, 326–27
Price, Martha 326
Price, Mary 326–27, 328, 335, 336, 340
"Primate of the Rose, The" 157
Prince Zaleski 13, 128, 134, 135, 136, 137, 140, 142–43, 144, 147, 157, 166, 167–70, 173–76, 178, 179, 180, 181, 182–83, 184, 193, 216, 237, 247, 272, 405, 448, 454, 455, 456, 461
Publisher's Weekly 320
Purple Cloud, The 11, 48, 61n28, 63, 100, 157–58, 159, 175, 216, 234, 235, 249, 252, 255–56, 257, 260, 265–66, 271, 342–43, 394, 428, 447, 448, 449, 452, 455
"Puzzling Case, A" 166

Queely, Margaret 23
Queen, Ellery 466
Queen 439
Queen for Redonda, The (Morse) 18n3
Queensbury, Marquess of 180

Rajah's Sapphire, The 134, 140, 175, 178, 179, 184, 185, 186–89, 190, 448
Ransome, Sir Arthur 42–43, 271–78, 289, 306, 307, 384
Rare Bits 127, 165
Rascoe, Burton 194, 448
Red Magazine 381, 386, 388, 391, 393, 403, 404, 411, 412
"Red Road" 462
Redonda 63, 70, 83–86, 110, 117, 233–34, 465
Renan, Ernest 99, 382
"Return of Cummings Monk, The" 347
"Rev. Augustus Stopford Brooke" 134
Review of Reviews 134, 182, 184–87, 201, 204, 270, 321, 328
Richards, Grant 12, 135, 185, 186–87, 209, 210, 211, 212, 216–18, 227, 228–29, 230, 232, 237–38, 239–40, 242–44, 246, 247–49, 252–54, 255–56, 258, 260, 264–66, 271–72, 278, 283, 289–91, 294, 297–300, 302–9, 319, 322, 324–25, 373, 386–90, 392, 393–94, 395–407, 408–9, 427–29, 431, 439, 448–49, 451, 452, 454
Richards Press 453, 455, 456, 460, 468
Richardson, Samuel 277
Ritson, Florence Eliza 338–39, 369–72, 373, 443
Ritson, Joseph 370, 372
Roberts, Llewelyn 405, 406
Robins, Elizabeth 344
Robinson, Sir William 128

Rolfe, Frederick. *See* Corvo, Baron
"Romance of the World from Day to Day, The" 184, 185–86, 188
Ross, Charlesworth 122–23, 125–26
Rota, Bertram 213
Rothermore, Lord 430
Royal Magazine 257, 265, 381, 452
Ruskin, John 140

"S. S., The" 135, 167, 169
Saba, J. M. 31
Salisbury, Lord 237
Saturday Evening Mail 372
Saturday Review 182
Schmitt, Heinrich 422
Schooling of the Future, The (Pankhurst) 425
Secker, Martin 454, 455
"Secret Panel, The" 151
Semper, Dudley 30, 31, 32, 33, 34–35, 84–85
Semper, Edmund 30, 32
Semper, Hugh 85
Semper, Michael 33, 35
Sergeant, Lewis 157
"Serpent Ship, The" 151
Seward, Annie 206, 207, 315–16
Seward, John Albert 206, 207
Seward, Nellie 159, 205, 206–7, 216, 243
Seymour, H. 382
Shakespear, Dorothy 153
Shakespear, Hope 153
Shakespear, Olivia 153, 154
Shakespeare, William 323n9
Shanks, Edward 429, 447
Shannon, J. H. 86
Shapes in the Fire 11, 125, 134, 137, 151, 153, 154, 155, 157, 166, 172, 173, 175, 182–83, 184, 193, 237, 253, 272, 405, 448
Shaw, George Bernard 343, 391
She (Haggard) 78
Shepherd, James L. 454–55
Sherman, Philip D. 448
Shiel, Ada Phipps Seward 159, 205, 206, 221, 225–26, 238–39, 243, 315–16
Shiel, Caesar Kenneth 328, 333, 334, 336, 404
Shiel, Carolina (Lina) 43, 159, 191, 197–99, 205, 212–16, 219–20, 222, 224, 235, 238, 240, 243, 244–46, 250–51, 252, 253, 258–67, 284–88, 292, 295–97, 306–7, 362, 373, 381
Shiel, Dolores (Lola) Katherine 43, 159, 222–23, 243, 255, 258–62, 264, 285, 296, 362, 369
Shiel, Lydia. *See* Jewson, Lydia Furley
Shiel, M[atthew] P[hipps]: early writings of, 78–79; education of, 77–78, 83, 86–88, 99–100, 122–27; employment of, 97–98, 103, 110, 114, 129, 163–65; finances of, 109–10, 114, 164–65, 235, 256, 259, 372, 416; move to London, 91–97; and plagiarism, 411–12; 421; racial heritage of, 46–48, 251–52, 431; rape conviction of, 407–11; readings of, 62, 77, 87, 430; translations by, 129, 131, 162, 228, 421–22; travels of, 62, 246, 297, 368, 381–82, 428–29
Shiel, Richard Lalor 127
Shiel in Diverse Hands (Morse) 13
Shiell, Ada Catherine 41, 42, 44, 71, 72, 100, 104, 113, 164
Shiell, Alberta Augusta ("Gussie") 41, 43–44, 46, 79–80, 85, 91, 95–96, 97, 98, 101, 103, 104, 106, 110, 115, 126, 137, 138, 154, 158, 164, 251–52, 254, 255, 258, 294, 322, 362, 402, 450
Shiell, Ann (Gordon) 24
Shiell, Elizabeth (Carey) 29
Shiell, Harriet 18, 19, 21, 38, 41, 42–43, 44, 46, 47, 71, 72, 77, 103, 104, 119–21, 139, 152, 242, 243, 253, 255, 258, 262–64, 267, 294, 322, 393
Shiell, James Phipps 19, 21, 23, 29–30, 32, 35, 36, 45, 122
Shiell, John 23, 24, 29, 36
Shiell, Luc 23
Shiell, Mary Cabey (Semper) 29, 33–34
Shiell, Matthew Dowdy 17–21, 29, 30, 35, 36, 37, 38, 41, 42, 44,

63, 80, 84, 86, 89, 101–10, 113, 114, 119–20, 133, 163–65
Shiell, Priscilla Ann (Blake) 18–20, 30–35, 36, 40, 41, 44, 71, 103, 113, 139, 158, 242, 321
Shiell, Queely 21, 23, 24, 27, 29, 34, 36
Shiell, Richard 12, 21, 26, 30, 32, 35, 37
Shiell, Sarah Ann (Sallie) 41, 42, 71–72, 102, 105, 106, 107, 108, 118, 120, 121, 151, 254, 362, 393
Shiell, William 21–22, 23, 24–28, 29, 30, 33–34, 35, 36, 37
Short Stories 190, 204, 209, 210, 211, 218, 227, 230
"Shot at the Sun, A" 49–50, 55–59
Silent House, The (Tracy–Shiel) 381, 389
Sircar, Dorothy 327, 336, 404, 407–8
Sircar, Eileen 327, 330, 408
Sircar, Elizabeth 404
Sircar, Elizabeth Price 326–27, 328, 330, 333, 335–36, 393, 396, 401, 404, 407–8, 411, 412
Sircar, Surja Kumar 327, 330, 332, 335, 411
Sister Teresa (Moore) 270
"16. Brook Street" 404
"Skin-the-Goat" 404
"Slap Bang" (Clarette [tr. Shiel]) 129, 165
Smith, Horace J. 284
"Song of the Cock" 475
Soviets or Parliament (Bukharin) 426
"Spectre-Ship, The" 151
Squires, John D. 12, 45n19, 134, 140, 141, 158–59, 169n9, 187, 191, 205, 228, 235, 249, 286, 317, 463
Stableford, Brian 167
Stead, W. T. 128, 134, 141, 178, 179, 184–88, 201, 204, 235, 270–71, 321
Stephens, E. 407, 408
Stephens, George 408
Stevenson, Robert Louis 124, 143, 169, 182
Stock, John R. 381, 386, 388–89, 391–92, 406, 411–12, 421
Stokes, John 169n9
Strand 129, 130, 131, 134, 151, 165, 166, 174, 205, 228
Strangest of All, The 429, 431
Sturge, Joseph 24
Sullivan, Sir Arthur 97
Sullivan, Mary 165
Sun (London) 189
Swinburne, Algernon Charles 424

T.P.'s Weekly 388
"Tale of Adam and Hannah, The" 381
"Tale of Henry and Rowena, The" 289
Tattooed Countess, The (Van Vechten) 449–50
Ten Contemporaries (Gawsworth) 391, 458, 459
Thaxter, Frederick 165, 280
Thaxter, Mary Sullivan 280
This Knot of Life 372, 383, 390, 399, 400
Thomas, Edward 326, 330
Three Impostors, The (Machen) 193
"Three Men and a Girl" 131, 166, 412, 421
Three Men and a Maid 286, 324
Thrills, Crimes and Mysteries (Gawsworth) 462, 467
Times (London) 82, 143, 144, 422, 431
Times Literary Supplement 439, 447, 453
Tit-Bits 130, 283, 286, 289
"To a Sailor Boy" (Wratislaw) 196
To Arms! 388, 393
Tokyo Nichi-Nichi 452, 458
"Torture by Hope, A" (Villiers de l'Isle-Adam) 129, 165, 205, 228
"Torture of Fear, The" 394
Tracy, Ethel 194
Tracy, Louis 140, 189–92, 194, 195, 196, 201–2, 234, 248, 252, 253, 254, 256–57, 278, 283, 286–87, 289, 294–95, 302–5, 307, 309–10, 317–18, 324, 325,

329, 347, 372, 373, 374–75, 381, 389–91, 393
Trent's Last Case (Bentley) 452
Trott, Percy 61, 76
"Tulsah" 151
"Two Fogs" 131, 166
"Two-Gun Man, The" (White) 411
Two Kings, The 386–87
"Two Lovely Black Eyes" (Coburn) 111–13
Tyhtheridge, Alan 452, 458

Under Quicken Boughs (Hopper) 323n9
Unto the Third Generation 289, 292–94, 295, 300, 309, 329, 399, 404
Unwin, T. Fisher 323n9

"Vaila" 151, 183
Valentine (Richards) 398
Van Vechten, Carl 193, 447–48, 449–51, 452, 453–54
Vanguard (publisher) 448, 449
Vestal Workers 358
Victoria (Queen of England) 260
Villiers de l'Isle Adam, Jean-Marie-Mathias-Philippe-Auguste, comte de 129, 165, 205, 228
Voice from the West Indies, A (Horsford) 23

"Waif, The" 404
Waite, A. E. 157
Wall, Florie 108, 121
Wall, John Clifford Llewellyn 108n7, 121
Walpole, Hugh 447, 450, 451–52, 453, 454
Ward, Lock 292, 294, 297–302, 305, 307, 309, 310, 311–15, 317–20, 322, 324, 353, 397, 398, 399
Watlington, John T. 21
Watt, A. P. 286, 292–94, 297–302, 310–15, 319–20
Way Stations (Robins) 344
"Wayward Love" 151
Week's Survey 306
Weekly Tale Teller 394, 404
Weird o' It, The 129, 130, 131, 132, 165, 205, 235, 271, 278–80, 283, 284, 286, 289–91, 300. *See also In Love's Whirlpool*
Welch, James 156
Wells, H. G. 182, 216, 284, 345
Westminster Gazette 265
"What Happened Behind the Locked Door" 289
Wheatland, Grace 72, 92
"Whiff of Violets, The" 324, 329
"Whirligig, The" 404
White, Stewart Edward 411–12, 421
White Wedding, The 61, 329, 330, 386, 399, 400, 406
Wilde, Oscar 142, 143, 155, 180–81, 183, 184, 193, 195, 196
Wilson, Sir John 181
Wilson, Patten 155, 182
Wings of the Morning (Tracy) 294
Woman Who Did, The (Allen) 140, 179
Workers Theatre Movement 454–55
Wratislaw, Theodore 183, 194–96, 235, 236–37, 240
Wynne-Tyson, Jon 19, 149n40

"Xélucha" 151

Yeats, W. B. 153, 322, 323n9
Yellow Book 135, 144, 149, 155, 172, 177, 182, 183, 193, 235
Yellow Danger, The 11, 158, 159, 202, 218, 227–29, 230, 232–33, 237, 238, 242, 243, 246, 247–48, 251, 252, 253, 255, 258, 260, 281, 282, 290, 306, 347, 384–85, 392, 394, 403, 405, 407, 428, 430
Yellow Deluge, The 423
Yellow Magazine 412, 421
Yellow Peril, The 392
Yellow Wave, The 45n19, 47, 233, 257, 306, 307–9, 310–12, 319, 322, 328, 353, 384, 392, 423

Zangwill, Israel 370
Zola, Émile 208–9, 211

THE AUTHOR

Harold Billings spent sixty years among libraries, books, and book people. He served for twenty-five years as director of General Libraries, The University of Texas at Austin. In 2002 the American Library Association awarded him its annual Hugh C. Atkinson Memorial Award for his "long commitment to innovation in automation, resource sharing, and creative management." He is the author of *Magic and Hypersystems: Constructing the Information Sharing Library* and editor of *Edward Dahlberg: American Ishmael of Letters,* Dahlberg's *The Leafless American,* and *A Bibliography of Edward Dahlberg.* He helped gather the remarkable archive of M. P. Shiel's works and documents for the Harry Ransom Humanities Research Center, The University of Texas at Austin that has served as a major resource for this biographical work.

www.ingramcontent.com/pod-product-compliance
Lightning Source LLC
LaVergne TN
LVHW020516100826
845148LV00010B/1252